COLIN DRURY

7TH EDITION

MANAGEMENT ACCOUNTING FOR BUSINESS

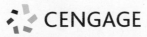

CENGAGE

Australia • Brazil • Mexico • Singapore • United Kingdom • United States

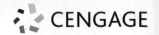

Management Accounting for Business,
Seventh Edition
Colin Drury

Publisher: Annabel Ainscow

List Manager: Jenny Grene

Marketing Manager: Sophie Clarke

Content Project Manager: Melissa Beavis

Manufacturing Manager: Eyvett Davis

Typesetter: Lumina Datamatics, Inc.

Text Design: Lumina Datamatics, Inc.

Cover Design: Simon Levy Associates

Cover Image(s): © Kalisson/Thinkstock Photos

For product information and technology assistance, contact us at
emea.info@cengage.com

For permission to use material from this text or product and for permission queries, email **emea.permissions@cengage.com**

British Library Cataloguing-in-Publication Data

A catalogue record for this book is available from the British Library.

ISBN: 978-1-4737-4911-5

Cengage Learning EMEA
Cheriton House, North Way
Andover, Hampshire, SP10 5BE
United Kingdom

Cengage Learning is a leading provider of customized learning solutions with employees residing in nearly 40 different countries and sales in more than 125 countries around the world. Find your local representative at: **www.cengage.co.uk.**

Cengage Learning products are represented in Canada by Nelson Education, Ltd.

For your course and learning solutions, visit **www.cengage.co.uk.**

Purchase any of our products at your local college store or at our preferred online store **www.cengagebrain.com.**

Printed in China by RR Donnelley
Print Number: 01   Print Year: 2018

BRIEF CONTENTS

CONTENTS

PART ONE   INTRODUCTION TO MANAGEMENT AND COST ACCOUNTING   2

1   INTRODUCTION TO MANAGEMENT ACCOUNTING   4

2   AN INTRODUCTION TO COST TERMS AND CONCEPTS   24

PART FOUR   INFORMATION FOR PLANNING, CONTROL AND PERFORMANCE MEASUREMENT   212

9   THE BUDGETING PROCESS   215

10   MANAGEMENT CONTROL SYSTEMS   250

PREFACE

The aim of this book is to provide an introduction to the theory and practice of management accounting and to emphasize its role in making business decisions. It is intended primarily for students who are not specializing in accounting and are pursuing a one- or two-semester basic management accounting course. The more advanced technical aspects that are required by specialist accounting students are not covered. These topics are examined in the author's successful *Management and Cost Accounting*, the tenth edition of which is also published by Cengage EMEA.

Feedback from lecturers in a large number of universities indicated that they had found the content, structure and presentation of *Management and Cost Accounting* extremely satisfactory and most appropriate for accounting students pursuing a 2-year management accounting course. They also indicated that there was a need for a book (based on *Management and Cost Accounting*) for students on shorter courses. This book is particularly suitable for students not specializing in accounting, studying management accounting on the following courses:

- a first-level management accounting course for undergraduate students
- higher national diploma in business and finance
- postgraduate introductory management accounting courses.

An introductory course in financial accounting is not a prerequisite, although many students will have undertaken such a course.

STRUCTURE AND PLAN OF THE BOOK

In writing this book I have adopted the same structure and included much of the introductory content of *Management and Cost Accounting*. The major theme is that different information is required for different purposes. The framework is based on the principle that there are three ways of constructing accounting information. One is conventional cost accounting with its emphasis on producing product costs for allocating costs between cost of goods sold and inventories to meet external and internal financial accounting inventory valuation and profit measurement requirements. The second is the notion of decision-relevant costs with the emphasis on providing information to help managers make good decisions. The third is responsibility accounting, cost control and performance management, which focuses on both financial and non-financial information, in particular the assignment of cost and revenues to responsibility centres. This book focuses mainly on the second and third of the above purposes. Less emphasis is given to conventional cost accounting because an in-depth understanding of this topic is not essential for those students who are not specializing in accounting.

This book consists of 16 chapters divided into five parts. Part One consists of two chapters and provides an introduction to management and cost accounting and a framework for studying the remaining chapters. Part Two consists of four chapters and is entitled 'Information for decision-making'. Here the focus is on measuring and identifying those costs that are relevant for different types of decisions. The title of Part Three is 'Cost assignment'. It consists of two chapters that provide an explanation of how costs are accumulated and assigned to cost objects, such as products or services. In particular, alternative approaches that can be used for measuring resources consumed by cost objects and the factors that should be considered in determining the sophistication of the cost accumulation system are described.

Part Four consists of five chapters and is entitled 'Information for planning, control and performance measurement'. This part concentrates on the process of translating organizational goals and objectives into specific activities and the resources that are required, via the short-term (budgeting) and long-term panning processes, to achieve the goals and objectives. In addition, the management control systems that organizations use are described and the role that management accounting control systems play within the overall control process is examined. The emphasis here is on the accounting process as a means of providing information to help managers control the activities for which they are responsible. Performance measurement and evaluation within different segments of the organization are also examined. The title of Part Five is 'Strategic performance and cost management and challenges for the future'. It consists of three chapters. The first chapter focuses on strategic performance management, the second on strategic cost management and value creation. The third chapter concentrates on the emerging issues that are likely to have an impact on management accounting and considers some potential future developments in management accounting.

MAJOR CHANGES IN THE CONTENT OF THE SEVENTH EDITION

The feedback relating to the structure and content of the previous editions has been extremely favourable and therefore no major changes have been made to the existing structure. The major objective in writing the seventh edition has been to produce a less complex and more accessible text and to incorporate recent development in the management accounting literature. This objective created the need to thoroughly review the entire content of the sixth edition and to rewrite, simplify and improve the presentation of much of the existing material. Many of the chapters have been rewritten and some new material has been added (e.g. environmental and sustainability issues, ethical considerations and the impact of the emergence of the knowledge base economy). In addition a new chapter (Challenges for the future) has been added that focuses on the emerging issues that are likely to have an impact on management accounting and considers some potential future developments in management accounting. The end result has been an extensive rewrite of the text.

Learning notes

In order to meet the different requirements of readers and different course curriculum, various topics are included as learning notes that can be accessed by students and lecturers on the digital support resources accompanying this book.

The learning notes relate to either specific topics that may be only applicable to the curriculum for a minority of the readers, or a discussion of topics where more complex issues are involved that not all readers may wish to pursue. All learning notes are appropriately cross-referenced within the text to the digital support resources. For example, at appropriate points within specific chapters the reader's attention is drawn to the fact that, for a particular topic, more complex issues exist and that a discussion of these issues can be found by referring to a specific learning note on the digital support resources accompanying this book.

Case studies

Case studies are available on the dedicated digital support resources for this book. Both lecturers and students can download these case studies from the digital support resources. Teaching notes for the case studies are only available for lecturers to download. The cases generally cover the content of several chapters and contain questions to which there is no ideal answer. They are intended to encourage independent thought and initiative and to relate and apply your understanding of the content of this book in more uncertain situations. They are also intended to develop your critical thinking and analytical skills.

International focus

The book has now become an established text in many different countries throughout the world. Because of this a more international focus has been adopted. A major feature is the presentation of boxed exhibits of surveys and practical applications of management accounting in companies in many different countries. To simplify the presentation, however, the UK pound monetary unit has been mostly used throughout the book, although examples of the euro, dollar and rand can be found in the assessment material at the end of each chapter. Most of the assessment material incorporates questions set within a UK context. These questions, however, are appropriate for worldwide use and contain the beneficial features described above for case study assignments.

Assessment material

Throughout this book I have kept the illustrations simple. You can check your understanding of each chapter by answering the review questions. Each review question is followed by page numbers within parentheses that indicate where in the text the answers to specific review questions can be found. More complex review problems are also set at the end of each chapter and within the digital online resources to enable students to pursue certain topics in more depth. Fully worked solutions to the review problems within the text are provided in a separate section at the end of the book.

SUPPLEMENTARY MATERIAL

The seventh edition of Colin Drury's *Management Accounting for Business* text is accompanied by the following dedicated digital support resources:

- Dedicated instructor resources only available to lecturers, who can register for access either at login.cengage.com or by speaking to their local Cengage representative.
- Cengage's MindTap helps students master the material. Dedicated content creates a learning path designed by the instructor to guide students through the course and focus on what's important. Instructors can find out more about accessing MindTap by speaking to their local Cengage representative.
- Cengage's Aplia, an online homework solution dedicated to improving learning by increasing student effort and engagement is embedded in the MindTap.

DEDICATED INSTRUCTOR RESOURCES

This includes the following resources for lecturers:

- Instructor's Manual with instructor's additional review problems
- Testbank provides approximately 500 extra questions and answers
- PowerPoint slides to use in your teaching
- Case Studies (internationally focused)
- Teaching Notes to accompany the Case Studies
- Downloadable figures and tables from the book to use in your teaching
- Quizzes
- Extra Real World Views
- Outline Solutions to all Real World View Questions
- Learning Notes (relating either to specific topics that may only be applicable to the curriculum for a minority of readers, or a discussion of topics where more complex issues are involved)
- Glossary
- Accounting and Finance definitions (handy introductions to Accounting and Finance techniques, disciplines and concepts)
- Guide to Excel
- Useful weblinks (links to the main accounting firms, magazines, journals, careers and job search pages)

MINDTAP

MindTap is a fully online digital learning platform of Cengage content, assignments and services that engages students with interactivity while also offering the lecturer choice in the configuration of coursework and enhancement of the curriculum via complimentary Web apps known as MindApps.

MindApps range from ReadSpeaker (which reads the text out loud to students), to ConnectYard (allowing the lecturer to create digital "yards" through social media).

APLIA

Cengage's Aplia is a fully tailored online homework solution embedded in the MindTap and dedicated to improving learning by increasing student effort and engagement. Aplia has been used by more than 1 million students at over 1300 institutions worldwide, and offers automatically graded assignments and detailed explanations for every question, to help students stay focused, alert and thinking critically.

ACKNOWLEDGEMENTS

I am indebted to many individuals for their ideas and assistance in preparing this and previous editions of the book. In particular, I would like to thank the following who have provided material for inclusion in the text and the book's accompanying digital support resources or who have commented on this and earlier editions of the book:

Magdy Abdel-Kader, University of Essex
Tony Abdoush, Bournemouth University
John Ahwere-Bafo, Royal Holloway, University of London
Karen Boyd, Newcastle University
Alison Broughton, Middlesex University
Anthony Atkinson, University of Waterloo
Stan Brignall, Aston Business School
Jose Manuel de Matos Carvalho, ISCA de Coimbra
Gin Chong, Southampton Institute
Peter Clarke, University College Dublin
Wayne Fiddler, University of Huddersfield
Ian G Fisher, John Moores University
Lin Fitzgerald, Loughborough University Business School
John Ford, Gordon Institute of Business Science, University of Pretoria
Keith Gainsley, Sheffield Hallam University
Olive Gardiner, Fife College
Alicia Gazely, Nottingham Trent University
Richard Grey, University of Strathclyde
David Grinton, University of Brighton
Antony Head, Sheffield Hallam University
Yu Lin Hou, University of Strathclyde
Lise Hunter, University of Plymouth

Mike Johnson, University of Dundee
Mohammed Sulaiman Hassan Kasbar, Queen Mary University of London
Michel Lebas, Groupe HEC
Pik Liew, London School of Economics
Kevan Lyons, University of New York in Prague
Phillip McCosker, University College, Worcester
Bhagwan Moorjani, University of Westminster
Ellertone Ndalama, University of Warwick
Lorenzo Neri, Queen Mary University of London
Peter Nordgaard Hansen, Copenhagen Business School
Deryl Northcott, Auckland University of Technology
Rona O'Brien, Sheffield Hallam University
Dan Otzen, Copenhagen Business School
Graham Parker, Kingston University
Breggie Van Der Poll, UNISA
Tony Rayman, University of Bradford
Jayne Rastrick, Sheffield Hallam University
Carsten Rohde, Copenhagen Business School
Robin Roslender, University of Stirling
George Sarpong, Nelson Mandela University
John Shank, The Amos Tuck School of Business, Dartmouth College
Helen Smith, Abertay University
Torkel Strömsten, Stockholm School of Economics
Mike Tayles, University of Hull
Chandres Tejura, University of North London
Ed Tew, University of Winchester
René Thamm, Technische Universität Dresden
Eric Tonner, Glasgow Caledonian Univeristy
Ben Ukaegbu, London Metropolitan University
Franco Visani, University of Bologna
John Williams, Rhodes University
Richard Wilson, M.S. Loughborough University Business School
Laura Zoni, Bocconi University
Nasiru Zubairu, University of Plymouth

I am also indebted to Martin Quinn for providing the new real world views that have been added to the seventh edition as well as Jenny Grene, Hannah Close, Sue Povey and Sophie Clarke at Cengage for their valuable publishing advice, support and assistance. My appreciation goes also to the Chartered Institute of Management Accountants, the Chartered Association of Certified Accountants, the Institute of Chartered Accountants in England and Wales, and the Association of Accounting Technicians for permission to reproduce examination questions. The answers in the text and accompanying website are my own and are in no way the approved solutions of the above professional bodies.

Finally, and most importantly I would like to thank my wife, Bronwen, for converting the original manuscript of the earlier editions into final typewritten form and for her continued help and support throughout the seven editions of this book.

ABOUT THE AUTHOR

Colin Drury was employed at Huddersfield University from 1970 until his retirement in 2004. He was awarded the title of professor in 1988 and emeritus professor in 2004. Colin is the author of three books published by Cengage: *Management and Cost Accounting*, which is Europe's bestselling management accounting textbook, *Management Accounting for Business* and *Cost and Management Accounting*. Colin has also been an active researcher and has published approximately 100 articles in professional and academic journals. In recognition for his contribution to accounting education and research, Colin was given a lifetime achievement award by the British Accounting Association in 2009.

LIST OF FIGURES

REAL WORLD VIEWS

CENGAGE

Teaching & Learning Support Resources

Cengage's peer reviewed content for higher and further education courses is accompanied by a range of digital teaching and learning support resources. The resources are carefully tailored to the specific needs of the instructor, student and the course. Examples of the kind of resources provided include:

- A password protected area for instructors with, for example, a testbank, PowerPoint slides and an instructor's manual.

- An open-access area for students including, for example, useful weblinks and glossary terms.

Lecturers: to discover the dedicated lecturer digital support resources accompanying this textbook please register here for access: login.cengage.com.

Students: to discover the dedicated student digital support resources accompanying this textbook, please search for **Management Accounting for Business** on: cengagebrain.com.

BE UNSTOPPABLE

PART ONE

INTRODUCTION TO MANAGEMENT AND COST ACCOUNTING

The objective of this section is to provide an introduction to management and cost accounting. In Chapter 1 we define accounting and distinguish between financial, management and cost accounting. This is followed by an examination of the role of management accounting in providing information to managers for decision-making, planning, control and performance measurement. We also consider the important changes that have taken place in the business environment. As you progress through the book you will learn how these changes have influenced management accounting systems. In Chapter 2 the basic cost terms and concepts that are used in the cost and management accounting literature are described.

1
INTRODUCTION TO MANAGEMENT ACCOUNTING

LEARNING OBJECTIVES After studying this chapter, you should be able to:

- distinguish between management accounting and financial accounting

- identify and describe the elements involved in the decision-making, planning and control process

- justify the view that a major objective of commercial organizations is to broadly seek to maximize future profits

- explain the important changes in the business environment that have influenced management accounting practice

- outline and describe the key success factors that directly affect customer satisfaction

- identify and describe the functions of a cost and management accounting system.

There are many definitions of accounting, but the one that captures the theme of this book is the definition formulated by the American Accounting Association. It describes accounting as:

> the process of identifying, measuring and communicating economic information to permit informed judgements and decisions by users of the information.

In other words, accounting is concerned with providing both financial and non-financial information that will help decision-makers to make good decisions. In order to understand accounting, you need to know something about the decision-making, planning and control process, and also to be aware of the various users of accounting information.

During the past two decades many organizations in both the manufacturing and service sectors have faced dramatic changes in their business environment. Deregulation and extensive competition from overseas companies in domestic markets has resulted in a situation where most companies now operate in a highly competitive global market. At the same time there has been a significant reduction in product life cycles arising from technological innovations and the need to meet increasingly discriminating customer demands. To succeed in today's highly competitive environment, companies have made customer satisfaction an overriding priority. They have also adopted new management approaches and manufacturing companies have changed their manufacturing systems and invested in new technologies. These changes have had a significant influence on management accounting systems.

The aim of this first chapter is to give you the background knowledge that will enable you to achieve a more meaningful insight into the issues and problems of cost and management accounting that are discussed in the book. We begin by looking at the users of accounting information and identifying their requirements. This is followed by a description of the decision-making process and the changing business environment. Finally, the different functions of management accounting are described.

THE USERS OF ACCOUNTING INFORMATION

Accounting is a language that communicates economic information to various parties (known as stakeholders) who have an interest in the organization. **Stakeholders** fall into several groups (e.g. managers, shareholders and potential investors, employees, creditors and the government) and each of these groups has its own requirements for information:

- Managers require information that will assist them in their decision-making and control activities; for example, information is needed on the estimated selling prices, costs, demand, competitive position and profitability of various products/ services that are provided by the organization.
- Shareholders require information on the value of their investment and the income that is derived from their shareholding.
- Employees require information on the ability of the firm to meet wage demands and avoid redundancies.
- Creditors and the providers of loan capital require information on a firm's ability to meet its financial obligations.
- Government agencies such as the Central Statistical Office collect accounting information and require such information as the details of sales activity, profits, investments, stocks (i.e. inventories), dividends paid, the proportion of profits absorbed by taxation and so on. In addition, government taxation authorities require information on the amount of profits that are subject to taxation. All this information is important for determining policies to manage the economy.

The need to provide accounting information is not confined to business organizations. Individuals sometimes have to provide information about their own financial situation; for example, if you want to obtain a mortgage or a personal loan, you may be asked for details of your private financial affairs. Non-profit-making organizations such as churches, charitable organizations, clubs and government units such as local authorities, also require accounting information for decision-making, and for reporting the results of their activities. For example, a tennis club will require information on the cost of undertaking its various activities so that a decision can be made as to the amount of the annual subscription that it will charge to its members. Similarly, municipal authorities, such as local government and public sector organizations, need information on the costs of undertaking specific activities so that decisions can be made as to which activities will be undertaken and the resources that must be raised to finance them.

As you can see, there are many different users of accounting information who require information for decision-making. The objective of accounting is to provide sufficient information to meet the needs of the various users at the lowest possible cost. Obviously, the benefit derived from using an information system for decision-making must be greater than the cost of operating the system.

The users of accounting information can be divided into two categories:

1   internal users within the organization

2   external users such as shareholders, creditors and regulatory agencies, outside the organization.

It is possible to distinguish between two branches of accounting, which reflect the internal and external users of accounting information. **Management accounting** is concerned with the provision of information to people within the organization to help them make better decisions and improve the efficiency and effectiveness of existing operations, whereas **financial accounting** is concerned with the provision of information to external parties outside the organization. Thus, management accounting could be called internal reporting and financial accounting could be called external reporting. This book concentrates on management accounting.

DIFFERENCES BETWEEN MANAGEMENT ACCOUNTING AND FINANCIAL ACCOUNTING

The major differences between these two branches of accounting are:

- *Legal requirements.* There is a statutory requirement for limited companies to produce annual financial accounts, regardless of whether or not management regards this information as useful. Management accounting, by contrast, is entirely optional and information should be produced only if it is considered that the benefits it offers management exceed the cost of collecting it.

- *Focus on individual parts or segments of the business.* Financial accounting reports describe the whole of the business, whereas management accounting focuses on small parts of the organization; for example, the cost and profitability of products, services, departments, customers and activities.

- *Generally accepted accounting principles.* Financial accounting statements must be prepared to conform with the legal requirements and the generally accepted accounting principles established by the regulatory bodies such as the International Financial Reporting Standards Board. These requirements are essential to ensure uniformity and consistency, which make intercompany and historical comparisons possible. Financial accounting data should be verifiable and objective. In contrast, management accountants are not required to adhere to generally accepted accounting principles when providing managerial information for internal purposes. Instead, the focus is on serving the management's needs and providing information that is useful to managers when they are carrying out their decision-making, planning and control functions.

- *Time dimension.* Financial accounting reports what has happened in the past in an organization, whereas management accounting is concerned with *future* information as well as past information. Decisions are concerned with *future* events and management, therefore require details of expected *future* costs and revenues.

- *Report frequency and less emphasis on precision.* A detailed set of financial accounts is published annually and less detailed accounts are published semi-annually. Management usually requires information more quickly than this if it is to act on it. Managers are often more concerned with timeliness than precision. They prefer a good estimate now rather than a precise answer much later. Consequently, management accounting reports on various activities may be prepared at daily, weekly or monthly intervals.

THE DECISION-MAKING, PLANNING AND CONTROL PROCESS

Information produced by management accountants must be judged in the light of its ultimate effect on the outcome of decisions. It is therefore important to have an understanding of the *decision-making, planning and control process*. Figure 1.1 presents a diagram of the decision-making, planning and control process. The first four stages represent the decision-making and planning process. The final two stages represent the **control process**, which is the process of measuring and correcting actual performance to ensure the best alternatives are chosen and the plans for implementing them are carried out. We will now examine the stages in more detail.

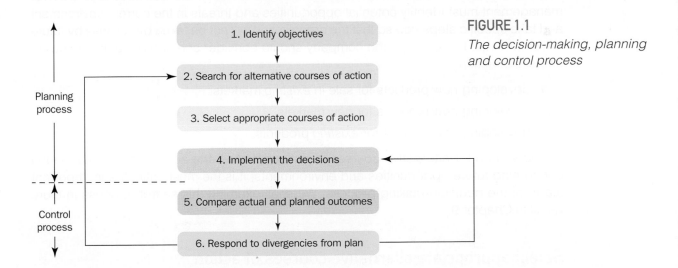

FIGURE 1.1

The decision-making, planning and control process

Identifying objectives

Before good decisions can be made there must be some guiding aim or direction that will enable the decision-makers to assess the desirability of choosing one course of action over another. Hence, the first stage in the decision-making process should be to specify the company's goals or organizational objectives.

This is an area where there is considerable controversy. Economic theory normally assumes that firms seek to maximize profits for the owners of the firm or, more precisely, the maximization of shareholders' wealth. Some writers (e.g. Simon, 1959) believe that many managers are content to find a plan that provides satisfactory profits rather than to maximize profits. Clearly it is too simplistic to say that the only objective of a business firm is to maximize profits. Some managers seek to establish a power base and build an empire. Another common goal is security, and the removal of uncertainty regarding the future may override the pure profit motive. Organizations may also pursue more specific objectives, such as producing high quality products or being the market leader within a particular market segment. Nevertheless, the view adopted in this book is that, *broadly*, firms seek to maximize future profits. There are two reasons for us to concentrate on this objective:

1 It is unlikely that any other objective is as widely applicable in measuring the ability of the organization to survive in the future.

2 It is unlikely that maximizing future profits can be realized in practice, but by establishing the principles necessary to achieve this objective you will learn how accounting information can highlight how profits can be increased.

The search for alternative courses of action

The second stage in the decision-making model is a search for a range of possible courses of action (or **strategies**) that might enable the objectives to be achieved. If the management of a company concentrates entirely on its present product range and markets, and market shares and profits are allowed to decline, there is a danger that the company will be unable to survive in the future. If the business is to survive, management must identify potential opportunities and threats in the current environment and take specific steps now so that the organization will not be taken by surprise by future developments. In particular, the company should consider one or more of the following courses of action:

1 developing *new* products for sale in *existing* markets

2 developing *new* products for *new* markets

3 developing *new* markets for *existing* products.

The search for alternative courses of action involves the acquisition of information concerning future opportunities and environments; it is the most difficult and important stage of the decision-making process. We shall examine this search process in more detail in Chapter 9.

Select appropriate alternative courses of action

In order for managers to make an informed choice of action, data about the different alternatives must be gathered. For example, managers might ask to see projected figures on:

● the potential growth rates of the alternative activities under consideration

● the market share the company is likely to achieve

● projected profits for each alternative activity.

The alternatives should be evaluated to identify which course of action best satisfies the objectives of an organization. The selection of the most advantageous alternative is central to the whole decision-making process and the provision of information that facilitates this choice is one of the major functions of management accounting. These aspects of management accounting are examined in Chapters 3–6.

Implement the decisions

Once the course of action has been selected, it should be implemented as part of the budgeting and long-term planning process. The **budget** is a financial plan for implementing the decisions that management has made. The budgets for all of the various decisions a company takes are expressed in terms of cash inflows and outflows, and sales revenues and expenses. These budgets are initially prepared at the departmental/responsibility centre level (i.e. a unit or department within an organization for whose performance a manager is held responsible) and merged together into a single unifying statement for the organization as a whole that specifies the organization's expectations for future periods. This statement is known as a **master budget** and consists of budgeted profit and cash flow statements. The budgeting process communicates to everyone in the organization the part that they are expected to play in implementing management's decisions. We shall examine the budgeting process in Chapter 9.

Comparing actual and planned outcomes and responding to divergencies from plan

The final stages in the process outlined in Figure 1.1 involve comparing actual and planned outcomes and responding to divergencies from plan. The managerial function of **control** consists of the measurement, reporting and subsequent correction of performance in an attempt to ensure that the firm's objectives and plans are achieved.

To monitor performance, the accountant produces **performance reports** and presents them to the managers who are responsible for implementing the various decisions. These reports compare actual outcomes (actual costs and revenues) with planned outcomes (budgeted costs and revenues) and should be issued at regular intervals. Performance reports provide feedback information and should highlight those activities that do not conform to plans, so that managers can devote their limited time to focusing mainly on these items. This process represents the application of **management by exception**. Effective control requires that corrective action is taken so that actual outcomes conform to planned outcomes. Alternatively, the plans may require modification if the comparisons indicate that the plans are no longer attainable.

The process of taking corrective action or modifying the plans if the comparisons indicate that actual outcomes do not conform to planned outcomes, is indicated by the arrowed lines in Figure 1.1 linking stages 6 and 4 and 6 and 2. These arrowed lines represent 'feedback loops'. They signify that the process is dynamic and stress the interdependencies between the various stages in the process. The feedback loop between stages 6 and 2 indicates that the plans should be regularly reviewed, and if they are no longer attainable then alternative courses of action must be considered for achieving the organization's objectives. The second loop stresses the corrective action taken so that actual outcomes conform to planned outcomes. Chapters 9–11 focus on the planning and control process.

What is management accounting?

Management accounting is the sourcing, analysis, communication and use of decision-relevant financial and non-financial information to generate and preserve value for organizations.

Management accounting combines accounting, finance and management with the business skills and techniques you'll need to add real value to any organization. Management accountants are qualified to work across the business, not just in finance, advising managers on the financial implications of big decisions, formulating business strategy and monitoring risk – much more than just crunching numbers.

Management accountants use information of all kinds, not just financial, to lead and inform business strategy and drive sustainable success. As a Chartered Global Management Accountant (CGMA), you will use this information to develop dynamic solutions to improve business.

CGMAs work in all areas of business, in all types of organizations in both the public and private sectors, all over the world. They work in finance, IT, marketing, HR, operations and senior management positions. They could be project managers, management consultants, finance directors or chief executives, and many go on to run their own business.

Question

1 How can management accounting be of assistance in an organization in which you are familiar?

Source

Extracted from the website of Chartered Institute of Management Accountants (www.cimaglobal.com/Starting-CIMA/Why-CIMA/what-is-management-accounting)

THE IMPACT OF THE CHANGING BUSINESS ENVIRONMENT ON MANAGEMENT ACCOUNTING

During the last few decades, global competition, deregulation, declines in product life cycles, advances in manufacturing and information technologies, environmental issues and a competitive environment requiring companies to become more customer driven, have changed the nature of the business environment. These changes have significantly altered the ways in which firms operate, which in turn have resulted in changes in management accounting practices.

Global competition

During the last few decades reductions in tariffs and duties on imports and exports, and dramatic improvements in transportation and communication systems, have resulted in many firms operating in a global market. Prior to this, many organizations operated in a protected competitive environment. Barriers of communication and geographical distance, and sometimes protected markets, limited the ability of overseas companies to compete in domestic markets. There was little incentive for firms to maximize efficiency and improve management practices, or to minimize costs, as cost increases could often be passed on to customers. During the 1990s, however, organizations began to encounter severe competition from overseas competitors that offered high quality products at low prices. Manufacturing companies can now establish global networks for acquiring raw materials and distributing goods overseas, and service organizations can communicate with overseas offices instantaneously using internet and digital technologies. These changes have enabled competitors to gain access to domestic markets throughout the world. Nowadays, organizations have to compete against the best companies in the world. This new competitive environment has increased the demand for information relating to quality and customer satisfaction, and cost information relating to cost management and profitability analysis by product/service lines and geographical locations.

Changing product life cycles

A **product's life cycle** is the period of time from initial expenditure on research and development to the time at which support to customers is withdrawn. Intensive global competition and technological innovation, combined with increasingly discriminating and sophisticated customer demands, have resulted in a dramatic decline in product life cycles. To be successful, companies must now speed up the rate at which they introduce new products to the market, and constantly develop new products and services. Being later to the market than the competitors with the introduction of new products can have a dramatic effect on product profitability.

In many industries a large fraction of a product's life cycle costs are determined by decisions made early in its life cycle. This has created a need for management accounting to place greater emphasis on providing information at the design stage because many of the costs are committed or locked in at this time. Therefore, to compete successfully, companies must be able to manage their costs effectively at the design stage, have the capability to adapt to new, different and changing customer requirements, and reduce the time to market of new and modified products.

REAL WORLD VIEWS 1.2

The Internet of things – new products and services

The Internet of things (IoT) refers to an ever-growing network of physical objects which are connected to the Internet. This includes household devices and many business and industrial applications. Take the example of lighting. For domestic use, companies such as TP Link offer smart bulbs which can be switched on and off via an app. A set on and off time is also possible and the user can monitor their power consumption. On an industrial scale, companies like Phillips offer smart lighting solutions to cities. These systems use analysis software, and through dashboards provide an overview of connected lighting systems which can be monitored, dimmed or switched on/off as required. In Buenos Aires, Argentina, such a system provided by Phillips reduced energy costs by 50% saving almost 24 000 tons of CO_2.

Question

1 Can you think of any barriers to entry for a business entering the IoT market?

Source

For more detail on smart lighting in Buenos Aires, see www.lighting.philips.com/main/inspiration/smart-cities/smart-cities-initiative/buenos-aires-smart-street-lighting and www.tp-link.com/uk for more detail on smart bulbs and plugs for the home.

Advances in manufacturing technologies

Excellence in manufacturing can provide a competitive weapon to compete in sophisticated worldwide markets. In order to compete effectively, companies must be capable of manufacturing innovative products of high quality at a low cost, and also provide a first-class customer service. At the same time, they must have the flexibility to cope with short product life cycles, demands for greater product variety from more discriminating customers and increasing international competition. World-class manufacturing companies have responded to these competitive demands by replacing traditional production systems with **lean manufacturing systems** that seek to reduce waste by implementing just-in-time (JIT) production systems, focusing on quality, simplifying processes and investing in advanced manufacturing technologies (AMTs). The major features of these new systems and their implications for management accounting will be described throughout the book.

REAL WORLD VIEWS 1.3

Medical devices in your hand, and at a low price

Devices such as heart monitors and blood pressure monitors have been traditionally the realm of hospitals and medical practices. In recent years however an increasing array of devices and apps have become available to end consumers. Such devices are quite effective and relatively low cost.

The availability of such devices, while possibly having health benefits for the end-consumer, is a challenge for medical device manufacturers. The price of medical equipment for hospital use is difficult to obtain publically, but to give an example a Phillips Intellivue portable heart monitor sells for about $2000–4000 second-hand on eBay. This would suggest a much higher price for a brand new device. Contrast this with an app called 'Instant Heart Rate' by Azumio Inc. which can be installed and used on a smartphone for free. The app uses the phone camera lens to detect minute changes in skin colour as the blood flows through the fingertip. Another example is a Fitbit (see fitbit.com) or similar wearable device. A Fitbit costing €120–150 can measure heart rate and cardio-fitness levels for example, to a reasonable level of accuracy. Or to give yet another example, a portable and accurate ECG machine by manufacturer OMRON can be purchased for a little over £200. Added to

this, apps like 'Instant Heart Rate' and the Fitbit type devices also come with various analytical tools which provide the user with trends over time. This is something which is arguably an advantage over devices used only in hospitals, and can contribute vastly to preventative medicine.

Questions

1 Do you think the costs of manufacturing a smart phone or wearable item which can be used as a consumer medical device are more or less than the costs of a specialized medical device?
2 How do you think the type of technologies mentioned above affect the manufacturers of specialized medical devices?

Source

Price of OMRON ECG at www.mistrymedical.com/item/3119/omron-heartscan-ecg-machine-without-software--hcg-801-e-

The impact of information technology

During the past two decades the use of information technology (IT) to support business activities has increased dramatically and the development of electronic business communication technologies known as **e-business**, **e-commerce** or **Internet commerce** have had a major impact. For example, consumers are more discerning in their purchases because they can access the Internet to compare the relative merits of different products and services. Internet trading also allows buyers and sellers to undertake transactions from diverse locations in different parts of the world. e-Commerce (such as barcoding) has allowed considerable cost savings to be made by streamlining business processes and has generated extra revenues from the adept use of online sales facilities (such as ticketless airline bookings and Internet banking). The proficient use of e-commerce has given many companies a competitive advantage.

The developments in IT have had a significant impact on the work of management accountants. They have substantially reduced the information gathering and processing of information. Instead of managers asking management accountants for information, they can access the system on their personal computers to derive the information they require directly and do their own analyses. This has freed accountants to adopt the role of advisers and internal consultants to the business. Management accountants have now become more involved in interpreting the information generated from the accounting system and providing business support for managers.

Environmental and sustainability issues

Increasing attention is now being given to making companies accountable for ethical, social and environmental issues and the need for organizations to be managed in a sustainable way. There is now a general recognition that environmental resources are limited and should be preserved for future generations.

Customers are no longer satisfied if companies simply comply with the legal requirements of undertaking their activities. They expect company managers to be more proactive in terms of their social responsibility, safety and environmental issues. Environmental management accounting is becoming increasingly important in many organizations. There are several reasons for this. First, environmental costs can be large for some industrial sectors. Second, regulatory requirements involving huge fines for non-compliance have increased significantly over the past decade. Therefore, selecting the least costly method of compliance has become a major objective. Third, society is demanding that companies focus on being more environmentally friendly. Companies are finding that becoming a good social citizen and being environmentally responsible improves their image and enhances their ability to sell their products and services.

These developments have created the need for companies to develop systems of measuring and reporting environmental costs, the consumption of scarce environmental resources and details of hazardous materials used or pollutants emitted to the environment. Knowledge of environmental costs, and their causes, provides the information that managers need to redesign processes to minimize the usage of scarce environmental resources and the emission pollutants and to also make more sensitive environmental decisions.

Pressures to adopt higher standards of ethical behaviour

Earlier in this chapter it was suggested that management accounting practices were developed to provide information that assists managers to maximize future profits. It was, however, pointed out that it is too simplistic to assume that the only objective of a business firm is to maximize profits. The profit maximization objective should be constrained by the need for firms to also give high priority to their social responsibilities and ensure that their employees adopt high standards of **ethical behaviour**. A code of ethics has now become an essential part of corporate culture.

Identification of what is acceptable ethical behaviour has attracted much attention in recent years with numerous examples of companies attracting negative coverage for ethical failings and their impact on reported profits. For example, Volkswagen (VW) Europe's biggest car maker has suffered a dramatic decline in its reputation after the revelation that it fitted software designed to cheat emission tests on 11 million cars worldwide. VW has set aside €18.4 billion to cover the costs of legal action, compensation and refits. Public distrust and protests against corporate misdemeanours have resulted in calls for increased regulation and the need to focus on improving ethical behaviour.

Management accountants have a critical part to play in the management of ethical performance and an obligation to uphold ethical standards. Professional accounting organizations play an important role in promoting a high standard of ethical behaviour by their members. Both of the professional bodies representing management accountants, in the UK (Chartered Institute of Management Accountants), and in the USA (The American Institute of Certified Public Accountants), have issued codes of ethical guidelines for their members and established mechanisms for monitoring and enforcing professional ethics. You can view each organization's ethical standards at www.cimaglobal.com/ethics and www.aicpa.org/research/standards/codeofconduct.html.

Deregulation and privatization

Before the 1990s many organizations, such as those operating in the airlines, utilities and financial service industries, were either government-owned monopolies or operated in a highly regulated, protected and non-competitive environment. These organizations were not subject to any great pressure to improve the quality and efficiency of their operations or to improve profitability by eliminating services or products that were making losses. Prices were set to cover operating costs and provide a predetermined return on capital. Hence cost increases could often be absorbed by increasing the prices of the products or services. Little attention was therefore given to developing management accounting systems that accurately measured the costs and profitability of individual products or services.

Privatization of government-controlled companies and deregulation have resulted in the elimination in pricing and competitive restrictions. Deregulation, intensive competition and an expanding product range create the need for these organizations to focus on cost management and develop management accounting information systems that enable them to understand their cost base and determine the sources of profitability for their products, customers and markets.

Focus on value creation

There is now an increasing recognition that management accounting needs to place greater emphasis on creating value rather than an overemphasis on managing and recording costs. Reducing cost is still important because it enables a company to remain competitive by reducing or maintaining selling prices and thus increasing customer value. You will see in Chapter 15 that recent developments have resulted in management accounting distinguishing between value-added and non-value-added activities with the former representing those activities that the customers perceive as adding value to the product or service and the latter adding costs but no value. Cost management seeks to eliminate or reduce non-value-added activities and to identify ways of performing the value-added activities in such a way that they enhance the value to the product or service.

Recently increasing attention has been given to the importance of **intellectual capital** (also known as intangible assets) arising from the observed dramatic differences between the book and market values of many companies, particularly the dotcom companies in the late 1990s. Examples of items that represent intellectual capital include resources such as the organization's reputation, the morale of its staff, customer satisfaction, knowledge and skills of employees, established relationships with suppliers, etc. It is important that intangible assets are taken into account in order to assess the value of future business opportunities. This presents a challenge to management accountants as to how to identify, measure and report on the value of intellectual capital.

Customer orientation

In order to survive in today's competitive environment, companies have had to become more customer-driven and recognize that customers are crucial to their future success. This has resulted in companies making customer satisfaction an overriding priority and focusing on identifying and achieving the key success factors that are necessary to be successful in today's competitive environment. These key success factors are discussed in the next section.

FOCUS ON CUSTOMER SATISFACTION AND NEW MANAGEMENT APPROACHES

The key success factors that organizations must concentrate on to provide customer satisfaction are cost, quality, reliability, delivery and the choice of innovative new products. In addition, firms are attempting to increase customer satisfaction by adopting a philosophy of continuous improvement to reduce costs and improve quality, reliability and delivery.

Cost efficiency

Keeping costs low and being cost-efficient provide an organization with a strong competitive advantage. Increased competition has also made decision errors due to poor cost information more potentially hazardous to an organization. Many companies have become aware of the need to improve their cost systems so that they can produce more accurate cost information to determine the cost of their products and services, monitor trends in costs over time, pinpoint loss-making activities and analyse profits by products, sales outlets, customers and markets.

Quality

In addition to demanding low costs, customers are demanding high quality products and services. Most companies are responding to this by focusing on **total quality management (TQM)**. TQM is a term used to describe a situation where *all* business functions are involved in a process of continuous quality improvement that focuses on delivering products or services of consistently high quality in a timely fashion. The emphasis on TQM has created fresh demands on the management accounting function to measure and evaluate the quality of products and services and the activities that produce them.

Time as a competitive weapon

Organizations are also seeking to increase customer satisfaction by providing a speedier response to customer requests, ensuring 100 per cent on-time delivery and reducing the time taken to develop and bring new products to market. For these reasons management accounting systems now place more emphasis on time-based measures, such as **cycle time**. This is the length of time from start to completion of a product or service. It consists of the sum of processing time, move time, wait time and inspection time. Only processing time adds value to the product, and the remaining activities are **non-value added activities** in the sense that they can be reduced or eliminated without altering the product's service potential to the customer. Organizations are therefore focusing on minimizing cycle time by reducing the time spent on such activities. The management accounting system has an important role to play in this process by identifying and reporting on the time devoted to value added and non-value added activities. Cycle time measures have also become important for service organizations. For example, the time taken to process mortgage loan applications by financial organizations can be considerable, involving substantial non-value added waiting time. Reducing the time to process applications enhances customer satisfaction and creates the potential for increasing sales revenue.

Innovation and continuous improvement

To be successful companies must develop a steady stream of innovative new products and services and have the capability to adapt to changing customer requirements. Management accounting information systems have begun to report performance measures relating to innovation. Examples include:

- the total launch time for new products/services
- an assessment of the key characteristics of new products relative to those of competitors
- feedback on customer satisfaction with the new features and characteristics of newly introduced products and the number of new products launched.

Organizations are also attempting to enhance customer satisfaction by adopting a philosophy of **continuous improvement**. Traditionally, organizations have sought to study activities and establish standard operating procedures. Management accountants developed systems and measurements that compared actual results with predetermined standards. This process created a climate whereby the predetermined standards represented a target to be achieved and maintained. In today's competitive environment, companies must adopt a philosophy of continuous improvement, an ongoing process that involves a continuous search to reduce costs, eliminate waste and improve the quality and performance of activities that increase customer value or satisfaction. Management accounting supports continuous improvement by identifying opportunities for change and then reporting on the progress of the methods that have been implemented.

Benchmarking is a technique that is increasingly being adopted as a mechanism for achieving continuous improvement. It is a continuous process of measuring a firm's products, services or activities against the other best performing organizations, either

REAL WORLD VIEWS 1.4

Key features of companies pursuing a low cost strategy

The following are examples of companies that pursue a low cost strategy:

- Southwest Airlines
  The airline industry has typically been an industry where profits are hard to come by without charging high ticket prices. Southwest Airlines challenged this concept by marketing itself as a cost leader. Southwest attempts to offer the lowest prices possible by being more efficient than traditional airlines. They minimize the time that their planes spend on the tarmac in order to keep them flying and to keep profits up. They also offer little in the way of additional frills to customers, but pass the cost savings on to them.

- Ikea
  The Swedish furniture retailer Ikea revolutionized the furniture industry by offering cheap but stylish furniture. Ikea is able to keep its prices low by sourcing its products in low-wage countries and by offering a very basic level of service. Ikea does not assemble furniture; customers must collect the furniture in the warehouse and assemble at home themselves, although they can pay extra for delivery. While this is less convenient than traditional retailers, it allows Ikea to offer lower prices that attract customers.

- McDonald's
  The restaurant industry is known for yielding low margins that can make it difficult to compete with a cost leadership marketing strategy. McDonald's has been extremely successful with this strategy by offering basic fast-food meals at low prices. They are able to keep prices low through a division of labour that allows it to hire and train inexperienced employees rather than trained cooks. It also relies on few managers, who typically earn higher wages. These staff savings allow the company to offer its foods for bargain prices

Question

1 How can the management accounting function provide information to support a low cost strategy?

Reference

K. Leonard, Examples of Cost Leadership & Strategy Marketing, smallbusiness.chron.com/examples-cost-leadership-strategy-marketing-12259.html

internal or external to the firm. The objective is to ascertain how the processes and activities can be improved. Ideally, benchmarking should involve an external focus on the latest developments, best practice and model examples that can be incorporated within various operations of business organizations. It therefore represents the ideal way of moving forward and achieving high competitive standards.

In their quest for the continuous improvement of organizational activities, managers have found that they need to rely more on the people closest to the operating processes and customers, to develop new approaches to performing activities. This has led to employees being provided with relevant information to enable them to make continuous improvements to the output of processes. Allowing employees to take such actions without the authorization by superiors has come to be known as **employee empowerment**. It is argued that by empowering employees and giving them relevant information they will be able to respond faster to customers, increase process flexibility, reduce cycle time and improve morale. Management accounting is therefore moving from its traditional emphasis on providing information to managers to monitor the activities of employees, to providing information to employees to empower them to focus on the continuous improvement of activities.

FUNCTIONS OF MANAGEMENT ACCOUNTING

A cost and management accounting system should generate information to meet the following requirements. It should:

1 allocate costs between cost of goods sold and inventories for internal and external profit reporting

2 provide relevant information to help managers make better decisions

3 provide information for planning, control, performance measurement and continuous improvement.

Financial accounting rules require that we match costs with revenues to calculate profit. Consequently, any unsold finished goods inventories (or partly completed work in progress) will *not* be included in the cost of goods sold, which is matched against sales revenue during a given period. In an organization that produces a wide range of different products it will be necessary, for inventory valuation purposes, to charge the costs to each individual product. The total value of the inventories of completed products and work in progress, plus any unused raw materials, forms the basis for determining the inventory valuation to be deducted from the current period's costs when calculating profit. This total is also the basis for determining the inventory valuation for inclusion in the balance sheet. Costs are therefore traced to each individual job or product for financial accounting requirements, in order to allocate the costs incurred during a period between cost of goods sold and inventories. (Note that the terms 'stocks' and 'inventories' are used synonymously throughout this book.) This information is required for meeting *external* financial accounting requirements, but most organizations also produce *internal* profit reports at monthly intervals. Thus, product costs are also required for periodic internal profit reporting. Many service organizations, however, do not carry any inventories and product costs are therefore not required by these organizations for valuing inventories.

The second requirement of a cost and management accounting system is to provide relevant financial information to managers to help them make better decisions. Information is required relating to the profitability of various segments of the business such as products, services, customers and distribution channels, in order to ensure that only profitable activities are undertaken. Information is also required for making resource allocation and product/service mix and discontinuation decisions. In some situations information extracted from the costing system also plays a crucial role in determining selling prices, particularly in markets where customized products and services that do not have readily available market prices are provided.

Management accounting systems should also provide information for planning, control, performance measurement and continuous improvement. Planning involves translating goals and objectives into the specific activities and resources that are required to achieve them. Companies develop both long-term and short-term plans and the management accounting function plays a critical role in this process. Short-term plans, in the form of the budgeting process, are prepared in more detail than the longer-term plans and are one of the mechanisms used by managers as a basis for control and performance evaluation. The control process involves the setting of targets or standards (often derived from the budgeting process) against which actual results are measured. The management accountant's role is to provide managers with feedback information in the form of periodic reports, suitably analysed, to enable them to determine if operations for which they are responsible are proceeding according to plan, and to identify those activities where corrective action is necessary. In particular, the management accounting function should provide economic feedback to managers to assist them in controlling costs and improving the efficiency and effectiveness of operations.

It is appropriate at this point to distinguish between **cost accounting** and management accounting. Cost accounting is concerned with cost accumulation for inventory valuation to meet the requirements of external reporting and internal profit measurement, whereas management accounting relates to the provision of appropriate information for decision-making, planning, control and performance evaluation. However, a study of the literature reveals that the distinction between cost accounting and management accounting is not clear-cut and the two terms are often used synonymously. In this book no further attempt will be made to distinguish between them.

You should now be aware that a management accounting system serves multiple purposes. The emphasis throughout this book is that costs must be assembled in different ways for different purposes. Most organizations record cost information in a single database, with costs appropriately coded and classified, so that relevant information can be extracted to meet the requirements of different users. We shall examine this topic in the next chapter.

SUMMARY OF THE CONTENTS OF THIS BOOK

This book is divided into five parts. Part One contains two chapters and provides an introduction to management and cost accounting and a framework for studying the remaining chapters. Part Two consists of four chapters and is titled 'Information for decision-making'. Here the focus is on measuring and identifying those costs that are relevant for different types of decisions. The title of Part Three is 'Cost assignment'. It consists of two chapters that seek to provide an understanding of how costs are accumulated and assigned to cost objects, such as different products or services. In particular, this part describes the alternative approaches that can be used for measuring resources consumed by cost objects and the factors that should be considered in determining the sophistication of the cost accumulation system.

The title of Part Four is 'Information for planning, control and performance measurement'. It consists of five chapters and concentrates on the process of translating goals and objectives into specific activities and the resources that are required, via the short-term (budgeting) and long-term planning processes, to achieve the goals and objectives. In addition, the management control systems that organizations use are described and the role that management accounting control systems play within the overall control process is examined. The emphasis here is on the accounting process as a means of providing information to help managers control the activities for which they are responsible. Performance measurement and evaluation within different segments of the organization is also examined.

Part Five contains three chapters and is titled 'Strategic Performance and Cost Management and Challenges for the Future.' The first chapter focuses on strategic performance management, the second on strategic cost management and value creation and the third chapter discusses the challenges for the future facing management accounting.

SUMMARY

The following items relate to the learning objectives listed at the beginning of the chapter.

- **Distinguish between management accounting and financial accounting.** Management accounting differs from financial accounting in several ways. Management accounting is concerned with the provision of information to internal users to help them make better decisions and improve the efficiency and effectiveness of operations. Financial accounting is concerned with the provision of information to external parties outside the organization. Unlike financial accounting there is no statutory requirement for management accounting to produce financial statements or follow externally imposed rules. Furthermore, management accounting provides information relating to different parts of the business whereas financial accounting reports focus on the whole business. Management accounting also tends to be more future oriented and reports are often published on a daily basis, whereas financial accounting reports are published semi-annually.

- **Identify and describe the elements involved in the decision-making, planning and control process.** The following elements are involved in the decision-making, planning and control process: (a) identify the objectives that will guide the business; (b) search for a range of possible courses of action that might enable the objectives to be achieved; (c) select appropriate alternative courses of action that will enable the objectives to be achieved;

(d) implement the decisions as part of the planning and budgeting process; (e) compare actual and planned outcomes; and (f) respond to divergencies from plan by taking corrective action so that actual outcomes conform to planned outcomes, or modify the plans if the comparisons indicate that the plans are no longer attainable.

- **Justify the view that a major objective of commercial organizations is to broadly seek to maximize future profits**. The reasons for identifying maximizing future profits as a major objective are: (a) it is unlikely that any other objective is as widely applicable in measuring the ability of the organization to survive in the future; (b) although it is unlikely that maximizing future profits can be realized in practice it is still important to establish the principles necessary to achieve this objective; and (c) it enables shareholders as a group in the bargaining coalition to know how much the pursuit of other goals is costing them by indicating the amount of cash distributed among the members of the coalition.

- **Explain the important changes that have taken place in the business environment that have influenced management accounting practice**. The important changes are: (a) globalization of world trade; (b) deregulation in various industries; (c) changing product life cycles; (d) advances in manufacturing and information technologies; (e) focus on environmental and ethical issues: (f) a greater emphasis on value creation, and (g) the need to become more customer driven.

- **Outline and describe the key success factors that directly affect customer satisfaction**. The key success factors are: cost-efficiency, quality, time and innovation and continuous improvement. Keeping costs low and being cost-efficient provides an organization with a strong competitive advantage. Customers also demand high quality products and services and this has resulted in companies making quality a key competitive variable. Organizations are also seeking to increase customer satisfaction by providing a speedier response to customer requests, ensuring 100 per cent on-time delivery and reducing the time taken to bring new products to the market. To be successful companies must be innovative and develop a steady stream of new products and services and have the capability to rapidly adapt to changing customer requirements.

- **Identify and describe the functions of a cost and management accounting system**. A cost and management accounting system should generate information to meet the following requirements: (a) allocate costs between cost of goods sold and inventories for internal and external profit reporting and inventory valuation; (b) provide relevant information to help managers make better decisions; and (c) provide information for planning, control and performance measurement.

KEY TERMS AND CONCEPTS

Each chapter includes a section like this. You should make sure that you understand each of the terms listed below before you proceed to the next chapter.

Benchmarking   A mechanism for achieving continuous improvement by measuring products, services or activities against those of other best performing organizations.

Budget   A financial plan for implementing management decisions.

Continuous improvement   An ongoing search to reduce costs, eliminate waste and improve the quality and performance of activities that increase customer value or satisfaction.

Control   A managerial function that consists of the measurement, reporting and subsequent correction of performance in order to achieve the organization's objectives.

Control process   The process of setting targets or standards against which actual results are measured.

Cost accounting   Accounting concerned with cost accumulation for inventory valuation to meet the requirements of external reporting and internal profit measurement.

Cycle time   The length of time from start to completion of a product or service and is the sum of processing time, move time, wait time and inspection time.

e-Business   The use of information and communication technologies to support any business activities, including buying and selling.

e-Commerce   The use of information and communication technologies to support the purchase, sale and exchange of goods.

Employee empowerment   Providing employees with relevant information to allow them to make continuous improvements to the output of processes without the authorization by superiors.

Ethical behaviour   Behaviour that is consistent with the standards of honesty, fairness and social responsibility that have been adopted by the organization.

Financial accounting   Accounting concerned with the provision of information to parties that are external to the organization.

Intellectual capital   The intangible benefits accessible by a firm from its workforce, and more broadly, from its established relationships with groups such as customers, suppliers and competitors. It is often used interchangeably with other terms such as 'knowledge capital', 'knowledge economy' and 'intangible assets.'

Internet commerce   The buying and selling of goods and services over the Internet.

Lean manufacturing systems   Systems that seek to reduce waste in manufacturing by implementing just-in-time production systems, focusing on quality, simplifying processes and investing in advanced technologies.

Management accounting   Accounting concerned with the provision of information to people within the organization to aid decision-making and improve the efficiency and effectiveness of existing operations.

Management by exception   A situation where management attention is focused on areas where outcomes do not meet targets.

Master budget   A single unifying statement of an organization's expectations for future periods comprising budgeted profit and cash flow statements.

Non-value added activities   Activities that can be reduced or eliminated without altering the product's service potential to the customer.

Performance reports   Regular reports to management that compare actual outcomes with planned outcomes.

Product's life cycle   The period of time from initial expenditure on research and development to the withdrawal of support to customers.

Stakeholders   Various parties that have an interest in an organization. Examples include managers, shareholders and potential investors, employees, creditors and the government.

Strategies   Courses of action designed to ensure that objectives are achieved.

Total quality management (TQM)   A customer-oriented process of continuous improvement that focuses on delivering products or services of consistent high quality in a timely fashion.

ASSESSMENT MATERIAL

The review questions are short questions that enable you to assess your understanding of the main topics included in the chapter. The numbers in parentheses provide you with the page numbers to refer to if you cannot answer a specific question.

The remaining chapters also contain review problems. These are more complex and require you to relate and apply the chapter content to various business problems. Fully worked solutions to the review problems are provided in a separate section at the end of the book.

The dedicated online digital support resources for this book includes over 30 case study problems.

REVIEW QUESTIONS

1.1 Identify and describe the different users of accounting information. *(pp. 5–6)*

1.2 Describe the differences between management accounting and financial accounting. *(pp. 6–7)*

1.3 Explain each of the elements of the decision-making, planning and control process. *(pp. 7–9)*

1.4 Describe what is meant by management by exception. *(p. 9)*

1.5 Explain how the business environment that businesses face has changed over the past decades and discuss how this has had an impact on management accounting. *(pp. 10–15)*

1.6 Describe each of the key success factors that companies should concentrate on to achieve customer satisfaction. *(pp. 15–18)*

1.7 Explain why firms are beginning to concentrate on social responsibility and corporate ethics. *(pp. 13–14)*

1.8 Describe the different functions of management accounting. *(pp. 18–19)*

2
AN INTRODUCTION TO COST TERMS AND CONCEPTS

LEARNING OBJECTIVES After studying this chapter you should be able to:

● explain why it is necessary to understand the meaning of different cost terms

● define and illustrate a cost object

● explain the meaning of each of the key terms highlighted in bold coloured type

● explain why in the short-term some costs and revenues are not relevant for decision-making

● describe the three purposes for which cost information is required.

In Chapter 1 it was pointed out that accounting systems measure costs which are used for profit measurement and inventory (i.e. stock) valuation, decision-making, performance measurement and control. The term cost is a frequently used word that reflects a monetary measure of the resources sacrificed or forgone to achieve a specific objective, such as acquiring a good or service. However, the term must be defined more precisely before the 'cost' can be determined. You will find that the word cost is rarely used without a preceding adjective to specify the type of cost being considered.

To understand how accounting systems calculate costs and to communicate accounting information effectively to others requires a thorough understanding of what cost means. Unfortunately, the term has multiple meanings and different types of costs are used in different situations. Therefore, a preceding term must be added to clarify the assumptions that underlie a cost measurement. A large terminology has emerged to indicate more clearly which cost meaning is being conveyed. Examples include variable cost, fixed cost, opportunity cost and sunk cost. The aim of this chapter is to provide you with an understanding of the basic cost terms and concepts that are used in the management accounting literature.

COST OBJECTS

A **cost object** is any activity for which a separate measurement of costs is desired. In other words, if the users of accounting information want to know the cost of something, this something is called a cost object. Examples of cost objects include the cost of a product, the cost of rendering a service to a bank customer or hospital patient, the cost of operating a particular department or sales territory, or indeed anything for which one wants to measure the cost of resources used.

We shall see that the cost collection system typically accounts for costs in two broad stages:

1 It accumulates costs by classifying them into certain categories such as by type of expense (e.g. direct labour, direct materials and indirect costs) or by cost behaviour (such as fixed and variable costs).

2 It then assigns these costs to cost objects.

In this chapter we shall focus on the following cost terms and concepts:

● direct and indirect costs
● period and product costs
● cost behaviour in relation to volume of activity
● relevant and irrelevant costs
● avoidable and unavoidable costs
● sunk costs
● opportunity costs
● incremental and marginal costs.

MANUFACTURING, MERCHANDISING AND SERVICE ORGANIZATIONS

To provide a better understanding of how different cost terms are used in organizations it is appropriate to describe the major features of activities undertaken in the manufacturing, merchandising and service organizations. Manufacturing organizations purchase raw materials from suppliers and convert these materials into tangible products through the use of labour and capital inputs (e.g. plant and machinery). This process results in manufacturing organizations having the following types of inventories:

● Raw material inventories consisting of purchased raw materials in stock awaiting use in the manufacturing process.

● Work in progress inventory (also called work in process) consisting of partially complete products awaiting completion.

● Finished goods inventory consisting of fully completed products that have not yet been sold.

Merchandising companies such as supermarkets, retail departmental stores and wholesalers sell tangible products that they have previously purchased in the same basic form from suppliers. Therefore, they have only finished goods inventories. Service organizations such as accounting firms, insurance companies, advertising agencies and hospitals provide tasks or activities for customers. A major feature of service organizations is that they provide perishable services that cannot be stored for future use. Therefore, service organizations do not have finished goods inventory but some service organizations do have work in process. For example, a firm of lawyers may have clients whose work is partially complete at the end of the accounting period.

DIRECT AND INDIRECT COSTS

Costs that are assigned to cost objects can be divided into two broad categories – direct and **indirect costs**. Both categories can be further divided into direct and indirect material costs, and direct and indirect labour costs.

Direct materials

Direct material costs represent those material costs that can be specifically and exclusively identified with a particular cost object. In manufacturing organizations, where the cost object is a product, physical observation can be used to measure the quantity consumed by each individual product. In other words, direct materials become part of a physical product or are used in providing a service. For example, wood used in the manufacture of different types of furniture can be directly identified with each specific type of furniture such as chairs, tables and bookcases.

The term direct materials is normally not applicable to merchandising and service organizations. The equivalent term in a merchandising organization is the purchase cost of the items that are for resale. For example, with a departmental store where the cost object is a department (e.g. televisions and DVD players, computers, clothing and furniture departments) the purchase cost of the goods from the suppliers will be directly charged to the appropriate department that resells the goods. Some service organizations do purchase materials or parts to provide a service. For example, a garage may purchase parts for vehicle repairs. These parts can be identified with the repair of each customer's vehicle (i.e. the cost object) and thus are equivalent to direct materials.

Direct labour

Direct labour costs represent those labour costs that can be specifically and exclusively identified with a particular cost object. Physical observation can be used to measure the quantity of labour used to produce a specific product or provide a service. The direct labour cost in producing a product includes the cost of converting the raw materials into a product, such as the cost of machine operatives engaged in the production process in the manufacture of televisions. The direct labour cost used to provide a service includes the labour costs in providing a service that can be specifically identified with an individual client in a firm of accountants or the labour costs that can be identified with a specific repair in a firm that repairs computers. The direct labour costs for a departmental store are the labour costs of the staff that can be attributed specifically to a department.

Indirect costs

Indirect costs cannot be identified specifically and exclusively with a given cost object. They consist of indirect labour, materials and expenses. In a manufacturing organization *where products are the cost object*, the wages of all employees whose time cannot be identified with a specific product represent indirect labour costs. Examples include the labour cost of staff employed in the maintenance and repair of production equipment and staff employed in the stores department. The cost of materials used to repair machinery cannot be identified with a specific product and can therefore be classified as indirect material costs. Examples of indirect expenses in manufacturing, service or a departmental store where products, the provision of a service or departments are the cost objectives include lighting and heating expenses and property taxes. These costs cannot be specifically identified with a particular product, service or department.

The term **overheads** is widely used instead of indirect costs. In a manufacturing organization overhead costs are categorized as either manufacturing, administration or marketing (or selling) overheads. Manufacturing overheads include all the costs of manufacturing apart from direct labour and material costs. Administrative overheads consist of all costs associated with the general administration of the organization that cannot be assigned to either manufacturing, marketing or distribution overheads. Examples of administrative overheads include top-executive salaries, general accounting, secretarial, and research and development costs. Those costs that are necessary to market and distribute a product or service are categorized as marketing (selling) costs. These costs are also known as order-getting and order-filling costs. Examples of marketing costs include advertising, sales personnel salaries/commissions, warehousing and delivery transportation costs.

Figure 2.1 illustrates the various classifications of manufacturing and non-manufacturing costs. You will see from this figure that two further classifications of manufacturing costs are sometimes used. **Prime cost** consists of all direct manufacturing costs (i.e. it is the sum of direct material and direct labour costs). **Conversion cost** is the sum of direct labour and manufacturing overhead costs. It represents the cost of converting raw materials into finished products.

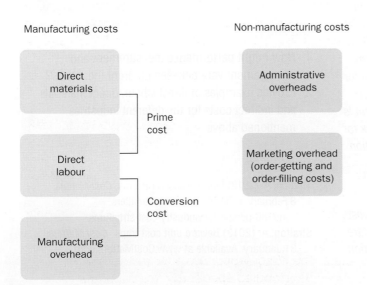

Manufacturing costs

Non-manufacturing costs

Direct materials	
Direct labour	— Prime cost
Manufacturing overhead	— Conversion cost

Administrative overheads

Marketing overhead (order-getting and order-filling costs)

FIGURE 2.1

Manufacturing and non-manufacturing costs

Distinguishing between direct and indirect costs

Sometimes, direct costs are treated as indirect because tracing costs directly to the cost object is not cost-effective. For example, the nails used to manufacture a particular desk can be identified specifically with the desk, but, because the cost is likely to be insignificant, the expense of tracing such items does not justify the possible benefits from calculating more accurate product costs.

The distinction between direct and indirect costs also depends on the cost object. A cost can be treated as direct for one cost object but indirect in respect of another. If the cost object is the cost of using different distribution channels, then the rental of warehouses and the salaries of storekeepers will be regarded as direct for each distribution channel. Also, consider a supervisor's salary in a maintenance department of a manufacturing company. If the cost object is the maintenance department, then the salary is a direct cost. However, if the cost object is the product, both the warehouse

---

REAL WORLD VIEWS 2.1

Industry cost structures

Allan Stratton is a cost management consultant with over 35 years of experience, who shares the benefit of his experience providing tools and resources via the Internet. The following information has been extracted from his website relating to one of his updates.

Some industries are labour intensive. Others are material or capital intensive. In distribution, regardless of industry, most of the costs are the acquisition of products purchased from manufacturers. The same is true for retail operations like a grocery store, where 70% or more of expenditures go towards the food and merchandise displayed in the stores. In a typical manufacturing organization, half the costs are raw materials or component parts purchased from suppliers. In the capital intensive semiconductor industry half the cost structure is depreciation of the capital investment. Once the investment is made, the depreciation cost is fixed and sunk for the foreseeable future. In a service organization, like a consulting firm or software developer, as much as 75% of the costs can be people and people related (offices, telephones and computers). For a company like Nike that invests heavily in its brand, the largest expenditures are related to marketing, advertising and promotion.

He concludes that performance management and measurement should differ between industries and reflect the cost structures of those businesses.

Questions

1 How might performance measurement and management vary between different industries?
2 Provide examples of direct labour, direct materials and indirect costs for the different industries mentioned above.

References

Stratton, A. (2012) Industry cost structures, *Cost Matters*, 8 February. Available at www.costmatters. com/180-perspective/industry-cost-structures/
Stratton, A. (2013) Beware unit cost traps, *Cost Matters*, 31 January. Available at www.CostMatters.com

rental and the salaries of the storekeepers and the supervisor will be an indirect cost because these costs cannot be specifically identified with the product.

Assigning direct and indirect costs to cost objects

Direct costs can be traced easily and accurately to a cost object. For example, where products are the cost object, direct materials and labour used can be physically identified with the different products that an organization produces. Therefore, it is a simple process to establish an information technology system that records the quantity and cost of direct labour and material resources used to produce specific products.

In contrast, indirect costs cannot be traced to cost objects. Instead, an estimate must be made of the resources consumed by cost objects using **cost allocations**. A cost allocation is the process of assigning costs when a direct measure does not exist for the quantity of resources consumed by a particular cost object. Cost allocations involve the use of surrogate rather than direct measures. For example, consider an activity such as receiving incoming materials. Assuming that the cost of receiving materials is strongly influenced by the number of receipts then costs can be allocated to products (i.e. the cost object) based on the number of material receipts each product requires. If 20 per cent of the total number of receipts for a period were required for a particular product then 20 per cent of the total costs of receiving incoming materials would be allocated to that product. Assuming that the product was discontinued, and not replaced, we would expect action to be taken to reduce the resources required for receiving materials by 20 per cent.

In this example the surrogate allocation measure is assumed to be a significant determinant of the cost of receiving incoming materials. The process of assigning indirect costs (overheads) and the accuracy of such assignments will be discussed in Chapters 7 and 8 but at this stage you should note that only direct costs can be accurately assigned to cost objects. Therefore, the more direct costs that can be traced to a cost object, the more accurate the cost assignment is.

PERIOD AND PRODUCT COSTS

For profit measurement and inventory/stock valuation (i.e. the valuation of completed unsold products and partly completed products or services) purposes it is necessary to classify costs as either product costs or period costs. **Product costs** are those costs that are identified with goods purchased or produced for resale. In a manufacturing organization they are costs that are attached to the product and that are included in the inventory valuation for finished goods, or for partly completed goods (work in progress), until they are sold; they are then recorded as expenses and matched against sales for calculating profit. **Period costs** are those costs that are not specifically related to manufacturing or purchasing a product or providing a service that generates revenues. Therefore they are not included in the inventory valuation and as a result are treated as expenses in the period in which they are incurred. *Hence no attempt is made to attach period costs to products for inventory valuation purposes.*

In a manufacturing organization all manufacturing costs are regarded as product costs and non-manufacturing costs are regarded as period costs. The treatment of period and product costs for a manufacturing organization is illustrated in Figure 2.2. You will see that both product and period costs are eventually classified as expenses. The major difference is the point in time at which they are so classified.

FIGURE 2.2

Treatment of period and product costs

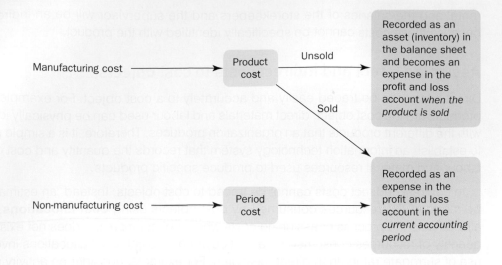

There are two reasons why non-manufacturing costs are treated as period costs and not included in the inventory valuation. First, inventories are assets (unsold production) and assets represent resources that have been acquired that are expected to contribute to future revenue. Manufacturing costs incurred in making a product can be expected to generate future revenues to cover the cost of production. There is no guarantee, however, that non-manufacturing costs will generate future revenue, because they do not represent value added to any specific product. Therefore, they are not included in the inventory valuation. Second, many non-manufacturing costs (e.g. distribution costs) are not incurred when the product is being stored. Hence it is inappropriate to include such costs within the inventory valuation.

You should now refer to Example 2.1, which provides an illustration of the accounting treatment of period and product costs for income (profit) measurement purposes for a manufacturing organization. Do merchandising and service organizations need to distinguish between product and period costs? The answer is yes. Companies operating in the merchandising sector purchase goods for resale without changing their basic form. The cost of the goods purchased is regarded as a product cost and all other costs, such as administration and selling and distribution expenses, are considered to be period costs. Therefore, the cost of goods sold for a merchandising company would consist of the beginning merchandise inventory, plus the purchase of merchandise during the period, less the closing merchandise inventory. Note that the opening and closing inventories would be valued at the purchase cost of acquiring the inventories. Service organizations do not have beginning and closing finished goods inventories since it is not possible to store services but they may have work in progress (WIP). The cost of direct materials (if applicable) plus direct labour and overheads that are assigned to cost objects (typically clients/customers) represent the product costs. All other costs represent the period costs. The beginning WIP, plus the cost assigned to the clients during the period, less the closing WIP represents the cost of the services sold for the period. This is equivalent to the cost of goods sold in a manufacturing organization.

EXAMPLE 2.1

The costs for Lee Manufacturing Company for period 1 are as follows:

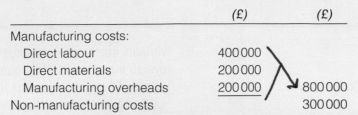

	(£)	(£)
Manufacturing costs:		
Direct labour	400 000	
Direct materials	200 000	
Manufacturing overheads	200 000	800 000
Non-manufacturing costs		300 000

The accounting records indicate that 70 per cent of the above costs were assigned to the cost of the goods that were sold during the period, 10 per cent to WIP and 20 per cent to finished goods inventory. Sales were £910 000 for the period. The opening and closing inventory of raw materials were identical and there were no opening WIP and finished goods inventories at the start of the period. The profit statement for period 1 will be as follows:

	(£)	(£)
Sales (50 000)		910 000
Manufacturing costs (product costs):		
Direct labour	400 000	
Direct materials	200 000	
Manufacturing overheads	200 000	
	800 000	
Less closing inventory: WIP (10%)	80 000	
Finished good inventory (20%)	160 000	240 000
Cost of goods sold (70%)		560 000
Gross profit		350 000
Less non-manufacturing costs (period costs)		300 000
Net profit		50 000

During the period 70 per cent of the production was sold and the remaining 30 per cent was produced for WIP and finished goods inventories. Seventy per cent of the product costs are therefore identified as an expense for the period and the remainder are included in the closing inventory valuations. If we assume that the closing inventory is sold in the next accounting period, the remaining 30 per cent of the product costs will become expenses in the next accounting period. However, all the period costs became an expense in this accounting period, because this is the period to which they relate. Note that only product costs form the basis for the calculation of cost of goods sold, and that period costs do not form part of this calculation.

COST BEHAVIOUR

A knowledge of how costs and revenues will vary with different levels of activity (or volume) is essential for decision-making. Managers might require information in order to answer questions such as these:

1 How will costs and revenues change if activity is increased (or decreased) by 15 per cent?

2 What will be the impact on profits if we reduce selling price by 10 per cent based on the estimate that this will increase sales volume by 15 per cent?

3   How do the cost and revenues change for a university if the number of students is increased by 5 per cent?

4   How do costs and revenues of a hotel change if a room and meals are provided for two guests for a 3-day stay?

5   How many tickets must be sold for a concert in order to break even?

REAL WORLD VIEWS 2.2

Cost structures in the airline sector

Low-cost carriers such as easyJet and Ryanair offer flights to customers at low prices. Despite this both continued to make good profits. For the year to September 2017, easyJet posted pre-tax profits of £408m and Ryanair €1470m for the year to March 2017. More traditional carriers like British Airways and Air France/KLM, who charge higher fares, reported a profit of £1566m (2016 calendar year) and a loss of €517m ((2017 calendar year) respectively. Why do low-cost carriers continue to do well even though they offer much lower fares? One reason is their cost structures.

You might be thinking, surely there is a cost of providing a seat to a passenger, so how can low-cost carriers sell seats so cheaply? To answer this, we need to consider the nature of their costs. Most costs are fixed in nature. First, the aircraft cost (of about US$75m–$90m for a Boeing 737) is fixed. Second, the salaries of the pilot, first officer and cabin crew are also fixed. Third, maintenance costs would also be considered as a fixed cost. And what about the fuel cost? This is also treated as a fixed cost, since it is incurred once the aircraft flies. Thus if one additional passenger flies with a low-cost carrier, the variable cost associated with this passenger is zero, and hence tickets can be sold cheaply.

Traditional carriers like Air France-KLM and British Airways have similar costs to the low-cost carriers – fuel, fleet purchase, maintenance and salaries, etc. – and these too are likely to be fixed. The difference is that these costs are probably at a higher level than low-cost carriers. For example, low-cost carriers typically use one model of aircraft, which reduces maintenance costs and adds buying leverage. Traditional airlines may have some

variable costs, e.g. passenger meals. Thus, with overall higher costs, it is more difficult to reduce prices. Of course, even for low-cost carriers, if sales volume is not attainable they cannot match their costs. The demise of Air Berlin in 2016 is a good example. Its sales growth was curtailed by the ongoing postponement of the opening of a new larger airport at Berlin.

Questions

1   Do you agree that the variable cost associated with a passenger can be zero? Can this be said for both low-cost and traditional carriers?

2   What options do more traditional carriers have to improve their fixed cost base?

References

Air France/KLM 2017 Annual Report. Available at www.airfranceklm.com/sites/default/files/124_afklm_consolidated_financial_statement_2017.pdf

British Airway 2016 Annual Report. Available at phx.corporate-ir.net/External.File?item=UGFyZW50SUQ9NjYzMTY0fENoaWWxkSUQ9MzcwNDUzfFR5cGU9MQ==&t=1

Easyjet 2017 Annual Report. Available at corporate.easyjet.com/~/media/Files/E/Easyjet/pdf/investors/results-centre/2017/2017-annualreport-and-accounts-v1.pdf

Ryanair 2017 Annual Report. Available at investor.ryanair.com/wp-content/uploads/2017/07/Ryanair-FY2017-Annual-Report.pdf

Activity or volume may be measured in terms of units of production or sales, hours worked, miles travelled, patients seen, students enrolled or any other appropriate measure of the activity of an organization. The terms 'variable', 'fixed', 'semi-variable' and 'semi-fixed' have traditionally been used in the management accounting literature to describe how a cost reacts to changes in activity. **Variable costs** vary in direct proportion to the volume of activity; that is, doubling the level of activity will double the total variable cost. Consequently, *total* variable costs are linear and *unit* variable cost is constant. Examples of variable costs in a manufacturing organization include direct materials, energy to operate the machines and sales commissions. Examples of variable costs in a merchandising company, such as a supermarket, include the purchase costs of all items that are sold. In a hospital variable costs include the costs of drugs and meals, which may be assumed to fluctuate with the number of patient days.

Consider the example of a bicycle manufacturer that purchases component parts. Assume that the cost of purchasing two wheels for a particular bicycle is £10 per bicycle. Figure 2.3(a) illustrates the concept of variable costs in graphic form. You can see that as the number of units of output of bicycles increases or decreases, the *total* variable cost of wheels increases and decreases proportionately. Look at Figure 2.3(b). This diagram shows that variable cost per *unit* of output is constant even though total variable cost increases/decreases proportionately with changes in activity.

Fixed costs remain constant over wide ranges of activity for a specified time period. They are not affected by changes in activity. Examples of fixed costs include depreciation

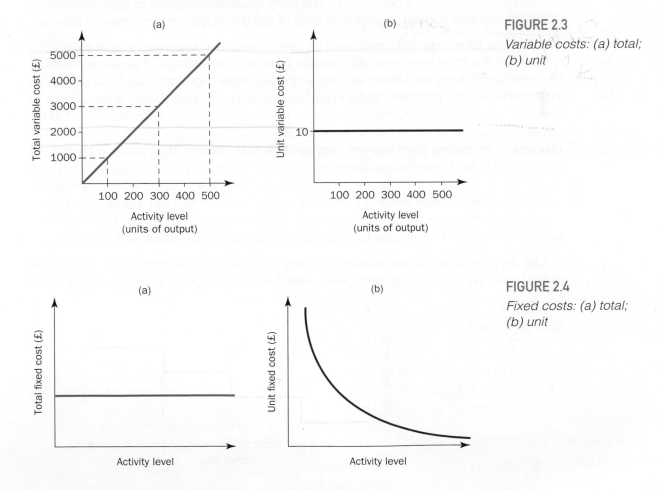

FIGURE 2.3

Variable costs: (a) total; (b) unit

FIGURE 2.4

Fixed costs: (a) total; (b) unit

of equipment, property taxes, insurance costs, supervisory salaries and leasing charges for cars used by the sales force. Figure 2.4 illustrates how *total* fixed costs and fixed cost per unit of activity react with changes in activity.

You will see from this diagram that *total* fixed costs are constant for all units of activity whereas *unit* fixed costs decrease proportionally with the level of activity. For example, if the total of the fixed costs is £50 000 for a month the fixed costs per *unit* of activity will be as follows:

Units produced	Fixed cost per unit (£)
1	50 000
10	5 000
100	500
1 000	50

Because unit fixed costs are not constant per unit they must be interpreted with caution. For decision-making, it is better to work with total fixed costs rather than unit costs.

The distinction between fixed and variable costs must be made relative to the time period under consideration. Over a sufficiently long time period of several years, virtually all costs are variable. During such a long period of time, contraction in demand will be accompanied by reductions in virtually all categories of costs. For example, senior managers can be released, machinery need not be replaced, and even buildings and land can be sold. Similarly, large expansions in activity will eventually cause all categories of costs to increase. Within shorter time periods, costs will be fixed or variable in relation to changes in activity.

Spending on some fixed costs, such as direct labour and supervisory salaries, can be adjusted in the short term to reflect changes in activity. For example, if production activity declines significantly then direct workers and supervisors might continue to be employed in the hope that the decline in demand will be temporary; however, if there is no upsurge in demand then staff might eventually be made redundant. If, on the other hand, production capacity expands to some critical level, additional workers might be employed, but the process of recruiting such workers may take several months. Thus within a short-term period, such as 1 year, labour costs can change in response to changes in demand in a manner similar to that depicted in Figure 2.5. Costs that behave in this manner are described as **semi-fixed costs** or **step-fixed costs**. The distinguishing feature of step fixed costs is that within a given time period they are fixed within specified activity levels, but they eventually increase or decrease by a constant amount at various critical activity levels.

Our discussion so far has assumed a 1-year time period. If we consider a shorter time period such as 1 month the step-fixed costs described in the previous paragraph will

FIGURE 2.5

Step-fixed costs

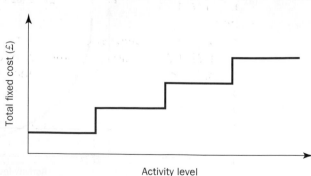

Activity level

not occur because it takes several months to respond to changes in activity and alter spending levels. Over very short-term periods, such as 1 month, spending on direct labour and supervisory salaries will be fixed in relation to changes in activity.

Even though fixed costs are normally assumed to remain unchanged in response to changes in the level of activity in the short term, they may change in response to other factors. For example, if price levels increase then some fixed costs such as management salaries will increase.

Before concluding our discussion of cost behaviour in relation to volume of activity, we must consider **semi-variable costs** (also known as **mixed costs**). These include both a fixed and a variable component. If you refer to your telephone account for your landline you will probably find that it consists of a fixed component (the line rental) plus a variable component (the number of telephone calls made multiplied by the cost per call). Similarly, the office photocopying costs may consist of a fixed rental charge for the photocopiers plus a variable cost (the cost of the paper multiplied by the number of photocopies). The cost of maintenance of equipment in a hospital may also be a semi-variable cost consisting of planned maintenance that is undertaken whatever the level of activity, and a variable element that is directly related to the level of usage of the equipment. We shall discuss how mixed costs can be separated into their fixed and variable elements in the next chapter.

RELEVANT AND IRRELEVANT COSTS AND REVENUES

For decision-making, costs and revenues can be classified according to whether they are relevant to a particular decision. **Relevant costs and revenues** are those *future* costs and revenues that will be changed by a decision, whereas **irrelevant costs and revenues** are those that will not be affected by the decision. For example, if you are faced with a choice of making a journey using your own car or by public transport, the car tax and insurance costs are irrelevant, since they will remain the same whatever alternative is chosen. However, fuel costs for the car will differ depending on which alternative is chosen, being zero if you use public transport but necessitating payment for extra fuel if you use the car. Therefore, fuel costs will be relevant for decision-making.

Let us now consider a further illustration of the classification of relevant and irrelevant costs. Assume that in the past a company purchased raw materials for £1000 per unit and then found that it was impossible to use them in future production or to sell them in their current state. A former customer is prepared to purchase a product that will require the use of all these materials, but is not prepared to pay more than £2500 for the product. The additional costs of converting these materials into the required product are £2000. Should the company accept the order for £2500? It appears that the cost of the order is £3000, consisting of £1000 material cost and £2000 conversion cost, but this is incorrect because the £1000 material cost will remain the same whether the order is accepted or rejected. The material cost is therefore irrelevant for the decision. If the order is accepted the conversion costs will change by £2000, and this conversion cost is a relevant cost. If we compare the revenue of £2500 with the relevant cost for the order of £2000, it means that the order should be accepted, assuming of course that no higher-priced orders can be obtained elsewhere. The following calculation shows that this is the correct decision:

	Do not accept order (£)	Accept order (£)
Materials	1 000	1 000
Conversion costs	—	2 000
Revenue	—	(2 500)
Net costs	1 000	500

The net costs of the company are £500 less, or alternatively the company is £500 better off as a result of accepting the order. This agrees with the £500 advantage that was suggested by the relevant cost method.

In this illustration the sales revenue was relevant to the decision because future revenue changed depending on which alternative was selected. However, in some circumstances sales revenue may also be irrelevant for decision-making. Consider a situation where a company can meet its sales demand by purchasing either machine A or machine B. The output of both machines is identical, but the operating costs and purchase costs of the machines are different. In this situation the sales revenue will remain unchanged irrespective of which machine is purchased (assuming of course that the quality of output is identical for both machines). Consequently, sales revenue is irrelevant for this decision; the relevant items are the operating costs and the cost of the machines. We have now established an important principle regarding the classification of cost and revenues for decision-making; namely, that in the short term not all costs and revenues are relevant for decision-making.

AVOIDABLE AND UNAVOIDABLE COSTS

Sometimes the terms **avoidable costs** and **unavoidable costs** are used instead of relevant and irrelevant cost. Avoidable costs are those costs that may be saved by not adopting a given alternative, whereas unavoidable costs cannot be saved. Only avoidable costs are relevant for decision-making purposes. In the example that we used to illustrate relevant and irrelevant costs the material costs of £1000 are unavoidable and irrelevant, but the conversion costs of £2000 are avoidable and hence relevant. The decision rule is to accept those alternatives that generate revenues in excess of the avoidable costs.

SUNK COSTS

These costs are the costs of resources already acquired where the total will be unaffected by the choice between various alternatives. They are costs that have been created by a decision made in the past and that cannot be changed by any decision that will be made now or in the future. The expenditure of £1000 on materials that were no longer required, referred to in the preceding section, is an example of a **sunk cost**. Similarly, the written down values of assets previously purchased are sunk costs. For example, if equipment was purchased 4 years ago for £100 000 with an expected life of 5 years and nil scrap value then the written down value will be £20 000 if straight line depreciation is used. This written down value will have to be written off, no matter what possible alternative future action might be chosen. If the equipment was scrapped, the £20 000 would be written off; if the equipment was used for productive purposes, the £20 000 would still have to be

REAL WORLD VIEWS 2.3

We must stop falling into the 'sunk costs' fallacy

An article written by Ben Chu published in *The Independent* newspaper in 2016 demonstrated why the classical economic view of humans as rational decision-makers is often very wide of the mark. When individuals evaluate a financial decision, when a business leader decides whether or not to continue with an investment project, when a politician decides on a policy, they are all supposed to weigh up the costs and benefits dispassionately. And those decisions are supposed to be made on the basis of future potential costs and benefits, not costs from the past. Anything spent to get to that point of decision should be irrelevant. They are sunk costs which cannot make a project a better or worse proposition.

Nevertheless, we find it very hard to avoid looking back. Business leaders will often plough on with dubious investments because they are so emotionally invested in the project. Fund managers have a tendency to hold on to bad company investments that they spent a great deal of time and effort researching. Football managers will play the hugely expensive striker they bought, even when the player is obviously misfiring.

Managers are often unable to make the decisions to scrap projects that are already up and running in order to cut their losses. For example, the sunk costs fallacy draws attention to how Sadiq Khan, the Mayor of London, originally opposed the construction of a new £175m Garden Bridge across the Thames but later changed his mind because 'the money [spent on the design] is spent. Cancelling would mean we lose that money and have nothing.'

This kind of behaviour is hard-wired into our psyches but nevertheless we should recognize when the sunk costs fallacy is leading us seriously astray.

Questions

1 What are the relevant costs and benefits relating to the Garden Bridge?
2 Why might managers be reluctant to abandon loss-making projects?

Reference

Chu, B. (2016) *We must stop falling into the 'sunk costs' fallacy*, Independent Print Ltd, London (UK). www.search.proquest.com/docview/178145 8259?accountid=11526

written off. This cost cannot be changed by any future decision and is therefore classified as a sunk cost.

Sunk costs are irrelevant for decision-making, but not all irrelevant costs are sunk costs. For example, a comparison of two alternative production methods may result in identical direct material expenditure for both alternatives, so the direct material cost is irrelevant because it will remain the same whichever alternative is chosen, but the material cost is not a sunk cost since it will be incurred in the future.

OPPORTUNITY COSTS

An **opportunity cost** is a cost that measures the opportunity that is lost or sacrificed when the choice of one course of action requires that an alternative course of action is given up. Consider the situation where a student is contemplating taking a gap year overseas after completing his or her studies. Assume that the student has an offer of a job upon completion of his or her studies. The lost salary is an opportunity cost of choosing the gap year that must be taken into account when considering the financial implications of the decision. For a further illustration of an opportunity cost you should now look at Example 2.2.

EXAMPLE 2.2

A company has an opportunity to obtain a contract for the production of a special component. This component will require 100 hours of processing on machine X. Machine X is working at full capacity on the production of product A, and the only way in which the contract can be fulfilled is by reducing the output of product A. This will result in a lost profit contribution of £200. The contract will also result in *additional* variable costs of £1000. If the company takes on the contract, it will sacrifice a profit contribution of £200 from the lost output of product A. This represents an opportunity cost, and should be included as part of the cost when negotiating for the contract. The contract price should at least cover the additional costs of £1000 plus the £200 opportunity cost to ensure that the company will be better off in the short term by accepting the contract.

Opportunity costs cannot normally be recorded in the accounting system since they do not involve cash outlays. They also only apply to the use of scarce resources. Where resources are not scarce, no sacrifice exists from using these resources. In Example 2.2, if machine X was operating at 80 per cent of its potential capacity and the decision to accept the contract would not have resulted in reduced production of product A there would have been no loss of revenue, and the opportunity cost would be zero.

REAL WORLD VIEWS 2.4

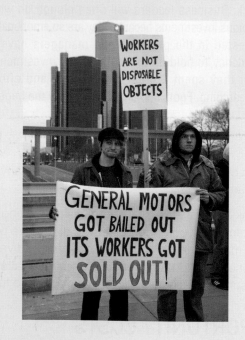

Opportunity costs and auto bail-outs

According to Andrew Coyne, the author of an article published in the National Post (Canada) the $14 billion in public funds handed out to General Motors and Chrysler by the governments of Canada and Ontario was one of the largest corporate bail-outs in the history of the country. The author claims that the question of opportunity costs (what else might have been done with the same money, what other investments might have been made or jobs created with the $14 billion governments taken out of the capital markets to lend to GM and Chrysler) never came up and that it never does. Instead, the focus tends to be only on the benefits, and that opportunity costs are neither counted nor understood.

Questions

1 Why might opportunity costs not be considered when making decisions?
2 Provide examples of opportunity costs that you might incur.

Reference

Andrew Coyne: On opportunity costs, $14B auto bail-outs and assuming a baseline level of competence. Available at nationalpost.com/opinion/andrew-coyne-on-opportunity-costs-14b-auto-bailouts-and-assuming-a-baseline-level-of-competence

Opportunity costs are of vital importance for decision-making. If no alternative use of resources exists then the opportunity cost is zero, but if resources have an alternative use, and are scarce, then an opportunity cost does exist.

INCREMENTAL AND MARGINAL COSTS

Incremental costs, which are also called **differential costs**, are the difference between costs of each alternative action that is being considered. For example, a university is evaluating the financial implications of increasing student numbers by 20 per cent. The two alternatives are:

1 No increase in the number of students.
2 A 20 per cent increase in the number of students.

If alternative 2 is chosen, the university will have to increase its budget for full-time lecturers on permanent contracts by £150 000 per annum. It will also need to employ additional part-time lecturers at a cost of £15 000 (300 hours at £50 per hour) per annum. The incremental/differential cost between the two alternatives is £165 000.

Incremental costs can include both fixed and variable costs. In the example above, the full-time staff represent a fixed cost and the part-time staff represent a variable cost. You will also meet the concept of incremental, or differential, revenues. These are the difference in revenues resulting from each alternative.

REAL WORLD VIEWS 2.5

Marginal costs of downloadable products

A distinguishing feature of today's digital technology is that it is characterized by zero (or near-zero) marginal costs. Once you've made the investment needed to create a digital good, it costs next to nothing to roll out and distribute millions of copies. Software, e-books and music are increasingly available as downloadable products. Each software, book or music download has no marginal cost. As download purchases are typically fully automated, there are no labour costs. Also, as the software development, publishing or music production costs are all in the past (i.e. sunk costs), there are no material or component type costs. There are, of course, fixed costs incurred with running servers and other components of the technology behind downloadable software and other media. Compare this with a purchase of an item of clothing from a leading high street retail outlet such as Zara. The purchase in this case is processed by a member of staff at the store. Going back along the supply chain, there may be logistical or delivery costs and, of course, the labour and material cost of the item of clothing itself.

Questions

1 Do you agree the marginal cost of downloaded software or music is nil?

2 What marginal costs, if any, might be incurred by the provider of the servers where software/music is downloaded from?

References

Prodham, B. 'The marginal cost of software', Enterprise Irregulars Blog, available at www.enterpriseirregulars.com/31274/the-marginal-cost-of-software Naughton, J. (2015), 'How Amazon took control of the cloud', The Observer, 4 November 2015 Guardian News & Media Limited, London (UK). search.proquest.com /docview/1729584646?accountid=11526

Ekeekwe, N (2017), Mechanics of start-up product pricing. Available at www.tekedia.com/mechanics-of-startup-product-pricing/

If you have studied economics you will have noticed that incremental costs and revenues are similar in principle to the economist's concept of **marginal cost** and **marginal revenue**. The main difference is that marginal cost/revenue represents the additional cost/revenue of one extra unit of output whereas incremental cost/revenue represents the additional cost/revenue resulting from a group of additional units of output. Because decisions normally entail identifying the change in costs and revenues arising from comparing two alternative courses of action, and where this involves a change in activity, it is likely that this will involve multiple, rather than single units of activity.

THE COST AND MANAGEMENT ACCOUNTING INFORMATION SYSTEM

In the previous chapter we noted that a cost and management accounting information system should generate information to meet the following requirements:

1 to allocate costs between cost of goods sold and inventories for internal and external profit measurement and inventory valuation

2 to provide relevant information to help managers make better decisions

3 to provide information for planning, control and performance measurement.

Modern information technology uses bar-coding or other electronic tags to gather cost information at source that is appropriately coded and classified to establish a database that enables data to be stored in a coherent way. Database software is now available from companies such as Oracle, Microsoft and IBM so that relevant cost information can be extracted in a different way to meet each of the above requirements according to the specific needs of the different users of cost information. A suitable coding system enables costs to be accumulated by the required cost objects (such as products or services, departments, responsibility centres, distribution channels, etc.) and also to be classified by appropriate categories of expenses (e.g. direct materials, direct labour and overheads) and also by cost behaviour (i.e. fixed and variable costs). In practice, direct materials will be accumulated by each individual type of material, direct labour by different grades of labour and overhead costs by different categories of indirect expenses (e.g. rent, depreciation, supervision, etc.).

For *inventory valuation* in a manufacturing organization, the costs of all partly completed products (i.e. WIP) and unsold finished products can be extracted from the database to ascertain the total cost assigned to inventories. The cost of goods sold that is deducted from sales revenues to compute the profit for the period can also be extracted by summing the manufacturing costs of all those products that have been sold during the period. We shall consider this process in more detail in Chapter 7.

Future costs, rather than past costs, are required for *decision-making*. Therefore costs extracted from the database should be adjusted for anticipated price changes. Where a company sells many products or services their profitability should be monitored at regular intervals so that potentially unprofitable products can be highlighted for a more detailed study of their future viability. This information is extracted from the database with costs reported by categories of expenses and divided into their fixed and variable elements. In Chapter 5 we shall focus in more detail on product/segmented profitability analysis.

For *cost control and performance measurement*, costs and revenues must be traced to the individuals who are responsible for incurring them. This system is known as responsibility accounting. **Responsibility accounting** involves the creation of responsibility centres. A **responsibility centre** is an organization unit or part of a business for whose performance a manager is held accountable. At this stage it may be easier to consider responsibility centres as being equivalent to separate departments within an organization. Responsibility accounting enables accountability for financial results and outcomes to be allocated to individuals (typically heads of departments) throughout the organization. Performance reports are produced at regular intervals for each responsibility centre. The reports are generated by extracting from the database costs analysed by responsibility centres and cost category, divided into controllable costs that can be influenced by the manager of the responsibility centre and those uncontrollable costs that cannot be influenced by the manager. Actual costs for each cost item listed on the performance report should be compared with budgeted costs so that those costs that do not conform to plan can be pinpointed and investigated. We shall examine responsibility accounting in more detail in Chapter 10.

SUMMARY

The following items relate to the learning objectives listed at the beginning of the chapter.

- **Explain why it is necessary to understand the meaning of different cost terms**. The term 'cost' has multiple meanings and different types of costs are used in different situations. Therefore, a preceding term must be added to clarify the assumptions that underlie a measurement. A knowledge of cost and management accounting depends on a clear understanding of the terminology it uses.

- **Define and illustrate a cost object**. A cost object is any activity for which a separate measurement of cost is required. In other words managers often want to know the cost of something and the 'thing' that they want to know the cost of is a cost object. Examples of cost objects include the cost of a new product, the cost of operating a sales outlet and the cost of operating a specific machine.

- **Explain the meaning of each of the key terms highlighted in bold coloured type**. You should check your understanding of each of the terms or concepts highlighted in bold coloured type by referring to the Key Terms and Concepts section.

- **Explain why in the short term some costs and revenues are not relevant for decision-making**. In the short term some costs and revenues may remain unchanged for all alternatives under consideration. For example, if you wish to determine the costs of driving to work in your own car or using public transport, the cost of the road fund licence and insurance will remain the same for both alternatives, assuming that you intend to keep your car for leisure purposes. Therefore the costs of these items are not relevant for assisting you in your decision to travel to work by public transport or using your own car. Costs that remain unchanged for all alternatives under consideration are not relevant for decision-making.

● **Describe the three purposes for which cost information is required.** A cost and management accounting system should generate information to meet the following requirements:

(a) to allocate costs between cost of goods sold and inventories for internal and external profit reporting and inventory valuation

(b) to provide relevant information to help managers make better decisions

(c) to provide information for planning, control and performance measurement.

A database should be maintained with costs appropriately coded or classified, so that relevant information can be extracted for meeting each of the above requirements.

KEY TERMS AND CONCEPTS

Avoidable costs Costs that may be saved by not adopting a given alternative.

Conversion cost The sum of direct labour and manufacturing overhead costs; it is the cost of converting raw materials in to finished products.

Cost allocations The process of assigning costs to cost objects where a direct measure of the resources consumed by these cost objects does not exist.

Cost object Any activity for which a separate measurement of costs is desired.

Differential costs The difference between the costs of each alternative action under consideration, also known as incremental costs.

Direct labour costs Labour costs that can be specifically and exclusively identified with a particular cost object.

Direct material costs Material costs that can be specifically and exclusively identified with a particular cost object.

Fixed costs Costs that remain constant for a specified time period and which are not affected by the volume of activity.

Incremental costs The difference between the costs of each alternative action under consideration, also known as differential costs.

Indirect costs Costs that cannot be identified specifically and exclusively with a given cost object, also known as overheads.

Irrelevant costs and revenues Future costs and revenues that will not be affected by a decision.

Marginal cost The additional cost of one extra unit of output.

Marginal revenue The additional revenue from one extra unit of output.

Mixed costs Costs that contain both a fixed and a variable component, also known as semi-variable costs.

Opportunity costs Costs that measure the opportunity that is sacrificed when the choice of one course of action requires that an alternative is given up.

Overheads Costs that cannot be identified specifically and exclusively with a given cost object, also known as indirect costs.

Period costs Costs that are not included in the inventory valuation of goods and which are treated as expenses for the period in which they are incurred.

Prime cost The sum of all direct manufacturing costs.

Product costs Costs that are identified with goods purchased or produced for resale and which are attached to products and included in the inventory valuation of goods.

Relevant costs and revenues Future costs and revenues that will be changed by a decision.

Responsibility accounting   Accounting that involves tracing costs and revenues to responsibility centres.

Responsibility centres   Units or departments within an organization for whose performance a manager is held responsible.

Semi-fixed costs   Costs that remain fixed within specified activity levels for a given amount of time but which eventually increase or decrease by a constant amount at critical activity levels; also known as step-fixed costs.

Semi-variable costs   Costs that contain both a fixed and a variable component, also known as mixed costs.

Step-fixed costs   Costs that remain fixed within specified activity levels for a given amount of time but which eventually increase or decrease by a constant amount at critical activity levels; also known as semi-fixed costs.

Sunk costs   Costs that have been incurred by a decision made in the past and that cannot be changed by any decision that will be made in the future.

Unavoidable costs   Costs that cannot be saved, whether or not an alternative is adopted.

Variable costs   Costs that vary in direct proportion to the volume of activity.

ASSESSMENT MATERIAL

The review questions are short questions that enable you to assess your understanding of the main topics included in the chapter. The page numbers in parentheses provide you with the page numbers to refer to if you cannot answer a specific question.

The review problems are more complex and require you to relate and apply the content to various business problems. Solutions to review problems are provided in a separate section at the end of the book. Additional review problems can be accessed by lecturers and students on the dedicated online support resources for this book. Solutions to these review problems are provided for lecturers in the *Instructor's Manual* accompanying this book that can be downloaded from the dedicated online instructor's resources (see Preface for details).

The dedicated online digital support resources for this book also includes over 30 case study problems.

REVIEW QUESTIONS

2.1 Define the meaning of the term 'cost object' and provide three examples of cost objects. *(p. 25)*

2.2 Distinguish between a direct and indirect cost. *(pp. 26–29)*

2.3 Describe how a given direct cost item can be both a direct and indirect cost. *(pp. 28–29)*

2.4 Provide examples of each of the following: (a) direct labour, (b) indirect labour, (c) direct materials, (d) indirect materials and (e) indirect expenses. *(pp. 26–27)*

2.5 Explain the meaning of the terms: (a) prime cost, (b) overheads and (c) cost allocations. *(pp. 27–29)*

2.6 Distinguish between product costs and period costs. *(pp. 29–31)*

2.7 Provide examples of decisions that require knowledge of how costs and revenues vary with different levels of activity. *(pp. 31–32)*

2.8 Explain the meaning of each of the following terms: (a) variable costs, (b) fixed costs, (c) semi-fixed costs and (d) semi-variable costs. Provide examples of costs for each of the four categories. *(pp. 33–35)*

2.9 Distinguish between relevant (avoidable) and irrelevant (unavoidable) costs and provide examples of each type of cost. *(pp. 35–36)*

2.10 Explain the meaning of the term 'sunk cost'. *(pp. 36–37)*

2.11 Distinguish between incremental and marginal costs. *(pp. 39–40)*

2.12 What is an opportunity cost? Give some examples. *(pp. 37–38)*

2.13 Explain responsibility accounting. *(p. 41)*

REVIEW PROBLEMS

2.14 Classify each of the following as being usually fixed (F), variable (V), semi-fixed (SF) or semi-variable (SV):

(a) direct labour
(b) depreciation of machinery
(c) factory rental
(d) supplies and other indirect materials
(e) advertising
(f) maintenance of machinery
(g) factory manager's salary
(h) supervisory personnel
(i) royalty payments.

2.15 Which of the following costs are likely to be controllable by the head of the production department?

(a) price paid for materials
(b) charge for floor space
(c) raw materials used
(d) electricity used for machinery
(e) machinery depreciation
(f) direct labour
(g) insurance on machinery
(h) share of cost of Human Resources (HR) department.

2.16 A direct cost is a cost that:

(a) is incurred as a direct consequence of a decision
(b) can be economically identified with the item being costed
(c) cannot be economically identified with the item being costed
(d) is immediately controllable
(e) is the responsibility of the board of directors.

2.17 Which of the following would be classed as indirect labour?

(a) assembly workers in a company manufacturing televisions
(b) a stores assistant in a factory store
(c) plasterers in a construction company
(d) an audit clerk in a firm of auditors.

2.18 Which one of the following costs would not be classified as a production overhead cost in a food processing company?

(a) the cost of renting the factory building
(b) the salary of the factory manager
(c) the depreciation of equipment located in the materials store
(d) the cost of ingredients.

2.19 Fixed costs are conventionally deemed to be:

(a) constant per unit of output
(b) constant in total when production volume changes
(c) outside the control of management
(d) those unaffected by inflation.

2.20 A manufacturing company has four types of cost (identified as T1, T2, T3 and T4). The total cost for each type at two different production levels is:

Cost type	Total cost for 125 units £	Total cost for 180 units £
T1	1 000	1 250
T2	1 750	2 520
T3	2 475	2 826
T4	3 225	4 644

Calculate the costs per unit. Which cost types would be classified as being semi-variable?

(a) T1
(b) T2
(c) T3
(d) T4

2.21 Data

	(£)
Cost of motor car	5 500
Trade-in price after 2 years or 60 000 miles is expected to be	1 500
Maintenance – 6-monthly service costing	60
Spares/replacement parts, per 1000 miles	20
Vehicle licence, per annum	80
Insurance, per annum	150
Tyre replacements after 25 000 miles, four at £37.50 each	
Petrol, per gallon	1.90

Average mileage from one gallon is 25 miles.

(a) From the above data you are required:
  (i) To prepare a schedule to be presented to management showing for the mileages of 5000, 10 000, 15 000 and 30 000 miles per annum:
    (1) total variable cost
    (2) total fixed cost
    (3) total cost
    (4) variable cost per mile (in pence to nearest penny)
    (5) fixed cost per mile (in pence to nearest penny)
    (6) total cost per mile (in pence to nearest penny).
    If, in classifying the costs, you consider that some can be treated as either variable or fixed, state the assumption(s) on which your answer is based together with brief supporting reason(s).
  (ii) On graph paper, plot the information given in your answer to (i) above for the costs listed against (1), (2), (3) and (6).
  (iii) To read off from your graph(s) in (ii) and state the approximate total costs applicable to 18 000 miles and 25 000 miles and the total cost per mile at these two mileages.
(b) 'The more miles you travel, the cheaper it becomes.' Comment briefly on this statement.

(25 marks)

2.22 Sunk and opportunity costs for decision-making

Mrs Johnston has taken out a lease on a shop for a down payment of €5000. Additionally, the rent under the lease amounts to €5000 per annum. If the lease is cancelled, the initial payment of €5000 is forfeit. Mrs Johnston plans to use the shop for the sale of clothing, and has estimated operations for the next 12 months as follows:

	(€)	(€)
Sales	120 000	
Less Value-added tax (VAT)	20 000	
Sales less VAT		100 000
Cost of goods sold	50 000	
Wages and wage-related costs	12 000	
Rent including the down payment	10 000	
Rates, heating, lighting and insurance	13 000	
Audit, legal and general expenses	2 000	
		87 000
Net profit before tax		13 000

In the figures no provision has been made for the cost of Mrs Johnston but it is estimated that one half of her time will be devoted to the business. She is undecided whether to continue with her plans because she knows that she can sub-let the shop to a friend for a monthly rent of €550 if she does not use the shop herself.

You are required to:

(a) explain and identify the 'sunk' and 'opportunity' costs in the situation depicted above

(b) state what decision Mrs Johnston should make according to the information given, supporting your conclusion with a financial statement.

(11 marks)

PART TWO

INFORMATION FOR DECISION-MAKING

The objective of Part Two, which contains four chapters, is to consider the provision of financial information that will help managers to make better decisions. Chapters 3–5 are concerned mainly with short-term decisions based on the environment of today, and the physical, human and financial resources that are currently available to a firm. These decisions are determined to a considerable extent by the quality of the firm's long-term decisions. An important distinction between long-term and short-term decisions is that the former cannot easily be reversed whereas the latter can often be changed. The actions that follow short-term decisions are frequently repeated, and it is possible for different actions to be taken in the future. For example, the setting of a particular selling price or product mix can often be changed fairly quickly. With regard to long-term decisions, such as capital investment, which involves, for example, the purchase of new plant and machinery, it is not easy to change such decisions in the short term. Resources may only be available for major investments in plant and machinery at lengthy intervals, and it is unlikely that plant replacement decisions will be repeated in the short term.

Chapters 3–5 concentrate mainly on how accounting information can be applied to different forms of short-term decisions. Chapter 3 focuses on what will happen to the financial results if a specific level of activity or volume fluctuates. This information is required for making optimal short-term output decisions. Chapter 4 focuses on the approaches that should be used to establish the relevant costs and revenues for a range of non-routine short-term and long-term decisions. Chapter 5 is concerned with profitability analysis and the provision of financial information for pricing decisions.

The final chapter is concerned with long-term decisions. It looks at the appraisal methods that are used for evaluating capital investment decisions, and introduces the concept of the time value of money.

3
COST–VOLUME–PROFIT ANALYSIS

LEARNING OBJECTIVES After studying this chapter you should be able to:

- justify the use of linear cost and revenue functions
- apply the numerical approach to answer questions similar to those listed in Example 3.1
- construct break-even, contribution and profit–volume graphs
- apply cost–volume–profit analysis in a multi-product setting
- explain the meaning of operating leverage and describe how it influences profits
- identify and explain the assumptions on which cost–volume–profit analysis is based.

You will remember from Chapter 1 that the decision-making process involves selecting from a range of possible courses of action. Before they make their choice, managers need to compare the likely effects of the options they are considering. This chapter looks at one technique that allows them to consider the consequences of particular courses of action. It provides answers to questions such as:

- How many units must be sold to break even?
- What would be the effect on profits if we reduce our selling price and sell more units?
- What sales volume is required to meet the additional fixed charges arising from an advertising campaign?
- Should we pay our sales people on the basis of a salary only, or on the basis of a commission only, or by a combination of the two?

These and other questions can be answered using cost–volume–profit (CVP) analysis.

CVP analysis examines the relationship between changes in activity (i.e. output) and changes in total sales revenue, costs and net profit. It allows us to predict what will happen to the financial results if a specified level of activity or volume fluctuates. This information is vital to management, since one of the most important variables influencing total sales revenue, total costs and profits is output or volume. Knowledge of this relationship will enable management to identify critical output levels, such as the level at which neither a profit nor a loss will occur (i.e. the **break-even point**).

CVP analysis is based on the relationship between volume and sales revenue, costs and profit in the short run. This is normally a period of 1 year, or less, a time in which the output of a firm is likely to be restricted to that available from the current operating capacity. In the short run some inputs can be increased, but others cannot. Additional supplies of materials and unskilled labour may be obtained at short notice, but operating capacity cannot be significantly changed. For example, it is not possible for a hospital to expand its facilities in the short run in order to increase the number of hospital beds. Similarly, a hotel cannot increase the number of rooms in the short run to increase the number of guests. It is also important to remember that most of the costs and prices of a firm's products or services will already have been predetermined over a short-run period, and the major area of uncertainty will be sales volume. Short-run profitability will therefore be most sensitive to sales volume. CVP analysis thus highlights the effects of changes in sales volume on the level of profits in the short run.

The term 'volume' is used within CVP analysis but this has multiple meanings. Different measures can be used to represent the term. For example, sales revenue is a generic term that can be used by most organizations. However, units of output, or activity, tend to be the most widely used terms. This raises the question of what constitutes a unit of output or activity. For a manufacturing organization, such as a car manufacturer, determining units of output is straightforward. It is the number of cars produced. For a computer manufacturer it is the number of computers produced. Service organizations face a more difficult choice. Hotels may define units as the number of guest nights, leisure centres may use the number of visitors as a measure of output/activity and airlines might use the number of passenger miles.

CVP analysis is dependent on the ability to estimate costs at different activity levels and to do this requires that costs are analysed into their fixed and variable elements. Cost estimation techniques are explained at the end of this chapter.

CURVILINEAR CVP RELATIONSHIPS

A diagram showing CVP behaviour is presented in Figure 3.1. You will see that the total revenue and total cost lines are curvilinear. The total revenue line (0E) initially resembles a straight line but then begins to rise less steeply and eventually starts to decline. This arises because the firm is only able to sell increasing quantities of output by reducing the selling price per unit; thus the total revenue line does not increase proportionately with output. To increase the quantity of sales, it is necessary to reduce the unit selling price, which results in the total revenue line rising less steeply, and eventually beginning to decline. The decline occurs because the adverse effect of price reductions outweighs the benefits of increased sales volume.

The total cost line (AD) illustrates cost behaviour in a manufacturing firm but similar cost behaviour also applies in non-manufacturing firms. At zero output level fixed costs equivalent to 0A are incurred. Between points A and B, total costs rise steeply at first as the firm operates at the lower levels of the volume range. This reflects the difficulties of efficiently using manufacturing facilities designed for much larger volume levels. Between points B and C, the total cost line begins to level out and rise less steeply because the firm is now able to operate its manufacturing facilities within the efficient operating range and can take advantage of economies of scale (e.g. specialization of labour, smooth production schedules and discounts for bulk purchases). Economists describe this situation as **increasing returns to scale**. In the upper portion of the volume range the total cost line

FIGURE 3.1

Curvilinear CVP relationships

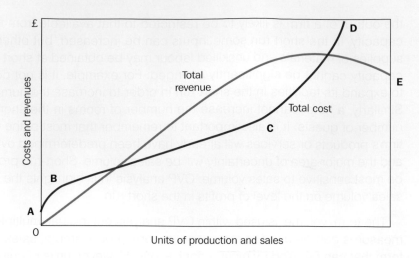

between points C and D rises more steeply as the cost per unit increases. This is because manufacturing facilities are being operated beyond their capacity. Bottlenecks develop, production schedules become more complex and equipment breakdowns begin to occur. The overall effect is that the cost per unit of output increases and causes the total cost line to rise steeply. Economists describe this situation as **decreasing returns to scale**.

It is also clear from Figure 3.1 that the shape of the total revenue line is such that it crosses the total cost line at two points. In other words, there are two output levels at which the total costs are equal to the total revenues; or, more simply, there are two break-even points.

LINEAR CVP RELATIONSHIPS

In Figure 3.2 the blue total cost line XY and the yellow total revenue line OV assume that variable cost and selling price are constant per unit of output. This results in a linear relationship (i.e. a straight line) for total revenue and total cost as output/volume changes. If you look at these two lines you will see that a linear relationship results in only one break-even point. You can also see that the profit area (i.e. the difference between the total revenue line OV and the total cost line XY) widens as volume increases. For comparative purposes the curvilinear relationships shown in Figure 3.1 are also reproduced in Figure 3.2 (with blue line AD and yellow line OE showing, respectively, curvilinear total cost and total revenue relationships).

Management accounting assumes linear CVP relationships when applying CVP analysis to short-run business problems. Curvilinear relationships appear to be more realistic of cost and revenue behaviour, so how can we justify CVP analysis based on the assumption of linear relationships? The answers are provided in the following sections.

Relevant range

Linear relationships are not intended to provide an accurate representation of total cost and total revenue throughout all ranges of output. The objective is to represent the

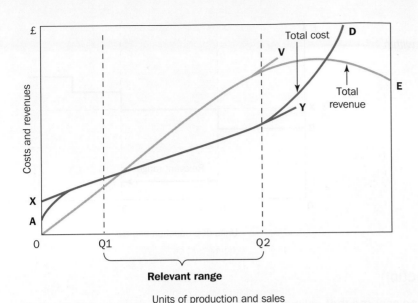

FIGURE 3.2

*Linear CVP
relationships*

behaviour of total cost and revenue over the range of output at which a firm expects to be operating within a short-term planning horizon. This range of output is represented by the output range between points Q1 and Q2 in Figure 3.2. The term **relevant range** is used to refer to the output range at which the firm expects to be operating within a short-term planning horizon. This relevant range also broadly represents the output levels that the firm has had experience of operating in the past and for which cost information is available.

It is clear from Figure 3.2 that, between points Q1 and Q2, the cost and revenue relationships are more or less linear. It would be unwise, however, to make this assumption for output levels outside the relevant range. CVP analysis should therefore only be applied within the relevant range. If the relevant range changes, different fixed and variable costs and selling prices must be used.

Fixed cost function

The linear fixed cost function line in Figure 3.2 indicates that at zero output level fixed costs equivalent to 0X would be incurred. This fixed cost level of 0X is assumed to be applicable to activity level Q1 to Q2, shown in Figure 3.3. If there were to be a prolonged economic recession then output might fall below Q1, and this could result in redundancies and shutdowns. Therefore, fixed costs may be reduced to 0B if there is a prolonged and significant decline in sales demand. Alternatively, additional fixed costs will be incurred if long-term sales volume is expected to be greater than Q2. Over a longer-term time horizon, the fixed cost line will consist of a series of step functions as shown in Figure 3.3. However, since within its short-term planning horizon the firm expects to be operating between output levels Q1 and Q2 (i.e. the relevant range), it will be committed, in the short term, to fixed costs of 0X. Thus the fixed cost of 0X shown in Figures 3.2 and 3.3 represent the fixed costs that would be incurred only for the relevant range.

FIGURE 3.3

*Fixed costs applicable within
the relevant range*

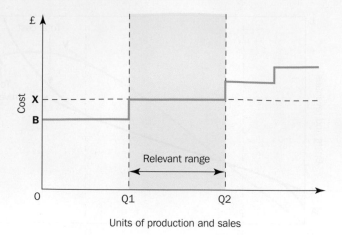

Units of production and sales

Total revenue function

Linear CVP relationships assume that selling price is constant over the relevant range of output, and therefore the total revenue line is a straight line. This is a realistic assumption in those firms that operate in industries where selling prices tend to be fixed in the short term. Also, beyond the relevant range, increases in output may only be possible by offering substantial reductions in price. As it is not the intention of firms to operate outside the relevant range it is appropriate to assume constant selling prices.

A NUMERICAL APPROACH TO COST–VOLUME–PROFIT ANALYSIS

As an alternative to using diagrams for CVP analysis we can also use a numerical approach. Diagrams are useful for presenting the outcomes in a more visual form to non-accounting managers, but the numerical approach is often a quicker and more flexible method for producing the appropriate information. Indeed, it is possible to express CVP relationships in a simple mathematical equation format so that they can form an input for computer financial models. To keep things simple we shall avoid mathematical formulae and use a simple numerical approach.

In the previous sections we pointed out that CVP analysis is based on the assumption that selling price and variable cost are constant per unit of output. In contrast, you will remember from Chapter 2 that over a short-run period fixed costs are a constant total amount whereas unit cost changes with output levels. As a result, profit per unit also changes with volume. For example, if fixed costs are £10 000 for a period and output is 10 000 units, the fixed cost will be £1 per unit. Alternatively, if output is 5000 units, the fixed cost will be £2 per unit. Profit per unit will not therefore be constant over varying output levels and it is incorrect to unitize fixed costs for CVP decisions.

Instead of using profit per unit we shall use contribution margins to apply the numerical approach. **Contribution margin** is equal to sales revenue minus variable costs. Because the variable cost per unit and the selling price per unit are assumed to be constant the contribution margin per unit is also assumed to be constant. We will use Example 3.1 to illustrate the application of the numerical approach to CVP analysis.

REAL WORLD VIEWS 3.1

Break-even rail fares

Many countries are noted for having high rail fares nowadays, which some commentators attribute to the fact that many railways are no longer in public ownership. However, even if a railway is in public ownership, it is not unreasonable to expect the fares to be set at a level which covers cost i.e. a break-even price. A cross border high-speed rail link between Hong Kong and China provides a good numerical example, as detailed in an article in the *South China Morning Post* (5 February 2018).

According to the article, 'the HK$84.4 billion cross-border high-speed rail link may become profitable eight years after its launch, Hong Kong's transport chief said yesterday'. Thus it will take about eight years to achieve a break-even scenario. The article's author provides some interesting calculations based on figures available for costs and revenues. He notes, 'now put it all together: operating income less operating costs, depreciation and interest charges, and we come to a loss of HK$3.18 billion a year'. He then takes this loss and calculates the fare needed to break-even – 'if we wanted this railway to break even, we would have to set the fare to Guangzhou at something like HK$662 and to Shenzen at about HK$230, crossing our fingers … that such extremely high ticket prices would have no dampening effect at all on passenger numbers'. The original planned fares were HK$45 to Shenzen, and HK$180 to Guangzhou.

Question

1 Can you think of some of the fixed costs associated with the railway described above which might contribute to high break-even level fares?

Reference

Jake Van Der Kamp, (2018) Dodgy mathematics puts the break-even point of Hong Kong's high-speed rail forever away, *South China Morning Post*, available at www.scmp.com/business/banking-finance/article/2132104/dodgy-mathematics-puts-break-even-point-hong-kongs-high

EXAMPLE 3.1

Norvik Enterprises operates in the leisure and entertainment industry and one of its activities is to promote concerts at locations throughout Europe. The company is examining the viability of a concert in Helsinki. Estimated fixed costs are £60 000. These include the fees paid to performers, the hire of the venue and advertising costs. Variable costs consist of the cost of a pre-packed buffet that will be provided by a firm of caterers at a price, which is currently being negotiated, but it is likely to be in the region of £10 per ticket sold. The proposed price for the sale of a ticket is £20. The management of Norvik have requested the following information:

1 The number of tickets that must be sold to break even (that is, the point at which there is neither a profit nor loss).

2 How many tickets must be sold to earn £30 000 target profit?

3 What profit would result if 8000 tickets were sold?

4 What selling price would have to be charged to give a profit of £30 000 on sales of 8000 tickets, fixed costs of £60 000 and variable costs of £10 per ticket?

5 How many additional tickets must be sold to cover the extra cost of television advertising of £8000?

Example 3.1 calculations

1. Break-even point in units (i.e. number of tickets sold)

You will see from Example 3.1 that each ticket sold generates a contribution of £10 (£20 selling price – £10 variable cost), which is available to cover fixed costs and, after they are covered, to contribute to profit. When we have obtained sufficient total contribution to cover fixed costs, the break-even point is achieved, and so:

$$\text{Break-even point in units} = \frac{\text{Fixed costs (£60 000)}}{\text{Contribution per unit (£10)}}$$

$$= 6\ 000 \text{ tickets}$$

2. Units to be sold to obtain a £30 000 profit

To achieve a profit of any size we must first obtain sufficient contribution to cover the fixed costs (i.e. the break-even point). If the total contribution is not sufficient to cover the fixed costs then a loss will occur. Once a sufficient total contribution has been achieved, any excess contribution represents profit. Thus to determine the total contribution to obtain a target profit we simply add the target profit to the fixed costs and divide by the contribution per unit so that:

$$\text{Units sold for the target profit} = \frac{\text{Fixed costs (£60 000) + Target profit (£30 000)}}{\text{Contribution per unit (£10)}}$$

$$= 9\ 000 \text{ tickets}$$

3. Profit from the sale of 8000 tickets

The total contribution from the sale of 8000 tickets is £80 000 (8000 × £10). To ascertain the profit, we deduct the fixed costs of £60 000 giving a net profit of £20 000. Let us now assume that we wish to ascertain the impact on profit if a further 1000 tickets are sold so that sales volume increases from 8000 to 9000 tickets. Assuming that fixed costs remain unchanged, the impact on a firm's profits resulting from a change in the number of units sold can be determined by multiplying the unit contribution margin by the change in units sold. Therefore, the increase in profits will be £10 000 (1000 units times a unit contribution margin of £10).

4. Selling price to be charged to show a profit of £30 000 on sales of 8000 tickets

First we must determine the total required revenue to obtain a profit of £30 000. This is £170 000, which is derived from the sum of the fixed costs (£60 000), variable costs (8000 × £10) and the target profit (£30 000). Dividing the required sales revenues of £170 000 by the sales volume (8000 tickets) gives a selling price of £21.25.

REAL WORLD VIEWS 3.2

Importance of break-even oil prices due to widely different costs of extraction

A break-even oil price is the price at which oil must be sold in order to recover the costs associated with its production. With the recent downturn in the global oil industry, break-even oil prices are an important measure of an oil extractor's ability to remain profitable. Break-even oil prices vary greatly throughout the world due to the widely differing costs associated with extracting different types of oil, the unique circumstances associated with oil extraction in different oil-producing regions, and so on.

In times of economic downturn, oil resources with higher break-even prices are the first to be discontinued. Unconventional oil resources, such as oil sands and shale oil, are more expensive to produce than conventional oil, and therefore suffer when oil prices drop. Since the oil glut began in 2014, even conventional oil deposits that are more expensive to extract are decreasing production. This has led to significant economic impacts in places where the economy is closely tied to oil, such as Venezuela, which has oil sands deposits in addition to conventional oil resources.

The chart below extracted from a 2015 publication reveals some interesting insights into the break-even price for producing crude oil. Petroleum extraction in the Arctic regions shows the highest break-even price of $75 per barrel. On the other hand, middle eastern countries have the lowest price at $27 per barrel. US shale oil producers have a break-even price of $65 per barrel. These estimates are average break-even prices. The costs may vary depending on the oil well and its location.

While oil prices have increased slightly since a record low in January 2016, it is uncertain how long it will take for oil prices to recover more substantially, if at all. According to the publication

WTI (*West Texas Intermediate*) crude oil was trading in 2015 at $45 per barrel, and Brent crude oil was trading at $46.4 per barrel. As of early 2018, these prices stood at $61, with Brent crude at $62. This suggests margins of high break-even-price US shale oil producers are not good, assuming the break-even prices from 2015 are still a good estimate. This in turn may mean that shale oil or oil from Arctic regions will see a fall in production, as oil prices during 2016 and 2017 have remained below the $75 mark.

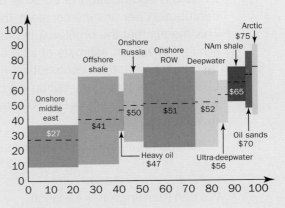

Breakeven Price of Crude Oil

Note: *Market Realist*
Source: Seadrill, Morgan Stanley Equity Research, International Energy Agency

Questions

1 Why does the break-even differ according to the location of the oil wells?
2 Is the break-even price of crude oil more important than the break-even volume?

References

Kristopher, G. (2015) A key investor's guide to the crude oil market (Part 4 of 1 of 15 Market Monitor). Available at marketrealist.com/2015/01/crude-oil-market-key-overview

Breakeven oil prices in Middle Eastern and North African countries in 2016. Available at www.statista.com/statistics/486086/breakeven-oil-prices-middleeast-northenafrica

5. Additional sales volume to meet £8000 additional fixed advertisement charges

The contribution per unit is £10 and fixed costs will increase by £8000. Therefore, an extra 800 tickets must be sold to cover the additional fixed costs of £8000.

THE PROFIT–VOLUME RATIO

The **profit–volume ratio** (also known as the **contribution margin ratio**) is the contribution divided by sales. It represents the proportion of each £1 of sales available to cover fixed costs and provide for profit. In Example 3.1 the contribution is £10 per unit and the selling price is £20 per unit; the profit–volume ratio is 0.5. This means that for each £1 sale a contribution of £0.50 is earned. Because we assume that selling price and contribution per unit are constant, the profit–volume ratio is also assumed to be constant. This means that the profit–volume ratio can be computed using either unit figures or total figures. Given an estimate of total sales revenue, it is possible to use the profit–volume ratio to estimate total contribution. For example, if total sales revenue is estimated to be £200 000, the total contribution will be £100 000 (£200 000 × 0.5). To calculate the profit, we deduct fixed costs of £60 000; thus a profit of £40 000 will be obtained from total sales revenue of £200 000.

This computation can be expressed in equation form:

$$\text{Profit} = (\text{Sales revenue} \times \text{PV ratio}) - \text{Fixed costs}$$

We can rearrange this equation:

$$\text{Profit} + \text{Fixed costs} = \text{Sales revenue} \times \text{PV ratio}$$

Therefore the break-even sales revenue (where profit = 0) = Fixed costs/PV ratio.

If we apply this approach to Example 3.1, the break-even sales revenue is £120 000 (£60 000 fixed costs/0.5 PV ratio).

RELEVANT RANGE

It is vital to remember that CVP analysis can only be used for decisions that result in outcomes within the relevant range. Outside this range the unit selling price and the variable cost are no longer deemed to be constant per unit, and any results obtained from the formulae that fall outside the relevant range will be incorrect. The concept of the relevant range is more appropriate for production settings but it can apply within non-production settings. Returning to Norvic Enterprises in Example 3.1, we shall assume that the caterers' charges will be higher per ticket if ticket sales are below 4000 but lower if sales exceed 12 000 tickets. Thus the £10 variable cost relates only to a sales volume within a range of 4000 to 12 000 tickets. Outside this range other costs apply. Also the number of seats made available at the venue is flexible and the hire cost will be reduced for sales of less than 4000 tickets and increased for sales beyond 12 000 tickets. In other words, we will assume that the relevant range is a sales volume of 4000 to 12 000 tickets and outside this range the results of our CVP analysis do not apply.

MARGIN OF SAFETY ✳

The **margin of safety** indicates by how much sales may decrease before a loss occurs. Using Example 3.1, where unit selling price and variable cost were £20 and £10 respectively and fixed costs were £60 000, we noted that the break-even point was 6000 tickets or £120 000 sales value. If sales are expected to be 8000 tickets or £160 000, the margin of safety will be 2000 tickets or £40 000. Alternatively, we can express the margin of safety in a percentage form based on the following ratio:

$$\text{Percentage margin of safety} = \frac{\text{Expected sales} - \text{Break-even sales}}{\text{Expected sales}}$$

$$= \frac{£16\,0000 - £120\,0000}{£160\,000} = 25\%$$

Note that higher margins of safety are associated with less risky activities.

REAL WORLD VIEWS 3.3

Guardian staff brace for more job cuts as part of break-even plan

According to an article published in the *Financial Times* the chief executive of *The Guardian* newspaper group and the paper's editor stated in a memo to staff that the publisher had 'made progress' and 'successfully' met its first year's objective of reducing losses as part of a three-year plan to break even. However, the memo warned that 'our operating costs remain too high, trading conditions remain tough and further changes and cost savings will be necessary if we are to meet our target of breaking even at an operating level by 2018/19.'

The article reported that *The Guardian* has been hit by declining print revenue and a digital advertising market where most revenues flow to Google and Facebook. This has prompted the Guardian Media Group, the parent company of the Guardian and Observer print and digital businesses, to reduce their print operations, shed jobs, move the newspapers from their Berliner formats to tabloid editions and to also outsource printing to Trinity Mirror.

Questions

1 Is break-even a good performance monitor over the longer term?
2 How do decreasing margins affect the break-even point and margin of safety?

Source

Financial Times March 22, 2017 www.ft.com/content/eb23fe42-63a8-3984-904f-4d6d4050fe09

CONSTRUCTING THE BREAK-EVEN CHART

Managers may obtain a clearer understanding of CVP behaviour if the information is presented in graphical format. Using the data in Example 3.1 we can construct the **break-even chart** for Norvik Enterprises (Figure 3.4). Note that activity/output is plotted on the horizontal axis and monetary amounts for total costs, total revenues and total profits (or loss) are recorded on the vertical axis. In constructing the graph, the fixed costs are plotted as a single horizontal line at the £60 000 level. Variable costs at the rate of £10 per unit of volume are added to the fixed costs to enable the total cost line to be plotted. Two points are required to insert the total cost line. At zero sales volume total cost will be equal to the fixed costs of £60 000. At 12 000 units sales volume total costs will be £180 000 consisting of £120 000 variable costs plus £60 000 fixed costs. The total revenue line is plotted at the rate of £20 per unit of volume. At zero output total sales are zero and at 12 000 units total sales revenue is £240 000. The total revenues for these two points are plotted on the graph and a straight line is drawn that joins these points. The constraints of the relevant range consisting of two vertical lines are then added to the graph; beyond these lines we have little assurance that the CVP relationships are valid.

The point at which the total sales revenue line cuts the total cost line is the point where the concert makes neither a profit nor a loss. This is the break-even point and is 6000 tickets or £120 000 total sales revenue. The distance between the total sales

FIGURE 3.4

Break-even chart for Example 3.1

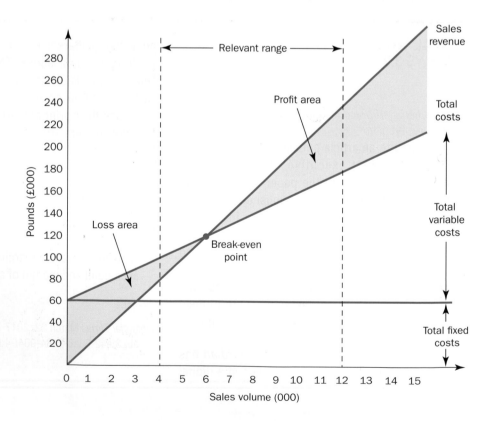

revenue line and the total cost line at a volume below the break-even point represents losses that will occur for various sales levels below 6000 tickets. Similarly, if the company operates at a sales volume above the break-even point, the difference between the total revenue and the total cost lines represents the profit that results from sales levels above 6000 tickets.

ALTERNATIVE PRESENTATION OF COST–VOLUME–PROFIT ANALYSIS

Contribution graph

In Figure 3.4 the fixed cost line is drawn parallel to the horizontal axis, and the variable cost is the difference between the total cost line and the fixed cost line. An alternative to Figure 3.4 for the data contained in Example 3.1 is illustrated in Figure 3.5. This alternative presentation is called a **contribution graph**. In Figure 3.5 the variable cost line is drawn first at £10 per unit of volume. The fixed costs are represented by the difference between the total cost line and the variable cost line. Because fixed costs are assumed to be a constant sum throughout the entire output range, a constant sum of £60 000 for fixed costs is added to the variable cost line, which results in the total cost line being drawn parallel to the variable cost line. The advantage of this form of presentation is that it emphasizes the total contribution which is represented by the difference between the total sales revenue line and the total variable cost line.

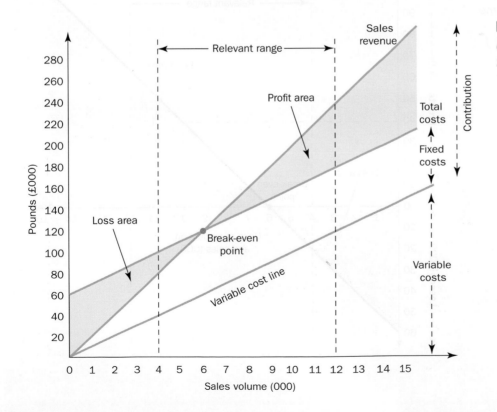

FIGURE 3.5

Contribution chart for Example 3.1

Profit–volume graph

Neither the break-even nor the contribution graphs highlight the profit or loss at different volume levels. To ascertain the profit or loss figures from a break-even graph, it is necessary to determine the difference between the total cost and total revenue lines. The **profit–volume graph** is a more convenient method of showing the impact of changes in volume on profit. Such a graph is illustrated in Figure 3.6. The horizontal axis represents the various levels of sales volume, and the profits and losses for the period are recorded on the vertical scale. You will see from Figure 3.6 that profits or losses are plotted for each of the various sales levels, and these points are connected by a profit line. Two points are required to plot the profit line. When units sold are zero a loss equal to the amount of fixed costs (£60 000) will be reported. At the break-even point (zero profits) sales volume is 6000 units. This is plotted at the point where the profit line intersects the horizontal line at a sales volume of 6000 tickets. The profit line is drawn between the two points. With each unit sold, a contribution of £10 is obtained towards the fixed costs, and the break-even point is at 6000 tickets, when the total contribution exactly equals the total of the fixed costs. With each additional unit sold beyond 6000 tickets, a surplus of £10 per ticket is obtained. If 10 000 tickets are sold, the profit will be £40 000 (4000 tickets at £10 contribution). You can see this relationship between sales and profit at 10 000 tickets from the dotted lines in Figure 3.6.

FIGURE 3.6

Profit–volume graph for Example 3.1

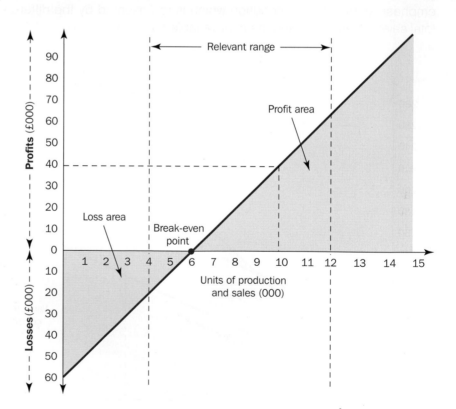

Alternative presentation of CVP – sales volumes and profits at Mazda

Auto manufacturers are keen to report their production and sales figures. This may be to assess market share or the data may be considered a key performance indicator given the high fixed costs an auto manufacturer may have to cover. Take Mazda for example. On their website (www.mazda.com) there are regular news releases providing investors with data on sales and production volumes by month and quarter, alongside the previous year data for comparison. Other auto companies like Ford, Honda and BMW also publish similar data.

Looking at the financial statements of Mazda for the year ended 31 March 2017, the company made a gross profit of approximately $1.2 billion and an operating (net) profit before interest and tax of $1.1 billion. The number of vehicles produced during the 2017 financial year was 1.56 million, the vast majority of which were passenger cars.

Questions

1 Do you think a profit–volume graph presentation of the relationships between costs volume and profits may be more useful than the typical break-even chart to auto manufacturers like Mazda?
2 Could you draw a rough profit–volume chart from the above data?

Reference

Mazda, 2017 Annual Report. Available at www.mazda.com/globalassets/en/assets/investors/library/annual/files/mazdaar17_e.pdf

MULTI-PRODUCT COST–VOLUME–PROFIT ANALYSIS

Our analysis so far has assumed a single-product setting. However, most firms produce and sell many products or services. In this section we shall consider how we can adapt CVP analysis to a multi-product setting. Consider the situation presented in Example 3.2. You will see that there are two types of fixed costs. Direct avoidable fixed costs can be specifically identified with each product and would not be incurred if the product was not made. For example, the deluxe and standard machines might be produced in different departments and the departmental supervisors' fixed salaries would represent fixed costs directly attributable to each machine. The common fixed costs relate to the costs of common facilities (e.g. factory rent) that cannot be specifically identified with either of the products since they can only be avoided if both products are not sold.

You might think that the break-even point for the firm as a whole can be derived if we allocate the common fixed costs to each individual product. However, this approach is inappropriate because the allocation will be arbitrary. The common fixed costs cannot be specifically identified with either of the products and can only be avoided if *both* products are not sold. The solution to our problem is to convert the sales volume measure of the individual products into standard batches of products based on the

EXAMPLE 3.2

The Super Bright Company sells two types of washing machines – a de-luxe model and a standard model. The financial controller has prepared the following information based on the sales forecast for the period:

Sales volume (units)	De-luxe machine 1 200 (£)	Standard machine 600 (£)	Total (£)
Unit selling price	300	200	
Unit variable cost	150	110	
Unit contribution	150	90	
Total sales revenues	360 000	120 000	480 000
Less: Total variable cost	180 000	66 000	246 000
Contribution to direct and common fixed costs[a]	180 000	54 000	234 000
Less: Direct avoidable fixed costs	90 000	27 000	117 000
Contribution to common fixed costs[a]	90 000	27 000	117 000
Less common (indirect) fixed costs			39 000
Operating profit			78 000

The common fixed costs relate to the costs of common facilities and can only be avoided if neither of the products is sold. The managing director is concerned that sales may be less than forecast and has requested information relating to the break-even point for the activities for the period.

Note

[a]Contribution was defined earlier in this chapter as sales less variable costs. Where fixed costs are divided into direct and common (indirect) fixed costs it is possible to identify two separate contribution categories. The first is described as contribution to direct and common fixed costs and this is identical to the conventional definition, being equivalent to sales less variable costs. The second is after a further deduction of direct fixed costs and is described as 'Contribution to common or indirect fixed costs'.

planned sales mix. You will see from Example 3.2 that Super Bright plans to sell 1200 de-luxe and 600 standard machines giving a sales mix of 1200:600. Reducing this sales mix to the smallest whole number gives a mix of 2:1. In other words, for the sale of every two de-luxe machines one standard machine is expected to be sold. We therefore define our standard batch of products as comprising two de-luxe and one standard machine giving a contribution of £390 per batch (two de-luxe machines at a contribution of £150 per unit sold plus one standard machine at a contribution of £90).

The break-even point in standard batches can be calculated by using the same break-even equation that we used for a single product, so that:

Break-even number of batches = Total fixed costs (£156 000)/Contribution margin per batch (£390)

= 400 batches

The sales mix used to define a standard batch (2:1) can now be used to convert the break-even point (measured in standard batches) into a break-even point expressed in terms of the required combination of individual products sold. Thus 800 de-luxe machines (2 × 400) and 400 (1 × 400) standard machines must be sold to break even. The following profit statement verifies this outcome:

Units sold	De-luxe machine 800 (£)	Standard machine 400 (£)	Total (£)
Unit contribution margin	150	90	
Contribution to direct and common fixed costs	120 000	36 000	156 000
Less: Direct fixed costs	90 000	27 000	117 000
Contribution to common fixed costs	30 000	9 000	39 000
Less: Common fixed costs			39 000
Operating profit			0

Let us now assume that the actual sales volume for the period was 1200 units, the same total volume as the break-even volume, but consisting of a sales mix of 600 units of each machine. Thus the actual sales mix is 1:1 compared with a planned sales mix of 2:1. The total contribution to direct and common fixed costs will be £144 000 ([£150 × 600 for de-luxe] + [£90 × 600 for standard]) and a loss of £12 000 (£144 000 contribution – £156 000 total fixed costs) will occur. It should now be apparent to you that *the break-even point (or the sales volumes required to achieve a target profit) is not a unique number: it varies depending upon the composition of the sales mix.* Because the actual sales mix differs from the planned sales mix, the sales mix used to define a standard batch has changed from 2:1 to 1:1 and the contribution per batch changes from £390 to £240 ([1 × £150] + [1 × £90]). This means that the revised break-even point will be 650 batches (£156 000 total fixed costs/£240 contribution per batch), which converts to a sales volume of 650 units of each machine based on a 1:1 sales mix. Generally, an increase in the proportion of sales of higher contribution margin products will decrease the break-even point whereas increases in sales of the lower margin products will increase the break-even point.

OPERATING LEVERAGE

Companies can sometimes influence the proportion of fixed and variable expenses in their cost structures. For example, they may choose to either rely heavily on automated facilities (involving high fixed and low variable costs) or on manual systems (involving high variable costs and low fixed costs). The chosen cost structure can have a significant impact on profits. Consider the situation presented in Exhibit 3.1 where the managers of an airline company are considering an investment in automated ticketing equipment.

You will see from Exhibit 3.1 that it is unclear which system should be chosen. If periodic sales exceed £960 000 the automated system will result in higher profits. Automation enables the company to lower its variable costs by increasing fixed costs. This cost structure results in a greater increase in profits as sales increase compared with

EXHIBIT 3.1 Sensitivity of profits arising from changes in sales for an automated and manual system

An airline company is considering investing in automated ticketing equipment. The estimated sales revenues and costs for the current manual system and the proposed automated system for a typical period are as follows:

	Automated system £	Manual system £
Sales revenue	1 000 000	1 000 000
Less: Variable expenses	300 000	800 000
Contribution	700 000 (70%)	200 000 (20%)
Less: Fixed expenses	600 000	120 000
Profit	100 000	80 000

The above cost structure suggests that the automated system yields the higher profits. However, if sales decline by 10 per cent the following calculations show that the manual system will result in the higher profits:

	Automated system £	Manual system £
Sales revenue	900 000	900 000
Less: Variable expenses	270 000	720 000
Contribution	630 000 (70%)	180 000 (20%)
Less: Fixed expenses	600 000	120 000
Profit	30 000	60 000

What will happen if sales are 10 per cent higher than the predicted sales for the period?

	Automated system £	Manual system £
Sales revenue	1 100 000	1 100 000
Less: Variable expenses	330 000	880 000
Contribution	770 000 (70%)	220 000 (20%)
Less: Fixed expenses	600 000	120 000
Profit	170 000	100 000

The sales revenue where both systems result in the same profits is £960 000. The automated system yields higher profits when periodic sales revenue exceeds £960 000 whereas the manual system gives higher profits when sales revenue is below £960 000.[a]

	Automated system £	Manual system £
Sales revenue	960 000	960 000
Less: Variable expenses	288 000	768 000
Contribution	672 000 (70%)	192 000 (20%)
Less: Fixed expenses	600 000	120 000
Profit	72 000	72 000

Note

[a] The profit–volume ratio is 0.7 for the automated system and 0.2 for the manual system. Let x = periodic sales revenue: the indifference point is where $0.7x - £600 000 = 0.2x - £120 000$, so $x = £960 000$.

the manual system. Unfortunately, it is also true that a high fixed cost and lower variable cost structure will result in a greater reduction in profits as sales decrease. The term **operating leverage** is used as a measure of the sensitivity of profits to changes in sales. The greater the **degree of operating leverage**, the more that changes in sales activity will affect profits. The degree of operating leverage can be measured for a given level of sales by the following formula:

Degree of operating leverage = Contribution margin/Profit

The degree of operating leverage in Exhibit 3.1 for sales of £1 million is 7 (£700 000/£100 000) for the automated system and 2.5 (£200 000/£80 000) for the manual system. This means that profits change by seven times more than the change in sales for the automated system and 2.5 times for the manual system. Thus, for a 10 per cent increase in sales from £1 million to £1.1 million profits increase by 70 per cent for the automated system (from £100 000 to £170 000) and by 25 per cent for the manual system (from £80 000 to £100 000). In contrast, you will see in Exhibit 3.1 that if sales decline by 10 per cent from £1 million, to £0.9 million, profits decrease by 70 per cent (from £100 000 to £30 000) for the automated system and by 25 per cent (from £80 000 to £60 000) for the manual system.

The degree of operating leverage provides useful information for the airline company in choosing between the two systems. Higher degrees of operating leverage can provide significantly greater profits when sales are increasing but higher percentage decreases will also occur when sales are declining. Higher operating leverage also results in a greater volatility in profits. The manual system has a break-even point of £600 000 sales (£120 000 fixed expenses/PV ratio of 0.2) whereas the break-even point for the automated system is £857 143 (£600 000 fixed expenses/PV ratio of 0.7). Thus, the automated system has a lower margin of safety. High operating leverage leads to higher risk arising from the greater volatility of profits and higher break-even point. On the other hand, the increase in risk provides the potential for higher profit levels (as long as sales exceed £960 000). We can conclude that if management are confident that sales will exceed £960 000 the automated system is preferable.

It is apparent from the above discussion that labour intensive organizations, such as McDonald's and Pizza Hut, have high variable costs and low fixed costs, and thus have low operating leverage. These companies can continue to report profits even when they experience wide fluctuations in sales levels. Conversely, organizations that are highly capital intensive, such as easyJet and Volkswagen, have high operating leverage. These companies must generate high sales volumes to cover fixed costs, but sales above the break-even point produce high profits. In general, these companies tend to be more vulnerable to sharp economic and business cycle swings.

COST–VOLUME–PROFIT ANALYSIS ASSUMPTIONS

It is essential that anyone preparing or interpreting CVP information is aware of the underlying assumptions on which the information has been prepared. If these assumptions are not recognized, or the analysis is modified, errors may result and incorrect conclusions

REAL WORLD VIEWS 3.5

The impact of operating leverage at Inktomi

Operating leverage can tell investors a lot about a company's risk profile, and although high operating leverage can often benefit companies, firms with high operating leverage are also vulnerable to sharp economic and business cycle swings. In good times, high operating leverage can supercharge profit. But companies with a lot of costs tied up in machinery, plants, real estate and distribution networks cannot easily cut expenses to adjust to a change in demand. So, if there is a downturn in the economy, earnings do not just fall, they can plummet.

Consider the software developer Inktomi. During the dotcom boom investors marvelled at the nature of its software business. The company spent tens of millions of dollars to develop each of its digital delivery and storage software programs. But thanks to the Internet, Inktomi's software could be distributed to customers at almost no cost. In other words, the company had close to zero cost of goods sold. After its fixed development costs were recovered, each additional sale was almost pure profit.

After the collapse of dotcom technology market demand, Inktomi suffered the dark side of operating leverage. As sales took a nosedive, profits swung dramatically to a staggering $58 million loss compared with the $1 million profit the company had enjoyed in the same period for the previous year. The high leverage involved in counting on sales to repay fixed costs can put companies and their shareholders at risk. High operating leverage during a downturn (such as the recession following the 2008 financial crisis) can be an Achilles heel, putting pressure on profit margins and making a contraction in earnings unavoidable.

Indeed, companies such as Inktomi with high operating leverage typically have larger volatility in their operating earnings and share prices. As a result, investors need to treat these companies with caution.

Discussion point

1 Provide examples of other companies that have high and low degrees of operating leverage.

Reference

Investopedia (nd) www.investopedia.com/articles/ stocks/06/opleverage.asp

may be drawn from the analysis. We shall now consider these important assumptions. They are as follows:

1 All other variables remain constant.
2 A single product or constant sales mix.
3 Total costs and total revenue are linear functions of output.
4 Costs can be accurately divided into their fixed and variable elements.
5 The analysis applies only to the relevant range.
6 The analysis applies only to a short-term time horizon.

COST–VOLUME–PROFIT ANALYSIS ASSUMPTIONS 67

1 All other variables remain constant

It has been assumed that all variables other than the particular one under consideration have remained constant throughout the analysis. In other words, it is assumed that volume is the only factor that will cause costs and revenues to change. However, changes in other variables such as production efficiency, sales mix and price levels can have an important influence on sales revenue and costs. If significant changes in these other variables occur the CVP analysis presentation will be incorrect and it will be necessary to revise the CVP calculations based on the projected changes to the other variables.

2 Single product or constant sales mix

CVP analysis assumes that either a single product is sold or, if a range of products is sold, that sales will be in accordance with a predetermined sales mix. When a predetermined sales mix is used, it can be depicted in the CVP analysis by measuring sales volume using standard batch sizes based on a planned sales mix. As we have discussed, any CVP analysis must be interpreted carefully if the initial product mix assumptions do not hold.

3 Total costs and total revenue are linear functions of output

The analysis assumes that unit variable cost and selling price are constant. This assumption is only likely to be valid within the relevant range of production described earlier in this chapter.

4 Costs can be accurately divided into their fixed and variable elements

CVP analysis assumes that costs can be accurately analysed into their fixed and variable elements. In practice, you will see later in this chapter that the separation of semi-variable costs into their fixed and variable elements is extremely difficult. Nevertheless, a reasonably accurate analysis is necessary if CVP analysis is to provide relevant information for decision-making. We shall briefly consider how costs can be divided into their fixed and variable elements at the end of this chapter.

5 Analysis applies only to the relevant range

Earlier in this chapter we noted that CVP analysis is appropriate only for decisions taken within the relevant production range, and that it is incorrect to project cost and revenue figures beyond the relevant range.

6 Analysis applies only to a short-term time horizon

CVP analysis is based on the relationship between volume and sales revenue, costs and profit in the short run, the short run typically being a period of 1 year in which the output of a firm is likely to be restricted to that available from the current operating capacity. During this period significant changes cannot be made to selling prices and fixed and variable costs. CVP analysis thus examines the effects of changes in sales volume on the level of profits in the short run. It is inappropriate to extend the analysis to long-term decision-making.

THE IMPACT OF INFORMATION TECHNOLOGY

The output from a CVP model is only as good as the input. The analysis will include assumptions about sales mix, production efficiency, price levels, total fixed costs, variable costs and selling price per unit. In practice, estimates regarding these variables will be subject to varying degrees of uncertainty.

Sensitivity analysis is one approach for coping with changes in the values of the variables. Sensitivity analysis focuses on how a result will be changed if the original estimates or the underlying assumptions change. With regard to CVP analysis, sensitivity analysis answers questions such as the following:

1 What will the profit be if the sales mix changes from that originally predicted?
2 What will the profit be if fixed costs increase by 10 per cent and variable costs decline by 5 per cent?

Today's information technology enables management accountants to build CVP computer-ized models and consider alternative plans by keying the information into a computer, which can quickly show changes both graphically and numerically. Thus managers can study various combinations of changes in selling prices, fixed costs, variable costs and product mix, and can react quickly without waiting for formal reports from the management accountant.

SEPARATION OF COSTS INTO THEIR FIXED AND VARIABLE ELEMENTS

CVP analysis assumes that costs can be accurately analysed into their fixed and variable elements, and mathematical techniques can be used to separate costs in this way. For a discussion of these techniques you should refer to Drury (2018, Chapter 24). However, first-year cost and management accounting courses sometimes require you to separate fixed and variable costs using a more simplistic non-mathematical technique called the **high–low method**.

The high–low method consists of examining past costs and activity, selecting the highest and lowest activity levels and comparing the changes in costs that result from the two levels. Assume that the following activity levels and costs are extracted:

	Volume of production (units)	Indirect costs (£)
Lowest activity	5 000	220 000
Highest activity	10 000	320 000

If variable costs are constant per unit and the fixed costs remain unchanged the increase in costs will be due entirely to an increase in variable costs. The variable cost per unit is therefore calculated as follows:

$$\frac{\text{Different in cost}}{\text{Difference in activity}} = \frac{\pounds100\ 000}{5000}$$

$$= \pounds20 \text{ variable cost per unit of activity}$$

The fixed cost can be estimated at any level of activity by subtracting the variable cost portion from the total cost. At an activity level of 5000 units the total cost is £220 000 and the total variable cost is £100 000 (5000 units at £20 per unit). The balance of £120 000 is assumed to represent the fixed cost.

SUMMARY

The following items relate to the learning objectives listed at the beginning of the chapter.

- **Justify the use of linear cost and revenue functions**. Within the relevant range it is generally assumed that cost and revenue functions are approximately linear. Outside the relevant range linearity is unlikely to apply. Care is therefore required in interpreting CVP relationships outside the relevant range.

- **Apply the numerical approach to answer questions similar to those listed in Example 3.1**. In Example 3.1, the break-even point was derived by dividing fixed costs by the contribution per unit. To ascertain the number of units sold to achieve a target profit the sum of the fixed costs and the target profit is divided by the contribution per unit.

- **Construct break-even, contribution and profit–volume graphs**. Managers may obtain a clearer understanding of CVP behaviour if the information is presented in graphical format. With the break-even chart the fixed costs are plotted as a single horizontal line. The total cost line is plotted by adding variable costs to fixed costs. The reverse situation applies with a contribution graph. The variable costs are plotted first and the fixed costs are added to variable costs to plot the total cost line. Because fixed costs are assumed to be a constant sum throughout the output range, the total cost line is drawn parallel to the variable cost line. The break-even and contribution graphs do not highlight the profit or loss at different output levels and must be ascertained by comparing the differences between the total cost and total revenue lines. The profit–volume graph shows the impact of changes in volume on profits. The profits and losses are plotted for each of the various sales levels and these are connected by a profit line. You should refer to Figures 3.4–3.6 for an illustration of the graphs.

- **Apply cost–volume–profit analysis in a multi-product setting**. Multi-product CVP analysis requires that an assumption is made concerning the expected sales mix. The approach that is used is to convert the multi-product CVP analysis into a single product analysis based on the assumption that output consists of standard batches of the multiple products based on the expected sales mix. However, you should note that the answers change as the sales mix changes.

● **Explain the meaning of operating leverage and describe how it influences profits.** Operating leverage measures the sensitivity of profits in relation to fluctuations in sales. It is measured by dividing total contribution by total profit. An operating leverage of four indicates that profits change by four times more than the change in sales. Therefore if sales increase/decrease by 10 per cent profits will increase/decrease by 40 per cent. High levels of operating leverage lead to higher risk arising from highly volatile profits but the increase in risk also provides the potential for higher profit levels when sales are expanding.

● **Identify and explain the assumptions on which cost–volume–profit analysis is based.** Cost–volume–profit analysis is based on the following assumptions: (a) all variables, other than volume, remain constant; (b) the sales mix remains constant; (c) total costs and revenues are linear functions of output; (d) costs can be accurately divided into their fixed and variable elements; (e) the analysis applies only to the relevant range; and (f) the analysis applies only to a short-term horizon.

KEY TERMS AND CONCEPTS

Break-even chart   A chart that plots total costs and total revenues against sales volume and indicates the break-even point.

Break-even point   The level of output at which costs are balanced by sales revenue and neither a profit nor a loss will occur.

Contribution graph   A graph that plots variable costs and total costs against sales volume, and fixed costs represent the difference between the total cost line and the variable cost line.

Contribution margin   The margin calculated by deducting variable expenses from sales revenue.

Contribution margin ratio   The proportion of sales available to cover fixed costs and provide for profit, calculated by dividing the contribution margin by the sales revenue, also known as profit–volume ratio.

Decreasing returns to scale   A situation that arises when unit costs rise as volume increases.

Degree of operating leverage   The contribution margin divided by the profit for a given level of sales.

High–low method   A method of analysing cost behaviour that consists of selecting the periods of highest and lowest activity levels and comparing the changes in costs that result from the two levels in order to separate fixed and variable costs.

Increasing returns to scale   A situation that arises when unit costs fall as volume increases.

Margin of safety   The amount by which sales may decrease before a loss occurs.

Operating leverage   A measure of the sensitivity of profits to changes in sales.

Profit–volume graph   A graph that plots profit/losses against volume.

Profit–volume ratio   The proportion of sales available to cover fixed costs and provide for profit, calculated by dividing the contribution margin by the sales revenue, also known as contribution margin ratio.

Relevant range   The output range at which an organization expects to be operating with a short-term planning horizon.

Sensitivity analysis   Analysis that shows how a result will be changed if the original estimates or underlying assumption changes.

ASSESSMENT MATERIAL

The review questions are short questions that enable you to assess your understanding of the main topics included in the chapter. The page numbers in parentheses provide you with the page numbers to refer to if you cannot answer a specific question.

The review problems are more complex and require you to relate and apply the content to various business problems. Solutions to review problems are provided in a separate section at the end of the book. Additional review problems can be accessed by lecturers and students in the dedicated online support resources for this book. Solutions to these review problems are provided for lecturers in the *Instructor's Manual* accompanying this book that can be downloaded from the dedicated online instructor's resources (see Preface for details).

The dedicated online digital support resources for this book also includes over 30 case study problems.

REVIEW QUESTIONS

3.1 Provide examples of how cost–volume–profit analysis can be used for decision-making. *(p. 48)*

3.2 Explain what is meant by the term 'relevant range'. *(pp. 50–51)*

3.3 Define the term 'contribution margin'. *(p. 52)*

3.4 Define the term 'profit–volume ratio' and explain how it can be used for cost–volume–profit analysis. *(p. 56)*

3.5 Describe and distinguish between the three different approaches to presenting cost–volume–profit relationships in graphical format. *(pp. 58–60)*

3.6 How can a company with multiple products use cost–volume–profit analysis? *(pp. 61–63)*

3.7 Explain why the break-even point changes when there is a change in sales mix. *(p. 63)*

3.8 Describe the assumptions underlying cost–volume–profit analysis. *(pp. 65–68)*

3.9 Define the term 'operating leverage' and explain how the degree of operating leverage can influence future profits. *(pp. 63–65)*

3.10 How can sensitivity analysis be used in conjunction with cost–volume–profit analysis? *(p. 68)*

REVIEW PROBLEMS

3.11 The following information is required for sub-questions (a) and (b)

The company expects to sell *h* units in the next accounting period.

(a) The margin of safety is shown on the diagram by:
   (i)   *k*
   (ii) *m*
   (iii) *n*
   (iv) *p*

(b) The effect of an increase in fixed costs, with all other costs and revenues remaining the same, will be:
   (i)   an increase in *m*
   (ii) an increase in *k*
   (iii) an increase in *f*
   (iv) a reduction in *p*

3.12 The diagram shows the profit–volume chart of Z Ltd for its last accounting period. The company made a profit of $*w* during the period.

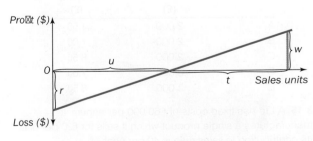

★ k is margin of safety ★

(a) An increase in the fixed costs per period (assuming the selling price per unit and the variable cost per unit remain unchanged), will result in:
  (i)   a reduction in r
  (ii) an increase in w
  (iii) a reduction in t
  (iv) no change in u
(b) The following results were achieved in the last accounting period:
  $r = \$50\,000$
  $w = \$16\,000$
  $t = 800$ units
  $u = 2500$ units
The company expects to make and sell an additional 1400 units in the next accounting period. If variable cost per unit, selling price per unit and total fixed costs remain unchanged, the effect on profit will be:

  (i)   an increase of $10 500
  (ii) an increase of $21 210
  (iii) an increase of $28 000
  (iv) an increase of $87 500

3.13 A company has established a budgeted sales revenue for the forthcoming period of £500 000 with an associated contribution of £275 000. Fixed production costs are £137 500 and fixed selling costs are £27 500.
   What is the break-even sales revenue?

(a) £75 625
(b) £90 750
(c) £250 000
(d) £300 000

3.14 The following details relate to product R:

Level of activity (units)	1 000 (£/unit)	2 000 (£/unit)
Direct materials	4.00	4.00
Direct labour	3.00	3.00
Production overhead	3.50	2.50
Selling overhead	1.00	0.50
	11.50	10.00

What are the total fixed cost and variable cost per unit?

	Total fixed cost (£)	Variable cost per unit (£)
A	2 000	1.50
B	2 000	7.00
C	2 000	8.50
D	3 000	7.00
E	3 000	8.50

3.15 A Ltd has fixed costs of €60 000 per annum. It manufactures a single product which it sells for €20 per unit. Its contribution to sales ratio is 40 per cent.
   A Ltd's break-even point in units is:

(a) 1200
(b) 1800

(c) 3000
(d) 5000
(e) 7500

3.16 A company manufactures a single product which it sells for £15 per unit. The product has a contribution to sales ratio of 40 per cent. The company's weekly break-even point is sales of £18 000.
   What would be the profit in a week when 1500 units are sold?

(a) £900
(b) £1800
(c) £2700
(d) £4500

3.17 A company's budget for the next period shows that it would break even at sales revenue of $800 000 and fixed costs of $320 000.
   The sales revenue needed to achieve a profit of $200 000 in the next period would be:

(a) $1 000 000
(b) $1 300 000
(c) $1 320 000
(d) $866 667

(2 marks)

3.18 An organization manufactures and sells a single product which has a variable cost of £24 per unit and a contribution to sales ratio of 40 per cent. Total monthly fixed costs are £720 000.
   What is the monthly break-even point (in units)?

(a) 18 000
(b) 20 000
(c) 30 000
(d) 45 000

3.19 Preparation of break-even and profit–volume graphs
ZED plc manufactures one standard product, which sells at £10. You are required to:

(a) prepare, from the data given below, a break-even and profit–volume graph showing the results for the 6 months ending 30 April and to determine:
  (i)   the fixed costs
  (ii) the variable cost per unit
  (iii) the profit–volume ratio
  (iv) the break-even point
  (v)   the margin of safety

Month	Sales (units)	Profit/(loss) (£)
November	30 000	40 000
December	35 000	60 000
January	15 000	(20 000)
February	24 000	16 000
March	26 000	24 000
April	18 000	(8 000)

(b) discuss the limitations of such a graph
(c) explain the use of the relevant range in such a graph.
(20 marks)

3.20 Preparation of a break-even chart with step fixed costs

Toowumba manufactures various products and uses CVP analysis to establish the minimum level of production to ensure profitability.

Fixed costs of $50 000 have been allocated to a specific product but are expected to increase to $100 000 once production exceeds 30 000 units, as a new factory will need to be rented in order to produce the extra units. Variable costs per unit are stable at $5 per unit over all levels of activity. Revenue from this product will be $7.50 per unit.

Required:

(a) Formulate the equations for the total cost at:
   (i) less than or equal to 30 000 units
   (ii) more than 30 000 units.

   (2 marks)

(b) Prepare a break-even chart and clearly identify the break-even point or points.

   (6 marks)

(c) Discuss the implications of the results from your graph in (b) with regard to Toowomba's production plans.

   (2 marks)

3.21 Non-graphical CVP analysis

The summarized profit and loss statement for Exewye plc for the last year is as follows:

	(£000)	(£000)
Sale (50 000 units)		1 000
Direct materials	350	
Direct wages	200	
Fixed production overhead	200	
Variable production overhead	50	
Administration overhead	180	
Selling and distribution overhead	120	
		1 100
Profit/(loss)		(100)

At a recent board meeting the directors discussed the year's results, following which the chairman asked for suggestions to improve the situation.

You are required, as management accountant, to evaluate the following alternative proposals and to comment briefly on each:

(a) Pay salesmen a commission of 10 per cent of sales and thus increase sales to achieve break-even point.

   (5 marks)

(b) Reduce selling price by 10 per cent, which it is estimated would increase sales volume by 30 per cent.

   (3 marks)

(c) Increase direct wage rates by 25 per cent per hour, as part of a productivity/pay deal. It is hoped that this would increase production and sales by 20 per cent, but advertising costs would increase by £50 000.

   (4 marks)

(d) Increase sales by additional advertising of £300 000, with an increased selling price of 20 per cent, setting a profit margin of 10 per cent.

   (8 marks)
   (Total 20 marks)

3.22

A company manufactures a single product. Budget and standard cost details for next year include:

Selling price per unit	$24.00
Variable production cost per unit	$8.60
Fixed production costs	$650 000
Fixed selling and distribution costs	$230 400
Sales commission	5% of selling price
Sales	90 000 units

Required:

(i) Calculate the break-even point in units.
(ii) Calculate the percentage by which the budgeted sales can fall before the company begins to make a loss.

The marketing manager has suggested that the selling price per unit can be increased to $25.00 if the sales commission is increased to 8 per cent of selling price and a further $10 000 is spent on advertising.

(iii) Calculate the revised break-even point based on the marketing manager's suggestion.

   (5 marks)

3.23 Changes in sales mix

XYZ Ltd produces two products and the following budget applies for the next year:

	Product X (£)	Product Y (£)
Selling price	6	12
Variable costs	2	4
Contribution margin	4	8
Fixed costs apportioned	100 000	200 000
Units sold	70 000	30 000

You are required to calculate the break-even points for each product and the company as a whole and comment on your findings.

3.24 Multi-product CVP analysis

Cardio Co manufactures three types of fitness equipment: treadmills (T), cross-trainers (C) and rowing machines (R). The budgeted sales prices and volumes for the next year are as follows:

	T	C	R
Selling price	$1 600	$1 800	$ 1 400
Units	420	400	380

The standard cost card for each product is shown below.

	T ($)	C ($)	R ($)
Material	430	500	360
Labour	220	240	190
Variable overheads	110	120	95

Labour costs are 60 per cent fixed and 40 per cent variable. General fixed overheads excluding any fixed labour costs are expected to be $55 000 for the next year.

Required:

(a) Calculate the weighted average contribution to sales ratio for Cardio Co.

(4 marks)

(b) Calculate the margin of safety in $ revenue for Cardio Co.

(3 marks)

(c) Assuming that the products are sold in a CONSTANT MIX, draw a multi-product break even chart for Cardio Co. Label fully both axes, any lines drawn on the graph and the break even point.

(6 marks)

(d) Explain what would happen to the break even point if the products were sold in order of the most profitable products first.
Note: You are NOT required to demonstrate this on the graph drawn in part (c).

(2 marks)

3.25 Operating leverage

The profit statements for two different companies in the same industry are as follows:

	Company A (€000)	Company B (€000)
Sales	10 000	10 000
Less: Variable costs	8 000	4 000
Contribution margin	2 000	6 000
Less: Fixed costs	1 000	5 000
Profit	1 000	1 000

Required:

(a) Compute the degree of operating leverage for each company.
(b) Compute the break-even point for each company. Explain why the break-even point for Company B is higher.
(c) Assume that both companies experience a 50 per cent increase in sales revenues. Explain why the percentage increase in Company B's profits is significantly larger than that of Company A.

3.26 Non-graphical CVP behaviour

Tweed Ltd is a company engaged solely in the manufacture of jumpers, which are bought mainly for sporting activities. Present sales are direct to retailers, but in recent years there has been a steady decline in output because of increased foreign competition. In the last trading year the accounting report indicated that the company produced the lowest profit for 10 years. The forecast for next year indicates that the present deterioration in profits is likely to continue. The company considers that a profit of £80 000 should be achieved to provide an adequate return on capital. The managing director has asked that a review be made of the present pricing and marketing policies. The marketing director has completed this review, and passes the proposals on to you for evaluation and recommendation, together with the profit and loss account for the last trading year.

Tweed Ltd profit and loss account for last trading year

	(£)	(£)	(£)
Sales revenue			
(100 000 jumpers at £10)			1 000 000
Factory cost of goods sold:			
Direct materials	100 000		
Direct labour	350 000		
Variable factory overheads	60 000		
Fixed factory overheads	220 000	730 000	
Administration overhead		140 000	
Selling and distribution overhead			
Sales commission			
(2% of sales)	20 000		
Delivery costs			
(variable per unit sold)	50 000		
Fixed costs	40 000	110 000	980 000
Profit			20 000

The information to be submitted to the managing director includes the following three proposals:

(i) To proceed on the basis of analyses of market research studies that indicate that the demand for the jumpers is such that a 10 per cent reduction in selling price would increase demand by 40 per cent.
(ii) To proceed with an enquiry that the marketing director has had from a mail order company about the possibility of purchasing 50 000 units annually if the selling price is right. The mail order company would transport the jumpers from Tweed Ltd to its own warehouse, and no sales commission would be paid on these sales by Tweed Ltd. However, if an acceptable price can be negotiated, Tweed Ltd would be expected

to contribute £60 000 per annum towards the cost of producing the mail order catalogue. It would also be necessary for Tweed Ltd to provide special additional packaging at a cost of £0.50 per jumper. The marketing director considers that in the next year sales from existing business would remain unchanged at 100 000 units, based on a selling price of £10 if the mail order contract is undertaken.

(iii) To proceed on the basis of a view held by the marketing director that a 10 per cent price reduction, together with a national advertising campaign costing £30 000, may increase sales to the maximum capacity of 160 000 jumpers.

Required:

(a) The calculation of break-even sales value based on the accounts for the last trading year.

(b) A financial evaluation of proposal (i) and a calculation of the number of units Tweed Ltd would require to sell at £9 each to earn the target profit of £80 000.

(c) A calculation of the minimum prices that would have to be quoted to the mail order company, first, to ensure that Tweed Ltd would at least break even on the mail order contract, secondly, to ensure that the same overall profit is earned as proposal (i) and, thirdly, to ensure that the overall target profit is earned.

(d) A financial evaluation of proposal (iii).

4

MEASURING RELEVANT COSTS AND REVENUES FOR DECISION-MAKING

LEARNING OBJECTIVES After studying this chapter you should be able to:

● distinguish between relevant and irrelevant costs and revenues

● explain the importance of qualitative factors

● distinguish between the relevant and irrelevant costs and revenues for the five decision-making problems described

● describe the key concept that should be applied for presenting information for product mix decisions when capacity constraints apply

● explain why the book value of equipment is irrelevant when making equipment replacement decisions

● describe the opportunity cost concept

● explain the misconceptions relating to relevant costs and revenues.

The provision of relevant information for decision-making is one of the most important functions of management accounting. Decision-making involves choosing between alternatives. For example, managers may be faced with decisions as to whether to discontinue a product or a channel of distribution, make a component within the company or buy from an outside supplier, introduce a new product or service and/or replace existing equipment. Something that these decisions have in common is that they are not routine. When decisions of this kind are being considered **special studies** are undertaken.

Making decisions requires that only those costs and revenues that are relevant to the alternatives are considered. If irrelevant cost and revenue data are included the wrong decisions may be made. Identifying and comparing relevant costs and revenues is crucial to decision-making. It is therefore essential to identify the relevant costs and revenues that are applicable to the alternatives being considered. The purpose of this chapter is to enable you to distinguish between relevant costs and revenues for various decision-making situations.

Special studies focus on whatever planning time horizon the decision-maker considers appropriate for a given situation. However, it is important not to focus excessively on the short term, because the objective is to maximize long-term benefits. We begin by explaining the concept of relevant cost and applying this principle to special studies relating to the following:

1 special selling price decisions

2 product mix decisions when capacity constraints exist

3 decisions on replacement of equipment

4 outsourcing (make or buy) decisions

5 discontinuation decisions.

IDENTIFYING RELEVANT COSTS AND REVENUES

The **relevant costs and revenues** required for decision-making are only those that will be affected by the decision. Costs and revenues that are independent of a decision are obviously not relevant and need not be considered when making that decision. The relevant financial inputs for decision-making purposes are therefore future cash flows, which will differ between the various alternatives being considered. In other words, only **differential** (or **incremental**) **cash flows** should be taken into account, and cash flows that will be the same for all alternatives are irrelevant. To keep things simple we shall focus on relevant costs. You should remember, however, that the same principles also apply to relevant revenues.

Because decision-making is concerned with choosing between future alternative courses of action, and nothing can be done to alter the past, then past costs (also known as **sunk costs**) are not relevant for decision-making. In Chapter 2 it was pointed out that sunk costs have already been incurred and cannot be avoided regardless of the alternatives being considered.

Allocated common fixed costs are also irrelevant for decision-making. **Facility sustaining costs** such as general administrative and property costs are examples of common costs. They are incurred to support the organization as a whole and generally will not change whichever alternative is chosen. They will only change if there is a dramatic change in organizational activity resulting in an expansion or contraction in the business facilities. Common fixed costs may be allocated (i.e. apportioned) to cost objects but they should be disregarded for decision-making. This is because decisions merely lead to a redistribution of the same sunk cost between cost objects – they do not affect the level of cost to the company as a whole.

We can illustrate the identification of relevant costs in a non-business setting. Consider a situation where an individual is uncertain as to whether he or she should purchase a monthly rail ticket to travel to work or use his or her car. Assuming that the individual already owns and keeps the car, whether or not he or she travels to work by train, the cost of the road fund licence and insurance will be irrelevant. They are sunk costs and will remain the same irrespective of the mode of travel. The cost of fuel will, however, be relevant, because this is a future cost that will differ depending on which alternative method of transport is chosen.

The following general principles can therefore be applied in identifying relevant and irrelevant costs:

1 relevant costs are future costs that differ between alternatives
2 irrelevant costs consist of sunk costs, allocated costs and future costs that do not differ between alternatives.

IMPORTANCE OF QUALITATIVE/NON-FINANCIAL FACTORS

In many situations it is difficult to quantify all the important elements of a decision in monetary terms. Those factors that cannot be expressed in monetary terms are classified as **qualitative or non-financial factors**. An example might be the decline in employee morale that results from redundancies arising from a closure decision. It is essential that qualitative factors be brought to the attention of management during the decision-making process, because otherwise there may be a danger that a wrong decision will be made. For example, the cost of manufacturing a component internally may be more expensive than purchasing from an outside supplier. However, the decision to purchase from an outside supplier could result in the closing down of the company's facilities for manufacturing the component. The effect of such a decision might lead to redundancies and a decline in employee morale, which could affect future output. In addition, the company will now be at the mercy of the supplier who might seek to increase prices on subsequent contracts and/or may not always deliver on time. The company may not then be in a position to meet customers' requirements. In turn, this could result in a loss of customer goodwill and a decline in future sales.

Qualitative factors such as these must be taken into account in the decision-making process. Management must consider the availability of future supplies and the likely effect on customer goodwill if there is a delay in meeting orders. If the component can be obtained from many suppliers and repeat orders for the company's products from customers are unlikely, then the company may give little weighting to these qualitative factors. However, if the component can be obtained from only one supplier and the company relies heavily on repeat sales to existing customers, then the qualitative factors will be of considerable importance. In the latter situation the company may consider that the quantifiable cost savings from purchasing the component from an outside supplier are insufficient to cover the risk of the qualitative factors occurring.

We shall now move on to apply the relevant cost approach to a variety of decision-making problems. We shall concentrate on measuring the financial outcomes but you should remember that they do not always provide the full story. Qualitative factors should also be taken into account in the decision-making process.

SPECIAL PRICING DECISIONS

Special pricing decisions relate to pricing decisions outside the main market. Typically they involve one-time only orders or orders at a price below the prevailing market price. Consider the information presented in Example 4.1.

EXAMPLE 4.1

The Caledonian Company is a manufacturer of clothing that sells its output directly to clothing retailers in the UK. One of its departments manufactures sweaters. The department has a production capacity of 50 000 sweaters per month. Because of the liquidation of one of its major customers the company has excess capacity. For the next quarter, current monthly production and sales volume is expected to be 35 000 sweaters at a selling price of £40 per sweater. Expected *monthly* costs and revenues for an activity level of 35 000 sweaters are as follows:

	(£)	(£ per unit)
Direct labour	420 000	12
Direct materials	280 000	8
Variable manufacturing overheads	70 000	2
Manufacturing fixed (non-variable) overheads	280 000	8
Marketing and distribution fixed (non-variable) costs	105 000	3
Total costs	1 155 000	33
Sales	1 400 000	40
Profit	245 000	7

Caledonian is expecting an upsurge in demand and considers that the excess capacity is temporary. Therefore, even though there is sufficient direct labour capacity to produce 50 000 sweaters, Caledonian intends to retain the temporary excess supply of direct labour for the expected upsurge in demand. A company located overseas has offered to buy 15 000 sweaters each month for the next 3 months at a price of £20 per sweater. The company would pay for the transportation costs and thus no additional marketing and distribution costs will be incurred. No subsequent sales to this customer are anticipated. The company would require its company logo inserting on the sweater and Caledonian has predicted that this will cost £1 per sweater. Should Caledonian accept the offer from the company?

At first glance it looks as if the order should be rejected since the proposed selling price of £20 is less than the total unit cost of £33. A study of the cost estimates, however, indicates that for the next quarter direct labour will remain unchanged. It is therefore a fixed cost for the period under consideration. Manufacturing fixed overheads and the marketing and distribution costs are also fixed costs for the period under consideration. These costs will thus remain the same irrespective of whether or not the order is accepted. Hence they are irrelevant for this decision. All of the variable costs (i.e. the direct material costs, variable manufacturing overheads and the cost of adding the leisure company's logo) will be different if the order is accepted. Therefore, they are relevant costs for making the decision. The relevant revenue and costs per unit for the decision are:

Selling price		20
Less: Direct materials	8	
Variable overheads	2	
Inserting company logo	1	11
Contribution to fixed costs and profit		9

For sales of 15 000 sweaters Caledonian will obtain an additional contribution of £135 000 per month (15 000 × £9). In Example 4.1 none of the fixed costs are relevant for the decision. It is appropriate to unitize variable costs because they are constant per unit but fixed costs should not be unitized since (you will recall from Chapter 2) they are not constant per unit of output. You should present unit relevant costs and revenues (as shown above) only when all fixed costs are irrelevant for decision-making. In most circumstances you are likely to be faced with situations where only some of the fixed costs are relevant. Therefore, it is recommended that you avoid using unit costs for decision-making and instead adopt the approach presented in Exhibit 4.1 where total costs are used.

Note from Exhibit 4.1 that in columns (1) and (2) both relevant and irrelevant *total* costs are shown for all alternatives under consideration. If this approach is adopted the *same* amounts for the irrelevant items (i.e. those items that remain unchanged as a result of the decision, which are direct labour, and manufacturing and marketing non-variable overheads) are included for all alternatives, thus making them irrelevant for decision-making. Alternatively, you can omit the irrelevant costs in columns (1) and (2) because they are the same for both alternatives. A third approach, which is shown in column (3), involves only presenting the relevant (i.e. differential) costs and revenues. Note that column (3) represents the difference between columns (1) and (2). You will see that a comparison of columns (1) and (2), or presenting only the relevant items in column (3), shows that the company is better off by £135 000 per month if the order is accepted.

Four important factors must be considered before recommending acceptance of the order. Most of them relate to the assumption that there are no long-run consequences of accepting the offer at a selling price of £20 per sweater. First, it is assumed that the future selling price will not be affected by selling some of the output at a price below the going market price. If this assumption is incorrect then competitors may engage in similar practices of reducing their selling prices in an attempt to unload spare capacity. This may lead to a fall in the market price, which in turn would lead to a fall in profits from future sales. The loss of future profits may be greater than the short-term gain obtained from accepting special orders at prices below the existing

EXHIBIT 4.1 Evaluation of the 3-month order from the overseas company

Monthly sales and production in units	(1) Do not accept order 35 000 (£)	(2) Accept the order 50 000 (£)	(3) Difference in relevant costs/ (revenues) 15 000 (£)
Direct labour	420 000	420 000	—
Direct materials	280 000	400 000	120 000
Variable manufacturing overheads	70 000	100 000	30 000
Manufacturing non-variable overheads	280 000	280 000	—
Inserting company logo		15 000	15 000
Marketing and distribution costs	105 000	105 000	—
Total costs	1 155 000	1 320 000	165 000
Sales revenues	1 400 000	1 700 000	(300 000)
Profit per month	245 000	380 000	135 000
Difference in favour of accepting the order		135 000	

REAL WORLD VIEWS 4.1

Contribution margin: what it is, how to calculate it and why do you need it?

An article by Joe Knight, author of *HBR Tools: Business Valuation* states that contribution margin is a common financial analysis tool that's not very well understood by managers. He states that when you make a product or deliver a service and deduct the variable cost of making and delivering that product/service, the balance left represents the contribution margin. Contribution margin therefore shows you the net revenue left after variable costs have been deducted that is available to cover fixed expenses and provide a profit to the company.

The author points out that identifying the contribution margin provides managers with the required information to make several types of decisions, such as whether to add or subtract a product line, how to price a product or service and how to structure sales commissions. It is frequently used for profitability analysis to compare products to determine which to retain and which to drop. If a product's contribution margin is negative, the company is losing money with each unit it produces, and it should either drop the product or increase prices. If a product has a positive contribution margin, it should normally be retained because it contributes to fixed costs and profit.

Knight points out that large companies have hundreds of products so managers need to decide where to allocate resources. They need to drop products that have negative or the lowest contribution margins so that they can focus resources on the higher contribution products that will result in higher profits.

Questions

1 Why are cost-volume-profit calculation based on contribution margins rather than profit margins?
2 What are the difficulties in calculating contribution margins?
3 What are the pitfalls of relying extensively on basing decisions solely on contribution margins?

References

Gallo, A. (2017) *Contribution Margin: What It Is, How to Calculate It, and Why You Need It*. Available at hbr.org/2017/10/contribution-margin-what-it-is-how-to-calculate-it-and-why-you-need-it
Knight, J. (2016) *HBR Tools: Business Valuation.* Available at hbr.org/product/hbr-tools-business-valuation/TLVAL1-ZIP-ENG

market price. However, given that Caledonian has found a customer outside its normal market it is unlikely that the market price would be affected. However, if the customer had been within Caledonian's normal retail market there would be a real danger that the market price would be affected. Second, the decision to accept the order prevents the company from accepting other orders that may be obtained during the period at the going price. In other words, it is assumed that no better opportunities will present themselves during the period. Third, it is assumed that the company has unused resources that have no alternative uses that will yield a contribution to profits in excess of £135 000 *per month*. Finally, it is assumed that the fixed costs are unavoidable for the period under consideration. In other words, we assume that the direct labour force and the fixed overheads cannot be reduced in the short term, or that they are to be retained for an upsurge in demand, which is expected to occur in the longer term.

Evaluation of a longer-term order

In Example 4.1 we focused on a short-term time horizon of 3 months. Capacity could not easily be altered in the short term and therefore direct labour and fixed costs were irrelevant costs with respect to the short-term decision. In the longer term, however, it may be possible to reduce capacity and spending on fixed costs and direct labour. Example 4.2 uses the same cost data as Example 4.1 but presents a revised scenario of a longer time horizon so that some of the costs that were fixed in the short term in Example 4.1 can now be changed in the longer term. You will see from Example 4.2 that Caledonian is faced with the following two alternatives:

1 do not accept the overseas order and reduce monthly capacity from 50 000 to 35 000 sweaters

2 accept the overseas order of 15 000 sweaters per month and retain capacity at 50 000 sweaters per month.

The appropriate financial data for the analysis is shown in Exhibit 4.2. Note that column (1) incorporates the reduction in direct labour and fixed costs if capacity is reduced from 50 000 to 35 000 sweaters. A comparison of the monthly outcomes reported in columns (1) and (2) of Exhibit 4.2 shows that the company is better off by £31 000 per month if it reduces capacity to 35 000 sweaters, assuming that there are no qualitative factors to be taken into consideration. Column (3) presents only the differential (relevant) costs and revenues. This approach also indicates that the company is better off by £31 000 per month.

Note that the entry in column (3) of £25 000 is the lost revenues from the rent of the unutilized capacity if the company accepts the orders. This represents the **opportunity cost** of accepting orders. In Chapter 2 it was pointed out that where the choice of one course

EXAMPLE 4.2

Assume that the department within Caledonian Company has a *monthly* production capacity of 50 000 sweaters. Liquidation of a major customer has resulted in expected future demand being 35 000 sweaters per *month*. Caledonian has not been able to find any customers for the excess capacity of 15 000 sweaters apart from a company located overseas that would be prepared to enter into a contractual agreement for a 3-year period for a supply of 15 000 sweaters per month at an agreed price of £25 per sweater. The company would require that a motif be added to each sweater and Caledonian has predicted that will cost £1 per sweater. The company would pay for the transportation costs and thus no additional marketing and distribution costs will be incurred.

Direct materials and variable overheads are predicted to be £8 and £2, respectively, per sweater (the same as Example 4.1) and fixed manufacturing (£280 000), marketing and distribution costs (£105 000) and direct labour (£420 000) are also currently the same as the costs used in Example 4.1. However, if Caledonian does not enter into a contractual agreement it will reduce the direct labour force by 30 per cent (to reflect a capacity reduction from 50 000 to 35 000 sweaters). Therefore, monthly direct labour costs will decline by 30 per cent, from £420 000 to £294 000. Further investigations indicate that manufacturing non-variable costs of £70 000 per month could be saved if a decision was made to reduce capacity by 15 000 sweaters per month. For example, the rental contracts for some of the machinery will not be renewed. Also some savings will be made in supervisory labour and support costs. Savings in marketing and distribution costs would be £20 000 per month. Assume also that if the capacity was reduced, factory rearrangements would result in part of the facilities being rented out at £25 000 per month. Should Caledonian accept the offer from the overseas company?

EXHIBIT 4.2   Evaluation of orders for the unutilized capacity over a 3-year time horizon

Monthly sales and production in units	(1) Do not accept order 35 000 (£)	(2) Accept the order 50 000 (£)	(3) Difference in relevant costs/ (revenues) 15 000 (£)
Direct labour	294 000	420 000	126 000
Direct materials	280 000	400 000	120 000
Variable manufacturing overheads	70 000	100 000	30 000
Manufacturing non-variable overheads	210 000	280 000	70 000
Inserting motif		15 000	15 000
Marketing and distribution costs	85 000	105 000	20 000
Total costs	939 000	1 320 000	381 000
Revenues from rental of facilities	25 000		25 000
Sales revenues	1 400 000	1 775 000	(375 000)
Profit per month	486 000	455 000	31 000
Difference in favour of rejecting the order		31 000	

of action requires that an alternative course of action is given up, the financial benefits that are foregone or sacrificed are known as opportunity costs. They only arise when resources are scarce and have alternative uses. Thus, in our illustration the capacity allocated to producing 15 000 sweaters results in an opportunity cost (i.e. the lost revenues from the rent of the capacity) of £25 000 per month.

In Exhibit 4.2 all of the costs and revenues are relevant to the decision because some of the costs that were fixed in the short term could be changed in the longer term. The relevance of a cost often depends on the time horizon under consideration. It is therefore important to make sure that the information presented for decision-making relates to the appropriate time horizon. If inappropriate time horizons are selected there is a danger that misleading information will be presented. Remember that our aim should always be to maximize *long-term* net cash inflows.

PRODUCT MIX DECISIONS WHEN CAPACITY CONSTRAINTS EXIST

In the short term, sales demand may be in excess of current productive capacity. For example, output may be restricted by a shortage of skilled labour, materials, equipment or space. When sales demand is in excess of a company's productive capacity, the resources responsible for limiting the output should be identified. These scarce resources are known as **limiting factors**. Within a short-term time period it is unlikely that constraints can be removed and additional resources acquired. Where limiting factors apply, profit is maximized when the greatest possible contribution to profit is obtained each time the scarce or limiting factor is used. Consider Example 4.3.

EXAMPLE 4.3

A farmer in Ruritania has 240 000 square metres (m²) of land on which he grows maize, barley, potatoes and wheat. He is planning his production for the next growing season. The following information is provided relating to the anticipated demand and productive capacity for the next season:

	Maize	Potatoes	Barley	Wheat
Contribution per tonne of output in Ruritanian dollars	$160	$112	$96	$80
m² required per tonne of output	80	32	24	16
Estimated sales demand (tonnes)	3 000	3 000	3 000	3 000
Required area to meet sales demand (m²)	240 000	96 000	72 000	48 000

It is not possible in the short run to increase the area of land beyond 240 000m² for growing the above crops. You have been asked to advise on the mix of crops that should be produced during the period.

In this situation the farmer's ability to increase output and profits/net cash inflows is limited in the short term by the availability of land for growing crops. At first glance you may think that the farmer should give top priority to producing maize, since this yields the highest contribution per tonne sold, but this assumption would be incorrect. To produce a tonne of maize, 80 scarce m² are required, whereas potatoes, barley and wheat require only 32m², 24m² and 16m² respectively of scarce land. By concentrating on growing potatoes, barley and wheat, the farmer can sell 3000 tonnes of each crop and still have some land left to grow maize. On the other hand if the farmer concentrates on growing maize it will only be possible to meet the maximum sales demand of maize, and there will be no land available to grow the remaining crops. The way in which you should determine the optimum output to maximize profits is to calculate the contribution per limiting factor (i.e. m² of land required per tonne of output) for each crop and then to rank the crops in order of profitability based on this calculation.

Using the figures in the present example the result would be as follows:

	Maize	Potatoes	Barley	Wheat
Contribution per tonne of output	$160	$112	$96	$80
m² required per tonne of output	80	32	24	16
Contribution per m²	$2	$3.50	$4	$5
Ranking	4	3	2	1

The farmer can now allocate the 240 000m² of land in accordance with the above rankings. The first choice should be to produce as much wheat as possible. The maximum sales are 3000 tonnes, and production of this quantity will result in 48 000m² of land being used. The second choice should be to grow barley and the maximum sales demand of 3000 tonnes will result in a further 72 000m² of land being used. The third choice is to grow potatoes. To meet the maximum sales demand for potatoes a further 96 000m² of land will be required. Growing 3000 tonnes of wheat, barley and potatoes requires 216 000m² of land, leaving a balance of 24 000m² for growing maize, which will enable 300 tonnes of maize to be grown.

REAL WORLD VIEWS 4.2

Multi-product quality competition: impact of resource constraints

According to an article authored by Yayla-Küllü *et al.*, multi-product firms account for 91 per cent of the output in US manufacturing and they often make short- to medium-term adjustments in their product-lines. For many of these product-line decisions, supply capacity constraints must be taken into account when making product-line decisions. The authors provide the following examples of supply capacity constraints.

Many furniture manufacturers produce custom and standard furniture using the same fixed capacity. In another example, the available capacity of a flexible machine (machining time) is allocated between high- and low-quality products where a higher-quality product requires slower machining speeds thereby taking a longer time to produce. The authors also provide an example of a firm in Finland that produces both mass-produced and custom-tailored suits in its factory where a custom-tailored suit uses more of the available limited factory time compared with a mass-produced suit.

The cruise line industry is another example where differentiated product-lines are the norm. They provide a wide range of staterooms ranging from small rooms to large luxurious suites. In this industry, supply capacity is limited because it takes time to refurbish existing ships or build new ships. In another example, airlines offer differentiated products such as economy, business and first-class seats. For airlines, changing the product mix by changing the seating configuration in an aircraft is a common short- to medium-term solution to increasing profitability without making investments for new aircrafts.

In all of the above-mentioned examples ignoring supply capacity while deciding the product-line can be sub-optimal. The authors point out that many firms often do not determine product-line decisions taking supply capacity constraints into account and provide evidence that shows when resources are limited firms' product-lines should be determined by considering the margin per unit capacity.

Questions

1 Provide examples of firms in the retail and merchandising sectors where supply capacity constraints should be taken into account when making product mix decisions.
2 What are the scarce/limiting factors that apply in the examples cited above?

Reference

Yayla-Küllü, H.M., Parlaktürk, A.K. and Swaminathan, J.M. (2013) Multiproduct quality competition: impact of resource constraints, *Production and Operations Management*, 22(3), 603–614.

We can now summarize the allocation of the 240 000m² of land:

Production	m² of land used	Balance of unused land (m²)
3000 tonnes of wheat	48 000	192 000
3000 tonnes of barley	72 000	120 000
3000 tonnes of potatoes	96 000	24 000
300 tonnes of maize	24 000	—

The above allocation results in the following total contribution:

	$
3000 tonnes of wheat at $80 per tonne contribution	240 000
3000 tonnes of barley at $96 per tonne contribution	288 000
3000 tonnes of potatoes at $112 per tonne contribution	336 000
300 tonnes of maize at $160 per tonne contribution	48 000
Total contribution	912 000

Contrast the above contribution with the contribution that would have been obtained if the farmer had ranked crop profitability by his or her contributions per tonne of output. This would have resulted in maize being ranked as the most profitable crop and all of the available land would have been used to grow 3000 tonnes of maize, giving a total contribution of $480 000 (3000 tonnes × $160).

Always remember to consider other qualitative factors before the final production programme is determined. For example, customer goodwill may be lost causing a fall in future sales if the farm is unable to supply all four crops to, say, 50 of its regular customers. Difficulties may arise in applying this procedure when there is more than one scarce resource. It could not be applied if, for example, labour hours were also scarce and maize had the highest contribution per scarce labour hour. In situations where more than one resource is scarce, it is necessary to resort to linear programming methods in order to determine the optimal production programme. For an explanation of how linear programming can be applied when there is more than one scarce resource you should refer to Drury (2018, Chapter 26).

Finally, it is important that you remember that the approach outlined in this section applies only to those situations where capacity constraints cannot be removed in the short term. In the longer term additional resources should be acquired if the contribution from the extra capacity exceeds the cost of acquisition.

REPLACEMENT OF EQUIPMENT – THE IRRELEVANCE OF PAST COSTS

Replacement of equipment is a capital investment or long-term decision that requires the use of discounted cash flow procedures. These procedures are discussed in detail in Chapter 6, but one aspect of asset replacement decisions that we will consider at this

EXAMPLE 4.4

Three years ago the Anytime Bank purchased a cheque sorting machine for £120 000. Depreciation using the straight line basis, assuming a life of 6 years and no salvage value, has been recorded each year in the financial accounts. The present written down value of the machine is £60 000 and it has a remaining life of 3 years. Recently a new sorting and imaging machine has been marketed that will cost £50 000 and have an expected life of 3 years with no scrap value. It is estimated that the new machine will reduce variable operating costs from £50 000 to £30 000 per annum. The current sales value of the old machine is £5000 and will be zero in 3 years' time.

stage is how to deal with the book value (i.e. the **written down value**) of old equipment. This is a problem that has been known to cause difficulty, but the correct approach is to apply relevant cost principles (i.e. past or sunk costs are irrelevant for decision-making). We shall now use Example 4.4 to illustrate the irrelevance of the book value of old equipment in a replacement decision.

You will see from an examination of Example 4.4 that the total costs over a period of 3 years for each of the alternatives are as follows:

	(1) Retain present machine (£)	(2) Buy replacement machine (£)	(3) Difference relevant costs/ (benefits) (£)
Variable/incremental operating costs:			
£50 000 for 3 years	150 000		
£30 000 for 3 years		90 000	(60 000)
Old machine book value:			
3-year annual depreciation charge	60 000		
Lump sum write-off		60 000	
Old machine disposal value		(5 000)	(5 000)
Initial purchase price of new machine		50 000	50 000
Total cost	210 000	195 000	(15 000)

You can see from the above analysis that the £60 000 book value of the old machine is irrelevant to the decision. Book values are not relevant costs because they are past or sunk costs and are therefore the same for all potential courses of action. If the present machine is retained, 3 years' depreciation at £20 000 per annum will be written off annually whereas if the new machine is purchased the £60 000 will be written off as a lump sum if it is replaced. Note that depreciation charges for the new machine are not included in the analysis since the cost of purchasing the machine is already included. The sum of the annual depreciation charges is equivalent to the purchase cost. Thus, including both items would amount to double counting.

The above analysis shows that the costs of operating the replacement machine are £15 000 less than the costs of operating the existing machine over the 3-year period. Again there are several different methods of presenting the information. They all show a £15 000 advantage in favour of replacing the machine. You can present the information shown in columns (1) and (2) above, as long as you ensure that the same amount for the irrelevant items is included for all alternatives. Alternatively you can present columns (1) and (2) with the irrelevant item (i.e. the £60 000) omitted or you can present the differential items listed in column (3). However, if you adopt the latter approach you will probably find it more meaningful to restate column (3) as follows:

	£
Savings on variable operating costs (3 years)	60 000
Sale proceeds of existing machine	5 000
	65 000
Less purchase cost of replacement machine	50 000
Savings on purchasing replacement machine	15 000

OUTSOURCING AND MAKE OR BUY DECISIONS

Outsourcing is the process of obtaining goods or services from outside suppliers instead of producing the same goods or providing the same services within the organization. Decisions on whether to produce components or provide services within the organization or to acquire them from outside suppliers are called outsourcing or 'make or buy' decisions. Many organizations outsource some of their activities such as their payroll and purchasing functions or the purchase of speciality components. Increasingly, municipal local services such as waste disposal, highways and property maintenance are being outsourced. Consider the information presented in Example 4.5 (Case A).

At first glance it appears that the component should be outsourced since the purchase price of £30 is less than the current total unit cost of manufacturing. However, the unit costs include some costs that will be unchanged whether or not the components are outsourced. These costs are therefore not relevant to the decision. We are also assuming that there are no alternative uses of the released capacity if the components are outsourced. The appropriate cost information is presented in Exhibit 4.3 (Section A). Alternative approaches to presenting relevant cost and revenue information are presented. In columns (1) and (2) of Exhibit 4.3 cost information is presented that includes both relevant and irrelevant costs for both alternatives under consideration. The same amount for non-manufacturing overheads, which are irrelevant, is included for both alternatives. By including the same amount in both columns the cost is made irrelevant. Alternatively, you can present cost information

REAL WORLD VIEWS 4.3

Potential adverse long-term consequences of outsourcing

Gary Kapanowski argues that for many organizations, undertaking activities internally yields many advantages that are not reflected in the standard make-versus buy analysis. He suggests that the negative impact of outsourcing on an organization's performance may not be solely attributable to the initial decision to outsource but to a cumulative effect over time. As we move decision-by-decision to outsource specific work, the organization's ability to perform tasks becomes more difficult at a specified point in time when expertise and efficiencies are lost. This is due to employees not performing the tasks routinely, and thus losing the ability to perform efficiently at high-volume levels. Employees performing the key activities leave over time, resulting in a death spiral effect when it comes to specific tasks and productivity, which jeopardizes the organization's ability to operate in the future.

The organization may lose the capability to replicate the outsourced activities and the inability to recover these lost skills may become a competitive disadvantage. Thus outsourcing can act as a death spiral of sorts, preventing the organization from achieving its goals, because of the lack of necessary skills and capabilities that were lost due to the outsourcing decision(s).

Questions

1 How can outsourcing change the cost structure of an organization?
2 What are the major benefits and limitations of outsourcing?

Reference

Kapanowski, G. (2017), The death spiral of outsourcing: A new view on the make-versus-buy analysis, *Cost Management*, September/October, 32-39.

EXAMPLE 4.5

Case A

One of the divisions within Rhine Autos is currently negotiating with another supplier regarding outsourcing component A that it manufactures. The division currently manufactures 10 000 units per annum of the component. The costs currently assigned to the components are as follows:

	Total costs of producing 10 000 components (£)	Unit cost (£)
Direct materials AB	120 000	12
Direct labour	100 000	10
Variable manufacturing overhead costs (power and utilities)	10 000	1
Fixed manufacturing overhead costs	80 000	8
Share of non-manufacturing overheads	50 000	5
Total costs	360 000	36

The above costs are expected to remain unchanged in the foreseeable future if the Rhine Autos division continues to manufacture the components. The supplier has offered to supply 10 000 components per annum at a price of £30 per unit guaranteed for a minimum of 3 years. If Rhine Autos outsources component A the direct labour force currently employed in producing the components will be made redundant. No redundancy costs will be incurred. Direct materials and variable overheads are avoidable if component A is outsourced. Fixed manufacturing overhead costs would be reduced by £10 000 per annum but non-manufacturing costs would remain unchanged. Assume initially that the capacity that is required for component A has no alternative use. Should the division of Rhine Autos make or buy the component?

Case B

Assume now that the extra capacity that will be made available from outsourcing component A can be used to manufacture and sell 10 000 units of component Z at a price of £34 per unit. All of the labour force required to manufacture component A would be used to make component Z. The variable manufacturing overheads, the fixed manufacturing overheads and non-manufacturing overheads would be the same as the costs incurred for manufacturing component A. Materials AB required to manufacture component A would not be required but additional materials XY required for making component Z would cost £13 per unit. Should Rhine Autos outsource component A?

in columns (1) and (2) that excludes any irrelevant costs and revenues. Adopting either approach will result in a difference of £60 000 in favour of making component A.

As in earlier exhibits the third approach is to list only the relevant costs, cost savings and any relevant revenues. This approach is shown in column (3) of Exhibit 4.3 (Section A). This column represents the differential costs or revenues and it is derived from the differences between columns (1) and (2). In column (3) only the information that is relevant to the

EXHIBIT 4.3   Evaluating a make or buy decision

Section A – Assuming there is no alternative use of the released capacity

	Total cost of continuing to make 10 000 components (1) (£ per annum)	Total cost of buying 10 000 components (2) (£ per annum)	Difference = Extra costs/ (savings) of buying (3) (£ per annum)
Direct materials AB	120 000		(120 000)
Direct labour	100 000		(100 000)
Variable manufacturing overhead costs (power and utilities)	10 000		(10 000)
Fixed manufacturing overhead costs	80 000	70 000	(10 000)
Non-manufacturing overheads	50 000	50 000	
Outside purchase cost incurred/(saved)		300 000	300 000
Total costs incurred/(saved) per annum	360 000	420 000	60 000

Extra costs of buying = 60 000

Section B – Assuming the released capacity can be used to make component Z

	Make component A and do not make component Z (1) (£ per annum)	Buy component A and make component Z (2) (£ per annum)	(3) Difference = Extra costs/ (benefits) of buying component A (£ per annum)
Direct materials XY		130 000	130 000
Direct materials AB	120 000		(120 000)
Direct labour	100 000	100 000	
Variable manufacturing overhead costs	10 000	10 000	
Fixed manufacturing overhead costs	80 000	80 000	
Non-manufacturing overheads	50 000	50 000	
Outside purchase cost incurred		300 000	300 000
Revenue from sales of component Z		(340 000)	(340 000)
Total net costs	360 000	330 000	(30 000)

Extra benefits from buying component A and using the released capacity to make component Z = £30 000

decision is presented. This approach shows the relevant costs of making directly against outsourcing. It indicates that the additional costs of buying component A are £300 000 but this enables costs of £240 000 associated with making component A to be saved. Therefore the company incurs an extra cost of £60 000 if it buys component A from the outside supplier.

We shall now explore what happens when the extra capacity created from not producing component A has an alternative use. Consider the information presented in

this will include opening 150 petrol stations and 1000 Click and Collect sites by 2018'.

Opening and closing new stores

In 2015, Asda was staging a major push south opening 11 new stores in the greater London region over the next few months with plans for a further 150 by 2018. Two of the new stores will be a trial of a new smaller format. These will be Asda's first 'High Street' stores, set on main thoroughfares at a time when many retailers are abandoning the heart of towns for retail parks. The retailer will also open seven standalone petrol filling stations, not attached to any existing stores, and two new superstores.

Also in 2015 arch rival Tesco had announced 43 store closures, Morrisons 23 stores and Sainsbury's has abandoned 40 new supermarket projects and cut 500 jobs. Discounters Aldi and Lidl are still growing. Aldi plans to open around 60 new shops.

Craig Bonnar, the Asda director responsible for store development, said: 'We have set out a clear five-year strategy which includes expanding further into London and the South East, and we anticipate

Questions

1 How might management of the above supermarkets determine which stores should be closed?
2 How might Asda management determine which stores to open?

Reference

Steiner, R. (2015) Asda in push south with smaller stores. *Daily Mail,* 23 Mar. 60. ISSN 03077578.

Example 4.5 (Case B). The management of Rhine Autos now should consider the following alternatives:

1 make component A and do not make component Z
2 outsource component A and make and sell component Z.

It is assumed that there is insufficient capacity to make both components A and Z. The appropriate financial information is shown in Exhibit 4.3 (Section B). You will see that the same costs will be incurred for both alternatives for direct labour and all of the overhead costs. Therefore these items are irrelevant and the same amount can be entered in columns (1) and (2) or they can be omitted from both columns. Note that direct materials AB (£120 000) will be incurred only if the company makes component A so an entry of £120 000 is shown in column (1) and no entry is made in column (2). However, if component A is bought from the supplier the capacity will be used to produce component Z and this will result in a purchase cost of £130 000 being incurred for materials XY that are required to produce product Z. Thus £130 000 is entered in column (2) and no entry is made in column (1) in respect of materials XY. Also note that the sales revenue arising from the sale of component Z is shown in parentheses in column (2). A comparison of the totals of columns (1) and (2) indicates that that there is a net benefit of £30 000 from buying component A if the released capacity is used to make component Z.

Instead of presenting the information in columns (1) and (2) you can present the relevant costs and benefits as shown by the differential items in column (3). This column indicates that the extra costs of buying component A and using the released capacity to make component Z are:

	£
Outside purchase cost incurred	300 000
Purchase of materials XY for component Z	130 000
	430 000

The extra benefits are:

	£
Revenues from the sale of component Z	340 000
Savings from not purchasing materials AB	120 000
	460 000

The above alternative analysis also shows that there is a net benefit of £30 000 from buying component A if the released capacity is used to make component Z.

DISCONTINUATION DECISIONS

Most organizations periodically analyse profits by one or more cost objects, such as products or services, customers and locations. Periodic profitability analysis can highlight unprofitable activities that require a more detailed appraisal (sometimes referred to as a special study) to ascertain whether or not they should be discontinued. In this section we shall illustrate how the principle of relevant costs can be applied to discontinuation decisions. Consider Example 4.6. You will see that it focuses on a decision whether to discontinue operating a sales territory, but the same principles can also be applied to discontinuing products, services or customers.

In Example 4.6 Euro Company analyses profits by locations. Profits are analysed by regions which are then further analysed by sales territories within each region. It is apparent from Example 4.6 that the Scandinavian region is profitable (showing a budgeted quarterly profit of £202 000) but the profitability analysis suggests that the Helsinki sales territory is unprofitable. A more detailed study is required to ascertain whether it should be discontinued. Let us assume that this study indicates that:

1 Discontinuing the Helsinki sales territory will eliminate cost of goods sold, salespersons' salaries and sales office rent.

2 Discontinuing the Helsinki sales territory will have no effect on depreciation of sales office equipment, warehouse rent, depreciation of warehouse equipment and regional and headquarters expenses. The same costs will be incurred by the company for all of these items even if the sales territory is discontinued.

Note that in the event of discontinuation the sales office will not be required and the rental will be eliminated whereas the warehouse rent relates to the warehouse for the region as a whole and, unless the company moves to a smaller warehouse, the rental will remain unchanged. It is therefore not a relevant cost. Discontinuation will result in the creation of additional space and if the extra space remains unused there are no financial consequences to take into account. However, if the additional space can be sublet to generate rental income the income would be incorporated as an opportunity cost for the alternative of keeping the Helsinki territory.

EXAMPLE 4.6

The Euro Company is a wholesaler that sells its products to retailers throughout Europe. Euro's headquarters is in Brussels. The company has adopted a regional structure with each region consisting of three-to-five sales territories. Each region has its own regional office and a warehouse that distributes the goods directly to the customers. Each sales territory also has an office where the marketing staff are located. The Scandinavian region consists of three sales territories with offices located in Stockholm, Oslo and Helsinki. The budgeted results for the next quarter are as follows:

	Stockholm (£000)	Oslo (£000)	Helsinki (£000)	Total (£000)
Cost of goods sold	920	1 002	1 186	3 108
Salespersons' salaries	160	200	240	600
Sales office rent	60	90	120	270
Depreciation of sales office equipment	20	30	40	90
Apportionment of warehouse rent	24	24	24	72
Depreciation of warehouse equipment	20	16	22	58
Regional and headquarters costs	360	400	340	1 100
Total costs assigned to each location	1 564	1 762	1 972	5 298
Reported profit/(loss)	236	238	(272)	202
Sales	1 800	2 000	1 700	5 500

Assuming that the above results are likely to be typical of future quarterly performance, should the Helsinki territory be discontinued?

Exhibit 4.4 shows the relevant cost and revenue computations. Column (1) shows the costs incurred and revenues derived by the company if the sales territory is kept open (i.e. the items listed in the final column of Example 4.6) and column (2) shows the costs and revenues that will occur if a decision is taken to drop the sales territory. Therefore, in column (2) only those costs that would be eliminated (i.e. those in item (1) on our list) are deducted from column (1). For example, Example 4.6 specifies that £240 000 salespersons' salaries will be eliminated if the Helsinki territory is closed, so the entry in column (2) is £360 000 (£600 000 – £240 000).

You can see that the company will continue to incur some of the costs (i.e. those in item (2) on our list) even if the Helsinki territory is closed and these costs are therefore irrelevant to the decision. Again you can either include, or exclude, the irrelevant costs in columns (1) and (2) as long as you ensure that the same amount of irrelevant costs is included for both alternatives if you adopt the first approach. Both approaches will show that future profits will decline by £154 000 if the Helsinki territory is closed. Alternatively, you can present just the relevant costs and revenues shown in column (3). This approach indicates that keeping the sales territory open results in additional sales revenues of £1 700 000 but additional costs of £1 546 000 are incurred giving a contribution of £154 000 towards fixed costs and profits. We can conclude that the Helsinki sales territory should not be closed.

EXHIBIT 4.4   Relevant cost analysis relating to the discontinuation of the Helsinki territory

Total costs and revenues to be assigned	(1) Keep Helsinki territory open (£000)	(2) Discontinue Helsinki territory (£000)	(3) Difference in incremental costs and revenues (£000)
Cost of goods sold	3 108	1 922	1 186
Salespersons' salaries	600	360	240
Sales office rent	270	150	120
Depreciation of sales office equipment	90	90	
Apportionment of warehouse rent	72	72	
Depreciation of warehouse equipment	58	58	
Regional and headquarters costs	1 100	1 100	
Total costs to be assigned	5 298	3 752	1 546
Reported profit	202	48	154
Sales	5 500	3 800	1 700

DETERMINING THE RELEVANT COSTS OF DIRECT MATERIALS

So far in this chapter we have assumed, when considering various decisions, that any materials required would not be taken from existing inventories but would be purchased at a later date, and so the estimated purchase price would be the relevant material cost. Where materials are taken from existing inventory, you should remember that the original purchase price represents a past or sunk cost and is therefore irrelevant for decision-making. However, if the materials are to be replaced then the decision to use them on an activity will result in additional acquisition costs compared with the situation if the materials were not used on that particular activity. Therefore, the future replacement cost represents the relevant cost of the materials.

Consider now the situation where the materials have no further use apart from being used on a particular activity. If the materials have some realizable value, the use of the materials will result in lost sales revenues, and this lost sales revenue will represent an opportunity cost that must be assigned to the activity. Alternatively, if the materials have no realizable value the relevant cost of the materials will be zero.

DETERMINING THE RELEVANT COSTS OF DIRECT LABOUR

Determining the direct labour costs that are relevant to short-term decisions depends on the circumstances. Where a company has temporary spare capacity and the labour force is to be maintained in the short term, the direct labour cost incurred will remain the same for all alternative decisions. The direct labour cost will therefore be irrelevant for short-term decision-making purposes. However, in a situation where casual labour is used and where workers can be hired on a daily basis, a company may then adjust the employment of labour to exactly the amount required to meet the production requirements. The labour cost will increase if the company accepts additional work, and will decrease if production is reduced. In this situation the labour cost will be a relevant cost for decision-making purposes.

In a situation where full capacity exists and additional labour supplies are unavailable in the short term, and where no further overtime working is possible, the only way that labour resources could then be obtained for a specific order would be to reduce existing production. This would release labour for the order, but the reduced production would result in a lost contribution, and this lost contribution must be taken into account when ascertaining the relevant cost for the specific order. The relevant labour cost per hour where full capacity exists is therefore the hourly labour rate plus an opportunity cost consisting of the contribution per hour that is lost by accepting the order. For a more detailed illustration explaining why this is the appropriate cost you should refer to Learning note 4.1 by accessing the supporting digital resources (see Preface for details).

INCORPORATING UNCERTAINTY INTO THE DECISION-MAKING PROCESS

In this and the previous chapter we have used a single representative set of estimates for predicting future costs and revenues for alternative courses of action. However, the outcome of a particular decision may be affected by an uncertain environment that cannot be predicted, and a single representative estimate does not therefore convey all the information that might reasonably influence a decision.

Consider a situation where a company has two mutually exclusive potential alternatives A and B so that only one alternative can be chosen. Both alternatives yield receipts of £50 000. The estimated costs of alternative A can be predicted with considerable confidence, and are expected to fall in the range of £40 000–£42 000; £41 000 might be considered a reasonable estimate of cost. The estimate for alternative B is subject to much greater uncertainty, since this alternative requires high-precision work involving operations that are unfamiliar to the company's labour force. The estimated costs are between £35 000 and £45 000, but £40 000 is selected as a representative estimate. If we consider single representative estimates alternative B appears preferable, since the estimated profit is £10 000 compared with an estimated profit of £9000 for alternative A, but a different picture may emerge if we take into account the range of possible outcomes.

Alternative A is expected to yield a profit of between £8000 and £10 000 whereas the range of profits for alternative B is between £5000 and £15 000. Management may consider it preferable to opt for a fairly certain profit of between £8000 and £10 000 for alternative A rather than take the chance of earning a profit of £5000 from alternative B (even though there is the possibility of earning a profit of £15 000 at the other extreme).

This example demonstrates that there is a need to incorporate the uncertainty relating to each alternative into the decision-making process. Decision-making under conditions of uncertainty is a topic that is normally included in second-level management accounting courses but some first-level courses do include this topic. Because this topic is likely to be relevant to a small percentage of the users of this book it is dealt with in Learning note 4.2 by accessing the dedicated digital resources. You should therefore check your course content to ascertain if you need to read Learning note 4.2

SUMMARY

The following items relate to the learning objectives listed at the beginning of the chapter.

- **Distinguish between relevant and irrelevant costs and revenues**. Relevant costs/revenues represent those future costs/revenues that will be changed by a particular decision, whereas irrelevant costs/revenues will not be affected by that decision. In the short term total profits will be increased (or total losses decreased) if a course of action is chosen where relevant revenues are in excess of relevant costs.

- **Explain the importance of qualitative factors**. Quantitative factors refer to outcomes that can be measured in numerical terms. In many situations it is difficult to quantify all the important elements of a decision. Those factors that cannot be expressed in numerical terms are called qualitative factors. Examples of qualitative factors include changes in employee morale and the impact of being at the mercy of a supplier when a decision is made to close a company's facilities and sub-contract components. Although qualitative factors cannot be quantified it is essential that they are taken into account in the decision-making process.

- **Distinguish between the relevant and irrelevant costs and revenues for the five decision-making problems described**. The five decision-making problems described were: (a) special selling price decisions; (b) product mix decisions when capacity constraints apply; (c) decisions on the replacement of equipment; (d) outsourcing (make or buy) decisions; and (e) discontinuation decisions. Different approaches can be used for presenting relevant cost and revenue information. Information can be presented that includes both relevant and irrelevant items for all alternatives under consideration. If this approach is adopted the same amount for the irrelevant items (i.e. those items that remain unchanged as a result of the decision) are included for all alternatives, thus making them irrelevant for the decision. Alternatively, information can be presented that lists only the relevant costs for the alternatives under consideration. Where only two alternatives are being considered a third approach is to present only the relevant (differential) items. You can adopt either approach. It is a matter of personal preference. All three approaches were illustrated for the five decision-making problems.

- **Describe the key concept that should be applied for presenting information for product mix decisions when capacity constraints apply**. The information presented should rank the products by the contribution per unit of the constraining or limiting factor (i.e. the scarce resource). The capacity of the scarce resource should be allocated according to this ranking.

- **Explain why the book value of equipment is irrelevant when making equipment replacement decisions**. The book value of equipment is a past (sunk) cost that cannot be changed for any alternative under consideration. Only future costs or revenues that will differ between alternatives are relevant for replacement decisions.
- **Describe the opportunity cost concept**. Where the choice of one course of action requires that an alternative course of action be given up the financial benefits that are foregone or sacrificed are known as opportunity costs. Opportunity costs thus represent the lost contribution to profits arising from the best alternative foregone. They arise only when the resources are scarce and have alternative uses. Opportunity costs must therefore be included in the analysis when presenting relevant information for decision-making.
- **Explain the misconceptions relating to relevant costs and revenues**. The main misconception relates to the assumption that only sales revenues and variable costs are relevant and that fixed costs are irrelevant for decision-making. Sometimes variable costs are irrelevant. For example, they are irrelevant when they are the same for all alternatives under consideration. Fixed costs are also relevant when they differ among the alternatives. For a more detailed discussion explaining the misconceptions relating to relevant costs and revenues you should refer to Learning note 4.3 by accessing the dedicated digital support resources (see Preface for details).

KEY TERMS AND CONCEPTS

Differential cash flows The cash flows that will be affected by a decision that is to be taken, also known as incremental cash flows.

Facility sustaining costs Common costs that are incurred to support the organization as a whole and which are normally not affected by a decision that is to be taken.

Incremental cash flows The cash flows that will be affected by a decision that is to be taken, also known as differential cash flows.

Limiting factors Scarce resources that constrain the level of output.

Non-financial factors Non-monetary factors that may affect a decision.

Opportunity cost Cost that measures the opportunity that is sacrificed when the choice of one course of action requires that an alternative is given up.

Outsourcing The process of obtaining goods or services from outside suppliers instead of producing the same goods or providing the same services within the organization.

Qualitative factors Non-monetary factors that may affect a decision.

Relevant costs and revenues Future costs and revenues that will be changed by a particular decision, whereas irrelevant costs and revenues will not be affected by that decision.

Special studies A detailed non-routine study that is undertaken relating to choosing between alternative courses of action.

Sunk costs Costs that have been incurred by a decision made in the past and that cannot be changed by any decision that will be made in the future.

Written down value The original cost of an asset minus depreciation.

ASSESSMENT MATERIAL

The review questions are short questions that enable you to assess your understanding of the main topics included in the chapter. The page numbers in parentheses provide you with the page numbers to refer to if you cannot answer a specific question.

The review problems are more complex and require you to relate and apply the content to various business problems. Solutions to review problems are provided in a separate section at the end of the book. Additional review problems can be accessed by lecturers and students on the dedicated online support resources for this book. Solutions to these review problems are provided for lecturers in the *Instructor's Manual* accompanying this book that can be downloaded from the dedicated online instructor's resources (see Preface for details).

The dedicated online digital support resources for this book also includes over 30 case study problems.

REVIEW QUESTIONS

4.1 What is a relevant cost? (p. 77)

4.2 Why is it important to recognize qualitative factors when presenting information for decision-making? Provide examples of qualitative factors. (p. 78)

4.3 What underlying principle should be followed in determining relevant costs for decision-making? (pp. 78–80)

4.4 Explain what is meant by special pricing decisions. (pp. 78–79)

4.5 Describe the important factors that must be taken into account when making special pricing decisions. (pp. 80–81)

4.6 Describe the dangers involved in focusing excessively on a short-run decision-making time horizon. (pp. 80–81)

4.7 Define limiting factors. (p. 83)

4.8 How should a company determine its optimal product mix when a limiting factor exists? (pp. 84–86)

4.9 Why is the written down value and depreciation of an asset being considered for replacement irrelevant when making replacement decisions? (p. 87)

4.10 Explain the importance of opportunity costs for decision-making. (p. 83)

4.11 Explain the circumstances when the original purchase price of materials are irrelevant for decision-making. (p. 94)

4.12 Why does the relevant cost of labour differ depending upon the circumstances? (pp. 94–95)

REVIEW PROBLEMS

4.13 All of a company's skilled labour, which is paid £8 per hour, is fully employed manufacturing a product to which the following data refer:

		£ per unit	£ per unit
Selling price			60
Less	Variable costs:		
	Skilled labour	20	
	Others	15	
			(35)
Contribution			25

The company is evaluating a contract which requires 90 skilled labour hours to complete. No other supplies of skilled labour are available.

What is the total relevant skilled labour cost of the contract?
(a) £720
(b) £900
(c) £1620
(d) £2160

4.14 A company requires 600 kg of raw material Z for a contract it is evaluating. It has 400 kg of material Z in stock which were purchased last month. Since then the purchase price of material Z has risen by 8 per cent to £27 per kg. Raw material Z is used regularly by the company in normal production.
What is the total relevant cost of raw material Z to the contract?

(a) £15 336
(b) £15 400
(c) £16 200
(d) £17 496

4.15 A company has the following production planned for the next four weeks. The figures reflect the full capacity level of operations. Planned output is equal to the maximum demand per product.

Product	A	B	C	D
	$	$	$	$
	per unit	per unit	per unit	per unit
Selling price	160	214	100	140
Raw material cost	24	56	22	40
Direct labour cost	66	88	33	22
Variable overhead cost	24	18	24	18
Fixed overhead cost	16	10	8	12
Profit	30	42	13	48
Planned output	300	125	240	400
Direct labour hours per unit	6	8	3	2

The direct labour force is threatening to go on strike for two weeks out of the coming four. This means that only 2160 hours will be available for production rather than the usual 4320 hours.

If the strike goes ahead, which product or products should be produced if profits are to be maximized?

(a) D and A
(b) B and D
(c) D only
(d) B and C

4.16 Equipment owned by a company has a net book value of €1800 and has been idle for some months. It could not be used on a 6 months contract which is being considered. If not used on this contract, the equipment would be sold now for a net amount of €2000. After use on the contract, the equipment would have no saleable value and would be dismantled. The cost of dismantling and disposing of it would be €800.

What is the total relevant cost of the equipment to the contract?

(a) €1200
(b) €1800
(c) €2000
(d) €2800

4.17 A company is considering accepting a 1-year contract that will require four skilled employees. The four skilled employees could be recruited on a 1-year contract at a cost of R40 000 per employee. The employees would be supervised by an existing manager who earns R60 000 per annum. It is expected that supervision of the contract would take 10 per cent of the manager's time.

Instead of recruiting new employees, the company could retrain some existing employees who currently earn R30 000 per year. The training would cost R15 000 in total. If these employees were used they would need to be replaced at a total cost of R100 000.

The relevant labour cost of the contract is:

(a) R100 000
(b) R115 000
(c) R135 000
(d) R141 000
(e) R166 000

4.18 A company which manufactures four components (A, B, C and D), using the same skilled labour, aims to maximize its profits. The following information is available:

	Component			
	A	B	C	D
Variable production cost per unit (£)	60	70	75	85
Purchase price per unit from another supplier (£)	108	130	120	124
Skilled labour hours per unit to manufacture	4	6	5	3

As it has insufficient skilled labour hours available to manufacture all the components required, the company will need to buy some units of one component from the other supplier.

Which component should be purchased from the other supplier?

(a) Component A
(b) Component B
(c) Component C
(d) Component D

4.19 A company has three shops (R, S and T) to which the following budgeted information relates:

	Shop R €000	Shop S €000	Shop T €000	Total €000
Sales	400	500	600	1 500
Contribution	100	60	120	280
Less: Fixed costs	(60)	(70)	(70)	(200)
Profit/loss	40	(10)	50	80

Sixty per cent of the total fixed costs are general company overheads. These are apportioned to the shops on the basis of sales value. The other costs are specific to each shop and are avoidable if the shop closes down.

If shop S closed down and the sales of the other two shops remained unchanged, what would be the revised budgeted profit for the company?

(a) €50 000
(b) €60 000
(c) €70 000
(d) €90 000

4.20 Relevant cost for minimum price for a contract
The Telephone Co. (T Co.) is a company specializing in the provision of telephone systems for commercial clients. There are two parts to the business:

- installing telephone systems in businesses, either first time installations or replacement installations
- supporting the telephone systems with annually renewable maintenance contracts.

T Co. has been approached by a potential customer, Push Co., who wants to install a telephone system in new offices it is opening. Whilst the job is not a particularly large one, T Co. is hopeful of future business in the form of replacement systems and support contracts for Push Co. T Co. is therefore keen to quote a competitive price for the job. The following information should be considered:

1   One of the company's salesmen has already been to visit Push Co. to give them a demonstration of the new system, together with a complimentary lunch, the costs of which totalled $400.

2   The installation is expected to take 1 week to complete and would require three engineers, each of whom is paid a monthly salary of $4000. The engineers have just had their annually renewable contract renewed with T Co. One of the three engineers has spare capacity to complete the work, but the other two would have to be moved from contract X in order to complete this one. Contract X generates a contribution of $5 per engineer hour. There are no other engineers available to continue with contract X if these two engineers are taken off the job. It would mean that T Co. would miss its contractual completion deadline on contract X by 1 week. As a result, T Co. would have to pay a one-off penalty of $500. Since there is no other work scheduled for their engineers in 1 week's time, it will not be a problem for them to complete contract X at this point.

3   T Co.'s technical advisor would also need to dedicate 8 hours of his time to the job. Je is working at full capacity, so he would have to work overtime in order to do this. He is paid an hourly rate of $40 and is paid all overtime at a premium of 50 per cent above his usual hourly rate.

4   Two visits would need to be made by the site inspector to approve the completed work. He is an independent contractor who is not employed by T Co. and charges Push Co. directly for the work. Hi cost is $200 for each visit made.

5   T Co.'s system trainer would need to spend 1 day at Push Co. delivering training. He is paid a monthly salary of $1500 but also receives commission of $125 for each day spent delivering training at a client's site.

6   One hundred and twenty telephone handsets would need to be supplied to Push Co. The current cost of these is $18.20 each, although T Co. already has 80 handsets in inventory. These were bought at a price of $16.80 each. The handsets are the most popular model on the market and are frequently requested by T Co.'s customers.

7   Push Co. would also need a computerized control system called 'Swipe 2'. The current market price of Swipe 2 is $10 800, although T Co. has an older version of the system, Swipe 1, in inventory, which could be modified at a cost of $4600. T Co. paid $5400 for Swipe 1 when it ordered it in error 2 months ago and has no other use for it. The current market price of Swipe 1 is $5450, although if T Co. tried to sell the one it has it would be deemed to be 'used' and therefore only worth $3000.

8   One thousand metres of cable would be required to wire up the system. The cable is used frequently by T Co. and it has 200 metres in inventory, which cost $1.20 per metre. The current market price for cable is $1.30 per metre.

9   You should assume that there are 4 weeks in each month and that the standard working week is 40 hours long.

Required:

(a) Prepare a cost statement, using relevant costing principles, showing the minimum cost that T Co. should charge for the contract. Make DETAILED notes showing how each cost has been arrived at and EXPLAINING why each of the costs above has been included or excluded from your cost statement.

(b) Explain the relevant costing principles used in part (a) and explain the implications of the minimum price that has been calculated in relation to the final price agreed with Push Co.

4.21 Deletion of a product

Blackarm Inc. makes three products and is reviewing the profitability of its product line. You are given the following budgeted data about the firm for the coming year.

Product	A	B	C
Sales (in units)	100 000	120 000	80 000
	($)	($)	($)
Revenue	1 500 000	1 440 000	880 000
Costs:			
Material	500 000	480 000	240 000
Labour	400 000	320 000	160 000
Overhead	650 000	600 000	360 000
	1 550 000	1 400 000	760 000
Profit/(Loss)	(50 000)	40 000	120 000

The company is concerned about the loss on product A. It is considering ceasing production of it and switching the spare capacity of 100 000 units to Product C.

You are told:

(i)   All production is sold.

(ii) Twenty-five per cent of the labour cost for each product is fixed in nature.

(iii) Fixed administration overheads of $900 000 in total have been apportioned to each product on the basis of units sold and are included in the overhead costs above. All other overhead costs are variable in nature.

(iv) Ceasing production of product A would eliminate the fixed labour charge associated with it and one-sixth of the fixed administration overhead apportioned to product A.

(v) Increasing the production of product C by 100 000 units would mean that the fixed labour cost associated with product C would double, the variable labour cost would rise by 20 per cent and its selling price would have to be decreased by $1.50 in order to achieve the increased sales.

Required:

(a) Prepare a marginal/incremental cost statement for a unit of each product on the basis of:
   (i) the original budget
   (ii) if product A is deleted.
   (12 marks)

(b) Prepare a statement showing the total contribution and profit for each product group on the basis of:
   (i) the original budget
   (ii) if product A is deleted.
   (8 marks)

(c) Using your results from (a) and (b) advise whether product A should be deleted from the product range, giving reasons for your decision.
   (5 marks)

4.22 Make or buy decision and limiting factors

Robber Co. manufactures control panels for burglar alarms, a very profitable product. Every product comes with a 1-year warranty offering free repairs if any faults arise in this period.

It currently produces and sells 80 000 units per annum, with production of them being restricted by the short supply of labour. Each control panel includes two main components – one keypad and one display screen. At present, Robber Co. manufactures both of these components in-house. However, the company is currently considering outsourcing the production of keypads and/or display screens. A newly established company based in Burgistan is keen to secure a place in the market, and has offered to supply the keypads for the equivalent of $4.10 per unit and the display screens for the equivalent of $4.30 per unit. This price has been guaranteed for 2 years.

The current total annual costs of producing the keypads and the display screens are:

	Keypads	Display screens
Production	80 000 units	80 000 units
	$000	$000
Direct materials	160	116
Direct labour	40	60
Heat and power costs	64	88
Machine costs	26	30
Depreciation and insurance costs	84	96
Total annual production costs	374	390

Notes:

1 Material costs for keypads are expected to increase by 5 per cent in 6 months time; material costs for display screens are only expected to increase by 2 per cent but with immediate effect.

2 Direct labour costs are purely variable and not expected to change over the next year.

3 Heat and power costs include an apportionment of the general factory overhead for head and power as well as the costs of heat and power directly used for the production of keypads and display screens. The general apportionment included is calculated using 50 per cent of the direct labour cost of each component and would be incurred irrespective of whether the components are manufactured in-house or not.

4 Machine costs are semi-variable; the variable element relates to set-up costs, which are based upon the number of batches made. The keypads machine has fixed costs of $4000 per annum and the display screens machine has fixed costs of $6000 per annum. Whilst both components are currently made in batches of 500, this would need to change with immediate effect to batches of 400.

5 Sixty per cent of depreciation and insurance costs relate to an apportionment of the general factory depreciation and insurance costs, the remaining 40 per cent is specific to the manufacture of keypads and display screens.

Required:

(a) Advise Robber Co. whether it should continue to manufacture the keypads and display screens in-house or whether it should outsource their manufacture in Burgistan, assuming it continues to adopt a policy to limit manufacture and sales to 80 000 control panels in the coming year.

(b) Robber Co. takes 0.5 labour hours to produce a keypad and 0.75 labour hours to produce a display screen. Labour hours are restricted to 100 000 hours and labour is paid at $1 per hour. Robber Co. wishes to increase its supply to 100 000 control panels (i.e. 100 000 each of keypads and display screens). Advise Robber Co. as to how many units of keypads and display panels it should either manufacture and/or outsource in order to minimize its costs.

(c) Discuss the non-financial factors that Robber Co. should consider when making a decision about outsourcing the manufacture of keypads and display screens.

4.23 Alternative uses of obsolete materials

Brown Ltd is a company that has in stock some materials of type XY that cost £75 000 but that are now obsolete and have a scrap value of only £21 000. Other than selling the material for scrap, there are only two alternative uses for them.

Alternative 1: Converting the obsolete materials into a specialized product, which would require the following additional work and materials:

Material A	600 units
Material B	1 000 units
Direct labour:	
5000 hours unskilled	
5000 hours semi-skilled	
5000 hours skilled	15 000 hours
Extra selling and delivery expenses	£27 000
Extra advertising	£18 000

The conversion would produce 900 units of saleable product, and these could be sold for £400 per unit.

Material A is already in stock and is widely used within the firm. Although present stocks together with orders already planned will be sufficient to facilitate normal activity, any extra material used by adopting this alternative will necessitate such materials being replaced immediately. Material B is also in stock, but it is unlikely that any additional supplies can be obtained for some considerable time because of an industrial dispute. At the present time material B is normally used in the production of product Z, which sells at £390 per unit and incurs total variable cost (excluding material B) of £210 per unit. Each unit of product Z uses four units of material B.

The details of materials A and B are as follows:

	Material A (£)	Material B (£)
Acquisition cost at time of purchase	100 per unit	10 per unit
Net realizable value	85 per unit	18 per unit
Replacement cost	90 per unit	—

Alternative 2: Adapting the obsolete materials for use as a substitute for a sub-assembly that is regularly used within the firm. Details of the extra work and materials required are as follows:

Material C	1 000 units
Direct labour:	
4000 hours unskilled	
1000 hours semi-skilled	
4000 hours skilled	9 000 hours

Twelve hundred units of the sub-assembly are regularly used per quarter, at a cost of £900 per unit. The adaptation of material XY would reduce the quantity of the sub-assembly purchased from outside the firm to 900 units for the next quarter only. However, since the volume purchased would be reduced, some discount would be lost, and the price of those purchased from outside would increase to £950 per unit for that quarter.

Material C is not available externally, but is manufactured by Brown Ltd. The 1000 units required would be available from stocks, but would be produced as extra production.

The standard cost per unit of material C would be as follows:

	(£)
Direct labour, 6 hours unskilled labour	48
Raw materials	1
Variable overhead, 6 hours at £1	6
Fixed overhead, 6 hours at £3	18
	73

The wage rates and overhead recovery rates for Brown Ltd are:

Variable overhead	£1 per direct labour hour
Fixed overhead	£3 per direct labour hour
Unskilled labour	£8 per direct labour hour
Semi-skilled labour	£9 per direct labour hour
Skilled labour	£10 per direct labour hour

The unskilled labour is employed on a casual basis and sufficient labour can be acquired to exactly meet the production requirements. Semi-skilled labour is part of the permanent labour force, but the company has temporary excess supply of this type of labour at the present time. Skilled labour is in short supply and cannot be increased significantly in the short term; this labour is presently engaged in meeting the demand for product L, which requires 4 hours of highly skilled labour. The contribution (sales less direct labour and material costs and variable overheads) from the sale of one unit of product L is £24.

Given this information, you are required to present cost information advising whether the stocks of material XY should be sold, converted into a specialized product (alternative 1) or adapted for use as a substitute for a sub-assembly (alternative 2).

4.24 Limiting factors and optimal production programme
A market gardener is planning his production for next season, and he has asked you, as a cost accountant, to recommend the optimal mix of vegetable production for the coming year. He has given you the following data relating to the current year.

	Potatoes	Turnips	Parsnips	Carrots
Area occupied (acres)	25	20	30	25
Yield per acre (tonnes)	10	8	9	12
Selling price per tonne (€)	100	125	150	135
Variable cost per acre (€):				
Fertilizers	30	25	45	40
Seeds	15	20	30	25
Pesticides	25	15	20	25
Direct wages	400	450	500	570
Fixed overhead per annum €54 000				

The land that is being used for the production of carrots and parsnips can be used for either crop, but not for potatoes or turnips. The land being used for potatoes and turnips can be used for either crop, but not for carrots or parsnips. In order to provide an adequate market service, the gardener must produce each year at least 40 tonnes each of potatoes and turnips and 36 tonnes each of parsnips and carrots.

(a) You are required to present a statement to show:
    (i) the profit for the current year
    (ii) the profit for the production mix that you would recommend

(b) Assuming that the land could be cultivated in such a way that any of the above crops could be produced and there was no market commitment, you are required to:

(i) advise the market gardener on which crop he should concentrate his production
(ii) calculate the profit if he were to do so
(iii) calculate in sterling the break-even point of sales.

(25 marks)

5
PRICING DECISIONS AND PROFITABILITY ANALYSIS

LEARNING OBJECTIVES After studying this chapter you should be able to:

- explain the relevant cost information that should be presented in price-setting firms for both short-term and long-term decisions

- describe product and customer profitability analysis and the information that should be included for managing the product and customer mix

- describe the target costing approach to pricing

- describe the different cost-plus pricing methods for deriving selling prices

- explain the limitations of cost-plus pricing

- justify why cost-plus pricing is widely used

- identify and describe the different pricing policies.

Accounting information is often an important input to pricing decisions. Organizations that sell products or services that are highly customized or differentiated from each other by special features, or who are market leaders, have some discretion in setting selling prices. In these organizations the pricing decision will be influenced by the cost of the product. The cost information that is accumulated and presented is therefore important for pricing decisions. In other organizations prices are set by overall market and supply and demand forces and they have little influence over the selling prices of their products and services. Nevertheless, cost information is still of considerable importance in these organizations for determining the relative profitability of different products and services so that management can determine the target product mix to which its marketing effort should be directed.

In this chapter we shall focus on both of the above situations. We shall consider the role that accounting information plays in determining the selling price by a price setting firm. Where prices are set by the market our emphasis will be on examining the cost information that is required for product mix decisions. In particular, we shall focus on both product and customer profitability analysis. The same approaches, however, can be applied to the provision of services such as financial or legal.

The theoretical solution to pricing decisions is derived from economic theory, which explains how the optimal selling price is determined. A knowledge of economic theory is not essential for understanding the content of this chapter but it does provide a theoretical background for the principles influencing pricing decisions. For a discussion of economic theory relating to pricing decisions you should refer to Learning note 5.1 that can be accessed from the dedicated digital support resources (see Preface for details).

THE ROLE OF COST INFORMATION IN PRICING DECISIONS

Most organizations need to make decisions about setting or accepting selling prices for their products or services. In some firms prices are set by overall market supply and demand forces and the firm has little or no influence over the selling prices of its products or services. This situation is likely to occur where there are many firms in an industry and there is little to distinguish their products from each other. No one firm can influence prices significantly by its own actions. For example, in commodity markets such as wheat, coffee, rice and sugar, prices are set for the market as a whole based on the forces of supply and demand. Also, small firms operating in an industry where prices are set by the dominant market leaders will have little influence over the price of their products or services. Firms that have little or no influence over the prices of their products or services are described as **price takers**.

In contrast, firms selling products or services that are highly customized or differentiated from each other by special features, or who are market leaders, have some discretion in setting prices. Here the pricing decision will be influenced by the cost of the product, the actions of competitors and the extent to which customers value the product. We shall describe those firms that have some discretion over setting the selling price of their products or services as **price setters**. In practice, firms may be price setters for some of their products and price takers for others.

Where firms are price setters cost information is often an important input into the pricing decision. Cost information is also of vital importance to price takers in deciding on the output and mix of products and services to which their marketing effort should be directed, given their market prices. For both price takers and price setters the decision time horizon determines the cost information that is relevant for product pricing or output mix decisions. We shall therefore consider the following four different situations:

1 a price-setting firm facing short-run pricing decisions
2 a price-setting firm facing long-run pricing decisions
3 a price-taking firm facing short-run product mix decisions
4 a price-taking firm facing long-run product mix decisions.

A PRICE-SETTING FIRM FACING SHORT-RUN PRICING DECISIONS

Companies can encounter situations where they have temporary un-utilized capacity and are faced with the opportunity of bidding for a one-time special order in competition with other suppliers. In this situation only the incremental costs of undertaking the order should be taken into account. It is likely that most of the resources required to fill the order will have already been acquired and the cost of these resources will be incurred whether or not the bid is accepted by the customer. Typically, the incremental costs are likely to consist of:

● extra materials that are required to fulfil the order

● any extra part-time labour, overtime or other labour costs

● the extra energy and maintenance costs for the machinery and equipment required to complete the order.

The incremental costs of one-off special orders in service companies are likely to be minimal. For example, the incremental cost of accepting one-off special business for a hotel may consist of only the cost of additional meals, laundering and bathroom facilities.

Bids should be made at prices that exceed incremental costs. Any excess of revenues over incremental costs will provide a contribution to committed fixed costs that would not otherwise have been obtained. Given the short-term nature of the decision, long-term considerations are likely to be non-existent and, apart from the consideration of bids by competitors, cost data are likely to be the dominant factor in determining the bid price.

Any bid for one-time special orders that is based on covering only short-term incremental costs must meet all of the following conditions:

● Sufficient capacity is available for all resources that are required to fulfil the order. If some resources are fully utilized, opportunity costs (see Chapter 4 for an illustration) of the scarce resources must be covered by the bid price.

● The bid price will not affect the future selling prices and the customer will not expect repeat business to be priced to cover short-term incremental costs.

● The order will utilize unused capacity for only a short period and capacity will be released for use on more profitable opportunities. If more profitable opportunities do not exist and a short-term focus is always adopted to utilize unused capacity then the effect of pricing a series of special orders over several periods to cover incremental costs constitutes a long-term decision. Thus, the situation arises whereby the decision to reduce capacity is continually deferred and short-term incremental costs are used for long-term decisions.

A PRICE-SETTING FIRM FACING LONG-RUN PRICING DECISIONS

In this section we shall focus on three approaches that are relevant to a price-setting firm facing long-run pricing decisions. They are:

1 pricing customized products/services

2 pricing non-customized products/services

3 pricing non-customized products/services using target costing

Pricing customized products/services

Customized products or services relate to situations where products or services tend to be unique so that no comparable market prices exist for them. Since sales revenues must cover costs for a firm to make a profit, many companies use product costs as an input to establish selling prices. Product costs are calculated and a desired profit margin is added to determine the selling price. This approach is called **cost-plus pricing**. For example, garages undertaking vehicle repairs establish the prices charged to customers using cost-plus pricing. Similarly, firms of accountants use cost-plus pricing to determine the price for the accountancy services that they have provided for their customers. Companies use different cost bases and mark-ups (i.e. the desired profit margin) to determine their selling prices. Consider the following information:

Cost base		Mark-up percentage (%)	Cost-plus selling price (£)
(1) Direct variable costs	200	150	500
(2) Direct fixed (non-variable) costs	100		
(3) Total direct costs	300	70	510
(4) Indirect (overhead) costs	80		
(5) Total cost	380	35	513

In the above illustration three different cost bases are used resulting in three different selling prices. In row (1) only direct variable costs are assigned to products for cost-plus pricing and a high percentage mark-up (150 per cent) is added to cover direct fixed costs and indirect (overhead) costs and also provide a contribution towards profit. The second cost base is row (3). Here a smaller percentage margin (70 per cent) is added to cover indirect costs and a profit contribution. The final cost base shown in row (5) includes the assignment of a share of company indirect (overhead) costs to each product, and when this is added to direct costs a total product cost is computed. This cost (also known as **full cost** or **long-run cost**) is the estimated sum of all those resources that are committed to a product in the long run. It represents an attempt to allocate a share of all costs to products to ensure that all costs are covered in the cost base. The lowest percentage mark-up (35 per cent) is therefore added since the aim is to provide only a profit contribution. We shall focus on cost assignment and the different cost bases in Chapters 7 and 8.

The above illustration is applicable to both manufacturing and non-manufacturing organizations. However, manufacturing organizations generally divide overhead costs (row 4) into manufacturing and non-manufacturing overheads. For example, if the overheads of £80 consist of £60 manufacturing and £20 non-manufacturing then £60 would be added to row (3) above to produce a total manufacturing cost of £360. Assuming that a profit margin of 40 per cent is added to the total manufacturing cost to provide a contribution to non-manufacturing costs and profit, the selling price would be £504.

Mark-ups are related to the demand for a product. A firm is able to command a higher mark-up for a product that has a high demand. Mark-ups are also likely to decrease when competition is intensive. Target mark-up percentages tend to vary from product line to product line to correspond with well-established differences in custom, competitive position and likely demand. For example, luxury goods with a low sales turnover may attract high profit margins whereas non-luxury goods with a high sales turnover (e.g. high volume products sold by supermarkets) may attract low profit margins.

Note that once the target selling price has been calculated, it is rarely adopted without amendment. The price is adjusted upwards or downwards depending on such factors as the future capacity that is available, the extent of competition from other firms, and management's general knowledge of the market. For example, if the price calculation is much lower than that which management considers the customer will be prepared to pay, the price may be increased.

REAL WORLD VIEWS 5.1

A price setting firm facing long-run pricing decisions – pricing cloud computing

Cloud computing is a term used to describe the delivery of information systems without, for example, the purchase of physical hardware or even software in some instances. What this means for an average business is that they can purchase processing capability, data storage or content delivery of large-scale computer systems, but at a fraction of the purchase price. Thus, expenditures move from a capital nature to an operational nature.

Amazon Web Services (aws.amazon.com) has been one of the pace setting firms in cloud computing. An arm of the well-known online retailer, the web services division offers a broad range of services from computing to database services, payments and billing, data storage and even a staffed support service. Pricing depends on the services required, and until more recently, competition was scarce. Around 2010, Microsoft released its cloud computing platform (Azure) and the immediate response of Amazon was to reduce all prices by $0.02 per gigabyte, which at the highest usage levels represented a price drop of 40 per cent. Pricing of most cloud providers now operates on a pay as you use basis – the more services used, the higher the cost – and there are many more operators such as Rackspace, Google Cloud and IBM.

In the accounting field, a number of providers offer cloud-based software services, charging a small monthly fee. For example, Quickbooks Online (http://quickbooksonline.intuit.com/) is available from $15–$50 per month depending on the product. Other examples include Billfaster (www.billfaster.com) at $25/€20/£16 per month, and Kashflow

(www.kashflow.com) ranging from £7–19 per month. Increasingly, such cloud software providers are providing more and more add-ons (e.g. Paypal integration) to retain customers. Almost all providers also offer a free trial period, typically 30 days. Some even offer totally free products, such as Wave Accounting (see www.waveapps.com/invoice).

Questions

1   Do you think large-scale providers like Amazon, Mircosoft an IBM can influence prices of cloud computing in the longer-term?

2   What is your opinion on a long-term price of zero, as currently offered by some cloud providers of accounting software? Is this model sustainable in the long run?

Reference

Rosenberg, D. (2010) Amazon Web Services continues to take the lead in cloud services, including pricing. Will 'free' be the only way to beat AWS?, cnet, 3 February. Available at www.cnet.com/news/already-a-pacesetter-amazon-drops-cloud-pricing

We may ask ourselves the question, 'Why should cost-based pricing formulae be used when the final price is likely to be altered by management?' The answer is that cost-based pricing formulae provide an initial approximation of the selling price. It is a target price and is important information, although by no means the only information that should be used when the final pricing decision is made. Management should use this information, together with their knowledge of the market and their intended pricing strategies, before the final price is set.

Pricing non-customized products/services

With highly customized products or services, sales are likely to be to a single customer with the pricing decision being based on direct negotiations with the customer for a known quantity. In contrast, a market leader must make a pricing decision, normally for large and unknown volumes, of a single product that is sold to thousands of different customers. To apply cost-plus pricing in this situation an estimate is required of sales volume to determine a unit cost, which will determine the cost-plus selling price. This circular process occurs because we are now faced with two unknowns that have a cause-and-effect relationship, namely selling price and sales volume. In this situation it is recommended that cost-plus selling prices are estimated for a range of potential sales volumes. Consider the information presented in Example 5.1 (Case A).

You will see that the Auckland Company has produced estimates of total costs for a range of activity levels. Instead of adding a percentage profit margin the Auckland Company has added a fixed lump sum target contribution of £2 million to cover fixed costs and provide a profit contribution.

The information presented indicates to management the sales volumes, and their accompanying selling prices, that are required to generate the required profit contribution. The unit cost calculation indicates the break-even selling price at each sales volume that is required to cover the cost of the resources committed at that particular volume. Management must assess the likelihood of selling the specified volumes at the designated prices and choose the price that they consider has the highest probability of generating at least the specified sales volume. If none of the sales volumes are likely to be achieved at the designated selling prices management must consider how demand can be stimulated and/or costs reduced to make the product viable. If neither of these, or other strategies, are successful the product should not be launched. The final decision must be based on management judgement and knowledge of the market.

The situation presented in Example 5.1 represents the most extreme example of the lack of market data for making a pricing decision. If we reconsider the pricing decision faced by the company it is likely that similar products are already marketed and information may be available relating to their market shares and sales volumes. Assuming that Auckland's product is differentiated from other similar products, a relative comparison should be possible of its strengths and weaknesses and whether customers would be prepared to pay a price in excess of the prices of similar products. It is therefore possible that Auckland may be able to undertake market research to obtain rough approximations of demand levels at a range of potential selling prices as illustrated in Example 5.1 (Case B). Let us assume that Auckland adopts this approach, and apart from this, the facts are the same as those given in Example 5.1 (Case A).

EXAMPLE 5.1

Case A

The Auckland Company is launching a new product. Sales volume will be dependent on the selling price and customer acceptance but because the product differs substantially from other products within the same product category it has not been possible to obtain any meaningful estimates of price/demand relationships. The best estimate is that demand is likely to range between 100 000 and 200 000 units provided that the selling price is less than £100. Based on this information the company has produced the following cost estimates and selling prices required to generate a target profit contribution of £2 million from the product.

Sales volume (000s)	100	120	140	160	180	200
Total cost (£000s)	10 000	10 800	11 200	11 600	12 600	13 000
Required profit contribution (£000s)	2 000	2 000	2 000	2 000	2 000	2 000
Required sales revenues (£000s)	12 000	12 800	13 200	13 600	14 600	15 000
Required selling price to achieve target profit contribution (£)	120.00	106.67	94.29	85.00	81.11	75.00
Unit cost (£)	100.00	90.00	80.00	72.50	70.00	65.00

Case B

Assume now an alternative scenario for the product in Case A. The same cost schedule applies but the £2 million minimum contribution no longer applies. In addition, Auckland now undertakes market research. Based on this research, and comparisons with similar product types and their current selling prices and sales volumes, estimates of sales demand at different selling prices have been made. These estimates, together with the estimates of total costs obtained in Case A are shown below:

Potential selling price	£100	£90	£80	£70	£60
Estimated sales volume at the potential selling price (000s)	120	140	180	190	200
Estimated total sales revenue (£000s)	12 000	12 600	14 400	13 300	12 000
Estimated total cost (£000s)	10 800	11 200	12 600	12 800	13 000
Estimated profit (loss) contribution (£000s)	1 200	1 400	1 800	500	(1 000)

Now look at Case B in Example 5.1. The demand estimates are given for a range of selling prices. In addition the projected costs, sales revenues and profit contribution are shown. You can see that profits are maximized at a selling price of £80. The information also shows the effect of pursuing other pricing policies. For example, a lower selling price of £70 might be selected to discourage competition and ensure that a larger share of the market is obtained in the future.

Pricing non-customized products/services using target costing

Instead of using the cost-plus pricing approach described in Example 5.1 (Case A) whereby cost is used as the starting point to determine the selling price, **target costing** is the reverse of this process. With target costing the starting point is the determination of the target selling price. Next a standard or desired profit margin is deducted to get a target cost for the product. The aim is to ensure that the future cost will not be higher than the target cost. The stages involved in target costing can be summarized as follows:

Stage 1: determine the target price that customers will be prepared to pay for the product

Stage 2: deduct a target profit margin from the target price to determine the target cost

Stage 3: estimate the actual cost of the product

Stage 4: if estimated actual cost exceeds the target cost investigate ways of driving down the actual cost to the target cost.

The first stage requires market research to determine the customers' perceived value of the product, its differentiation value relative to competing products and the price of competing products. The target profit margin depends on the planned return on investment for the organization as a whole and profit as a percentage of sales. This is then decomposed into a target profit for each product that is then deducted from the target price to give the target cost. The target cost is compared with the predicted actual cost. If the predicted actual cost is above the target cost, intensive efforts are made to close the gap. Product designers focus on modifying the design of the product so that it becomes cheaper to produce. Manufacturing engineers also concentrate on methods of improving production processes and efficiencies.

The aim is to drive the predicted actual cost down to the target cost, but if the target cost cannot be achieved at the pre-production stage the product may still be launched if management are confident that the process of continuous improvement will enable the target cost to be achieved early in the product's life. If this is not possible the product will not be launched.

The major attraction of target costing is that marketing factors and customer research provide the basis for determining selling price whereas cost tends to be the dominant factor with cost-plus pricing. A further attraction is that the approach requires the collaboration of product designers, production engineers, marketing and finance staff whose focus is on managing costs at the product design stage. At this stage costs can be most effectively managed because a decision committing the firm to incur costs will not have been made.

Target costing is most suited for setting prices for non-customized and high sales volume products. It is also an important mechanism for managing the cost of future products. We shall therefore look at target costing in more detail when we focus on cost management in Chapter 15.

A PRICE-TAKING FIRM FACING SHORT-RUN PRODUCT MIX DECISIONS

Price-taking firms with a temporary excess capacity may be faced with opportunities of taking on short-term business at *a market-determined selling price*. In this situation the cost information that is required is no different from that of a price-setting firm making a short-run pricing decision. In other words, accepting short-term business where the market-determined incremental sales revenues exceed incremental short-run costs will provide a contribution towards committed fixed costs that would not otherwise have been obtained. However, such business is acceptable only if the same conditions as those specified for a price-setting firm apply. You should remember that these conditions are:

● sufficient capacity is available for all resources that are required from undertaking the business (if some resources are fully utilized, opportunity costs of the scarce resources must be covered by the selling price)

● the company will not commit itself to repeat longer-term business that is priced to cover only short-term incremental costs

● the order will utilize unused capacity for only a short period and capacity will be released for use on more profitable opportunities.

Besides considering new short-term opportunities organizations may, in certain situations, review their existing product-mix over a short-term time horizon. Consider a situation where a firm has excess capacity which is being retained for an expected upsurge in demand. If committed resources are to be maintained then the product profitability analysis of existing products should be based on a comparison of incremental revenues with short-term incremental costs. The same principle applies as that which applied for accepting new short-term business where spare capacity exists. That is, in the short term, products should be retained if their incremental revenues exceed their incremental short-term costs.

A PRICE-TAKING FIRM FACING LONG-RUN PRODUCT MIX DECISIONS

When prices are set by the market a firm has to decide which products or services to sell given their market prices. In the longer term a firm can adjust the supply of resources committed to a product. Therefore, the sales revenue from a product should exceed the cost of all the resources that are committed to it. Hence there is a need to undertake periodic profitability analysis to distinguish between profitable and unprofitable products in order to ensure that only profitable products are sold. Exhibit 5.1 presents an illustration of hierarchical profitability analysis for a company that has three product lines and three individual products within each product line. For example, product line A has three individual products called A1, A2 and A3 within its product line. A similar format has been applied to product lines B and C. A product line consists of a group of similar products. For example, banks have product lines such as savings accounts, lending services, currency services, insurance services and brokering services. Each product line contains individual product variants. The savings product line would include low balance/low interest savings accounts, high balance/high interest accounts, postal and Internet savings accounts and other product variants. The lending services product line would include personal loans, house mortgage loans, business loans and other product variants within the product line.

You will see in Exhibit 5.1 that three different hierarchical levels have been identified. In row (3) the contribution to product line fixed costs is derived for each individual product by deducting direct variable and direct fixed costs (e.g. advertising for a specific individual product) from sales revenue. Next, in row (4), avoidable fixed costs that can be directly traced to each product line, but not the individual products, are deducted to derive the total contribution for each product line that is reported in row (5).

EXHIBIT 5.1   An illustration of hierarchical profitability analysis

| | Product line A | | | | Product line B | | | | Product line C | | | | Company |
| | A1 | A2 | A3 | Total | B1 | B2 | B3 | Total | C1 | C2 | C3 | Total | total |
	(£000s)	(£000s)	£000s	£000s	£000s	£000s	£000s	£000s	£000s	£000s	£000s	£000s	£000s
(1) Sales	100	200	300	600	400	500	600	1 500	700	800	900	2 400	
(2) Less direct variable and fixed costs	20	60	120	200	200	550	360	1 110	680	240	600	1 520	
(3) Contribution to product line fixed costs	80	140	180	400	200	(50)	240	390	20	560	300	880	1 670
(4) Fixed costs directly attributable to the product line				350				300				500	1 150
(5) Contribution to business sustaining fixed costs				50				90				380	520
(6) Business/ facility sustaining fixed costs													200
(7) Overall company profit													320

Finally, in row (6) the costs of sustaining the business that cannot be specifically identified with individual products or product lines are deducted from the sum of the product line contributions to compute the profit for the company as a whole. Business sustaining costs, such as general administrative and property costs, are incurred to support the organization as a whole and cannot be directly attributed to individual products or product lines.

To illustrate how profitability analysis can be used, look at product B2. It provides a negative contribution of £50 000 to product line fixed costs. The analysis indicates that the contribution of product line B will increase by £50 000 if product B2 is discontinued. However, periodic profitability analysis as illustrated in Exhibit 5.1 should not be used directly for decision-making. Instead, the profitability analysis represents a periodical strategic review of the costs and profitability of a firm's products/services (or other cost objects, such as customers and sales outlets). In particular, profitability analysis should be used to highlight those products or services that require more detailed special studies.

Before discontinuing product B2 other alternatives or considerations must be taken into account at the special study stage. In some situations it is important to maintain a full product line for marketing reasons. For example, if customers are not offered a full product line to choose from they may migrate to competitors who offer a wider choice. By reporting individual product profitability the cost of maintaining a full product line, being the sum of unprofitable products within the product line, is highlighted. Where maintaining a full product line is not required managers should consider other options before dropping unprofitable products. They should consider re-engineering or redesigning the products to reduce their resource consumption.

You will see from the profitability analysis shown in Exhibit 5.1 that product C1 generates a very small contribution margin (£20 000) relative to other products within the product line. This low contribution margin might trigger the need to undertake a special study. Such a study might reveal that although none of product line C direct fixed costs of £500 000 are traceable to individual products, a decision to discontinue product C1 would enable the product line fixed costs to be reduced by £50 000. Thus, discontinuing product C1 would result in the product line contribution (shown in row (5)) and total company profits increasing by £30 000 (£50 000 – £20 000).

The profitability analysis shown in Exhibit 5.1 is based on **direct costing** principles whereby all costs can be specifically identified with a cost objective at a particular level within the hierarchy of reported profits. Those fixed costs (row 4) that cannot be specifically identified with individual products, but which can be identified with product lines, are only assigned at the product line level. Similarly those fixed costs (row 6) that cannot be specifically identified with individual products or product lines are assigned at the overall company level. Therefore, none of the costs are categorized as indirect within the profit reporting hierarchy. An alternative costing system, known as the **absorption costing system**, is used by many companies whereby the product line fixed costs (row 4) and the business/ facility sustaining fixed costs (row 6) are allocated to the individual products, often on an arbitrary basis. Where absorption costing principles are used such costs represent indirect costs at the individual product level. At this stage the aim is to highlight the role of profitability analysis within price-taking firms and not to focus on the different cost assignment methods. We shall look at the mechanisms for assigning costs to cost objects in Chapters 7 and 8.

Finally, you should note that in practice firms may have hundreds of products and many individual product lines. It will not be feasible to present a product profitability analysis, similar to that shown in Exhibit 5.1, in hard copy format. Instead, the necessary information will be maintained on a database. With hundreds of products, managers will seek to avoid information overload and may extract the relevant information that they require only when they are examining the profitability of a particular product line. In addition, the database may be designed so that periodically only individual loss-making products are routinely reported. Managers can then decide whether they need to initiate more detailed studies to ascertain if such products are viable in the long run.

SURVEYS OF PRACTICE RELATING TO PRICING DECISIONS

Generally companies should concentrate on long-run pricing decisions and short-run decisions should be viewed as representing abnormal situations. In the previous sections cost-plus pricing and periodic profitability analysis were examined for price-setting and price-taking firms facing long-run pricing and product mix decisions. To what extent are these approaches used in practice? Exhibit 5.2 summarizes surveys that have been undertaken relating to pricing practices and profitability analysis. A survey of 186 UK companies by Drury and Tayles (2006) reported that 91 per cent of respondents used periodic profitability analysis to monitor the profitability of products, services or customers. The study also indicated that 60 per cent of the respondents used cost-plus pricing even though this practice has been widely criticized. A more recent survey by the Chartered Institute of Management Accountants based on the responses of 439 respondents located world-wide reported that approximately 75 per cent of manufacturing organizations and 60 per cent of service organizations used cost-plus pricing. In the following sections the criticisms of cost-plus pricing and the reasons for its widespread use are examined.

EXHIBIT 5.2   Surveys of practice

A survey of 187 UK organizations by Drury and Tayles (2006) indicated that 91 per cent of respondents analysed profits at least on an annual basis and that 60 per cent used cost-plus pricing. Most of the organizations that used cost-plus pricing indicated that it was applied selectively. It accounted for less than 10 per cent of total sales revenues for 26 per cent of the respondents and more than 50 per cent for 39 per cent of the organizations. Most of the firms (85 per cent) used full cost and the remaining 15 per cent used direct cost as the pricing base. The survey also indicated that 74 per cent analysed profits either by customers or customer categories. In terms of factors influencing the importance of cost-plus pricing a survey of UK and Australian companies by Guilding et al. (2005) reported that the intensity of competition was positively related to the importance of cost-plus pricing.

An earlier UK study by Innes and Mitchell (1995) reported that 50 per cent of respondents had used customer profitability analysis and a further 12 per cent planned to do so in the future. Of those respondents that ranked customer profitability, 60 per cent indicated that the Pareto 80/20 rule broadly applied (that is, 20 per cent of the customers were generating 80 per cent of the profits).

Dekker and Smidt (2003) undertook a survey of 32 Dutch firms on the use of costing practices that resembled the Japanese target costing concept. They reported that 19 out of the 32 firms used these practices, although they used different names for them. Adoption was highest among assembling firms and was related to a competitive and unpredictable environment.

LIMITATIONS OF COST-PLUS PRICING

The main criticism that has been made against cost-plus pricing is that demand is ignored. The price is set by adding a mark-up to cost, and this may bear no relationship to the price–demand relationship. It is assumed that prices should depend solely on costs. For example, a cost-plus formula may suggest a price of £20 for a product where the demand is 100 000 units, whereas at a price of £25 the demand might be 80 000 units. Assuming that the variable cost for each unit sold is £15, the total contribution will be £500 000 at a selling price of £20, compared with a total contribution of £800 000 at a selling price of £25. Thus cost-plus pricing formulae might lead to incorrect decisions.

It is often claimed that cost-based pricing formulae serve as a pricing 'floor' shielding the seller from a loss. This argument, however, is incorrect since it is quite possible for a firm to lose money even though every product is priced higher than the estimated unit cost. The reason for this is that if sales demand falls below the activity level that was used to calculate the fixed cost per unit, the total sales revenue may be insufficient to cover the total fixed costs. Cost-plus pricing will only ensure that all the costs will be met, and the target profits earned, if the sales volume is equal to, or more than, the activity level that was used to estimate total unit costs.

Consider a hypothetical situation where all of the costs attributable to a product are fixed in the short term and amount to £1 million. Assume that the cost per unit is £100 derived from an estimated volume of 10 000 units. The selling price is set at £130 using the cost-plus method and a mark-up of 30 per cent. If actual sales volume is 7000 units,

---

REAL WORLD VIEWS 5.2

Cost-plus pricing at City Steel in Thailand
In the first quarter of the year 2015/2016, City Steel's total revenues (THB 135.44 million) decreased by 35 per cent compared with the previous year. Adverse economic conditions caused the Group's products to decrease substantially and made price competition become more intense. A drop in steel price of more than 30 per cent from the previous year had contributed to a decrease in the Group's total revenues. Since the Group employed cost-plus pricing strategy to determine products selling prices, once material costs decreased, the Group's sales revenues would decline, which caused the Group's net profits to decrease correspondingly. The Group had to reduce some mark-ups on the selling price in order to maintain sales revenues and retain customers. Also, the Group incurred some fixed expenses that did not vary according to a decrease in revenues.

Questions

1 To what extent did cost-plus pricing contribute to the decline in total sales revenues?

2 How might City Steel determine the price at which it sells steel?

Reference

Anonymous (2015) Thailand: CITY – Management Discussion and Analysis Quarter 1 Ending 31 Oct 2015. *Asia News Monitor* 16 Dec.

sales revenues will be £910 000 compared with total costs of £1 million. Therefore the product will incur a loss of £90 000 even though it is priced above full cost.

REASONS FOR USING COST-PLUS PRICING

Considering the limitations of cost-plus pricing, why is it that these techniques are frequently used in practice? The most frequently cited reasons were made by Baxter and Oxenfeldt (1961) in a classic article that was published many years ago. They suggest the following reasons:

Cost-plus pricing offers a means by which plausible prices can be found with ease and speed, no matter how many products the firm handles. Moreover, its imposing computations look factual and precise, and its prices may well seem more defensible on moral grounds than prices established by other means. Thus a monopolist threatened by a public inquiry might reasonably feel that he is safeguarding his case by cost-plus pricing.

Another major reason for the widespread use of cost-plus pricing methods is that they may help a firm to predict the prices of other firms. For example, if a firm has been operating in an industry where average mark-ups have been 40 per cent in the past, it may be possible to predict that competitors will be adding a 40 per cent mark-up to their costs. Assuming that all the firms in the industry have similar cost structures, it will be possible to predict the price range within which competitors may price their products. If all the firms in an industry price their products in this way, it may encourage price stability.

In response to the main objection that cost-based pricing formulae ignore demand, we have noted that the actual price that is calculated by the formula is rarely adopted without amendments. The price is adjusted upwards or downwards after taking account of the number of sales orders on hand, the extent of competition from other firms, the importance of the customer in terms of future sales, and the policy relating to customer relations. Therefore, it is argued that management attempts to adjust the mark-up based on the state of sales demand and other factors that are of vital importance in the pricing decision.

PRICING POLICIES

Cost information is only one of many variables that must be considered in the pricing decision. The final price that is selected will depend upon the pricing policy of the company. A price-skimming or penetration pricing policy might be selected.

A **price-skimming policy** is an attempt to exploit those sections of the market that are relatively insensitive to price changes. For example, high initial prices may be charged to take advantage of the novelty appeal of a new product when demand is not very sensitive to price changes. A skimming pricing policy offers a safeguard against unexpected future increases in costs, or a large fall in demand after the novelty appeal has declined. Once the market becomes saturated, the price can be reduced to attract that part of the market that has not yet been exploited. A skimming pricing policy should not, however, be

REAL WORLD VIEWS 5.3

Pricing policies – pricing iPhones and similar devices

Apple Inc. is well known for developing innovative products like the iPhone, iPad and Apple Watch. Such devices are manufactured with complex electronic components and incur substantial design and development costs. The actual cost of manufacture of these products is a closely guarded secret. While cost is an important factor in setting a price for such devices, other factors affect pricing policy too, according to industry analysts and reviewers.

Taking the iPhone as an example, a major factor is the features and capability of the device. For example, the price increases according to the storage capacity or screen quality. As the iPhone has developed through to the current iPhone X (launched September 2017), additional functionality has been offered. The iPhone X introduced a better display, Face ID and can be charged wirelessly. Previous iPhones have similarly added new features. While such additional functionality may have increased manufacturing costs, in general end-consumer pricing has remained relatively static for each new iPhone model at about $600–700. The iPhone X is the first to surpass the $1000 price mark, and some analysts suggest Apple will lose money on each iPhone X, and so are subsidising the price. How has Apple kept prices low, despite increasing costs? The answer lies, at least partly, in a pricing policy which forces mobile phone operators to offer heavy subsidies to customers wanting an iPhone. Operators typically comply with this as demand for iPhones remains high – for example, UK demand outstripped supply in late 2017 according to *The Guardian*.

Questions

1. Do devices like iPhones have differing prices during various stages of their life cycle?
2. Can companies like Apple adopt price-skimming policies? Why or why not?

References

Hern, A. (2017) iPhone X: most expensive Apple smartphone sells out in minutes, The Guardian, 28 October. Available at www.theguardian.com/technology/2017/oct/27/iphone-x-shipping-most-expensive-apple-smartphone-sells-out-in-minutes-iphone-8

Solomon, B. (2016) Apple Earnings, iPhone Sales Keep Falling, Forbes, 25 October. Available at www.forbes.com/sites/briansolomon/2016/10/25/apple-reports-4th-quarter-earnings-iphone-7

Su, J.B. (2016) Apple iPhone 6s Crowned World's Best-Selling Smartphone, Forbes, 7 September. Available at www.forbes.com/sites/jeanbaptiste/2016/09/07/apple-iphone-6s-was-worlds-top-selling-smartphone-last-quarter-report

Zimbardo, P. (2010) What's behind Apple's iPhone pricing strategy?, Seeking Alpha, 21 June. Available at seekingalpha.com/article/211063-whats-behind-apples-iphone-pricing-strategy

adopted when a number of close substitutes are already being marketed. Here demand is likely to be very sensitive to price changes, and any price in excess of that being charged for a substitute product by a competitor is likely to lead to a large reduction in sales.

A **penetration pricing policy** is based on the concept of charging low prices initially with the intention of gaining rapid acceptance of the product. Such a policy is appropriate when close substitutes are available or when the market is easy to enter. The low price discourages potential competitors from entering the market and enables a company to establish a large share of the market. This can be achieved more easily when the product is new, rather than later on when buying habits have become established.

Many products have a product life cycle consisting of four stages: introductory, growth, maturity and decline. At the introductory stage the product is launched and there is minimal awareness and acceptance of it. Sales begin to expand rapidly at the growth stage because of introductory promotions and greater customer awareness, but this begins to taper off at the maturity stage as potential new customers are exhausted. At the decline stage sales diminish as the product is gradually replaced with new and better versions.

Sizer (1989) suggests that in the introductory stage it may be appropriate to shade upwards or downwards the price found by normal analysis to create a more favourable demand in future years. For example, if there is no production capacity constraint, a lower price than that suggested by normal analysis may be preferred. Such a price may result in a higher sales volume and a slow competitive reaction, which will enable the company to establish a large market share and to earn higher profits in the long term.

When the product moves from the introduction to the growth stage the product will have less of a novelty appeal as competitors introduce their versions of the product. Competitors can be discouraged from entering the market by lowering the price. The move from the introduction to the growth stage should also result in a reduction in unit costs because of reduced material costs from bulk buying, reduced labour costs arising from increased efficiency due to the learning effect and lower unit fixed costs arising from fixed production costs being spread over a greater volume.

The move from the growth stage to the maturity stage means that the product has become established and the selling price is likely to be fairly constant, but periodically special offers may be made to tempt customers to buy the product. Unit production costs are likely to be fairly constant as there will be no further benefits arising from economies of scale. At the maturity stage a firm also will be less concerned with the future effects of current selling prices and should adopt a selling price that maximizes short-run profits.

CUSTOMER PROFITABILITY ANALYSIS

In the past, management accounting reports have tended to concentrate on analysing profits by products. Increasing attention is now being given to analysing profits by customers using an activity-based costing approach. **Customer profitability analysis** provides important information that can be used to determine which classes of customers should be emphasized or de-emphasized and the price to charge for customer services.

Let us now look at an illustration of customer profitability analysis. Consider the information presented in Example 5.2. Note that the cost driver rate referred to in Example 5.2 represents the costing rates that have been computed by the company

EXAMPLE 5.2

The Darwin Company has recently adopted customer profitability analysis. It has undertaken a customer profitability review for the past 12 months. Details of the activities and the cost driver rates relating to those expenses that can be attributed to customers are as follows:

Activity	Cost driver rate
Sales order processing	£300 per sales order
Sales visits	£200 per sales visit
Normal delivery costs	£1 per delivery kilometre travelled
Special (urgent) deliveries	£500 per special delivery
Credit collection costs	10% per annum on average payment time

Details relating to four of the firm's customers are as follows:

Customer	A	B	Y	Z
Number of sales orders	200	100	50	30
Number of sales visits	20	10	5	5
Kilometres per delivery	300	200	100	50
Number of deliveries	100	50	25	25
Total delivery kilometres	30 000	10 000	2 500	1 250
Special (urgent deliveries)	20	5	0	0
Average collection period (days)	90	30	10	10
Annual sales	£1 million	£1 million	£0.5 million	£2 million
Annual operating profit contribution[a]	£90 000	£120 000	£70 000	£200 000

Note

[a]Consists of sales revenues less variable cost of sales.

for the different activities. An explanation of how these rates are derived will be provided in Chapter 8. The profitability analysis in respect of the four customers is as follows:

	A (£)	B (£)	Y (£)	Z (£)
Customer attributable costs:				
Sales order processing	60 000	30 000	15 000	9 000
Sales visits	4 000	2 000	1 000	1 000
Normal deliveries	30 000	10 000	2 500	1 250
Special (urgent) deliveries	10 000	2 500	0	0
Credit collection[a]	24 658	8 220	1 370	5 480
	128 658	52 720	19 870	16 730
Operating profit contribution	90 000	120 000	70 000	200 000
Contribution to higher level sustaining expenses	(38 658)	67 280	50 130	183 270

Note

[a](Annual sales revenue × 10%) × (Average collection period/365)

REAL WORLD VIEWS 5.4

Measuring and managing customer profitability

In an article in *Strategic Finance* Garry Cokins states that many companies' managerial accounting systems are not able to report customer profitability information to support analysis for how to rationalize which types of customers to retain, grow or win back, and which types of new customers to acquire. Some customers purchase a mix of mainly low-profit margin products and, after adding the non-product-related costs to serve for those customers to the product costs, they may be unprofitable. Conversely, customers who purchase a mix of relatively high-profit-margin products may demand so much in extra services that they may be unprofitable. The danger of maintaining unprofitable customers is further exacerbated by basing compensation incentives to the sales force that are based exclusively on sales revenues rather than profitable sales after taking into account the associated costs to serve the customers.

Cokins distinguishes between low-maintenance 'good' customers who place standard orders with no fuss and high-maintenance 'bad' customers who demand non-standard offers and services, such as special delivery requirements. The extra expenses for high-maintenance customers add up. Cokins advocates the use of activity-based customer profitability analysis (see Chapter 8) to turn loss-making customers into profit-making customers.

Questions

1 Can you think of any reason why two customers who purchase equal volumes of equivalent products might be more or less profitable?
2 What actions should a company take with its unprofitable customers?

Reference

Cokins, G. (2015) Measuring and managing customer profitability, *Strategic Finance*, 23–29 February. Available at customerthink.com/measuring-and-managing-customer-profitability/

You can see from the above analysis that A and B are high cost to serve whereas Y and Z are low cost to serve customers. Customer A provides a positive operating profit contribution but is unprofitable when customer attributable costs are taken into account. This is because customer A requires more sales orders, sales visits, and normal and urgent deliveries than the other customers. In addition, the customer is slow to pay and has higher delivery costs than the other customers. Customer profitability analysis identifies the characteristics of high cost and low cost to serve customers and shows how customer profitability can be increased. The information should be used to persuade high cost to serve customers to modify their buying behaviour away from placing numerous small orders and/or purchasing non-standard items that are costly to make. For example, customer A can be made profitable if action is taken to persuade the customer to place a smaller number of larger quantity orders, avoid special deliveries and reduce the credit period. If unprofitable customers cannot be persuaded to change their buying behaviour selling prices should be increased (or discounts on list prices reduced) to cover the extra resources consumed.

Customer profitability analysis can also be used to rank customers by order of profitability using **Pareto analysis**. This type of analysis is based on observations by Pareto that a very small proportion of items usually account for the majority of the value. For example, the Darwin Company might find that 20 per cent of customers account for 80 per cent of profits. Special attention can then be given to enhancing the relationships with the most profitable customers to ensure that they do not migrate to other competitors. In addition, greater emphasis can be given to attracting new customers that have the same attributes as the most profitable customers.

Organizations, such as banks, often with a large customer base of millions of customers cannot apply customer profitability analysis at the individual customer level. Instead, they concentrate on customer segment profitability analysis by combining groups of customers into meaningful segments. This enables profitable segments to be highlighted where customer retention is particularly important and provides an input for determining the appropriate marketing strategies for attracting the new customers that have the most profit potential. Segment groupings that are used by banks include income classes, age bands, socioeconomic categories and family units.

SUMMARY

The following items relate to the learning objectives listed at the beginning of the chapter.

- **Explain the relevant cost information that should be presented in price-setting firms for both short-term and long-term decisions**. For short-term decisions the incremental costs of accepting an order should be presented. Bids should then be made at prices that exceed incremental costs. For short-term decisions many costs are likely to be fixed and irrelevant. Short-term pricing decisions should meet the following conditions: (a) spare capacity should be available for all of the resources that are required to fulfil an order; (b) the bid price should represent a one-off price that will not be repeated for future orders; and (c) the order will utilize unused capacity for only a short period and capacity will be released for use on more profitable opportunities. For long-term decisions a firm can adjust the supply of virtually all of the resources. Therefore, cost information should be presented providing details of all of the resources that are committed to a product or service. Since business facility sustaining costs should be covered in the long term by sales revenues there are strong arguments for allocating such costs for long-run pricing decisions. To determine an appropriate selling price a mark-up is added to the total cost of the resources assigned to the product/service to provide a contribution to profits. If facility sustaining costs are not allocated, the mark-up must be sufficient to provide a contribution to covering facility sustaining costs and a contribution to profit.

- **Describe product and customer profitability analysis and the information that should be included for managing the product and customer mix**. Price-taking firms have to decide which products to sell, given their market prices. A mechanism is therefore required that ascertains whether or not the sales revenues from a product/service (or customer) exceeds the cost of resources that are committed to it. Periodic profitability analysis meets this requirement. Ideally, hierarchical profitability analysis should be used that categorizes costs according to their variability at different hierarchical levels to report different hierarchical contribution levels. The aim of the hierarchical analysis should be to directly assign all organizational expenses to the particular hierarchical or organizational level where they become avoidable, so that arbitrary apportionments are avoided. The approach is illustrated in Exhibit 5.1.

- **Describe the target costing approach to pricing.** Target costing is the reverse of cost-plus pricing. With target costing the starting point is the determination of the target selling price – the price that customers are willing to pay for the product (or service). Next a target profit margin is deducted to derive a target cost. The target cost represents the estimated long-run cost of the product (or service) that enables the target profit to be achieved. Predicted actual costs are compared with the target cost and, where the predicted actual cost exceeds the target cost, intensive efforts are made through value engineering methods to achieve the target cost. If the target cost is not achieved the product/service is unlikely to be launched.

- **Describe the different cost-plus pricing methods for deriving selling prices.** Different cost bases can be used for cost-plus pricing. Bases include direct variable costs, total direct costs and total cost based on an assignment of a share of all organizational costs to the product or service. Different percentage profit margins are added depending on the cost base that is used. If direct variable cost is used as the cost base, a high percentage margin will be added to provide a contribution to cover a share of all of those costs that are not included in the cost base plus profits. Alternatively if total cost is used as the cost base a lower percentage margin will be added to provide only a contribution to profits.

- **Explain the limitations of cost-plus pricing.** Cost-plus pricing has three major limitations. First, demand is ignored. Secondly, the approach requires that some assumption be made about future volume prior to ascertaining the cost and calculating the cost-plus selling prices. This can lead to an increase in the derived cost-plus selling price when demand is falling and vice-versa. Thirdly, there is no guarantee that total sales revenue will be in excess of total costs even when each product is priced above 'cost'.

- **Justify why cost-plus pricing is widely used.** There are several reasons why cost-plus pricing is widely used. First, it offers a means by which prices can be determined with ease and speed in organizations that produce hundreds of products. Cost-plus pricing is likely to be particularly applicable to those products that generate relatively minor revenues that are not critical to an organization's success. A second justification is that cost-based pricing methods may encourage price stability by enabling firms to predict the prices of their competitors. Also, target mark-ups can be adjusted upwards or downwards according to expected demand, thus ensuring that demand is indirectly taken into account.

- **Identify and describe the different pricing policies.** Cost information is only one of the many variables that must be considered in the pricing decision. The final price that is selected will depend upon the pricing policy of a company. A price-skimming policy or a penetration pricing policy might be selected. A price-skimming policy attempts to charge high initial prices to exploit those sections of the market where demand is initially insensitive to pricing changes. In contrast, a penetration pricing policy is based on the concept of charging low prices, initially with the intention of gaining rapid acceptance of the product (or service).

KEY TERMS AND CONCEPTS

Absorption costing system   A costing system that allocates all manufacturing costs, including fixed manufacturing costs, to products and values unsold stocks at their total cost of manufacture.

Cost-plus pricing   An approach to pricing customized products and services that involves calculating product costs and adding the desired profit margin.

Customer profitability analysis   The analysis of profits by individual customers or customer categories.

Direct costing   A costing system that assigns only direct costs to products or services and includes them in the inventory valuation.

Full cost   The estimated sum of all resources that are committed to a product or service in the long run, also known as long-run cost.

Long-run cost   The estimated sum of all resources that are committed to a product or service in the long run, also known as full cost.

Pareto analysis   A type of analysis based on the observation that a very small proportion of items account for the majority of value.

Penetration pricing policy   An approach to pricing that involves charging low prices initially with the intention of gaining rapid acceptance of the product.

Price setters   Firms that have some discretion over setting the selling price of their products or services.

Price takers   Firms that have little or no influence over setting the selling price of their products or services.

Price-skimming policy   An approach to pricing that attempts to exploit sections of the market that are relatively insensitive to price changes.

Target costing   A technique that focuses on managing costs during a product's planning and design phase by establishing the target cost for a product or service that is derived from starting with the target selling price and deducting a desired profit margin.

ASSESSMENT MATERIAL

The review questions are short questions that enable you to assess your understanding of the main topics included in the chapter. The page numbers in parentheses provide you with the page numbers to refer to if you cannot answer a specific question.

The review problems are more complex and require you to relate and apply the content to various business problems. Solutions to review problems are provided in a separate section at the end of the book. Additional review problems can be accessed by lecturers and students on the dedicated online support resources for this book. Solutions to these review problems are provided for lecturers in the *Instructor's Manual* accompanying this book that can be downloaded from the dedicated online instructor's resources (see Preface for details).

The dedicated online digital support resources for this book also includes over 30 case study problems.

REVIEW QUESTIONS

5.1   Distinguish between a price taker and a price setter. *(p. 105)*

5.2   What costs are likely to be relevant for (a) a short-run pricing decision, and (b) a long-run pricing decision? *(pp. 105–106)*

5.3   What is meant by the term 'full cost'? *(p. 107)*

5.4   What is meant by cost-plus pricing? *(pp. 107–108)*

5.5   Distinguish between cost-plus pricing and target costing. *(pp. 110–111)*

5.6 Describe the four stages involved with target costing. *(pp. 110–111)*

5.7 What role does cost information play in price-taking firms? *(pp. 112–113)*

5.8 Describe the alternative cost bases that can be used with cost-plus pricing. *(p. 107)*

5.9 What are the limitations of cost-plus pricing? *(p. 116)*

5.10 Why is cost-plus pricing frequently used in practice? *(p. 117)*

5.11 Describe the different kinds of pricing policies that an organization can apply. *(pp. 117–119)*

5.12 Why is customer profitability analysis important? *(pp. 119–121)*

REVIEW PROBLEMS

5.13 ABC plc is about to launch a new product. Facilities will allow the company to produce up to 20 units per week. The marketing department has estimated that at a price of €8000 no units will be sold, but for each €150 reduction in price one additional unit per week will be sold.

Fixed costs associated with manufacture are expected to be €12 000 per week.

Variable costs are expected to be €4000 per unit for each of the first 10 units; thereafter each unit will cost €400 more than the preceding one.

The most profitable level of output per week for the new product is:

(a) 10 units
(b) 11 units
(c) 13 units
(d) 14 units
(e) 20 units

(3 marks)

5.14 Calculation of an optimal selling price
A company manufactures a single product, product Y. It has documented levels of demand at certain selling prices for this product as follows:

Demand	Selling price per unit	Cost per unit
Units	£	£
1 100	48	24
1 200	46	21
1 300	45	20
1 400	42	19

Required:

Using a tabular approach, calculate the incremental revenues and incremental costs for product Y at the different levels of demand, and so determine the selling price at which the company profits are maximized.

(10 marks)

5.15 Calculation of different cost-plus prices
Albany has recently spent some time on researching and developing a new product for which they are trying to establish a suitable price. Previously they have used cost plus 20 per cent to set the selling price.

The standard cost per unit has been estimated as follows:

	£	
Direct materials		
Material 1	10	(4 kg at £2.50/kg)
Material 2	7	(1 kg at £7/kg)
Direct labour	20	(2 hours at £10/hour)
Fixed overheads	7	(2 hours at £3.50/hour)
	44	

Required:

(a) Using the standard costs calculate two different cost-plus prices using two different bases and explain an advantage and disadvantage of each method.

(6 marks)

(b) Give two other possible pricing strategies that could be adopted and describe the impact of each one on the price of the product.

(4 marks)

(Total 10 marks)

5.16 Preparation of full cost and variable cost information
A small company is engaged in the production of plastic tools for the garden.

Sub-totals on the spreadsheet of budgeted overheads for a year reveal:

	Moulding department	Finishing department	General factory overhead
Variable overhead (£000)	1 600	500	1 050
Fixed overhead (£000)	2 500	850	1 750
Budgeted activity			
Machine hours (000)	800	600	
Practical capacity			
Machine hours (000)	1 200	800	

For the purposes of reallocation of general factory overhead it is agreed that the variable overheads accrue in line with the machine hours worked in each department. General factory fixed overhead is to be reallocated on the basis of the practical machine hour capacity of the two departments.

It has been a longstanding company practice to establish selling prices by applying a mark-up on full manufacturing cost of between 25 per cent and 35 per cent.

A possible price is sought for one new product that is in a final development stage. The total market for this product is estimated at 200 000 units per annum. Market research indicates that the company could expect to obtain and hold about 10 per cent of the market. It is hoped the product will offer some improvement over competitors' products, which are currently marketed at between £90 and £100 each.

The product development department have determined that the direct material content is £9 per unit. Each unit of the product will take one labour hour (four machine hours) in the moulding department and two labour hours (three machine hours) in finishing. Hourly labour rates are £10 and £8.25 respectively.

Management estimate that the annual fixed costs that would be specifically incurred in relation to the product are: supervision £20 000, depreciation of a recently acquired machine £120 000 and advertising £27 000. It may be assumed that these costs are included in the budget given above. Given the state of development of this new product, management do not consider it necessary to make revisions to the budgeted activity levels given above, for any possible extra machine hours involved in its manufacture.

Required:

(a) Briefly explain the role of costs in pricing.

(6 marks)

(b) Prepare full cost and variable cost information that may help with the pricing decision.

(9 marks)

(c) Comment on the cost information and suggest a price range that should be considered.

(5 marks)

(Total 20 marks)

5.17 Minimum selling price based on relevant costs

DLW is a company that builds innovative, environmentally friendly housing. DLW's houses use high quality materials and the unique patented energy saving technology used in the houses has been the result of the company's own extensive research in the area.

DLW is planning to expand into another country and has been asked by a prominent person in that country for a price quotation to build them a house. The Board of Directors believes that securing the contract will help to launch their houses in the country and has agreed to quote a price for the house that will exactly cover its relevant cost.

The following information has been obtained in relation to the contract:

1 The Chief Executive and Marketing Director recently met with the potential client to discuss the house. The meeting was held at a restaurant and DLW provided food and drinks at a cost of $375.

2 Twelve hundred kg of Material Z will be required for the house. DLW currently has 550 kg of Material Z in its inventory purchased at a price of $58 per kg. Material Z is regularly used by DLW in its houses and has a current replacement cost of $65 per kg. The resale value of the Material Z in inventory is $35 per kg.

3 Four hundred hours of construction worker time are required to build the house. DLW's construction workers are paid an hourly rate of $22 under a guaranteed wage agreement and currently have spare capacity to build the house.

4 The house will require 90 hours of engineer time. DLW engineers are paid a monthly salary of $4750 each and do not have any spare capacity. In order to meet the engineering requirement for the house, DLW can choose one of the two options:

(i) Pay the engineers an overtime rate of $52 per hour to perform the additional work.

(ii) Reduce the number of engineers' hours available for their existing job, the building of Product Y. This would result in lost sales of Product Y.

Summary details of the existing job the engineers are working on:

Information for one unit of Product Y

Sales revenue	$4 860
Variable costs	$3 365
Engineers' time required per unit	30 hours

5 A specialist machine would be required for 7 weeks for the house build. DLW has 4 weeks remaining on the 15-week specialist machine rental contract that cost $15 000. The machine is currently not in use. The machine can be rented for an additional 15 weeks at a cost of $15 250. The specialist machine can only be rented in blocks of 15 weeks.

Alternatively, a machine can be purchased for $160 000 and sold after the work on the house has been completed for $140 000.

6 The windows required for the house have recently been developed by DLW and use the latest environmentally friendly insulating material. DLW produced the windows at a cost of $34 950 and they are currently the only ones of their type. DLW was planning to exhibit the windows at a house building conference. The windows would only be used for display purposes at the conference and would not be for sale to prospective clients.

DLW has had assurances from three separate clients that they would place an order for 25 windows each if they saw the technology demonstrated at the conference. The contribution from each window is $10 450. If the windows are used for the contract, DLW would not be able to attend the conference. The conference organizers will charge a penalty fee of $1500 for non-attendance by DLW. The Chief Executive of DLW can meet the clients directly and still secure the orders for the windows. The meetings would require 2 days of the Chief Executive's time. The Chief Executive is paid an annual salary of $414 000 and contracted to work 260 days per year.

7   The house build requires 400 kg of other materials. DLW currently has none of these materials in its inventory. The total current purchase price for these other materials is $6000.

8   DLW's fixed overhead absorption rate is $37 per construction worker hour.

9   DLW's normal policy is to add a 12 per cent mark-up to the cost of each house.

Required:

(a) Produce a schedule that shows the minimum price that could be quoted for the contract to build the house.
Your schedule should show the relevant cost of each of the nine items identified above. You should also explain each relevant cost value you have included in your schedule and why any values you have excluded are not relevant.

(b) Explain two reasons why relevant costing may not be a suitable approach to pricing houses in the longer term for DLW.

(c) Recommend with justifications a pricing strategy for DLW to use to price the innovative, environmentally friendly houses when they are launched in the new country.

(4 marks)

5.18 Profit maximizing pricing decision based on demand/price relationships

The McIntyre Resort (MR), which is privately owned, is a world famous luxury hotel and golf complex. It has been chosen as the venue to stage 'The Robyn Cup', a golf tournament which is contested by teams of golfers from across the globe, which is scheduled to take place during July. MR will offer accommodation for each of the five nights on which guests would require accommodation.

The following information is available regarding the period of the tournament:

1   Hotel data:

Total rooms	2 400
Room mix:	
Double rooms	75%
Single rooms	15%
Family rooms	10%
Fee per room per night ($):	
Double rooms	400
Single rooms	300
Family rooms	600
Number of guests per room:	
Double rooms	2
Single rooms	1
Family rooms	4

When occupied, all rooms will contain the number of guests as above.

Costs:	
Variable cost per guest per night	$100
Attributable fixed costs for the five-day period:	
Double rooms	$516 000
Single and family rooms (total)	$300 000

2   Accommodation for guests is provided on an all-inclusive basis (meals, drinks, entertainment, etc.).

3   The objective of the hotel management is to maximize profit.

4   The hotel management expect all single and family rooms to be 'sold out' for each of the five nights of the tournament. However, they are unsure whether the fee in respect of double rooms should be increased or decreased. At a price of $400 per room per night they expect an occupancy rate of 80 per cent of available double rooms. For each $10 increase/decrease they expect the number of rooms to decrease/increase by 40.

Required:

(a)

(i) Calculate the profit-maximizing fee per double room that MR should charge per night during the Tournament;

(6 marks)

(ii) Calculate how much profit would be earned from staging the tournament as a consequence of charging that fee.

(4 marks)

(b) The management of the hotel are concerned by the level of variable costs per guest night to be incurred in respect of the tournament, A recent review of proposed operational activities has concluded that variable cost per guest per night in all rooms in the hotel would be reduced by 20 per cent if proposed changes in operational activities were made. However, this would result in additional attributable fixed costs amounting to $200 000 in respect of the 5-day period.

Required:

Advise management whether, on purely financial grounds, they should make the proposed changes in operational activities.

(6 marks)

(c) Discuss TWO initiatives that management might consider in order to further improve the profit from staging the golf tournament.

(4 marks)

6
CAPITAL INVESTMENT DECISIONS: APPRAISAL METHODS

LEARNING OBJECTIVES After studying this chapter you should be able to:

- explain the opportunity cost of an investment

- distinguish between compounding and discounting

- explain the concepts of net present value (NPV), internal rate of return (IRR), payback method and accounting rate of return (ARR)

- calculate NPV, IRR, the payback period and ARR

- justify the superiority of NPV over the IRR

- explain the limitations of payback and ARR

- justify why the payback and ARR methods are widely used in practice

- describe the effect of performance measurement on capital investment decisions.

Capital investment decisions are those decisions that involve current outlays in return for a stream of benefits in future years. It is true to say that all of a firm's expenditures are made in expectation of realizing future benefits. The distinguishing feature between short-term decisions and capital investment (long-term) decisions is time. Generally, we can classify short-term decisions as those that involve a relatively short time horizon, say 1 year, from the commitment of funds to the receipt of the benefits. On the other hand, capital investment decisions are those decisions where a significant period of time elapses between the outlay and the recoupment of the investment. We shall see that this commitment of funds for a significant period of time involves an interest cost, which must be brought into the analysis. With short-term decisions, funds are committed only for short periods of time, and the interest cost is normally so small that it can be ignored.

Capital investment decisions normally represent the most important decisions that an organization makes, since they commit a substantial proportion of a firm's resources to actions that are likely to be irreversible. For example, the projected capital expenditure for Sainsbury plc and Tesco plc (two UK supermarket chains) for 2016/17 was around £600 million and £1.2 billion respectively.

Capital investment decisions normally are applicable to all sectors of society. Business firms' investment decisions include investments in plant and machinery, research and development, advertising and warehouse facilities. Investment decisions in the public sector include new roads, schools and airports. Individuals' investment decisions include house-buying and the purchase of consumer durables. In this chapter we shall examine the economic evaluation of the desirability of investment proposals. We shall concentrate on the investment decisions of business firms, but the same principles, with modifications, apply to individuals and the public sector.

For most of this chapter we shall assume that the investments appraised are in firms that are all equity financed. In other words, projects are financed by the issue of new ordinary shares or from retained earnings. Later in the chapter we shall relax this assumption and assume that projects are financed by a combination of debt (i.e. borrowed funds) and equity capital. You will find throughout the chapter that mathematical formulae and simple arithmetic are used to compute the values that are used to evaluate investments. You can use either approach. If you have an aversion to mathematical formulae you should ignore the formulae calculations. All of the calculations are repeated using non-formulae approaches.

THE OPPORTUNITY COST OF AN INVESTMENT

Investors can invest in securities traded in financial markets. If you prefer to avoid risk, you can invest in government securities, which will yield a *fixed* return. On the other hand, you may prefer to invest in *risky* securities such as the ordinary shares of companies quoted on the stock exchange. If you invest in the ordinary shares of a company, you will find that the return will vary from year to year, depending on the performance of the company and its future expectations. Investors normally prefer to avoid risk if possible, and will generally invest in risky securities only if they believe that they will obtain a greater return for the increased risk. In the past **risk-free gilt-edged securities** issued by governments in many countries have yielded returns varying from 0.5 to 15 per cent but in 2018 they were generally in the region of 1 per cent. To simplify the calculations we shall assume that government securities yield a return of 10 per cent. You will therefore be prepared to invest in ordinary shares if you expect a return in excess of 10 per cent; let us assume that you require an *expected* return of 15 per cent to induce you to invest in ordinary shares in preference to a risk-free security. Note that expected return means the estimated average future return. You would expect to earn, on average, 15 per cent, but in some years you might earn more and in others considerably less.

Suppose you invest in company X ordinary shares. Would you want company X to invest your money in a capital project that gives less than 15 per cent? Surely not, assuming the project has the same risk as the alternative investments in shares of other companies that are yielding a return of 15 per cent. You would prefer company X to invest in other companies' ordinary shares at 15 per cent or, alternatively, to repay your investment so that you could invest yourself at 15 per cent.

The rates of return that are available from investments in securities in financial markets such as ordinary shares and government gilt-edged securities represent the **opportunity cost of an investment** in capital projects; that is, if cash is invested in the capital project, it cannot be invested elsewhere to earn a return. A firm should therefore invest in capital projects only if they yield a return in excess of the opportunity cost of the investment. The opportunity cost of the investment is also known as the **minimum required rate of return**, **cost of capital**, **discount rate** or **interest rate**.

The return on securities traded in financial markets provides us with the opportunity costs, that is the required rates of return available on securities. The expected returns that investors require from the ordinary shares of different companies vary because some companies' shares are more risky than others. The greater the risk, the greater the expected returns. Consider Figure 6.1. You can see that as the risk of a security increases the return that investors require to compensate for the extra risk increases. Consequently, investors will expect to receive a return in excess of 15 per cent if they invest in securities that have a higher risk than company X ordinary shares. If this return was not forthcoming, investors would not purchase high-risk securities. It is therefore important that companies investing in high-risk capital projects earn higher returns to compensate investors for this risk. You can also see that a risk-free security such as a gilt-edged government security yields the lowest return, i.e. 10 per cent. Consequently, if a firm invests in a project with zero risk, it should earn a return in excess of 10 per cent. If the project does not yield this return and no other projects are available then the funds earmarked for the project should be repaid to shareholders as dividends. The shareholders could then invest the funds themselves at 10 per cent.

FIGURE 6.1
Risk–return trade-off

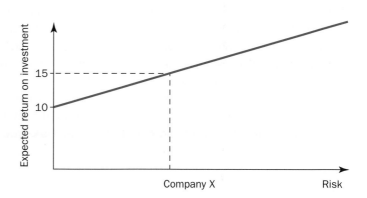

COMPOUNDING AND DISCOUNTING

Our objective is to calculate and compare returns on an investment in a capital project with an alternative equal risk investment in securities traded in the financial markets. This comparison is made using a technique called **discounted cash flow (DCF)** analysis. Because a DCF analysis is the opposite of the concept of **compounding interest**, we shall initially focus on compound interest calculations.

Suppose you are investing £100 000 in a risk-free security yielding a return of 10 per cent payable at the end of each year. Exhibit 6.1 shows that if the interest is re-invested, your investment will accumulate to £146 410 by the end of year 4. Period 0 in the first

REAL WORLD VIEWS 6.1

Capital investment in energy generation

All businesses have to continually engage in capital investment to improve and maintain processes, equipment and facilities. Governments also invest in infrastructure projects like roads, rail and utilities provision. Whether a private or public organization, when capital investment is not undertaken, the effects will cause problems.

In South Africa, no power generation plants had been built for about 20 years from the early 1990s. With a growing economy since then, this has caused problems for many businesses. In 2008, the country exceeded its generation capability which caused power blackouts. The power problems hit one business sector particularly hard, namely the mining sector. Ore smelters and mines consume vast quantities of power and the South African economy is hugely dependent on this sector. Why no investment in new generation capacity? The *Financial Times* website (10 April 2010), stated that a major problem was low electricity prices, which in turn implied little cash for re-investment. According to a Bloomberg article, investment of R500 billion from 2013 to 2017 was needed to overcome an electricity shortage. To help overcome this issue, electricity prices were increased from just under 20 cent per kw/h to 75 cent between 2008 and 2016. However, additional power generation capacity takes time to build and Eskom, who produce 95 per cent of South Africa's power, had spent R265 billion up to 2015. In response, smelting operations like International Ferro Metals invested in their own onsite generation facility. The company produces some of its power requirements by recycling heat from its smelters. This not only helps protect the company from power outages, but also protects to some degree against rising costs. A sound investment in the longer term it would seem.

Questions

1 When evaluating an investment in energy generation solely on cost considerations, can a manager make the right decision?

2 Thinking about the International Ferro Metals example given above, what non-financial benefits might arise other than protecting against power outages?

References

Deloitte (2012) The economic impact of electricity price increases on various sectors of the South African economy. Available at www.eskom.co.za/CustomerCare/MYPD3/Documents/Economic_Impact_of_Electrcity_Price_Increases_Document1.pdf

Eskom Price Tariff, available at www.eskom.co.za/CustomerCare/TariffsAndCharges/Pages/Tariff_History.aspx

Eskom 2015 annual report results summary, available at www.eskom.co.za/IR2015/Documents/Eskom_advert_2015.pdf

MacNamara, W. (2010) Energy crisis: Big push to make sure that power stays on, Financial Times, 10 April. Available at www.ft.com/content/aaaec744-4c0e-11df-a217-00144feab49a

column of Exhibit 6.1 means that no time has elapsed or the time is *now*, period 1 means 1 year later and so on. The values in Exhibit 6.1 can also be obtained by using the formula:

$$FV_n = V_0 (1 + K)^n \qquad (6.1)$$

where FV_n denotes the future value of an investment in n years, V_0 denotes the amount invested at the beginning of the period (year 0), K denotes the rate of return on the investment and n denotes the number of years for which the money is invested. The calculation for £100 000 invested at 10 per cent for 2 years is:

$$FV_2 = £100\ 000\ (1 + 0.10)^2 = £121\ 000$$

EXHIBIT 6.1   The value of £100 000 invested at 10 per cent, compounded annually, for 4 years

End of year	Interest earned (£)	Total investment (£)
0		100 000
	0.10 × 100 000	10 000
1		110 000
	0.10 × 110 000	11 000
2		121 000
	0.10 × 121 000	12 100
3		133 100
	0.10 × 133 100	13 310
4		146 410

In Exhibit 6.1 all of the year-end values are equal as far as the time value of money is concerned. For example, £121 000 received at the end of year 2 is equivalent to £100 000 received today and invested at 10 per cent. Similarly, £133 100 received at the end of year 3 is equivalent to £121 000 received at the end of year 2, because £121 000 can be invested at the end of year 2 to accumulate to £133 100. Unfortunately, none of the amounts are directly comparable at any single moment in time, because each amount is expressed at a different point in time.

When making capital investment decisions, we must convert cash inflows and outflows for different years into a common value. This is achieved by converting the cash flows into their respective values at the same point in time. Mathematically, any point in time can be chosen, since all four figures in Exhibit 6.1 are equal to £100 000 at year 0, £110 000 at year 1, £121 000 at year 2 and so on. However, it is preferable to choose the point in time at which the decision is taken, and this is the present time or year 0. All of the values in Exhibit 6.1 can therefore be expressed in values at the present time (i.e. **present value**) of £100 000.

The process of converting cash to be received in the future into a value at the present time by the use of an interest rate is termed **discounting** and the resulting present value is the **discounted present value**. Compounding is the opposite of discounting, because it is the future value of present value cash flows. Equation (6.1) for calculating future values can be rearranged to produce the present value formula:

$$V_0 \text{ (Present value)} = \frac{FV_n}{(1 + K)^n} \qquad (6.2)$$

By applying this equation, the calculation for £121 000 received at the end of year 2 can be expressed as:

$$\text{Present value} = \frac{£121\,000}{(1 + 0.10)^2} = £100\,000$$

You should now be aware that £1 received today is not equal to £1 received 1 year from today. No rational person will be equally satisfied with receiving £1 a year from now as opposed to receiving it today, because money received today can be used to earn interest over the ensuing year. Thus, 1 year from now an investor can have the original £1 plus 1 year's interest on it. For example, if the interest rate is 10 per cent each £1 invested now will yield £1.10 1 year from now. That is, £1 received today is equal to £1.10 1 year from today at 10 per cent interest. Alternatively, £1 1 year from today is equal to £0.9091 today, its present value because £0.9091 plus 10 per cent interest for 1 year amounts to £1. The concept that £1 received in the future is not equal to £1 received today is known as the **time value of money**.

We shall now consider four different methods of appraising capital investments: the net present value (NPV), internal rate of return (IRR), accounting rate of return and payback methods. We shall see that the first two methods take into account the time value of money, whereas the accounting rate of return and payback methods ignore this factor.

THE CONCEPT OF NET PRESENT VALUE

By using discounted cash flow techniques and calculating present values, we can compare the return on an investment in capital projects with an alternative equal risk investment in securities traded in the financial market. Suppose a firm is considering four projects (all of which are risk-free) as shown in Exhibit 6.2. You can see that each of the projects is identical with the investment in the risk-free security shown in Exhibit 6.1 because you can cash in this investment for £110 000 in year 1, £121 000 in year 2, £133 100 in year 3 and £146 410 in year 4. In other words, your potential cash receipts from the risk-free security are identical to the net cash flows for projects A, B, C and D shown in Exhibit 6.2. Consequently, the firm should be indifferent as to whether it uses the funds to invest in the projects or invests the funds in securities of identical risk traded in the financial markets.

The most straightforward way of determining whether a project yields a return in excess of the alternative equal risk investment in traded securities is to calculate the **net present value (NPV)**. This is the present value of the net cash inflows less the project's initial investment outlay. If the rate of return from the project is greater

EXHIBIT 6.2 Evaluation of four risk-free projects

	A (£)	B (£)	C (£)	D (£)
Project investment outlay	100 000	100 000	100 000	100 000
End of year cash flows:				
Year 1	110 000	0	0	0
2	0	121 000	0	0
3	0	0	133 100	0
4	0	0	0	146 410
Present value =	$\dfrac{110\,000}{1.10}$	$\dfrac{121\,000}{(1.10)^2}$	$\dfrac{133\,100}{(1.10)^3}$	$\dfrac{146\,410}{(1.10)^4}$
	= 100 000	= 100 000	= 100 000	= 100 000

than the return from an equivalent risk investment in securities traded in the financial market, the NPV will be positive. Alternatively, if the rate of return is lower, the NPV will be negative. A positive NPV therefore indicates that an investment should be accepted, while a negative value indicates that it should be rejected. A zero NPV calculation indicates that the firm should be indifferent to whether the project is accepted or rejected.

You can see that the present value of each of the projects shown in Exhibit 6.2 is £100 000. You should now deduct the investment cost of £100 000 to calculate the project's NPV. The NPV for each project is zero. The firm should therefore be indifferent to whether it accepts any of the projects or invests the funds in an equivalent risk-free security. This was our conclusion when we compared the cash flows of the projects with the investment in a risk-free security shown in Exhibit 6.1.

You can see that it is better for the firm to invest in any of the projects shown in Exhibit 6.2 if their initial investment outlays are less than £100 000. This is because we have to pay £100 000 to obtain an equivalent stream of cash flows from a security traded in the financial markets. Conversely, we should reject the investment in the projects if their initial investment outlays are greater than £100 000. You should now see that the NPV rule leads to a direct comparison of a project with an equivalent risk security traded in the financial market. Given that the present value of the net cash inflows for each project is £100 000, their NPVs will be positive (thus signifying acceptance) if the initial investment outlay is less than £100 000 and negative (thus signifying rejection) if the initial outlay is greater than £100 000.

CALCULATING NET PRESENT VALUES

You should now have an intuitive understanding of the NPV rule. We shall now learn how to calculate NPVs. The NPV can be expressed as:

$$NPV = \frac{FV_1}{1 + K} + \frac{FV_2}{(1 + K)^2} + \frac{FV_3}{(1 + K)^3} + \dots + \frac{FV_n}{(1 + K)^n} - I_0 \qquad (6.3)$$

where I_0 represents the investment outlay and FV represents the future values received in years 1 to n. The rate of return K used is the return available on an equivalent risk security in the financial market. Consider the situation in Example 6.1.

The NPV calculation for Project A is:

$$NPV = \frac{£300\,000}{(1.10)} + \frac{£1\,000\,000}{(1.10)^2} + \frac{£400\,000}{(1.10)^3} - £1\,000\,000 = +£399\,700$$

Alternatively, the NPV can be calculated by referring to a published table of present values. You will find examples of such a table if you refer to Appendix A (see pages 449–450). To use the table, simply find the discount factors by referring to each year of the cash flows and the appropriate interest rate.

For example, if you refer to year 1 in Appendix A, and the 10 per cent column, this will show a discount factor of 0.909. For years 2 and 3 the discount factors are 0.826 and 0.751.

You then multiply the cash flows by the discount factors to find the present value of the cash flows. The calculation is as follows:

Year	Amount (£000)	Discount factor	Present value (£)
1	300	0.9091	272 730
2	1 000	0.8264	826 400
3	400	0.7513	300 520
			1 399 650
		Less initial outlay	1 000 000
		Net present value	399 650

In order to reconcile the NPV calculations derived from Formula 6.3 and the discount tables, the discount factors used in this chapter are based on four decimal places. Normally the factors given in Appendix A based on three decimal places will suffice. The difference between the two calculations shown above is due to rounding differences.

Note that the discount factors in the present value table shown in Appendix A are based on £1 received in n years time calculated according to the present value formula (equation 6.2). For example, £1 received in years 1, 2 and 3 when the interest rate is 10 per cent is calculated (based on four decimal places) as follows:

$$\text{Year 1} = £1/1.10 = 0.9091$$

$$\text{Year 2} = £1(1.10)^2 = 0.8264$$

$$\text{Year 3} = £1(1.10)^3 = 0.7513$$

The positive NPV represents the potential increase in present consumption that the project makes available to the ordinary shareholders, after any funds used have been repaid with interest. For example, assume that the firm finances the investment of £1 million in Example 6.1 by borrowing £1 399 700 at 10 per cent and repays the loan and interest out of the project's proceeds as they occur. You can see from the repayment schedule in Exhibit 6.3 that £399 700 received from the loan is available for current consumption, and the remaining £1 000 000 can be invested in the project. The cash flows from the project are just sufficient to repay the loan. Therefore, acceptance of the project enables the ordinary shareholders' present consumption to be increased by the

EXAMPLE 6.1

The Bothnia Company is evaluating two projects with an expected life of 3 years and an investment outlay of £1 million. The estimated net cash inflows for each project are as follows:

	Project A (£)	Project B (£)
Year 1	300 000	600 000
Year 2	1 000 000	600 000
Year 3	400 000	600 000

The opportunity cost of capital for both projects is 10 per cent. You are required to calculate the NPV for each project.

EXHIBIT 6.3 The pattern of cash flows assuming that the loan is repaid out of the proceeds of the project

Year	Loan outstanding at start of year (1) (£)	Interest at 10% (2) (£)	Total amount owed before repayment (3) = (1) + (2) (£)	Proceeds from project (4) (£)	Loan outstanding at year end (5) = (3) − (4) (£)
1	1 399 700	139 970	1 539 670	300 000	1 239 670
2	1 239 670	123 967	1 363 637	1 000 000	363 637
3	363 637	36 363	400 000	400 000	0

NPV of £399 700. Hence the acceptance of all available projects with a positive NPV should lead to the maximization of shareholders' wealth.

We shall now calculate the NPV for Project B shown in Example 6.1. The cash flows for project B represent an **annuity**. An annuity is an asset that pays a fixed sum each period for a specific number of periods. You can see for project B that the cash flows are £600 000 per annum for 3 years. When the annual cash flows are equivalent to an annuity, the calculation of NPV is simplified. The discount factors for an annuity are set out in Appendix B (see pages 451–452). We need to find the discount factor for 10 per cent for 3 years. If you refer to Appendix B, you will see that it is 2.487. The NPV is calculated as follows:

Annual cash inflow	Discount factor	Present value (£)
£600 000	2.487	1 492 200
	Less investment cost	1 000 000
	Net present value	492 200

You will see that the total present value for the period is calculated by multiplying the cash inflow by the discount factor. It is important to note that the annuity tables shown in Appendix B can only be applied when the annual cash flows are the same each year. Annuities are also based on the assumption that cash flows for the first period are received at the end of the period, and not at the start of the period, and that all subsequent cash flows are received at the end of each period. Sometimes, to simplify the calculations, examination questions are set based on the assumption that constant cash flows occur into perpetuity (i.e. for a very long time, typically over 50 years). In this situation the present value is determined by dividing the cash flow by the discount rate. For example, the present value of a cash flow of £100 per annum into perpetuity at a discount rate of 10 per cent is £1000 (£100/0.10). Again the present value calculation is based on the assumption that the first cash flow is received one period hence.

INTERNAL RATE OF RETURN

The **internal rate of return (IRR)** is an alternative technique for use in making capital investment decisions that also takes into account the time value of money. The IRR represents the true interest rate earned on an investment over the course of its economic life. This measure is sometimes referred to as the **discounted rate of return**. The IRR is the interest rate K that when used to discount all cash flows resulting from an investment, will equate the present value of the cash receipts to the present value of the cash outlays.

In other words, it is the discount rate that will cause the NPV of an investment to be zero. Alternatively, the IRR can be described as the maximum cost of capital that can be applied to finance a project without causing harm to the shareholders. The IRR is found by solving for the value of K from the following formula:

$$I_0 = \frac{FV_1}{1 + K} + \frac{FV_2}{(1 + K)^2} + \frac{FV_3}{(1 + K)^3} + \dots + \frac{FV_n}{(1 + K)^n} \qquad (6.4)$$

It is easier, however, to use the discount tables. Let us now calculate the IRR (using discount factors based on four decimal places) for Project A in Example 6.1.

The IRR can be found by trial and error by using a number of discount factors until the NPV equals zero. For example, if we use a 25 per cent discount factor, we get a positive NPV of £84 800. We must therefore try a higher figure. Applying 35 per cent gives a negative NPV of £66 530. We know then that the NPV will be zero somewhere between 25 per cent and 35 per cent. In fact, the IRR is between 30 per cent and 31 per cent but closest to 30 per cent, as indicated by the following calculation:

Year	Net cash flow (£)	Discount factor (30%)	Present value of cash flow (£)
1	300 000	0.7692	230 760
2	1 000 000	0.5917	591 700
3	400 000	0.4552	182 080
		Net present value	1 004 540
		Less initial outlay	1 000 000
		Net present value	4 540

The decision rule is that if the IRR is greater than the opportunity cost of capital, the investment is profitable and will yield a positive NPV. Alternatively, if the IRR is less than the cost of capital, the investment is unprofitable and will result in a negative NPV. The calculation of the IRR is illustrated in Figure 6.2.

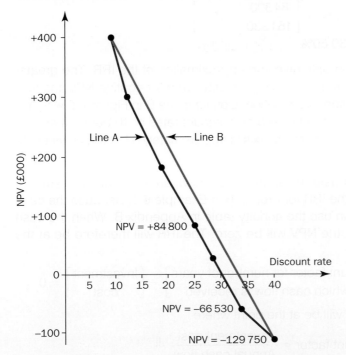

FIGURE 6.2

Interpretation of the internal rate of return

The dots in the graph represent the NPV at different discount rates. The point where the line joining the dots cuts the horizontal axis indicates the IRR (the point at which the NPV is zero). Figure 6.2 indicates that the IRR is approximately 30 per cent, and you can see from this diagram that the interpolation method can be used to calculate the IRR without carrying out trial and error calculations. When we use interpolation, we infer the missing term (in this case the discount rate at which NPV is zero) from a known series of numbers. For example, at a discount rate of 25 per cent the NPV is +£84 800 and for a discount rate of 35 per cent the NPV is –£66 530. The total distance between these points is £151 330 (+£84 800 and –£66 530). The calculation for the approximate IRR is therefore:

$$25\% + \frac{84\,800}{151\,330} \times (35\% - 25\%) = 30.60\%$$

In other words, if you move down line A in Figure 6.2 from a discount rate of 25 per cent by £84 800, you will reach the point at which NPV is zero. The distance between the two points on line A is £151 330, and we are given the discount rates of 25 per cent and 35 per cent for these points. Therefore 84 800/151 330 represents the distance that we must move between these two points for the NPV to be zero. This distance in terms of the discount rate is 5.60 per cent [(84 800/151 330) × 10 per cent], which, when added to the starting point of 25 per cent, produces an IRR of 30.60 per cent. The formula using the interpolation method is as follows:

$$A + \frac{C}{C - D}(B - A) \tag{6.5}$$

where A is the discount rate of the low trial, B is the discount rate of the high trial, C is the NPV of cash inflow of the low trial and D is the NPV of cash inflow of the high trial. Thus:

$$25\% + \left[\frac{84\,800}{84\,800 - (-66\,530)} \times 10\% \right]$$

$$= 25\% + \left[\frac{84\,800}{151\,330} \times 10\% \right]$$

$$= 30.60\%$$

Note that the interpolation method only gives an approximation of the IRR. The greater the distance between any two points that have a positive and a negative NPV, the less accurate is the IRR calculation using interpolation. Consider line B in Figure 6.2 which is based on using the interpolation method based on discount rates of 10 per cent and 40 per cent. The point where it cuts the horizontal axis is approximately 33 per cent, whereas the actual IRR is 30.60 per cent.

The calculation of the IRR is easier when the cash flows are of a constant amount each year. Let us now calculate the IRR for Project B in Example 6.1. Because the cash flows are equal each year, we can use the annuity table in Appendix B. When the cash flows are discounted at the IRR, the NPV will be zero. The IRR will therefore be at the point where

$$[\text{Annual cash flow}] \times \left[\begin{array}{c} \text{Discount factor for number of years} \\ \text{for which cash flow is received} \end{array} \right] - \left[\begin{array}{c} \text{Investment} \\ \text{cost} \end{array} \right] = 0$$

Rearranging this formula, the IRR will be at the point where

$$\text{Discount factor} = \frac{\text{Investment cost}}{\text{Annual cash flow}}$$

REAL WORLD VIEWS 6.2

The results of a prefeasibility study by Ironveld plc in South Africa

The *Africa Research Bulletin* reported the results of a prefeasibility study by Ironveld plc stating that the grades for pig iron and ferro vanadium were better than expected at its project on the Northern Limb of the Bushveld Complex in South Africa. The prefeasibility study demonstrated the viability of developing the Ironveld pig-iron project delivering 1 Mt/y of pig iron and 9670 t/y of ferro vanadium

production for 25 years starting from 2019. The capital cost of the project is estimated at about US$938 million. The prefeasibility study estimated a post-tax internal rate of return of 28.8 per cent and a net present value of US$1.07 billion, assuming a 10 per cent discount rate. The prefeasibility study was based on pig-iron prices of US$450/t and US$35/kg for ferro vanadium, yielding total annual revenue of R6500 million (US$657 million) at full production.

Questions

1   Why has the company used both net present value and internal rate of return, but ignored the payback, when undertaking the prefeasibility study?
2   What steps can the company take to ensure that there is less likelihood that incorrect estimates will result in the project not having an acceptable net present value and internal rate of return?

Reference

Iron Ore: South Africa (2013) Africa Research Bulletin: Economic, Financial and Technical Series, 50(5): 19999B–20000A. Available at onlinelibrary.wiley.com/doi/10.1111/j.1467-6346.2013.05209.x/pdf

Substituting the figures for Project B in Example 6.1:

$$\text{Discount factor} = \frac{\pounds1\,000\,000}{\pounds600\,000} = 1.666$$

We now examine the entries for the year 3 row in Appendix B to find the figures closest to 1.666. They are 1.673 (entered in the 36 per cent column) and 1.652 (entered in the 37 per cent column). We can therefore conclude that the IRR is between 36 per cent and 37 per cent. However, because the cost of capital is 10 per cent, an accurate calculation is unnecessary; the IRR is far in excess of the cost of capital. The calculation of the IRR can be rather tedious (as the cited examples show), but the trial-and-error approach can be programmed for fast and accurate solution by a computer or calculator.

RELEVANT CASH FLOWS

Investment decisions, like all other decisions, should be analysed in terms of the cash flows that can be directly attributable to them. These cash flows should include the incremental cash flows that will occur in the future following acceptance of the investment.

The cash flows will include cash inflows and outflows, or the inflows may be represented by savings in cash outflows. For example, a decision to purchase new machinery may generate cash savings in the form of reduced out-of-pocket operating costs. For all practical purposes such cost savings are equivalent to cash receipts.

It is important to note that depreciation is not included in the cash flow estimates for capital investment decisions, since it is a non-cash expense. This is because the capital investment cost of the asset to be depreciated is included as a cash outflow at the start of the project, and depreciation is merely a financial accounting method for allocating past capital costs to future accounting periods. Any inclusion of depreciation will lead to double counting.

TIMING OF CASH FLOWS

To simplify the presentation our calculations have been based on the assumption that any cash flows in future years will occur in one lump sum at the year-end. Obviously, this is an unrealistic assumption, since cash flows are likely to occur at various times throughout the year, and a more realistic assumption is to assume that cash flows occur at the end of each month and use monthly discount rates. Discount and interest rates are normally quoted as rates per annum using the term **annual percentage rate (APR)**. Discount tables, such as those provided in the Appendix at the end of this book, also assume that cash flows occur in one lump sum at the end of the year. If you wish to use monthly discount rates it is necessary to convert annual discount rates to monthly rates. An approximation of the monthly discount rate can be obtained by dividing the annual rate by 12. However, this simplified calculation ignores the compounding effect whereby each monthly interest payment is reinvested to earn more interest each month. To convert the annual discount rate to a monthly discount rate that takes into account the compounding effect we must use the following formula:

$$Monthly\ discount\ rate = (\sqrt[12]{1 + APR})-1 \tag{6.6}$$

Assume that the annual percentage discount rate is 12.68 per cent. Applying Formula 6.6 gives a monthly discount rate of:

$$(\sqrt[12]{1.1268}) - 1 = 1.01 - 1 = .01\ (i.e.\ 1\ per\ cent\ per\ month)$$

Therefore the monthly cash flows would be discounted at 1 per cent. In other words, 1 per cent compounded monthly is equivalent to 12.68 per cent compounded annually. Formula 6.2 can be used to ascertain the present value using monthly discount rates with k denoting the monthly discount rate and n denoting the number of months. Note that the monthly discount rates can also be converted to annual percentage rates using the formula:

$$(1 + k)^{12} - 1\ (where\ k = the\ monthly\ discount\ rate) \tag{6.7}$$

Assuming a monthly rate of 1 per cent the annual rate is $(1.01)^{12} - 1 = 0.1268$ (i.e. 12.68 per cent per annum). Instead of using formulae (6.6) and (6.7) you can divide the annual percentage rate by 12 to obtain an approximation of the monthly discount rate or multiply the monthly discount rate by 12 to approximate the annual percentage rate.

COMPARISON OF NET PRESENT VALUE AND INTERNAL RATE OF RETURN

In many situations the IRR method will result in the same decision as the NPV method. In the case of conventional projects (in which an initial cash outflow is followed by a series of cash inflows) that are independent of each other (i.e. where the selection of a particular project does not preclude the choice of the other), both NPV and IRR rules will lead to the same accept/reject decisions. However, there are also situations where the IRR method may lead to different decisions being made from those that would follow the adoption of the NPV procedure.

Mutually exclusive projects

Where projects are **mutually exclusive**, it is possible for the NPV and the IRR methods to suggest different rankings as to which project should be given priority. Mutually exclusive projects exist where the acceptance of one project excludes the acceptance of another project, for example the choice of one of several possible factory locations, or the choice of one of many different possible machines. When evaluating mutually exclusive projects, the IRR method can incorrectly rank projects, because of its reinvestment assumptions, and in these circumstances it is recommended that the NPV method is used.

Percentage returns

Another problem with the IRR rule is that it expresses the result as a percentage rather than in monetary terms. Comparison of percentage returns can be misleading; for example, compare an investment of £10 000 that yields a return of 50 per cent with an investment of £100 000 that yields a return of 25 per cent. If only one of the investments can be undertaken, the first investment will yield £5000 but the second will yield £25 000. If we assume that the cost of capital is 10 per cent, and that no other suitable investments are available, any surplus funds will be invested at the cost of capital (i.e. the returns available from equal risk securities traded in financial markets). Choosing the first investment will leave a further £90 000 to be invested, but this can only be invested at 10 per cent, yielding a return of £9000. Adding this to the return of £5000 from the £10 000 investment gives a total return of £14 000. Clearly, the second investment, which yields a return of £25 000, is preferable. Thus, NPV provides the correct measure.

Reinvestment assumptions

The assumption concerning the reinvestment of interim cash flows from the acceptance of projects provides another reason for supporting the superiority of the NPV method. The implicit assumption if the NPV method is adopted is that the cash flows generated from an investment will be reinvested immediately at the cost of capital (i.e. the returns available from equal risk securities traded in financial markets). However, the IRR method makes a different implicit assumption about the reinvestment of the cash flows. It assumes that all the proceeds from a project can be reinvested immediately to earn a return equal to the IRR of the original project. This assumption is likely to be unrealistic because a firm should have accepted all projects that offer a return in excess of the cost of capital, and any other funds that become available can only be reinvested at the cost of capital. This is the assumption that is implicit in the NPV rule.

Unconventional cash flows

Where a project has unconventional cash flows, the IRR has a technical shortcoming. Most projects have conventional cash flows that consist of an initial negative investment cash flow followed by positive cash inflows in later years. In this situation the algebraic sign changes, being negative at the start and positive in all future periods. If the sign of the net cash flows changes in successive periods, it is possible for the calculations to produce as many internal rates of return as there are sign changes. While multiple rates of return are mathematically possible, only one rate of return is economically significant in determining whether or not the investment is profitable.

Fortunately, the majority of investment decisions consist of conventional cash flows that produce a single IRR calculation. However, the problem cannot be ignored, since unconventional cash flows are possible (such as open cast mining where cash outflows occur at the end of the project arising from the need to rectify the land after mining) and, if the decision-maker is unaware of the situation, serious errors may occur at the decision-making stage.

TECHNIQUES THAT IGNORE THE TIME VALUE OF MONEY

In addition to those methods that take into account the time value of money, two other methods that ignore this factor are frequently used in practice. These are the payback method and the accounting rate of return method. Methods that ignore the time value of money are theoretically weak, and they will not necessarily lead to the maximization of the market value of ordinary shares. Nevertheless, the fact that they are frequently used in practice means that we should be aware of these techniques and their limitations.

PAYBACK METHOD

The **payback method** is one of the simplest and most frequently used methods of capital investment appraisal. It is defined as the length of time that is required for a stream of cash proceeds from an investment to recover the original cash outlay required by the investment. If the stream of cash flows from the investment is constant each year, the payback period can be calculated by dividing the total initial cash outlay by the amount of the expected annual cash proceeds. Therefore, if an investment requires an initial outlay of £60 000 and is expected to produce annual cash inflows of £20 000 per year for 5 years, the payback period will be £60 000 divided by £20 000, or 3 years. If the stream of expected proceeds is not constant from year to year, the payback period is determined by adding up the cash inflows expected in successive years until the total is equal to the original outlay. Example 6.2 illustrates two projects, A and B, that require the same initial outlay of £50 000 but that display different time profiles of benefits.

REAL WORLD VIEWS 6.3

Use your crystal ball

An article published in the Irish Times by Olive Keogh cites the following comments by Patrick Gibbons, Professor of strategic management at the UCD Michael Smurfit Graduate Business School:

The one thing we know about most forecasts is that they are wrong. At a minimum, in making forecasts, firms should think about a range of key parameters, such as market shares, growth

rates and so on, as opposed to single-point estimates. The amount of resources devoted to forecasting are predicated on how easily reversible the decisions are. Where investment requirements are low, the investment/capital is extremely flexible, or the payback period is very fast, then extensive market forecasting may not be required. Where investment requirements are high, capital is extremely specialized and inflexible, and where the lead-time to bring investment on-stream is very long, then more extensive forecasting is necessary.

Questions

1 How can more extensive and less extensive forms of forecasting be applied to appraising capital investment projects?
2 What is the difference between estimates based on a range of key parameters and single-point estimates?

Reference

Keogh, O. (2012) Use your crystal ball, Irish Times, 30 March. Available at www.irishtimes.com/business/economy/ireland/use-your-crystal-ball-1.492272

In Example 6.2 project A pays back its initial investment cost in 3 years, whereas project B pays back its initial cost in 4 years. Therefore, project A would be ranked in preference to project B because it has the fastest payback period. However, project B has a higher NPV, and the payback method incorrectly ranks project A in preference to project B. Two obvious deficiencies are apparent from these calculations. First, the payback method does not take into account cash flows that are earned after the payback period and, second, it fails to take into account the differences in the timing of the proceeds which are earned before the payback period. Payback computations ignore the important fact that future cash receipts cannot be validly compared with an initial outlay until they are discounted to their present values.

Not only does the payback period incorrectly rank project A in preference to project B, but the method can also result in the acceptance of projects that have a negative NPV. Consider the cash flows for project C in Example 6.3.

The payback period for project C is 3 years, and if this was within the time limit set by management, the project would be accepted in spite of its negative NPV. Note also that the payback method would rank project C in preference to project B in Example 6.2, despite the fact that B would yield a positive NPV.

The payback period can only be a valid indicator of the time that an investment requires to pay for itself if all cash flows are first discounted to their present values and

EXAMPLE 6.2

The cash flows and NPV calculations for two projects are as follows:

	Project A (£)	(£)	Project B (£)	(£)
Initial cost				
Net cash inflows		50 000		50 000
Year 1	10 000		10 000	
Year 2	20 000		10 000	
Year 3	20 000		10 000	
Year 4	20 000		20 000	
Year 5	10 000		30 000	
Year 6	–		30 000	
Year 7	–	80 000	30 000	140 000
NPV at 10% cost of capital		10 500		39 460

EXAMPLE 6.3

The cash flows and NPV calculation for project C are as follows:

	(£)	(£)
Initial cost		
Net cash inflows		50 000
Year 1	10 000	
Year 2	20 000	
Year 3	20 000	
Year 4	3 500	
Year 5	3 500	
Year 6	3 500	
Year 7	3 500	64 000
NPV at 10% cost of capital		(–1 036)

the discounted values are then used to calculate the payback period. This adjustment gives rise to what is known as the adjusted or **discounted payback method**. Even when such an adjustment is made, the adjusted payback method cannot be a complete measure of an investment's profitability. It can estimate whether an investment is likely to be profitable, but it cannot estimate how profitable the investment will be.

Despite the theoretical limitations of the payback method it is the method most widely used in practice (see Exhibit 6.4). Why, then, is payback the most widely applied formal

EXHIBIT 6.4 Surveys of practice

A survey by Brounen *et al.* (2004) in mainland Europe reported that the usage of the payback method was 65 per cent in the Netherlands, 50 per cent in Germany and 51 per cent in France. NPV was used by 70 per cent of German respondents compared with 56 per cent using IRR. Usage of IRR exceeded that of NPV in the Netherlands and France. A more recent survey based on 439 respondents (60 per cent UK and 40 per cent non-UK) by the Chartered Institute of Management Accountants (2009) reported that net present value was used by 62 per cent of the companies surveyed followed by 55 per cent using payback, 42 per cent using internal rate of return, 34 per cent using discounted payback and 18 per cent using accounting rate of return. The larger companies used all of the appraisal techniques to a greater extent than the smaller companies.

REAL WORLD VIEWS 6.4

Payback from domestic wind and solar energy

Increasingly, householders and small businesses are considering renewable power generation to decrease their energy costs. Most of the UK, Ireland and Scandinavia are suited to generating energy from wind, whereas more central European countries are more suited to solar power. While larger businesses typically appraise all investments using solid techniques and criteria, smaller businesses (and households) do not have either the knowledge or resources to do a full investment appraisal.

For wind energy generation, an investment outlay is necessary. This may range from a few thousand pounds for a small domestic wind turbine to about £70 000 for a 15 kW turbine capable of meeting the power requirements of a small farm or office complex. In terms of measuring whether an investment is worthwhile, the typical evaluation method used is the payback period. Most suppliers of wind turbines provide payback calculators on their websites. The UK's Energy Saving Trust also provides such a tool (see the link below). According to its calculator, a wind turbine rated with a 15 kW generation capability, assuming 75 per cent of the power is sold to the national grid and an average wind speed greater than 5 m/s, will have a lifetime benefit of just over £92 000

at 2018 rates. If the cost is £70 000, the net gain is thus £22 000, giving a payback period of about 15 years assuming a 20 year lifespan.

Questions

1 What might affect the payback calculations on wind energy investments for a business and/or a household?
2 In making a decision, should the business or householder look beyond the payback period?

References

Energy Saving Trust (2016) Cashback calculator. Available at www.nonpvfitcalculator.energysavingtrust. org.uk, accessed 23 February 2018.

The Renewable Energy Hub, www.renewableenergyhub. co.uk/wind-turbines/how-much-does-wind-turbines-cost.html, accessed 23 February 2018.

investment appraisal technique? It is a particularly useful approach for ranking projects where a firm faces liquidity constraints and requires a fast repayment of investments. The payback method may also be appropriate in situations where risky investments are made in uncertain markets that are subject to fast design and product changes or where future cash flows are extremely difficult to predict. The payback method assumes that risk is time-related: the longer the period, the greater the chance of failure. By concentrating on the early cash flows, payback uses data in which managers have greater confidence. Thus, the payback period can be used as a rough measure of risk, based on the assumption that the longer it takes for a project to pay for itself, the riskier it is. Managers may also choose projects with quick payback periods because of self-interest. If a manager's performance is measured using short-term criteria, such as net profits, there is a danger that he or she may choose projects with quick paybacks to show improved net profits as soon as possible. The payback method is also frequently used in conjunction with the NPV or IRR methods. It serves as a simple first-level screening device that identifies those projects that should be subject to more rigorous investigation. A further attraction of payback is that it is easily understood by all levels of management and provides an important summary measure: how quickly will the project recover its initial outlay? Ideally, the payback method should be used in conjunction with the NPV method, and the cash flows discounted before the payback period is calculated.

ACCOUNTING RATE OF RETURN

The **accounting rate of return** (also known as the **return on investment** and **return on capital employed**) is calculated by dividing the average annual profits from a project into the average investment cost. It differs from other methods in that profits rather than cash flows are used. Assuming that depreciation represents the only non-cash expense, profit is equivalent to cash flows less depreciation. The use of accounting rate of return can be attributed to the wide use of the return on investment measure in financial statement analysis.

When the average annual net profits are calculated, only additional revenues and costs that follow from the investment are included in the calculation. The average annual net profit is therefore calculated by dividing the difference between incremental revenues and costs by the estimated life of the investment. The incremental costs include either the *net* investment cost or the total depreciation charges, these figures being identical. The average investment figure that is used in the calculation depends on the method employed to calculate depreciation. If straight line depreciation is used, it is presumed that investment will decline in a linear fashion as the asset ages. The average investment under this assumption is one-half of the amount of the initial investment plus one-half of the scrap value at the end of the project's life (see Note 1 at the end of the chapter for an explanation).

For example, the three projects described in Examples 6.2 and 6.3 for which the payback period was computed required an initial outlay of £50 000. If we assume that the projects have no scrap values and that straight line depreciation is used, the average investment for each project will be £25 000. The calculation of the accounting rate of return for each of these projects is as follows:

$$\text{Accounting rate of return} = \frac{\text{Average annual profits}}{\text{Average investment}}$$

$$\text{project A} = \frac{6000}{25000} = 24\%$$

$$\text{project B} = \frac{12857}{25000} = 51\%$$

$$\text{project C} = \frac{2000}{25000} = 8\%$$

For project A the total profit over its 5-year life is £30 000 (£80 000 − £50 000), giving an average annual profit of £6000. The average annual profits for projects B and C are calculated in a similar manner.

It follows that the accounting rate of return is superior to the payback method in one respect; that is, it allows for differences in the useful lives of the assets being compared. For example, the calculations set out above reflect the high earnings of project B over the whole life of the project, and consequently it is ranked in preference to project A. Also, projects A and C have the same payback periods, but the accounting rate of return correctly indicates that project A is preferable to project C.

However, the accounting rate of return suffers from the serious defect that it ignores the time value of money. When the method is used in relation to a project where the cash inflows do not occur until near the end of its life, it will show the same accounting rate of return as it would for a project where the cash inflows occur early in its life, providing that the average cash inflows are the same. For this reason the accounting rate of return cannot be recommended. Nevertheless, the accounting rate of return is employed in practice (see Exhibit 6.4). This is probably due to the fact that the annual accounting rate of return is frequently used to measure the managerial performance of different business units within a company. Therefore, managers are likely to be interested in how any new investment contributes to the business unit's overall accounting rate of return.

THE EFFECT OF PERFORMANCE MEASUREMENT ON CAPITAL INVESTMENT DECISIONS

The way that the performance of a manager is measured is likely to have a profound effect on the decisions he or she will make. There is a danger that, because of the way performance is measured, a manager may be motivated to take the wrong decision and not follow the NPV rule. Consider the information presented in Exhibit 6.5 in respect of the net cash inflows and the annual reported profits or losses for projects J and K. The figures without the parentheses refer to the cash inflows whereas the figures within parentheses refer to annual reported profit. You will see that the total cash inflows over the 5-year lives for projects J and K are £11 million and £5 million respectively. Both projects require an initial outlay of £5 million. Assuming a cost of capital of 10 per cent, without undertaking any calculations it is clear that project J will have a positive NPV and project K will have a negative NPV.

If the straight line method of depreciation is used the annual depreciation for both projects will be £1 million (£5 million investment cost/5 years). Therefore, the reported

EXHIBIT 6.5   Annual net cash inflows (profits/losses) for two projects, each with an initial outlay of £5 million

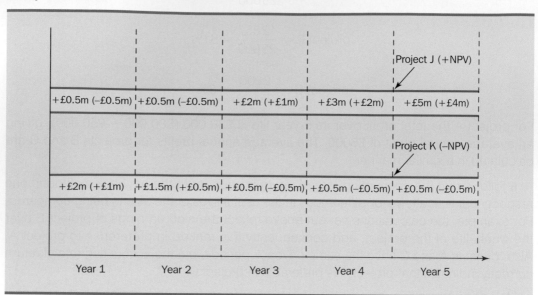

profits (shown in parentheses) are derived from deducting the annual depreciation charge from the annual net cash inflows. For decision-making the focus is on the entire life of the projects. Our objective is to ascertain whether the present value of the cash inflows exceeds the present value of the cash outflows over the entire life of a project, and not allocate the NPV to different accounting periods as indicated by the dashed vertical lines in Exhibit 6.5. In other words we require an answer to the question: will the project add value?

In contrast, a company is required to report on its performance externally at annual intervals and managerial performance is also often evaluated on an annual or more frequent basis. Evaluating managerial performance at the end of the 5-year project lives is clearly too long a timescale because managers are unlikely to remain in the same job for such lengthy periods. Therefore, if a manager's performance is measured using short-term criteria, such as annual profits, he or she may choose projects that have a favourable impact on short-term financial performance. Because project J will have a negative impact on performance in its early years (i.e. it contributes losses) there is a danger that a manager who is anxious to improve his or her short-term performance might reject project J even though it has a positive impact on the performance measure in the long term.

The reverse may happen with project K. This has a favourable impact on the short-term profit performance measure in years 1 and 2 but a negative impact in the longer term, so the manager might accept the project to improve his or her short-term performance measure.

It is thus important to avoid an excessive focus on short-term profitability measures because this can have a negative impact on long-term profitability. Emphasis should also be given to measuring a manager's contribution to an organization's long-term objectives. These issues are discussed in Chapter 12 when we look at performance measurement in more detail. However, at this point you should note that the way in which managerial performance is measured will influence managers' decisions and may motivate them to work in their own best interests, even when this is not in the best interests of the organization.

Appraising water irrigation systems

The globe is facing an increase in water demand resulting in the need for additional agricultural land and irrigation water. Elyamany and El-Nashar (2013) provided an illustration of a financial appraisal of four alternative methods of water irrigation in Egypt. They were a traditional system of open canals which allow a high percentage of water dissipation and evaporation, a pipeline with one pump at the canal head, a pipeline with one pump at the head and one pump at the middle, and a lined open canal. Three appraisal methods were used to evaluate the alternatives. They were NPV, IRR and the payback method. All three methods provide the same conclusion and support the decision that the best design alternative was one pump at the intake of the canal.

Questions

1 Can you provide some examples of the costs and benefits that would be included in the investment appraisal?

2 What are the disadvantages of using IRR and payback to evaluate the above alternatives?

Reference

Elnashar, W. and Elyamany, A.H. (2013), 'Estimating Life Cycle Cost of Improved Field Irrigation Canal', *Water Resource Management*, 30, 99–113

QUALITATIVE FACTORS

Not all investment projects can be described completely in terms of monetary costs and benefits (e.g. expenditure on facilities for employees, or expenditure to avoid unpleasant environmental effects from the company's manufacturing process). There is a danger that those aspects of a new investment that are difficult to quantify may be omitted from the financial appraisal.

One approach that has been suggested for overcoming these difficulties is not to attempt to place a value on those benefits that are difficult to quantify. Instead, the process can be reversed by estimating how large these benefits must be in order to justify the proposed investment. Assume that a project with an estimated life of ten years and a cost of capital of 20 per cent has a negative NPV of £1 million. To achieve a positive NPV, or in other words to obtain the required rate of return of 20 per cent, additional cash flows would need to be achieved that when discounted at 20 per cent, would amount to at least £1 million. The project lasts for ten years, and the discount factor for an annuity over ten years at 20 per cent is 4.192. Therefore the additional cash flows from the benefits that have not been quantified must be greater than £238 550 per annum (note that £1 million divided by an annuity factor (Appendix B) for ten years at 20 per cent (4.192) equals £238 550) in order to justify the proposed investment. Discussions should then take place to consider whether benefits that have not been quantified, such as improved flexibility, rapid customer service, market adaptability and reduction in environmental impact are worth more than £238 550 per year.

Capital investment decisions are particularly difficult in non-profit organizations such as public sector organizations, since it is not always possible to quantify the costs and benefits of a project. **Cost-benefit analysis (CBA)** has been developed to resolve this problem. It is an investment appraisal technique for analysing and measuring the costs and benefits to the community arising from capital projects. CBA defines the costs and benefits in much wider terms than those that would be included in investment appraisals undertaken in the pursuit of profit maximization. For example, the application of CBA to an investment in a public transportation system would incorporate the benefits of the travelling time saved by users of the system.

WEIGHTED AVERAGE COST OF CAPITAL

So far we have assumed that firms are financed only by equity finance (i.e. ordinary share capital and retained earnings). However, most companies are likely to be financed by a combination of debt (i.e. borrowed funds) and equity capital. These companies aim to maintain target proportions of debt and equity.

The cost of *new* debt (i.e borrowed funds) capital is simply the after-tax interest cost of raising new debt. Assume that the after-tax cost of new debt capital is 6 per cent and the required rate of return on equity capital is 14 per cent and that the company intends to maintain a capital structure of 50 per cent debt and 50 per cent equity. The overall cost of capital for the company is calculated as follows:

$$= \begin{bmatrix} \text{proportion of debt capital} \\ \times \;\; \text{cost of debt capital} \\ (0.5 \times 6\%) \end{bmatrix} + \begin{bmatrix} \text{proportion of equity capital} \\ \times \;\; \text{cost of equity capital} \\ (0. \times 14\%) \end{bmatrix} = 10\%$$

The overall cost of capital is also called the **weighted average cost of capital**. Can we use the weighted average cost of capital as the discount rate to calculate a project's NPV? The answer is yes, provided that the project is of equivalent risk to the firm's existing assets and the firm intends to maintain its target capital structure of 50 per cent debt and 50 per cent equity.

We have now established how to calculate the discount rate for projects that are of similar risk to the firm's existing assets and to incorporate the financing aspects. It is the weighted average cost of equity and debt capital.

TAXATION AND INVESTMENT DECISIONS

In our discussion so far we have ignored the impact of taxation. Generally, in most countries net cash inflows are subject to taxation, but taxation allowances that enable the amount of taxation payable to be reduced are available on investment outlays. A knowledge of the impact of taxation on capital investment appraisal is unlikely to be a requirement of non-specialist management accounting courses. You can, however, refer to Learning note 6.1 by accessing the dedicated digital support resources (see Preface for details) for an explanation of the impact of taxation on investment appraisal.

SUMMARY

The following items relate to the learning objectives listed at the beginning of the chapter.

- **Explain the opportunity cost of an investment**. The rates of return that are available from investments in financial markets in securities with different levels of risk (e.g. company shares, company and government bonds) represent the opportunity cost of an investment. In other words, if cash is invested in a capital project it cannot be invested elsewhere to earn a return. A firm should therefore only invest in projects that yield a return in excess of the opportunity cost of investment.

- **Distinguish between compounding and discounting**. The process of converting cash invested today at a specific interest rate into a future value is known as compounding. Discounting is the opposite of compounding and refers to the process of converting cash to be received in the future into the value at the present time. The resulting present value is called the discounted present value.

- **Explain the concepts of net present value (NPV), internal rate of return (IRR), payback method and accounting rate of return (ARR)**. Both NPV and IRR are methods of determining whether a project yields a return in excess of an equal risk investment in traded financial securities. A positive NPV provides an absolute value of the amount by which an investment exceeds the return available from an alternative investment in financial securities of equal risk. Conversely, a negative value indicates the amount by which an investment fails to match an equal risk investment in financial securities. In contrast, the IRR indicates the true percentage return from an investment after taking into account the time value of money. To ascertain whether an investment should be undertaken, the percentage IRR on investment should be compared with the returns available from investing in equal risk in financial securities. Investing in all projects that have positive NPVs or IRRs in excess of the opportunity cost of capital should maximize net cash flow. The payback method is the length of time that is required for a stream of cash proceeds from an investment to recover the original cash outflow required by the investment. The ARR expresses the annual average profits arising from a project as a percentage return on the average investment required for the project.

- **Calculate NPV, IRR, the payback period and ARR**. The NPV is calculated by discounting the net cash inflows from a project and deducting the investment outlay. The IRR is calculated by ascertaining the discount rate that will cause the NPV of a project to be zero. The payback period is calculated by adding up the cash flows expected in successive years until the total is equal to the original outlay. The ARR is calculated by dividing the average annual profits estimated from a project by the average investment cost. The calculation of NPV and IRR was illustrated using Example 6.1, while Examples 6.2 and 6.3 were used to illustrate the calculations of the payback period and the ARR.

● **Justify the superiority of NPV over the IRR**. NPV is considered to be theoretically superior to IRR because: (a) unlike the NPV method the IRR method cannot be guaranteed to rank mutually exclusive projects correctly; (b) the percentage returns generated by the IRR method can be misleading when choosing between alternatives; (c) the IRR method makes incorrect reinvestment assumptions by assuming that the interim cash flows can be reinvested at the IRR rather than the cost of capital; and (d) where unconventional cash flows occur multiple IRRs are possible.

● **Explain the limitations of payback and ARR**. The major limitations of the payback method are that it ignores the time value of money and it does not take into account the cash flows that are earned after the payback period. The ARR also fails to take into account the time value of money and relies on a percentage return rather than an absolute value.

● **Justify why the payback and ARR methods are widely used in practice**. The payback method is frequently used in practice because (a) it is considered useful when firms face liquidity constraints and require a fast repayment of their investments; (b) it serves as a simple first-level screening device that identifies those projects that should be subject to more rigorous investigations; and (c) it provides a rough measure of risk, based on the assumption that the longer it takes for a project to pay for itself, the riskier it is. The ARR is a widely used financial accounting measure of managerial and company performance. Therefore, managers are likely to be interested in how any new investment contributes to the business unit's overall accounting rate of return.

● **Describe the effect of performance measurement on capital investment decisions**. Managerial and company performance is normally evaluated using short-term financial criteria whereas investment appraisal decisions should be based on the cash flows over the whole life of the projects. Thus, the way that performance is evaluated can have a profound influence on investment decisions and there is a danger that managers will make decisions on the basis of an investment's impact on the short-term financial performance evaluation criteria rather than using the NPV decision rule.

KEY TERMS AND CONCEPTS

Accounting rate of return   A method of appraising capital investments where the average annual profits from a project are divided into the average investment cost, also known as return on investment and return on capital employed.

Annual percentage rate (APR)   A discount or interest rate quoted as a rate per annum.

Annuity   An asset that pays a fixed sum each period for a specific number of periods.

Compounding interest   The concept of adding the interest earned to the original capital invested so that further interest is generated.

Cost of capital   The financial return that an organization could receive if, instead of investing cash in a capital project, it invested the same amount in securities on the financial markets, also known as the opportunity cost of an investment, the minimum required rate of return, the discount rate and the interest rate.

Cost-benefit analysis (CBA)   An investment appraisal technique developed for use by non-profit-making organizations that defines the costs and benefits of a project in much wider terms than those included in investment appraisals undertaken in the pursuit of profit maximization.

Discount rate   The financial return that an organization could receive if, instead of investing cash in a capital project, it invested the same amount in securities on the financial markets, also known as the opportunity cost of an investment, the minimum required rate of return, the cost of capital and the interest rate.

Discounted cash flow (DCF)   A technique used to compare returns on investments that takes account of the time value of money.

Discounted payback method   A version of the payback method of appraising capital investments in which future cash flows are discounted to their present values.

Discounted present value   The value today of cash to be received in the future, calculated by discounting.

Discounted rate of return   A technique used to make capital investment decisions that takes into account the time value of money, representing the true interest rate earned on an investment over the course of its economic life, also known as internal rate of return (IRR).

Discounting   The process of converting cash to be received in the future into a value at the present time by the use of an interest rate.

Interest rate   The financial return that an organization could receive if, instead of investing cash in a capital project, it invested the same amount in securities on the financial markets, also known as the opportunity cost of an investment, the minimum required rate of return, the cost of capital and the discount rate.

Internal rate of return (IRR)   A technique used to make capital investment decisions that takes into account the time value of money, representing the true interest rate earned on an investment over the course of its economic life, also known as discounted rate of return.

Minimum required rate of return   The financial return that an organization could receive if,

instead of investing cash in a capital project, it invested the same amount in securities on the financial markets, also known as the opportunity cost of an investment, the cost of capital, the discount rate and the interest rate.

Mutually exclusive   In the context of comparing capital investments, a term used to describe projects where the acceptance of one project excludes the acceptance of another.

Net present value (NPV)   The present value of the net cash inflows from a project less the initial investment outlay.

Opportunity cost of an investment   The financial return that an organization could receive if, instead of investing cash in a capital project, it invested the same amount in securities on the financial markets, also known as the minimum required rate of return, the cost of capital, the discount rate and the interest rate.

Payback method   A simple method to appraise capital investments, defined as the length of time that is required for a stream of cash proceeds from an investment to recover the original cash outlay.

Present value   The value today of cash to be received in the future.

Return on capital employed   A method of appraising capital investments where the average annual profits from a project are divided into the average investment cost, also known as the accounting rate of return and return on investment.

Return on investment (ROI)   A method of appraising capital investments where the average annual profits from a project are divided into the average investment cost, also known as the accounting rate of return and return on capital employed.

Risk-free gilt-edged securities   Bonds issued by governments in many countries for set periods of time with fixed interest rates.

Time value of money   The concept that a specific amount of cash is worth more now than it will be in the future.

Weighted average cost of capital   The overall cost of capital to an organization, taking into account the proportion of capital raised by debt and equity.

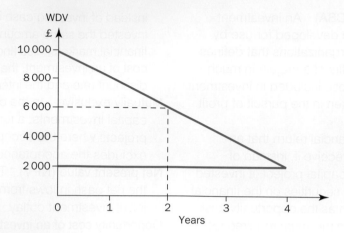

Note

1 Consider a project that costs £10 000 and has a life of 4 years and an estimated scrap value of £2000. The above diagram (using straight line depreciation to calculate the written down values) illustrates why the project's scrap value is added to the initial outlay to calculate the average capital employed. You can see that at the mid point of the project's life the capital employed is equal to £6000 (i.e. ½ (10 000 + £2000)).

ASSESSMENT MATERIAL

The review questions are short questions that enable you to assess your understanding of the main topics included in the chapter. The page numbers in parentheses provide you with the page numbers to refer to if you cannot answer a specific question.

The review problems are more complex and require you to relate and apply the content to various business problems. Solutions to review problems are provided in a separate section at the end of the book. Additional review problems can be accessed by lecturers and students on the dedicated online support resources for this book. Solutions to these review problems are provided for lecturers in the *Instructor's Manual* accompanying this book that can be downloaded from the dedicated online instructor's resources (see Preface for details).

The dedicated online digital support resources for this book also includes over 30 case study problems.

REVIEW QUESTIONS

6.1 What is meant by the opportunity cost of an investment? What role does it play in capital investment decisions? *(pp. 129–130)*

6.2 Distinguish between compounding and discounting. *(pp. 130–133)*

6.3 Explain what is meant by the term 'time value of money'. *(p. 133)*

6.4 Describe the concept of net present value (NPV). *(pp. 133–134)*

6.5 Explain what is meant by the internal rate of return (IRR). *(pp. 136–137)*

6.6 Distinguish between independent and mutually exclusive projects. *(p. 141)*

6.7 Explain the theoretical arguments for preferring NPV to IRR when choosing among mutually exclusive projects. *(pp. 141–142)*

6.8 Why might managers choose to use IRR in preference to NPV? *(pp. 136–139)*

6.9 Describe the payback method. What are its main strengths and weaknesses? *(pp. 142–146)*

6.10 Describe the accounting rate of return. What are its main strengths and weaknesses? *(pp. 146–147)*

6.11 Distinguish between the payback method and discounted payback method. *(pp. 143–144)*

6.12 What impact can the way in which a manager's performance is measured have on capital investment decisions? *(pp. 147–148)*

REVIEW PROBLEMS

6.13 Dalby is currently considering an investment that gives a positive net present value of £3664 at 15 per cent. At a discount rate of 20 per cent it has a negative net present value of £21 451.
What is the internal rate of return of this investment?

(a) 15.7%
(b) 16.0%
(c) 19.3%
(d) 19.9%

6.14 Ayr is planning on paying £300 into a fund on a monthly basis, starting 3 months from now, for 12 months. The interest earned will be at a rate of 3 per cent per month.
Note that the annuity factor for 12 periods at 3 per cent is 9.954 and the discount factors for periods 1, 2 and 3 are respectively 0.9709, 0.9426 and 0.9151.
What is the present value of these payments?

(a) £2816
(b) £2733
(c) £2541
(d) £2986

6.15 An investment has the following cash inflows and cash outflows:

Time	Cash flow per annum €000
0	(20 000)
1–4	3 000
5–8	7 000
10	(10 000)

What is the net present value of the investment at a discount rate of 8 per cent?

(a) €2416
(b) €7046
(c) €6981
(d) €2351

6.16 Sydney is considering making a monthly investment for his son who will be 5 years old on his next birthday. He wishes to make payments until his 18th birthday and intends to pay $50 per month into an account yielding an APR of 12.68 per cent. He plans to start making payments into the account the month after his son's fifth birthday.
How much will be in the account immediately after the final payment has been made?

(a) $18 847
(b) $18 377
(c) $17 606
(d) $18 610

6.17 Sydney wishes to make an investment on a monthly basis starting next month for 5 years. The payments into the fund would be made on the first day of each month.
The interest rate will be 0.5 per cent per month. Sydney needs a terminal value of £7000.
What should be the monthly payments into the fund to the nearest £?

(a) £75
(b) £86
(c) £100
(d) £117

6.18 Augustine wishes to take out a loan of €2000. The interest rate on this loan would be 10 per cent per annum and Augustine wishes to make equal monthly repayments, comprising interest and principal, over 3 years starting one month after the loan is taken out.
What would be the monthly repayment on the loan to the nearest €?

(a) €56
(b) €64
(c) €66
(d) €67

6.19 Calculation of payback, ARR and NPV

The following data are supplied relating to two investment projects, only one of which may be selected:

	Project A (£)	Project B (£)
Initial capital expenditure	50 000	50 000
Profit (loss) year 1	25 000	10 000
2	20 000	10 000
3	15 000	14 000
4	10 000	26 000
Estimated resale value at end of year 4	10 000	10 000

Notes:
1 Profit is calculated after deducting straight line depreciation.
2 The cost of capital is 10 per cent.

Required:
(a) Calculate for each project:
 (i) average annual rate of return on average capital invested
 (ii) payback period
 (iii) net present value.

(12 marks)

(b) Briefly discuss the relative merits of the three methods of evaluation mentioned in (a) above.

(10 marks)

(c) Explain which project you would recommend for acceptance.

(3 marks)

(Total 25 marks)

6.20 A project requires an initial investment of $150 000 and has an expected life of five years. The required rate of return on the project is 12 per cent per annum.

The project's estimated cash flows each year are as follows:

	$000
Sales revenue	101
Variable costs	30
Incremental fixed costs	5

The selling price, costs and activity levels are expected to remain the same for each year of the project.

Ignore taxation and inflation.

Required:

Calculate the percentage change in the selling price that would result in the project being rejected.

(4 marks)

6.21 Determination of relevant cash flows

Cab Co. owns and runs 350 taxis and had sales of $10 million in the last year. Cab Co. is considering introducing a new computerized taxi tracking system.

The expected costs and benefits of the new computerized tracking system are as follows:

(i)   The system would cost $2 100 000 to implement.

(ii) Depreciation would be provided at $420 000 per annum.

(iii) $75 000 has already been spent on staff training in order to evaluate the potential of the new system. Further training costs of $425 000 would be required in the first year if the new system is implemented.

(iv) Sales are expected to rise to $11 million in year 1 if the new system is implemented, thereafter increasing by 5 per cent per annum. If the new system is not implemented, sales would be expected to increase by $200 000 per annum.

(v)   Despite increased sales, savings in vehicle running costs are expected as a result of the new system. These are estimated at 1 per cent of total sales.

(vi) Six new members of staff would be recruited to manage the new system at a total cost of $120 000 per annum.

(vii) Cab Co. would have to take out a maintenance contract for the new system at a cost of $75 000 per annum for five years.

(viii) Interest on money borrowed to finance the project would cost $150 000 per annum.

(ix) Cab Co.'s cost of capital is 10 per cent per annum.

Required:

(a) State whether each of the following items are relevant or irrelevant cashflows for a net present value (NPV) evaluation of whether to introduce the computerized tracking system.

(i)   Computerized tracking system investment of $2 100 000;

(ii) Depreciation of $420 000 in each of the five years;

(iii) Staff training costs of $425 000;

(iv) New staff total salary of $120 000 per annum;

(v)   Staff training costs of $75 000;

(vi) Interest cost of $150 000 per annum.

(5 marks)

(b) Calculate the following values if the computerized tracking system is implemented.

(i)   Incremental sales in year 1;

(ii) Savings in vehicle running costs in year 1;

(iii) Present value of the maintenance costs over the life of the contract.

(3 marks)

6.22 A machine with a purchase price of £14 000 is estimated to eliminate manual operations costing £4000 per year. The machine will last 5 years and have no residual value at the end of its life.

You are required to calculate:

(a) the internal rate of return (IRR)

(b) the level of annual saving necessary to achieve a 12 per cent IRR

(c) the net present value if the cost of capital is 10 per cent.

6.23 Relevant cash flows and calculation of NPV and IRR.
(This question requires a knowledge of the term 'expected value.' This term is explained in detail in Learning Note 4.2 that can be accessed by referring to the digital online support resources supporting this book - see Preface for details). A car manufacturer has been experiencing financial difficulties over the past few years. Sales have reduced significantly as a result of the worldwide economic recession. Costs have increased due to quality issues that led to a recall of some models of its cars.

Production volume last year was 50 000 cars and it is expected that this will increase by 4 per cent per annum each year for the next 5 years.

The company directors are concerned to improve profitability and are considering two potential investment projects.

Project 1 – implement a new quality control process

The company has paid a consultant process engineer $50 000 to review the company's quality processes. The consultant recommended that the company implement a new quality control process. The new process will require a machine costing $20 000 000. The machine is expected to have a useful life of 5 years and no residual value.

It is estimated that raw material costs will be reduced by $62 per car and that both internal and external failure costs from quality failures will be reduced by 80 per cent.

Estimated internal and external failure costs per year without the new process, based on last year's production volume of 50 000 cars, and their associated probabilities are shown below:

Internal failure costs		External failure costs	
$	Probability	$	Probability
300 000	50%	1 300 000	60%
500 000	30%	1 900 000	30%
700 000	20%	3 000 000	10%

Internal and external failure costs are expected to increase each year in line with the number of cars produced.

The company's accountant has calculated that this investment will result in a net present value (NPV) of $1 338 000 and an internal rate of return of 10.5 per cent.

Project 2 – in-house component manufacturing

The company could invest in new machinery to enable in-house manufacturing of a component that is currently made by outside suppliers. The new machinery is expected to cost $15 000 000 and have a useful life of 5 years and no residual value. Additional working capital of $1 000 000 will also be required as a result of producing the component in-house.

The price paid to the current supplier is $370 per component. It is estimated that the in-house variable cost of production will be $260 per component. Each car requires one component. Fixed production costs, including machinery depreciation, are estimated to increase by $5 000 000 per annum as a result of manufacturing the component in-house.

Depreciation is calculated on a straight line basis.

Additional Information

The company is unable to raise enough capital to carry out both projects. The company will therefore have to choose between the two alternatives.

Taxation and inflation should be ignored.

The company uses a cost of capital of 8 per cent per annum.

Required:

(a) Calculate for Project 1 the relevant cash flows that the accountant should have used for year 1 when appraising the project.

All workings should be shown in $000.

(6 marks)

(b) Calculate for Project 2:
   (i) the net present value (NPV)
   (ii) the internal rate of return (IRR)
   All workings should be shown in $000.

(10 marks)

(c) Advise the company directors which of the two investment projects should be undertaken.

(4 marks)

(d) A company is considering two alternative investment projects both of which have a positive net present value.

The projects have been ranked on the basis of both net present value (NPV) and internal rate of return (IRR). The result of the ranking is shown below:

	Project A	Project B
NPV	1st	2nd
IRR	2nd	1st

Discuss potential reasons why the conflict between the NPV and IRR ranking may have arisen.

(5 marks)

6.24 Calculation of NPV and IRR with taxes and inflation

DP is considering whether to purchase a piece of land close to a major city airport. The land will be used to provide 600 car parking spaces. The cost of the land is $6 000 000 but further expenditure of $2 000 000 will be required immediately to develop the land to provide access roads and suitable surfacing for car parking. DP is planning to operate the car park for 5 years after which the land will be sold for $10 000 000 at Year 5 prices. A consultant has prepared a report detailing projected revenues and costs.

Revenues

It is estimated that the car park will operate at 75 per cent capacity during each year of the project.

Car parking charges will depend on the prices being charged by competitors. There is a 40 per cent chance that the price will be $60 per week, a 25 per cent chance the price will be $50 per week and a 35 per cent chance the price will be $70 per week.

DP expects that it will earn a contribution to sales ratio of 80 per cent.

Fixed operating costs

DP will lease a number of vehicles to be used to transport passengers to and from the airport. It is expected that the lease costs will be $50 000 per annum.

Staff costs are estimated to be $350 000 per annum.

The company will hire a security system at a cost of $100 000 per annum.

Inflation

All of the values above, other than the amount for the sale of the land at the end of the 5-year period, have been expressed in terms of current prices. The vehicle leasing costs of $50 000 per annum will apply throughout the 5 years and is not subject to inflation.

Car parking charges and variable costs are expected to increase at a rate of 5 per cent per annum starting in Year 1.

All fixed operating costs excluding the vehicle leasing costs are expected to increase at a rate of 4 per cent per annum starting in Year 1.

Other information

The company uses net present value based on the expected values of cash flow when evaluating projects of this type.

DP has a money cost of capital of 8 per cent per annum.

DP's Financial Director has provided the following taxation information:

● Tax depreciation is not available on either the initial cost of the land or the development costs.
● Taxation rate: 30 per cent of taxable profits. Half of the tax is payable in the year in which it arises, the balance is payable in the following year.

All cash flows apart from the initial investment of $8 000 000 should be assumed to occur at the end of the year.

Required:

(a) Evaluate the project from a financial perspective. You should use net present value as the basis of your evaluation and show your workings in $000.
(14 marks)

(b) Calculate the internal rate of return (IRR) of the project.
(5 marks)

The main reason why discounted cash flow methods of investment appraisal are considered theoretically superior is that they take account of the time value of money.

Required:

(c) Explain the three elements that determine the 'time value of money' and why it is important to take it into consideration when appraising investment projects.
(6 marks)

6.25 Calculation of payback, ARR and NPV

Stadler is an ambitious young executive who has recently been appointed to the position of financial director of Paradis plc, a small listed company. Stadler regards this appointment as a temporary one, enabling him to gain experience before moving to a larger organization. His intention is to leave Paradis plc in 3-years' time, with its share price standing high. As a consequence, he is particularly concerned that the reported profits of Paradis plc should be as high as possible in his third and final year with the company.

Paradis plc has recently raised £350 000, and the directors are considering three ways of using these funds. Three projects (A, B and C) are being considered, each involving the immediate purchase of equipment costing £350 000.

One project only can be undertaken, and the equipment for each project will have a useful life equal to that of the project, with no scrap value. Stadler favours project C because it is expected to show the highest accounting profit in the third year. However, he does not wish to reveal his real reasons for favouring project C, and so, in his report to the chairman, he recommends project C because it shows the highest internal rate of return. The following summary is taken from his report:

Project %	\multicolumn{9}{c}{Net cash flows (£000) Years}	Internal rate of return
	0	1	2	3	4	5	6	7	8	
A	−350	100	110	104	112	138	160	180	–	27.5
B	−350	40	100	210	260	160	–	–	–	26.4
C	−350	200	150	240	40	–	–	–	–	33.0

The chairman of the company is accustomed to projects being appraised in terms of payback and accounting rate of return, and he is consequently suspicious of the use of internal rate of return as a method of project selection. Accordingly, the chairman has asked for an independent report on the choice of project. The company's cost of capital is 20 per cent and a policy of straight line depreciation is used to write off the cost of equipment in the financial statements.

Required:

(a) Calculate the payback period for each project.
(3 marks)

(b) Calculate the accounting rate of return for each project.
(5 marks)

(c) Prepare a report for the chairman with supporting calculations indicating which project should be preferred by the ordinary shareholders of Paradis plc.
(12 marks)

(d) Discuss the assumptions about the reactions of the stock market that are implicit in Stadler's choice of project C.
(5 marks)
(Total 25 marks)

Note: Ignore taxation.

PART THREE

COST ASSIGNMENT

P art Three seeks to provide an understanding of how costs are accumulated and assigned to cost objects. Chapter 7 describes the alternative approaches that can be used for measuring resources consumed by cost objects and the factors that should be considered in determining the sophistication of the cost accumulation system. In addition, traditional costing systems that were designed primarily for meeting financial accounting stock (inventory) valuation and profit measurement requirements are described. The cost information generated by traditional costing systems may not be sufficiently accurate for decision-making purposes. In Chapter 8 a more refined cost accumulation system for measuring resources consumed by cost objects is described. This approach is called activity-based costing.

7
COST ASSIGNMENT

LEARNING OBJECTIVES After studying this chapter you should be able to:

- distinguish between cause-and-effect and arbitrary cost allocations

- explain why different cost information is required for different purposes

- describe how cost systems differ in terms of their level of sophistication

- understand the factors influencing the choice of an optimal cost system

- explain why departmental overhead rates should be used in preference to a single blanket overhead rate

- construct an overhead analysis sheet and calculate cost centre allocation rates

- justify why budgeted overhead rates should be used in preference to actual overhead rates

- calculate and explain the accounting treatment of the under-/over-recovery of overheads

- explain how the cost assignment approach described for manufacturing organizations can be extended to non-manufacturing organizations.

The aim of this chapter is to provide an understanding of how costs are accumulated and assigned to cost objects. Remember from Chapter 2 that a cost object is anything for which a separate measurement of cost is desired. For most of this chapter we shall assume that products are the cost object but towards the end of the chapter we shall look at situations where products are not the cost object. However, the same cost assignment approaches can be applied to all cost objects.

Why do we need to assign costs to products or other cost objects? You will remember that in Chapter 5 it was pointed out that cost-plus pricing and product profitability analysis are extensively used by organizations. Cost-plus pricing requires that costs are assigned to each product to ascertain the product cost for adding a profit margin to determine the selling price. With product profitability analysis we need to assign costs to products to distinguish between profitable and unprofitable products in order to ensure that only profitable products are sold.

Costs must also be assigned to products for internal and external profit measurement and inventory valuation. Profit measurement requires that the costs incurred for a period should be allocated between cost of goods sold and inventories. The cost of goods sold that is deducted from sales revenues to compute the profit for the period is derived by summing the manufacturing costs that have been assigned to all those individual products that have been sold during the period. The inventory (stock) valuation is derived from the sum of the costs assigned to all of the partly completed products (i.e. work in progress (WIP)) and unsold finished products. Inventory valuation is mainly applicable to manufacturing organizations, particularly in those organizations that produce individual products or unique batches of products and where products or batches of products incur different costs. Thus there is a need to keep track of the cost of each product or batch.

Inventory valuation is not an issue for many service organizations. They do not carry inventories and therefore a costing system is required mainly for providing relevant decision-making information for cost-plus pricing and for distinguishing between profitable and unprofitable activities. Later in the chapter, however, we shall look at how the approaches that have been described for inventory valuation can be applied to non-manufacturing organizations. We shall also consider how they can be adapted to providing decision-making information for distinguishing between profitable and unprofitable activities.

We begin with a brief description of the two different types of costing systems (i.e. direct and absorption costing) that are used to assign costs to cost objects.

ASSIGNMENT OF DIRECT AND INDIRECT COSTS

Costs that are assigned to cost objects can be divided into two categories – direct costs and indirect costs. Sometimes the term **overheads** is used instead of indirect costs. Direct costs can be accurately traced to cost objects because they can be specifically and exclusively traced to a particular cost object whereas indirect costs cannot. Where a cost can be directly assigned to a cost object the term **direct cost tracing** is used. With direct cost tracing cost assignment merely involves the implementation of suitable data processing procedures that identify and record the cost of those resources that can be specifically and exclusively identified with a particular cost object. In contrast, direct cost tracing cannot be applied to indirect costs because they are usually common to several cost objects. Indirect costs are therefore assigned to cost objects using cost allocations.

A **cost allocation** is the process of assigning costs when the quantity of resources consumed by a particular cost object cannot be directly measured. Cost allocations involve the use of surrogate rather than direct measures. For example, consider an activity such as receiving incoming materials. Assuming that the cost of receiving materials is strongly influenced by the number of receipts, then costs can be allocated to products (i.e. the cost object) based on the number of material receipts each product requires. The basis that is used to allocate costs to cost objects (i.e. the number of material receipts in our example) is called an **allocation base** or **cost driver**. If 20 per cent of the total number of receipts for a period were required for a particular product then 20 per cent of the total costs of receiving incoming materials would be allocated to that product. Assuming that the product was discontinued, and not replaced, we would expect action to be taken to reduce the resources required for receiving materials by 20 per cent.

In the above illustration the allocation base is assumed to be a significant determinant of the cost of receiving incoming materials. Where allocation bases are significant determinants of the costs the terms **cause-and-effect allocations** or **driver tracing** are used. Where a cost allocation base is used that is not a significant determinant of its cost the term **arbitrary allocation** will be used. An example of an **arbitrary allocation** would be if direct labour hours were used as the allocation base to allocate the costs of materials receiving. If a labour-intensive product required a large proportion of direct labour hours (say 30 per cent) but few material receipts it would be allocated with a large proportion of the costs of materials receiving. The allocation would be an inaccurate assignment of the resources consumed by the product. Furthermore, if the product were discontinued, and not replaced, the cost of the material receiving activity would not decline by 30 per cent because the allocation base is not a significant determinant of the costs of the materials receiving activity. Arbitrary allocations are therefore likely to result in inaccurate allocations of indirect costs to cost objects. For the accurate assignment of indirect costs, cause-and-effect allocations should be used.

Figure 7.1 provides a summary of the three methods of assigning costs to cost objects. You can see that direct costs are assigned to cost objectives using direct cost tracing whereas indirect costs are assigned using either cause-and-effect or arbitrary cost allocations. For accurate assignment of indirect costs to cost objects, cause-and-effect allocations should be used. Two types of systems can be used to assign costs to cost objects. They are direct and **absorption costing systems**. A **direct costing system** (also known as a marginal or variable costing system) assigns only direct costs to cost objects whereas an absorption costing system assigns both direct and indirect costs to cost objectives. Absorption costing systems can be sub-divided into **traditional costing systems** and **activity-based-costing (ABC)** systems. Traditional costing systems were developed in the early 1900s and are still widely used today. They tend to use arbitrary cost allocations. ABC systems only began to be implemented in the 1990s. One of the major aims of ABC systems is to use mainly cause-and-effect cost allocations and avoid arbitrary allocations. Both cost systems adopt identical approaches to assigning direct costs to cost objects. We shall focus on traditional costing systems in this chapter and ABC systems in the next chapter.

FIGURE 7.1

Cost assignment methods

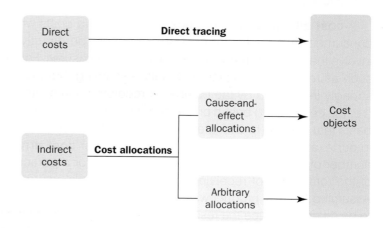

DIFFERENT COSTS FOR DIFFERENT PURPOSES

Manufacturing organizations assign costs to products for two purposes: first, for internal profit measurement and external financial accounting requirements in order to allocate the manufacturing costs incurred during a period between cost of goods sold and inventories; and, second, to provide useful information for managerial decision-making requirements. In order to meet financial accounting requirements, it may not be necessary to accurately assign costs to *individual* products. Consider a situation where a firm produces 1000 different products and the costs incurred during a period are £10 million. A well-designed product costing system should accurately analyse the £10 million costs incurred between cost of sales and inventories. Let us assume the true figures are £7 million and £3 million. Approximate but inaccurate *individual* product costs may provide a reasonable approximation of how much of the £10 million should be attributed to cost of sales and inventories. Some product costs may be overstated and others may be understated, but this would not matter for financial accounting purposes as long as the *total* of the individual product costs assigned to cost of sales and inventories was approximately £7 million and £3 million.

For decision-making purposes, however, more accurate product costs are required so that we can distinguish between profitable and unprofitable products. By more accurately measuring the resources consumed by products, or other cost objects, a firm can identify its sources of profits and losses. If the cost system does not capture sufficiently accurately the consumption of resources by products, the reported product costs will be distorted, and there is a danger that managers may drop profitable products or continue production of unprofitable products.

Besides different levels of accuracy, different cost information is required for different purposes. For meeting external financial accounting requirements, financial accounting regulations and legal requirements in most countries require that inventories should be valued at manufacturing cost. Therefore only manufacturing costs are assigned to products for meeting external financial accounting requirements. For decision-making, non-manufacturing costs must be taken into account and assigned to products. Not all costs, however, may be relevant for decision-making. For example, depreciation of plant and machinery will not be affected by a decision to discontinue a product. Such costs were described in the previous chapter as irrelevant and sunk for decision-making. Thus depreciation of plant must be assigned to products for inventory valuation but it should not be assigned for discontinuation decisions.

COST–BENEFIT ISSUES AND COST SYSTEM DESIGN

Until the 1990s most organizations were relying on traditional costing systems that had been designed primarily for meeting external financial accounting requirements. These systems were designed decades ago when information processing costs were high and precluded the use of more sophisticated methods of assigning indirect costs to products. Such systems are still widely used today. They rely extensively on arbitrary cost allocations, which may be sufficiently accurate for meeting external financial accounting requirements but not for meeting decision-making requirements.

FIGURE 7.2

Absorption costing systems – varying levels of sophistication for cost assignment

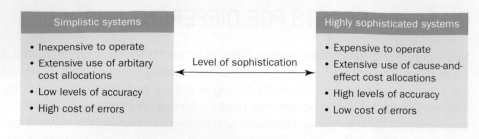

In the late 1980s ABC systems were promoted as a mechanism for more accurately assigning indirect costs to cost objects. Surveys in many countries suggest that between 20 and 30 per cent of the surveyed organizations currently use ABC systems. The majority of organizations therefore continue to operate traditional systems. Both traditional and ABC systems vary in their level of sophistication but, as a general rule, traditional systems tend to be simplistic whereas ABC systems tend to be sophisticated. What determines the chosen level of sophistication of a costing system? The answer is that the choice should be made on costs versus benefits criteria. Simplistic systems are inexpensive to operate, but they are likely to result in inaccurate cost assignments and the reporting of inaccurate costs. Managers using cost information extracted from simplistic systems are more likely to make important mistakes arising from using inaccurate cost information. The end result may be a high cost of errors. Conversely, sophisticated systems are more expensive to operate but they minimize the cost of errors.

Figure 7.2 illustrates the above points with costing systems ranging from simplistic to sophisticated. In practice, cost systems in most organizations are not located at either of these extreme points but are positioned somewhere within the range shown in Figure 7.2. The aim should not be to have the most accurate cost system. Improvements should be made in the level of sophistication of the costing system up to the point where the marginal/incremental cost of improvement equals the marginal/incremental benefit from the improvement.

The optimal cost system is different for different organizations. For example, the optimal costing system will be located towards the extreme left for an organization whose indirect costs are a low percentage of total costs and that also has a fairly standardized product range, all consuming organizational resources in similar proportions. In these circumstances simplistic systems may not result in the reporting of inaccurate costs. In contrast, the optimal costing system for organizations with a high proportion of indirect costs, whose products consume organizational resources in different proportions, will be located towards the extreme right. More sophisticated costing systems are required to capture the diversity of consumption of organizational resources and accurately assign the high level of indirect costs to different cost objects.

PLANT-WIDE (BLANKET) OVERHEAD RATES

The most simplistic traditional costing system assigns indirect costs (overheads) to cost objects using a single overhead rate for the organization as a whole. Such a costing system would be located at the extreme left of the level of sophistication shown in Figure 7.2.

The terms **blanket overhead rate** or **plant-wide rate** are used to describe a single overhead rate that is established for the organization as a whole. Let us assume that the total manufacturing overheads for the manufacturing plant of Arcadia are £9 million and that the company has selected direct labour hours as the allocation base for assigning overheads to products. Assuming that the total number of direct labour hours are 600 000 for the period, the plant-wide overhead rate for Arcadia is £15 per direct labour hour (£9 million/600 000 direct labour hours). This calculation consists of two stages. First, overheads are accumulated in one single plant-wide pool for a period. Second, a plant-wide rate is computed by dividing the total amount of overheads accumulated (£9 million) by the selected allocation base (600 000 direct labour hours). The overhead costs are assigned to products by multiplying the plant-wide rate by the units of the selected allocation base (direct labour hours) used by each product.

Assume now that Arcadia is considering establishing separate overheads for each of its three production departments. Further investigations reveal that the products made by the company require different operations and some products do not pass through all three departments. These investigations also indicate that the £9 million total manufacturing overheads and 600 000 direct labour hours can be analysed as follows:

	Department A	Department B	Department C	Total
Overheads	£2 000 000	£6 000 000	£1 000 000	£9 000 000
Direct labour hours	200 000	200 000	200 000	600 000
Overhead rate per direct labour hour	£10	£30	£5	£15

Consider now a situation where product Z requires 20 direct labour hours in department C but does not pass through departments A and B. If a plant-wide overhead rate is used then overheads of £300 (20 hours at £15 per hour) will be allocated to product Z. On the other hand, if a departmental overhead rate is used, only £100 (20 hours at £5 per hour) would be allocated to product Z. Which method should be used? The logical answer must be to establish separate departmental overhead rates, since product Z only consumes overheads in department C. If the plant-wide overhead rate were applied, all the factory overhead rates would be averaged out and product Z would be indirectly allocated with some of the overheads of department B. This would not be satisfactory, since product Z does not consume any of the resources and this department incurs a large amount of the overhead expenditure.

Where some departments are more 'overhead-intensive' than others, products spending more time in these departments should be assigned more overhead costs than those spending less time. Departmental rates capture these possible effects but plant-wide rates do not, because of the averaging process. We can conclude that a plant-wide rate will generally result in the reporting of inaccurate product costs and can only be justified when all products consume departmental overheads in approximately the same proportions (i.e. low product diversity applies). In the above illustration each department accounts for one-third of the total direct labour hours. If all products spend approximately one-third of their time in each department, a plant-wide overhead rate can be safely used. Consider a situation where product X spends 1 hour in each department and product Y spends 5 hours in each department. Overheads of £45 and £225 respectively would be allocated to products X and Y using either a plant-wide rate (3 hours at £15 and 15 hours at £15) or separate departmental overhead rates. However, if a diverse product range

REAL WORLD
VIEWS 7.1

Three cost allocation myths

Allan Stratton is a cost management consultant with over 35 years of experience who shares the benefit of his experience providing tools and resources via the internet. In one of his articles he debunks three myths on cost allocation.

All sorts of businesses and government organizations use cost allocation. It is a way of dividing and assigning the money that an entity spends. Sometimes this means spreading costs incurred by one department amongst others who also benefitted from the expense, sometimes it means distributing a cost across all products. Over time, several dangerous myths about cost allocation have developed.

First, that allocating costs improves decision-making; this is the intent but the outcome depends on the way it is done. Attention must be paid to cause and effect and/or the actual operating relationships, otherwise those using the data to make decisions may be misled.

Second, that all costs must be allocated. There is no reason to allocate a cost that will not influence a decision.

Third, that idle capacity cost must be allocated to actual products and services. A dangerous downward spiral could be started if idle capacity cost is allocated to products because this would result in higher product costs. If higher product costs are reported then the company may raise their prices in order to continue making the same profit margin.

Questions

1 Explain how applying each of the above three myths can lead to bad decisions.
2 What changes should be made to cost allocations to avoid the bad decisions?

Reference

Stratton, A. (2012) *Three Cost Allocation Myths*. Available at www.costmatters.com/2012/06/three-cost-allocation-myths/#more-415 (accessed 30 March, 2017).

is produced with products spending different proportions of time in each department, separate departmental overhead rates should be established.

Surveys indicate that less than 5 per cent of the surveyed organizations use a single plant-wide overhead rate. In Scandinavia only 5 per cent of Finnish companies (Lukka and Granlund, 1996), one Norwegian company (Bjornenak, 1997) and none of the Swedish companies sampled (Ask *et al.*, 1996) used a single plant-wide rate. Zero usage of plant-wide rates was also reported from a survey of Greek companies (Ballas and Venieris, 1996). In a more recent study of UK organizations Al-Omiri and Drury (2007) reported that a plant-wide rate was used by 4 per cent of the surveyed organizations.

THE TWO-STAGE ALLOCATION PROCESS

It is apparent from the previous section that separate departmental overhead rates should normally be established. To establish departmental overhead rates, an approach known as the two-stage allocation process is used. This process applies to assigning costs to other cost objects, besides products, and is applicable to all organizations that assign indirect costs to cost objects.

The two-stage allocation process is illustrated in Figure 7.3 for a traditional costing system. You can see that in the *first stage* overheads are assigned to **cost centres**

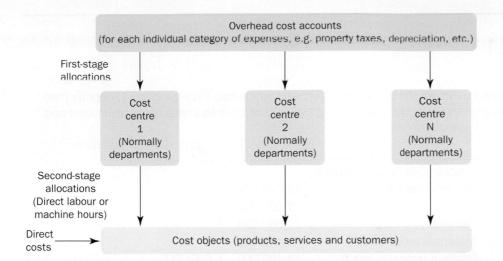

FIGURE 7.3

An illustration of the two-stage allocation process for traditional absorption costing systems

(also called **cost pools**). The terms cost centres or cost pools are used to describe a location to which overhead costs are initially assigned. Normally, cost centres consist of departments, but in some cases they consist of smaller segments such as separate work centres within a department. In the *second stage* the costs accumulated in the cost centres are allocated to cost objects using selected allocation bases (note that allocation bases are also called cost drivers). Traditional costing systems tend to use a small number of second-stage allocation bases, typically direct labour hours or machine hours. In other words, traditional systems assume that direct labour or machine hours have a significant influence in the long term on the level of overhead expenditure. Other allocation bases used to a lesser extent by traditional systems are direct labour cost, direct materials cost and units of output.

How many cost centres should a firm establish? If only a small number of cost centres are established it is likely that activities within a cost centre will not be homogeneous and, if the consumption of the activities by products/services within the cost centres varies, activity resource consumption will not be accurately measured. Therefore, in most situations, increasing the number of cost centres increases the accuracy of measuring the indirect costs consumed by cost objects. The choice of the number of cost centres should be based on cost–benefit criteria using the principles described on pages 165–166. A survey by Drury and Tayles (2005) of 170 UK organizations reported that 35 per cent of the organizations used less than 11 cost centres whereas 36 per cent used more than 20 cost centres. In terms of the number of different types of second-stage cost drivers/allocation bases, 59 per cent of the responding organizations used less than three.

AN ILLUSTRATION OF THE TWO-STAGE PROCESS FOR A TRADITIONAL COSTING SYSTEM

We shall now use Example 7.1 to provide a more detailed illustration of the two-stage allocation process for a traditional absorption costing system. Note that a manufacturing company is used to illustrate the process. We shall also assume that

EXAMPLE 7.1

The annual overhead costs for the Enterprise Company, which has three production centres (two machine centres and one assembly centre) and two service centres (materials procurement and general factory support), are as follows:

	(£)	(£)
Indirect wages and supervision		
Machine centres: X	1 000 000	
Y	1 000 000	
Assembly	1 500 000	
Materials procurement	1 100 000	
General factory support	1 480 000	6 080 000
Indirect materials		
Machine centres: X	500 000	
Y	805 000	
Assembly	105 000	
Materials procurement	0	
General factory support	10 000	1 420 000
Lighting and heating	500 000	
Property taxes	1 000 000	
Insurance of machinery	150 000	
Depreciation of machinery	1 500 000	
Insurance of buildings	250 000	
Salaries of works management	800 000	4 200 000
		11 700 000

The following information is also available:

	Book value of machinery (£)	Area occupied (sq. metres)	Number of employees	Direct labour hours	Machine hours
Machine shop: X	8 000 000	10 000	300	1 000 000	2 000 000
Y	5 000 000	5 000	200	1 000 000	1 000 000
Assembly	1 000 000	15 000	300	2 000 000	
Stores	500 000	15 000	100		
Maintenance	500 000	5 000	100		
	15 000 000	50 000	1 000		

Details of total materials issues (i.e. direct and indirect materials) to the production centres are as follows:

	£
Machine shop X	4 000 000
Machine shop Y	3 000 000
Assembly	1 000 000
	8 000 000

To allocate the overheads listed above to the production and service centres we must prepare an overhead analysis sheet, as shown in Exhibit 7.1.

the aim is to calculate product costs that are required for inventory valuation and profit measurement purposes. To keep the illustration manageable it is assumed that the company has only five cost centres – machine departments X and Y, an assembly department, and materials handling and general factory support cost centres. The illustration focuses on manufacturing costs but we shall look at non-manufacturing costs later in the chapter. Applying the two-stage allocation process requires the following four steps:

1 assigning all manufacturing overheads to production and service cost centres
2 reallocating the costs assigned to service cost centres to production cost centres
3 computing separate overhead rates for each production cost centre
4 assigning cost centre overheads to products or other chosen cost objects.

Steps 1 and 2 comprise stage one and steps 3 and 4 relate to the second stage of the two-stage allocation process. Let us now consider each of these steps in detail.

Step 1 – Assigning all manufacturing overheads to production and service cost centres

Using the information given in Example 7.1 our initial objective is to assign all manufacturing overheads to production and service cost centres. To do this requires the preparation of an **overhead analysis sheet** which is shown in Exhibit 7.1. In most organizations it will exist only in computer form.

If you look at Example 7.1 you will see that the indirect labour and indirect material costs have been directly traced to cost centres. Although these items cannot be directly assigned to products they can be directly assigned to the cost centres. In other words, they are indirect costs when products are the cost objects and direct costs when cost centres are the cost object. Therefore, they are traced directly to the cost centres shown in the overhead analysis sheet in Exhibit 7.1. The remaining costs shown in Example 7.1 cannot be traced directly to the cost centres and must be allocated to the cost centre using appropriate allocation bases. The term **first-stage allocation bases** is used to describe allocations at this point. The following list summarizes commonly used first-stage allocation bases:

Cost	Basis of allocation
Property taxes, lighting and heating	Area
Employee-related expenditure: works management, works canteen, payroll office	Number of employees
Depreciation and insurance of plant and machinery	Value of items of plant and machinery

Where utility consumption, such as lighting and heating, can be measured by separate meters located in each department, departmental consumption can be measured and the costs directly traced to the user departments.

Applying the allocation bases to the data given in respect of the Enterprise Company in Example 7.1 it is assumed that property taxes, lighting and heating, and insurance of buildings are related to the total floor area of the buildings, and the benefit obtained by each cost centre can therefore be ascertained according to the proportion of floor area that it occupies. The total floor area of the factory shown in Example 7.1 is 50 000 square

EXHIBIT 7.1 Overhead analysis sheet

| | | | Production centres | | | Service centres | |
Item of expenditure	Basis of allocation	Total (£)	Machine centre X (£)	Machine centre Y (£)	Assembly (£)	Materials procurement (£)	General factory support (£)
Indirect wage and supervision	Direct	6 080 000	1 000 000	1 000 000	1 500 000	1 100 000	1 480 000
Indirect materials	Direct	1 420 000	500 000	805 000	105 000		10 000
Lighting and heating	Area	500 000	100 000	50 000	150 000	150 000	50 000
Property taxes	Area	1 000 000	200 000	100 000	300 000	300 000	100 000
Insurance of machinery	Book value of machinery	150 000	80 000	50 000	10 000	5 000	5 000
Depreciation of machinery	Book value of machinery	1 500 000	800 000	500 000	100 000	50 000	50 000
Insurance of buildings	Area	250 000	50 000	25 000	75 000	75 000	25 000
Salaries of works management	Number of employees	800 000	240 000	160 000	240 000	80 000	80 000
Step 1 of stage 1		11 700 000	2 970 000	2 690 000	2 480 000	1 760 000	1 800 000
Reallocation of service centre costs							
Materials procurement	Value of materials issued	—	880 000	660 000	220 000	1 760 000	
General factory support	Direct labour hours	—	450 000	450 000	900 000		1 800 000
Step 2 of stage 1		11 700 000	4 300 000	3 800 000	3 600 000	—	—
Machine hours and direct labour hours			2 000 000	1 000 000	2 000 000		
Machine hour overhead rate (Step 3)			£2.15	£3.80			
Direct labour hour overhead rate (Step 3)					£1.80		

metres; machine centre X occupies 20 per cent of this and machine centre Y a further 10 per cent. Therefore, if you refer to the overhead analysis sheet in Exhibit 7.1 you will see that 20 per cent of property taxes, lighting and heating and insurance of buildings are allocated to machine centre X, and 10 per cent are allocated to machine centre Y.

The insurance premium paid and depreciation of machinery are generally regarded as being related to the book value of the machinery. Because the book value of machinery for machine centre X is 8/15 of the total book value and machine centre Y is 5/15 of the total book value then 8/15 and 5/15 of the insurance and depreciation of machinery is allocated to machine centres X and Y.

It is assumed that the amount of time that works management devotes to each cost centre is related to the number of employees in each centre; since 30 per cent of the total employees are employed in machine centre X, 30 per cent of the salaries of works management will be allocated to this centre.

If you now look at the overhead analysis sheet shown in Exhibit 7.1, you will see in the row labelled 'step 1 of stage 1' that all manufacturing overheads for the Enterprise Company have been assigned to the three production and two service cost centres.

Step 2 – Reallocating the costs assigned to service cost centres to production cost centres

The next step is to reallocate the costs that have been assigned to service cost centres to production cost centres. **Service departments** (i.e. service cost centres) are those departments that exist to provide services of various kinds to other units within the organization. They are sometimes called **support departments**. The Enterprise Company has two service centres. They are materials procurement and general factory support, which includes activities such as production scheduling and machine maintenance. These service centres render essential services that support the production process, but they do not deal directly with the products. Therefore, service centre costs are not allocated to products passing through these centres. Nevertheless, the cost of providing support services are part of the total product costs and therefore should be assigned to products. To assign costs to products, traditional costing systems reallocate service centre costs to production centres that actually work on the product. The method that is chosen to allocate service centre costs to production centres should be related to the benefits that the production centres derive from the service rendered.

We shall assume that the value of materials issued (shown in Example 7.1) provides a suitable approximation of the benefit that each of the production centres receives from materials procurement. Therefore, 50 per cent of the value of materials is issued to machine centre X, resulting in 50 per cent of the total costs of materials procurement being allocated to this centre. If you refer to Exhibit 7.1 you will see that £880 000 (50 per cent of material procurement costs of £1 760 000) has been reallocated to machine centre X. It is also assumed that direct labour hours provides an approximation of the benefits received by the production centres from general factory support resulting in the total costs for this centre being reallocated to the production centres proportionate to direct labour hours. Therefore, since machine centre X consumes 25 per cent of the direct labour hours, £450 000 (25 per cent of the total costs of £1 800 000 assigned to general factory support) has been reallocated to machine centre X. You will see in the row labelled 'step 2 of stage 1' in Exhibit 7.1 that all manufacturing costs have now been assigned to the three production centres. This completes the first stage of the two-stage allocation process.

Step 3 – Computing separate overhead rates for each production cost centre

The second stage of the two-stage process is to allocate overheads of each production centre to products passing through that centre. It is necessary to establish departmental overhead rates because multiple products are worked on by each producing department. If each department worked only on one product all of the costs allocated to that department would be assigned to the product and step 3 would not be required. The allocation bases most frequently used employed by traditional costing systems for computing production cost centre rates are based on the amount of time products spend in each production centre – for example, direct labour hours, machine hours and direct wages. In respect of non-machine centres, direct labour hours is the most frequently used allocation base. This implies that the overheads incurred by a production centre are closely related to direct labour hours worked. In the case of machine centres a machine hour overhead rate is preferable because most of the overheads (e.g. depreciation) are likely to be more closely related to machine hours. We shall assume that the Enterprise Company uses a **machine hour rate** for the machine production centres and a **direct labour hour rate** for the assembly centre. The overhead rates are calculated by applying the following formula:

$$\frac{\text{Cost centre overheads}}{\text{Cost centre direct labour hours or machine hours}}$$

The calculations (i.e. step 3 of the four steps of the two-stage allocation process) using the information given in Exhibit 7.1 are as follows:

$$\text{Machine centre X} = \frac{\pounds4\,300\,000}{2\,000\,000 \text{ machine hours}} = \pounds2.15 \text{ per machine hour}$$

$$\text{Machine centre Y} = \frac{\pounds3\,800\,000}{1\,000\,000 \text{ machine hours}} = \pounds3.80 \text{ per machine hour}$$

$$\text{Assembly department} = \frac{\pounds3\,600\,000}{2\,000\,000 \text{ direct labour hours}} = \pounds1.80 \text{ per direct labour hour}$$

Step 4 – Assigning cost centre overheads to products or other chosen cost objects

The final step is to allocate the overheads to products passing through the production centres. Therefore, if a product spends 10 hours in machine cost centre A, overheads of £21.50 (10 × £2.15) will be allocated to the product. We shall compute the manufacturing costs of two products. Product A is a low sales volume product with direct costs of £100. It is manufactured in batches of 100 units and each unit requires 5 hours in machine centre A, 10 hours in machine centre B and 10 hours in the assembly centre. Product B is a high sales volume product thus enabling it to be manufactured in larger batches. It is manufactured in batches of 200 units and each unit requires 10 hours in machine centre A, 20 hours in machine centre B and 20 hours in the assembly centre. Direct costs of £200 have been assigned to product B. The calculations of the manufacturing costs assigned to the products are as follows:

Product A	£
Direct costs (100 units × £100)	10 000
Overhead allocations	
Machine centre A (100 units × 5 machine hours × £2.15)	1 075
Machine centre B (100 units × 10 machine hours × £3.80)	3 800
Assembly (100 units × 10 direct labour hours × £1.80)	1 800
Total cost	16 675
Cost per unit (£16 675/100 units) = £166.75	

Product B	£
Direct costs (200 units × £200)	40 000
Overhead allocations	
Machine centre A (200 units × 10 machine hours × £2.15)	4 300
Machine centre B (200 units × 20 machine hours × £3.80)	15 200
Assembly (200 units × 20 direct labour hours × £1.80)	7 200
Total cost	66 700
Cost per unit (£66 700/200 units) = £333.50	

The overhead allocation procedure is more complicated where service cost centres serve each other. In Example 7.1 it was assumed that materials procurement does not provide any services for general factory support and that general factory support does not provide any services for materials procurement. An understanding of situations where service cost centres do serve each other is not, however, necessary for a general understanding of the overhead procedure, and the problem of service centre reciprocal cost allocations is therefore not covered in this book. For an explanation of how to deal with service centre reciprocal cost allocations you should refer to Drury (2018, Chapter 3).

EXTRACTING RELEVANT COSTS FOR DECISION-MAKING

The cost computations relating to the Enterprise Company for products A and B represent the costs that should be generated for meeting inventory valuation and profit measurement requirements. For decision-making, non-manufacturing costs should also be taken into account. In addition, some of the costs that have been assigned to the products may not be relevant for certain decisions. For example, if you look at the overhead analysis sheet in Exhibit 7.1 you will see that property taxes, depreciation of machinery and insurance of buildings and machinery have been assigned to cost centres, and thus included in the costs assigned to products. If these costs are unaffected by a decision to discontinue a product they should not be assigned to products when undertaking product discontinuation reviews. However, if cost information is used to determine selling prices such costs may need to be assigned to products to ensure that the selling price of a customer's order covers a fair share of all organizational costs. It is therefore necessary to ensure that the costs incorporated in the overhead analysis are suitably coded so that different overhead rates can be extracted for different combinations of costs. This will enable relevant cost information to be extracted from the database for meeting different requirements. For an illustration of this approach, see the answer to Review problem 7.20.

REAL WORLD
VIEWS 7.2

Product diversity and costing system design choice

Two Australian firms, one with three divisions (HC1, HC2 and HC3), and the second with two divisions (FT1 and FT2) were studied. HC1 and FT1 had the simplest costing systems with all of the overheads accumulated into a single cost pool. In other words, a plant-wide overhead rate was used. HC2 and HC3 established separate 'work centre cost pools' that reflect manufacturing processes (e.g. HC2 had three cost pools and HC3 two cost pools). Overheads such as power were directly traced to the work centres. The remaining overheads were allocated to the work centres based on their levels of direct labour hours (DLHs) usage. The work centre overhead was then determined by dividing the work centre cost pool by the number of DLHs and allocating the costs to the product according to the consumption of DLHs in each of the work centres.

FT2 was the only research site that had a highly sophisticated costing system consisting of many different cost pools. The overheads for each cost pool were allocated to products on the basis of two cost drivers, namely direct labour hours and machine hours. The overheads allocated based on DLHs included indirect labour associated with materials handling, packers and factory foremen. Overheads allocated on the basis of machine hours include costs that vary with machine hours (e.g. power and electricity) as well as fixed costs such as factory management and depreciation.

HC1, HC2 and FT1 all had low product diversity (i.e. products consumed organizational resources in similar proportions) and users were satisfied with the information provided by the costing system. Both HC3 and FT2 had high levels of product diversity. FT2 had a relatively sophisticated costing system while HC3 maintained a simplistic system. The users of the costing system at FT2 were very satisfied with the system whereas there was much dissatisfaction with HC3's system. Costing information at HC3 was particularly important for determining product costs. However, management believed that the costs were highly inaccurate and were inadequate for setting prices. Overheads were large and product diversity was high creating the need for a relatively sophisticated costing system. However, a simplistic costing system was implemented. This absence of 'fit' was a major dissatisfaction with the existing costing system. In contrast, there was a 'fit' between the costing systems and the level of product diversity in the four other business units and a general satisfaction with the costing systems.

Discussion points

1 Why might increasing the number of cost centres (pools) result in the reporting of more accurate product costs?
2 What other factors, besides product diversity, might enable a simplistic product costing system to report reasonably accurate product costs?

Reference

Adapted from Abernethy, M.A. et al. (2001) Product diversity and costing system design: Field study evidence, *Management Accounting Research*, 12(3), 261–80. Reproduced with permission from Elsevier.

BUDGETED OVERHEAD RATES

Our discussion in this chapter has assumed that the *actual* overheads for an accounting period have been allocated to the products. However, the use of actual figures can be problematic. This is because the product cost calculations have to be delayed until the end of the accounting period, because the overhead rate calculations cannot be obtained before this date. However, information on product costs is required more quickly if it is to

EXAMPLE 7.2

The fixed overheads for Euro are £24 million per annum, and monthly production varies from 400 000 to 1 million direct labour hours. The monthly overhead rate for fixed overhead will therefore fluctuate as follows:

Monthly overhead	£2 000 000	£2 000 000
Monthly production	400 000 hours	1 000 000 hours
Monthly overhead rate	£5 per hour	£2 per hour

Overhead expenditure that is fixed in the short term remains constant each month, but monthly production fluctuates because of holiday periods and seasonal variations in demand. Consequently, the overhead rate varies from £2 to £5 per hour. It would be unreasonable for a product worked on in one month to be allocated overheads at a rate of £5 per hour and an identical product worked on in another month allocated at a rate of only £2 per hour.

be used for monthly profit calculations and inventory valuations or as a basis for setting selling prices. One may argue that the timing problem can be resolved by calculating actual overhead rates at more frequent intervals, say on a monthly basis, but the difficulty here is that a large amount of overhead expenditure is fixed in the short term whereas activity will vary from month to month, giving large fluctuations in the overhead rates.

Consider Example 7.2. The monthly overhead rates of £2 and £5 per hour computed in Example 7.2 are not representative of typical, normal production conditions. Management has committed itself to a specific level of fixed costs in the light of foreseeable needs for beyond one month. Thus, where production fluctuates, monthly overhead rates may be volatile. Furthermore, some costs such as repairs, maintenance and heating are not incurred evenly throughout the year. Therefore, if monthly overhead rates are used, these costs will not be allocated fairly to units of output. For example, heating costs would be charged only to winter production so that products produced in winter would be more expensive than those produced in summer.

An average, annualized rate based on the relationship of total annual overhead to total annual activity is more representative of typical relationships between total costs and volume than a monthly rate. What is required is a normal product cost based on average long-term production rather than an actual product cost, which is affected by month-to-month fluctuations in production volume. Taking these factors into consideration, it is preferable to establish a **budgeted overhead rate** based on annual *estimated* overhead expenditure and activity.

UNDER- AND OVER-RECOVERY OF OVERHEADS

The effect of calculating overhead rates based on budgeted annual overhead expenditure and activity is that it will be most unlikely that the overhead allocated to products manufactured during the period will be the same as the actual overhead incurred.

Consider a situation where the estimated annual fixed overheads are £2 000 000 and the estimated annual activity is 1 000 000 direct labour hours. The estimated fixed overhead rate will be £2 per hour. Assume that actual overheads are £2 000 000 and are therefore identical with the estimate, but that actual activity is 900 000 direct labour hours instead of the estimated 1 000 000 hours. In this situation only £1 800 000 will be charged to production. This calculation is based on 900 000 direct labour hours at £2 per hour, giving an under-recovery of overheads of £200 000.

Consider an alternative situation where the actual overheads are £1 950 000 instead of the estimated £2 000 000, and actual activity is 1 000 000 direct labour hours, which is identical to the original estimate. In this situation 1 000 000 direct labour hours at £2 per hour will be charged to production giving an over-recovery of £50 000. This example illustrates that there will be an **under- or over-recovery of overheads** whenever actual

REAL WORLD VIEWS 7.3

Overheads in cafés

Bubble tea cafés are becoming increasingly popular across Malaysia and in recent years, many new chains have been formed, opening cafés in mainly urban locations.

Leading bubble tea firms provide some interesting information on the rapid growth of the product in recent years. According to Bryan Loo of Chatime (which is quoted on the Taiwan stock exchange), the rationale for setting up a bubble tea business was that there is a strong demand for tea in Malaysia, but no tea businesses as such – in the coffee business names like Starbucks are already in situ. Bubble tea is also more appealing to health-conscious consumers. Globally, Chatime has more than 800 outlets as of 2016, 116 of which are in Malaysia.

The primary business model for the new cafés is a franchise model. The cost of setting up a café in Malaysia is at least RM200 000 (about £45 000), depending on factors such as location, size and renovation costs. According to Billy Koh, the franchisor for Gong Cha brand bubble tea, overhead costs of running a café are typically higher in a shopping mall franchise than in a normal high-street type shop. However, the profit margins are reasonable at approximately 30 per cent for a typical franchise operation. The lower margin is attributable to the high materials cost.

Questions

1 Can you think of some examples of overhead costs that might be incurred by cafés such as those described above?
2 How would these overheads affect profit if sales declined?

References

Wei-Shen, W. (2012) Bubble tea craze leads to a flurry of stores opening in Klang Valley, *The Star* (Malaysia), 19 March. Available at www.thestar.com.my/news/community/2012/03/19/bubble-tea-craze-leads-to-a-flurry-of-stores-opening-in-klang-valley/
Chatime (2015) Nothing but bubbling good … Available at www.chatime.com.my/main/story.php

activity or overhead *expenditure* is different from the budgeted overheads and activity used to estimate the budgeted overhead rate. This under- or over-recovery of *fixed* overheads arising from actual activity differing from budgeted activity, is also called a **volume variance** and any under- or over-recovery arising from actual fixed overhead expenditure differing from budget is also called a **fixed overhead expenditure variance**.

Accounting regulations in most countries recommend that the under- or over-recovery of overheads should be regarded as a period cost adjustment (see Chapter 2 for an explanation of period costs). The accounting procedure is illustrated in Figure 7.4. Note that any under- or over-recovery of overhead is not allocated to products. Also note that the under-recovery is recorded as an expense in the current accounting period whereas an over-recovery is recorded as a reduction in the expenses for the period. Finally, you should note that our discussion here is concerned with how to treat any under- or over-recovery for the purpose of financial accounting and its impact on inventory valuation and profit measurement.

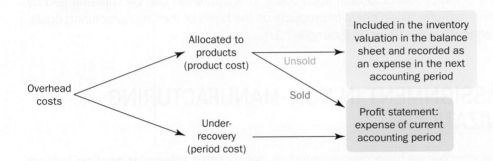

FIGURE 7.4

Illustration of under-recovery of factory overheads

NON-MANUFACTURING OVERHEADS

For financial accounting purposes only manufacturing costs are allocated to products. Non-manufacturing overheads are regarded as period costs and are treated in exactly the same way as the under- or over-recovery of manufacturing overheads outlined in Figure 7.4. For external reporting it is therefore unnecessary to allocate non-manufacturing overheads to products. However, for decision-making it may be necessary to assign non-manufacturing costs to products. For example, in many organizations it is not uncommon for selling prices to be based on estimates of total cost or even actual cost. Housing contractors and garages often charge for their services by adding a percentage profit margin to actual cost.

Some non-manufacturing costs may be a direct cost of the product. Delivery costs, salesmen's salaries and travelling expenses may be directly identifiable with the product, but it is likely that many non-manufacturing overheads cannot be allocated directly to specific products. On what basis should we allocate non-manufacturing overheads? The answer is that we should select an allocation base/cost driver that corresponds most closely to non-manufacturing overheads. The problem is that cause-and-effect allocation bases often cannot be established for many non-manufacturing overheads. Therefore, an allocation base must be used which, although is arbitrary, allocates costs on a reasonable basis as possible. A widely used approach is to allocate non-manufacturing overheads

EXAMPLE 7.3

The estimated non-manufacturing and manufacturing costs of a company for the year ending 31 December are £500 000 and £1 million respectively. The non-manufacturing overhead absorption rate is calculated as follows:

$$\frac{\text{Estimated non-manufacturing overhead}}{\text{Estimated manufacturing cost}}$$

In percentage terms each product will be allocated with non-manufacturing overheads at a rate of 50 per cent of its total manufacturing cost.

on the ability of the products to bear such costs. This approach can be implemented by allocating non-manufacturing costs to products on the basis of their manufacturing costs, and this procedure is illustrated in Example 7.3.

COST ASSIGNMENT IN NON-MANUFACTURING ORGANIZATIONS

So far in this chapter we have concentrated on describing a **job-order costing system** that is used in manufacturing firms where the products incur different costs resulting in the need to keep track of the cost of each product or batch of products. In particular, we have focused on cost assignment for allocating costs between cost of goods sold and inventories for profit reporting. Many service organizations also use a job-order costing system. For example, accounting, law, printing, automotive and appliance repair firms provide unique services to customers resulting in the need to track the costs of the services provided to each customer. The costs assigned to each customer are also often used to determine the prices of the services that have been provided. These firms may also have inventories consisting of work partially completed (i.e. WIP) at the end of the accounting period. The same basic concepts and procedures that are used by manufacturing organizations can therefore be applied where the cost of a service provided to customer differs.

However, a job-order costing system is inappropriate for many non-manufacturing organizations for the following reasons:

1 They do not provide unique services for customers. Instead, they provide similar services for a large number of customers. Consider a bank whose principal activities include mortgage lending, personal lending, variable interest and fixed interest savings accounts, insurance, foreign currency, etc. It is not feasible or useful to track the costs of undertaking these activities to individual customers. Instead, costs are assigned to each activity so that the total costs incurred can be deducted from sales revenue to periodically determine the profits/losses of each activity.

2 They do not need to assign costs to individual customers to determine prices of the services provided because prices are determined by market forces rather than cost.

3 They do not convert purchased materials into finished products or have WIP. Therefore, there is no legal requirement to assign indirect costs to cost objects for inventory valuation.

Instead of using job-order costing systems, the above organizations require costing systems that support profitability analysis. They need to undertake periodic profitability analysis that analyses profits by appropriate activities (e.g. products, services, departments, locations, etc.) so that they can distinguish between profitable and unprofitable activities in order to ensure that only profitable activities are undertaken. Consider a merchandising company such as a departmental store that analyses profits by departments (e.g. televisions and DVD players, computers, clothing and furniture departments). The company does not have to adhere to legal requirements for assigning indirect costs to goods processed for inventory valuation. It may choose not to assign indirect costs to departments where they are a small proportion of total costs or are common to all departments resulting in arbitrary allocations not having to be relied upon. In other words, only direct costs are assigned to departments so that departmental profits cannot be reported. Instead, departmental profit contributions to indirect costs (i.e. sales revenues less direct costs) are reported.

Alternatively, indirect costs can be assigned to departments using suitable allocation bases. For example, utility and property costs may be allocated based on the floor area occupied by each department. Other indirect costs may initially be assigned to relevant support departments such as payroll, data processing and personnel and then reallocated to the user departments (i.e. television, computing, clothing, etc.) using appropriate allocation bases. This approach enables all costs (direct and indirect) to be assigned to departments so that departmental profits can be reported.

SUMMARY

The following items relate to the learning objectives listed at the beginning of the chapter.

● **Distinguish between cause-and-effect and arbitrary cost allocations**. Allocation bases which are significant determinants of costs that are being allocated are described as cause-and-effect allocations whereas arbitrary allocations refer to allocation bases that are not the significant determinants of the costs. To accurately measure the cost of resources used by cost objects cause-and-effect allocations should be used.

● **Explain why different cost information is required for different purposes**. Manufacturing organizations assign costs to products for two purposes: first for external (financial accounting) profit measurement and inventory valuation purposes in order to allocate manufacturing costs incurred during a period to cost of goods sold and inventories; second to provide useful information for managerial decision-making requirements. Financial accounting regulations specify that only manufacturing costs should be assigned to products for meeting inventory and profit measurement requirements. Both manufacturing and non-manufacturing costs, however, may be relevant for decision-making. In addition, not all costs that are assigned to products for inventory valuation and profit measurement are relevant for decision-making. For example, costs that will not be affected by a decision (e.g. depreciation) are normally not relevant for product/service discontinuation decisions.

● **Describe how cost systems differ in terms of their level of sophistication.** Cost systems range from simplistic to sophisticated. Simplistic systems are inexpensive to operate, involve extensive use of arbitrary allocations, have a high likelihood of reporting inaccurate product costs and generally result in a high cost of errors. Sophisticated costing systems are more expensive to operate, rely more extensively on cause-and-effect allocations, generally report more accurate product costs and have a low cost of errors. Further distinguishing features are that simplistic costing systems have a small number of first-stage cost centres/pools and use a single second-stage cost driver. In contrast, sophisticated costing systems use many first-stage cost centres/ pools and many different types of second-stage drivers.

● **Understand the factors influencing the choice of an optimal cost system.** The optimal costing system is different for different organizations and should be determined on a costs versus benefits basis. Simplistic costing systems are appropriate in organizations whose indirect costs are a low percentage of total costs and which also have a fairly standardized product range, all consuming organizational resources in similar proportions. Under these circumstances simplistic costing systems may report costs that are sufficiently accurate for decision-making purposes. Conversely, organizations with a high proportion of indirect costs, whose products consume organizational resources in different proportions, are likely to require sophisticated costing systems. Relying on sophisticated costing systems under these circumstances is likely to result in the additional benefits from reporting more accurate costs exceeding the costs of operating more sophisticated systems.

● **Explain why departmental overhead rates should be used in preference to a single blanket overhead rate.** A blanket (also known as plant-wide) overhead rate establishes a single overhead rate for the organization as a whole whereas departmental rates involve indirect costs being accumulated by different departments and a separate overhead rate being established for each department. A blanket overhead rate can only be justified when all products or services consume departmental overheads in approximately the same proportions. Such circumstances are unlikely to be applicable to most organizations resulting in blanket overheads generally reporting inaccurate product/service costs.

● **Construct an overhead analysis sheet and calculate cost centre allocation rates.** Cost centre overhead allocation rates are established and assigned to cost objects using the two-stage allocation overhead procedure. In the first stage, an overhead analysis sheet is used to (a) allocate overheads to production and service centres or departments and (b) to reallocate the total service department overheads to production departments. The second stage involves (a) the calculation of appropriate departmental overhead rates and (b) the allocation of overheads to products passing through each department. These steps were illustrated using data presented in Example 7.1.

- **Justify why budgeted overhead rates should be used in preference to actual overhead rates.** Because the uses of actual overhead rates causes a delay in the calculation of product or service costs, and the establishment of monthly rates results in fluctuations in the overhead rates throughout the year, it is recommended that annual budgeted overhead rates should be used.

- **Calculate and explain the accounting treatment of the under-/over-recovery of overheads.** The use of annual budgeted overhead rates gives an under- or over-recovery of overheads whenever actual overhead expenditure or activity is different from budget. Any under- or over-recovery is generally regarded as a period cost adjustment and written off to the profit and loss statement and thus not allocated to products.

- **Explain how the cost assignment approach described for manufacturing organizations can be extended to non-manufacturing organizations.** The same basic cost assignment procedures that are used by manufacturing organizations can be applied where there is a need to track the cost of the services provided to each individual customer. Where a job-order costing system is inappropriate, cost information is required for profitability analysis by products, services, departments, etc. Organizations may choose to assign only direct costs to cost objects using a direct costing system. Alternatively, they may also use only the first stage of the two-stage overhead allocation procedure to assign indirect costs to departments that are synonymous with the products/services that are sold by the organization.

KEY TERMS AND CONCEPTS

Absorption costing system   A costing system that allocates all manufacturing costs, including fixed manufacturing costs, to products and values unsold stocks at their total cost of manufacture.

Activity-based costing (ABC)   A system of cost allocation that aims to use mainly cause-and-effect cost allocations by assigning costs to activities.

Allocation base   The basis used to allocate costs to cost objects.

Arbitrary allocation   The allocation of costs using a cost base that is not a significant determinant of cost.

Blanket overhead rate   An overhead rate that assigns indirect costs to cost objects using a single overhead rate for the whole organization, also known as plant-wide rate.

Budgeted overhead rate   An overhead rate based on estimated annual expenditure on overheads and levels of activity.

Cause-and-effect allocation   The use of an allocation base that is a significant determinant of cost, also known as driver tracing.

Cost allocation   The process of assigning costs to cost objects where a direct measure of the resources consumed by these cost objects does not exist.

Cost centre   A location to which costs are assigned, also known as a cost pool.

Cost driver   The basis used to allocate costs to cost objects in an ABC system.

Cost pool   A location to which overhead costs are assigned, also known as a cost centre.

Direct cost tracing   The process of assigning a cost directly to a cost object.

Direct costing system   A costing system that assigns only direct manufacturing costs, not fixed manufacturing costs, to products or services, also known as variable costing system or marginal costing system.

Direct labour hour rate   An hourly overhead rate calculated by dividing the cost centre overheads by the number of direct labour hours.

Driver tracing   The use of an allocation base that is a significant determinant of cost, also known as cause-and-effect allocation.

First stage allocation bases   The various bases, such as area, book value of machinery and number of employees, used to allocate indirect costs to production and service centres.

Fixed overhead expenditure variance   The difference between the budgeted fixed overheads and the actual fixed overhead spending.

Job-order costing system   A system of assigning costs to products or services that is used in situations where many different products or services are produced.

Machine hour rate   An hourly overhead rate calculated by dividing the cost centre overheads by the number of machine hours.

Overhead analysis sheet   A document used to assign manufacturing overheads to production and service cost centres.

Overheads   Another term for indirect costs, which are costs that cannot be specifically traced to a particular cost object.

Plant-wide rate   An overhead rate that assigns indirect costs to cost objects using a single overhead rate for the whole organization, also known as a blanket overhead rate.

Service departments   Departments that exist to provide services to other units within the organization, also known as support departments.

Support departments   Departments that exist to provide services to other units within the organization, also known as service departments.

Traditional costing systems   Widely used costing systems that tend to use arbitrary allocations to assign indirect costs to cost objects.

Under- or over-recovery of overheads   The difference between the overheads that are allocated to products or services during a period and the actual overheads that are incurred.

Volume variance   The difference between actual production and budgeted production for a period multiplied by the standard fixed overhead rate.

ASSESSMENT MATERIAL

The review questions are short questions that enable you to assess your understanding of the main topics included in the chapter. The page numbers in parentheses provide you with the page numbers to refer to if you cannot answer a specific question.

The review problems are more complex and require you to relate and apply the content to various business problems. Solutions to review problems are provided in a separate section at the end of the book. Additional review problems can be accessed by lecturers and students on the dedicated online support resources for this book. Solutions to these review problems are provided for lecturers in the *Instructor's Manual* accompanying this book that can be downloaded from the dedicated online instructor's resources (see Preface for details).

The dedicated online digital support resources for this book also includes over 30 case study problems.

REVIEW QUESTIONS

7.1 Why are indirect costs not directly traced to cost objects in the same way as direct costs? *(pp. 163–164)*

7.2 Define cost tracing, cost allocation, allocation base and cost driver. *(pp. 163–164)*

7.3 Distinguish between arbitrary and cause-and-effect allocations. *(p. 164)*

7.4 Explain how cost information differs for profit measurement/inventory valuation requirements compared with decision-making requirements. *(p. 165)*

7.5 Explain why cost systems should differ in terms of their level of sophistication. *(pp. 165–166)*

7.6 Why are separate departmental or cost centre overhead rates preferred to a plant-wide (blanket) overhead rate? *(pp. 167–168)*

7.7 Describe the two-stage overhead allocation procedure. *(pp. 168–169)*

7.8 Why are some overhead costs sometimes not relevant for decision-making purposes? *(p. 175)*

7.9 Why are budgeted overhead rates preferred to actual overhead rates? *(pp. 176–177)*

7.10 Give two reasons for the under- or over-recovery of overheads at the end of the accounting period. *(pp. 178–179)*

7.11 Explain how the cost assignment approach described for manufacturing organizations can be extended to non-manufacturing organizations. *(pp. 180–181)*

REVIEW PROBLEMS

7.12 A company uses a predetermined overhead recovery rate based on machine hours. Budgeted factory overhead for a year amounted to £720 000, but actual factory overhead incurred was £738 000. During the year, the company absorbed £714 000 of factory overhead on 119 000 actual machine hours.

What was the company's budgeted level of machine hours for the year?

(a) 116 098
(b) 119 000
(c) 120 000
(d) 123 000

7.13 A company uses an overhead absorption rate of $3.50 per machine hour, based on 32 000 budgeted machine hours for the period. During the same period the actual total overhead expenditure amounted to $108 875 and 30 000 machine hours were recorded on actual production.

By how much was the total overhead under- or over-absorbed for the period?

(a) Under-absorbed by $3875
(b) Under-absorbed by $7000
(c) Over-absorbed by $3875
(d) Over-absorbed by $7000

7.14 The following data are to be used for sub-questions (i) and (ii) below:

Budgeted labour hours	8500
Budgeted overheads	$148 750
Actual labour hours	7928
Actual overheads	$146 200

(i) Based on the data given above, what is the labour hour overhead absorption rate?
A $17.50 per hour
B $17.20 per hour
C $18.44 per hour
D $18.76 per hour

(ii) Based on the data given above, what is the amount of overhead under-/over-absorbed?
A $2550 under-absorbed
B $2529 over-absorbed
C $2550 over-absorbed
D $7460 under-absorbed

7.15 A firm makes special assemblies to customers' orders and uses job costing. The data for a period are:

	Job no. AA10 (€)	Job no. BB15 (€)	Job no. CC20 (€)
Opening work in progress	26 800	42 790	—
Material added in period	17 275	—	18 500
Labour for period	14 500	3 500	24 600

The budgeted overheads for the period were €126 000.
(i) What overhead should be added to job number CC20 for the period?
A €24 600
B €65 157
C €72 761
D €126 000

(ii) Job number BB15 was completed and delivered during the period and the firm wishes to earn 33$^{1}/_{3}$ per cent profit on sales.
What is the selling price of job number BB15?

A €69 435

B €75 521

C €84 963

D €138 870

(iii) What was the approximate value of closing work in progress at the end of the period?

A €58 575

B €101 675

C €147 965

D €217 323

7.16 A company absorbs overheads on machine hours. In a period, actual machine hours were 17 285, actual overheads were £496 500 and there was under-absorption of £12 520.
What was the budgeted level of overheads?

(a) £483 980

(b) £496 500

(c) £509 020

(d) it cannot be calculated from the information provided

7.17 Canberra has established the following information regarding fixed overheads for the coming month:

Budgeted information:

Fixed overheads	£180 000
Labour hours	3 000
Machine hours	10 000
Units of production	5 000

Actual fixed costs for the last month were £160 000.

Canberra produces many different products using highly automated manufacturing processes and absorbs overheads on the most appropriate basis.
What will be the predetermined overhead absorption rate?

(a) £16

(b) £18

(c) £36

(d) £60

7.18 Overhead analysis and calculation of product costs

A furniture-making business manufactures quality furniture to customers' orders. It has three production departments and two service departments. Budgeted overhead costs for the coming year are as follows:

	Total ($)
Rent and rates	12 800
Machine insurance	6 000
Telephone charges	3 200
Depreciation	18 000
Production supervisors' salaries	24 000
Heating/lighting	6 400
	70 400

The three production departments – A, B and C, and the two service departments – X and Y, are housed in the new premises, the details of which, together with other statistics and information, are given below.

	Departments				
	A	B	C	X	Y
Floor area occupied (sq. metres)	3 000	1 800	600	600	400
Machine value ($000)	24	10	8	4	2
Direct labour hours budgeted	3 200	1 800	1 000		
Labour rates per hour	$8.80	$8.50	$8.40	$7.50	$7.50
Allocated overheads:					
Specific to each department ($000)	2.8	1.7	1.2	0.8	0.6
Service department X's costs apportioned	50%	25%	25%		
Service department Y's costs apportioned	20%	30%	50%		

Required:

(a) Prepare a statement showing the overhead cost budgeted for each department, showing the basis of apportionment used. Also calculate suitable overhead absorption rates.

(9 marks)

(b) Two pieces of furniture are to be manufactured for customers. Direct costs are as follows:

	Job 123	Job 124
Direct material	$125	$79.70
Direct labour	10 hours Dept A	8 hours Dept A
	6 hours Dept B	5 hours Dept B
	5 hours Dept C	7 hours Dept C

Calculate the total costs of each job.

(5 marks)

(c) If the firm quotes prices to customers that reflect a required profit of 25 per cent on selling price, calculate the quoted selling price for each job.

(2 marks)

(Total 16 marks)

7.19 Calculation of product overhead costs

Bookdon plc manufactures three products in two production departments, a machine shop and a fitting section; it also has two service departments, a canteen and a machine maintenance section. Shown below are next year's budgeted production data and manufacturing costs for the company.

	Product X	Product Y	Product Z
Production	4 200 units	6 900 units	1 700 units
Prime cost:			
Direct materials	£11 per unit	£14 per unit	£17 per unit
Direct labour:			
Machine shop	£6 per unit	£4 per unit	£2 per unit
Fitting section	£12 per unit	£3 per unit	£21 per unit
Machine hours per unit	6 hours per unit	3 hours per unit	4 hours per unit

	Machine shop	Fitting section	Canteen	Machine maintenance section	Total
Budgeted overheads (£):					
Allocated overheads	27 660	19 470	16 600	26 650	90 380
Rent, rates, heat and light					17 000
Depreciation and insurance of equipment					25 000
Additional data:					
Gross book value of equipment (£)	150 000	75 000	30 000	45 000	
Number of employees	18	14	4	4	
Floor space occupied (sq. metres)	3 600	1 400	1 000	800	

It has been estimated that approximately 70 per cent of the machine maintenance section's costs are incurred servicing the machine shop and the remainder incurred servicing the fitting section.

Required:

(a) (i) Calculate the following budgeted overhead absorption rates:
A machine hour rate for the machine shop.
A rate expressed as a percentage of direct wages for the fitting section.
All workings and assumptions should be clearly shown.

(12 marks)

(ii) Calculate the budgeted manufacturing overhead cost per unit of product X.

(2 marks)

(b) The production director of Bookdon plc has suggested that 'as the actual overheads incurred and units produced are usually different from the budgeted and as a consequence profits of each month-end are distorted by over-/under-absorbed overheads, it would be more accurate to calculate the actual overhead cost per unit each month-end by dividing the total number of all units actually produced during the month into the actual overheads incurred.'
Critically examine the production director's suggestion.

(8 marks)

(Total 22 marks)

7.20 Make or buy decision
Shown below is next year's budget for the forming and finishing departments of Tooton Ltd. The departments manufacture three different types of component, which are incorporated into the output of the firm's finished products.

	Component		
	A	B	C
Production (units)	14 000	10 000	6 000
Prime cost (€ per unit):			
Direct materials			
Forming department	8	7	9
Direct labour			
Forming department	6	9	12
Finishing department	10	15	8
	24	31	29
Manufacturing times (hours per unit):			
Machining			
Forming department	4	3	2
Direct labour			
Forming department	2	3	4
Finishing department	3	10	2

	Forming department (€)	Finishing department (€)
Variable overheads	200 900	115 500
Fixed overheads	401 800	231 000
	€602 700	€346 500
Machine time required and available	98 000 hours	—
Labour hours required and available	82 000 hours	154 000 hours

The forming department is mechanized and employs only one grade of labour; the finishing department employs several grades of labour with differing hourly rates of pay.

Required:

(a) Calculate suitable overhead absorption rates for the forming and finishing departments for the next year and include a brief explanation for your choice of rates.

(6 marks)

(b) Another firm has offered to supply next year's budgeted quantities of the above components at the following prices:

Component A €30 Component B €65
Component C €60

Advise management whether it would be more economical to purchase any of the above components from the outside supplier. You must show your workings and, considering cost criteria only, clearly state any assumptions made or any aspects that may require further investigation.

(8 marks)

(c) Critically consider the purpose of calculating production overhead absorption rates.

(8 marks)

(Total 22 marks)

8
ACTIVITY-BASED COSTING

LEARNING OBJECTIVES After studying this chapter you should be able to:

● describe the differences between activity-based and traditional costing systems

● explain why traditional costing systems can provide misleading information for decision-making

● compute product costs using an activity-based costing system

● identify and explain each of the four stages involved in designing ABC systems

● describe the ABC cost hierarchy.

In the previous chapter the cost assignment process for a traditional costing system was described. From the late 1980s until the end of the 1990s the limitations of traditional product costing systems began to be widely publicized. These systems were designed decades ago when most companies marketed a narrow range of products. Indirect costs were relatively small, and the distortions arising from inappropriate overhead allocations were not significant. Information processing costs were high and it was therefore difficult to justify more sophisticated methods of assigning indirect costs to cost objects.

By the 1990s companies were marketing a wide range of products, indirect costs were no longer relatively unimportant and information processing costs had ceased to be a barrier to introducing more sophisticated systems. Furthermore, the intense global competition of the 1990s resulted in decision errors from poor cost information becoming more probable and more costly. It is against this background that a new, and more sophisticated costing system, called activity-based costing (ABC), emerged in the late 1980s. Recent studies (see Exhibit 8.1) suggest that approximately 30 per cent of organizations in various countries have implemented ABC systems.

In this chapter we shall focus on ABC systems – in particular, the measurement of indirect costs for decision-making using ABC techniques. The major aims of the chapter are to explain how an ABC system operates and provide a conceptual understanding of ABC. You should note that ABC can also be used for managing and controlling costs. These aspects are considered in Chapter 15.

Unless otherwise stated, we will assume that products are the cost objects, but the techniques used and the principles established can be applied to other cost objects such as customers, services and locations. We begin with a comparison of traditional and ABC systems.

EXHIBIT 8.1   Surveys of company practice

Surveys indicate that service companies are more likely to implement ABC than manufacturing companies. This is because most of the costs in service organizations are indirect. In contrast, manufacturing companies can trace important components (such as direct materials and direct labour) of costs to individual products. Therefore, indirect costs are likely to be a much smaller proportion of total costs.

A UK survey by Drury and Tayles (2005) reported that 51 per cent of the financial and service organizations surveyed, compared with 15 per cent of manufacturing organizations, had implemented ABC. The international survey by the Chartered Institute of Management Accountants (2009) reported that approximately 28 per cent of the respondents used ABC. Both surveys report a higher rate of adoption in larger companies compared with smaller companies.

A more recent survey by Al-Sayed and Dugdale (2016) adopted a wider definition of ABC and focused on activity-based innovations (defined as 'any management accounting practice that uses the concept of "activities" as its hard core'). They reported that 32 per cent were serious users of activity-based innovations (ABI) and that 72 per cent of the business units sampled have had experience or interest in ABI. Based on these findings the authors concluded that ABI can now be regarded as mainstream management accounting practice.

COMPARISON OF TRADITIONAL AND ABC SYSTEMS

Figure 8.1 illustrates the major differences between traditional and ABC systems. The upper panel of this diagram is identical to Figure 7.3 used in the previous chapter to describe a traditional costing system. Both systems use a two-stage allocation process. In the first stage a traditional system allocates overheads to production and service cost centres (typically departments) and then reallocates service department/cost centre costs to the production departments. You will see from the lower panel of Figure 8.1 that an ABC system assigns overheads to each major activity (rather than cost centres or departments). With ABC systems, many activity-based cost centres (alternatively known as activity cost pools) are established, whereas with traditional systems overheads tend to be pooled by departments, although they are normally described as cost centres.

Activities consist of the aggregation of many different tasks, events or units of work that cause the consumption of resources. They tend to consist of verbs associated with objects. Typical support activities include: schedule production, set up machines, move materials, purchase materials, inspect items, process supplier records, expedite and process customer orders. Production process activities include machine products and assemble products. Within the production process, **activity cost centres** are sometimes identical to the cost centres used by traditional cost systems. Support activities are also sometimes identical to cost centres used by traditional systems, such as when the purchasing department and activity are both treated as cost centres. Overall, however, ABC systems will normally have a greater number of activity cost centres compared with traditional systems.

You will see from Figure 8.1 that the second stage of the two-stage allocation process allocates costs from cost centres (pools) to products or other chosen cost objects. Traditional costing systems trace overheads to products using a small number of second-stage allocation bases (normally described as overhead allocation rates), which

FIGURE 8.1

An illustration of the two-stage allocation for traditional and activity-based costing systems

(a) Traditional costing systems

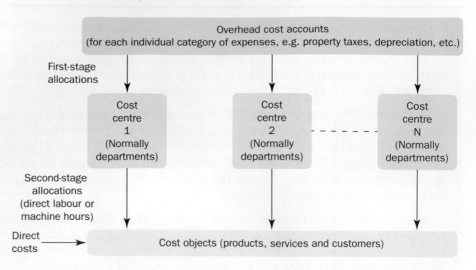

(b) Activity-based costing systems

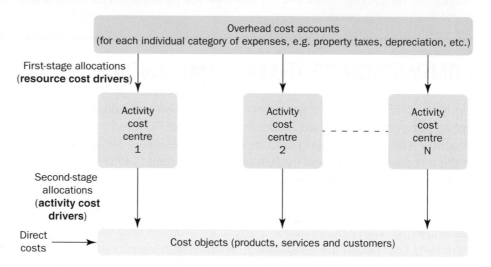

vary directly with the volume produced. Instead of using the terms 'allocation bases' or 'overhead allocation rates' the term '**cost driver**' is used by ABC systems. You should be able to remember from the previous chapter that a cost driver represents a measure that exerts the major influence on the cost of a particular activity. Direct labour and machine hours are the allocation bases that are normally used by traditional costing systems. In contrast, ABC systems use many different types of second-stage cost drivers, including non-volume-based drivers, such as the number of production runs for production scheduling and the number of purchase orders for the purchasing activity.

Therefore, the major distinguishing features of ABC systems are that within the two-stage allocation process they rely on:

1 a greater number of cost centres

2 a greater number and variety of second-stage cost drivers.

By using a greater number of cost centres and different types of cost drivers that cause activity resource consumption, and assigning activity costs to cost objects on the

REAL WORLD VIEWS 8.1

ABC in China – Xu Ji Electric Co Ltd

Until recently, Xu Ji Electric Co Ltd was a typical stateowned Chinese enterprise manufacturing electrical products such as relays. From an accounting point of view, this implied a manual book-keeping system which was primarily designed to meet extenal reporting requirements. This was to the detriment of management accounting information, and product costing was not accurate.

The company underwent several changes under Chinese free market developments. If the company were to compete and introduce new products, it needed to invest in more modern production control and testing methods, increase its marketing, increase its research and development, as well as improve its costing system. It decided to adopt an activity-based costing (ABC) system which would trace labour costs directly to products and customer contracts and allocate manufacturing overheads. It took some years for Xu Ji Electric Co Ltd to get the ABC system up and running, but the eventual result was monthly ABC cost reports in some divisions. For example, at the Relays Division which manufactures many types

of electrical relay, these reports allocatcd costs like after-sales service, technical support, warehousing, marketing and production planning to products and customer contracts. At the Relays Division, the activity cost centres included activities such as wiring, labelling, installation, electrical testing and materials management. The Relays division operated in a highly competitive and saturated market and the resulting ABC system assisted the division managers in obtaining more accurate costs and improving divisional performance.

Questions

1 Do you think Xu Ji Electric Co Ltd is a good example of a business where ABC might be useful?

2 Can you think of some activities of Xu Ji Electric Co Ltd other than those stated above?

Reference

Liu, L.Y.J. and Pan, F. (2011) 'Activity based costing in China: A case study of Xu Ji Electric Co. Ltd', *Research Executive Summary* Series, Vol. 7, No. 13, CIMA, London. Available at www.cimaglobal.com/Thought-leadership/Research-topics/Management-accounting-in-different-sectors/Activity-based-costing-in-China/

basis of cost driver usage, ABC systems can more accurately measure the resources consumed by cost objects. Traditional cost systems tend to report less accurate costs because they use cost drivers where no cause-and-effect relationships exist to assign support costs to cost objects.

VOLUME-BASED AND NON-VOLUME-BASED COST DRIVERS

Our comparison of ABC systems with traditional costing systems indicated that ABC systems rely on a greater number and variety of second-stage cost drivers. The term 'variety of cost drivers' refers to the fact that ABC systems use both volume-based and non-volume-based cost drivers. In contrast, traditional systems use only volume-based cost drivers. **Volume-based cost drivers** assume that a product's consumption of overhead resources is directly related to units produced. In other words, they assume that the overhead consumed by products is highly correlated with the number of units produced. Typical volume-based cost drivers used by traditional systems are units of output, direct labour hours and machine hours. These cost drivers are appropriate for measuring the consumption of expenses such as machine energy costs, indirect labour employed in production centres and inspection costs where each item produced is subject to final inspection. For example, machine hours are an appropriate cost driver for energy costs since if volume is increased by 10 per cent, machine hours are likely to increase by 10 per cent, thus causing 10 per cent more energy costs to be consumed.

Volume-based drivers are appropriate in the above circumstances because activities are performed each time a unit of the product or service is produced. In contrast, non-volume-related activities are not performed each time a unit of the product or service is produced. Consider, for example, the activity of setting up a machine. Set-up resources are consumed each time a machine is changed from one product to another. It costs the same to set up a machine for 10 or 5000 items. As more set-ups are done more set-up resources are consumed. The number of set-ups, rather than the number of units produced, is a more appropriate measure of the resources consumed by the set-up activity. A **non-volume-based cost driver**, such as number of set-ups, is needed for the accurate assignment of the costs of this activity.

Using only volume-based cost drivers to assign non-volume-related overhead costs can result in the reporting of distorted product costs. The extent of distortion depends on what proportion of total overhead costs the non-volume-based overheads represent and the level of product diversity. If a large proportion of an organization's costs are unrelated to volume there is a danger that inaccurate product costs will be reported with a traditional costing system. Conversely, if non-volume-related overhead costs are only a small proportion of total overhead costs, the distortion of product costs will not be significant. In these circumstances traditional product costing systems are likely to be acceptable.

Product diversity applies when products consume different overhead activities in dissimilar proportions. Differences in product size, product complexity, sizes of batches and set-up times cause product diversity. If all products consume overhead resources in similar proportions product diversity will be low and products will consume non-volume-related activities in the same proportion as volume-related activities. Hence, product cost distortion will not occur with traditional product costing systems. Two conditions are therefore necessary for product cost distortion:

● non-volume-related overhead costs are a large proportion of total overhead costs, and

● product diversity applies.

Where these two conditions exist, traditional product costing systems can result in the overcosting of high-volume products and undercosting of low-volume products. Consider the information presented in Example 8.1. The reported product costs and profits for the two products are as follows:

	Traditional system		ABC system	
	Product HV (£)	Product LV (£)	Product HV (£)	Product LV (£)
Direct costs	310 000	40 000	310 000	40 000
Overheads allocated[a]	300 000 (30%)	50 000 (5%)	150 000 (15%)	150 000 (15%)
Reported profits/(losses)	(10 000)	60 000	140 000	(40 000)
Sales revenues	600 000	150 000	600 000	150 000

Note
[a]Allocation of £1 million overheads using direct labour hours as the allocation base for the traditional system and number of batches processed as the cost driver for the ABC system.

EXAMPLE 8.1

Assume that the Balearic Company has only one overhead cost centre or cost pool. It currently operates a traditional costing system using direct labour hours to allocate overheads to products. The company produces several products, two of which are products HV and LV. Product HV is made in high volumes whereas product LV is made in low volumes. Product HV consumes 30 per cent of the direct labour hours and product LV consumes only 5 per cent. Because of the high-volume production product HV can be made in large production batches but the irregular and low level of demand for product LV requires it to be made in small batches. A detailed investigation indicates that the number of batches processed causes the demand for overhead resources. The traditional system is therefore replaced with an ABC system using the number of batches processed as the cost driver. You ascertain that each product accounts for 15 per cent of the batches processed during the period and the overheads assigned to the cost centre that fluctuate in the long term according to the demand for them amount to £1 million. The direct costs and sales revenues assigned to the products are as follows:

	Product HV (£)	Product LV (£)
Direct costs	310 000	40 000
Sales revenues	600 000	150 000

Show the product profitability analysis for products HV and LV using the traditional and ABC systems.

Because product HV is a high-volume product that consumes 30 per cent of the direct labour hours whereas product LV, the low-volume product, consumes only 5 per cent, the traditional system that uses direct labour hours as the allocation base allocates six times more overheads to product HV. However, ABC systems recognize that overheads are caused by other factors, besides volume. In our example, all of the overheads are assumed to be volume unrelated. They are caused by the number of batches processed and the ABC system establishes a cause-and-effect allocation relationship by using the number of batches processed as the cost driver. Both products require 15 per cent of the total number of batches so they are allocated with an equal amount of overheads.

It is apparent from the consumption ratios of the two products that the traditional system based on direct labour hours will overcost high-volume products and undercost low-volume products. **Consumption ratios** represent the proportion of each activity consumed by a product. The consumption ratios if direct labour hours are used as the cost driver are 0.30 for product HV and 0.05 for product LV so that six times more overheads will be assigned to product HV. When the number of batches processed are used as the cost driver the consumption ratios are 0.15 for each product and an equal amount of overhead will be assigned to each product. Distorted product costs are reported with the traditional costing system that uses the volume-based cost driver because the two conditions specified above apply:

1 non-volume related overheads are a large proportion of total overheads, being 100 per cent in our example

2 product diversity exists because the product consumption ratios for the two identified cost drivers are significantly different.

The illustration above shows that if the consumption ratios for batches processed had been the same as the ratios for direct labour, the traditional and ABC systems would report identical product costs.

With the traditional costing system, misleading information is reported. A small loss is reported for product HV and if it were discontinued the costing system mistakenly gives the impression that overheads will decline in the longer term by £300 000. The message from the costing system is to concentrate on the more profitable speciality products like product LV. In reality this strategy would be disastrous because low-volume products like product LV are made in small batches and require more people for scheduling production, performing set-ups, inspection of the batches and handling a large number of customer requests for small orders. The long-term effect would be escalating overhead costs.

In contrast, the ABC system allocates overheads on a cause-and-effect basis and more accurately measures the relatively high level of overhead resources consumed by product LV. The message from the profitability analysis is the opposite from the traditional system; that is, product HV is profitable and product LV is unprofitable. If product LV is discontinued, and assuming that the cost driver (the number of batches processed) is the cause of all the overheads then a decision to discontinue product LV should result in the reduction in resource spending on overheads by £150 000.

Example 8.1 is very simplistic. It is assumed that the organization has established only a single cost centre or cost pool, when in reality many will be established with a traditional system, and even more with an ABC system. Furthermore, the data have been deliberately biased to show the superiority of ABC. The aim of the illustration has been to highlight the potential cost of errors that can occur when information extracted from simplistic and inaccurate cost systems is used for decision-making.

AN ILLUSTRATION OF THE TWO-STAGE ALLOCATION PROCESS FOR ABC

We shall now use the data presented in Example 7.1 (the Enterprise Company) from the previous chapter to illustrate ABC in more detail. This example was used to compute the product costs shown in Exhibit 7.1 for a traditional costing system. To refresh your memory you should now refer back to Example 7.1 in the previous chapter and also read pages 171–175 relating to steps 1–4 of the two-stage allocation process.

Exhibit 8.2 provides a *summary* of the two-stage overhead allocation process for a traditional costing system for Example 7.1. You will see the entries in row 1 are identical to the entries in the row labelled 'step 1 of stage 1' shown in Exhibit 7.1 whereby all of the manufacturing overheads of £11 700 000 have been assigned to the three production departments and two service (support departments). In row 2 the service department overheads are reallocated to the production departments so that row 3 shows that all manufacturing overheads have now been assigned to the three production cost centres.

EXHIBIT 8.2 Overheads assigned to the production of 1000 units of products A and B (traditional costing system)

		Production centres			Service centres	
	Total (£)	Machine centre X (£)	Machine centre Y (£)	Assembly (£)	Material procurement (£)	General factory support (£)
1. Step 1 of stage 1	11 700 000	2 970 000	2 690 000	2 480 000	1 760 000	1 800 000
2. Reallocation of service centre costs						
Materials procurement		880 000	660 000	220 000	1 760 000	
General factory support		450 000	450 000	900 000		1 800 000
3. Step 2 of stage 1	11 700 000	4 300 000	3 800 000	3 600 000	–	–
4. Machine hours and direct labour hours (DLH)		2 000 000	1 000 000	2 000 000		
5. Machine hour overhead rate		£2.15	£3.80			
6. Direct labour hour overhead rate				£1.80		
7. Quantity of machine hours/DLH for 100 units of product A		500	1 000	1 000		
8. Quantity of machine hours/DLH for 200 units of product B		2 000	4 000	4 000		
9. Product A total overhead cost (£)		£1 075	£3 800	£1 800		
10. Product B total overhead cost (£)		£4 300	£15 200	£7 200		

The second stage of the two-stage process allocates overheads of each production centre to products passing through that centre by establishing departmental overhead rates. You will see from rows 5 and 6 of Exhibit 8.2 that separate machine hour overhead rates have been established for the two machine production centres and a direct labour hour rate has been established for the assembly department. In other words, two allocation bases (machine hours and direct labour hours) are used by the traditional system in the second stage of the two-stage allocation process. Overheads are assigned to products (e.g. products A and B in our illustration) by multiplying the overhead rates by the quantity of the allocation base used by each product. This process is shown in rows 7–10 in Exhibit 8.2.

Exhibit 8.3 shows how the product costs are computed using an ABC system. You should remember from Figure 8.1 that a major distinguishing feature of ABC is that overheads are assigned to each major activity, rather than departments, which normally represent cost centres with traditional systems. When costs are accumulated by activities they are known as **activity cost centres**. Production process activities include machine products and assemble products. Thus within the production process, activity cost centres may be identical to the cost centres used by traditional cost systems. In contrast, service (support) department cost centres are established for traditional systems, whereas with an ABC system these centres are often decomposed into many different activity centres.

ABC systems have a greater number of cost centres, but to keep things simple we shall assume in Exhibit 8.3 that the three production centres (i.e. the two machining centres and the assembly cost centre) established for the traditional costing system have also been identified as activity cost centres with the ABC system. Therefore, the production activity cost centres are identical to the cost centres used by traditional cost systems. Look at row 1 in both Exhibits 8.2 and 8.3. You will see that the same amounts have been assigned to the three production cost centres. However, we shall assume that three activity centres have been established for each of the two support functions. For the materials procurement support function the following activity centres have been established:

Activity	£	Activity cost driver
Purchasing materials	960 000	Number of purchase orders
Receiving materials	600 000	Number of material receipts
Disburse materials	200 000	Number of production runs
	1 760 000	

Therefore, the assignment of £1 760 000 to the materials procurement department in Exhibit 8.2 is replaced by the assignments to the above three activities totalling £1 760 000 that are shown in Exhibit 8.3. For the second support department (i.e. general factory support) used as a cost centre with the traditional costing system we shall assume that the following three activity cost centres have been identified:

Activity	£	Activity cost driver
Production scheduling	1 000 000	Number of production runs
Set-up machines	600 000	Number of set-up hours
Quality inspection	200 000	Number of first item inspections
	1 800 000	

EXHIBIT 8.3   Overheads assigned to the production of 1000 units of products A and B (ABC system)

	Machine centre X	Machine centre Y	Assembly	Purchasing components	Receiving components	Disburse materials	Production scheduling	Set-up machines	Quality inspection
1. Stage 1 assignment (£)	2 970 000	2 690 000	2 480 000	960 000	600 000	200 000	1 000 000	600 000	200 000
2. Activity cost driver	Machine hours	Machine hours	Direct labour hours	Number of purchase orders	Number of material receipts	Number of production runs	Number of production runs	Number of set-up hours	Number of first item inspections
3. Quantity of activity cost driver	2 000 000	1 000 000	2 000 000	10 000	5 000	2 000	2 000	12 000	1 000
4. Activity cost driver rate (£)	£1.485	£2.69	£1.24	£96	£120	£100	£500	£50	£200
5. Quantity of activity cost driver for 100 units of product A	500 hours	1 000 hours	1 000 hours	1 purchased component	1 component received	5 production runs	5 production runs	50 set-up hours	1 inspection
6. Quantity of activity cost driver for 200 units of product B	2 000 hours	4 000 hours	4 000 hours	1 purchased component	1 component received	1 production run	1 production run	10 set-up hours	1 inspection
7. Overheads assigned to Product A (£)	742.50	2 690.00	1 240.00	96.00	120.00	500.00	2 500.00	2 500.00	200.00
8. Overheads assigned to Product B (£)	2 970.00	10 760.00	4 960.00	96.00	120.00	100.00	500.00	500.00	200.00
9. Product A total overhead cost = £10 588.50 (sum of row 7)									
10. Product B total overhead cost = £20 206.00 (sum of row 8)									

You can see that the total costs assigned to the production scheduling, set-up machines and quality inspection activities shown in row 1 in Exhibit 8.3 total £1 800 000, the same as the total allocated to the general factory support cost centre with the traditional costing system in row 1 of Exhibit 8.2. The process of allocating the costs of £11 700 000 to the activity cost centres is the same as that used to allocate these costs with the traditional costing system. To simplify the presentation the stage 1 cost assignments for the ABC system are not shown. We have now completed the first stage of the two-stage allocation process for both the traditional and ABC systems. Row 3 of Exhibit 8.2 indicates that overhead costs are assigned to three cost centres with the traditional system whereas row 1 of Exhibit 8.3 indicates that overheads are assigned to nine activity cost centres. Thus a major distinguishing feature between the two exhibits is that the ABC system use a greater number of cost centres than traditional systems in the first stage of the two-stage allocation process.

We shall now compare the second stage of the two-stage allocation process for the traditional and ABC system. You will remember that earlier in this section it was pointed out that in rows 5 and 6 of Exhibit 8.2 that separate machine hour overhead rates have been established for the two machine production centres and a direct labour hour rate has been established for the assembly department. Overheads are assigned to products A and B (see rows 7–10 in Exhibit 8.2) by multiplying the overhead rates by the quantity of the allocation base used by each product.

The same approach is used in Exhibit 8.3 with the ABC system. You will see from row 2 that seven different second-stage cost drivers have been established for the ABC system. Cost driver rates are computed in row 4 by dividing the costs assigned to the activity cost centres in row 1 by the estimated quantity of the cost drivers for the period shown in row 3. Activity centre costs are assigned to products by multiplying the cost driver rate by the quantity of the cost driver used by products. These calculations are shown in rows 5–8 of Exhibit 8.3. For example £960 000 has been assigned to the purchasing activity for processing 10 000 purchasing orders resulting in a cost driver rate of £96 per purchasing order. Rows 5 and 6 indicate that a batch of 100 units of product A, and 200 units of product B, each require one purchased component and thus one purchase order. Therefore, purchase order costs of £96 are allocated to each batch. Now look at the production scheduling column in Exhibit 8.3. You will see that £1 000 000 has been assigned to this activity for 2000 production runs resulting in a cost driver rate of £500 per production run. Rows 5 and 6 show that a batch of 100 units of product A requires five production runs whereas a batch of 200 units of product B requires one production run. Therefore production scheduling activity costs of £2500 (5 × £500) are allocated to a batch of product A and £500 to a batch of product B. The same approach is used to allocate the costs of the remaining activities shown in Exhibit 8.3. You should now work through Exhibit 8.3 and study the product cost calculations.

Exhibits 8.2 and 8.3 highlight the major differences between traditional and ABC systems. They are:

1 ABC systems have a greater number of cost centres than traditional costing systems. Exhibit 8.2 indicates that three cost centres are used with the traditional costing system, whereas Exhibit 8.3 indicates that nine cost centres are used with the ABC system.

2 ABC systems use a greater number and variety of second-stage cost drivers (Exhibit 8.3 shows that nine cost drivers consisting of seven different types are

used with the ABC system whereas three cost drivers consisting of two different types are used by the traditional system shown in Exhibit 8.2).

3 The traditional costing system reallocates service/support department costs to production cost centres and allocates these costs within the production cost centre overhead rates (see rows 2, 5 and 6 in Exhibit 8.2) whereas the ABC system does not reallocate these costs. Instead, the ABC system establishes separate cost driver rates for the support activities (see row 4 relating to the final six columns in Exhibit 8.3).

Exhibits 8.2 and 8.3 indicate that the overhead costs assigned to products A and B are as follows:

	Traditional costing system £	ABC system £
Batch of 100 units of product A	6 675	10 588.50
Batch of 200 units of product B	26 700	20 206.00
Product A cost per unit	66.75 (£6 675/100 units)	105.88 (£10 588.50/100 units)
Product B cost per unit	133.50 (£26 700/200 units)	101.03 (£20 206/200 units)

Compared with the ABC system the traditional system undercosts product A and overcosts product B. By reallocating the service centre costs to the production centres and allocating the costs to products on the basis of either machine hours or direct labour hours the traditional system incorrectly assumes that these allocation bases are the cause of the costs of the support activities. Compared with product A, product B consumes twice as many machine and direct labour hours per unit of output. Therefore, relative to product A, the traditional costing system allocates twice the amount of support costs to product B.

In contrast, ABC systems create separate cost centres for each major support activity and allocate costs to products using cost drivers that are the significant determinants of the cost of the activities. The ABC system recognizes that a batch of both products consume the same quantity of purchasing, receiving and inspection activities and, for these activities, allocates the same costs to both products. Because product B is manufactured in batches of 200 units, and product A in batches of 100 units, the cost per unit of output for product B is half the amount of product A for these activities. Product A also has five unique machined components, whereas product B has only one, resulting in a batch of product A requiring five production runs whereas a batch of product B only requires one. Therefore, relative to product B, the ABC system assigns five times more costs to product A for the production scheduling and disbursement of materials activities (see rows 5–8 for these activities in Exhibit 8.3). Because product A is a more complex product it requires relatively more support activity resources and the cost of this complexity is captured by the ABC system.

It should be apparent from the computation of the product costs that traditional and ABC systems use the same basic approach. It is unfortunate that the terms traditional and ABC systems have emerged. They have now become the conventional terms used in the literature but using these terms gives the impression that they are two separate systems, when in reality they represent a single cost assignment system. If you re-examine the workings it will become apparent that one approach (ABC systems) merely uses more cost centres and different types of cost drivers. Rather than viewing the approaches as two separate systems it is preferable to view ABC systems as sophisticated or complex cost assignment systems and traditional systems as simple or unsophisticated cost assignment systems.

DESIGNING ABC SYSTEMS

We shall now examine in more detail the ABC system that was illustrated in Exhibit 8.2. Four steps are involved in designing ABC/sophisticated costing systems. They are:

1 identifying the major activities that take place in an organization
2 assigning costs to cost pools/cost centres for each activity
3 selecting appropriate cost drivers for assigning the cost of activities to cost objects
4 assigning the cost of activities to products according to the product's demand for activities.

The first two steps relate to the first stage, and the final two steps to the second stage, of the two-stage allocation process shown in Figure 8.1. Let us now consider each of these stages in more detail.

Step 1: Identifying activities

Activities are the aggregation of many different tasks, events or units of work that cause the consumption of resources. For example, purchasing of materials might be identified as a separate activity. This activity consists of the aggregation of many different tasks, such as receiving a purchase request, identifying suppliers, preparing purchase orders, mailing purchase orders and performing follow-ups.

The activities chosen should be at a reasonable level of aggregation based on costs versus benefits criteria. For example, rather than classifying purchasing of materials as an activity, each of its constituent tasks could be classified as separate activities. However, this level of decomposition would involve the collection of a vast amount of data and is likely to be too costly for product costing purposes. Alternatively, the purchasing activity might be merged with the materials receiving, storage and issuing activities to form a single materials procurement and handling activity. This is likely to represent too high a level of aggregation because a single cost driver is unlikely to provide a satisfactory determinant of the cost of the activity. For example, selecting the number of purchase orders as a cost driver may provide a good explanation of purchasing costs but may be entirely inappropriate for explaining costs relating to receiving and issuing. Therefore, instead of establishing materials procurement and handling as a single activity it may be preferable to decompose it into three separate activities; namely purchasing, receiving and issuing activities, and to establish separate cost drivers for each activity. You will remember that in Exhibit 8.2 materials procurement represented a single cost centre for the traditional costing system whereas with the ABC system shown in Exhibit 8.3 it was decomposed into three separate activities (the purchasing, receiving and issuing of materials).

The final choice of activities must be a matter of judgement but it is likely to be influenced by factors such as the total cost of the activity centre (it must be of significance to justify separate treatment) and the ability of a single driver to provide a satisfactory determinant of the cost of the activity. Where the latter is not possible further decomposition of the activity will be necessary.

Step 2: Assigning costs to activity cost centres

After the activities have been identified the cost of resources consumed over a specified period must be assigned to each activity. The aim is to determine how much the organization is spending on each of its activities. Many of the resources will be directly attributable to specific activity centres but others (such as labour, and lighting and heating costs) may be indirect and jointly shared by several activities. These costs should be assigned to activities on the basis of cause-and-effect cost drivers. Employee surveys are frequently used to estimate the amount of time they spend on different activities in order to assign costs to activities. In large organizations this process can be very time-consuming and expensive and has deterred many organizations from adopting ABC. Arbitrary allocations should be minimized. The greater the amount of costs traced to activity centres by cost apportionments at this stage, the more arbitrary and less reliable will be the product cost information generated by ABC systems. Cause-and-effect cost drivers used at this stage to allocate shared resources to individual activities are called **resource cost drivers**.

Step 3: Selecting appropriate cost drivers for assigning the cost of activities to cost objects

In order to assign the costs attached to each activity cost centre to products, a cost driver must be selected for each activity centre. Cost drivers used at this stage are called **activity cost drivers**. Several factors must be borne in mind when selecting a suitable cost driver. First, it should provide a good explanation of costs in each activity cost centre. Second, a cost driver should be easily measurable, the data should be relatively easy to obtain and be identifiable with products. The costs of measurement must therefore be taken into account.

Activity cost drivers consist of transaction and duration drivers. **Transaction drivers**, such as the number of purchase orders processed, number of customer orders processed, number of inspections performed and the number of set-ups undertaken, all count the number of times an activity is performed. Transaction drivers are the least expensive type of cost driver to measure, but they are also likely to be the least accurate because they assume that the same quantity of resources is required every time an activity is performed. However, if the variation in the amount of resources required by individual cost objects is not great, transaction drivers will provide a reasonably accurate measurement of activity resources consumed. If this condition does not apply then duration cost drivers should be used.

Duration drivers represent the amount of time required to perform an activity. Examples of duration drivers include set-up hours and inspection hours. For example, if one product requires a short set-up time and another requires a long time then using set-up hours as the cost driver will more accurately measure activity resource consumption than the transaction driver (number of set-ups) which assumes that an equal amount of activity resources are consumed by both products. Using the number of set-ups will result in the product that requires a long set-up time being undercosted whereas the product that requires a short set-up will be overcosted. This problem can be overcome by using set-up hours as the cost driver, but this will increase the measurement costs.

Step 4: Assigning the cost of the activities to products

The final step involves applying the cost driver rates to products. This means that the cost driver must be measurable in a way that enables it to be identified with individual products. Thus, if set-up hours are selected as a cost driver, there must be a mechanism for measuring the set-up hours consumed by each product. Alternatively, if the number of set-ups is selected as the cost driver, measurements by products are not required since all products that require a set-up are charged with a constant set-up cost. The ease and cost of obtaining data on cost driver consumption by products is therefore a factor that must be considered during the third step when an appropriate cost driver is being selected.

ACTIVITY HIERARCHIES

Manufacturing activities can be classified along a cost hierarchy dimension consisting of:

1 unit-level activities
2 batch-level related activities
3 product-sustaining activities
4 facility sustaining activities.

Unit-level activities (also known as volume-related activities) are performed each time a unit of the product or service is produced. Expenses in this category include direct labour, direct materials, energy costs and expenses that are consumed in proportion to machine processing time (such as maintenance). Unit-level activities consume resources in proportion to the number of units of production and sales volume. For example, if a firm produces 10 per cent more units it will consume 10 per cent more labour cost, 10 per cent more machine hours and 10 per cent more energy costs. Typical cost drivers for unit-level activities include labour hours, machine hours and the quantity of materials processed. These cost drivers are also used by traditional costing systems. Traditional systems are therefore also appropriate for assigning the costs of unit-level activities to cost objects.

Batch-related activities, such as setting up a machine or processing a purchase order, are performed each time a batch of goods is produced. The cost of batch-related activities varies with the number of batches made, but is common (or fixed) for all units within the batch. For example, set-up resources are consumed when a machine is changed from one product to another. As more batches are produced, more set-up resources are consumed. It costs the same to set up a machine for 10 or 5000 items. Thus the demands for the set-up resources are not determined by the number of units produced after completing the set-up. Similarly, purchasing resources are consumed each time a purchasing order is processed, but the resources consumed are not determined by the number of units included in the purchase order. Other examples of batch-related costs include resources devoted to production scheduling, first-item inspection and materials movement. Traditional costing systems treat batch-related expenses as fixed costs, whereas ABC systems assume that batch-related expenses vary with the number of batches processed.

Product sustaining activities or **service sustaining activities** are performed to enable the production and sale of individual products (or services). Examples of product sustaining activities include maintaining and updating product specifications and the technical support provided for individual products and services. Other examples

REAL WORLD VIEWS 8.2

Activity-based costing in a regional bank

Austill and Kocakülâh (2017) illustrate how ABC can be effectively used in measuring the profitability of commercial lending operations in a USA regional bank. Compared with the traditional costing method that had been used, the ABC analysis indicated that the bank had been underpricing its commercial loans, and that commercial lending operations were not as profitable as management had been led to believe. The authors concluded that with the traditional costing system operating units generating revenue, such as mortgage lending and consumer lending, were being unfairly allocated higher indirect costs whereas commercial lending activities have been allocated fewer indirect costs. Switching to ABC could re-evaluate those activities necessary for its commercial lending operations, as well as other activities in its operations, and reduce costs by eliminating activities that do not add value. By more accurately knowing its costs of operations in commercial lending, the bank was in a position to make better management decisions in pricing,

promotional strategy and managing its employees in commercial lending operations.

Questions

1 An ABC system requires that the major activities and cost drivers are identified. Provide examples of a bank's activities and cost drivers.
2 What action should an organization take when the ABC analysis identifies loss-making activities?

Reference

M.A., Austill, A.D., and Kocakülâh, M.C. (2017), *Cost Management*, September/October, 19-31

---

are the resources to prepare and implement engineering change notices (ECNs), to design processes and test routines for individual products, and to perform product enhancements. The costs of product sustaining activities are incurred irrespective of the number of units of output or the number of batches processed and their expenses will tend to increase as the number of products manufactured is increased. ABC uses product-level bases such as number of active part numbers and number of ECNs to assign these costs to products. Where customers are the cost objects with the equivalent term for product sustaining is **customer sustaining activities**. Customer market research and support for an individual customer, or groups of customers if they represent the cost object, are examples of customer sustaining activities.

The final activity category is **facility sustaining** (or **business-sustaining**) **activities**. They are performed to support the facility's general manufacturing process and include general administrative staff, plant management and property costs. They are incurred to support the organization as a whole and are common and joint to all products manufactured in the plant. There would have to be a dramatic change in activity, resulting in an expansion or contraction in the size of the plant, for facility sustaining costs to change. Such events are most unlikely in most organizations. Therefore, these costs should not be assigned to products since they are unavoidable and irrelevant for most decisions. Instead, they are regarded as common costs to *all* products made in the plant and deducted as a lump sum from the total of the operating margins from *all* products.

COST VERSUS BENEFIT CONSIDERATIONS

In the previous chapter it was pointed out that the design of a cost system should be based on cost versus benefit considerations. A sophisticated ABC system should generate the most accurate product costs. Implementing and operating an ABC system is significantly more expensive than operating a direct costing or a traditional costing system. In particular, the training and software requirements may prohibit its adoption by small organizations. However, the partial costs reported by direct costing systems,

REAL WORLD VIEWS 8.3

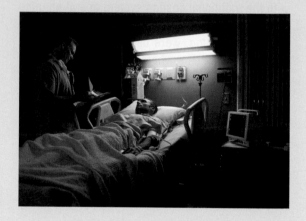

ABC in health care

The remuneration system that is applied in health care organizations in several countries (e.g. Australia, the USA, Switzerland, Spain and Italy) enables ABC profitability analysis to be applied in hospitals. These countries apply the Diagnosis Related Groups (DRGs) reimbursement system to fund hospital activities. With this system, diagnoses requiring similar treatments are assumed to require similar resources resulting in reimbursement at a standard unit price by the National Health System for the health care services. Diagnostic-Therapeutic Pathways (DTPs) identify all the services needed to diagnose and treat a specific disease from the first access of the patient into the health care system and are made comparable with the DRG.

Cannavacciuolo *et al.* (2015) report on how ABC was used in an Italian hospital to determine the amount of resources used by each activity included in the DTP and thus develop a DTP cost. The DTP cost was derived from the sum of activity cost pools needed to perform a DTP. Thus it is possible to determine the profitability of each DTP by comparing its cost with the DRG tariff. Where the DTP cost exceeded the DRG tariff activities are examined with a view to performing them more efficiently. ABC also enabled the most cost-consuming activities to be identified. The

determination of the cost of each activity of a DTP also provided the potential to compare the costs of DTPs with those in other hospitals and thus highlight potential for carrying out the activities more effectively and efficiently.

Questions

1. In some countries revenues may be received in a lump sum and are not assignable to individual diagnosis related groups. What role can ABC play in such organizations?
2. Do you think many business organizations utilize ABC techniques? Why or why not?

Reference

Cannavacciuolo, L., Illario, M., Ippolito, A. and Ponsiglione, C. (2015) An activity-based costing approach for detecting inefficiencies of healthcare processes, *Business Process Management Journal*, 21(1), 55–79. Available at dx.doi.org/10.1108/BPMJ-11-2013-0144

and the distorted costs reported by traditional (unsophisticated) systems, may result in significant mistakes in decisions (such as selling unprofitable products or dropping profitable products) arising from the use of this information. If the cost of errors arising from using partial or distorted information generated from using these systems exceeds the additional costs of implementing and operating an ABC system then an ABC (sophisticated) system ought to be implemented.

The optimal costing system is different for different organizations. A simplistic traditional costing system may report reasonably accurate product costs in organizations that have the following characteristics:

1 low levels of competition

2 non-volume-related indirect costs that are a low proportion of total indirect costs

3 a fairly standardized product range all consuming organizational resources in similar proportions (i.e. low product diversity).

In contrast, a sophisticated (ABC) system may be optimal for organizations having the following characteristics:

1 intensive competition

2 non-volume-related indirect costs that are a high proportion of total indirect costs

3 a diverse range of products, all consuming organizational resources in significantly different proportions (i.e. high product diversity).

ABC COST MANAGEMENT APPLICATIONS

Our aim in this chapter has been to look at how ABC can be used to provide information for decision-making by more accurately assigning costs to cost objects, such as products, customers and locations. In addition, ABC can be used for a range of strategic cost management applications. They include cost reduction, activity-based budgeting, performance measurement, benchmarking of activities and business process re-engineering.

The decision to implement ABC should not, therefore, be based only on its ability to produce more accurate and relevant decision-making information. A survey by Innes *et al.* (2000) on ABC applications reported that the strategic cost management applications tend to outweigh the product costing applications that were central to ABC's initial development. We shall examine ABC applications to cost management in Chapter 15.

SUMMARY

The following items relate to the learning objectives listed at the beginning of the chapter.

● **Describe the differences between activity-based and traditional costing systems**. The major differences relate to the two-stage allocation process. In the first stage, traditional systems allocate indirect costs to cost centres (normally departments) whereas activity-based systems allocate indirect costs to cost centres based on activities rather than departments. Since there are many more activities than departments a distinguishing feature is that activity-based systems will have a greater number of cost centres in the first stage of the allocation process. In the second stage, traditional systems use a limited number of different types of second-stage volume-based allocation bases (cost drivers) whereas activity-based systems use many different types of volume-based and non-volume-based cause-and-effect second-stage drivers.

● **Explain why traditional costing systems can provide misleading information for decision-making**. Traditional systems often tend to rely on arbitrary allocations of indirect costs. In particular, they rely extensively on volume-based allocations. Many indirect costs are not volume-based but, if volume-based allocation bases are used, high-volume products are likely to be assigned with a greater proportion of indirect costs than they have consumed whereas low-volume products will be assigned a lower proportion. In these circumstances traditional systems will overcost high-volume products and undercost low-volume products. In contrast, ABC systems recognize that many indirect costs vary in proportion to changes other than production volume. By identifying the cost drivers that cause the costs to change and assigning costs to cost objects on the basis of cost driver usage, costs can be more accurately traced. It is claimed that this cause-and-effect relationship provides a superior way of determining relevant costs.

● **Compute product costs using an activity-based costing system**. The computation of product costs was illustrated in Exhibit 8.3 using data derived from Example 7.1 in the previous chapter.

● **Identify and explain each of the four stages involved in designing ABC systems**. The design of ABC systems involves the following four stages: (a) identify the major activities that take place in the organization; (b) create a cost centre/cost pool for each activity; (c) determine the cost driver for each major activity; and (d) trace the cost of activities to the product according to a product's demand (using cost drivers as a measure of demand) for activities.

● **Describe the ABC cost hierarchy**. ABC systems classify activities along a cost hierarchy consisting of unit-level, batch-level, product sustaining and facility sustaining activities. Unit-level activities are performed each time a unit of the product or service is produced. Examples include direct labour and energy costs. Batch-level activities are performed each time a batch is produced. Examples include setting up a machine or processing a purchase order. Product sustaining activities are performed to enable the production and sale of individual products. Examples include the technical support provided for individual products and the resources required performing product enhancements. Facility sustaining activities are performed to support the facility's general manufacturing process. They include general administrative staff and property support costs.

KEY TERMS AND CONCEPTS

Activities   The aggregation of many different tasks, events or units of work that cause the consumption of resources.

Activity cost centres   Cost centres in which costs are accumulated by activities.

Activity cost drivers   A cost driver used to assign the costs assigned to an activity cost centre to products.

Batch-related activities   Activities that are performed each time a batch of goods is produced.

Business-sustaining activities   Activities performed to support the organization as a whole, also known as facility-sustaining activities.

Consumption ratio   The proportion of each activity consumed by a product.

Cost driver   The basis used to allocate costs to cost objects in an ABC system. It is also a measure that exerts a major influence on the cost of a particular activity.

Customer-sustaining activities   Activities that are performed to support the relationship with customers.

Duration drivers   A cost driver used to assign the costs assigned to an activity cost centre to products that is based on the amount of time required to perform an activity.

Facility-sustaining activities   Activities performed to support the organization as a whole, which are normally not affected by a decision that is to be taken. Also known as business-sustaining activities.

Non-volume-based cost drivers   A method of allocating indirect costs to cost objects that uses alternative measures instead of assuming that a product's consumption of overhead resources is directly related to the number of units produced.

Product-sustaining activities   Support activities that are performed to enable the production and sale of individual products and which are not related to the volume of each product.

Resource cost driver   A cause-and-effect cost driver used to allocate shared resources to individual activities.

Service-sustaining activities   Support activities that are performed to enable the production and sale of individual services and which are not related to the volume of each service provided.

Transaction drivers   A cost driver used to assign the costs assigned to an activity cost centre to products that is based on the number of times an activity is performed.

Unit-level activities   Activities that are performed each time a unit of the product or service is produced.

Volume-based cost drivers   A method of allocating indirect costs to cost objects that correlates a product's consumption of overhead resources with the number of units produced.

ASSESSMENT MATERIAL

The review questions are short questions that enable you to assess your understanding of the main topics included in the chapter. The page numbers in parentheses provide you with the page numbers to refer to if you cannot answer a specific question.

The review problems are more complex and require you to relate and apply the content to various business problems. Solutions to review problems are provided in a separate section at the end of the book. Additional review problems can be accessed by lecturers and students on the dedicated online support resources for this book. Solutions to these review problems are provided for lecturers in the *Instructor's Manual* accompanying this book that can be downloaded from the dedicated online instructor's resources (see Preface for details).

The dedicated online digital support resources for this book also includes over 30 case study problems.

REVIEW QUESTIONS

8.1 What are the fundamental differences between a traditional and an ABC system? *(pp. 189–194)*

8.2 Define activities and cost drivers. *(pp. 189–190)*

8.3 What factors led to the emergence of ABC systems? *(p. 188)*

8.4 Distinguish between volume-based and non-volume-based cost drivers. *(pp. 191–194)*

8.5 Describe the circumstances when traditional costing systems are likely to report distorted costs. *(pp. 193–194)*

8.6 Explain how low-volume products can be undercosted and high-volume products overcosted when traditional costing systems are used. *(pp. 192–194)*

8.7 What is meant by 'product diversity' and why is it important for product costing? *(p. 192)*

8.8 Describe each of the four stages involved in designing ABC systems. *(pp. 200–202)*

8.9 Distinguish between resource cost drivers and activity cost drivers. *(p. 201)*

8.10 Distinguish between transaction and duration cost drivers. *(p. 201)*

8.11 Describe the ABC manufacturing cost hierarchy. *(pp. 202–204)*

8.12 Explain the circumstances when ABC is likely to be preferred to traditional costing systems. *(pp. 204–205)*

REVIEW PROBLEMS

8.13 Calculation of gross profit using ABC. MS manufactures three types of skincare product for sale to retailers. MS currently operates a standard absorption costing system. Budgeted information for next year is given below:

Products	Anti-ageing cream ($000)	Facial masks ($000)	Collagen fillers ($000)	Total ($000)
Sales	60 000	38 000	22 000	120 000
Direct material	11 800	6 200	4 000	22 000
Direct labour	3 700	2 400	1 900	8 000
Fixed production overheads				15 400
Gross profit				74 600

	Anti-ageing cream	Facial masks	Collagen fillers
Production and sales (units)	1 000 000	1 200 000	600 000

Fixed production overheads are absorbed using a direct material cost percentage rate.

The management accountant of MS is proposing changing to an activity-based costing system. The main activities and their associated cost drivers and overhead cost have been identified as follows:

Activity	Cost driver	Production overhead cost ($000)
Machine set up	Number of set ups	3 600
Quality inspection	Number of quality inspections	1 200
Processing	Processing time	6 500
Purchasing	Number of purchase orders	1 800
Packaging	Number of units of product	2 300
		15 400

Further details have been ascertained as follows:

	Anti-ageing cream	Facial masks	Collagen fillers
Batch size (units)	1 000	2 000	1 500
Machine set-ups per batch	3	3	4
Purchase orders per batch	2	2	1
Processing time per unit (minutes)	2	3	4
Quality inspections per batch	1	1	1

Required:

Calculate for each product:

(i) the total fixed production overhead costs using the current absorption costing system;

(2 marks)

(ii) the total gross profit using the proposed activity-based costing system.

(13 marks)

8.14 Calculation of ABC product cost and discussion as to whether ABC should be implemented. Beckley Hill (BH) is a private hospital carrying out two types of procedures on patients. Each type of procedure incurs the following direct costs:

Procedure	A ($)	B ($)
Surgical time and materials	1 200	2 640
Anaesthesia time and materials	800	1 620

BH currently calculates the overhead cost per procedure by taking the total overhead cost and simply dividing it by the number of procedures, then rounding the cost to the nearest two decimal places. Using this method, the total cost is $2 475.85 for Procedure A and $4 735.85 for Procedure B.

Recently, another local hospital has implemented activity-based costing (ABC). This has led the finance director at BH to consider whether this alternative costing technique would bring any benefits to BH. He has obtained an analysis of BH's total overheads for the last year and some additional data, all of which is shown below:

Cost	Cost driver	($)
Administrative costs	Administrative time per procedure	1 870 160
Nursing costs	Length of patient stay	6 215 616
Catering costs	Number of meals	966 976
General facility costs	Length of patient stay	8 553 600
Total overhead costs		17 606 352

Procedure	A	B
No. of procedures	14 600	22 400
Administrative time per procedure (hours)	1	1.5
Length of patient stay per procedure (hours)	24	48
Average no. of meals required per patient	1	4

Required:

(a) Calculate the full cost per procedure using activity-based costing.

(6 marks)

(b) Making reference to your findings in part (a), advise the finance director as to whether activity-based costing should be implemented at BH.

(4 marks)

8.15 Preparation of conventional costing and ABC profit statements

The following budgeted information relates to Brunti Inc. for the forthcoming period:

	XYI (000)	YZT (000)	ABW (000)
Sales and production (units)	50	40	30
	($)	($)	($)
Selling price (per unit)	45	95	73
Prime cost (per unit)	32	84	65
	Hours	Hours	Hours
Machine department (machine hours per unit)	2	5	4
Assembly department (direct labour hours per unit)	7	3	2

Overheads allocated and apportioned to production departments (including service cost centre costs) were to be recovered in product costs as follows:

Machine department at $1.20 per machine hour
Assembly department at $0.825 per direct labour hour

You ascertain that the above overheads could be reanalyzed into 'cost pools' as follows:

Cost pool	$000	Cost driver	Quantity for the period
Machining services	357	Machine hours	420 000
Assembly services	318	Direct labour hours	530 000
Set-up costs	26	Set-ups	520
Order processing	156	Customer orders	32 000
Purchasing	84	Suppliers' orders	11 200
	941		

You have also been provided with the following estimates for the period:

	XYI	YZT	ABW
Number of set-ups	120	200	200
Customer orders	8 000	8 000	16 000
Suppliers' orders	3 000	4 000	4 200

Required:

(a) Prepare and present profit statements using:
(i) conventional absorption costing

(5 marks)

(ii) activity-based costing

(10 marks)

(b) Comment on why activity-based costing is considered to present a fairer valuation of the product cost per unit.

(5 marks)
(Total 20 marks)

8.16 Calculation of traditional and ABC product costs and a discussion of their impact on selling prices and sales volume.

Duff Co manufactures three products, X, Y and Z. Demand for products X and Y is relatively elastic whilst demand for product Z is relatively inelastic. Each product uses the same materials and the same type of direct labour but in different quantities. For many years, the company has been using full absorption costing and absorbing overheads on the basis of direct labour hours. Selling prices are then determined using cost plus pricing. This is common within this industry, with most competitors applying a standard mark-up.

Budgeted production and sales volumes for X, Y and Z for the next year are 20 000 units, 16 000 units and 22 000 units respectively.

The budgeted direct costs of the three products are shown below:

Product	X $ per unit	Y $ per unit	Z $ per unit
Direct materials	25	28	22
Direct labour ($12 per hour)	30	36	24

In the next year, Duff Co also expects to incur indirect production costs of $1 377 400, which are analysed as follows:

Cost pools	$	Cost drivers
Machine set up costs	280 000	Number of batches
Material ordering costs	316 000	Number of purchase orders
Machine running costs	420 000	Number of machine hours
General facility costs	361 400	Number of machine hours
	1 377 400	

The following additional data relate to each product:

Product	X	Y	Z
Batch size (units)	500	800	400
No of purchase orders per batch	4	5	4
Machine hours per unit	1.5	1.25	1.4

Duff Co wants to boost sales revenue in order to increase profits but its capacity to do this is limited because of its use of cost plus pricing and the application of the standard mark-up. The finance director has suggested using activity-based costing (ABC) instead of full absorption costing, since this will alter the cost of the products and may therefore enable a different price to be charged.

Required:

(a) Calculate the budgeted full production cost per unit of each product using Duff Co's current method of absorption costing. All workings should be to two decimal places.

(3 marks)

(b) Calculate the budgeted full production cost per unit of each product using activity-based costing. All workings should be to two decimal places.

(11 marks)

(c) Discuss the impact on the selling prices and the sales volumes OF EACH PRODUCT which a change to activity based costing would be expected to bring about.

(6 marks)

8.17 Traditional and ABC profitability analysis comparisons.
FG specializes in the manufacture of tablets, laptops and desktop PCs. FG currently operates a standard absorption costing system. Budgeted information for next year is given below:

Products	Tablets $000	Laptops $000	Desktop PCs $000	Total $000
Sales revenue	3 640	12 480	9 880	26 000
Direct material	800	2 800	2 200	5 800
Direct labour	300	1 200	800	2 300
Fixed production overheads	1 456	4 992	3 952	10 400
Gross profit	1 084	3 488	2 928	7 500

Fixed production overheads are currently absorbed based on a percentage of sales revenue.

FG is considering changing to an activity-based costing system. The main activities and their associated cost drivers and overhead cost have been identified as follows:

Activity	Cost driver	Production overhead cost $000
Manufacturing scheduling	Number of orders	162
Parts handling	Number of parts	2 464
Assembly	Assembly time	4 472
Software installation and testing	Number of software applications	2 000
Packaging	Number of units	1 302
		10 400

Further details have also been ascertained as follows:

	Tablets	Laptops	Desktop PCs
Budgeted production for next year (units)	10 000	12 000	6 000
Average number of units per order	10	6	4
Number of parts per unit	20	35	25
Assembly time per unit (minutes)	20	40	30
Number of software applications per unit	2	3	4

Required:

(a) Calculate the total gross profit for each product using the proposed activity-based costing system.

(13 marks)

(b) Discuss the differences between the gross profit figures calculated in part (a) compared with those calculated under the current absorption costing system.

(8 marks)

(c) Explain how the information obtained from the activity-based costing system could be used for cost management purposes.

(4 marks)

8.18 Hierarchical profitability analysis
WTL manufactures and sells four products: W, X, Y and Z from a single factory. Each of the products is manufactured in batches of 100 units using a just-in-time manufacturing process and consequently there is no inventory of any product. This batch size of 100 units cannot be altered without significant cost implications. Although the products are manufactured in batches of 100 units, they are sold as single units at the market price. WTL has a significant number of competitors and is forced to accept the market price for each of its products. It is currently reviewing the profit it makes from each product, and for the business as a whole, and has produced the following statement for the latest period:

Product	W	X	Y	Z	Total
Number of units sold	100 000	130 000	80 000	150 000	
Machine hours	200 000	195 000	80 000	300 000	775 000
Direct labour hours	50 000	130 000	80 000	75 000	335 000
	$	$	$	$	$
Sales	1 300 000	2 260 000	2 120 000	1 600 000	7 280 000
Direct materials	300 000	910 000	940 000	500 000	2 650 000
Direct labour	400 000	1 040 000	640 000	600 000	2 680 000
Overhead costs	400 000	390 000	160 000	600 000	1 550 000
Profit/(loss)	200 000	(80 000)	380 000	(100 000)	400 000

WTL is concerned that two of its products are loss making and has carried out an analysis of its products and costs. This analysis shows:

1 The sales of each product are completely independent of each other.
2 The overhead costs have been absorbed into the above product costs using an absorption rate of $2 per machine hour.
3 Further analysis of the overhead cost shows that some of it is caused by the number of machine hours used, some is caused by the number of batches produced and some of the costs are product specific fixed overheads that would be avoided if the product were discontinued. Other general fixed overhead costs would be avoided only by the closure of the factory. Details of this analysis are as follows:

Required:

(a) Prepare a columnar statement that is more useful for decision-making than the profit statement prepared by WTL. Your statement should also show the current total profit for the business.
(8 marks)

(b) Prepare a report to the Board of WTL that:
  (i) Explains why your statement is suitable for decision-making
  (4 marks)

  (ii) Advises WTL which, if any, of its four products should be discontinued in order to maximize its company profits.
  (4 marks)

(c) Calculate the break-even volume (in batches) for Product W.
4 marks)

(d) Explain how WTL could use value analysis to improve its profits.
(5 marks)

8.19 Large service organizations, such as banks and hospitals, used to be noted for their lack of standard costing systems, and their relatively unsophisticated budgeting and control systems compared with large manufacturing organizations. But this is changing and many large service organizations are now revising their use of management accounting techniques.

Required:

(a) Explain which features of large-scale service organizations encourage the application of activity-based approaches to the analysis of cost information.
(6 marks)

(b) Explain which features of service organizations may create problems for the application of activity-based costing.
(4 marks)

(c) Explain the uses for activity-based cost information in service industries.
(4 marks)

(d) Many large service organizations were at one time state-owned, but have been privatized. Examples in some countries include electricity supply and telecommunications. They are often regulated. Similar systems of regulation of prices by an independent authority exist in many countries, and are designed to act as a surrogate for market competition in industries where it is difficult to ensure a genuinely competitive market.

Explain which aspects of cost information and systems in service organizations would particularly interest a regulator, and why these features would be of interest.
(6 marks)
(Total 20 marks)

PART FOUR

INFORMATION FOR PLANNING, CONTROL AND PERFORMANCE MEASUREMENT

The objective in Part Four is to consider the implementation of decisions through the planning and control process. Planning involves systematically looking at the future so that decisions can be made today that will bring the company its desired results. Control can be defined as the process of measuring and correcting actual performance to ensure that plans for implementing the chosen course of action are carried out.

Part Four contains five chapters. Chapter 9 considers the role of budgeting within the planning process and the relationship between the long-range plan and the budgeting process. Chapters 10 and 11 are concerned with the control process. To fully understand the role that management accounting control systems play in the control process, it is necessary to be aware of how they relate to the entire array of control mechanisms used by organizations. Chapter 10 describes the different types of controls that are used by companies. The elements of management accounting control systems are described within the context of the overall control process. Chapter 11 focuses on the technical aspects of accounting control systems. It describes the major features of a standard costing system: a system that enables the differences between planned and actual outcomes to be analysed in detail. Chapter 11 also describes the operation of a standard costing system and explains the procedure for calculating variances.

Chapters 9–11 focus on management accounting control systems within cost centres at lower management levels within an organization rather than at the business unit level. Chapter 12 considers financial performance measurement at higher organization levels relating to divisionalized business units. Our focus in this chapter is on financial measures of divisional performance, but you should note at this point that financial measures alone cannot adequately measure all those factors that are critical to the success of a division. Emphasis should also be given to reporting key non-financial measures relating to such areas as competitiveness, quality, delivery performance, innovation and flexibility to respond to changes in demand. In particular, a range of financial and non-financial performance measures should be developed that support the objectives and strategies of the organization. We shall examine these aspects in Chapter 14 where our focus will be on strategic performance management.

A major feature of divisionalized companies is that they engage in inter-divisional trading of goods and services involving financial transactions with each other, which creates the need to establish transfer prices. The established transfer price is a cost to the receiving division and revenue to the supplying division, which means that whatever transfer price is set will affect the divisional financial performance measures. Chapter 13 focuses on the transfer pricing problem and examines how transfer prices can be established that will motivate managers to make optimal decisions and also ensure that the performance measures derived from using transfer prices represent a fair reflection of managerial performance.

9
THE BUDGETING PROCESS

LEARNING OBJECTIVES After studying this chapter you should be able to:

● explain how budgeting fits into the overall strategic planning and control framework

● identify and describe the six different purposes of budgeting

● identify and describe the various stages in the budget process

● prepare functional and master budgets

● describe the limitations of incremental budgeting

● describe activity-based budgeting (ABB)

● describe zero-based budgeting (ZBB)

● describe the criticisms relating to traditional budgeting.

In the previous chapters we have considered how management accounting can assist managers in making decisions. The actions that follow managerial decisions normally involve several aspects of the business, such as the marketing, production, purchasing and finance functions, and it is important that management should coordinate these various interrelated aspects of decision-making. If they fail to do this, there is a danger that managers may individually make decisions that they believe are in the best interests of the organization when, in fact, taken together they are not; for example, the marketing department may introduce a promotional campaign that is designed to increase sales demand to a level beyond that which the production department can handle. The various activities within a company should be coordinated by the preparation of plans of actions for future periods. These detailed plans are usually referred to as **budgets**. Our objective in this chapter is to examine the planning process within a business organization and to consider the role of budgeting within this process.

THE STRATEGIC PLANNING, BUDGETING AND CONTROL PROCESS

To help you understand the budgetary process we shall begin by looking at how it fits into an overall general framework of planning and control. The framework outlined in Figure 9.1 provides an overview of an organization's planning and control process. The first stage involves establishing the objectives and supporting strategies of the organization within the strategic planning process.

Strategic planning process

Before the budgeting process begins an organization should have prepared a **long-term plan** (also known as a **strategic plan**). Strategic planning begins with the specification of an organization's vision, mission and objectives towards which future operations should be directed. The vision and mission of an organization are normally specified in short statements that consist of a few sentences (see Exhibit 9.1 for an illustration). A **vision statement** clarifies the beliefs and governing principles of an organization, what it wants to be in the future or how it wants the world in which it operates to be. In contrast, a **mission statement** is more action oriented. It includes a description in very general terms of what the organization does to achieve its vision, its broad purpose and reason for its existence, the nature of the business(es) it is in and the customers it seeks to serve and satisfy. Both vision and mission statements are a visionary projection of the central and overriding concepts on which the organization is based.

   Corporate objectives relate to the organization as a whole. Objectives tend to be more specific, and represent desired states or results to be achieved. They are normally measurable and are expressed in financial terms such as desired profits or sales levels, return on capital employed, rates of growth or market share. Objectives must also be developed for the different parts of an organization. **Unit objectives** relate to the specific objectives of individual business units within the organization, such as a division or one company within a holding company. Corporate objectives are normally set for the organization as a whole and are then translated into unit objectives, which become the targets for the individual units. It is important that senior managers in an organization understand clearly where their company is going, and why and how their own role contributes to the attainment of corporate objectives. The strategic planning process should also specify how the objectives of the organization will be achieved.

Creation of long-term plan

The term **strategy** is used to describe the courses of action that need to be taken to achieve the objectives set. When management has identified those strategic options that have the greatest potential for achieving the company's objectives, long-term plans should be created to implement the strategies. A long-term plan is a statement of the preliminary targets and activities required by an organization to achieve its strategic plan together with a broad estimate for each year of the resources required and revenues expected. Because long-term planning involves 'looking into the future' for several years ahead (typically at least 5 years) the plans tend to be uncertain, general in nature, imprecise and subject to change.

Preparation of the annual budget within the context of the long-term plan

Budgeting is concerned with the implementation of the long-term plan for the year ahead. Because of the shorter planning horizon, budgets are more precise and detailed. Budgets are a clear indication of what is expected to be achieved during the budget period whereas long-term plans represent the broad directions that top management intend to follow.

   The budget is not something that originates 'from nothing' each year – it is developed within the context of ongoing business and is ruled by previous decisions that have

EXHIBIT 9.1   Vision and mission statements for Singapore Airlines

Singapore Airlines vision statement

Singapore Airlines has a responsibility not only to be an excellent company, but also to be an excellent citizen of the world by enhancing the lives of the people we touch. With that aim in mind, we have made many commitments to the arts and education, to our communities, and the health and welfare of our country's citizens, and those in countries we fly to. With this goal in mind, we've also made a strong commitment to preserving the environment – and our world for future generations.

Singapore Airlines mission statement

Singapore Airlines is a global company dedicated to providing air transportation services of the highest quality and to maximizing returns for the benefit of its shareholders and employees.

been taken within the long-term planning process. When the activities are initially approved for inclusion in the long-term plan, they are based on uncertain estimates that are projected for several years. These proposals must be reviewed and revised in the light of more recent information. This review and revision process frequently takes place as part of the annual budgeting process, and it may result in important decisions being taken on possible activity adjustments within the current budget period. The budgeting process cannot therefore be viewed as being purely concerned with the current year – it must be considered as an integrated part of the long-term planning process.

Monitor actual outcomes and respond to deviations from planned outcomes

The final stages in the strategic planning, budgeting and control process outlined in Figure 9.1 are to compare the actual and the planned outcomes, and to respond to any deviations from the plan. These stages represent the **budgetary control process** of budgeting. Planning and control are closely linked. Planning involves looking ahead to determine the actions required to achieve the objectives of the organization. Control involves looking back to ascertain what actually happened and comparing it with the planned outcomes. Effective control requires that corrective action is taken so that actual outcomes conform to planned outcomes. Alternatively, the plans may require modification if the comparisons indicate that the plans are no longer attainable. The corrective action is indicated by the arrowed lines in Figure 9.1 linking stages 5 and 2 and 5 and 3. These arrowed lines represent **feedback loops**. They signify that the process is dynamic and stress the inter-dependencies between the various stages in the process. The feedback loops between the stages indicate that the plans should be regularly reviewed, and if they are no longer attainable then alternative courses of action must be considered for achieving the organization's objectives. The loop between stages 5 and 3 also stresses the corrective action that may be taken so that actual outcomes conform to planned outcomes.

A detailed discussion of the control process will be deferred until the next chapter. We shall now consider the short-term budgeting process in more detail.

FIGURE 9.1

Strategic planning, budgeting and control process

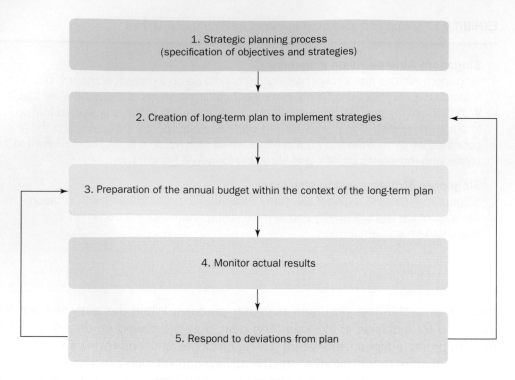

1. Strategic planning process (specification of objectives and strategies)

2. Creation of long-term plan to implement strategies

3. Preparation of the annual budget within the context of the long-term plan

4. Monitor actual results

5. Respond to deviations from plan

THE MULTIPLE FUNCTIONS OF BUDGETS

Budgets serve a number of useful purposes. They include:

1 *planning* annual operations
2 *coordinating* the activities of the various parts of the organization and ensuring that the parts are in harmony with each other
3 *communicating* plans to the various responsibility centre managers
4 *motivating* managers to strive to achieve the organizational goals
5 *controlling* activities
6 *evaluating* the performance of managers.

Let us now examine each of these six factors.

Planning

The major planning decisions will already have been made as part of the long-term planning process. However, the annual budgeting process leads to the refinement of those plans, since managers must produce detailed plans for the implementation of the long-range plan. Without the annual budgeting process, the pressures of day-to-day operating problems may tempt managers not to plan for future operations. The budgeting process ensures that managers do plan for future operations, and that they consider how conditions in the next year might change and what steps they should take now to respond to these changed conditions. This process encourages managers to anticipate problems before they arise, and to respond to changing conditions with reasoned judgement, instead of making hasty decisions that are based on expediency.

Coordinating

The budget serves as a vehicle through which the actions of the different parts of an organization can be brought together and reconciled into a common plan. Without any guidance, managers may each make their own decisions, believing that they are working in the best interests of the organization. For example, the purchasing manager may prefer to place large orders so as to obtain large discounts; the production manager will be concerned with avoiding high inventory levels; and the accountant will be concerned with the impact of the decision on the cash resources of the business. It is the aim of budgeting to reconcile these differences for the good of the organization as a whole, rather than for the benefit of any individual area. Budgeting therefore compels managers to examine the relationship between their own operations and those of other departments, and, in the process, to identify and resolve conflicts.

Communicating

If an organization is to function effectively, there must be definite lines of communication so that all the parts will be kept fully informed of the plans and the policies, and constraints, to which the organization is expected to conform. Everyone in the organization should have a clear understanding of the part they are expected to play in achieving the annual budget. This process will ensure that the appropriate individuals are made accountable for implementing the budget. Through the budget, top management communicates its expectations to lower level management, so that all members of the organization may understand these expectations and can coordinate their activities to attain them. It is not just the budget itself that facilitates communication – much vital information is communicated in the actual act of preparing it.

Motivating

The budget can be a useful device for influencing managerial behaviour and motivating managers to perform in line with the organizational objectives. A budget provides a standard that, under the right circumstances, a manager will be motivated to strive to achieve. However, budgets can also encourage inefficiency and conflict between managers. If individuals have actively participated in preparing the budget, and it is used as a tool to assist managers in managing their departments, it can act as a strong motivational device by providing a challenge. However, if the budget is dictated from above, and imposes a threat rather than a challenge, it may be resisted and do more harm than good. We shall discuss the dysfunctional motivational consequences of budgets in the next chapter.

Controlling

A budget assists managers in managing and controlling the activities for which they are responsible. By comparing the actual results with the budgeted amounts for different categories of expenses, managers can identify costs that do not conform to the original plan and thus require their attention. This process enables management to operate a system of **management by exception**, which means that a manager's attention and effort can be concentrated on significant deviations from the expected results. By investigating the reasons for the deviations, managers may be able to identify inefficiencies such as the purchase of inferior quality materials. When the reasons for the inefficiencies have been found, appropriate control action should be taken to remedy the situation.

Evaluating performance

A manager's performance is often evaluated by measuring his or her success in meeting the budgets. In some companies bonuses are awarded on the basis of an employee's ability to achieve the targets specified in the periodic budgets, or promotion may be partly dependent upon a manager's budget record. In addition, the manager may wish to evaluate his or her own performance. The budget thus provides a useful means of informing managers of how well they are performing in meeting targets that they have previously helped to set. The use of budgets as a method of performance evaluation also influences human behaviour, and for this reason we shall consider the behavioural aspects of performance evaluation in Chapter 10.

CONFLICTING ROLES OF BUDGETS

Because a single budget system is normally used to serve several purposes there is a danger that these purposes may conflict with each other. For instance, the planning and motivation roles may be in conflict with each other. Demanding budgets that may not be achieved may be appropriate to motivate maximum performance, but they are unsuitable for planning purposes. For these a budget should be set based on easier and more realistic targets that are expected to be met.

There can also be a conflict between the planning and performance evaluation roles. For planning purposes budgets are set in advance of the budget period and are based on an anticipated set of circumstances or environment. Performance evaluation should be based on a comparison of actual performance with an adjusted budget to reflect the circumstances under which managers actually operated. In practice, many firms compare actual performance with the original budget (adjusted to the actual level of activity, i.e. a flexible budget), but if the circumstances envisaged when the original budget was set have changed then there will be a planning and evaluation conflict.

THE BUDGET PERIOD

The conventional approach is that once a year the manager of each budget centre prepares a detailed budget for 1 year. For control purposes the budget is divided into either 12 monthly or 13 four-weekly periods. The preparation of budgets on an annual basis has been strongly criticized on the grounds that it is too rigid and ties a company to a 12-month commitment, which can be risky because the budget is based on uncertain forecasts.

An alternative approach is for the annual budget to be broken down by months for the first 3 months, and by quarters for the remaining 9 months. The quarterly budgets are then developed on a monthly basis as the year proceeds. For example, during the first quarter, the monthly budgets for the second quarter will be prepared; and during the second quarter, the monthly budgets for the third quarter will be prepared. The quarterly budgets may also be reviewed as the year unfolds. For example, during the first quarter, the budget for the next three quarters may be changed as new information becomes available. A new budget for a fifth quarter will also be prepared. This process is known as **continuous** or **rolling budgeting**, and ensures that a 12-month budget is always available by adding a quarter in the future as the quarter just ended is dropped. Contrast this with a budget prepared once per year. As the year goes by, the period for which a budget is available will shorten until the budget for next year is prepared. Rolling budgets also ensure that planning is not something that takes place once a year when the budget is being formulated. Instead, budgeting is a continuous process, and managers are encouraged to constantly look ahead and review future plans. Another advantage is that actual performance will be compared with a more realistic target, because budgets are being constantly reviewed and updated. The main disadvantage of a rolling budget is that it can create uncertainty for managers because the budget is constantly being changed.

Irrespective of whether the budget is prepared on an annual or a continuous basis, monthly or four-weekly budgets are normally used for *control* purposes.

ADMINISTRATION OF THE BUDGETING PROCESS

It is important that suitable administration procedures exist to ensure that the budget process works effectively. In practice, the procedures should be tailor-made to the requirements of the organization, but as a general rule a firm should ensure that procedures are established for approving the budgets and that the appropriate staff support is available for assisting managers in preparing their budgets.

REAL WORLD VIEWS 9.1

Rolling budgets in a health care organization

An article by Larry Hill reported that in 2014, Mission Health decided to leave the annual budgeting process behind and embark upon a new approach involving a rolling forecast. A rolling forecast differs fundamentally from a traditional annual budget in terms of its time frame and the level of detail required for its analysis. First, a traditional budget calls for financial planning once a year while a rolling forecast uses a continuous planning cycle, such as monthly or quarterly (depending on available manpower). Because the traditional budgeting process occurs only once annually, performance is compared with financial targets that are set at the beginning of the fiscal year. By contrast, Mission's rolling forecast is updated each quarter and compares to desired outcomes for the current and following year. This approach allows an organization to monitor continuous improvement with the expectation of year-over-year growth and productivity improvement. Frontline managers are required to shift their mindset from 'meeting my budget' on an annual basis to meeting productivity and cost efficiency targets on a continuous basis. The organization must become more agile to adjust to changing conditions.

Questions

1 Identify three significant advantages of rolling budgets.
2 Identify three problems that are likely to be encountered when using rolling budgets.

Reference

Hill, L.E. (2016), Pioneering a rolling forecast, *Healthcare Financial Management*; November, 58–62

The budget committee

The budget committee should consist of high-level executives who represent the major segments of the business. Its main task is to ensure that budgets are realistic and that they are coordinated satisfactorily. The normal procedure is for the functional heads to present their budget to the committee for approval. If the budget does not reflect a reasonable level of performance, it will not be approved and the functional head will be required to adjust the budget and resubmit it for approval. It is important that the person whose performance is being measured should agree that the revised budget can be achieved or it will not act as a motivational device. If budget revisions are made, the budgetees should at least feel that they were given a fair hearing by the committee. We shall discuss budget negotiation in more detail later in this chapter.

Accounting staff

The accounting staff will normally assist managers in the preparation of their budgets. They will, for example, circulate instructions and offer advice about budget preparation, provide past information that may be useful for preparing the present budget, and ensure that managers submit their budgets on time. The accounting staff do not determine the content of the various budgets, but they do provide a valuable advisory service for line managers. They will also coordinate the individual budgets into a budget for the whole organization.

STAGES IN THE BUDGETING PROCESS

The important stages are as follows:

1 communicating details of the budget policy and guidelines to those people responsible for the preparation of budgets

2 determining factor that restricts performance

3 preparation of the sales budget

4 initial preparation of budgets

5 negotiation of budgets

6 coordination and review of budgets

7 final acceptance of budgets

8 ongoing review of budgets.

Let us now consider each of these stages in more detail.

Communicating details of the budget policy

Many decisions affecting the budget year will already have been taken as part of the long-term planning process. The long-range plan is therefore the starting point for the preparation of the annual budget. Thus top management must communicate the policy effects of the long-term plan to those responsible for preparing the current year's budgets. Policy effects might include planned changes in sales mix, or the expansion or contraction of certain activities. Any other important guidelines that are to govern the preparation of the budget should also be specified – for example, the allowances that are to be made for price and wage increases, and the expected changes in productivity. Also, any expected changes in the environment such as industry demand and output should be communicated by top management to the managers responsible for budget preparation.

Determining the factor that restricts performance

In every organization there is some factor that restricts performance for a given period. In the majority of organizations this factor is sales demand. However, it is possible for production capacity to restrict performance when sales demand is in excess of available capacity. Prior to the preparation of the budgets, top management needs to determine the factor that restricts performance, since this factor will in turn determine the point at which the annual budgeting process should begin.

Preparation of the sales budget

When sales demand is the factor that restricts output, it is the volume of sales and the sales mix that determine output. For this reason, the sales budget is the most important plan in the annual budgeting process. This budget is also the most difficult plan to produce, because sales demand will be influenced by the state of the economy or the actions of competitors.

Initial preparation of budgets

The managers who are responsible for meeting the budgeted performance should prepare the budget for those areas for which they are responsible. The preparation of the budget should be a 'bottom-up' process. This means that the budget should originate at the lowest levels of management and be refined and coordinated at higher levels. The justification for this approach is that it enables managers to participate in the preparation of their budgets and increases the probability that they will accept the budget and strive to achieve the budget targets.

Negotiation of budgets

Budgetting should be a participative process. The budget should originate at the lowest level of management and managers at this level should submit their budget to their superiors for approval. The superior should then incorporate this budget with other budgets for which he or she is responsible and then submit this budget for approval to his or her superior. The manager who is the superior then becomes the budgetee at the next higher level. The process is illustrated in Figure 9.2. Sizer (1989) describes this approach as a two-way process of a top-down statement of objectives and strategies, bottom-up budget preparation and top-down approval by senior management.

The lower-level managers are represented by boxes 1–8. Managers 1 and 2 will prepare their budgets in accordance with the budget policy and the guidelines laid down by top management. The managers will submit their budget to their supervisor, who is in charge of the whole department (department A). Once these budgets have been agreed by the manager of department A, they will be combined by the departmental manager, who will

FIGURE 9.2

An illustration of budgets moving up the organization

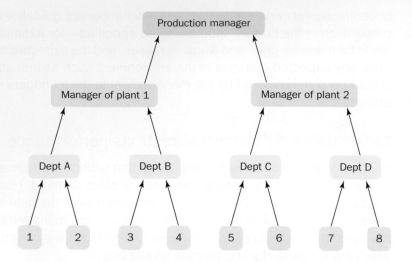

then present this budget to his or her superior (manager of plant 1) for approval. The manager of plant 1 is also responsible for department B, and will combine the agreed budgets for departments A and B before presenting the combined budget to his or her supervisor (the production manager). The production manager will merge the budget for plants 1 and 2, and this final budget will represent the production budget that will be presented to the budget committee for approval.

At each of these stages the budgets will be negotiated between the budgetees and their superiors, and eventually be agreed by both parties. Hence, the figures that are included in the budget are the result of a bargaining process between a manager and his or her superior. It is important that the budgetees should participate in arriving at the final budget and that the superior does not revise the budget without giving full consideration to the subordinates' arguments for including any of the budgeted items. Otherwise, real participation will not be taking place, and it is unlikely that the subordinate will be motivated to achieve a budget that he or she did not accept.

It is also necessary to be watchful that budgetees do not deliberately attempt to obtain approval for easily attainable budgets. It is equally unsatisfactory for a superior to impose difficult targets in the hope that an authoritarian approach will produce the desired results. The desired results may be achieved in the short term, but only at the cost of a loss of morale and increased labour turnover in the future.

Coordination and review of budgets

As the individual budgets move up the organizational hierarchy in the negotiation process, they must be examined in relation to each other. This examination may reveal that some budgets are out of balance with others and need modifying so that they will be compatible with conditions, constraints and plans that are beyond a manager's knowledge or control. This process may lead to the budgets being recycled from the bottom to the top for a second or even a third time until all the budgets are coordinated and are acceptable to all the parties involved. During the coordination process, a budgeted profit statement, a balance sheet and a cash flow statement should be prepared to ensure that all the parts combine to produce an acceptable whole. Otherwise, further adjustments and budget recycling will be necessary until the final outcome is acceptable.

Final acceptance of budgets

When all the budgets are in harmony with each other, they are summarized into a **master budget** consisting of a budgeted profit and loss statement, a balance sheet and a cash flow statement. After the master budget has been approved, the budgets are then passed down through the organization to the appropriate responsibility centres. The approval of the master budget is the authority for the manager of each responsibility centre to carry out the plans contained in each budget.

Ongoing review of budgets

The budget process should not stop when the budgets have been agreed. Periodically, the actual results should be compared with the budgeted results in the form of a regular performance report. These comparisons should normally be made on a monthly basis and a report should be available online immediately following the month end so that management can investigate the reasons for the differences. If these differences are within the control of management, corrective action can be taken to avoid similar inefficiencies occurring again in the future.

During the budget year, the budget committee should periodically evaluate the actual performance and reappraise the company's future plans. If there are any changes in the actual conditions from those originally expected, this will normally mean that the budget plans should be adjusted. This revised budget then represents a revised statement of formal operating plans for the remaining portion of the budget period. The important point to note is that the budgetary process does not end for the current year once the budget has begun; budgeting should be seen as a continuous and dynamic process.

A DETAILED ILLUSTRATION

Let us now look at an illustration of the procedure for constructing budgets in a manufacturing company, using the information contained in Example 9.1. Note that the level of detail included here is much less than that which would be presented in practice. A truly realistic illustration would fill many pages, with detailed budgets being analysed in various ways. We shall consider an annual budget, whereas a realistic illustration would analyse the annual budget into 12 monthly periods. Monthly analysis would considerably increase the size of the illustration, but would not give any further insight into the basic concepts or procedures. In addition, we shall assume in this example that the budgets are prepared for only two responsibility centres (namely departments 1 and 2). In practice, many responsibility centres are likely to exist.

Sales budget

The sales budget shows the quantities of each product that the company plans to sell and the intended selling price. It provides the predictions of total revenue from which cash receipts from customers will be estimated, and it also supplies the basic data for constructing budgets for production costs, and for selling, distribution and administrative expenses. The sales budget is therefore the foundation of all other budgets, since all expenditure is ultimately dependent on the volume of sales. If the sales budget is not accurate, the other budget estimates will also be unreliable. We will assume that the

EXAMPLE 9.1

The Enterprise Company manufactures two products, known as alpha and sigma. Alpha is produced in department 1 and sigma in department 2. The following information is available for the next financial year:

	(£)
Material X	7.20 per unit
Material Y	16.00 per unit
Direct labour	12.00 per hour

Overhead is recovered on a direct labour hour basis.

The standard material and labour usage for each product is as follows:

	Model alpha	Model sigma
Material X	10 units	8 units
Material Y	5 units	9 units
Direct labour	10 hours	15 hours

The balance sheet for the previous year end was as follows:

	(£)	(£)	(£)
Fixed assets:			
Land		170 000	
Buildings and equipment	1 292 000		
Less depreciation	255 000	1 037 000	1 207 000
Current assets:			
Inventories, finished goods	99 076		
raw materials	189 200		
Debtors	289 000		
Cash	34 000		
	611 276		
Less current liabilities			
Creditors	248 800		362 476
Net assets			1 569 476
Represented by shareholders' interest:			
1 200 000 ordinary shares of £1 each		1 200 000	
Reserves		369 476	
			1 569 476

Other relevant budgeted data are as follows for the year:

	Finished product	
	Model alpha	Model sigma
Forecast sales (units)	8 500	1 600
Selling price per unit	£400	£560
Ending inventory required (units)	1 870	90
Beginning inventory (units)	170	85

	Direct material	
	Material X	Material Y
Beginning inventory (units)	8 500	8 000
Ending inventory required (units)	10 200	1 700

	Department 1 (£)	Department 2 (£)
Budgeted variable overhead rates (per direct labour hour):		
Indirect materials	1.20	0.80
Indirect labour	1.20	1.20
Power (variable portion)	0.60	0.40
Maintenance (variable portion)	0.20	0.40
Budgeted fixed overheads		
Depreciation	100 000	80 000
Supervision	100 000	40 000
Power (fixed portion)	40 000	2 000
Maintenance (fixed portion)	45 600	3 196

	(£)
Estimated non-manufacturing overheads:	
Stationery etc. (Administration)	4 000
Salaries	
Sales	74 000
Office	28 000
Commissions	60 000
Car expenses (Sales)	22 000
Advertising	80 000
Miscellaneous (Office)	8 000
	276 000

Budgeted cash flows are as follows:

	Quarter 1 (£)	Quarter 2 (£)	Quarter 3 (£)	Quarter 4 (£)
Receipts from customers	1 000 000	1 200 000	1 120 000	985 000
Payments:				
Materials	400 000	480 000	440 000	547 984
Payments for wages	400 000	440 000	480 000	646 188
Other costs and expenses	120 000	100 000	72 016	13 642

You are required to prepare a master budget for the next year and the following budgets:

1 sales budget
2 production budget
3 direct materials usage budget
4 direct materials purchase budget
5 direct labour budget
6 production overhead budget
7 selling and administration budget
8 cash budget.

Enterprise Company has completed a marketing analysis and that the following annual sales budget is based on the result:

Schedule 1 – Annual sales budget

Product	Units sold	Selling price (£)	Total revenue (£)
Alpha	8 500	400	3 400 000
Sigma	1 600	560	896 000
			4 296 000

Schedule 1 represents the *total* sales budget for the year. In practice, the *total* sales budget will be supported by detailed *subsidiary* sales budgets where sales are analysed by areas of responsibility, such as sales territories, and into monthly periods analysed by products.

Production budget and budgeted inventory levels

When the sales budget has been completed, the next stage is to prepare the production budget. This budget is expressed in *quantities only* and is the responsibility of the production manager. The objective is to ensure that production is sufficient to meet sales demand and that economic stock levels are maintained. The production budget (schedule 2) for the year will be as follows:

Schedule 2 – Annual production budget

	Department 1 (alpha)	Department 2 (sigma)
Units to be sold	8 500	1 600
Planned closing inventory	1 870	90
Total units required for sales and inventories	10 370	1 690
Less planned opening inventories	170	85
Units to be produced	10 200	1 605

The total production for each department should also be analysed on a monthly basis.

Direct materials usage budget

The supervisors of departments 1 and 2 will prepare estimates of the materials required to meet the production budget. The materials usage budget for the year will be as follows:

Schedule 3 – Annual direct material usage budget

	Department 1			Department 2					
	Units	Unit price (£)	Total (£)	Units	Unit price (£)	Total (£)	Total units	Total unit price (£)	Total (£)
Material X	102 000[a]	7.20	734 400	12 840[c]	7.20	92 448	114 840	7.20	826 848
Material Y	51 000[b]	16.00	816 000	14 445[d]	16.00	231 120	65 445	16.00	1 047 120
			1 550 400			323 568			1 873 968

[a] 10 200 units production at ten units per unit of production.
[b] 10 200 units production at five units per unit of production.
[c] 1605 units production at eight units per unit of production.
[d] 1605 units production at nine units per unit of production.

Direct materials purchase budget

The direct materials purchase budget is the responsibility of the purchasing manager, since it will be he or she who is responsible for obtaining the planned quantities of raw materials to meet the production requirements. The objective is to purchase these materials at the right time at the planned purchase price. In addition, it is necessary to take into account the planned raw material inventory levels. The annual materials purchase budget for the year will be as follows:

Schedule 4 – Direct materials purchase budget	Material X (units)	Material Y (units)
Quantity necessary to meet production requirements as per material usage budget	114 840	65 445
Planned closing inventory	10 200	1 700
	125 040	67 145
Less planned opening inventory	8 500	8 000
Total units to be purchased	116 540	59 145
Planned unit purchase price	£7.20	£16
Total purchases	£839 088	£946 320

Note that this budget is a summary budget for the year, but for detailed planning and control it will be necessary to analyse the annual budget on a monthly basis.

Direct labour budget

The direct labour budget is the responsibility of the respective managers of departments 1 and 2. They will prepare estimates of their departments' labour hours required to meet the planned production. Where different grades of labour exist, these should be specified separately in the budget. The budget rate per hour should be determined by the Human Resources (HR) department. The direct labour budget will be as follows:

Schedule 5 – Annual direct labour budget	Department 1	Department 2	Total
Budgeted production (units)	10 200	1 605	
Hours per unit	10	15	
Total budgeted hours	102 000	24 075	126 075
Budgeted wage rate per hour	£12	£12	
Total wages	£1 224 000	£288 900	£1 512 900

Production overhead budget

The production overhead budget is also the responsibility of the respective production department managers. The total of the overhead budget will depend on the behaviour of the costs of the individual overhead items in relation to the anticipated level of production. The overheads must also be analysed according to whether they are controllable or non-controllable for the purpose of cost control. The production overhead budget will be as follows:

Schedule 6 – Annual production overhead budget
Anticipated activity – 102 000 direct labour hours (department 1)
24 075 direct labour hours (department 2)

	Variable overhead rate per direct labour hour		Overheads		
	Department 1 (£)	Department 2 (£)	Department 1 (£)	Department 2 (£)	Total (£)
Controllable overheads:					
Indirect material	1.20	0.80	122 400	19 260	
Indirect labour	1.20	1.20	122 400	28 890	
Power (variable portion)	0.60	0.40	61 200	9 630	
Maintenance (variable portion)	0.20	0.40	20 400	9 630	
			326 400	67 410	393 810
Non-controllable overheads:					
Depreciation			100 000	80 000	
Supervision			100 000	40 000	
Power (fixed portion)			40 000	2 000	
Maintenance (fixed portion)			45 600	3 196	
			285 600	125 196	410 796
Total overhead			612 000	192 606	804 606
Budgeted departmental overhead rate			£6.00[a]	8.00[b]	

[a]£612 000 total overheads divided by 102 000 direct labour hours.
[b]£192 606 total overheads divided by 24 075 direct labour hours.

The budgeted expenditure for the variable overhead items is determined by multiplying the budgeted direct labour hours for each department by the budgeted variable overhead rate per hour. It is assumed that all variable overheads vary in relation to direct labour hours.

Selling and administration budget

The selling and administration budgets have been combined here to simplify the presentation. In practice, separate budgets should be prepared: the sales manager will be responsible for the selling budget, the distribution manager will be responsible for the distribution expenses and the chief administrative officer will be responsible for the administration budget.

Schedule 7 – Annual selling and administration budget

	(£)	(£)
Selling:		
Salaries	74 000	
Commission	60 000	
Car expenses	22 000	
Advertising	80 000	236 000
Administration:		
Stationery	4 000	
Salaries	28 000	
Miscellaneous	8 000	40 000
		276 000

Departmental budgets

For cost control the direct labour budget, materials usage budget and production overhead budget are combined into separate departmental budgets known as responsibility centres. These budgets are normally broken down into 12 separate monthly budgets, and the actual monthly expenditure is compared with the budgeted amounts for each of the items concerned. This comparison is used for judging how effective managers are in controlling the expenditure for which they are responsible. The departmental budget for department 1 will be as follows:

Department 1 – Annual departmental operating budget

	(£)	Budget (£)	Actual (£)
Direct labour (from schedule 5):			
102 000 hours at £12		1 224 000	
Direct materials (from schedule 3):			
102 000 units of material X at £7.20 per unit	734 400		
51 000 units of material Y at £16 per unit	816 000	1 550 400	
Controllable overheads (from schedule 6):			
Indirect materials	122 400		
Indirect labour	122 400		
Power (variable portion)	61 200		
Maintenance (variable portion)	20 400	326 400	
Uncontrollable overheads (from schedule 6):			
Depreciation	100 000		
Supervision	100 000		
Power (fixed portion)	40 000		
Maintenance (fixed portion)	45 600	285 600	
		3 386 400	

Master budget

When all the budgets have been prepared, the budgeted profit statement and balance sheet provide the overall picture of the planned performance for the budget period.

Budgeted profit statement for the year

	(£)	(£)
Sales (schedule 1)		4 296 000
Opening inventory of raw materials	189 200	
(from opening balance sheet)		
Purchases (schedule 4)	1 785 408[a]	
	1 974 608	
Less inventory stock of raw materials (schedule 4)	100 640[b]	
Cost of raw materials consumed	1 873 968	
Direct labour (schedule 5)	1 512 900	
Factory overheads (schedule 6)	804 606	
Total manufacturing cost	4 191 474	
Add opening inventory of finished goods	99 076	
(from opening balance sheet)		
Less closing inventory of finished goods	665 984[c]	
		(566 908)
Cost of sales		3 624 566
Gross profit		671 434
Selling and administration expenses (schedule 7)		276 000
Budgeted operating profit for the year		395 434

ª £839 088 (X) + £946 320 (Y) from schedule 4.
ᵇ 10 200 units at £7.20 plus 1700 units at £16 from schedule 4.
ᶜ 1870 units of alpha valued at £332 per unit, 90 units of sigma valued at £501.60 per unit. The product unit costs are calculated as follows:

	Alpha		Sigma	
	Units	(£)	Units	(£)
Direct materials				
X	10	72.00	8	57.60
Y	5	80.00	9	144.00
Direct labour	10	120.00	15	180.00
Factory overheads:				
Department 1	10	60.00	—	—
Department 2	—	—	15	120.00
		332.00		501.60

Budgeted balance sheet as at 31 December

	(£)	(£)
Fixed assets:		
Land		170 000
Building and equipment	1 292 000	
Less depreciationª	435 000	857 000
		1 027 000
Current assets:		
Raw material inventory	100 640	
Finished good inventory	665 984	
Debtorsᵇ	280 000	
Cashᶜ	199 170	
	1 245 794	
Current liabilities:		
Creditorsᵈ	307 884	937 910
		1 964 910
Represented by shareholders' interest:		
1 200 000 ordinary shares of £1 each	1 200 000	
Reserves	369 476	
Profit and loss account	395 434	1 964 910

ª £255 000 + £180 000 (schedule 6) = £435 000.
ᵇ £289 000 opening balance + £4 296 000 sales – £4 305 000 cash.
ᶜ Closing balance as per cash budget.
ᵈ £248 800 opening balance + £1 785 408 purchases + £141 660 indirect materials – £1 867 984 cash.

Cash budgets

The objective of the **cash budget** is to ensure that sufficient cash is available at all times to meet the level of operations that are outlined in the various budgets. The cash budget for Example 9.1 is presented below and is analysed by quarters, but in practice monthly or weekly budgets will be necessary. Because cash budgeting is subject to uncertainty, it is necessary to provide for more than the minimum amount required to allow for some margin of error in planning. Cash budgets can help a firm to avoid cash balances that are surplus to its requirements by enabling management to take steps in advance to invest the surplus cash in short-term investments. Cash deficiencies can also be identified in advance, and steps can be taken to ensure that bank loans will be available to meet any temporary shortfalls. For example, when management examines the cash budget for the Enterprise Company, they may consider that the cash balances are higher than necessary in the second and third quarters of the year, and they may decide to invest part of the cash balance in short-term investments.

The overall aim should be to manage the cash of the firm to attain maximum cash availability and maximum interest income on any idle funds.

Cash budget for the year

	Quarter 1 (£)	Quarter 2 (£)	Quarter 3 (£)	Quarter 4 (£)	Total (£)
Opening balance	34 000	114 000	294 000	421 984	34 000
Receipts from debtors	1 000 000	1 200 000	1 120 000	985 000	4 305 000
	1 034 000	1 314 000	1 414 000	1 406 984	4 339 000
Payments:					
Purchase of materials	400 000	480 000	440 000	547 984	1 867 984
Payment of wages	400 000	440 000	480 000	646 188	1 966 188
Other costs and expenses	120 000	100 000	72 016	13 642	305 658
	920 000	1 020 000	992 016	1 207 814	4 139 830
Closing balance	114 000	294 000	421 984	199 170	199 170

Final review

The budgeted profit statement, the balance sheet and the cash budget will be submitted by the accountant to the budget committee, together with a number of budgeted financial ratios such as the return on capital employed, working capital, liquidity and gearing ratios. If these ratios prove to be acceptable, the budgets will be approved. In Example 9.1 the return on capital employed is approximately 20 per cent, but the working capital ratio (current assets:current liabilities) is over 4:1, so management should consider alternative ways of reducing investment in working capital before finally approving the budgets.

COMPUTERIZED BUDGETING

In the past, budgeting was a task dreaded by many management accountants. You will have noted from Example 9.1 that many numerical manipulations are necessary to prepare the budget. In the real world the process is far more complex and, as the budget is being formulated, it is usually revised many times.

In today's world, the budgeting process is computerized, and instead of being primarily concerned with numerical manipulations, the accounting staff can now become more involved in the real planning process. Computer-based financial models enable management to evaluate many different options before the budget is finally agreed. 'What-if?' analysis can be employed. For example, answers to the following questions can be displayed in the form of a master budget: What if sales increase or decrease by 10 per cent? What if unit costs increase or decrease by 5 per cent? What if the credit terms for sales were reduced from 30 to 20 days?

Big data and budgeting

Big data and analytics is more often associated with big business, but this need not be so. The problem is often that expensive tools and hardware are needed for big data collection, and analytics is the realm of larger business. However, the increasing availability of technologies and tools as a service now means many medium and smaller companies can afford to analyse data for planning and forecasting purposes. For example, IBM's Watson Analytics platform is a simple and self-service application, within the reach of small and medium business.

According to an IBM blog post, using analytic tools as a service is useful for smaller or start-up companies who may not be able to afford software or an extra accountant/analyst needed to do the analysis or forecasting. The blog post suggests that advanced data analytics can support what it terms dynamic budgeting. To paraphrase the post, volatile markets mean few companies can prepare an annual budget and follow it. However, powerful tools are available (as a service) to help companies cope with this volatility. These tools include big data access and analysis, fast in-memory computing, location information and data visualization to depict the business world. There are of course service providers other than IBM, for example Adobe (www. adobe.com), SAS (www.sas.com/en_us/solutions/cloud-analytics.html) and LatentView Analytics (www.latentview.com).

From a budgeting perspective, having access to such data and tools can provide valuable insights to improve budgets and forecasts. For example, it may help companies identify consumer trends or reveal how customers interact with a company's products or services. Such examples can alter how resources are allocated in budgets, normally for the better.

Questions

1 Can you think of an example of a business process/area where data analytics could help a small/medium company budget/plan better and achieve cost savings?
2 Could big data/data analytics help in the preparation of production budgets in small/medium companies?

Reference

IBM Big Data and Analytics Hub Blog "Budgeting and forecasting on a small business budget", available at www.ibmbigdatahub.com/blog/budgeting-and-forecasting-small-business-budget

In addition, such models can incorporate actual results, period by period, and carry out the necessary calculations to produce budgetary *control* reports. It is also possible to adjust the budgets for the remainder of the year when it is clear that the circumstances on which the budget was originally set have changed.

ACTIVITY-BASED BUDGETING

The conventional approach to budgeting that was illustrated using Example 9.1 is appropriate for unit-level activities (see Chapter 8), such as the direct labour and direct materials budgets, where the consumption of resources varies proportionately with the volume of final output of products or services. However, for those indirect costs and support activities where there are no clearly identified input–output relationships, conventional budgets merely serve as authorization levels for the budgeted level of spending for each item of expense. They can only indicate whether the budget has been exceeded and thus provide little relevant information for managing the costs of the support activities.

With conventional budgeting indirect costs and support activities are prepared on an incremental basis. This means that existing operations and the current budgeted allowance for existing activities are taken as the starting point for preparing the next annual budget. The base is then adjusted for changes (such as changes in product mix, volumes and prices) which are expected to occur during the new budget period. This approach is called **incremental budgeting**, since the budget process is concerned mainly with the increment in operations or expenditure that will occur during the forthcoming budget period. For example, the allowance for budgeted expenses may be based on the previous budgeted allowance plus an increase to cover higher prices caused by inflation. The major disadvantage of the incremental approach is that the majority of expenditure, which is associated with the 'base level' of activity, remains unchanged. Thus the cost of the support activities become fixed. Past inefficiencies and waste inherent in the current way of doing things are perpetuated.

To manage costs more effectively organizations have adopted **activity-based budgeting (ABB)**. The aim of ABB is to authorize the supply of only those resources that are needed to perform activities required to meet the budgeted production and sales volume. ABB involves the following stages:

1 estimate the production and sales volume by individual products or customers
2 estimate the demand for organizational activities
3 determine the resources that are required to perform organizational activities
4 estimate for each resource the quantity that must be supplied to meet the demand
5 take action to adjust the capacity of resources to match the projected supply.

The *first stage* is identical to conventional budgeting. Details of budgeted production and sales volumes for individual products and customer types will be contained in the sales and production budgets. Next, ABB extends conventional budgeting to support activities such as ordering, receiving, scheduling production and processing customers' orders. To implement ABB the activities that are necessary to produce and sell the products and services and service customers must be identified. In the *second stage*, estimates of the quantity of activity cost drivers must be derived for each activity. For example, the number of purchase orders, the number of receipts, the number of set-ups and the number of customer orders processed are estimated using the same approach as that used by conventional budgeting to determine the quantity of direct labour and materials that are incorporated into the direct labour and materials purchase budgets.

The *third stage* is to estimate the resources that are required for performing the quantity of activity drivers demanded. In particular, estimates are required of each type of resource, and their quantities required, to meet the demanded quantity of activities. For example, if the number of customer orders to be processed is estimated to be 5000 and each order takes 30 minutes processing time, then 2500 labour hours of the customer processing activity must be supplied.

EXHIBIT 9.2　Activity-based budget for an order receiving process

Activities →	Handle import goods	Execute express orders	Special deliveries	Distribution administration	Order receiving (standard products)	Order receiving (non-standard products)	Execute rush orders	Total cost
Resource expense accounts:								
Office supplies								
Telephone								
Expenses								
Salaries								
Travel								
Training								
Total cost								
Activity cost driver → measures	Number of customs documents	Number of customer bills	Number of letters of credit	Number of consignment notes	Number of standard orders	Number of non-standard orders	Number of rush orders	

In the *fourth stage* the resources demanded (derived from the third stage) are converted into an estimate of the total resources that must be supplied for each type of resource used by an activity. The quantity of resources supplied depends on the cost behaviour of the resource. For flexible resources where the supply can be matched exactly to meet demand, the quantity of resources supplied will be identical to the quantity demanded. For example, if customer processing were a flexible resource exactly 2500 hours would be purchased. However, a more likely assumption is that customer processing labour will be a step cost function in relation to the volume of the activity (see Chapter 2 for a description of step cost functions). Assuming that each person employed is contracted to work 1500 hours per year then 1.67 persons (2500/1500) represents the quantity of resources required, but because resources must be acquired in whole amounts, two persons must be employed. For other resources, such as equipment, resources will tend to be fixed and committed over a very wide range of volume for the activity. As long as demand is less than the capacity supplied by the committed resource no additional spending will be required.

The *final stage* is to compare the estimates of the quantity of resources to be supplied for each resource with the quantity of resources that are currently committed. If the estimated demand for a resource exceeds the current capacity additional spending must be authorized within the budgeting process to acquire additional resources. Alternatively, if the demand for resources is less than the projected supply, the budgeting process should result in management taking action to either redeploy or reduce those resources that are no longer required.

Exhibit 9.2 illustrates an activity-based budget for an order receiving process or department. You will see that the budget is presented in a matrix format with the major activities being shown for each of the columns and the resource inputs listed by rows. The cost driver activity levels are also highlighted. A major feature of ABB is the enhanced visibility arising from highlighting the cost of activities and showing the outcomes, in terms of cost drivers, from the budgeted expenditure. This information is particularly useful for planning and estimating future expenditure.

ZERO-BASED BUDGETING

Zero-based budgeting (also known as **priority-based budgeting**) emerged as an attempt to overcome the limitations of **incremental budgets**. This approach requires that projected expenditure for existing activities should start from base zero rather than last year's budget. In other words, managers are required to justify all budgeted expenditure rather than just the changes from the previous year. Besides adopting a 'zero-based' approach, zero-based budgeting (ZBB) also focuses on programmes or activities instead of functional departments, which is a feature of traditional budgeting. Programmes normally relate to various activities undertaken by municipal or government organizations. Examples include extending childcare facilities, improvement of health care for senior citizens and the extension of nursing facilities.

ZBB is best suited to discretionary costs and support activities. With **discretionary costs** management has some discretion as to the amount it will budget for the particular activity in question. Examples of discretionary costs include advertising, research and development and training costs. There is no optimum relationship between inputs (as measured by the costs) and outputs (measured by revenues or some other objective function) for these costs. Furthermore, they are not predetermined by some previous commitment. In effect, management can determine what quantity of service it wishes to purchase and there is no established method for determining the appropriate amount to be spent in particular periods. ZBB has mostly been applied in municipal and government organizations where the predominant costs are of a discretionary nature.

ZBB involves the following three stages:

- a description of each organizational activity in a decision package
- the evaluation and ranking of decision packages in order of priority
- allocation of resources based on order of priority up to the spending cut-off level.

Decision packages are identified for each decision unit. Decision units represent separate programmes or groups of activities that an organization undertakes. A decision package represents the operation of a particular programme with incremental packages reflecting different levels of effort that may be expended on a specific function. One package is usually prepared at the 'base' level for each programme. This package represents the minimum level of service or support consistent with the organization's objectives. Service or support higher than the base level is described in one or more incremental packages. For example, managers might be asked to specify the base package in terms of level of service that can be provided at 70 per cent of the current cost level and incremental packages identify higher activity or cost levels.

Once the decision packages have been completed, management is ready to start to review the process. To determine how much to spend and where to spend it, management will rank all packages in order of decreasing benefits to the organization. Theoretically, once management has set the budgeted level of spending, the packages should be accepted down to the spending level based on cost–benefit principles.

The benefits of ZBB over traditional methods of budgeting are claimed to be as follows:

1 Traditional budgeting tends to extrapolate the past by adding a percentage increase to the current year. ZBB avoids the deficiencies of incremental budgeting

and represents a move towards the allocation of resources by need or benefit. Thus, unlike traditional budgeting the level of previous funding is not taken for granted.

2 ZBB creates a questioning attitude rather than one that assumes that current practice represents value for money.

3 ZBB focuses attention on outputs in relation to value for money.

ZBB was first applied in Texas Instruments. It quickly became one of the fashionable management tools of the 1970s and, according to Phyrr (1976), there were 100 users in the USA in the early 1970s. ZBB never achieved the widespread adoption that its proponents envisaged. The major reason for its lack of success would appear to be that it is too costly and time-consuming. The process of identifying decision packages and determining their purpose, cost and benefits is extremely time-consuming. Furthermore, there are often too many decision packages to evaluate and there is frequently insufficient information to enable them to be ranked.

Research suggests that many organizations tend to approximate the principles of ZBB rather than applying the full-scale approach outlined in the literature. For example, it does not have to be applied throughout the organization. It can be applied selectively to those areas about which management is most concerned and used as a one-off cost reduction programme. Some of the benefits of ZBB can be captured by using **priority-based incremental budgets**. Priority incremental budgets require managers to specify what incremental activities or changes would occur if their budgets were increased or decreased by a specified percentage (say 10 per cent). Budget allocations are made by comparing the change in costs with the change in benefits. Priority incremental budgets thus represent an economical compromise between ZBB and incremental budgeting.

CRITICISMS OF BUDGETING

In recent years criticisms of traditional budgeting have attracted much publicity. The most outspoken critics of traditional budgeting have been Hope and Fraser. In a series of articles Hope and Fraser (1999a, 1999b, 2001, 2003a, 2003b) have argued that companies should abandon traditional budgeting. They advocate that companies should move beyond budgeting. According to Hope and Fraser (1999a), a number of innovative companies, such as Svenska Handelsbanken (a Swedish bank) and Volvo, are in the process of abandoning traditional budgeting. The major criticism is that the annual budgeting process is incapable of meeting the demands of the competitive environment in today's information age. Ekholm and Wallin (2000) and Dugdale and Lyne (2006) have reviewed the literature relating to annual budgets. They have identified the following criticisms relating to the annual budgeting process:

- encouraging rigid planning and incremental thinking whereby budgets are derived from last year's activities plus an adjustment for the current year rather than adopting a zero-based budgeting approach

- being time-consuming taking up an enormous amount of management time which results in a situation where the benefits may not be worth their cost. Hope and Fraser (2003a, 2003b) claim that budgeting is a protracted and expensive process, absorbing up to 30 per cent of management's time. They cite a study indicating that global companies invested more than 25 000 person-days per $1 billion of revenue in the planning and performance-measurement processes

- ignoring key drivers of shareholder value (e.g. innovation, developing new products and markets and responding to competitor threats) by focusing too much attention on short-term financial numbers

- being a yearly rigid ritual that impedes firms from being flexible and adaptive in the increasingly unpredictable fast-changing environment facing contemporary organizations, Hope and Fraser (2003a, 2003b) argue that budgeting conflicts with the new competitive environment and stifles innovation because, once set, budgets are not typically changed resulting in plans and targets that become quickly out of date

- tying the company to a 12-month commitment, which is risky since it is based on uncertain forecasts derived from a fast-changing environment

- meeting only the lowest targets and not attempting to beat the targets. Hope and Fraser argue that budgets often serve as a 'fixed performance contract' whereby targets are set at the beginning of the period. If the actual performance meets or exceeds the pre-specified static budget target, performance is deemed to be satisfactory. They argue that a fixed contract represents a poor standard of performance evaluation when the factors underlying the targets may have changed during the budget period. They also argue that the use of fixed performance contracts encourages managers to engage in dysfunctional behaviour (see 'Harmful side-effects of controls' in Chapter 10) to achieve the budget even if this results in undesirable actions that do not contribute to the organization's objectives

- spending what is in the budget even if this is not necessary in order to guard against next year's budget being reduced

- being disconnected from strategy whereby budgets are typically prepared in isolation from, and not aligned with, the strategic objectives of the organization.

Beyond budgeting

The term **beyond budgeting** is used by Hope and Fraser (2003a, 2003b) to relate to alternative approaches that should be used instead of annual budgeting. Beyond budgeting consists of similar activities as budgeting but dispenses with the annual budgeting process whereby resources are allocated in advance only on an annual basis. Instead, rolling forecasts, ambitious target setting, more decentralized decision behaviour and relative external performance evaluation are advocated.

Quarterly rolling forecasts are advocated that typically cover five to eight quarters. Such forecasts are regularly revised, thus supporting managers' ability to determine strategies that continuously adapt to the fast changing market conditions. Rolling forecasts are considered to provide more accurate information because they are constantly updated by the latest estimates of economic trends, customer demand and data from the most recent quarter. Hope and Fraser (2003a, 2003b) also argue that rolling forecasts avoid the dysfunctional behaviour that occurs with annual budgets because performance evaluation is no longer based on achieving fixed targets since the targets are continuously changed and updated.

Instead of evaluating performance against a static outdated budget, Hope and Fraser advocate abandoning budget targets and replacing them with relative external performance measures. These performance measures are based on comparisons of a small number of key performance indicators with competitors and similar units within the company, thus ensuring that they are based on the economic conditions prevailing at the time. Because the use of relative comparisons means managers do not know how successful they have been until the period is over, they must strive to ensure that their performance (in terms of a comparison of the key performance indicators) is better than the external and internal competitors. Hope and Fraser suggest that this approach results in managers having the confidence to stretch their performance. According to Bourmistrov and Kaarbøe (2013), one of the main problems of budgets is the establishment of 'comfort zones' whereas relative performance evaluation moves managers to so-called 'stretch zones' whereby they strive for continuous improvement.

Advocates of the beyond budgeting philosophy claim that it supports decentralization and employee empowerment initiatives that are required for firms to compete in today's fast-changing environment. In empowered organizations, managers have wide discretion in making decisions and can obtain resources more quickly without being dependent on resources being centrally allocated in advance as part of the annual budgeting process. Empowered organizations trust their managers to claim the resources they need to seize the opportunities that they identify in an ever-changing environment.

Beyond budgeting also places greater emphasis on team-based (or business unit) rewards rather than individual rewards because of the difficulty in identifying the incremental contribution of individuals and the need to demonstrate that everyone is pulling together in the same direction, each dependent on the other.

Surveys relating to the criticisms of budgeting

Because of the criticisms of budgeting, and the beyond budgeting movement, Dugdale and Lyne (2006) surveyed financial and non-financial managers in 40 UK companies. Their main conclusion was that budgeting is alive and well. All of the companies surveyed used budgets and, generally, both financial and non-financial managers thought they were important for planning, control, performance measurement, coordination and communication. To find out how problematic the respondents viewed their budgets, they were asked whether they agreed with 20 critical propositions. The respondents tended to disagree with the propositions. Ekholm and Wallin also surveyed 168 Finnish companies. They reported that relatively few companies were planning to abandon the annual budget. However, in contrast to the UK findings by Dugdale and Lyne (2006), there was strong agreement with many of the criticisms relating to budgeting. Comments by several respondents also indicated that complementary systems, such as rolling forecasts and monitoring systems similar to the balanced scorecard, already exist and are run in parallel with the annual budget.

A more recent study of budgeting practices in North American organizations was undertaken by Libby and Lindsay (2010). Their findings indicate that budgeting systems continue to play a key role in firms' control systems and that only 5 per cent of the 558 surveyed firms were considering possibly abandoning budgeting, although many were taking steps to improve their systems to overcome some of the common criticisms. They also found that:

- budgets were revised much more often than expected and new resources were allocated outside the budget process in order to respond in changes in the competitive environment
- the budget was explicitly linked to strategy implementation in the majority of firms surveyed and that the criticism that budgets are not linked to strategy was not supported by the responses by the majority of firms
- few of the sampled firms used budgets as fixed performance contracts. Instead, subjective considerations and allowances for uncontrollable events were extensively used when using the budget for performance evaluation.

Libby and Lindsay (2010) conclude that instead of going beyond budgeting, most firms have chosen to improve the process and that claims that budgets are flawed are probably overstated. The international survey undertaken by the Chartered Institute of Management Accountants (2009) reported that only around 5 per cent of the responding organizations used beyond budgeting and around 90 per cent used annual financial forecasts.

SUMMARY

The following items relate to the learning objectives listed at the beginning of the chapter.

- **Explain how budgeting fits into the overall strategic planning and control framework.** The annual budget should be set within the context of longer-term plans, which are likely to exist even if they have not been made explicit. A long-term plan is a statement of the preliminary targets and activities required by an organization to achieve its strategic plans together with a broad estimate for each year of the resources required. Because long-term planning involves 'looking into the future' for several years, the plans tend to be uncertain, general in nature, imprecise and subject to change. Annual budgeting is concerned with the detailed implementation of the long-term plan for the year ahead.

● **Identify and describe the six different purposes of budgeting.** Budgets are used for the following purposes: (a) planning annual operations; (b) coordinating the activities of the various parts of the organization and ensuring that the parts are in harmony with each other; (c) communicating the plans to the managers of the various responsibility centres; (d) motivating managers to strive to achieve organizational goals; (e) controlling activities; and (f) evaluating the performance of managers.

● **Identify and describe the various stages in the budget process.** The important stages are as follows: (a) communicating details of the budget policy and guidelines to those people responsible for the preparation of the budgets; (b) determining the factor that restricts performance (normally sales volume); (c) preparation of the sales budget (assuming that sales demand is the factor that restricts output); (d) initial preparation of the various budgets; (e) negotiation of budgets with superiors; (f) coordination and review of budgets; (g) final acceptance of budgets; and (h) ongoing review of budgets. Each of the above stages is described in the chapter.

● **Prepare functional and master budgets.** When all of the budgets have been prepared they are summarized into a master budget consisting of a budgeted profit and loss account, a balance sheet and a cash budget statement. The preparation of functional and master budgets was illustrated using Example 9.1.

● **Describe the limitations of incremental budgeting.** With incremental budgeting, indirect costs and support activities are prepared on an incremental basis. This means that existing operations and the current budgeted allowance for existing activities are taken as the starting point for preparing the next annual budget. The base is then adjusted for changes which are expected to occur during the new budget period. When this approach is adopted the concern is mainly with the increment in operations or expenditure that will occur during the forthcoming budget period. The major disadvantage of the incremental approach is that the majority of expenditure, which is associated with the 'base level' of activity, remains unchanged. Thus, past inefficiencies and waste inherent in the current way of doing things are perpetuated.

● **Describe activity-based budgeting.** Activity-based budgeting (ABB) aims to manage costs more effectively by authorizing the supply of only those resources that are needed to perform activities required to meet the budgeted production and sales volume. Whereas ABC assigns resource expenses to activities and then uses activity cost drivers to assign activity costs to cost objects (such as products, services or customers) ABB is the reverse of this process. Cost objects are the starting point. Their budgeted output determines the necessary activities that are then used to estimate the resources required for the budget period. ABB involves the following stages: (a) estimate the production and sales volume by individual products and customers; (b) estimate the demand for organizational activities; (c) determine the resources that are required to perform organizational activities; (d) estimate for each resource the quantity that must be supplied to meet the demand; and (e) take action to adjust the capacity of resources to match the projected supply.

- **Describe zero-based budgeting (ZBB).** ZBB is a method of budgeting that is mainly used in non-profit organizations but it can also be applied to discretionary costs and support activities in profit organizations. It seeks to overcome the deficiencies of incremental budgeting. ZBB works from the premise that projected expenditure for existing programmes should start from base zero, with each year's budgets being compiled as if the programmes were being launched for the first time.

- **Describe the criticisms relating to traditional budgeting.** Criticisms relating to traditional budgeting include encouraging rigid planning and incremental thinking, being time-consuming, a failure to encourage continuous improvement, achieving the target even if this results in undesirable actions and being a yearly rigid ritual. The beyond budgeting movement advocates that budgeting should be replaced with rolling forecasts that embrace key performance indicators and also incorporate exception-based monitoring and benchmarking.

KEY TERMS AND CONCEPTS

Activity-based budgeting (ABB)   An approach to budgeting that takes cost objects as the starting point, determines the necessary activities and then estimates the resources that are required for the budget period.

Beyond budgeting   A term used to describe alternative approaches, such as rolling forecasts, that can be used instead of annual budgeting.

Budget   A financial plan for implementing management decisions.

Budgetary control process   The process of comparing actual and planned outcomes, and responding to any deviations from the plan.

Budgeting   The implementation of the long-term plan for the year ahead through the development of detailed financial plans.

Cash budget   A budget that aims to ensure that sufficient cash is available at all times to meet the level of operations that are outlined in all other budgets.

Continuous budgeting   An approach to budgeting in which the annual budget is broken down into months for the first 3 months and into quarters for the rest of the year, with a new quarter being added as each quarter ends, also known as rolling budgeting.

Corporate objectives   Specific, measurable statements, often expressed in financial terms, of what the organization as a whole wishes to achieve.

Decision packages   A decision package represents the incremental packages reflecting different levels of effort that may be expended to undertake a specific group of activities within an organization.

Discretionary costs   Costs such as advertising and research where management has some discretion as to the amount it will budget.

Feedback loops   Parts of a control system that allow for review and corrective action to ensure that actual outcomes conform with planned outcomes.

Incremental budgeting   An approach to budgeting in which existing operations and the current budgeted allowance for existing activities are taken as the starting point for preparing the next annual budget and are then adjusted for anticipated changes.

Long-term plan   A top level plan that sets out the objectives that an organization's future activities will be directed towards, also known as a strategic plan.

Management by exception A system in which a manager's attention and effort can be concentrated on significant deviations from the expected results.

Master budget A document that brings together and summarizes all lower level budgets and which consists of a budgeted profit and loss account, a balance sheet and cash flow statement.

Mission statement A statement that provides in very general terms what the organization does to achieve its vision, its broad purpose and reason for its existence, the nature of the business(es) it is in and the customers it seeks to serve and satisfy.

Priority-based budgeting An approach to budgeting in which projected expenditure for existing activities starts from base zero rather than last year's budget, forcing managers to justify all budget expenditure, also known as zero-based budgeting.

Priority-based incremental budgets Budgets in which managers specify what incremental activities or changes would occur if their budgets were increased or decreased by a specified percentage, leading to budget allocations being made by comparing the change in costs with the change in benefits.

Rolling budgeting An approach to budgeting in which the annual budget is broken down into months for the first 3 months and into quarters for the rest of the year, with a new quarter being added as each quarter ends, also known as continuous budgeting.

Strategic plan A top level plan that sets out the objectives that an organization's future activities will be directed towards, also known as a long-term plan.

Strategy The courses of action that must be taken to achieve an organization's overall objectives.

Unit objectives Specific, measurable statements, often expressed in financial terms, of what individual units within an organization wish to achieve.

Vision statement A statement that clarifies the beliefs and governing principles of an organization, what it wants to be in the future or how it wants the world in which it operates to be

Zero-based budgeting An approach to budgeting in which projected expenditure for existing activities starts from base zero rather than last year's budget, forcing managers to justify all budget expenditure, also known as priority-based budgeting.

ASSESSMENT MATERIAL

The review questions are short questions that enable you to assess your understanding of the main topics included in the chapter. The page numbers in parentheses provide you with the page numbers to refer to if you cannot answer a specific question.

The review problems are more complex and require you to relate and apply the content to various business problems. Solutions to review problems are provided in a separate section at the end of the book. Additional review problems can be accessed by lecturers and students on the dedicated online support resources for this book. Solutions to these review problems are provided for lecturers in the *Instructor's Manual* accompanying this book that can be downloaded from the dedicated online instructor's resources (see Preface for details).

The dedicated online digital support resources for this book also includes over 30 case study problems.

REVIEW QUESTIONS

9.1 Define the term 'budget'. How are budgets used in planning? *(pp. 215–218)*

9.2 Describe the different stages in the planning and control process. *(pp. 215–216)*

9.3 Distinguish between budgeting and long-range planning. How are they related? *(pp. 216–217)*

9.4 Describe the different purposes of budgeting. *(pp. 218–220)*

9.5 Explain what is meant by the term 'management by exception'. *(p. 219)*

9.6 Describe how the different roles of budgets can conflict with each other. *(p. 220)*

9.7 Distinguish between continuous and rolling budgets. *(pp. 220–221)*

9.8 Describe the different stages in the budgeting process. *(pp. 222–225)*

9.9 All budgets depend on the sales budget. Do you agree? Explain. *(p. 223)*

9.10 What is a master budget? *(p. 225)*

9.11 Define incremental budgeting. *(p. 235)*

9.12 What are the distinguishing features of activity-based budgeting? *(pp. 235–236)*

9.13 Describe the five different stages that are involved with activity-based budgeting. *(pp. 235–236)*

9.14 How does zero-based budgeting differ from traditional budgeting? *(pp. 237–238)*

9.15 What are discretionary costs? *(p. 237)*

9.16 Distinguish between zero-based budgeting and priority-based incremental budgeting. *(p. 238)*

REVIEW PROBLEMS

9.17 X Co uses rolling budgeting, updating its budgets on a quarterly basis. After carrying out the last quarter's update to the cash budget, it projected a forecast cash deficit of $400000 at the end of the year. Consequently, the planned purchase of new capital equipment has been postponed.

Which of the following types of control is the manager's actions an example of?

(a) Feed-forward control
(b) Negative feedback control
(c) Positive feedback control
(d) Double loop feedback control

9.18 Preparation of functional budgets

Wollongong wishes to calculate an operating budget for the forthcoming period. Information regarding products, costs and sales levels is as follows:

Product	A	B
Materials required		
X (kg)	2	3
Y (litres)	1	4
Labour hours required		
Skilled (hours)	4	2
Semi-skilled (hours)	2	5
Sales level (units)	2 000	1 500
Opening inventory (units)	100	200

Closing inventory of materials and finished goods will be sufficient to meet 10 per cent of demand. Opening inventory of material X was 300 kg and for material Y was 1000 litres. Material prices are $10 per kg for material X and $7 per litre for material Y. Labour costs are $12 per hour for the skilled workers and $8 per hour for the semi-skilled workers.

Required:

Produce the following budgets:

(a) production (units)
(b) materials usage (kg and litres)
(c) materials purchases (kg, litres and $), and
(d) labour (hours and $).

(10 marks)

9.19 Budget preparation and comments on sales forecasting methods

You have recently been appointed as the management accountant to Alderley Ltd, a small company manufacturing two products, the Elgar and the Holst. Both products use the same type of material and labour but in different proportions. In the past, the company has had poor control over its working capital. To remedy this, you have recommended to the directors that a budgetary control system be introduced. This proposal has, now, been agreed.

Because Alderley Ltd's production and sales are spread evenly over the year, it was agreed that the annual budget should be broken down into four periods, each of 13 weeks, and commencing with the 13 weeks ending 4 April. To help you in this task, the sales and production directors have provided you with the following information:

1   Marketing and production data

	Elgar	Holst
Budgeted sales for 13 weeks (units)	845	1 235
Material content per unit (kilograms)	7	8
Labour per unit (standard hours)	8	5

2   Production labour
The 24 production employees work a 37-hour, 5-day week and are paid £8 per hour. Any hours in excess of

this involve Alderley in paying an overtime premium of 25 per cent. Because of technical problems, which will continue over the next 13 weeks, employees are only able to work at 95 per cent efficiency compared to standard.

3 Purchasing and opening inventory

The production director believes that raw materials will cost £12 per kilogram over the budget period. He also plans to revise the amount of inventory being kept. He estimates that the inventory levels at the commencement of the budget period will be as follows:

Raw materials	Elgar	Holst
2 328 kilograms	163 units	361 units

4 Closing inventory

At the end of the 13-week period closing stocks are planned to change. On the assumption that production and sales volumes for the second budget period will be similar to those in the first period:

● raw materials stocks should be sufficient for 13 days' production

● finished stocks of the Elgar should be equivalent to 6 days' sales volume

● finished stocks of the Holst should be equivalent to 14 days' sales volume.

Task 1

Prepare in the form of a statement the following information for the 13-week period to 4 April:

(a) the production budget in units for the Elgar and Holst

(b) the purchasing budget for Alderley Ltd in units

(c) the cost of purchases for the period

(d) the production labour budget for Alderley Ltd in hours

(e) the cost of production labour for the period.

Note: Assume a 5-day week for both sales and production.

The managing director of Alderley Ltd, Alan Dunn, has also only recently been appointed. He is keen to develop the company and has already agreed to two new products being developed. These will be launched in 18 months' time. While talking to you about the budget, he mentions that the quality of sales forecasting will need to improve if the company is to grow rapidly. Currently, the budgeted sales figure is found by initially adding 5 per cent to the previous year's sales volume and then revising the figure following discussions with the marketing director. He believes this approach is increasingly inadequate and now requires a more systematic approach.

A few days later, Alan Dunn sends you a memo. In that memo, he identifies three possible strategies for increasing sales volume. They are:

● more sales to existing customers

● the development of new markets

● the development of new products.

He asks for your help in forecasting likely sales volumes from these sources.

Task 2

Write a brief memo to Alan Dunn. Your memo should:

(a) identify *four* ways of forecasting future sales volume

(b) show how each of your four ways of forecasting can be applied to *one* of the sales strategies identified by Alan Dunn, and justify your choice

(c) give *two* reasons why forecasting methods might not prove to be accurate.

9.20 Preparation of cash budgets

The management of Beck plc have been informed that the union representing the direct production workers at one of their factories, where a standard product is produced, intends to call a strike. The accountant has been asked to advise the management of the effect the strike will have on cash flow.

The following data has been made available:

	Week 1	Week 2	Week 3
Budgeted sales	400 units	500 units	400 units
Budgeted production	600 units	400 units	Nil

The strike will commence at the beginning of week 3 and it should be assumed that it will continue for at least 4 weeks. Sales at 400 units per week will continue to be made during the period of the strike until inventory of finished goods are exhausted. Production will stop at the end of week 2. The current inventory level of finished goods is 600 units. Inventories of work in progress are not carried.

The selling price of the product is £60 and the budgeted manufacturing cost is made up as follows:

	(£)
Direct materials	15
Direct wages	7
Variable overheads	8
Fixed overheads	18
Total	£48

Direct wages are regarded as a variable cost. The company operates a full absorption costing system and the fixed overhead absorption rate is based upon a budgeted fixed overhead of £9000 per week. Included in the total fixed overheads is £700 per week for depreciation of equipment. During the period of the strike direct wages and variable overheads would not be incurred and the cash expended on fixed overheads would be reduced by £1500 per week.

The current inventory of raw materials are worth £7500; it is intended that these stocks should increase to £11 000 by the end of week 1 and then remain at this level during the period of the strike. *All direct materials are paid for 1 week after they have been received. Direct wages are paid 1 week in arrears. It should be assumed that all relevant overheads are paid for immediately the expense is incurred.* All sales are on credit, 70 per cent of the sales value is received in cash from the debtors at the end of the first week after the sales have been made and the balance at the end of the second week.

The current amount outstanding to material suppliers is £8000 and direct wage accruals amount to £3200. Both of these will be paid in week 1. The current balance owing from debtors is £31 200, of which £24 000 will be received during week 1 and the remainder during week 2. The current balance of cash at the bank and in hand is £1000.

Required:

(a)

(i) Prepare a cash budget for weeks one to six showing the balance of cash at the end of each week together with a suitable analysis of the receipts and payments during each week.

(13 marks)

(ii) Comment upon any matters arising from the cash budget which you consider should be brought to management's attention.

(4 marks)

(b) Explain why the reported profit figure for a period does not normally represent the amount of cash generated in that period.

(5 marks)

(Total 22 marks)

9.21 Rolling budgets

Designit is a small company providing design consultancy to a limited number of large clients. The business is mature and fairly stable year on year. It has 30 employees and is privately owned by its founder. Designit prepares an annual fixed budget. The company's accounts department consists of one part-qualified accountant, who has a heavy workload. He prepares the budget using spreadsheets. The company has a November year-end.

Designit pays each of its three sales managers an annual salary of $150 000, plus an individual bonus based on a lower and an upper level of income. For the year ended 30 November, for example, each of the sales managers was given a lower target of securing $1.5 million of fee income each, to be required by an individual bonus equating to 20 per cent of salary. If any of the managers secured a further $1.5 million of fee income, their bonus would increase by 5 per cent to the upper target of 25 per cent. None of the managers achieved the upper target but all of them achieved the lower one.

This is the same every year and Designit finds that often the managers secure work from several major clients early in the year and reach the $1.5 million target well before the year has ended. They then make little effort to secure extra fees for the company, knowing that it would be almost impossible to hit the second target. This, together with a few other problems that have arisen, has made the company consider whether its current budgeting process could be improved and whether the bonus scheme should also be changed.

Designit is now considering replacing the fixed budget with a monthly rolling budget, which Designit believes will make the budgeting process more relevant and timely and encourage managers to focus on the future rather than the past. It would also prevent the problem of targets being met too early on in the year by the sales managers because the targets would be set for monthly performance rather than annual performance. For example, a manager could be given a target of securing $200 000 fee income in the first month for a reward of 2 per cent of salary. Then, depending on what is happening both within the business and in the economy as a whole, at the end of the first month, a different target fee income could be set for the second month.

Required:

(a) Explain what a monthly rolling budget is and how it would operate at Designit.

(4 marks)

(b) Discuss the problems that may be encountered if Designit decides to introduce monthly rolling budgets together with a new bonus scheme, such as the one outlined above.

(5 marks)

(c) Discuss the problems with the current bonus scheme and, assuming that the company decides against introducing rolling budgets, describe and justify an alternative, more effective bonus scheme that could be introduced.

(6 marks)

(d) Discuss the risk of using the company accountant's own spreadsheets for budgeting.

(4 marks)

9.22 Incremental and zero base budgeting.
Newtown School's head teacher has prepared the budget for the year ending 31 May. The government pays the school $1050 for each child registered at the beginning of the school year, which is June 1, and $900 for any child joining the school part-way through the year. The school does not have to refund the money to the government if a child leaves the school part-way through the year. The number of pupils registered at the school on 1 June at the beginning of the budget year is 690, which is 10 per cent lower than the previous year. Based on past experience, the probabilities for the number of pupils starting the school part-way through the year are as follows:

Probability	No. of pupils joining late
0.2	50
0.3	20
0.5	26

The head teacher admits to being 'poor with numbers' and does not understand probabilities so, when calculating budgeted revenue, he just calculates a simple average for the number of pupils expected to join late. His budgeted revenue for the year ending 31 May is therefore as follows:

	Pupils	Rate per pupil	Total income
Pupils registered at beginning of school year	690	$1 050	$724 500
Average expected number of new joiners	32	$900	$28 800
			$753 300

The head teacher uses incremental budgeting to budget for his expenditure, taking actual expenditure for the previous year as a starting point and simply adjusting it for inflation, as shown below.

	Note	Actual cost for y/e 31 May $	Inflationary adjustment	Budgeted cost for y/e 31 May $
Repairs and maintenance	1	44 000	+3%	45 320
Salaries	2	620 000	+2%	632 400
Capital expenditure	3	65 000	+6%	68 900
Total budgeted expenditure				746 620
Budget surplus				6 680

Notes:

1 $30 000 of the costs for the year ended 31 May related to standard maintenance checks and repairs that have to be carried out by the school every year in order to comply with government health and safety standards. These are expected to increase by 3 per cent in the coming year. In the year ended 31 May $14 000 was also spent on redecorating some of the classrooms. No redecorating is planned for the coming year.

2 One teacher earning a salary of $26 000 left the school on 31 May and there are no plans to replace her. However, a 2 per cent pay rise will be given to all staff with effect from 1 December.

3 The full $65 000 actual costs for the year ended 31 May related to improvements made to the school gym. This year, the canteen is going to be substantially improved, although the extent of the improvements and level of service to be offered to pupils is still under discussion. There is a 0.7 probability that the cost will be $145 000 and a 0.3 probability that it will be $80 000. These costs must be paid in full before the end of the year ending 31 May.

The school's board of governors, who review the budget, are concerned that the budget surplus has been calculated incorrectly. They believe that it should have been calculated using expected income, based on the probabilities provided, and using expected expenditure, based on the information provided in Notes 1 to 3. They believe that incremental budgeting is not proving a reliable tool for budget setting in the school since, for the last three years, there have been shortfalls of cash despite a budget surplus being predicted. Since the school has no other source of funding available to it, these shortfalls have had serious consequences, such as the closure of the school kitchen for a considerable period in the last school year, meaning that no hot meals were available to pupils. This is thought to have been the cause of the 10 per cent fall in the number of pupils registered at the school on 1 June.

Required:

(a) Considering the views of the board of governors, recalculate the budget surplus/deficit for the year ending 31 May.

(6 marks)

(b) Discuss the advantages and disadvantages of using incremental budgeting.

(4 marks)

(c) Briefly outline the three main steps involved in preparing a zero-based budget.

(6 marks)

(d) Discuss the extent to which zero-based budgeting could be used by Newtown School to improve the budgeting process.

9.23 Some commentators argue that: 'With continuing pressure to control costs and maintain efficiency, the time has come for all public sector organizations to embrace zero-based budgeting. There is no longer a place for incremental budgeting in any organization, particularly public sector ones, where zero-based budgeting is far more suitable anyway.'

Required:

(a) Discuss the particular difficulties encountered when budgeting in public sector organizations compared with budgeting in private sector organizations, drawing comparisons between the two types of organizations.

(5 marks)

(b) Explain the terms 'incremental budgeting' and 'zero-based budgeting'.

(4 marks)

(c) State the main stages involved in preparing zero-based budgets.

(3 marks)

(d) Discuss the view that 'there is no longer a place for incremental budgeting in any organization, particularly public sector ones,' highlighting any drawbacks of zero-based budgeting that need to be considered.

(8 marks)

9.24 Budgeting has been criticized as:

- a cumbersome process that occupies considerable management time
- concentrating unduly on short term financial control
- having undesirable effects on the motivation of managers
- emphasizing formal organization structure.

Required:

(a) Explain these criticisms.

(8 marks)

(b) Explain what changes can be made in response to these criticisms to improve the budgeting process.

(12 marks)

(Total 20 marks)

10
MANAGEMENT CONTROL SYSTEMS

LEARNING OBJECTIVES After studying this chapter you should be able to:

● describe the three different types of controls used in organizations

● distinguish between feedback and feed-forward controls

● explain the potential harmful side-effects of results controls

● define the four different types of responsibility centres

● explain the different elements of management accounting control systems

● describe the controllability principle and the methods of implementing it

● discuss how the level of difficulty of targets impacts on motivation and performance

● describe the influence of participation in the budgeting process.

Control is the process of ensuring that a firm's activities conform to its plans and that its objectives are achieved. There can be no control without objectives and plans, since these predetermine and specify the desirable behaviour and set out the procedures that should be followed by members of the organization to ensure that a firm is operated in a desired manner.

In an article published many years ago, Drucker (1964) distinguished between 'controls' and 'control'. **Controls** are measurement and information, whereas control means direction. In other words, 'controls' are purely a means to an end; the end is control. '**Control**' is the function that makes sure that actual work is done to fulfil the original intention, and 'controls' are used to provide information to assist in determining the control action to be taken. For example, material costs may be greater than budget. 'Controls' will indicate that costs exceed budget and that this may be because the purchase of inferior quality materials causes excessive wastage. 'Control' is the action that is taken to purchase the correct quality materials in the future to reduce excessive wastage.

'Controls' encompasses all the methods and procedures that direct employees towards achieving the organization objectives. Many different control mechanisms are used in organizations and the management accounting control system represents only one aspect of the various control mechanisms that companies use to control their managers and employees. To fully understand the role that management accounting control systems play in the control process, it is necessary to be aware of how they relate to the entire array of control mechanisms used by organizations. Note that the term **management control system** is used to refer to the entire array of controls used by an organization

This chapter begins by describing the different types of controls that are used by companies. The elements of management accounting control systems will then be described within the context of the overall control process.

CONTROL AT DIFFERENT ORGANIZATIONAL LEVELS

Control is applied at different levels within an organization. Merchant and van der Stede (2017) distinguish between strategic control and management control. **Strategic control** has an external focus. The emphasis is on how a firm, given its strengths and weaknesses and limitations, can compete with other firms in the same industry. We shall explore some of these issues in Chapter 14 within the context of strategic performance management. In this, and the next four chapters, our emphasis will be on management control systems which consist of a collection of control mechanisms that primarily have a shorter-term internal focus. The aim of management control systems is to influence employee behaviours in desirable ways in order to increase the probability that an organization's objectives will be achieved. Merchant and van der Stede define management control as dealing with employees' behaviour. They state:

It is people in the organization that make things happen. Management controls are necessary to guard against the possibilities that people will do something the organizations do not want them to do or fail to do something they should do. If all employees could always be relied on to do what is best for the organization there would be no need for management control systems.

The terms 'management accounting control systems', 'accounting control systems' and 'management control systems' are often used interchangeably. Both management accounting and accounting control systems refer to the collection of practices such as budgetary planning and control, standard costing and periodic performance reporting that are normally administered by the management accounting function. Management control systems represent a broader term that encompasses management accounting/accounting control systems but it also includes other controls such as action, personnel and social controls. These controls are described in the following section.

DIFFERENT TYPES OF CONTROLS

Companies use many different control mechanisms to cope with the problem of organizational control. To make sense of the vast number of controls that are used we shall classify them into three categories using approaches that have been adopted by Ouchi (1979) and Merchant and van der Stede (2017). They are:

1 action (or behavioural) controls
2 personnel, cultural and social controls
3 results (or output) controls.

You should note that management accounting systems are normally synonymous with output controls whereas management control systems encompass all of the above categories of controls.

Action or behavioural controls

Behavioural controls (also known as **action controls**) involve observing the actions of individuals as they go about their work. They are appropriate where cause-and-effect relationships are well understood, so that if the correct actions are followed, the desired outcomes will occur. Under these circumstances effective control can be achieved by having superiors watch and guide the actions of subordinates. For example, if the supervisor watches the workers on the assembly line and ensures that the work is done exactly as prescribed then the expected quality and quantity of work should ensue. Forms of action controls described by Merchant and van der Stede include behavioural constraints, preaction reviews and action accountability.

The aim of *behavioural constraints* is to prevent people from doing things that should not be done. They include physical constraints, such as computer passwords that restrict accessing or updating information sources to authorized personnel, and administrative constraints, such as ceilings on the amount of capital expenditure that managers may authorize.

Preaction reviews involve the scrutiny and approval of action plans of the individuals being controlled before they can undertake a course of action. Examples include the approval by municipal authorities of plans for the construction of properties prior to building commencing or the approval by a tutor of a dissertation plan prior to the student being authorized to embark on the dissertation.

Action accountability involves defining actions that are acceptable or unacceptable, observing the actions and rewarding acceptable or punishing unacceptable actions. Examples of action accountability include establishing work rules and procedures and company codes of conduct that employees must follow. Budgets are another form of action accountability whereby an upper limit on an expense category is given for the budget period. If managers exceed these limits they are held accountable and are required to justify their actions.

Personnel, cultural and social controls

Social or cultural controls involve the selection of people who have already been socialized into adopting particular norms and patterns of behaviour required to achieve an organization's objectives. For example, if the only staff promoted to managerial level are those who display a high commitment to the firm's objectives then the need for other forms of controls can be reduced. Social/cultural controls represent a set of values, social norms and beliefs that are shared by members of the organization and that influence their actions. Control is exercised by individuals over one another – for example, procedures used by groups within an organization to regulate performance of their own members and to bring them into line when they deviate from group norms.

Personnel controls involve helping employees do a good job by building on employees' natural tendencies to control themselves. In particular, they ensure that the employees have the capabilities (in terms of intelligence, qualifications and experience) and the resources needed to do a good job. This requires appropriate training to ensure that employees know how to perform the assigned tasks and to make them fully aware of the results and actions that are expected from them.

Cultural controls represent a set of values, social norms and beliefs that are shared by members of the organization and that influence their actions. Cultural controls are exercised by individuals over one another – for example, procedures used by groups within an organization to regulate performance of their own members and to bring them into line when they deviate from group norms. It is apparent from the above description that cultural controls are virtually the same as social controls.

Results or output controls

Output or **results controls** involve collecting and reporting information about the outcomes of work effort. The major advantage of results controls is that senior managers do not have to be knowledgeable about the means required to achieve the desired results or be involved in directly observing the actions of subordinates. They merely rely on performance reports to ascertain whether or not the desired outcomes have been achieved. Management accounting control systems can be described as a form of output controls. They are mostly defined in monetary terms such as revenues, costs, profits and ratios (e.g. return on investment). Results measures also include non-accounting measures such as the number of units of defective production, the number of loan applications processed or ratio measures such as the number of customer deliveries on time as a percentage of total deliveries.

Results controls involve the following stages:

1 establishing performance measures for the activities that the organization wishes to monitor
2 establishing performance targets
3 measuring performance
4 providing rewards or punishment.

The *first stage* involves selecting performance measures for those aspects of activities that the organization wishes to monitor. Ideally, desirable behaviour should improve the performance measure and undesirable behaviour should have a detrimental effect on the measure.

The *second-stage* requirement of a preset performance target informs individuals what to aim for and enables employees or their superiors to interpret performance. The *third stage* specified above relates to measuring performance. Ability to measure some outputs effectively constrains the use of results measures. Consider a personnel department. The accomplishments of the department can be difficult to measure and other forms of control are likely to be preferable. To encourage the right behaviours, results measures should also be timely and understandable. Significant delays in reporting will result in the measures losing most of their motivational impact and a lengthy delay in taking remedial action when outcomes deviate from target. Also, if measures are not understandable it is unlikely that managers will know how their actions will affect the measure and there is a danger that the measures will lose their motivational impact.

The *final stage* of results controls involves encouraging employees to achieve organizational goals by having rewards (or punishments) linked to their success (or failure) in achieving the results measures. Organizational rewards include salary increases, bonuses, promotions and recognition. Employees can also derive intrinsic rewards through a sense of accomplishment and achievement. Punishments include demotions, failure to obtain the rewards and possibly the loss of one's job.

FEEDBACK AND FEED-FORWARD CONTROLS

Feedback control involves monitoring outputs achieved against desired outputs and taking corrective action if a deviation exists. In **feed-forward control**, instead of actual outputs being compared against desired outputs, predictions are made of what outputs are expected to be at some future time. If these expectations differ from what is desired, control actions are taken that will minimize these differences. The objective is for control to be achieved before any deviations from desired outputs actually occur. In other words, with feed-forward controls likely errors can be anticipated and steps taken to avoid them, whereas with feedback controls actual errors are identified after the event and corrective action is taken to implement future actions to achieve the desired outputs.

A major limitation of feedback control is that errors are identified after they have occurred. However, this is not usually a significant problem when there is a short time lag between the occurrence of an error and the identification and implementation of corrective action. Feed-forward control is therefore preferable when a significant time lag occurs. The budgeting process is a feed-forward control system. To the extent that outcomes fall short of what is desired, alternatives are considered until a budget is produced that is expected to achieve what is desired. The comparison of actual results with budget, in identifying **variances** and taking remedial action to ensure that future outcomes will conform with budgeted outcomes is an illustration of a feedback control system. Thus accounting control systems consist of both feedback and feed-forward controls.

HARMFUL SIDE-EFFECTS OF CONTROLS

Harmful side-effects occur when the controls motivate employees to engage in behaviour that is not organizationally desirable. In this situation the control system leads to a lack of **goal congruence**. Alternatively, when controls motivate behaviour that is organizationally desirable they are described as encouraging goal congruence.

Results controls can lead to a lack of goal congruence if the results that are required can only be partially specified. Here there is a danger that employees will concentrate only on what is monitored by the control system, regardless of whether or not it is organizationally desirable. In other words, they will seek to maximize their individual performance according to the rules of the control system irrespective of whether their actions contribute to the organization's objectives. In addition, they may ignore other important areas, if they are not monitored by the control system. The phrase 'What you measure is what you get' applies in these circumstances.

Figure 10.1, derived from Emmanual *et al.* (1990), illustrates the problems that can arise when the required results can only be partially specified. You will see that those aspects of

REAL WORLD VIEWS 10.1

Defining success on what is spent rather than what is achieved

The British government has pledged to spend 0.7 per cent of national income on foreign aid, resulting in £13 billion being allocated to the Department for International Development's (DfID's) aid budget, despite the Independent Commission on Aid Impact publishing a scathing report on DfID's efforts to help developing countries. The report concluded that the programmes had unrealistic targets and their performances were not properly assessed.

'There is almost nothing better designed to perpetuate wastefulness than the knowledge that the overall budget is guaranteed come what may,' writes Dominic Lawson in *the Sunday Times*. He cites that in 2012 the House of Lords' economic affairs committee warned that this target 'wrongly prioritizes the amount spent rather than the result achieved; it makes the achievement of the spending target more important than the overall effectiveness of the programme'. More recently a National Audit Office (NAO) report raised concerns that money is being wasted because of the 'rush' by civil servants to hit the legal requirement of spending 0.7 per cent of the nation's income on overseas aid. The report revealed five out of 11 departments responsible for spending on foreign aid spent more than half their annual aid budget in the last few weeks of the year to meet financial deadlines. An article in the *Daily Telegraph* quotes a Government MP as stating that 'We really need to the abandon the 0.7 per cent target as soon as possible. The Government departments are spending money to meet these artificial targets, not on the basis of need.'

Questions

1 What are the advantages and disadvantages of using a fixed budget as outlined above?
2 What approaches can be taken to overcome the problems relating to fixed budgets?

References

Lawson, D. (2015) This is one target our armed forces can afford to miss, *Sunday Times*, 8 March.
Anonymous (2017), Government departments 'struggling' to spend their foreign aid budgets. *Telegraph.co.uk*. July 17 2017. Available at www.telegraph.co.uk/news/2017/07/17/government-departments-struggling-spend-foreign-aid-budgets/

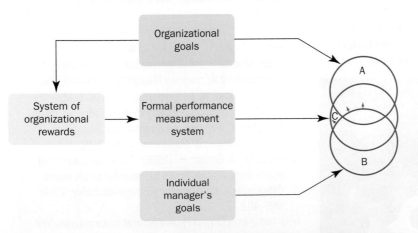

FIGURE 10.1

The measurement and reward process with imperfect measures

A Behaviour necessary to achieve organizational goals
B Behaviour actually engaged in by an individual manager
C Behaviour formally measured by control systems

behaviour on which subordinates are likely to concentrate to achieve their personal goals (circle B) do not necessarily correspond with those necessary for achieving the wider organizational goals (circle A). In an ideal system the measured behaviour (represented by circle C) should completely cover the area of desired behaviour (represented by circle A). Therefore, if a manager maximizes the performance measure, he or she will also maximize his or her contribution to the goals of the organization. In other words, the performance measures encourage goal congruence. In practice, it is unlikely that perfect performance measures can be constructed that measure all desirable organizational behaviour, and so it is unlikely that all of circle C will cover circle A. Assuming that managers desire the rewards offered by circle C, their actual behaviour (represented by circle B) will be altered to include more of circle C and, to the extent that C coincides with A, more of circle A.

However, organizational performance will be improved only to the extent that the performance measure is a good indicator of what is desirable to achieve the firm's goals.

REAL WORLD VIEWS 10.2

Targets and controls in police forces

Some academic literature has noted the positive outcomes of budgeting and other forms of performance measurement systems in police forces (see for example Collier, 2001; Drake and Simper, 2005; Donnelly et al. 2006). However, setting targets for a police force can also have a negative side, and lead to dysfunctional behaviour or even corruption. The Irish police force, known as the Garda, provide an interesting example.

During 2017, a 'scandal' emerged whereby the number of road-side alcohol breath tests conducted by the Garda appeared to have been incorrectly reported. According to an article in the *Irish Independent* 'from 2009 to 2016 … 3 498 400 tests were recorded on the Garda's internal Pulse computer system, but only 2 040 179 were carried out'.

The head officer of the Garda (known as the Commissioner) said this showed failures in systems, processes, supervision and management of the force. The article also notes that while no criminality on the part of any Garda had been found at the time, Garda management may have set overly ambitious targets for the rank-and-file Garda in terms of driver breath tests. Mention is also made of budget cuts in the period 2008.

Questions

1 Do you think management control systems (including budgets or performance measures) are likely to be as effective in a police force as in a typical commercial organization?
2 Based on the facts above, is this an example of failure of the management control systems?

References

Collier, P. M. (2001). The power of accounting: a field study of local financial management in a police force. *Management Accounting Research*, 12(4), 465–486

Donnelly, M., Kerr, N. J., Rimmer, R., & Shiu, E. M. (2006). Assessing the quality of police services using SERVQUAL. *Policing: An International Journal of Police Strategies & Management*, 29(1), 92–105

Drake, L. M., & Simper, R. (2005). The measurement of police force efficiency: An assessment of UK Home Office policy. *Contemporary Economic Policy*, 23(4), 465–482

Irish Independent (2017). Available at www.independent. ie/breaking-news/irish-news/fake-breath-test-reports-unacceptable-garda-commissioner-36106609.html

Unfortunately, performance measures are not perfect, and ideal measures of overall performance are unlikely to exist. Some measures may encourage goal congruence or organizationally desirable behaviour (the part of circle C that coincides with A), but other measures will not encourage goal congruence (the part of circle C that does not coincide with A). Consequently, there is a danger that subordinates will concentrate only on what is measured, regardless of whether or not it is organizationally desirable. Furthermore, actual behaviour may be modified so that desired results appear to be obtained, although they may have been achieved in an undesirable manner that is detrimental to the firm.

It is clear that flaws in the performance measurement sytems used by banks contributed to the financial crisis in the banking sector in 2008. Bonuses and performance measures were based on short-term, rather than long-term performance, that did not take risk into account. These performance measures encouraged managers to take actions to increase sales or profits when such actions resulted in providing high risk loans. The performance measures motivated managers to increase the reported sales revenues and profits, and thus their bonus, without considering the adverse long-term implications of their actions. They were not engaging in organizationally desirable behaviour because the performance measurement and reward system strongly encouraged them not to do so. Many would argue that the managers were acting in an unethical manner but clearly the performance measurement and the reward system was also at fault. We shall discuss how such dysfunctional behaviour may be reduced in Chapters 12 and 14.

MANAGEMENT ACCOUNTING CONTROL SYSTEMS

Up to this point in the chapter we have been looking at the broad context of management control systems. We shall now concentrate on management accounting control systems, which represent the predominant controls in most organizations.

Why are management accounting controls the predominant controls? There are several reasons. First, all organizations need to express and aggregate the results of a wide range of dissimilar activities using a common measure. The monetary measure meets this requirement. Second, profitability and liquidity are essential to the success of all organizations and financial measures relating to these and other areas are closely monitored by stakeholders. It is therefore natural that managers will wish to monitor performance in monetary terms. Third, financial measures also enable a common decision rule to be applied by all managers when considering alternative courses of action. That is, a course of action will normally benefit a firm only if it results in an improvement in its financial performance. Finally, measuring results in financial terms enables managers to be given more autonomy. Focusing on the outcomes of managerial actions, summarized in financial terms, gives managers the freedom to take whatever actions they consider to be appropriate to achieve the desired results.

RESPONSIBILITY CENTRES

The complex business environment of today makes it virtually impossible for most firms to be controlled centrally. It is simply not possible for central management to have all the relevant information and time to determine the detailed plans for the entire organization.

Some degree of decentralization is essential for all but the smallest firms. Organizations decentralize by creating **responsibility centres**. A responsibility centre may be defined as a unit of a firm such as a department or division where an individual manager is held responsible for the unit's performance. There are four types of responsibility centre:

1 cost or expense centres
2 revenue centres
3 profit centres
4 investment centres.

The creation of responsibility centres is a fundamental part of management accounting control systems. It is therefore important that you can distinguish between the various forms of responsibility centres.

Cost or expense centres

Cost or **expense centres** are responsibility centres whose managers are normally accountable for only those costs that are under their control. We can distinguish between two types of cost centres – **standard cost centres** and discretionary cost centres (also known as discretionary expense centres). The main features of standard cost centres are that output can be measured and the input required to produce each unit of output can be specified. Control is exercised by comparing the standard cost (that is, the cost of the inputs that *should* have been consumed in producing the output) with the cost that was *actually* incurred. The difference between the actual cost and the standard cost is described as the variance. Standard cost centres and variance analysis will be discussed extensively in the next chapter.

Discretionary expense centres are those responsibility cost centres where output cannot be measured in financial terms and there are no clearly observable relationships between inputs (the resources consumed) and the outputs (the results achieved). Control normally takes the form of ensuring that actual expenditure adheres to budgeted expenditure for each expense category and also ensuring that the tasks assigned to each centre have been successfully accomplished. Examples of discretionary centres include advertising and publicity and research and development departments. One of the major problems arising in discretionary expense centres is measuring the effectiveness of expenditures. For example, the marketing support department may not have exceeded an advertising budget but this does not mean that the advertising expenditure has been effective. The advertising may have been incorrectly timed, it may have been directed to the wrong audience, or it may have contained the wrong message. Determining the effectiveness and efficiency of discretionary expense centres is one of the most difficult areas of management control.

Revenue centres

Revenue centres are responsibility centres where managers are mainly accountable for financial outputs in the form of generating sales revenues. Typical examples of revenue centres are where regional sales managers are accountable for sales within their regions. Revenue centre managers may also be held accountable for selling expenses, such as salesperson salaries, commissions and order-getting costs. They are not, however, made accountable for the cost of the goods and services that they sell.

Profit centres

Both cost and revenue centre managers have limited decision-making authority. Cost centre managers are accountable only for managing inputs (costs) of their centres. Revenue centres are accountable for selling the products or services but they have no control over their manufacture. A significant increase in managerial autonomy occurs when unit managers are given responsibility for both production and sales. In this situation managers are normally free to set selling prices, choose which markets to sell in, make product mix and output decisions and select suppliers. Units within an organization whose managers are accountable for both revenues and costs are called **profit centres** or **business units**. As the name implies profit centres tend to be larger independent units within an organization.

Investment centres

Investment centres are responsibility centres whose managers are responsible for both sales revenues and costs and, in addition, have responsibility and authority to make capital investment decisions. Typical investment centre performance measures include return on investment and economic value added. These measures are influenced by revenues, costs and assets employed and thus reflect the responsibility that managers have for both generating profits and managing the investment base. Investment centres represent the highest level of managerial autonomy. They include the company as a whole, operating subsidiaries, business units and divisions. Investment and profit centres will be discussed extensively in Chapter 12.

THE NATURE OF MANAGEMENT ACCOUNTING CONTROL SYSTEMS

Management accounting control systems have two core elements. The first is the formal planning processes such as budgeting and long-term planning that were described in the previous chapter. These processes are used for establishing performance expectations for evaluating performance. The second is responsibility accounting, which involves the creation of responsibility centres. Responsibility centres enable accountability for financial results and outcomes to be allocated to heads of responsibility centres throughout the organization. The objective of **responsibility accounting** is to accumulate costs and revenues for each individual responsibility centre so that the deviations from a performance target (typically the budget) can be attributed to the individual who is accountable for the responsibility centre. For each responsibility centre the process involves setting a performance target, measuring performance, comparing performance against the target, analysing the variances and taking action where significant variances exist between actual and target performance. In the remainder of the chapter we shall focus on responsibility accounting within cost centres at lower management levels rather than at the business unit level. We shall consider control and performance measurement at higher organization levels relating to business units (profit centres and investment centres) in Chapters 12 and 14 where our focus will be on strategic performance measurement and management.

Responsibility accounting relating to cost and revenue centres at lower management levels is implemented by issuing **performance reports** at frequent intervals (normally monthly) that inform responsibility centre managers of the deviations from budgets for which they are accountable and are required to take action. An example of a performance report issued to a cost centre manager is presented in the lower section of Exhibit 10.1. You should note that at successively higher levels of management less detailed information is reported. You can see from the upper sections of Exhibit 10.1 that the information is condensed and summarized as the results relating to the responsibility centre are reported at higher levels. Exhibit 10.1 only includes financial information. In addition, important non-financial measures such as those relating to quality and timeliness may be reported. We shall look at non-financial measures in more detail in Chapter 14.

Responsibility accounting involves:

- distinguishing between those items that managers can control and for which they should be held accountable and those items over which they have no control and for which they are not held accountable (i.e. applying the controllability principle)

EXHIBIT 10.1 Responsibility accounting monthly performance reports

		Budget		Variance[a] F (A)	
		Current month (€)	Year to date (€)	This month (€)	Year to date (€)
	Performance report to managing director				
Managing director	▶ Factory A	453 900	6 386 640	80 000(A)	98 000(A)
	Factory B	X	X	X	X
	Factory C	X	X	X	X
	Administration costs	X	X	X	X
	Selling costs	X	X	X	X
	Distribution costs	X	X	X	X
		2 500 000	30 000 000	400 000(A)	600 000(A)
	Performance report to production manager of factory A				
Production manager	Works manager's office	X	X	X	X
	▶ Machining department 1	165 600	717 600	32 760(A)	89 180(A)
	Machining department 2	X	X	X	X
	Assembly department	X	X	X	X
	Finishing department	X	X	X	X
		453 900	6 386 640	80 000(A)	98 000(A)
	Performance report to head of responsibility centre				
Head of responsibility centre	Direct materials	X	X	X	X
	Direct labour	X	X	X	X
	Indirect labour	X	X	X	X
	Indirect materials	X	X	X	X
	Power	X	X	X	X
	Maintenance	X	X	X	X
	Idle time	X	X	X	X
	Other	X	X	X	X
		165 600	717 600	32 760(A)	89 180(A)

[a] F indicates a favourable variance (actual cost less than budgeted cost) and (A) indicates an adverse budget (actual cost greater than budget cost). Note that, at the lowest level of reporting, the responsibility centre head's performance report contains detailed information on operating costs. At successively higher levels of management less detail is reported. For example, the managing director's information on the control of activities consists of examining those variances that represent significant departures from the budget for each factory and functional area of the business and requesting explanations from the appropriate managers.

- setting performance targets and determining how challenging the targets should be
- determining how much influence managers should have in the setting of targets.

We shall now examine each of these items in detail.

THE CONTROLLABILITY PRINCIPLE

Responsibility accounting is based on the application of the **controllability principle**, which means that it is appropriate to assign only those costs to responsibility centres that can be significantly influenced by the manager of that responsibility centre. The controllability principle can be implemented by either eliminating the uncontrollable items from the areas for which managers are held accountable or calculating their effects so that the reports distinguish between controllable and uncontrollable items.

Applying the controllability principle is difficult in practice because many areas do not fit neatly into either controllable or uncontrollable categories. Instead, they are partially controllable. Even when outcomes are affected by occurrences outside a manager's control – such as competitors' actions, price changes and supply shortages – a competent manager can take action to reduce their adverse effects. He or she can substitute alternative materials where the prices of raw materials change or monitor and respond to competitors' actions. If these factors are categorized as uncontrollables managers will not be motivated to try and influence them.

Dealing with the distorting effects of uncontrollable factors before the measurement period

Management can attempt to deal with the distorting effects of uncontrollables by making adjustments either before or after the measurement period. Uncontrollable and controllable factors can be determined prior to the measurement period by specifying which budget line items are to be regarded as controllable and uncontrollable. Uncontrollable items can either be excluded from performance reports or shown in a separate section within the performance report so that they are clearly identifiable. The latter approach has the advantage of drawing managerial attention to those costs that a company incurs to support their activities. Managers may be able to indirectly influence these costs if they are made aware of the sums involved.

Dealing with the distorting effects of uncontrollable factors after the measurement period

Merchant and van der Stede (2017) identify four methods of removing the effects of uncontrollable factors from the results measures after the measurement period and before the rewards are assigned:

1 variance analysis
2 flexible performance standards
3 relative performance evaluations
4 subjective performance evaluations.

EXAMPLE 10.1

An item of expense that is included in the budget for a responsibility centre varies directly in relation to activity at an estimated cost of £5 per unit of output. The budgeted monthly level of activity was 20 000 units and the actual level of activity was 24 000 units at a cost of £105 000.

Variance analysis seeks to analyse the factors that cause the actual results to differ from pre-determined budgeted targets. In particular, it helps to distinguish between controllable and uncontrollable items and identify those individuals who are accountable for the variances. For example, variances analysed by each type of cost, and by their price and quantity effects, enables variances to be traced to accountable individuals and also to isolate those variances that are due to uncontrollable factors. Variance analysis will be discussed extensively in the next chapter.

Flexible performance standards apply when targets are adjusted to reflect variations in uncontrollable factors arising from the circumstances not envisaged when the targets were set. The most widely used flexible performance standard is to use **flexible budgets** in which the uncontrollable volume effects on cost behaviour are removed from the manager's performance reports. Because some costs vary with changes in the level of activity, it is essential when applying the controllability principle to take into account the variability of costs. For example, if the actual level of activity is greater than the budgeted level of activity then those costs that vary with activity will be greater than the budgeted costs purely because of changes in activity. Let us consider the simplified situation presented in Example 10.1.

Assuming that the increase in activity was due to the sales volume being greater than that anticipated when the budget was set then the increases in costs arising from the volume change are beyond the control of the responsibility centre manager. It is clearly inappropriate to compare actual *variable* costs of £105 000 from an activity level of 24 000 units with budgeted *variable* costs of £100 000 from an activity level of 20 000 units. This would incorrectly suggest an overspending of £5 000. If managers are to be made responsible for their costs, it is essential that they are responsible for performance under the conditions in which they worked, and not for a performance based on conditions when the budget was drawn up. In other words, it is misleading to compare actual costs at one level of activity with budgeted costs at another level of activity. At the end of the period the original budget must be adjusted to the actual level of activity to take into account the impact of the uncontrollable volume change on costs. This procedure is called flexible budgeting. In Example 10.1 the performance report should be as follows:

Budgeted expenditure	Actual expenditure
(flexed to 24 000 units)	(24 000 units)
£120 000	£105 000

The budget is adjusted to reflect what the costs should have been for an actual activity of 24 000 units. This indicates that the manager has incurred £15 000 less expenditure than would have been expected for the actual level of activity, and a favourable variance of £15 000 should be recorded on the performance report, not an adverse variance of £5000, which would have been recorded if the original budget had not been adjusted.

In Example 10.1 it is assumed that there was only one variable item of expense, but in practice the budget will include many different expenses including fixed, semi-variable and variable expenses. You should note that fixed expenses do not vary in the short term with activity and therefore the budget should remain unchanged for these expenses. The budget should be flexed only for variable and semi-variable expenses.

Budgets may also be adjusted to reflect other uncontrollable factors besides volume changes. Budgets are normally set based on the environment that is anticipated during the budget setting process. If the budget targets are then used throughout the duration of the annual budget period for performance evaluation the managers will be held accountable for uncontrollable factors arising from forecasting errors. To remove the managerial exposure to uncontrollable risks arising from forecasting errors **ex post budget adjustments** can be made whereby the budget is adjusted to the environmental and economic conditions that the managers actually faced during the period.

Relative performance evaluation relates to the situations where the performance of a responsibility centre is evaluated relative to the performance of similar centres within the same company or to similar units outside the organization. To be effective, responsibility centres must perform similar tasks and face similar environmental and business conditions with the units that they are being benchmarked against. Such relative comparisons with units facing similar environmental conditions neutralizes the uncontrollable factors because they are in effect held constant when making the relative comparisons. The major difficulty relating to relative performance evaluations is finding benchmark units that face similar conditions and uncertainties.

REAL WORLD VIEWS 10.3

Budgetary control in a state owned enterprise in China

An article by Dai *et al.* (2017) provides insights into the budgetary control practices at Superhydro, a Chinese state-owned enterprise. Budgets are used as a planning tool and target setting is an important step in preparing budgets. The company determines the targets for its master budget in light of the twelfth Five-Year Plan issued by the Chinese central government. These targets serve as one of the benchmarks against which the performance of divisions, business units and subsidiaries are assessed and monitored. Progress in achieving the targets is continuously checked and followed up using variance analysis reports. Appropriate key performance indicators were established to assess the financial performance of its divisions, business units and subsidiaries. These key performance indicators were also used to measure and evaluate the performance of individual employees so that their performance could be better linked to rewards.

Questions

1 What types of rewards or punishments should be used when comparing target and actual performance?
2 What are the limitations of linking bonuses with achievement of key financial performance indicators?

Reference

Dai, N.T., Tan, Z.S., Tang, G. and Xiao, J.Z. (2017), IPOs, institutional complexity, and management accounting in hybrid organisations: A field study in a state-owned enterprise in China, *Management Accounting Research*, 36, 2–23

Instead of making the formal and quantitative adjustments that are a feature of the methods that have been described so far, **subjective judgements** can be made in the evaluation process based on the knowledge of the outcome measures and the circumstances faced by the responsibility centre heads. The disadvantages of subjective evaluations are that they are not objective, they tend not to provide the person being evaluated with a clear indication of how performance has been evaluated, they can create conflict with superiors resulting in a loss of morale and a decline in motivation and they are expensive in terms of management time.

Guidelines for applying the controllability principle

Dealing with uncontrollables represents one of the most difficult areas for the design and operation of management accounting control systems. The following guidelines published by the Report of the Committee of Cost Concepts and Standards in the USA in 1956 still continues to provide useful guidance:

1 If a manager *can control the quantity and price paid* for a service then the manager is responsible for all the expenditure incurred for the service.

2 If the manager *can control the quantity of the service but not the price paid* for the service then only that amount of difference between actual and budgeted expenditure that is due to usage should be identified with the manager.

3 If the manager *cannot control either the quantity or the price paid* for the service then the expenditure is uncontrollable and should not be identified with the manager.

An example of the latter situation is when the costs of a Human Resources (HR) department are apportioned to a department on some arbitrary basis; such arbitrary apportionments on an arbitrary basis that results in an allocation of expenses that the managers of responsibility centres may not be able to influence. In addition to the above guidelines Merchant and van der Stede (2017) suggest a general rule should also be used as a guide – 'Hold employees accountable for the performance areas you want them to pay attention to.'

SETTING PERFORMANCE TARGETS AND DETERMINING HOW CHALLENGING THEY SHOULD BE

There is substantial evidence from a large number of studies that the existence of a defined, quantitative goal or target is likely to motivate higher levels of performance than when no such target is stated. People perform better when they have a clearly defined goal to aim for and are aware of the standards that will be used to interpret their performance. The fact that a target represents a specific quantitative goal gives it a strong motivational potential, but the targets set must be accepted if managers are to be motivated to achieve higher levels of performance. Unfortunately, it is not possible to specify exactly the optimal degree of difficulty for targets, since task uncertainty and cultural, organizational and personality factors all affect an individual manager's reaction to a financial target.

Figure 10.2, derived from Emmanuel *et al.* (1990), shows the theoretical relationship between budget difficulty, aspiration levels and performance. In Figure 10.2 it is assumed that performance and aspiration levels are identical. Note that the **aspiration level** relates to the personal goal of the budgetee (that is, the person who is responsible for the budget).

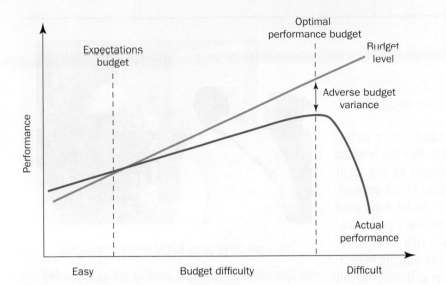

FIGURE 10.2

The effect of budget difficulty on performance

In other words, it is the level of performance that they hope to attain. You will see from Figure 10.2 that as the level of budget difficulty is increased both the budgetees' aspiration level and performance increases. However, there comes a point where the budget is perceived as impossible to achieve and the aspiration level and performance decline dramatically. It can be seen from Figure 10.2 that the budget level that motivates the best level of performance may not be achievable. In contrast, the budget that is expected to be achieved (that is, the expectations budget in Figure 10.2) motivates a lower level of performance.

To motivate the highest level of actual performance, demanding budgets should be set and small adverse variances should be regarded as a healthy sign and not as something to be avoided. If budgets are always achieved with no adverse variances, this indicates that the standards are too loose to motivate the best possible results.

It appears from our previous discussion that tight budgets should be established to motivate maximum performance, although this may mean that the budget has a high probability of not being achieved. However, budgets are not used purely as a motivational device to maximize performance. They are also used for planning purposes and it is most unlikely that tight budgets will be suitable for planning purposes. Why? Tight budgets that have a high probability of not being achieved are most unsuitable for cash budgeting and for harmonizing the company plans in the form of a master budget. Most companies use the same budgets for planning and motivational purposes. If only one set of budgets is used it is most unlikely that one set can, at the same time, perfectly meet both the planning and the motivational requirements.

Budgets with a high probability of being achieved are widely used in practice. They provide managers with a sense of achievement and self-esteem that can be beneficial to the organization in terms of increased levels of commitment and aspirations. Rewards such as bonuses, promotions and job security are normally linked to budget achievement so that the costs of failing to meet budget targets can be high. The greater the probability of the failure to meet budget targets the greater is the probability that managers will be motivated to distort their performance by engaging in behaviour that will result in the harmful side-effects described earlier in this chapter.

REAL WORLD VIEWS 10.4

Community participation in local budget spend

Some years ago in a BBC documentary called *Power to the People*, Michael Portillo visited a 'You Decide' session organized by the local council in Tower Hamlets, London. At this session, local people decided what was to be done with £250 000 of council money. They were given fully costed options under headings like healthcare, the elderly and local policing. The options in each category could be debated for a time, then all present 'voted' for their preferred option using an electronic voting system. This continued until all funds were used up. This, it could be argued, saves the council some time and allocates resources to where residents deem most appropriate. Of course £250 000 is a long way off a council's full budget, but at least there is participation in how the money is spent. This idea developed into a 'You Choose' budget simulator website that encourages the public to consider where council budget cuts might fall, where efficiencies might be made, where income might be generated and effects of changes in budget allocation. This latter point is particularly relevant, as local councils are expected to produce a balanced budget, and with the simulator, the public can see what happens if more or less money is allocated to particular areas of expenditure. As an example, here is an extract from the webpages of Tameside Council:

There are three parts to the budget simulator:

- Use the sliding budget lines to tell us if you feel individual service budgets should go up or down. As you make changes, 'consequences' start to appear - you can change your mind as many times as you like until you are ready to 'submit' your thoughts.
- Read about 'how we can bring money in' and 'how we can save money' and tick the ideas you like.
- Give us your comments on your budget priorities and any suggestions on saving money by clicking the 'suggestions' button in the bottom left of the screen.

Questions

1 Can you think of any advantages of schemes or tools like those mentioned above?
2 Can you think of any disadvantages?

Reference

Tameside Council "You Choose" simulator, available at youchoose.esd.org.uk/TamesideMBC

DETERMINING HOW MUCH INFLUENCE MANAGERS SHOULD HAVE IN SETTING TARGETS

Participation relates to the extent that subordinates or budgetees are able to influence the figures that are incorporated in their budgets or targets. Participation is sometimes referred to as **bottom-up budget setting** whereas a non-participatory approach whereby subordinates have little influence on the target setting process is sometimes called **top-down budget setting**.

Allowing individuals to participate in the setting of performance targets has several advantages. First, individuals are more likely to accept the targets and be committed to achieving them if they have been involved in setting them. Second, participation can reduce the information asymmetry gap that can occur when standards are imposed from above. Budgetees have more information than their superiors on the relationships between outputs and inputs and the constraints that exist at the operating level whereas the superiors have a broader view of the organization as a whole and the resource constraints that apply. This information-sharing process enables more effective targets to be set that reflect both operational and organizational constraints. Finally, imposed standards can encourage negative attitudes and result in demotivation and alienation. This in turn can lead to a rejection of the targets and poor performance.

Participation has been advocated by many writers as a means of making tasks more challenging and giving individuals a greater sense of responsibility. For many years participation in decision-making was thought to be a panacea for effective organizational effort but this school of thought was later challenged. The debate has never been resolved. The believers have never been able to demonstrate that participation really does have a positive effect on productivity and the sceptics have never been able to prove the opposite.

Because of the conflicting findings relating to the effectiveness of participation, research has tended to concentrate on studying how various factors influence the effectiveness of participation. If participation is used selectively and in the right circumstances it has an enormous potential for encouraging the commitment to organizational goals, improving attitudes towards the budgeting system and increasing subsequent performance. Note, however, at this stage that there are some limitations on the positive effects of participation in standard setting and circumstances where top-down budget setting is preferable. They are:

1 Performance is measured by precisely the same standard that the budgetee has been involved in setting. This gives the budgetee the opportunity to negotiate lower targets that increase the probability of target achievement and the accompanying rewards. Therefore an improvement in performance – in terms of comparison with the budget – may result merely from a lowering of the standard.

2 Participation by itself is not adequate in ensuring commitment to standards. The manager must also believe that he or she can significantly influence the results and be given the necessary feedback about them.

3 A top-down approach to budget setting is likely to be preferable where a process is highly programmable, and there are clear and stable input–output relationships. Here there is no need to negotiate targets using a bottom-up process.

SUMMARY

The following items relate to the learning objectives listed at the beginning of the chapter.

● **Describe the three different types of controls used in organizations.**
Three different categories of controls are used – action/behavioural controls, personnel/cultural controls and results/output controls. With action controls the actions themselves are the focus of controls. Personnel controls help

employees do a good job by building on employees' natural tendencies to control themselves. They include selection and placement, training and job design. Cultural controls represent a set of values, social norms and beliefs that are shared by members of the organization and that influence their actions. Output or results controls involve collecting and reporting information about the outcomes of work effort.

● **Distinguish between feedback and feed-forward controls.** Feedback control involves monitoring outputs achieved against desired outputs and taking whatever corrective action is necessary if a deviation exists. In feed-forward control, instead of actual outputs being compared against desired outputs, predictions are made of what outputs are expected to be at some future time. If these expectations differ from what is desired, control actions are taken that will minimize these differences.

● **Explain the potential harmful side-effects of results controls.** Results controls can promote a number of harmful side-effects. They can lead to a lack of goal congruence when employees seek to achieve the performance targets in a way that is not organizationally desirable. They can also lead to data manipulation and negative attitudes, which can result in a decline in morale and a lack of motivation.

● **Define the four different types of responsibility centres.** A responsibility centre may be defined as a unit of a firm where an individual manager is held accountable for the unit's performance. There are four types of responsibility centres – cost or expense centres, revenue centres, profit centres and investment centres. Cost or expense centres are responsibility centres whose managers are normally accountable for only those costs that are under their control. Revenue centres are responsibility centres where managers are accountable only for financial outputs in the form of generating sales revenues. Units within an organization whose managers are accountable for both revenues and costs are called profit centres. Investment centres are responsibility centres whose managers are responsible for both sales revenues and costs and, in addition, have responsibility and authority to make capital investment decisions.

● **Explain the different elements of management accounting control systems.** Management accounting control systems have two core elements. The first is the formal planning processes such as budgeting and long-term planning. These processes are used for establishing performance expectations for evaluating performance. The second is responsibility accounting, which involves the creation of responsibility centres. Responsibility centres enable accountability for financial results/outcomes to be allocated to individuals throughout the organization.

● **Describe the controllability principle and the methods of implementing it.** The controllability principle states that it is appropriate to charge to an area of responsibility only those costs that are significantly influenced by the manager of that responsibility centre. The controllability principle can be implemented by either eliminating the uncontrollable items from the areas that managers are held accountable for or calculating their effects so that the reports distinguish between controllable and uncontrollable items.

● **Discuss how the level of difficulty of targets impacts on motivation and performance.** Different types of financial performance targets can be set ranging from easily achievable to difficult to achieve. Targets that are considered moderately difficult to achieve (called highly achievable targets) are recommended because they can be used for planning purposes and they also have a motivational impact.

● **Describe the influence of participation in the budgeting process.** Participation relates to the extent that budgetees are able to influence the figures that are incorporated in their budgets or targets. Allowing individuals to participate in the setting of performance targets results in individuals being more likely to accept the targets and be committed to achieving them. Participation, however, is subject to the limitation that performance is measured by precisely the same standard that the budgetee has been involved in setting. Participation must be used selectively; but if it is used in the right circumstances, it has an enormous potential for encouraging the commitment to organizational goals.

KEY TERMS AND CONCEPTS

Action controls Observing the actions of individuals as they go about their work, also known as behavioural controls.

Aspiration level The level of performance that the person responsible for the budget hopes to attain.

Behavioural controls Controls that involve observing the actions of individuals as they go about their work, also known as action controls.

Bottom-up budget setting Allowing individuals to participate in the setting of budgets and targets.

Business units Responsibility centres where managers are accountable for both revenues and costs, also known as profit centres.

Control The process of ensuring that a firm's activities conform to its plan and that its objectives are achieved.

Controllability principle The principle that it is appropriate to charge to an area of responsibility only those costs that are significantly influenced by the manager of that responsibility centre.

Controls Measurement and information used to help determine what control action needs to be taken.

Cost centres Responsibility centres whose managers are normally accountable for only those costs that are under their control, also known as expense centres.

Cultural controls A set of values, social norms and beliefs that are shared by members of the organization and that influence their actions.

Discretionary expense centres Cost centres where output cannot be measured in financial terms and there are no clearly observable relationships between inputs and outputs.

Ex post budget adjustments The adjustment of a budget to the environmental and economic conditions that the managers actually faced during the period.

Expense centres Responsibility centres whose managers are normally accountable for only those costs that are under their control, also known as cost centres.

Feedback control Monitoring outputs achieved against desired outputs and taking whatever corrective action is necessary if a deviation exists.

Feed-forward control   Comparing predictions of expected outputs with the desired outputs and taking prior corrective action to minimize any differences.

Flexible budgets   Budgets in which the uncontrollable volume effects on cost behaviour are removed from the managers' performance reports.

Goal congruence   The situation that exists when controls motivate employees to behave in a way that is in tune with the organization's goals.

Investment centres   Responsibility centres whose managers are responsible for both sales revenues and costs and also have responsibility and authority to make capital investment decisions.

Management control system   The entire array of controls used by an organization.

Output controls   Collecting and reporting information about the outcomes of work effort, also known as results controls.

Participation   The extent that individuals are able to influence the figures that are incorporated in their budgets or targets.

Performance reports   Performance reports show budget and actual performance (normally listed by items of expenses) at frequent intervals (normally monthly) for each responsibility centre.

Personnel controls   Helping employees to perform well through the use of selection and placement, training, job design and the provision of necessary resources.

Profit centres   Responsibility centres where managers are accountable for both revenues and costs, also known as business units.

Relative performance evaluation   The evaluation of the performance of a responsibility centre relative to the performance of similar centres within the same company or of similar units outside the organization.

Responsibility accounting   The creation of responsibility centres and the accumulation of costs and revenues so that the deviations from budget can be attributed to the individual who is accountable for the responsibility centre.

Responsibility centre   A unit of a firm where an individual manager is held responsible for the unit's performance.

Results controls   Collecting and reporting information about the outcomes of work effort, also known as output controls.

Revenue centres   Responsibility centres where managers are mainly accountable for financial outputs in the form of generating sales revenues.

Social or cultural controls   The selection of people who have already been socialized into adopting particular norms and patterns of behaviour to perform particular tasks.

Standard cost centres   Cost centres where output can be measured and the input required to produce each unit of output can be specified.

Strategic control   Control that focuses outside the organization, looking at how a firm can compete with other firms within the same industry.

Subjective judgements   Judgements made by senior managers of a responsibility head's performance based on the senior manager's own experience, knowledge and interpretation of the performance level achieved.

Top-down budget setting   Imposing budgets and targets from above, without the participation of the individuals involved.

Variance   The difference between the actual cost and the standard cost.

Variance analysis   The analysis of factors that cause the actual results to differ from predetermined budgeted targets.

ASSESSMENT MATERIAL

The review questions are short questions that enable you to assess your understanding of the main topics included in the chapter. The page numbers in parentheses provide you with the page numbers to refer to if you cannot answer a specific question.

The review problems are more complex and require you to relate and apply the content to various business problems. Solutions to review problems are provided in a separate section at the end of the book. Additional review problems can be accessed by lecturers and students on the dedicated online support resources for this book. Solutions to these review problems are provided for lecturers in the *Instructor's Manual* accompanying this book that can be downloaded from the dedicated online instructor's resources (see Preface for details).

The dedicated online digital support resources for this book also includes over 30 case study problems.

REVIEW QUESTIONS

10.1 Distinguish between 'controls' and 'control'. *(p. 250)*

10.2 Identify and describe three different types of control mechanisms used by companies. *(pp. 251–254)*

10.3 Provide examples of behavioural, action, social, personnel and cultural controls. *(pp. 251–253)*

10.4 Describe the different stages that are involved with output/results controls. *(pp. 253–254)*

10.5 Distinguish between feedback and feed-forward controls. Provide an example of each type of control. *(p. 254)*

10.6 Describe some of the harmful side-effects that can occur with output/results controls. *(pp. 254–257)*

10.7 Describe the four different types of responsibility centres. *(pp. 257–259)*

10.8 Explain what is meant by the term 'responsibility accounting'. *(pp. 259–261)*

10.9 What factors must be taken into account when operating a responsibility accounting system? *(pp. 261–264)*

10.10 What is the 'controllability principle'? Describe the different ways in which the principle can be applied. *(pp. 261–264)*

10.11 What are flexible budgets? Why are they preferred to fixed (static) budgets? *(p. 262)*

10.12 What is meant by the term 'aspiration level'? *(pp. 264–265)*

10.13 Describe the effect of the level of budget difficulty on motivation and performance. *(pp. 264–265)*

10.14 Distinguish between participation and top-down budget setting. *(pp. 266–267)*

10.15 Describe the factors influencing the effectiveness of participation in the budget process. *(pp. 266–267)*

10.16 What are the limitations of participation in the budget process? *(pp. 266–267)*

REVIEW PROBLEMS

10.17 Preparation of a flexible budget performance report
The Viking Smelting Company established a division, called the reclamation division, 2 years ago, to extract silver from jewellers' waste materials. The waste materials are processed in a furnace, enabling silver to be recovered. The silver is then further processed into finished products by three other divisions within the company.

A performance report is prepared each month for the reclamation division which is then discussed by the management team. Sharon Houghton, the newly appointed financial controller of the reclamation division, has recently prepared her first report for the 4 weeks to 31 May. This is shown below:

Performance Report Reclamation Division
4 weeks to 31 May

	Actual	Budget	Variance	Comments
Production (tonnes)	200	250	50 (F)[a]	
	(£)	(£)	(£)	
Wages and social security costs	46 133	45 586	547 (A)	Overspend
Fuel	15 500	18 750	3 250 (F)	
Consumables	2 100	2 500	400 (F)	
Power	1 590	1 750	160 (F)	
Divisional overheads	21 000	20 000	1 000 (A)	Overspend
Plant maintenance	6 900	5 950	950 (A)	Overspend
Central services	7 300	6 850	450 (A)	Overspend
Total	100 523	101 386	863 (F)	

[a](A) = adverse, (F) = favourable

In preparing the budgeted figures, the following assumptions were made for May:

- the reclamation division was to employ four teams of six production employees
- each employee was to work a basic 42-hour week and be paid £7.50 per hour for the 4 weeks of May
- social security and other employment costs were estimated at 40 per cent of basic wages
- a bonus, shared amongst the production employees, was payable if production exceeded 150 tonnes. This varied depending on the output achieved, as follows:
  1. if output was between 150 and 199 tonnes, the bonus was £3 per tonne produced
  2. if output was between 200 and 249 tonnes, the bonus was £8 per tonne produced
  3. if output exceeded 249 tonnes the bonus was £13 per tonne produced
- the cost of fuel was £75 per tonne
- consumables were £10 per tonne
- power comprised a fixed charge of £500 per 4 weeks plus £5 per tonne for every tonne produced
- overheads directly attributable to the division were £20 000
- plant maintenance was to be apportioned to divisions on the basis of the capital values of each division
- the cost of Viking's central services was to be shared equally by all four divisions.

You are the deputy financial controller of the reclamation division. After attending her first monthly meeting with the board of the reclamation division, Sharon Houghton arranges a meeting with you. She is concerned about a number of issues, one of them being that the current report does not clearly identify those expenses and variances that are the direct responsibility of the reclamation division.

Task 1
Sharon Houghton asks you to prepare a flexible budget report for the reclamation division for May in a form consistent with responsibility accounting.

On receiving your revised report. Sharon tells you about the other questions raised at the management meeting when the original report was presented. These are summarized below:
(i) Why are the budget figures based on 2-year-old data taken from the proposal recommending the establishment of the reclamation division?
(ii) Should the budget data be based on what we were proposing to do or what we actually did do?
(iii) is it true that the less we produce the more favourable our variances will be?
(iv) Why is there so much maintenance in a new division with modern equipment and why should we be charged with the actual costs of the maintenance department even when they overspend?
(v) Could the comments, explaining the variances, be improved?
(vi) Should all the variances be investigated?
(vii) Does showing the cost of central services on the divisional performance report help control these costs and motivate the divisional managers?

Task 2
Prepare a memo for the management of the reclamation division. Your memo should answer their queries and justify their comments.

10.18 Comments on a performance report
The Victorial Hospital is located in a holiday resort that attracts visitors to such an extent that the population of the area is trebled for the summer months of June, July and August. From past experience, this influx of visitors doubles the activity of the hospital during these months. The annual budget for the hospital's laundry department is broken down into four quarters, namely April–June, July–September, October–December and January–March, by dividing the annual budgeted figures by four. The budgeting work has been done for the current year by the secretary of the hospital using the previous year's figures and adding 3 per cent for inflation. It is realized by the Hospital Authority that management information for control purposes needs to be improved, and you have been recruited to help to introduce a system of responsibility accounting.

You are required, from the information given, to:

(a) comment on the way in which the quarterly budgets have been prepared and to suggest improvements that could be introduced when preparing the budgets for the next year
(b) state what information you would like to flow from the actual against budget comparison (note that calculated figures are not required)
(c) state the amendments that would be needed to the current practice of budgeting and reporting to enable the report shown below to be used as a measure of the efficiency of the laundry manager.

Victorial Hospital – Laundry Department
Report for quarter ended 30 September

	Budget	Actual
Patients days	9 000	12 000
Weight processed (kg)	180 000	240 000
	(£)	(£)
Costs:		
Wages	8 800	12 320
Overtime premium	1 400	2 100
Detergents and other supplies	1 800	2 700
Water, water softening and heating	2 000	2 500
Maintenance	1 000	1 500
Depreciation of plant	2 000	2 000
Manager's salary	1 250	1 500
Overhead, apportioned:		
for occupancy	4 000	4 250
for administration	5 000	5 750

(15 marks)

10.19 Flexible budgets and the motivational role of budgets

Club Atlantic is an all-weather holiday complex providing holidays throughout the year. The fee charged to guests is fully inclusive of accommodation and all meals. However, because the holiday industry is so competitive, Club Atlantic is only able to generate profits by maintaining strict financial control of all activities.

The club's restaurant is one area where there is a constant need to monitor costs. Susan Green is the manager of the restaurant. At the beginning of each year she is given an annual budget which is then broken down into months. Each month she receives a statement monitoring actual costs against the annual budget and highlighting any variances. The statement for the month ended 31 October is reproduced below along with a list of assumptions:

Club Atlantic Restaurant Performance Statement
Month to 31 October

	Actual	Budget	Variance (over)/ under
Number of guest days	11 160	9 600	(1 560)
	(€)	(€)	(€)
Food	20 500	20 160	(340)
Cleaning materials	2 232	1 920	(312)
Heat, light and power	2 050	2 400	350
Catering wages	8 400	7 200	(1 200)
Rent rates, insurance and depreciation	1 860	1 800	(60)
	35 042	33 480	(1 562)

Assumptions:

(a) The budget has been calculated on the basis of a 30-day calendar month with the cost of rents,

insurance and depreciation being an apportionment of the fixed annual charge.

(b) The budgeted catering wages assume that:
   (i) there is one member of the catering staff for every 40 guests staying at the complex
   (ii) the daily cost of a member of the catering staff is €30.

(c) All other budgeted costs are variable costs based on the number of guest days.

Task 1
Using the data above, prepare a revised performance statement using flexible budgeting. Your statement should show both the revised budget and the revised variances. Club Atlantic uses the existing budgets and performance statements to motivate its managers as well as for financial control. If managers keep expenses below budget they receive a bonus in addition to their salaries. A colleague of Susan is Brian Hilton. Brian is in charge of the swimming pool and golf course, both of which have high levels of fixed costs. Each month he manages to keep expenses below budget and in return enjoys regular bonuses. Under the current reporting system, Susan Green only rarely receives a bonus.

At a recent meeting with Club Atlantic's directors Susan Green expressed concern that the performance statement was not a valid reflection of her management of the restaurant. You are currently employed by Hall and Co., the club's auditors, and the directors of Club Atlantic have asked you to advise them whether there is any justification for Susan Green's concern.

At the meeting with the Club's directors, you were asked the following questions:

(a) Do budgets motivate managers to achieve objectives?
(b) Does motivating managers lead to improved performance?
(c) Does the current method of reporting performance motivate Susan Green and Brian Hilton to be more efficient?

Task 2
Write a *brief* letter to the directors of Club Atlantic addressing their question and justifying your answers.
Note: You should make use of the data given in this task plus your findings in Task 1.

10.20 Recommendations for improvements to a performance report and a review of the management control system

Your firm has been consulted by the managing director of Inzone Inc., which owns a chain of retail stores. Each store has departments selling furniture, tableware and kitchenware. Departmental managers are responsible to a store manager, who is in turn responsible to head office (HO).

All goods for sale are ordered centrally and stores sell at prices fixed by HO. Store managers (aided by departmental managers) order stocks from HO and stores are charged interest based on month-end stock levels. HO appoints all permanent staff and sets all pay levels. Store managers can engage or dismiss temporary workers, and are responsible for store running expenses.

The introduction to Inzone Inc.'s management accounting manual states:

Budgeting starts 3 months before the budget year, with product sales projections which are developed by HO buyers in consultation with each store's departmental managers. Expense budgets, adjusted for expected inflation, are then prepared by HO for each store. Inzone Inc's accounting year is divided into 13 four-weekly control periods, and the budgeted sales and expenses are assigned to periods with due regard to seasonal factors. The budgets are completed 1 month before the year begins on 1 January.

All HO expenses are recharged to stores in order to give the clearest indication of the 'bottom line' profit of each store. These HO costs are mainly buying expenses, which are recharged to stores according to their square footage.

Store reports comparing actual results with budgets are on the desks of HO and store management 1 week after the end of each control period. Significant variations in performance are then investigated, and appropriate action taken.

Ms Lewis is manager of an Inzone Inc. store. She is eligible for a bonus equal to 5 per cent of the amount by which her store's 'bottom-line' profit exceeds the year's budget. However, Ms Lewis sees no chance of a bonus this year, because major roadworks near the store are disrupting trade. Her store report for the 4 weeks ending 21 June is as follows:

	Actual ($)	Budget ($)
Sales	98 850	110 000
Costs:		
Cost of goods (including stock losses)	63 100	70 200
Wages and salaries	5 300	5 500
Rent	11 000	11 000
Depreciation of store fittings	500	500
Distribution costs	4 220	4 500
Other store running expenses	1 970	2 000
Interest charge on stocks	3 410	3 500
Store's share of HO costs	2 050	2 000
Store profit	7 300	10 800
	98 850	110 000
Stocks held at end of period	341 000	350 000
Store fittings at written down value	58 000	58 000

Required:

(a) Make recommendations for the improvement of Inzone Inc.'s store report, briefly justifying each recommendation.
(11 marks)

(b) Prepare a report for the managing director of Inzone Inc. reviewing the company's responsibility delegation, identifying the major strengths and weaknesses of Inzone Inc.'s management control system, and recommending any changes you consider appropriate.
(14 marks)
(Total 25 marks)

10.21 Comments on budget and control practices

The Rubber Group (TRG) manufactures and sells a number ol rubber-based products. Its strategic focus is channelled through profit centres which sell products transferred from production divisions that are operated as cost centres. The profit centres are the primary value-adding part of the business, whose commercial profit centre managers are responsible for the generation of a contribution margin sufficient to earn the target return of TRG. The target return is calculated after allowing for the sum of the agreed budgeted cost of production at production divisions, plus the cost of marketing, selling and distribution costs and central services costs.

The Bettamould Division is part of TRG and manufactures moulded products that it transfers to profit centres at an agreed cost per tonne. The agreed cost per tonne is set following discussion between management of the Bettamould Division and senior management of TRG.

The following information relates to the agreed budget for the Bettamould Division for the year ending 30 June:

1 The budgeted output of moulded products to be transferred to profit centres is 100 000 tonnes. The budgeted transfer cost has been agreed on a two-part basis as follows:
   (i) A standard variable cost of $200 per tonne of moulded products.
   (ii) A lump sum annual charge of $50 000 000 in respect of fixed costs, which is charged to profit centres, at $500 per tonne of moulded products.

2 Budgeted standard variable costs (as quoted in 1 above) have been set after incorporating each of the following:
   (i) A provision in respect of processing losses amounting to 15 per cent of material inputs. Materials are sourced on a JIT basis from chosen suppliers who have been used for some years. It is felt that the 15 per cent level of losses is necessary because the ageing of the machinery will lead to a reduction in the efficiency of output levels.
   (ii) A provision in respect of machine idle time amounting to 5 per cent. This is incorporated into variable machine costs. The idle time allowance is held at the 5 per cent level partly through elements of 'real-time' maintenance undertaken by the machine operating teams as part of their job specification.

3 Quality checks are carried out on a daily basis on 25 per cent of throughput tonnes of moulded products.

4 All employees and management have contracts based on fixed annual salary agreements. In addition, a bonus of 5 per cent of salary is payable as long as the budgeted output of 100 000 tonnes has been achieved;

5 Additional information relating to the points in (2) above (but NOT included in the budget for the year ending 30 June) is as follows:
   (i) There is evidence that materials of an equivalent specification could be sourced for 40 per cent of the annual requirement at the Bettamould

Division, from another division within TRG which has spare capacity.

(ii) There is evidence that a move to machine maintenance being outsourced from a specialist company could help reduce machine idle time and hence allow the possibility of annual output in excess of 100 000 tonnes of moulded products.

(iii) It is thought that the current level of quality checks (25 per cent of throughput on a daily basis) is vital, although current evidence shows that some competitor companies are able to achieve consistent acceptable quality with a quality check level of only 10 per cent of throughput on a daily basis.

The directors of TRG have decided to investigate claims relating to the use of budgeting within organizations which have featured in recent literature. A summary of relevant points from the literature is contained in the following statement.

'The use of budgets as part of a 'performance contract' between an organization and its managers may be seen as a practice that causes management action which might lead to the following problems:

(a) Meeting only the lowest targets
(b) Using more resources than necessary
(c) Making the bonus–whatever it takes
(d) Competing against other divisions, business units and departments
(e) Ensuring that what is in the budget is spent
(f) Providing inaccurate forecasts
(g) Meeting the target, but not beating it
(h) Avoiding risks.

Required:

(a) Explain the nature of any SIX of the eight problems listed above relating to the use of budgeting.
(12 marks)

(b) Illustrate EACH of the six problems chosen in (a) using the data from the Bettamould division TRG scenario.
(6 marks)

(c) Suggest ways in which each of the six problems chosen in (a) above may be overcome.
(6 marks)

10.22 Discussion of the weaknesses of a budget system and beyond budgeting. Perkin manufactures electronic components for export worldwide, from factories in Ceeland, for use in smartphones and hand held gaming devices. These two markets are supplied with similar components by two divisions, Phones Division (P) and Gaming Division (G). Each division has its own selling, purchasing, IT and research and development functions, but separate IT systems. Some manufacturing facilities, however, are shared between the two divisions.

Perkin's corporate objective is to maximize shareholder wealth through innovation and continuous technological improvement in its products. The manufacturers of smartphones and gaming devices, who use Perkin's components, update their products frequently and constantly compete with each other to launch models which are technically superior.

Perkin has a well established incremental budgeting process. Divisional managers forecast sales volumes and costs months in advance of the budget year. These divisional budgets are then scrutinized by the main board, and revised significantly by them in line with targets they have set for the business. The finalized budgets are often approved after the start of the accounting year. Under pressure to deliver consistent returns to institutional shareholders, the board does not tolerate failure by either division to achieve the planned net profit for the year once the budget is approved. Last year's results were poor compared to the annual budget. Divisional managers, who are appraised on the financial performance of their own division, have complained about the length of time that the budgeting process takes and that the performance of their divisions could have been better but was constrained by the budgets which were set for them.

In P Division, managers had failed to anticipate the high popularity of a new smartphone model incorporating a large screen designed for playing games, and had not made the necessary technical modifications to the division's own components. This was due to the high costs of doing so, which had not been budgeted for. Based on the original sales forecast, P Division had already committed to manufacturing large quantities of the existing version of the component and so had to heavily discount these in order to achieve the planned sales volumes.

A critical material in the manufacture of Perkin's products is silver, which is a commodity which changes materially in price according to worldwide supply and demand. During the year, supplies of silver were reduced significantly for a short period of time and G Division paid high prices to ensure continued supply. Managers of G Division were unaware that P Division held large inventories of silver which they had purchased when the price was much lower.

Initially, G Division accurately forecasted demand for its components based on the previous years' sales volumes plus the historic annual growth rate of 5 per cent. However, overall sales volumes were much lower than budgeted. This was due to a fire at the factory of their main customer, which was then closed for part of the year. Reacting to this news, managers at G Division took action to reduce costs, including closing one of the three R&D facilities in the division.

However, when the customer's factory reopened, G Division was unwilling to recruit extra staff to cope with increased demand; nor would P Division re-allocate shared manufacturing facilities to them, in case demand increased for its own products later in the year. As a result, Perkin lost the prestigious preferred supplier status from their main customer who was unhappy with G Division's failure to effectively respond to the additional demand. The customer had been forced to purchase a more expensive, though technically superior, component from an alternative manufacturer.

The institutional shareholders' representative, recently appointed to the board, has asked you as a performance management expert for your advice. 'We need to know whether Perkin's budgeting process is appropriate for the business, and how this contributed to last year's poor performance', she said, 'and more importantly, how do we need to change the process to prevent this happening in the future, such as a move to beyond budgeting.'

Required:

(a) Evaluate the weaknesses in Perkin's current budgeting system and whether it is suitable for the environment in which Perkin operates. *(13 marks)*

(b) Evaluate the impact on Perkin of moving to beyond budgeting. *(12 marks)*

10.23 A college is preparing its annual budget. In previous years the director of the college has prepared the college budget without the participation of senior staff and presented it to the college board for approval.

Last year the college board criticized the director over the lack of participation of his senior staff in the preparation of the budget and requested this year the senior staff should be involved.

Required:

Discuss the potential advantages and disadvantages to the college of involving the senior staff in the budget preparation process.

10.24 A firm of solicitors is using budgetary control. The senior partner estimated the demand for the year for each of the firm's four divisions: Civil, Criminal, Corporate and Property. A separate partner is responsible for each division.

Each divisional partner then prepared a cost budget based on the senior partner's demand estimate for the division. These budgets were then submitted to the senior partner for his approval. He then amended them as he thought appropriate before issuing each divisional partner with the final budget for the division. He did not discuss these amendments with the respective divisional partners. Actual performance is then measured against the final budgets for each month and each divisional partner's performance is appraised by asking the divisional partner to explain the reasons for any variances that occur.

The Corporate partner has been asked to explain why her staff costs exceeded the budgeted costs for last month while the chargeable time was less than budgeted. Her reply is below:

'My own original estimate of staff costs was higher than the final budgeted costs shown on my divisional performance report. In my own cost budget I allowed for time to be spent developing new services for the firm's corporate clients and improving the clients' access to their own case files. This would improve the quality of our services to clients and therefore increase client satisfaction. The trouble with our present system is that it focuses on financial performance and ignores the other performance indicators found in modem performance management systems.'

Required:

(a) Discuss the present budgeting system and its likely effect on divisional partner motivation.

(6 marks)

(b) Explain two non-financial performance indicators (other than client satisfaction and service quality) that could be used by the firm.

(4 marks)

10.25 You are required to:

(i) discuss the factors that are likely to cause managers to submit budget estimates of sales and costs that do not represent their best estimates or expectations of what will actually occur

(8 marks)

(ii) suggest, as a budget accountant, what procedures you would advise in order to minimize the likelihood of such biased estimates arising.

(4 marks)

10.26 (a) Explain the ways in which the attitudes and behaviour of managers in a company are liable to pose more threat to the success of its budgetary control system than are minor technical inadequacies that may be in the system.

(15 marks)

(b) Explain briefly what the management accountant can do to minimize the disruptive effects of such attitudes and behaviour.

(5 marks)

11
STANDARD COSTING AND VARIANCE ANALYSIS

In the previous chapter the major features of management accounting control systems were examined. The different types of controls used by companies were explained so that the elements of management accounting control systems could be described within the context of the overall control process. A broad approach to control was adopted and the detailed procedures of financial controls were not examined. In this chapter we shall focus on the detailed financial controls that are used by organizations.

We shall describe a financial control system that enables the deviations from budget to be analysed in detail, thus enabling costs to be controlled more effectively. This system of control is called standard costing. In particular, we shall examine how a standard costing system operates and how the variances are calculated. Standard costing systems are applied in cost centres where the output can be measured and the input required to produce each unit of output can be specified. In manufacturing organizations standard costing is generally applied to manufacturing activities, and non-manufacturing activities are not incorporated within the standard costing system. However, the sales variances that are described in this chapter can also be applied in revenue centres. In the next chapter we shall look at performance measures that are appropriate for measuring the performance of profit and investment centres.

Standard costs are predetermined costs; they are target costs that should be incurred under efficient operating conditions. They are not the same as **budgeted costs**. A budget relates to an entire activity or operation; a standard presents the same information on a *per unit* basis. A standard therefore provides cost expectations per unit of activity and a budget provides the cost expectation for the total activity. If the budget output for a product is for 10 000 units and the standard cost is £3 per unit, budgeted cost will be £30 000. We shall see that establishing standard costs for each unit produced enables a detailed analysis to be made of the difference between the budgeted cost and the actual cost so that costs can be controlled more effectively.

OPERATION OF A STANDARD COSTING SYSTEM

Standard costing is most suited to an organization whose activities consist of a series of *common* or *repetitive* operations where the input required to produce each unit of output can be specified. It is therefore relevant in manufacturing companies, since the processes involved are often of a repetitive nature. Standard costing procedures can also be applied in service industries such as units within banks, where output can be measured in terms of the number of cheques or the number of loan applications processed, and there are also well-defined input–output relationships (see Exhibit 11.1 for surveys relating to the usage of standard costing systems). In fast-food restaurants, such as Burger King, the standard input required to produce a single hamburger can be specified. It is therefore possible to specify the standard inputs required for a given output of hamburgers because there is a physical relationship between the ingredients such as meat, buns, condiments and packaging and the number of hamburgers made. Standard costing cannot, however, be applied to activities of a non-repetitive nature, since there is no basis for observing repetitive operations and consequently standards cannot be set.

A standard costing system can be applied to organizations that produce many different products, as long as production consists of a series of common operations. For example, if the output from a factory is the result of five common operations, it is possible to produce many different product variations from these operations. It is therefore possible that a large product range may result from a small number of common operations. Standard costs are developed for repetitive operations as product standard costs can be derived simply by combining the standard costs from the operations that are necessary to make the product. This process is illustrated in Exhibit 11.2.

EXHIBIT 11.1   Surveys of company practice

Since its introduction in the early 1900s standard costing has flourished and is now one of the most widely used management accounting techniques. Surveys of UK manufacturing companies by Drury *et al.* (1993) and New Zealand companies by Guilding *et al.* (1998) reported that approximately 75 per cent of the companies used standard costing.

A CIMA sponsored study of 41 UK manufacturing organizations by Dugdale *et al.* (2006) reported that 30 of the firms employed standard costing. The majority of these firms (26) set standard costs for materials and labour and a smaller majority (20) also set standard overhead costs. They conclude that despite the huge changes in the manufacturing environment standard costing is alive and well. The international survey conducted by the Chartered Institute of Management Accountants (2009) reported that approximately 45 per cent of the respondents used standard costing. This survey included manufacturing and non-manufacturing companies, so it is likely that the usage rate was much higher for manufacturing companies.

EXHIBIT 11.2 Standard costs analysed by operations and products

Responsibility centre	Operation no. and standard cost No. (£)	Products 100	101	102	103	104	105	106	Total standard cost (£)	Actual cost
A	1 200	●	●		●	●	●	●	1 200	
B	2 300		●		●		●		900	
C	3 400	●		●		●			1 200	
D	4 500	●	●	●				●	2 000	
Standard product cost		£1 100	£1 000	£900	£500	£600	£500	£700	5 300	

It is assumed that the standard costs are £200, £300, £400 and £500 for each of the operations 1 to 4. The standard cost for *product* 100 is therefore £1100, which consists of £200 for operation 1, plus £400 and £500 for operations 3 and 4. The standard costs for each of the other products are calculated in a similar manner. In addition, the total standard cost for the total output of each operation for the period has been calculated. For example, six items of operation number 1 have been completed, giving a total standard cost of £1200 for this operation (six items at £200 each). Three items of operation 2 have been completed, giving a total standard cost of £900 and so on.

Variances allocated to responsibility centres

You can see from Exhibit 11.2 that different responsibility centres are responsible for each operation. For example, responsibility centre A is responsible for operation 1, responsibility centre B for operation 2 and so on. Consequently, there is no point in comparing the actual cost of *product* 100 with the standard cost of £1100 for the purposes of control, since responsibility centres A, C and D are responsible for the variance. None of the responsibility centres is solely answerable for the variance. Cost control requires that responsibility centres be identified with the standard cost for the output achieved. Therefore, if the actual costs for responsibility centre A are compared with the standard cost of £1200 for the production of the six items (see first row of Exhibit 11.2), the manager of this responsibility centre will be answerable for the full amount of the variance. Only by comparing total actual costs with total standard costs *for each operation or responsibility centre* for a period can control be effectively achieved. A comparison of standard *product* costs (i.e. the columns in Exhibit 11.2) with actual costs that involves several different responsibility centres is clearly inappropriate.

Figure 11.1 provides an overview of the operation of a standard costing system. You will see that the standard costs for the actual output for a particular period are traced to the managers of responsibility centres who are responsible for the various operations. The actual costs for the same period are also charged to the responsibility centres. Standard and actual costs are compared and the variance is reported. For example, if the actual cost for the output of the six items produced in responsibility centre A during the period is £1300 and the standard cost is £1200 (Exhibit 11.2), a variance of £100 will be reported.

FIGURE 11.1

An overview of a standard costing system

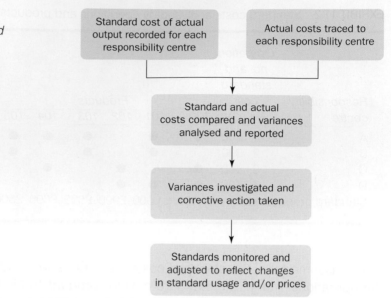

Standard cost of actual output recorded for each responsibility centre

Actual costs traced to each responsibility centre

Standard and actual costs compared and variances analysed and reported

Variances investigated and corrective action taken

Standards monitored and adjusted to reflect changes in standard usage and/or prices

Detailed analysis of variances

The box below the first arrow in Figure 11.1 indicates that the operation of a standard costing system also enables a detailed analysis of the variances to be reported. Variances for each responsibility centre can be identified by each element of cost and analysed according to the price and quantity content because different managers may be responsible for the price and quantity elements. For example, the purchasing manager may be responsible for material prices whereas the production manager may be responsible for the quantities used. The accountant assists managers by pinpointing where the variances have arisen and the responsible managers would then undertake to carry out the appropriate investigations to identify the reasons for the variance. For example, the accountant might identify the reason for a direct materials variance as being excessive usage of a certain material in a particular process, but the responsibility centre manager must investigate this process and identify the reasons for the excessive usage. Such an investigation should result in appropriate remedial action being taken or, if it is found that the variance is due to a permanent change in the standard, the standard should be changed.

Actual product costs are not required

It is questionable whether the allocation of actual costs to products serves any useful purpose. Because standard costs represent *future* target costs, they are preferable to actual *past* costs for decision-making. Also, the external financial accounting regulations in most countries specify that if standard product costs provide a reasonable approximation of actual product costs, they are acceptable for inventory valuation calculations for external reporting.

There are therefore strong arguments for not producing actual *product* costs when a standard costing system exists, since this will lead to a large reduction in information processing costs. However, it must be stressed that actual costs must be accumulated periodically for each operation or responsibility centre, so that comparisons can be made with standard costs. Nevertheless, there will be considerably fewer responsibility centres than products, and the accumulation of actual costs is therefore much less time-consuming.

ESTABLISHING COST STANDARDS

Control over costs is best effected through action at the point where the costs are incurred. Hence, the standards should be set for the quantities of material, labour and services to be consumed in performing an *operation*, rather than the complete *product* cost standards. Variances from these standards should be reported to show causes and responsibilities for deviations from standard. Product cost standards are derived by listing and adding the standard costs of operations required to produce a particular product. For example, you will see by referring to Exhibit 11.2 that the standard cost of product 100 is £1100 and is derived from the sum of the standard costs of operations 1, 3 and 4.

There are two approaches that can be used to set standard costs. First, past historical records can be used to estimate labour and material usage. Second, standards can be set based on **engineering studies**. This involves a detailed study of each operation based on careful specifications of materials, labour and equipment, and on controlled observations of operations. If historical records are used to set standards, there is a danger that the past inefficiencies will effect the standards. If historical standards are used, standards are set based on average past performance for the same or similar operations. The disadvantage of this method is that, unlike the engineering method, it does not focus attention on finding the best combination of resources, production methods and product quality. Nevertheless, standards derived from average historical usage do appear to be widely used in practice.

We shall now consider how standards are established for each operation for direct labour, direct materials and overheads using the engineering studies approach. Note that the standard cost for each operation is derived from multiplying the quantity of input that should be used per unit of output (i.e. the quantity standard) by the amount that should be paid for each unit of input (i.e. the price standard).

Direct material standards

These are based on product specifications derived from an intensive study of the input *quantity* necessary for each operation. This study should establish the most suitable materials for each product/operation, based on product design and quality policy, and also the optimal quantity that should be used after taking into account any unavoidable wastage or loss. Material quantity standards are usually recorded on a **bill of materials**. This states the required quantity of materials for each operation to complete the product. A separate bill of materials is maintained for each product. The standard material product cost is then found by multiplying the standard quantities by the appropriate standard prices.

The standard *prices* are obtained from the purchasing department. The standard material prices are based on the assumption that the purchasing department has carried out a suitable search of alternative suppliers and has selected suppliers who can provide the required quantity of sound quality materials at the most competitive price. Standard prices then provide a suitable base against which actual prices paid for materials can be evaluated.

REAL WORLD VIEWS 11.1

Establishing standard costs – using an ERP to update standard costs

Once standard costs have been established and used by a business, they should be updated on a regular basis. Actual costs are frequently used as basis for any updates. SAP, a leading enterprise resource planning (ERP) system, provides tools and data with which actual costs can be used to establish and update standards. A component of SAP called Product Costing (PC) is a very useful starting point for the exercise. This module captures the cost of manufacture and the costs of goods sold (including sales and administration overhead). Cost of manufacture as defined by SAP is composed of material and production costs, process costs and production overhead. The PC module can feed actual data to another component of SAP called cost object controlling (COO). This module in turn is used to calculate material usage costs, value work in progress and calculate variances. The PC module can also pass actual material cost data to material records in the system, thereby keeping the standard cost of material up-to-date automatically.

Questions

1 Can you think of any type of business that might need to frequently update the standard cost of its materials?
2 Do you think variance reporting would be more relevant to managers if standard costs are regularly updated?

References

Duncan, T. (2013) 5 steps to understanding product costing – Part 3 quantity structure, SAP Community Network, 2 January. Available at www.scribd.com/document/263894845/5-steps-to-understanding-product-costing-part-3-quantity-structure-pdf

SAP (2015) Product cost by period, SAP. Available at help.sap.com/doc/21ccd8530439414de10000000a174cb4/3.6/en-US/b8a839531d37e447e10000000a441470.html

Direct labour standards

To set labour standards, activities should be analysed by the different operations. Each operation is studied and an allowed time computed. The normal procedure for such a study is to analyse each operation to eliminate any unnecessary elements and to determine the most efficient production method. The most efficient methods of production, equipment and operating conditions are then standardized. This is followed by an estimate of the number of standard hours required by an average worker to complete the job. Unavoidable delays such as machine breakdowns and routine maintenance are included in the standard time. The contractual wage rates are applied to the standard time to determine the standard labour cost for each operation. Where an operation requires a mix of workers paid at different wage rates the average wage rate may be used.

Overhead standards

The procedure for establishing standard manufacturing overhead rates for a standard costing system is the same as that which is used for establishing *predetermined* overhead rates as described in Chapter 7. Separate rates for fixed and variable overheads are essential for planning and control. With traditional costing systems the standard overhead rate will be based on a rate per direct labour hour or machine hour of input.

Fixed overheads are largely independent of changes in activity, and remain constant over wide ranges of activity in the short term. It is therefore inappropriate to unitize fixed overheads for short-term cost control purposes. However, in order to meet the external financial reporting inventory valuation requirements, fixed manufacturing overheads must be traced to products. It is therefore necessary to unitize fixed overheads for inventory valuation purposes.

The main difference with the treatment of overheads under a standard costing system as opposed to a non-standard costing system is that the product overhead cost is based on the hourly overhead rates multiplied by the *standard hours* (that is, hours that should have been used) rather than the *actual hours* used.

A standard cost card should be maintained for each product and operation. It reveals the quantity of each unit of input that should be used to produce one unit of output. A typical product standard cost card is illustrated in Exhibit 11.3. In most organizations standard cost cards will be stored on a computerized database. Standards should be continuously reviewed, and, where significant changes in production methods or input prices occur, they should be changed in order to ensure that standards reflect current targets.

Standard hours produced

It is not possible to measure *output* in terms of units produced for a department making several different products or operations. For example, if a department produces 100 units of product X, 200 units of product Y and 300 units of product Z, it is not possible

EXHIBIT 11.3   An illustration of a standard cost card

Date standard set ....   Product: sigma

Direct materials

Operation no.	Item code	Quantity (kg)	Standard price (£)	A	B	C	D	Totals (£)
1	5.001	5	3	£15				
2	7.003	4	4		£16			
								31

Direct labour

Operation no.	Standard hours	Standard rate (£)					
1	7	9	£63				
2	8	9		£72			
							135

Factory overhead

Operation no.	Standard hours	Standard rate (£)					
1	7	3	£21				
2	8	4		£32			
							53

Total manufacturing cost per unit (£)   219

to add the production of these items together, since they are not homogeneous. This problem can be overcome by ascertaining the amount of time, working under efficient conditions, it should take to make each product. This time calculation is called **standard hours produced**. In other words, **standard hours** are an *output* measure that can act as a common denominator for adding together the production of unlike items.

Let us assume that the following standard times are established for the production of one unit of each product:

Product X	5 standard hours
Product Y	2 standard hours
Product Z	3 standard hours

REAL WORLD VIEWS 11.2

The effect of standards on product and service quality

Setting standards in an organization may be primarily to assist in the calculation of a standard cost for the product or service for management accounting purposes. Standards are also relevant for operational and customer service managers as they may affect the manufacture of the product or the quality of the service.

Take McDonald's, Burger King or Coca-Cola for example. All three companies produce products that adhere to standard ingredients, albeit with some minimal regional variation. A Big Mac or Whopper, for example, will contain a beef pattie that is manufactured to an exact uncooked weight. Similarly, every bottle of Coca-Cola will contain a similar amount of cola concentrate. As the ingredients are standardized according to 'recipes', a standard cost can be readily calculated and used for cost control and performance reporting. Perhaps more importantly, the customer is confident of getting a similar product on each purchase.

In comparison, consider a car-hire company like Hertz or a bank like HSBC. Most service organizations will have a customer care (HSBC) or reservations (Hertz) call centre. Staff at these centres will have a standard customer handling time to adhere

to –perhaps 3 minutes. It is not always possible to deal with customer issues or make a sale in the allotted time. Exceeding the standard handling time ultimately increases cost as more staff may be needed to handle customer call volume. On the other hand, by strictly adhering to a standard handling time, customer satisfaction and quality of service may be reduced. Thus, in a service company scenario, a fine balance between standards and quality must be achieved to ensure customer satisfaction in the longer term.

Discussion points

1 Do you think it is plausible to set standards for delivery of a service, which are primarily dictated by cost?
2 Is it possible to measure the delivery of a service (e.g. a mortgage application) against a set standard?

This means that it should take 5 hours to produce one unit of product X under efficient production conditions. Similar comments apply to products Y and Z. The production for the department will be calculated in standard hours as follows:

Product	Standard time per unit produced (hours)	Actual output (units)	Standard hours produced
X	5	100	500
Y	2	200	400
Z	3	300	900
			1 800

Remember that standard hours produced is an output measure, and flexible budget allowances should be based on this. In the illustration we should expect the *output* of 1800 standard hours to take 1800 direct labour hours of *input* if the department works at the prescribed level of efficiency. The department will be inefficient if 1800 standard hours of output are produced using, say, 2000 direct labour hours of input. The flexible budget allowance should therefore be based on 1800 standard hours produced to ensure that no extra allowance is given for the 200 excess hours of input. Otherwise, a manager will obtain a higher budget allowance through being inefficient.

PURPOSES OF STANDARD COSTING

Standard costing systems are widely used because they provide cost information for many different purposes, such as the following:

- Providing a prediction of future costs that can be used for *decision-making purposes*. Standard costs can be derived from either traditional or activity-based costing systems. Because standard costs represent *future* target costs based on the elimination of avoidable inefficiencies they are preferable to estimates based on adjusted past costs which may incorporate inefficiencies. For example, in markets where competitive prices do not exist products may be priced on a bid basis. In these situations standard costs provide more appropriate information because efficient competitors will seek to eliminate avoidable costs. It is therefore unwise to assume that inefficiencies are recoverable within the bid price.

- Providing a *challenging target* that individuals are motivated to achieve. For example, research evidence suggests that the existence of a defined quantitative goal or target is likely to motivate higher levels of performance than would be achieved if no such target was set.

- Assisting in *setting budgets* and evaluating managerial performance. Standard costs are particularly valuable for budgeting because they provide a reliable and convenient source of data for converting budgeted production into physical and monetary resource requirements. Budgetary preparation time is considerably reduced if standard costs are available because the standard costs of operations and products can be readily built up into total costs of any budgeted volume and product mix.

- Acting as a *control device* by highlighting those activities that do not conform to plan and thus alerting managers to those situations that may be 'out of control' and in need of corrective action. With a standard costing system variances are analysed in great detail such as by element of cost, and price and quantity elements. Useful feedback is therefore provided to help pinpoint the areas where variances have arisen.

● Simplifying the task of tracing costs to products for *profit measurement and inventory valuation* purposes. Besides preparing annual financial accounting profit statements most organizations also prepare monthly internal profit statements. If actual costs are used a considerable amount of time is required in tracking costs so that monthly costs can be allocated between cost of sales and inventories. A data processing system is required that can track monthly costs in a resource efficient manner. Standard costing systems meet this requirement. You will see from Figure 11.2 that product costs are maintained at standard cost. Inventories and cost of goods sold are recorded at standard cost and a conversion to actual cost is made by writing off all variances arising during the period as a period cost. Note that the variances from standard cost are extracted by comparing actual with standard costs at the responsibility centre level, and not at the product level, so that actual costs are not assigned to individual products.

FIGURE 11.2

Standard costs for inventory valuation and profit measurement

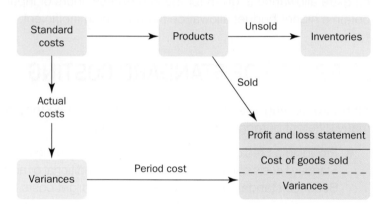

A SUMMARY OF VARIANCE ANALYSIS FOR A VARIABLE COSTING SYSTEM

It is possible to compute variances simply by committing to memory a series of variance formulae. If you adopt this approach, however, it will not help you to understand what a variance is intended to depict and what the relevant variables represent. In our discussion we shall therefore concentrate on the fundamental meaning of the variance, so that you can logically deduce the variance formulae as we go along.

All of the variances presented in this chapter are illustrated from the information contained in Example 11.1. Note that the level of detail presented is highly simplified. A truly realistic situation would involve many products, operations and responsibility centres but would not give any further insights into the basic concepts or procedures.

Figure 11.3 shows the breakdown of the profit variance (the difference between budgeted and actual profit) into the component cost and revenue variances that can be calculated for a standard variable costing system. We shall now calculate the variances set out in Figure 11.3 using the data presented in Example 11.1.

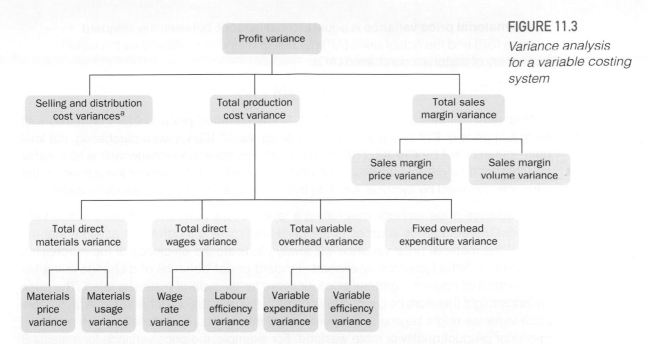

FIGURE 11.3

Variance analysis for a variable costing system

aSelling and distribution cost variances are not presented in this chapter. If activities are of a repetitive nature, standards can be established and variances can be calculated in a similar manner to production cost variances. If standards cannot be established, costs should be controlled by comparing budgeted and actual costs.

MATERIAL VARIANCES

The costs of the materials used in a manufactured product are determined by two basic factors: the price paid for the materials, and the quantity of materials used in production. This gives rise to the possibility that the actual cost will differ from the standard cost because the *actual price* paid will be different from the *standard price* and/or that the *actual quantity* of materials used will be different from the *standard quantity*. We can therefore calculate a price variance (called a material price variance for materials) and a quantity variance (called a material usage variance).

Material price variances

The starting point for calculating this variance is simply to compare the standard price per unit of materials with the actual price per unit. You should now read Example 11.1. You will see that the standard price for material A is £10 per kg, but the actual price paid was £11 per kg. The price variance is £1 per kg. This is of little consequence if the excess purchase price has been paid only for a small number of units or purchases. But the consequences are important if the excess purchase price has been paid for a large number of units, since the effect of the variance will be greater.

The difference between the standard material price and the actual price per unit should therefore be multiplied by the quantity of materials purchased. For material A the price variance is £1 per unit; but since 19 000 kg were purchased, the excess price was paid out 19 000 times. Hence the total material price variance is £19 000 adverse. The formula for the material price variance now follows logically:

The **material price variance** is equal to the difference between the standard price (SP) and the actual price (AP) per unit of materials multiplied by the actual quantity of materials purchased (AQ):

$$(SP - AP) \times AQ$$

Now refer to material B in Example 11.1. The standard price is £15, compared with an actual price of £14 giving a £1 saving per kg. As 10 100 kg were purchased, the total price variance will be £10 100 (10 100 kg at £1). The variance for material B is favourable and that for material A is adverse. The normal procedure is to present the amount of the variances followed by symbols A or F to indicate either adverse or favourable variances.

An adverse price variance may reflect a failure by the purchasing department to seek the most advantageous sources of supply. However, it is incorrect to assume that the level of the material price variance will always indicate the efficiency of the purchasing department. Actual prices may exceed standard prices because of a change in market conditions that causes a general price increase for the type of materials used. The price variance might therefore be beyond the control of the purchasing department. A favourable price variance might be due to the purchase of inferior quality materials, which may lead to inferior product quality or more wastage. For example, the price variance for material B is favourable, but we shall see in the next section that this is offset by excess usage. If the reason for this excess usage is the purchase of inferior quality materials then the material usage variance should be assigned to the purchasing department.

Calculation of quantity purchased or quantity used

It is important that variances are reported as quickly as possible so that any inefficiencies can be identified and remedial action taken. A problem occurs, however, with material purchases in that there may be a considerable delay before materials are actually used; materials may be purchased in one period and used in subsequent periods. For example, if 10 000 units of a material are purchased in period 1 at a price of £1 per unit over standard and 2000 units are used in each of periods 1 to 5, the following alternatives are available for calculating the price variance:

1 The full amount of the price variance of £10 000 is reported in *period 1* with quantity being defined as the *actual quantity purchased*.

2 The price variance is calculated with quantity being defined as the *actual quantity used*. The unit price variance of £1 is multiplied by the quantity used (i.e. 2000 units), which means that a price variance of £2000 will be reported for each of *periods 1 to 5*.

Method 1 is recommended, because the price variance can be reported in the period in which it is incurred, and reporting of the total price variance is not delayed until months later when the materials are used. Also, adopting this approach enables corrective action to be taken earlier. For the sake of simplicity we shall assume in Example 11.1 that the actual purchases are identical with the actual usage.

Material usage variance

The starting point for calculating this quantity variance is simply to compare the standard quantity that should have been used with the actual quantity that has been used. Refer again to Example 11.1. You will see that the standard usage for the production of one

EXAMPLE 11.1

Alpha manufacturing company produces a single product, which is known as sigma. The product requires a single operation, and the standard cost for this operation is presented in the following standard cost card:

Standard cost card for product sigma	(£)
Direct materials:	
2 kg of A at £10 per kg	20.00
1 kg of B at £15 per kg	15.00
Direct labour (3 hours at £9 per hour)	27.00
Variable overhead (3 hours at £2 per direct labour hour)	6.00
Total standard variable cost	68.00
Standard contribution margin	20.00
Standard selling price	88.00

Alpha Ltd plans to produce 10 000 units of sigma in the month of April, and the budgeted costs based on the information contained in the standard cost card are as follows:

Budget based on the above standard costs and an output of 10 000 units	(£)	(£)	(£)
Sales (10 000 units of sigma at £88 per unit)			880 000
Direct materials:			
A: 20 000 kg at £10 per kg	200 000		
B: 10 000 kg at £15 per kg	150 000	350 000	
Direct labour (30 000 hours at £9 per hour)		270 000	
Variable overheads (30 000 hours at £2 per direct labour hour)		60 000	680 000
Budgeted contribution			200 000
Fixed overheads			120 000
Budgeted profit			80 000

Annual budgeted fixed overheads are £1 440 000 and are assumed to be incurred evenly throughout the year. The company uses a direct (variable) costing system for internal profit measurement purposes.

The actual results for April are:

	(£)	(£)
Sales (9 000 units at £90)		810 000
Direct materials:		
A: 19 000 kg at £11 per kg	209 000	
B: 10 100 kg at £14 per kg	141 400	
Direct labour (28 500 hours at £9.60 per hour)	273 600	
Variable overheads	52 000	676 000
Contribution		134 000
Fixed overheads		116 000
Profit		18 000

Manufacturing overheads are charged to production on the basis of direct labour hours. Actual production and sales for the period were 9 000 units.

unit of sigma is 2 kg for material A. As 9000 units of sigma are produced, 18 000 kg of material A should have been used; however, 19 000 kg are actually used, which means there has been an excess usage of 1000 kg.

The importance of this excess usage depends on the price of the materials. For example, if the price is £0.01 per kg then an excess usage of 1000 kg will not be very significant, but if the price is £10 per unit then an excess usage of 1000 kg will be very significant. It follows that to assess the importance of the excess usage, the variance should be expressed in monetary terms.

Should the standard material price per kg or the actual material price per kg be used to calculate the variance? The answer is the standard price. If the *actual* material price is used, the usage variance will be affected by the efficiency of the purchasing department, since any excess purchase price will be assigned to the excess usage. It is therefore necessary to remove the price effects from the usage variance calculation, and this is achieved by valuing the variance at the standard price. Hence, the 1000 kg excess usage of material A is multiplied by the standard price of £10 per unit, which gives an adverse usage variance of £10 000. The formula for the variance is:

The **material usage variance** is equal to the difference between the standard quantity (SQ) required for actual production and the actual quantity (AQ) used multiplied by the standard material price (SP):

$$(SQ - AQ) \times SP$$

For material B you will see from Example 11.1 that the standard quantity is 9000 kg (9000 units × 1 kg), but 10 100 kg have been used. The excess usage of 1100 kg is multiplied by the standard price of £15 per kg, which gives an adverse variance of £16 500. Note that the principles of flexible budgeting described in the previous chapter also apply here, with *standard quantity being based on actual production and not budgeted production*. This ensures that a manager is evaluated under the conditions in which he or she actually worked and not those envisaged at the time the budget was prepared.

The material usage variance is normally controllable by the manager of the appropriate production responsibility centre. Common causes of material usage variances include the careless handling of materials by production personnel, the purchase of inferior quality materials, pilferage, changes in quality control requirements, or changes in methods of production. Separate material usage variances should be calculated for each type of material used and allocated to each responsibility centre.

Total material variance

From Figure 11.3 you will see that this variance is the total variance before it is analysed into the price and usage elements. The formula for the variance is:

The **total material variance** is the difference between the standard material cost (SC) for the actual production and the actual cost (AC):

$$SC - AC$$

To compute the total material variance we need to determine what the standard cost of materials should be for the actual production. For material A the standard material cost is £20 per unit (see Example 11.1), giving a total standard material cost of £180 000 (9000 units × £20). The actual cost is £209 000, and therefore the variance is £29 000 adverse.

The price variance of £19 000 plus the usage variance of £10 000 agrees with the total material variance. Similarly, the total material variance for material B is £6400, consisting of a favourable price variance of £10 100 and an adverse usage variance of £16 500.

Note that if the price variance is calculated on the actual quantity *purchased* instead of the actual quantity *used*, the price variance plus the usage variance will agree with the total variance only when the quantity purchased is equal to the quantity that is used in the particular accounting period. Reconciling the price and usage variance with the total variance is merely a reconciliation exercise, and you should not be concerned if reconciliation of the sub-variances with the total variance is not possible.

LABOUR VARIANCES

The cost of labour is determined by the price paid for labour and the quantity of labour used. Thus a price variance (wage rate variance) and a quantity variance (labour efficiency variance) will also arise for labour.

Wage rate variance

The price (wage rate) variance is calculated by comparing the standard price per hour with the actual price paid per hour. In Example 11.1 the standard wage rate per hour is £9 and the actual wage rate is £9.60 per hour, giving a wage rate variance of £0.60 per hour. To determine the importance of the variance, it is necessary to ascertain how many times the excess payment of £0.60 per hour is paid. As 28 500 labour hours are used (see Example 11.1), we multiply 28 500 hours by £0.60. This gives an adverse wage rate variance of £17 100. The formula for the **wage rate variance** is:

The wage rate variance is equal to the difference between the standard wage rate per hour (SR) and the actual wage rate (AR) multiplied by the actual number of hours worked (AH):

$$(SR - AR) \times AH$$

Note the similarity between this variance and the material price variance. Both variances multiply the difference between the standard price and the actual price paid for a unit of a resource by the actual quantity of resources used. The wage rate variance is probably the one that is least subject to control by management. In most cases the variance is due to wage rate standards not being kept in line with changes in actual wage rates, and for this reason it is not normally controllable by departmental managers.

Labour efficiency variance

The labour efficiency variance represents the quantity variance for direct labour. The quantity of labour that should be used for the actual output is expressed in terms of *standard hours produced*. In Example 11.1 the standard time for the production of one unit of sigma is 3 hours. Thus a production level of 9000 units results in an output of 27 000 standard hours. In other words, working at the prescribed level of efficiency, it should take 27 000 hours to produce 9000 units. However, 28 500 direct labour hours are actually required to produce this output, which means that 1500 excess direct labour hours are used. We multiply the excess direct labour hours by the *standard* wage rate of £9 per hour to calculate the variance. This gives an adverse variance of £13 500. The formula for calculating the **labour efficiency variance** is.

The labour efficiency variance is equal to the difference between the standard labour hours for actual production (SH) and the actual labour hours worked (AH) during the period multiplied by the standard wage rate per hour (SR):

$$(SH - AH) \times SR$$

This variance is similar to the material usage variance. Both variances multiply the difference between the standard quantity and actual quantity of resources consumed by the standard price. The labour efficiency variance is normally controllable by the manager of the appropriate production responsibility centre and may be due to a variety of reasons. For example, the use of inferior quality materials, different grades of labour, failure to maintain machinery in proper condition, the introduction of new equipment or tools and changes in the production processes will all affect the efficiency of labour. An efficiency variance may not always be controllable by the production managers; it may be due, for example, to poor production scheduling by the planning department, or to a change in quality control standards.

Total labour variance

From Figure 11.3 you will see that this variance represents the total variance before analysis into the price and quantity elements. The formula for the variance is:

The **total labour variance** is the difference between the standard labour cost (SC) for the actual production and the actual labour cost (AC):

$$SC - AC$$

In Example 11.1 the actual production was 9000 units, and, with a standard labour cost of £27 per unit, the standard cost is £243 000 (9000 × £27). The actual cost is £273 600, which gives an adverse variance of £30 600.

VARIABLE OVERHEAD VARIANCES

A total variable overhead variance is calculated in the same way as the total direct labour and material variances. In Example 11.1 the output is 9000 units and the standard variable overhead cost is £6 *per unit* produced. The standard cost for the production of 9000 units for variable overheads is thus £54 000. The actual variable overheads incurred are £52 000, giving a favourable variance of £2000. The formula for the variance is:

The **total variable overhead variance** is the difference between the standard variable overheads charged to production (SC) and the actual variable overheads incurred (AC):

$$SC - AC$$

Where variable overheads vary with direct labour or machine hours of *input* the total variable overhead variance will be due to one or both of the following:

1 A *price* variance arising from actual expenditure being different from budgeted expenditure.

2 A *quantity* variance arising from actual direct labour or machine hours of input being different from the hours of input, which *should* have been used.

These reasons give rise to the two sub-variances, which are shown in Figure 11.3: the variable overhead expenditure variance and the variable overhead efficiency variance.

Variable overhead expenditure variance

To compare the actual overhead expenditure with the budgeted expenditure, it is necessary to flex the budget (see Chapter 10 for an explanation of flexible budgeting). Because it is assumed in Example 11.1 that variable overheads will vary with direct labour hours of *input* the budget is flexed on this basis. Actual variable overhead expenditure is £52 000, resulting from 28 500 direct labour hours of input. For this level of activity variable overheads of £57 000, which consist of 28 500 input hours at £2 per hour, should have been spent. Spending was £5000 less than it should have been, and the result is a favourable variance.

If we compare the budgeted and the actual overhead costs for 28 500 direct labour hours of input, we shall ensure that any efficiency content is removed from the variance. This means that any difference must be due to actual variable overhead spending being different from the budgeted variable overhead spending. The formula for the variance is:

> The **variable overhead expenditure variance** is equal to the difference between the budgeted flexed variable overheads (BFVO) for the actual direct labour hours of input and the actual variable overhead costs incurred (AVO):

$$BFVO - AVO$$

Because it is assumed that variable overheads vary with the actual direct labour hours of input the budgeted flexed variable overheads (BFVO) has been derived from multiplying the actual quantity of direct labour hours of input by the standard variable overhead rate.

Variable overhead represents the aggregation of a large number of individual items, such as indirect labour, indirect materials, electricity, maintenance and so on. The variable overhead variance can arise because the prices of individual items have changed. It can also be affected by how efficiently the individual variable overhead items are used. Waste or inefficiency, such as using more kilowatt-hours of power than should have been used will increase the cost of power and, thus, the total cost of variable overhead. The variable overhead expenditure on its own is therefore not very informative. Any meaningful analysis of this variance requires a comparison of the actual expenditure for each individual item of variable overhead expenditure against the budget.

Variable overhead efficiency variance

In Example 11.1 it is assumed that variable overheads vary with direct labour hours of input. The variable overhead efficiency variance arises because 28 500 direct labour hours of input were required to produce 9000 units. Working at the prescribed level of efficiency (3 hours per unit of output), it should take 27 000 hours to produce 9000 units of output. Therefore, an extra 1500 direct labour hours of input were required. Because variable overheads are assumed to vary with direct labour hours of input, an additional 3000 (1500 hours at £2) variable overheads will be incurred. The formula for the variance is:

> The **variable overhead efficiency variance** is the difference between the standard hours of output (SH) and the actual hours of input (AH) for the period multiplied by the standard variable overhead rate (SR):

$$(SH - AH) \times SR$$

You should note that if it is assumed that variable overheads vary with direct labour hours of input, this variance is identical to the labour efficiency variance, apart from the fact that the standard variable overhead rate is used instead of the wage rate.

The reasons for the variance are the same as those described previously for the labour efficiency variance. If you refer again to Figure 11.3, you will see that the variable overhead expenditure variance (£5000 favourable) plus the variable efficiency variance (£3000 adverse) add up to the total variable overhead variance of £2000 favourable.

A GENERIC ROUTINE APPROACH TO VARIANCE ANALYSIS

In our discussion of each of the variable cost variances in the preceding sections, a theoretical approach was adopted that began by explaining the fundamental meaning of each variance so that you could logically deduce the formula for each variance. Although it is the author's recommendation that you adopt this approach, feedback indicates that

REAL WORLD VIEWS 11.3

Standard costing variance analysis is obsolete for lean manufacturers

Andrew Bargerstock argues that standard costing variance analysis is obsolete for lean manufacturers. He identifies the following three key flaws relating to standard costing for lean manufacturers:

Inconsistent updates of standards. Companies establish standards at the beginning of the year, often as enterprise resource planning (ERP) data inputs. But many later forget to make periodic updates as commodity markets move during the year. Labour rates may also change as industry and economic factors change. Therefore, variances may contain a significant degree of error—not because of inefficiencies but because the company updated the standards inconsistently.

Time-lagged data. Variance reports frequently are developed and investigated weeks after the data is generated, creating a time lag. Cost accountants investigating the root causes of unfavourable variances often find that production people don't remember clearly the events that generated the data, hampering any investigation. From the perspective of production teams, the standard costing variance analysis (SCVA) reports come too late. Instead, more real time feedback is needed to correct inefficiencies quickly.

Need for more granular feedback. The classic model of standard costing spans an entire production process—from the point that the company first introduces materials and labour until workers complete the finished product. But standard costing doesn't provide data showing how much value is added by each work cell (that is, each small group of workers who perform a set of coordinated activities). Instead, traditional SCVA aggregates the data, and mathematical averaging actually hides the kind of specific, detailed information that production work cell teams need to optimize production efficiencies. Therefore, lean production teams using SCVA lack the work cell level data that tells them how well they are creating value for customers. So it's clear that SCVA doesn't deliver work cell level data promptly enough to aid lean decision making.

Questions

1 Explain the arguments in favour of the relevance of standard costing and variance analysis in a modern manufacturing environment.
2 Suggest methods that might be used by management accountants to control costs and evaluate efficiency as alternatives to complements to standard costing and variance analysis.

Reference

Bargerstock, A., and Shi, Y. (2016), Leaning away from standard costing, *Strategic Finance*, June, 37–45.

some readers prefer to use an alternative routine generic approach that is presented in Appendix 11.1. You should only read Appendix 11.1 if you have found the variance calculations in the previous section confusing and wish to adopt the alternative routine generic approach.

FIXED OVERHEAD EXPENDITURE OR SPENDING VARIANCE

The final production variance shown in Figure 11.3 is the fixed overhead expenditure variance. With a direct costing system, fixed manufacturing overheads are not unitized and allocated to products. Instead, the total fixed overheads for the period are charged as an expense to the period in which they are incurred. Fixed overheads are assumed to remain unchanged in the short term in response to changes in the level of activity, but they may change in response to other factors. For example, price increases may cause expenditure on fixed overheads to increase. The **fixed overhead expenditure variance** therefore explains the difference between budgeted fixed overheads and the actual fixed overheads incurred. The formula for the fixed overhead expenditure variance is the difference between the budgeted fixed overheads (BFO) and the actual fixed overhead (AFO) spending:

$$BFO - AFO$$

In Example 11.1 budgeted fixed overhead expenditure is £120 000 and actual fixed overhead spending £116 000. Therefore the fixed overhead expenditure variance is £4000. Whenever the actual fixed overheads are less than the budgeted fixed overheads, the variance will be favourable. The total of the fixed overhead expenditure variance on its own is not particularly informative. Any meaningful analysis of this variance requires a comparison of the actual expenditure for each individual item of fixed overhead expenditure against the budget. The difference may be due to a variety of causes, such as changes in salaries paid to employees, or the appointment of additional supervisors. Only by comparing individual items of expenditure and ascertaining the reasons for the variances, can one determine whether the variance is controllable or uncontrollable. Generally, this variance is likely to be uncontrollable in the short term.

SALES VARIANCES

Sales variances can be used to analyse the performance of the sales function or revenue centres on broadly similar terms to those for manufacturing costs. The most significant feature of sales variance calculations is that they are calculated in terms of profit contribution margins rather than sales values. Consider Example 11.2.

EXAMPLE 11.2

The budgeted sales for a company are £110 000 consisting of 10 000 units at £11 per unit. The standard cost per unit is £7. Actual sales are £120 000 (12 000 units at £10 per unit) and the actual cost per unit is £7.

You will see that when the variances are calculated on the basis of sales *value*, it is necessary to compare the budgeted sales *value* of £110 000 with the actual sales of £120 000. This gives a favourable variance of £10 000. This calculation, however, ignores the impact of the sales effort on profit. The budgeted profit contribution is £40 000, which consists of 10 000 units at £4 per unit, but the actual impact of the sales effort in terms of profit margins indicates a profit contribution of £36 000, which consists of 12 000 units at £3 per unit, indicating an adverse variance of £4000. If we examine Example 11.2, we can see that compared with the budget the selling prices have been reduced, and that this has led not only to an increase in the total sales revenue but also to a reduction in total profits. The objective of the selling function is to influence favourably total profits. Thus a more meaningful performance measure will be obtained by comparing the results of the sales function in terms of profit contribution margins rather than sales revenues. Let us now calculate the sales variances from the information contained in Example 11.1.

Total sales margin variance

The total sales margin variance seeks to identify the influence of the sales function on the difference between budget and actual profit contribution. In Example 11.1 the budgeted contribution to fixed overheads and profit is £200 000, which consists of budgeted sales of 10 000 units at a contribution of £20 per unit. This is compared with a contribution derived from the actual sales volume of 9000 units. Because the sales function is responsible for the sales volume and the unit selling price, but not the unit manufacturing costs, the standard cost of sales and not the actual cost of sales is deducted from the actual sales revenue. The calculation of the contribution for ascertaining the total sales margin variance will therefore be as follows:

	(£)
Actual sales revenue (9000 units at £90)	810 000
Standard variable cost of sales for actual sales volume (9000 units at £68)	612 000
Profit contribution margin	198 000

To calculate the total sales margin variance we deduct the budgeted contribution for the period of £200 000 from the above profit contribution of £198 000. This gives an adverse variance of £2000.

The formula for calculating the variance is as follows:

The **total sales margin variance** is the difference between actual sales revenue (ASR) less the standard variable cost of sales (SCOS) and the budgeted contribution (BC):

$$(ASR - SCOS) - BC$$

Using the standard cost of sales in the above formula and calculation ensures that production variances do not distort the calculation of the sales variances. This means that sales variances arise only because of changes in those variables controlled by the sales function (i.e. selling prices and sales quantity). Figure 11.3 indicates that it is possible to analyse the total sales margin variance into two sub-variances – a sales margin price variance and a sales margin volume variance.

Sales margin price variance

In Example 11.1 the actual selling price is £90 and the standard selling price is £88. In order to ensures that production variances do not distort the calculation of the sales margin price variance the standard unit variable cost of £68 should be deducted from both the actual and the standard selling prices. This gives a contribution of £22 that is derived from the actual selling price and a contribution of £20 derived from the standard selling price. Because the actual sales volume is 9000 units, the increase in selling price means that the increase in contribution of £2 per unit is obtained 9000 times giving a favourable sales margin variance of £18 000. In formula terms the variance is calculated as follows:

[(Actual selling price − Standard variable cost) − (Standard selling price − Standard variable cost)] × Actual sales volume

Since the standard variable cost is deducted from both the actual and standard selling price the above formula can be simplified by omitting standard variable cost so that:

The **sales margin price variance** is the difference between the actual selling price (ASP) and the standard selling price (SSP) multiplied by the actual sales volume (AV):

$$(ASP − SSP) × AV$$

Sales margin volume variance

To ascertain the effect of changes in the sales volume on the difference between the budgeted and the actual contribution, we must compare the budgeted sales volume with the actual sales volume. You will see from Example 11.1 that the budgeted sales are 10 000 units but the actual sales are 9000 units, and to enable us to determine the impact of this reduction in sales volume on profit, we must multiply the 1000 units by the standard contribution margin of £20. This gives an adverse variance of £20 000.

The use of the standard margin (standard selling price less standard cost) ensures that the volume variance will not be affected by any *changes* in the actual selling prices. The formula for calculating the variance is:

The **sales margin volume variance** is the difference between the actual sales volume (AV) and the budgeted volume (BV) multiplied by the standard contribution margin (SM):

$$(AV − BV) × SM$$

Difficulties in interpreting sales margin variances

The favourable sales margin price variance of £18 000 plus the adverse volume variance of £20 000 add up to the total adverse sales margin variance of £2000. It may be argued that it is not very meaningful to analyse the total sales margin variance into price and volume components, since changes in selling prices are likely to affect sales volume. A favourable price variance will tend to be associated with an adverse volume variance, and vice versa. It may be unrealistic to expect to sell more than the budgeted volume when selling prices have increased.

A further problem with sales variances is that the variances may arise from external factors and may not be controllable by management. For example, changes in selling prices may be a reaction to changes in selling prices of competitors. Alternatively, a reduction in both selling prices and sales volume may be the result of an economic recession that was not foreseen when the budget was prepared. For control and performance appraisal it may be preferable to compare actual market share with target market share for each product. In addition, the trend in market shares should be monitored and selling prices should be compared with competitors' prices.

RECONCILING BUDGETED PROFIT AND ACTUAL PROFIT

Top management will be interested in the reason for the actual profit being different from the budgeted profit. By adding the favourable production and sales variances to the budgeted profit and deducting the adverse variances, the reconciliation of budgeted and actual profit shown in Exhibit 11.4 can be presented in respect of Example 11.1.

Example 11.1 assumes that Alpha Ltd produces a single product consisting of a single operation and that the activities are performed by one responsibility centre. In practice, most companies make many products, which require operations to be carried out in different responsibility centres. A reconciliation statement such as that presented in Exhibit 11.4 will therefore normally represent a summary of the variances for many responsibility centres. The reconciliation statement thus represents a broad picture to top management that explains the major reasons for any difference between the budgeted and actual profits.

EXHIBIT 11.4   Reconciliation of budgeted and actual profits for a standard variable costing system

	(£)	(£)	(£)
Budgeted net profit			80 000
Sales variances:			
Sales margin price	18 000F		
Sales margin volume	20 000A	2 000A	
Direct cost variances:			
Material: Price	8 900A		
Usage	26 500A	35 400A	
Labour: Rate	17 100A		
Efficiency	13 500A	30 600A	
Manufacturing overhead variances:			
Fixed overhead expenditure	4 000F		
Variable overhead expenditure	5 000F		
Variable overhead efficiency	3 000A	6 000F	62 000A
Actual profit			18 000

SUMMARY

The following items relate to the learning objectives listed at the beginning of the chapter.

- **Explain how a standard costing system operates.** Standard costing is most suited to an organization whose activities consist of a series of repetitive operations and the input required to produce each unit of output can be specified. A standard costing system involves the following: (a) the standard costs for the actual output are recorded for each operation for each responsibility centre; (b) actual costs for each operation are traced to each responsibility centre; (c) the standard and actual costs are compared; (d) variances are investigated and corrective action is taken where appropriate; and (e) standards are monitored and adjusted to reflect changes in standard usage and/or prices.

- **Explain how standard costs are set.** Standards should be set for the quantities and prices of materials, labour and services to be consumed in performing each operation associated with a product. Product standard costs are derived by listing and adding the standard costs of operations required to produce a particular product. Two approaches are used for setting standard costs. First, past historical records can be used to estimate labour and material usage. Secondly, standards can be set based on engineering studies. With engineering studies a detailed study of each operation is undertaken under controlled conditions, based on high levels of efficiency, to ascertain the quantities of labour and materials required. Target prices are then applied to ascertain the standard costs.

- **Explain the meaning of standard hours produced.** It is not possible to measure output in terms of units produced for a department making several different products or operations. This problem is overcome by ascertaining the amount of time, working under efficient operating conditions, it should take to make each product. This time calculation is called standard hours produced. Standard hours thus represents an output measure that acts as a common denominator for adding together the production of unlike items.

- **Identify and describe the purposes of a standard costing system.** Standard costing systems can be used for the following purposes: (a) providing a prediction of future costs that can be used for decision-making; (b) providing a challenging target that individuals are motivated to achieve; (c) providing a reliable and convenient source of data for budget preparation; (d) acting as a control device by highlighting those activities that do not conform to plan and thus alerting managers to those situations that may be 'out of control' and in need of corrective action; and (e) simplifying the task of tracing costs to products for profit measurement and inventory valuation purpose.

- **Calculate labour, material, overhead and sales margin variances and reconcile actual profit with budgeted profit.** To reconcile actual profit with budget profit the favourable variances are added to the budgeted profit and adverse variances are deducted. The end result should be the actual profit. A summary of the formulae for the computation of the variances is presented in Exhibit 11.5. In each case the formula is presented so that a positive variance is favourable and a negative variance unfavourable. Alternatively, you can use the routine generic approach shown in Appendix 11.1.

EXHIBIT 11.5   Summary of the formulae for the computation of variances

The following variances are reported for both variable and absorption costing systems:

Materials and labour

1	Material price variance	=	(Standard price per unit of material – Actual price) × Quantity of materials purchased
2	Material usage variance	=	(Standard quantity of materials for actual production – Actual quantity used) × Standard price per unit
3	Total materials cost variance	=	(Actual production × Standard material cost per unit of production) – Actual materials cost
4	Wage rate variance	=	(Standard wage rate per hour – Actual wage rate) × Actual labour hours worked
5	Labour efficiency variance	=	(Standard quantity of labour hours for actual production – Actual labour hours) × Standard wage rate
6	Total labour cost variance	=	(Actual production × Standard labour cost per unit of production) – Actual labour cost

Fixed production overhead

7	Fixed overhead expenditure	=	Budgeted fixed overheads – Actual fixed overheads

Variable production overhead

8	Variable overhead expenditure variance	=	(Budgeted variable overheads for actual input volume – Actual variable overhead cost)
9	Variable overhead efficiency variance	=	(Standard quantity of input hours for actual production – Actual input hours) × Variable overhead rate
10	Total variable overhead variance	=	(Actual production × Standard variable overhead rate per unit) – Actual variable overhead cost

Sales margins

11	Sales margin price variance	=	(Actual selling price – Budgeted selling price) × Actual sales volume
12	Sales margin volume variance	=	(Actual sales volume – Budgeted sales volume) × Standard contribution margin
13	Total sales margin variance	=	(Actual sales revenue – Standard variable cost of sales) – Total budgeted contribution

● Identify the causes of labour, material, overhead and sales margin variances. Quantities cost variances arise because the actual quantity of resources consumed exceeds actual usage. Examples include excess usage of materials and labour arising from the usage of inferior materials, careless handling of materials and failure to maintain machinery in proper condition. Price variances arise when the actual prices paid for resources exceed the standard prices. Examples include the failure of the purchasing function to seek the most efficient sources of supply or the use of a different grade of labour to that incorporated in the standard costs.

APPENDIX 11.1: A GENERIC ROUTINE APPROACH TO VARIANCE ANALYSIS

In this appendix an alternative approach is presented for calculating the materials, labour and variable cost variances. The disadvantage with adopting this alternative approach is that you will not have a theoretical understanding of each variance. The advantage of the alternative approach is its simplicity because all of the variable cost variances can be derived from a single worksheet. You should therefore only read this section and Exhibit 11.A1 if you found the theoretical approach confusing and your preference is to use the generic approach.

To compute the price variances (material price, wage rate and variable overhead expenditure variances) we noted that the price variances were due to the differences between the standard prices (SP) and the actual prices (AP) multiplied by the actual quantity (AQ) of the resource used giving the formula:

$$(SP - AP) \times AQ \text{ which can be restated as:}$$
$$(AQ \times SP) - (AQ \times AP)$$

The first term in the above formula is entered in the first column of Exhibit 11.A1 and the second term is entered in the second column so that the variance is the difference between columns 1 and 2. Adopting this approach for material A the actual quantity of materials purchased (19 000 kg) at the standard price (£10) is entered in column 1 and the actual quantity of materials purchased (19 000 kg) at the actual price (£11) is entered in column 2. The difference between columns 1 and 2 is the adverse price variance of £19 000 (£190 000 − £209 000). If you now refer to Exhibit 11.A1 you will see that the same approach is used to compute the price variances for labour and variable overhead. All of the variances are derived from the differences between columns 1 and 2. In order to present a generic approach the terms 'actual quantity of materials purchased' and 'actual hours' have been replaced with the generic term 'actual quantity of inputs' in Exhibit 11.A1.

We shall now calculate the quantity variances (material usage, labour and overhead efficiency) using the generic approach. Look at the material usage variance. We used the following formula:

$$(SQ - AQ) \times SP \text{ which can be restated as:}$$
$$(SQ \times SP) - (AQ \times SP)$$

EXHIBIT 11.A1 Variance analysis adopting the generic routine approach

	(1) Actual quantity of inputs at standard price (AQ × SP)	(2) Actual quantity of inputs at actual price (AQ × AP)	(3) Standard inputs required for actual output at standard prices (SQ × SP)
	Price variance 5 (1 – 2)		*Quantity variance (3 – 1)*
Material A price and usage variances	19 000 kg × £10 = £190 000	19 000 kg × £11 = £209 000 = £19 000A	(9 000 × 2 kg) × £10 = £180 000 = £10 000A
Material B price and usage variances	10 100 kg × £15 = £151 500	10 100 kg × £14 = £141 400 = £10 100F	(9 000 × 1 kg) × £15 = £135 000 = £16 500A
Wage rate and labour efficiency variance	28 500 hours × £9 = £256 500	28 500 hours × £9.60 = £273 600 = £17 100A	(9 000 × 3 hours) × £9 = £243 000 = £13 500A
Variable overhead expenditure and efficiency variance	28 500 hours × £2 = £57 000	£52 000 = £5 000F	(9 000 × 3 hours) × £2 = £54 000 = £3 000A

Total variances (3 2 2)
Material A (£180 000 − £209 000) = £29 000A
Material B (£135 000 − £141 400) = £6 400A
Labour (£243 000 − £273 600) = £30 600A
Variable overheads (£54 000 − £52 000) = £2 000F

The first term in the above formula is entered in the third column of Exhibit 11.A1 and the second term is already entered in the first column so the variance is the difference between columns 3 and 1. Adopting this approach for material A the standard quantity required for the actual production (9000 × 2 kg) at the standard price (£10) is entered in column 3 and the actual quantity used (19 000kg) at the standard price (£10) is entered in column 1. The difference between column 3 and column 1 is the adverse usage variance of £10 000 (£180 000 − £190 000). You will see by referring to Exhibit 11.A1 that the same approach has also been used to calculate the usage variances for labour and variable overheads (labour and variable overhead efficiency). All of the quantity variances are therefore derived from the differences between columns 3 and 1.

In our earlier calculations in the main body of the chapter we noted that the total variances for materials, labour and variable overheads were the difference between the standard cost for the actual production and the actual cost. The first item is shown in column 3 of Exhibit 11.A1 and the second in column 2. Therefore the total variance for each element of cost is the difference between columns 3 and 2.

KEY TERMS AND CONCEPTS

Bill of materials A document stating the required quantity of materials for each operation to complete the product.

Budgeted costs Expected costs for an entire activity or operation.

Engineering studies Detailed studies of each operation, based on careful specifications of materials, labour and equipment and on controlled observations of operations.

Fixed overhead expenditure variance The difference between the budgeted fixed overheads and the actual fixed overhead spending.

Labour efficiency variance The difference between the standard labour hours for actual production and the actual labour hours worked during the period multiplied by the standard wage rate per hour.

Material price variance The difference between the standard price and the actual price per unit of materials multiplied by the quantity of materials purchased.

Material usage variance The difference between the standard quantity required for actual production and the actual quantity used multiplied by the standard material price.

Sales margin price variance The difference between the actual selling price and the standard selling price multiplied by the actual sales volume.

Sales margin volume variance The difference between the actual sales volume and the budgeted volume multiplied by the standard contribution margin.

Standard costs Target costs that are predetermined and should be incurred under efficient operating conditions.

Standard hours The number of hours a skilled worker should take working under efficient conditions to complete a given job.

Standard hours produced A calculation of the amount of time, working under efficient conditions, it should take to make each product.

Total labour variance The difference between the standard labour cost for the actual production and the actual labour cost.

Total material variance The difference between the standard material cost for the actual production and the actual cost.

Total sales margin variance The difference between actual sales revenue less the standard variable cost of sales and the budgeted contribution.

Total variable overhead variance The difference between the standard variable overheads charged to production and the actual variable overheads incurred.

Variable overhead efficiency variance The difference between the standard hours of output and the actual hours of input for the period multiplied by the standard variable overhead rate.

Variable overhead expenditure variance The difference between the budgeted flexed variable overheads for the actual direct labour hours of input and the actual variable overhead costs incurred.

Wage rate variance The difference between the standard wage rate per hour and the actual wage rate, multiplied by the actual number of hours worked.

ASSESSMENT MATERIAL

The review questions are short questions that enable you to assess your understanding of the main topics included in the chapter. The page numbers in parentheses provide you with the page numbers to refer to if you cannot answer a specific question.

The review problems are more complex and require you to relate and apply the content to various business problems. Solutions to review problems are provided in a separate section at the end of the book. Additional review problems can be accessed by lecturers and students on the dedicated online support resources for this book. Solutions to these review problems are provided for lecturers in the *Instructor's Manual* accompanying this book that can be downloaded from the dedicated online instructor's resources (see Preface for details).

The dedicated online digital support resources for this book also includes over 30 case study problems.

REVIEW QUESTIONS

11.1 Describe the difference between budgeted and standard costs. *(pp. 277–278)*

11.2 Explain how a standard costing system operates. *(pp. 278–280)*

11.3 Describe how standard costs are established using engineering studies. *(pp. 281–283)*

11.4 Explain what is meant by the term 'standard hours produced?' *(pp. 283–285)*

11.5 Describe the different purposes of a standard costing system. *(pp. 285–286)*

11.6 What are the possible causes of (a) material price and (b) material usage variances? *(pp. 288–291)*

11.7 Explain why it is preferable for the material price variance to be computed at the point of purchase rather than the point of issue. *(p. 288)*

11.8 What are the possible causes of (a) wage rate and (b) labour efficiency variances? *(pp. 291–292)*

11.9 Explain how variable overhead efficiency and expenditure variances are computed. What are the possible causes of each of these variances? *(pp. 292–294)*

11.10 Why are sales variances based on contribution margins rather than sales revenues? *(pp. 295–296)*

REVIEW PROBLEMS

11.11 The following details relate to the standard material cost for a product produced by a company:

8 kg at £0.80/kg = £6.40 per unit
Budgeted production in April was 850 units

The following details relate to actual materials purchased and issued to production during April, when actual production was 870 units:

Materials purchased	8200 kg costing £6888
Materials issued to production	7150 kg

Which of the following correctly states the material price and usage variance to be reported?

	Price	Usage
A	£286 (A)	£152 (A)
B	£286 (A)	£280 (A)
C	£286 (A)	£294 (A)
D	£328 (A)	£152 (A)
E	£328 (A)	£280 (A)

11.12 PQ Limited operates a standard costing system for its only product. The standard cost card is as follows:

Direct material (4 kg at £2/kg)	$8.00
Direct labour (4 hours at £8/hour)	$32.00
Variable overhead (4 hours at £3/hour)	$12.00
Fixed overhead (4 hours at £5/hour)	$20.00

Fixed overheads are absorbed on the basis of labour hours. Fixed overhead costs are budgeted at £120 000 per annum, arising at a constant rate during the year.

Activity in period 3 is budgeted to be 10 per cent of total activity for the year. Actual production during period 3 was 500 units, with actual fixed overhead costs incurred being £9800 and actual hours worked being 1970.

The fixed overhead expenditure variance for period 3 was:

A   £2200 (F)
B   £200 (F)
C   £50 (F)
D   £200 (A)
E   £2200 (A)

11.13 J Limited operates a standard cost accounting system. The following information has been extracted from its standard cost card and budgets:

Budgeted sales volume	5000 units
Budgeted selling price	$10.00 per unit
Standard variable cost	$5.60 per unit
Standard total cost	$7.50 per unit

If the actual sales were 4500 units at a selling price of £12.00, its sales volume variance would be:

A $1250 adverse
B $2200 adverse
C $2250 adverse
D $3200 adverse
E $5000 adverse

11.14 Labour, material and variable overhead variances

Casilda Ltd manufactures gonds, which have a standard selling price of £120 per gond. The company operates a standard costing system and values stocks at standard cost. The standard variable cost of a gond is as follows:

	£ per gond
Direct material	20
Direct labour (6 hours at £8 per hour)	48
Production overhead	24
	92

The budgeted and actual activity levels for last month were as follows:

	Budget units	Actual units
Sales	25 000	25 000
Production	25 000	26 000

The actual sales and variable costs for last month were as follows:

	£
Sales	2 995 000
Direct labour (purchased and used)	532 800
Direct labour (150 000 hours)	1 221 000
Variable production overhead	614 000

Required:

(a) Calculate the following cost variances for last month:
(i) Total direct materials
(ii) Total variable production overhead
(iii) Direct labour rate
(iv) Direct labour efficiency.
(4 marks)

(b) Prepare a statement that reconciles the budgeted contribution with the actual contribution for last month and which incorporates the variances calculated in (a).
(6 marks)

(c) Suggest ONE possible explanation of how the direct labour variance calculated in (a) could be interrelated.
(2 marks)

11.15 Sales variances

Fairfax Ltd manufactures a single product which has a standard selling price of £22 per unit. It operates a standard costing system. The standard variable production cost is £9 per unit. Budgeted annual production is 360 000 units and budgeted non-production costs of £1 152 000 per annum are all fixed.

The following data relate to last month:

	Budget units	Actual units
Production	30 000	33 000
Sales	32 000	34 000

Required:

(a) Calculate the sales price and sales volume contribution variances for last month showing clearly whether each variance is favourable or adverse.
(4 marks)

(b) Prepare a statement that reconciles the budgeted contribution with the actual contribution for last month and which incorporates the variances calculated in (a).
(6 marks)

11.16 Variance analysis and reconciliation of actual and budgeted profit

BS Limited manufactures a single product and operates a standard costing system. Using the data given below, you are required to prepare the operating statement for the month ended 31 October to show the budgeted profit; the variances for direct materials, direct wages, overhead and sales, each analysed into causes; and actual profit.

Budgeted and standard cost data:

Budgeted sales and production for the month: 10 000 units

Standard cost for each unit of product:
Direct material: X: 10 kg at €1 per kg
Y: 5 kg at €5 per kg
Direct wages: 5 hours at €8 per hour
Budgeted fixed overheads are €300 000

Budgeted sales price has been calculated to give a contribution of 50 per cent of the selling price.

Actual data for the month ended 31 October:

Production: 9500 units sold at a price of €160
Direct materials consumed:
X: 96 000 kg at €1.20 per kg
Y: 48 000 kg at €4.70 per kg

Direct wages incurred 46 000 hours at €8.20 per hour
Fixed production overhead incurred €290 000
(25 marks)

11.17 Calculation of actual input data working back from variances

The following data relate to actual output, costs and variances for the 4-weekly accounting period number 4 of a company that makes only one product. Opening and closing work in progress figures were the same.

	(£000)
Actual production of product XY	18 000 units
Actual costs incurred:	
Direct materials purchased and used (150 000 kg)	210
Direct wages for 32 000 hours	328
Variable production overhead	38

	(£000)
Variances:	
Direct materials price	15 F
Direct materials usage	9 A
Direct labour rate	8 A
Direct labour efficiency	40 F
Variable production overhead expenditure	6 A
Variable production overhead efficiency	4 F

Variable production overhead varies with labour hours worked.

A standard marginal costing system is operated.

You are required to:

present a standard product cost sheet for one unit of product XY.

(16 marks)

11.18 Interpretation of variances and calculation of materials, labour and sales variances

Sticky Wicket (SW) manufactures cricket bats using high quality wood and skilled labour using mainly traditional manual techniques. The manufacturing department is a cost centre within the business and operates a standard costing system based on marginal costs.

At the beginning of April the production director attempted to reduce the cost of the bats by sourcing wood from a new supplier and de-skilling the process a little by using lower grade staff on parts of the production process. The standards were not adjusted to reflect these changes.

The variance report for April is shown below (extract).

Variances	Adverse $	Favourable $
Material price		5 100
Material usage	7 500	
Labour rate		43 600
Labour efficiency	48 800	
Labour idle time	5 400	

The production director pointed out in his April board report that the new grade of labour required significant training in April and this meant that productive time was lower than usual. He accepted that the workers were a little slow at the moment but expected that an improvement would be seen in May. He also mentioned that the new wood being used was proving difficult to cut cleanly, resulting in increased waste levels.

Sales for April were down 10 per cent on budget and returns of faulty bats were up 20 per cent on the previous month. The sales director resigned after the board meeting, stating that SW had always produced quality products but the new strategy was bound to upset customers and damage the brand of the business.

Required:

(a) Assess the performance of the production director using all the information above, taking into account both the decision to use a new supplier and the decision to de-skill the process.

(7 marks)

In May the budget sales were 19 000 bats and the standard cost card is as follows:

	Std cost $	Std cost $
Materials (2 kg at $5/kg)	10	
Labour (3 hrs at $12/per hr)	36	
Marginal cost		46
Selling price		68
Contribution		22

In May the following results were achieved:

Forty thousand kg of wood were bought at a cost of $196 000, this produced 19 200 cricket bats. No inventory of raw materials is held. The labour was paid for 62 000 hours and the total cost was £694 000. Labour worked for 61 500 hours.

The sales price was reduced to protect the sales levels. However, only 18 000 cricket bats were sold at an average price of $65.

Required:

(b) Calculate the materials, labour and sales variances for May in as much detail as the information allows. You are not required to comment on the performance of the business.

11.19 Calculation of labour variances and actual material inputs working backwards from variances

A company manufactures two components in one of its factories. Material A is one of several materials used in the manufacture of both components.

The standard direct labour hours per unit of production and budgeted production quantities for a 13-week period were:

	Standard direct labour hours	Budgeted production quantities
Component X	0.40 hours	36 000 units
Component Y	0.56 hours	22 000 units

The standard wage rate for all direct workers was €9.00 per hour. Throughout the 13-week period 53 direct workers were employed, working a standard 40-hour week.

The following actual information for the 13-week period is available:

Production:
   Component X, 35 000 units
   Component Y, 25 000 units
Direct wages paid, €248 740
Material A purchases, 47 000 kg costing €85 110
Material A price variance, €430 F
Material A usage (component X), 33 426 kg
Material A usage variance (component X), €320.32 A

Required:

(a) Calculate the direct labour variances for the period.
(5 marks)

(b) Calculate the standard purchase price for material A for the period and the standard usage of material A per unit of production of component X.
(8 marks)

(c) Describe the steps, and information, required to establish the material purchase quantity budget for material A for a period.
(7 marks)
(Total 20 marks)

12

DIVISIONAL FINANCIAL PERFORMANCE MEASURES

LEARNING OBJECTIVES After studying this chapter you should be able to:

- distinguish between non-divisionalized and divisionalized organizational structures

- explain why it is preferable to distinguish between managerial and economic performance

- explain the factors that should be considered in designing financial performance measures for evaluating divisional managers

- explain the meaning of return on investment, residual income and economic value added (EVA$^{(TM)}$)

- compute economic value added (EVA$^{(TM)}$)

- identify and explain the approaches that can be used to reduce the dysfunctional consequences of short-term financial measures.

Large global companies produce and sell a wide variety of products throughout the world. Because of the complexity of their operations, it is difficult for top management to directly control operations. It may therefore be appropriate to divide a company into separate self-contained segments or divisions and to allow divisional managers to operate with a great deal of independence. Divisional managers have responsibility for both the production and marketing activities of the division. The danger in creating autonomous divisions is that divisional managers might not pursue goals that are in the best interests of the company as a whole. The objective of this chapter is to consider divisional financial performance measures that aim to motivate divisional managers to pursue those goals that will best benefit the company as a whole. In other words, the objective is to develop divisional performance measures that will achieve goal congruence.

A major feature of divisionalized companies is that they engage in inter-divisional trading of goods and services involving financial transactions with each other, which creates the need to establish transfer prices. The established transfer price is a cost to the receiving division and revenue to the supplying division, which means that whatever transfer price is set will affect the divisional financial performance measures. In the next chapter, we shall examine the various approaches that can be adopted to arrive at transfer prices between divisions. Our focus in this chapter is on financial measures of divisional performance, but you should note at this point that financial measures alone cannot adequately measure all those factors that are critical to the success of a division. Emphasis should also be given to reporting key non-financial measures relating to such areas as competitiveness, quality, delivery performance, innovation and flexibility to respond to changes in demand. In particular, a range of financial and non-financial performance measures should be developed that support the objectives and strategies of the organization. We shall examine these aspects in Chapter 14 where our focus will be on strategic performance management.

DIVISIONAL ORGANIZATIONAL STRUCTURES

A **functional organizational structure** is one in which all activities of a similar type within a company are placed under the control of the appropriate departmental head. A simplified organization chart for a functional organizational structure is illustrated in Figure 12.1(a). It is assumed that the company illustrated consists of five separate departments – production, marketing, financial administration, purchasing and research and development. In a typical functional organization none of the managers of the five departments is responsible for more than a part of the process of acquiring the raw materials, converting them into finished products, selling to customers, and administering the financial aspects of this process. You will see from Figure 12.1 (a) that the marketing function is a revenue centre and the remaining departments are cost centres. Revenues and costs (including the cost of investments) are combined together only at the chief executive, or corporate level, which is classified as an investment centre.

Let us now consider Figure 12.1(b), which shows a simplified **divisionalized organizational structure**, which is split up into divisions in accordance with the products that are made. Alternatively, many global companies may establish divisions according to geographical regions (e.g. European division, North African division, Asian division etc.). You will see from the diagram that each divisional manager is responsible for all of the operations relating to his or her particular product. To reflect this greater autonomy each division is either an investment centre or a profit centre.

Note that there are also multiple cost and revenue centres at lower management levels within each division. The planning and control systems described in the previous chapters should be applied to the cost and revenue centres. Also, in practice only parts of a company may be divisionalized. For example, in the simplified structure shown in Figure 12.1(b) administration and shared services would represent one of the functional cost cost centres with responsibility for providing services to all of the divisions. In practice rather than combining all shared services under one centre there would be several centres such as research and development, legal services, financial services etc., all reporting to the chief executive and providing services to all divisions. Figure 12.1(b) also shows that each divisional manager reports to a chief executive or top management team that will normally be located at corporate headquarters who are responsible for the activities of all of the divisions. In this chapter we shall focus on financial measures and controls at the profit or investment centre (i.e. divisional) level.

Generally, a divisionalized organizational structure will lead to decentralization of the decision-making process. For example, divisional managers will normally be free to set

FIGURE 12.1

A divisionalized and functional organizational structure

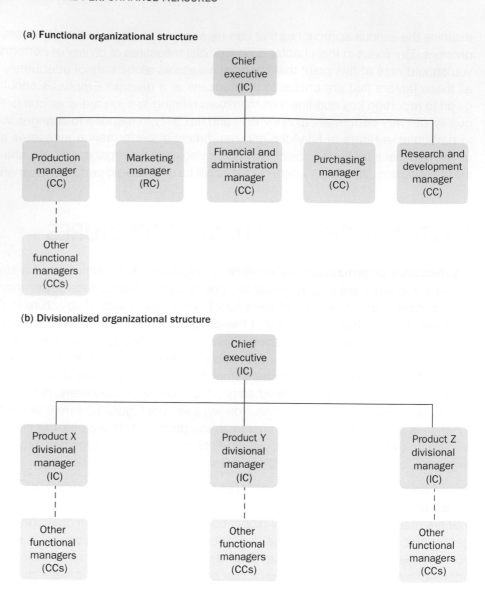

(a) Functional organizational structure

(b) Divisionalized organizational structure

IC = Investment centres, CC = Cost centres, RC = Revenue centres

selling prices, choose which market to sell in, make product mix and output decisions and select suppliers (this may include buying from other divisions within the company or from other companies). In non-divisionalized organizations pricing, product mix and output decisions will be made by central management. Consequently, managers in non-divisionalized organizations will have far less independence than divisional managers. Thus divisional managers have profit responsibility whereas managers in non-divisionalized companies do not have profit responsibility.

Profit centres and investment centres

The creation of separate divisions may lead to the delegation of different degrees of authority; for example, in some organizations a divisional manager may also have responsibility for making capital investment decisions. Where this situation occurs, the division is known as an **investment centre**. Alternatively, where a manager cannot control the investment and is responsible only for the profits obtained from operating the assets assigned to him or her by corporate headquarters, the segment is referred to as a **profit centre**. In contrast, the term **cost centre** is used to describe a responsibility centre where a manager is responsible for costs but not profits.

ADVANTAGES AND DISADVANTAGES OF DIVISIONALIZATION

Divisionalization can improve the decision-making process both from the point of view of the quality of the decision and the speed of the decision. The quality of the decisions should be improved because decisions can be made by the person who is familiar with the situation and who should therefore be able to make more informed judgements than central management who cannot be intimately acquainted with all the activities of the various segments of the business. Speedier decisions should also occur because information does not have to pass along the chain of command to and from top management. Decisions can be made on the spot by those who are familiar with the product lines and production processes and who can react to changes in local conditions in a speedy and efficient manner. In addition, delegation of responsibility to divisional managers provides them with greater freedom, thus making their activities more challenging and providing the opportunity to achieve self-fulfilment. This process should mean that motivation will be increased not just at the divisional manager level but throughout the whole division.

The major potential disadvantage of divisionalization is that there is a danger that divisions may compete with each other excessively and that divisional managers may be encouraged to take action that will increase their own profits at the expense of the profits of other divisions and the company as a whole. This may adversely affect cooperation between the divisions and lead to a lack of harmony in achieving the overall organizational goals of the company.

PREREQUISITES FOR SUCCESSFUL DIVISIONALIZATION

A divisionalized structure is most suited to companies engaged in several dissimilar activities. Examples of companies with divisionalized structures include Unilever, Siemens AG, Mitsubishi Group and Samsung. The reason is that it is difficult for top management to be intimately acquainted with all the diverse activities of the various segments of the business. On the other hand, when the major activities of a company are closely related, these activities should be carefully coordinated, and this coordination is more easily achieved in a centralized organizational structure.

For successful divisionalization it is important that the activities of a division be as independent as possible of other activities. However, the comments by Solomons (1965) many years ago are still relevant today. He states that even though substantial independence of divisions from each other is a necessary condition for divisionalization, if carried to the limit it would destroy the very idea that such divisions are an integral part of any single business. Divisions should be more than investments – they should contribute not only to the success of the company but to the success of each other.

DISTINGUISHING BETWEEN THE MANAGERIAL AND ECONOMIC PERFORMANCE OF THE DIVISION

Before discussing the factors to be considered in determining how divisional profitability should be measured, we must decide whether the primary purpose is to measure the performance of the division or that of the divisional manager. The messages transmitted from these two measures may be quite different. For example, a manager may be assigned to an ailing division to improve performance, and might succeed in substantially improving the performance of the division. However, the division might still be unprofitable because of industry factors, such as overcapacity and a declining market. The future of the division might be uncertain, but the divisional manager may well be promoted as a result of the outstanding managerial performance. Conversely, a division might report

REAL WORLD VIEWS 12.1

Prerequisites for successful divisionalization – divisions at Siemens AG

German global company Siemens AG had a turnover of almost €83 billion in 2017, recording a profit after taxes of €6.1 billion, according to its annual report. The company operates globally, with 377 000 employees globally. Siemens is a diverse organization. Looking at the home page of the company's website, we get an idea of how diverse. The web page lists ten divisions:

- Power and Gas
- Power Generation Services
- Energy Management
- Building Technologies
- Mobility
- Digital Factory
- Process Industries and Drives
- Healthineers
- Siemens Gamesa Renewable Energy
- Financial Services

Each division is further broken down. For example, the Process Industries and Drives division includes process automation, sensor systems, integrated drive systems and plant engineering software. This level of information suggests a quite detailed organizational structure and the 2017 Annual Report notes 'as global entrepreneurs our Divisions

and Strategic Units carry business responsibility worldwide, including with regard to their operating results'. While the website does not tell us the exact internal structures, we could expect that some activities (e.g. financial services) may be cross-sector and/or cross-divisional. The annual reports for example suggest that the Financial Services division supports the activities of other divisions, and per the 2017 Annual Report 'also conducts its own business with external customers'.

Questions

1 What advantages does a divisionalized structure have for decision-making at Siemens?
2 Would a divisionalized structure be suited to fast-food giant McDonalds?

References

Siemens (2017) Annual Report 2017, Siemens AG. Available at www.siemens.com/investor/pool/en/ investor_relations/Siemens_AR2017.pdf
Siemens (2017) Siemens at a Glance. Available at www. siemens.com/investor/en/company_overview.htm

significant profits but, because of management deficiencies, the performance may be unsatisfactory when the favourable economic environment is taken into account.

It the purpose is to evaluate the divisional manager then only those items directly controllable by the manager should be included in the divisional financial performance measure. Thus all allocations of indirect costs, such as central service and central administration costs, which cannot be influenced by divisional managers, ought not to be included in the profitability measure. Such costs can only be controlled where they are incurred; which means that central service managers should be held accountable for them.

Corporate headquarters, however, will also be interested in evaluating a division's economic performance for decision-making purposes, such as expansion, contraction and divestment decisions. In this situation a measure that includes only those amounts directly controllable by the divisional manager would overstate the economic performance of the division. Therefore, to measure the economic performance of the division many items that the divisional manager cannot influence, such as interest expenses, taxes and the allocation of some central administrative staff expenses, should be included in the profitability measure.

ALTERNATIVE DIVISIONAL PROFIT MEASURES

There are strong arguments for two measures of divisional profitability – one to evaluate managerial performance and the other to evaluate the economic performance of the division. In this chapter we shall focus on both measures. Exhibit 12.1 presents a divisional profit statement that contains three different measures that we can use to measure divisional performance. For measuring *managerial performance* the application of the controllability principle (see Chapter 10) suggests that **controllable profit** is the most appropriate measure. This is computed by deducting from divisional revenues all those costs that are controllable by a divisional manager. Controllable profit provides a measure of divisional managerial performance based on their ability to use only those resources under their control effectively. It should not be interpreted in isolation if it is used to evaluate the performance of a divisional manager. Instead, it should be evaluated relative to a budgeted performance, so that market conditions and size (in terms of assets employed) are taken into account.

EXHIBIT 12.1 Alternative divisional profit measures

	£
Total sales revenues	xxx
Less controllable costs	xxx
1 *Controllable profit*	xxx
Less non-controllable avoidable costs	xxx
2 *Divisional profit contribution*	xxx
Less allocated corporate expenses	xxx
3 *Divisional net profit before taxes*	xxx

Controllable profit provides an incomplete measure of the *economic performance* of a division, since it does not include those costs that are attributable to the division but which are not controllable by the divisional manager. For example, depreciation of divisional assets, and head office finance and legal staff who are assigned to providing services for specific divisions, would fall into this category. These expenses would be avoidable if a decision were taken to close the division. Those non-controllable expenses that are attributable to a division, and which would be avoidable if the division was closed, are deducted from controllable profit to derive the **divisional profit contribution**. This is clearly a useful figure for evaluating the *economic contribution* of the division, since it represents the contribution that a division is making to corporate profits and overheads. It should not be used, however, to evaluate managerial performance, because it includes costs that are not controllable by divisional managers.

Many companies allocate all corporate general and administrative expenses to divisions to derive a **divisional net profit before taxes**. From a theoretical point of view, it is difficult to justify such allocations since they tend to be arbitrary and do not have any connection with the manner in which divisional activities influence the level of these corporate expenses. Divisional profit contribution would therefore seem to be the most appropriate measure of the *economic* performance of divisions, because it is not distorted by arbitrary allocations. We have noted, however, that corporate headquarters may wish to compare a division's economic performance with that of comparable firms operating in the same industry. The divisional profit contribution would overstate the performance of the division, because if the division were independent, it would have to incur the costs of those services performed by head office. The apportioned head office costs are an approximation of the costs that the division would have to incur if it traded as a separate company. Consequently, companies may prefer to use divisional net profit when comparing the economic performance of a division with similar companies.

SURVEYS OF PRACTICE

Despite the many theoretical arguments against divisional net profit, survey evidence indicates that this measure is used widely to evaluate both divisional economic and managerial performance (Reece and Cool, 1978; Fremgen and Liao, 1981; Drury and El-Shishini, 2005; Chartered Institute of Management Accountants, 2009). The CIMA (2009) study also reported profit before tax was the most widely used performance measurement tool, being used by approximately 90 per cent of the organizations. The UK study by Drury and El-Shishini (2005) asked the respondents to rank in order of importance the factors influencing organizations to allocate the cost of shared corporate resources to divisions. In rank order the highest rankings were attributed to the following factors:

1 to show divisional managers the total costs of operating their divisions
2 to make divisional managers aware that such costs exist and must be covered by divisional profits
3 divisional managers would incur such costs if they were independent units.

REAL WORLD VIEWS 12.2

Distinguishing between the managerial and economic performance of the division – performance at Siemens

From Real World Views 12.1, you know that Siemens operates in many countries and has quite a diverse product offering. With such complex and broad operations, there are many factors that can affect the performance of a business sector or division. In its 2017 Annual Report, Siemens refers to its performance under a number of headings derived from Vision 2020. The performance measures are under seven headings: stringent corporate governance, sustainable value creation, financial, global management, partner of choice for customers, be employer of choice and an ownership culture. Throughout Annual Reports from 2014 to 2017, the targets set under the Vision 2020 programme are mentioned and/or performance is reported on.For example:

For example, we expect to create sustainable value from productivity measures in connection with our "Vision 2020" concept. Moreover, in course of the digital transformation, we seek to standardize, automate and digitize our processes and make them leaner and more efficient (Annual Report 2017).

Therein, we expect execution of "Vision 2020" measures to improve our cost position by an additional approximately €0.4 billion to €0.5 billion in fiscal 2016, following cost savings of approximately €0.4 billion already achieved in fiscal 2015 (Annual Report 2015).

Questions

1 If the performance of a divisional manager at Siemens falls short of target due to external factors such as economic recession, should the manager be held accountable?
2 How might the actual assessment of divisional performance differ in recessionary times?

References

Siemens (2017) Annual Report 2017, Siemens AG. Available at www.siemens.com/investor/pool/en/investor_relations/Siemens_AR2017.pdf
Siemens (2017) Strategy overview. Available at www.siemens.com/about/en/strategic-overview.htm
Siemens (2015) Annual Report 2015, Siemens AG. Available at www.siemens.com/investor/pool/en/investor_relations/Siemens_AR2015.pdf

The counter-argument to item 2 above is that if central management wishes to inform managers that divisions must be profitable enough to cover not only their own operations but corporate expenses as well, it is preferable to set a high budgeted controllable profit target that takes account of these factors. Divisional managers can then concentrate on increasing controllable profit by focusing on those costs and revenues that are under their control, and not be concerned with costs that they cannot control.

There is also some evidence to suggest that companies hold managers accountable for divisional net profit because this is equivalent to the measure that financial markets focus on to evaluate the performance of the company as a whole (Joseph *et al.*, 1996; Ezzamel *et al.*, 2008) Top management therefore require their divisional managers to concentrate on the same measures as those used by financial markets. A further reason to justify the use of divisional net profit as a managerial performance measure is that it represents the application of the controllability principle by the use of relative performance evaluations that were described in Chapter 10. You should remember from Chapter 10 that with relative performance evaluations the performance of a responsibility centre is evaluated relative to the performance of similar centres within the same company or to similar units outside the organization.

RETURN ON INVESTMENT

Instead of focusing purely on the absolute size of a division's profits most organizations focus on the **return on investment (ROI)** of a division. Note that ROI is also referred to as **return on capital employed** or **accounting rate of return**. ROI expresses divisional profit as a percentage of the assets employed in a division. Any three of the alternative divisional profit measures described earlier (i.e. divisional controllable profit, divisional profit contribution and net profit before taxes) can be used as the measure of divisional profit, while assets employed can be defined as assets controllable by the divisional manager, total divisional assets or net assets.

To illustrate the attraction of ROI consider a situation where division A earns a profit of £10 million and division B a profit of £20 million. Can we conclude that division B is more profitable than division A? The answer is no, since we should consider whether the divisions are returning a sufficiently high return on the capital invested in the division. Assume that £40 million capital is invested in division A and £200 million in division B. Division A's ROI is 25 per cent (£10 million/£40 million) whereas the return for division B is 10 per cent (£20 million/£200 million). Capital invested has alternative uses, and corporate management will wish to ascertain whether the returns being earned on the capital invested in a particular division exceed the division's opportunity cost of capital (i.e. the returns available from the alternative use of the capital). If, in the above illustration, the return available on similar investments to that in division B is 15 per cent then the economic viability of division B is questionable if profitability cannot be improved. In contrast, the ROI measure suggests that division A is very profitable.

A major attraction of ROI is that because it is a ratio measure it can be used as a common denominator for comparing the returns of dissimilar businesses, such as other divisions within the group or outside competitors.

Despite the widespread use of ROI, a number of problems exist when this measure is used to evaluate the performance of divisional managers. For example, it is possible that divisional ROI can be increased by actions that will make the company as a whole worse off, and conversely, actions that decrease the divisional ROI may make the company as a whole better off. In other words, evaluating divisional managers on the basis of ROI may not encourage goal congruence. Consider the following example:

	Division X	Division Y
Investment project available	£10 million	£10 million
Controllable profit	£2 million	£1.3 million
Return on the proposed project	20%	13%
ROI of divisions at present	25%	9%

It is assumed that neither project will result in any changes in non-controllable costs and that the overall cost of capital for the company is 15 per cent. The manager of division X would be reluctant to invest the additional £10 million because the return on the proposed project is 20 per cent, and this would reduce the existing overall ROI of 25 per cent. The manager of Division Y would, however, wish to invest the £10 million because the return on the proposed project of 13 per cent is in excess of the present return of 9 per cent, and it would increase the division's overall ROI. Consequently, the managers of both divisions would make decisions that would not be in the best interests of the company. The company should accept only those projects where the return is in excess of the cost of capital of 15 per cent, but the manager of division X would reject a potential return of 20 per cent and the manager of division Y would accept a potential return of 13 per cent. ROI can therefore lead to a lack of goal congruence.

RESIDUAL INCOME

To overcome some of the dysfunctional consequences of ROI, the **residual income** approach can be used. For the purpose of evaluating the performance of *divisional managers*, residual income is defined as controllable profit less a cost of capital charge on the investment controllable by the divisional manager. For evaluating the *economic performance* of the division residual income can be defined as divisional profit contribution (see Exhibit 12.1) less a cost of capital charge on the total investment in assets employed by the division. If residual income is used to measure the managerial performance of investment centres, there is a greater probability that managers will be encouraged, when acting in their own best interests, also to act in the best interests of the company. Returning to our previous illustration in respect of the investment decision for divisions X and Y, the residual income calculations are as follows:

	Division X (£)	Division Y (£)
Proposed investment	10 million	10 million
Controllable profit	2 million	1.3 million
Cost of capital charge (15% of the investment cost)	1.5 million	1.5 million
Residual income	0.5 million	– 0.2 million

This calculation indicates that the residual income of division X will increase and that of division Y will decrease if both managers accept the projects. Therefore the manager of division X would invest, whereas the manager of division Y would not. These actions are in the best interests of the company as a whole.

Residual income suffers from the disadvantages of being an absolute measure, which means that it is difficult to compare the performance of a division with that of other divisions or companies of a different size. For example, a large division is more likely to earn a larger residual income than a small division. To overcome this deficiency, targeted or budgeted levels of residual income should be set for each division that are consistent with asset size and the market conditions of the divisions.

Surveys of methods used by companies to evaluate the performance of divisional managers indicate a strong preference for ROI over residual income. For example, the international CIMA survey (2009) reported that approximately 70 per cent of the respondents' organizations used ROI compared with around 10 per cent using residual income.

Why is ROI preferred to residual income? Skinner (1990) found evidence to suggest that firms prefer to use ROI because, being a ratio, it can be used for inter-division and inter-firm comparisons where the size of the divisions or firms differs. ROI for a division can be compared with the return from other divisions within the group or with whole companies outside the group, whereas absolute monetary measures such as residual income are not appropriate in making such comparisons. A second possible reason for the preference for ROI is that 'outsiders' tend to use ROI as a measure of a company's overall performance. Corporate managers therefore want their divisional managers to focus on ROI so that their performance measure is congruent with outsiders' measure of the company's overall economic performance.

ECONOMIC VALUE ADDED (EVA(TM))

During the 1990s residual income was refined, improved and renamed as **economic value added (EVA(TM))** by the Stern Stewart consulting organization, and they have registered EVA((TM)) as their trademark. Stern Stewart advocate that EVA(TM) can be used to measure the performance of companies as a whole or different divisions within a divisionalized company. *The Economist* (1997) reported that more than 300 firms worldwide had adopted EVA(TM) including Coca-Cola, AT&T, ICL, Siemens, Boots and the Burton Group. A UK study by Drury and El-Shishini (2005) reported that 23 per cent of the responding organizations used EVA(TM) to evaluate divisional performance. More recently the CIMA (2009) international survey reported a usage rate of around 15–20 per cent.

Stern Stewart developed EVA(TM) with the aim of producing an overall financial measure that encourages senior managers to concentrate on the delivery of shareholder value. It considers that the major aim of managers of companies, whose shares are traded in the stock market, should be to maximize shareholder value. This management principle of maximizing shareholder value is also known as **value based-management (VBM)**. VBM states that management should first and foremost consider the interests of shareholders in its business decisions. It is therefore important that the key financial measure that is used to measure divisional or company performance should be congruent with shareholder value. VBM focuses on value as opposed to profit thus reducing the tendency to make decisions which have positive short-term impact but may be detrimental in the long term. Stern Stewart claims that, compared with other financial measures, EVA(TM) is more likely to meet this requirement than traditional profit measures.

The EVA(TM) concept extends the traditional residual income measure by incorporating adjustments to the traditional profit performance measure for distortions that can arise in measuring economic value added arising from measuring profit using generally accepted accounting principles (GAAP). EVA(TM) can be defined as:

$$\text{EVA}^{(TM)} = \text{Conventional divisional profit} \pm \text{Accounting adjustments} - \text{Cost of capital charge on divisional assets}$$

The cost of capital charge is incorporated in the above calculation because traditional profit measures ignore the cost of equity capital (i.e. the opportunity cost of funds provided by shareholders). Companies only create shareholder value when they generate a return in excess of the return required by the providers of capital (i.e. both debt and equity). Traditional profit measures include the cost of debt finance but ignore the cost of equity finance. Also, by making the cost of capital visible, managers are made aware that capital has a cost so that they need to generate sufficient income to cover their cost of capital.

Adjustments are made to the chosen conventional divisional profit measure in order to replace historical accounting data with a measure that attempts to approximate economic profit and asset values. Stern Stewart has stated that it has developed approximately 160 accounting adjustments that may need to be made to convert the conventional accounting profit into a sound measure of EVA(TM) but has indicated that most organizations will only need to use about ten of the adjustments. These adjustments result in the capitalization of many discretionary expenditures, such as research and development, marketing and advertising, by spreading these costs over

REAL WORLD VIEWS 12.3

The rise and fall of EVA™ in three New Zealand Companies

McLaren *et al.* (2016) undertook a longitudinal study of three New Zealand companies that had implemented EVA™. Stern Stewart consultants were employed to assist with the comprehensive introduction of EVA. Initially around 10 adjustments were made to the conventional accounting records. Following Stern Stewart recommendations EVA was calculated initially at the overall firm level, followed by mapping to the business unit level after a period of time. This means that full implementation of the system, in terms of its embedding in the organization and its use for planning, investment decisions, control and remuneration, may take several years. Full implementation took 1–2 years in one company and up to 5 years in the other two companies.

In all three firms, full implementation resulted in EVA being pushed down to the business units, where managers had their own balance sheets and remuneration was based on their unit's EVA (together with a corporate EVA element). Initially, EVA projections and outcomes were presented alongside existing measures so that managers had time to understand the system and see how EVA tracks against the conventional numbers. Most of the capital was directly traceable but cost allocation methodologies had to be used to allocate debtors and creditors to business units. Because the companies were not listed on the Stock Exchange the cost of capital charge was estimated for each business unit using data for similar companies that were listed abroad.

The incentives created by the EVA system did not work as expected. The incentives resulted in conflict, disunity and lack of managerial coordination and cooperation, manifested in managers attempting to improve their own result at the expense of others via the transfer pricing mechanism. EVA was pulled back to the corporate level, followed by the removal of the EVA bonus bank for remuneration. However, the removal of incentives at the business unit level resulted in EVA being no longer in the forefront of managers' minds. About 12 years after its introduction EVA was abandoned in all three companies.

Questions

1 What approaches should a company take in ensuring that EVA™ is successfully implemented?
2 Can you provide examples of accounting adjustments required to compute EVA™?

Reference

McLaren, J., Appleyard, T. and Mitchell, F. (2016), The rise and fall of management accounting systems: A case study investigation of EVA™, *The British Accounting Review*, 48, 341–358.

the periods in which the benefits are received. Therefore, managers will not bear the full costs of the discretionary expenditures in the period in which they are incurred. Instead, the cost will be spread across the periods when the benefits from the expenditure are estimated to be received.

An illustration of the calculation of EVA(™)

We shall now compute EVA(™) using the information shown in Example 12.1. To compute EVA(™) an amended accounting profit is calculated by making adjustments to the conventional accounting profit and then deducting a cost of capital charge. The cost of capital charge is derived from multiplying the percentage cost of capital by an amended capital employed computation that incorporates adjustments of historical accounting values to estimate economic values. Given that capital employed should

EXAMPLE 12.1

The summarized profit statement for the past year for Atlantic plc is shown below:

	£000
Operating profit before tax and interest	15 000
Interest expenses	1 000
Profit before tax	14 000
Taxation at 20%	2 800
Profit after tax and interest	11 200

Further information is as follows:

1   Research and development costs of £500 000 were incurred during the current financial year and £400 000 in the previous financial year, and the full amount was included in the profit computations for both years. The expenditure in both years is expected to yield benefits in future years.

2   Non-cash expenses of £50 000 in the current year and £40 000 in the previous year were included in the calculation of operating profit.

3   Economic depreciation is estimated to be £210 000 in the current financial year, whereas historical depreciation included in the above profit calculation was £160 000. In previous years it can be assumed that economic and accounting depreciation were the same;

4   The capital employed (debt plus equity capital) recorded in the published financial statements at the start of the financial year was £80 million.

5   The before tax cost of debt was 5 per cent and the estimated cost of equity was 10 per cent. The rate of corporation tax was 20 per cent.

6   The company's capital structure was 60 per cent equity and 40 per cent debt.

You are required to calculate the EVA(TM) for the period.

relate to the investment for the full period, our aim is to estimate the capital employed *at the start* of the period. The calculations of adjusted profit, adjusted capital employed and EVA(TM) are shown in Exhibit 12.2. An explanation of the calculations in Exhibit 12.2 is shown below:

● The EVA(TM) calculation seeks to ascertain whether value is being added for shareholders in terms of whether the funds invested in the business generate a return in excess of the cost of capital. To do this the adjusted profit excludes any cost of capital charges (e.g. interest on debt capital) because it is incorporated in the EVA(TM) cost of capital adjustment. The tax charge should also be adjusted because it includes the tax benefit arising from interest being a tax deductible expense. The inclusion of interest in the profit statement results in the tax charge being lower. Since the adjusted profit excludes the interest cost, it is also necessary to remove the interest tax benefit from the taxation charge. You will see from Exhibit 12.2 that instead of making profit before interest and tax (£15 million)

EXHIBIT 12.2   Calculation of EVA(TM) for example 12.1

Adjusted profit

	£000
Operating profit before tax and interest	15 000
Less: Tax charges adjusted to exclude the tax benefit	
on interest (£2800 + (£1000 × 20%)	(3 000)
	12 000
Add: Research and development costs recorded as an expense	500
Non-cash expenses	50
Accounting depreciation	160
	12 710
Less: Economic depreciation	(210)
Adjusted profit	12 500

Adjusted capital employed

	£000
Capital employed at the *start* of the year (see Note 4 in Example 12.1)	80 000
Add: Capitalization of research and development (incurred in the previous financial year)	400
Non-cash expenses incurred in the previous financial year	40
Adjusted capital employed at the start of the year	80 440

Weighted average cost of capital

Cost of equity (60% × 10%) + After-tax cost of debt 40% × (5% × (1- 0.2)) = 7.6%

Economic value added EVA(TM)

Adjusted profit (£12.5m) − cost of capital charge (7.6% × 80.440m) = £6.387m

the starting point the above adjustment could also have been incorporated by making profit after tax (£11.2 million) the starting point in the adjusted profit calculation and adding back the after- tax cost of interest of £0.8 million (£1m × (1 – the tax rate)). This agrees with the sub-total of £12 million shown by the approach adopted in Exhibit 12.2.

● The expenses on research and development (£500 000) incurred in the current period represents an investment that yields future benefits so the costs should be assigned to the future periods that benefit from this expenditure. Therefore, £500 000 should be added back to profit and capitalized by adding to capital employed in the year in which the expenses were incurred. This means that capital employed will be increased by £500 000 in the *current accounting period* but our objective is to calculate the adjusted capital employed at *the start of the current accounting period* so the research and development expenses incurred in the previous period (£400 000) are added back to determine the adjusted capital employed at the start of the period.

- Non-cash expenses of £50 000 that are recorded as expenses in the current accounting period are added back to current profits since EVA$^{(TM)}$ seeks to convert figures derived from accrual accounting to cash flows because cash flows provide a better measure of economic value added. These items should also be capitalized so the previous year's non-cash expense (£40 000) is added back to determine the adjusted capital employed at *the start of the current accounting period*.

- Economic depreciation represents an estimate of the true change in the value of assets during a period. Therefore, depreciation of £160 000 based on historical book values is added back to profits. Instead, a charge for economic depreciation of £210 000 based on economic values, rather than historical values, is deducted in the adjusted profit calculation. Given that note 3 in Example 12.1 indicates that economic and accounting depreciation were the same in previous years, no adjustment is required to the adjusted capital employed at the start of the current accounting period.

- Finally, a cost of capital charge consisting of the weighted average cost of capital (see Chapter 6) is applied to the adjusted capital employed and deducted from the adjusted profit to calculate EVA$^{(TM)}$.

Our earlier discussion relating to which of the conventional alternative divisional profit measures listed in Exhibit 12.1 should be used to evaluate managerial performance, also applies to the calculation of EVA$^{(TM)}$. There are strong theoretical arguments for using controllable profit as the starting point for calculating EVA$^{(TM)}$ for evaluating managerial performance. Many companies, however, use divisional net profit (after allocated costs) to calculate EVA$^{(TM)}$ and use this measure to evaluate both divisional managerial and economic performance.

ADDRESSING THE DYSFUNCTIONAL CONSEQUENCES OF SHORT-TERM FINANCIAL PERFORMANCE MEASURES

Ideally, divisional financial performance measures should report economic income rather than accounting profit. To calculate economic income all future cash flows should be estimated and discounted to their present value (see Chapter 6 for an explanation of present values). This calculation should be made for a division at the beginning and end of a measurement period. The difference between the beginning and ending values represents economic income. Economic income represents a theoretical ideal since in practice it is extremely difficult to approximate. The main problem with using estimates of economic income to evaluate performance is that it lacks precision and objectivity. It is also inconsistent with external financial accounting information that is used by financial markets to evaluate the performance of the company as a whole. It is likely that corporate managers may prefer their divisional managers to focus on the same financial reporting measures that are used by financial markets to evaluate the company as a whole.

The financial performance measures described in this chapter are used as surrogates for economic income. Their main weaknesses are that they are backward-looking and short-term oriented. Such weaknesses have been widely publicized in recent years and highlighted as a major contributory factor to the collapse of the banking sector in 2008. The performance measures encouraged senior bankers to engage in risky behaviour

REAL WORLD VIEWS 12.4

Tesco fiasco fuels fears that executive pay equation can skew priorities

As a result of the recent financial troubles at Tesco its shares declined to an 11-year low in 2014. This trend continued into 2015, with the price recovering somewhat from 2016. Terry Smith, chief executive of investment house Fundsmith stated in an article published in *The Financial Times* that investors had long ignored warning signs that Tesco's return on capital employed/return on investment (ROCE/ROI) had fallen sharply between 1995 and 2011. This trend continued to 2015, where ROCE was at 4 per cent. Some improvement has since occurred with 2017 ROCE at 8 per cent (see Tesco 2017). While ROCE declined, investors had reacted favourably to Tesco's reported results because they had become fixated on its rising earnings per share (EPS) which had quadrupled. This raises questions about the metrics Tesco uses to calculate executive remuneration, and whether this might have led managers to prioritize EPS over ROCE. Deloitte's annual review of FTSE 100 directors' executive remuneration reported an 'over- emphasis on measures such as EPS, total shareholder return (a combination of share price changes and dividend payouts over a period of time) and return measures such as ROCE/ROI'.

The article highlights comments from a major asset management company for Dutch pension scheme members (APG) and Homes Equity Ownership Services which advises more than 30 institutional investors. APG recently issued remuneration guidelines for the companies it invests in. The guidelines express concerns about incentives that seem vulnerable to the risk of manipulation of corporate activity to improve payouts. 'In the most basic terms, we believe that long-term value creation to shareholders is the added economic value over and above the cost of capital. We believe pay policies should be set to reflect and support this.' APG is also in favour of the additional use of non-financial factors, such as customer satisfaction, human capital, health and safety, and sustainability performance, in determining pay.

The director of Homes Equity Ownership Services stated that ROCE can produce 'a very profitable business, but a very small business. For instance, if a company has a ROCE of 30 per cent, this figure will fall if it embarks on a project with an estimated ROCE of 20 per cent. A ROCE maximize would therefore avoid this investment. Yet if the company's cost of capital is 10 per cent, taking on this project would still increase its profitability.' The director recommends that ROCE should be used in combination with a measure of profit, such as economic value added or economic profit.

Questions

1 Why might measures such as ROCE (also called ROI) continue to be used to determine executive remuneration even though the limitations of such measures have been highlighted for many years?
2 Why is the use of additional non-financial measures recommended to determine executive remuneration and what are the disadvantages of incorporating such measures?

References

Collis, S., McGee, H. and Carswell, S. (2014) *Financial Times*, 29 September.
Tesco share price from Google Finance. Available at www.google.com/search?q=LON:TSCO&tbm=fin#scso=uid_zeiXWuv1OtKAgQa5kqzwDQ_5:0
Tesco (2017) Five Year Record. Available at www.tescoplc.com/investors/reports-results-and-presentations/financial-performance/five-year-record/

REAL WORLD VIEWS 12.5

Airport security performance measurements – and bonus payments

Following events of September 2001, airport security screening in the US and globally increased dramatically. As we all know, this led to increasing queues at airports which, while inconvenient, are paramount to the safety and security of passengers.

Since 2001, many airports have used technology to speed things up to some extent at the security checks. For example, automated conveyors delivering crates for our hand luggage through x-ray machines and full body scanners are now quite common. Anonymous tracking of smart devices (smart phones and tablets) in the security queue is also a commonly used method of predicting the length of the queue. With such developments, as you may imagine, the time spent at security has become a performance measurement at many airports. For example, Heathrow Airport in London

reported less than 5 minutes' security waiting time at least 96 per cent of the time in December 2017, and 99 per cent less than10 minutes waiting time.

While waiting time is an important measurement, is it the correct measure to consider in the longer term? An article on revealnews.org provide some insights. In the US, the Transportation Security Administration (TSA) are responsible for airport security. The article reports how undercover officials were able to get weapons and other items through security undetected 95 per cent of the time. The article mentions how 'the findings weren't surprising to current and former TSA officials, who say that the security operations office had come to focus on efficiency and reduced wait times.' It also suggests that managers in charge received bonuses for achieving these targets.

Questions

1   Based on the above, is time waiting for or being processed through airport security a shorter term target or longer term? Could it ever be a shorter term performance measure?
2   Do you think performance on an issue such as airport security should be measured and rewarded by bonuses performance-based payments?

References

Becker, A (2016) TSA official responsible for security lapses earned big bonuses, reveal.com. Available at www.revealnews.org/article/tsa-official-responsible-for-security-lapses-earned-big-bonuses/

"How are we performing" December 2017. Available at www.heathrow.com/file_source/Company/Static/PDF/Companynewsandinformation/Central_Security_Performance_Feb18.pdf

because risk was not reflected in the short-term performance measures. Indeed, the short-term impact of marketing high risk loans and trading in high risk complex financial products can initially result in the reporting of favourable performance measures. The longer the measurement period, the more congruent accounting measures of performance are with economic income. For example, profits over a 3-year measurement period are a better indicator of economic income than profits over a 6-month period. The longer the measurement period the more likely the adverse long-term consequences of the risky activities of the banks would have been reflected in the performance measurement system. The disadvantage of lengthening the measurement period is that rewards are often tied to the performance evaluation, and if they are provided a long time after actions are taken, there is a danger that they will lose much of their motivational effects. Also feedback information is required at frequent intervals to enable managers to respond to deviations from plan.

Probably the most widely used approach to mitigate against the dysfunctional consequences that can arise from relying excessively on short-term financial performance measures is to supplement them with non-financial measures that measure those factors that are critical to the long-term success and profits of the organization. These measures focus on areas such as competitiveness, product/service leadership, productivity, quality, delivery performance, innovation and flexibility in responding to changes in demand. If managers focus excessively on the short term, the benefits from improved short-term financial performance may be counter-balanced by a deterioration in the non-financial measures. Such non-financial measures should provide a broad indication of the contribution of a divisional manager's current actions to the long-term success of the organization.

The incorporation of non-financial measures creates the need to link financial and non-financial measures of performance. The balanced scorecard emerged in the 1990s to meet this requirement. The **balanced scorecard** will be covered extensively in Chapter 14 where our focus will be on strategic performance management, but at this stage you should note that the divisional financial performance evaluation measures discussed in this chapter ought to be seen as one of the elements within the balanced scorecard. Divisional performance evaluation should be based on a combination of financial and non-financial measures.

SUMMARY

The following items relate to the learning objectives listed at the beginning of the chapter.

- **Distinguish between non-divisionalized and divisionalized organizational structures**. In non-divisionalized organizations the organization as a whole is an investment centre. With a divisionalized structure, the organization is split up into divisions that consist of either investment centres or profit centres. Thus, the distinguishing feature is that in a non-divisionalized structure only the organization as a whole is an investment centre and below this level a functional structure consisting of cost centres and revenue centres applies throughout. In contrast, in a divisionalized structure the organization is divided into separate profit or investment centres, and a functional structure applies below this level.

- **Explain why it is preferable to distinguish between managerial and economic performance**. Divisional economic performance can be influenced by many factors beyond the control of divisional managers. For example, good or bad economic performance may arise mainly from a favourable or unfavourable economic climate faced by the division rather than the specific contribution of the divisional manager. To evaluate the performance of divisional managers an attempt ought to be made to distinguish between economic and managerial performance.

- **Explain the factors that should be considered in designing financial performance measures for evaluating divisional managers**. To evaluate the performance of a divisional manager only those items directly controllable by the manager should be included in the divisional managerial performance financial measures. Thus, all allocations of indirect costs, such as those central service and administration costs that cannot be influenced by divisional managers, ought not to be included in the performance measure. Such costs can only be controlled where they are incurred, which means those central service managers should be held accountable for them.

- **Explain the meaning of return on investment, residual income and economic value added (EVA(™))**. ROI expresses divisional profit as a percentage of the assets employed in a division. Residual income is defined as divisional profit less a cost of capital charge on divisional investment (e.g. net assets or total assets). During the 1990s, residual income was refined and renamed as EVA™. It extends the traditional residual income measure by incorporating adjustments to the divisional financial performance measure for distortions introduced by using generally accepted accounting principles that are used for external financial reporting. Thus, EVA™ consists of a divisional profit measure plus or minus the accounting adjustments less a cost of capital charge. All three measures can be used either as measures of managerial or economic performance.

- **Compute economic value added (EVA(™))**. EVA(™) is computed by starting with a conventional divisional profit measure and (a) adding or deducting adjustments for any distortions to divisional profit measures arising from using generally accepted accounting principles for external reporting, and (b) deducting a cost of capital charge on divisional assets. Typical accounting adjustments include the capitalization of discretionary expenditures, such as research and development expenditure. A detailed calculation of EVA(™) was presented in Exhibit 12.2.

- **Identify and explain the approaches that can be used to reduce the dysfunctional consequences of short-term financial measures**. Methods suggested for reducing the dysfunctional consequences include (a) use of improved financial performance measures such as EVA(™) that incorporate accounting adjustments that attempt to overcome the deficiencies of conventional accounting measures; (b) lengthening the performance measurement period; and (c) focusing on both financial and non-financial measures using the balanced scorecard approach described in Chapter 14.

KEY TERMS AND CONCEPTS

Accounting rate of return   A method of appraising capital investments where the average annual profits from a project are divided into the average investment cost, also known as the return on capital employed and return on investment.

Balanced scorecard   A strategic management tool that integrates financial and non-financial measures of performance in a single concise report, with the aim of incorporating performance management within the strategic management process.

Controllable profit   A profit figure that is computed by deducting from divisional revenues all those costs that are controllable by a divisional manager.

Cost centre   A location to which costs are assigned, also known as a cost pool.

Divisional net profit before taxes   A profit figure obtained by allocating all general and administrative expenses to divisions.

Divisional profit contribution   Controllable profit, less any non-controllable expenses that are attributable to a division, and which would be avoidable if the division was closed.

Divisionalized organizational structure   A decentralized organizational structure in which a firm is split into separate divisions.

Economic value added (EVA(TM))   A refinement of the residual income measure that incorporates adjustments to the divisional financial performance measure for distortions introduced by generally accepted accounting principles, trademarked by the Stern Stewart consulting organization.

Functional organizational structure   An organization in which all activities of a similar type within a company are placed under the control of the appropriate departmental head, who is responsible for only that part of the organization's activities.

Investment centre   Responsibility centre whose managers are responsible for both sales revenues and costs and also have responsibility and authority to make capital investment decisions.

Profit centre   A division or part of an organization where the manager does not control the investment and is responsible for only the profits obtained from operating the assets assigned by corporate headquarters.

Residual income   Controllable profit less a cost of capital charge on the investment controllable by the divisional manager.

Return on capital employed   A method of appraising capital investments where the average annual profits from a project are divided into the average investment cost, also known as the accounting rate of return and return on investment.

Return on investment (ROI)   A method of appraising capital investments where the average annual profits from a project are divided into the average investment cost, also known as the accounting rate of return and return on capital employed.

Value-based-management (VBM)   A management principle that states that management should first and foremost consider the interests of shareholders in its business decisions.

ASSESSMENT MATERIAL

The review questions are short questions that enable you to assess your understanding of the main topics included in the chapter. The page numbers in parentheses provide you with the page numbers to refer to if you cannot answer a specific question.

The review problems are more complex and require you to relate and apply the content to various business problems. Solutions to review problems are provided in a separate section at the end of the book. Additional review problems can be accessed by lecturers and students on the dedicated online support resources for this book. Solutions to these review problems are provided for lecturers in the *Instructor's Manual* accompanying this book that can be downloaded from the dedicated online instructor's resources (see Preface for details).

The dedicated online digital support resources for this book also includes over 30 case study problems.

REVIEW QUESTIONS

12.1 Distinguish between a divisionalized and a non-divisionalized organizational structure. *(pp. 309–310)*

12.2 Distinguish between profit centres and investment centres. *(pp. 310–311)*

12.3 What are the advantages and disadvantages of divisionalization? *(p. 311)*

12.4 What are the prerequisites for successful divisionalization? *(p. 311)*

12.5 Why might it be appropriate to distinguish between the managerial and economic performance of a division? *(p. 312)*

12.6 Describe three alternative profit measures that can be used to measure divisional performance. Which measures are preferable for (a) measuring divisional managerial performance and (b) measuring divisional economic performance? *(pp. 313–314)*

12.7 Why is it common practice not to distinguish between managerial and economic performance? *(p. 314)*

12.8 Why is it common practice to allocate central costs to measure divisional managerial performance? *(pp. 314–315)*

12.9 Distinguish between return on investment, residual income and economic value added. *(pp. 316–322)*

12.10 How does the use of return on investment as a performance measure lead to bad decisions? How do residual income and economic value added overcome this problem? *(pp. 316–317)*

12.11 Explain how economic value added is calculated. *(pp. 318–322)*

12.12 Explain the approaches that can be used to reduce the dysfunctional consequences of short-term financial measures. *(pp. 322–325)*

REVIEW PROBLEMS

12.13 Bollon uses residual income to appraise its divisions using a cost of capital of 10 per cent. It gives the managers of these divisions considerable autonomy although it retains the cash control function at head office.

The following information was available for one of the divisions:

	Net profit after tax R000	Profit before interest and tax R000	Divisional net assets R000	Cash/ (overdraft) R000
Division 1	47	69	104	(21)

What is the residual income for this division based on controllable profit and controllable net assets?

(a) R36 600
(b) R56 500
(c) R58 600
(d) R60 700

12.14 A company has reported annual operating profits for the year of £89.2 million after charging £9.6 million for the full development costs of a new product that is expected to last for the current year and two further years. The cost of capital is 13 per cent per annum. The balance sheet for the company shows fixed assets with a historical cost of £120 million.

A note to the balance sheet estimates that the replacement cost of these fixed assets at the beginning of the year is £168 million. The assets have been depreciated at 20 per cent per year.

The company has a working capital of £27.2 million. Ignore the effects of taxation.

The ecomonic valued added (EVA(™)) of the company is closest to:

(a) £64.16 million
(b) £70.56 million
(c) £83.36 million
(d) £100.96 million

12.15 Division L has reported a net profit after tax of £8.6 million for the year ended 30 April 2016. Included in the costs used to calculate this profit are the following items:

● interest payable of £2.3 million
● development costs of £6.3 million for a new product that was launched in May 2015, and is expected to have a life of 3 years
● advertising expenses of £1.6 million that relate to the relaunch of a product in June 2016.

The net assets invested in Division L are £30 million. The cost of capital for Division L is 13 per cent per year.

Calculate the economic valued added(™) for Division L for the year ended 30 April 2016.

(3 marks)

12.16 A division is considering investing in capital equipment costing $2.7m. The useful economic life of the equipment is expected to be 50 years, with no resale value at the end of the period. The forecast return on the initial investment is 15 per cent per annum before depreciation. The division's cost of capital is 7 per cent.

What is the expected annual residual income of the initial investment?

(a) $0

(b) ($270 000)

(c) $162 000

(d) $216 000

(2 marks)

12.17 Return on investment and residual income

Southe plc has two divisions, A and B, whose respective performances are under review.

Division A is currently earning a profit of £35 000 and has net assets of £150 000.

Division B currently earns a profit of £70 000 with net assets of £325 000.

South plc has a current cost of capital of 15 per cent.

Required:

(a) Using the information above, calculate the return on investment and residual income figures for the two divisions under review and comment on your results.

(5 marks)

(b) State which method of performance evaluation (i.e. return on investment or residual income) would be more useful when comparing divisional performance and why.

(2 marks)

(c) List three general aspects of performance measures that would be appropriate for a service sector company.

(3 marks)

12.18 Calculation of ROI and RI and conflict between NPV and performance measurement

The Biscuits division (Division B) and the Cakes division (Division C) are two divisions of a large manufacturing company. Whilst both divisions operate in almost identical markets, each division operates separately as an investment centre. Each month, operating statements must be prepared by each division and these are used as a basis for performance measurement for the divisions.

Last month, senior management decided to recharge head office costs to the divisions. Consequently, each division is now going to be required to deduct a share of head office costs in its operating statement before arriving at net profit, which is then used to calculate return on investment (ROI).

Prior to this, ROI has been calculated using controllable profit only. The company's target ROI, however, remains unchanged at 20 per cent per annum. For each of the last 3 months, Divisions B and C have maintained ROIs of 22 per cent per annum and 23 per cent per annum respectively, resulting in healthy bonuses being awarded to staff. The company has a cost of capital of 10 per cent.

The budgeted operating statement for the month of July is shown below:

	B $000	C $000
Sales revenue	1 300	1 500
Less variable costs	(700)	(800)
Contribution	600	700
Less controllable fixed costs	(134)	(228)
Controllable profit	466	472
Less apportionment of head office costs	(155)	(180)
Net profit	311	292
Divisional net assets	$23.2m	$22.6m

Required:

(a) Calculate the expected annualized return on investment (ROI) using the new method as preferred by senior management, based on the above budgeted operating statements, for each of the divisions.

(2 marks)

(b) The divisional managing directors are unhappy about the results produced by your calculations in (a) and have heard that a performance measure called residual income may provide more information.

Calculate the annualized residual income (RI) for each of the divisions, based on the net profit figures for the month of July.

(3 marks)

(c) Discuss the expected performance of each of the two divisions, using both ROI and RI, and making any additional calculations deemed necessary. Conclude as to whether, in your opinion, the two divisions have performed well.

(4 marks)

(d) Division B has now been offered an immediate opportunity to invest in new machinery at a cost of $2.12 million. The machinery is expected to have a useful economic life of 4 years, after which it could be sold for $200 000. Division B's policy is to depreciate all of its machinery on a straight line basis over the life of the asset. The machinery would be expected to expand Division B's production capacity, resulting in an 8.5 per cent increase in contribution per month.

Recalculate Division B's expected annualized ROI and annualize RI based on July's budgeted operating statement after adjusting for the investment. State whether the managing director will be making a decision that is in the best interests of the company as a whole if ROI is used as the basis of the decision.

(5 marks)

(e) Explain any behavioural problems that will result if the company's senior management insist on using solely ROI, based on net profit rather than controllable profit, to assess divisional performance and reward staff.

(4 marks)

ACCA F5 Performance Measurement

12.19 Computation and discussion of economic value added

The managers of Toutplut Inc were surprised at a recent newspaper article which suggested that the company's performance in the last 2 years had been poor. The CEO commented that turnover had increased by nearly 17 per cent and pre-tax profit by 25 per cent between the last 2 financial years, and that the company compared well with others in the same industry.

$ million

Profit and loss account extracts for the year

	2018	2019
Turnover	326	380
Pre-tax accounting profit[1]	67	84
Taxation	23	29
Profit after tax	44	55
Dividends	15	18
Retained earnings	29	37

Balance sheet extracts for the year ending

	2018	2019
Fixed assets	120	156
Net current assets	130	160
	250	316
Financed by:		
Shareholders' funds	195	236
Medium- and long-term bank loans	55	80
	250	316

[1]After deduction of the economic depreciation of the company's fixed assets. This is also the depreciation used for tax purposes.

Other information:

(i) Toutplut had non-capitalized leases valued at $10 million in each year 2017–2019.

(ii) Balance sheet capital employed at the end of 2017 was $223 million.

(iii) The company's pre-tax cost of debt was estimated to be 9 per cent in 2018, and 10 per cent in 2019.

(iv) The company's cost of equity was estimated to be 15 per cent in 2018 and 17 per cent in 2019.

(v) The target capital structure is 60 per cent equity, 40 per cent debt.

(vi) The effective tax rate was 35 per cent in both 2018 and 2019.

(vii) Economic depreciation was $30 million in 2018 and $35 million in 2019.

(viii) Other non-cash expenses were $10 million per year in both 2018 and 2019.

(ix) Interest expense was $4 million in 2018 and $6 million in 2019.

Required:

(a) Estimate the economic valued added (EVA(TM)) for Toutplut Inc for both 2018 and 2019. State clearly any assumptions that you make.

Comment upon the performance of the company.

(7 marks)

(b) Briefly discuss the advantages and disadvantages of EVA(TM).

(6 marks)

(Total 13 marks)

12.20 Value based management and EVA™

LOL Co. is a chain of shops selling cards and gifts throughout its country. It has been listed on the stock exchange for 10 years and enjoys a fairly high profile in the retail sector of the national economy. You have been asked by the chief executive officer (CEO) to advise the company on value-based management (VBM), as a different approach to performance management. The CEO has read about this method as a way of focusing on shareholder interests and in the current tough economic climate, she thinks that it may be a useful development for LOL.

The company has traditionally used earnings per share (EPS) growth and share price in order to assess performance. The changes being proposed are considered significant and the CEO wants to be briefed on the implications of the new analysis and also how to convince both the board and the major investors of the benefits.

Financial data for LOL

	2018 $m	2019 $m
Profit before interest and tax	50.7	43.5
Interest paid	4.0	7.8
Profit after interest and tax	35.0	26.8
Average number of shares in issue (millions)	160	160

Capital employed at the end of the year was	(in $m)
2017	99.2
2018	104.1
2019	97.8

LOL aims for a capital structure of 50:50 debt to equity.

Costs of capital

	2018	2019
Equity	12.70%	15.30%
Debt (post tax cost)	4.20%	3.90%

Corporation tax is at the rate of 25%.

Stock market information

	2018	2019
Stock market all-share index	2 225.4	1 448.9
Retailing sector index	1 225.6	907.1
LOL (average share price) ($)	12.20	10.70

Required:

(a) Explain to the CEO what value-based management involves and how it can be used to focus the company on shareholder interests.

(4 marks)

(b) Perform an assessment of the financial performance of LOL using Economic Value Added (EVA™) and evaluate your results compared with those of earnings per share (EPS) growth and share price performance. You should state any assumptions made.

(12 marks)

(c) Evaluate VBM measures against traditional profit-based measures of performance.

(4 marks)

12.21 A long-established, highly centralized company has grown to the extent that its chief executive, despite having a good supporting team, is finding difficulty in keeping up with the many decisions of importance in the company.

Consideration is therefore being given to reorganizing the company into profit centres. These would be product divisions, headed by a divisional managing director, who would be responsible for all the divisions' activities relating to its products.

You are required to explain, in outline:

(a) the types of decision areas that should be transferred to the new divisional managing directors if such a reorganization is to achieve its objectives

(b) the types of decision areas that might reasonably be retained at company head office

(c) the management accounting problems that might be expected to arise in introducing effective profit centre control.

(20 marks)

12.22 (a) Explain the meaning of each of the undernoted measures that may be used for divisional performance measurement and investment decision-making. Discuss the advantages and problems associated with the use of each.

(i) Return on capital employed.
(ii) Residual income.
(iii) Discounted future earnings.

(9 marks)

(b) Comment on the reasons why the measures listed in (a) above may give conflicting investment decision responses when applied to the same set of data. Use the following figures to illustrate the conflicting responses that may arise:
Additional investment of £60 000 for a 6-year life with nil residual value.

Average net profit per year: £9000 (after depreciation).

Cost of capital: 14 per cent.

Existing capital employed: £300 000 with ROCE of 20 per cent.

(8 marks)

(Solutions should ignore taxation implications.)

(Total 17 marks)

13
TRANSFER PRICING IN DIVISIONALIZED COMPANIES

LEARNING OBJECTIVES After studying this chapter you should be able to:

● describe the different purposes of a transfer pricing system

● identify and describe five different transfer pricing methods

● explain why the correct transfer price is the external market price when there is a perfectly competitive market for the intermediate product

● explain why cost-plus transfer prices will not result in the optimum output being achieved

● explain a method of transfer pricing that has been advocated to resolve the conflicts between the decision-making and performance evaluation objectives

● describe the additional factors that must be considered when setting transfer prices for multinational transactions.

I n the previous chapter alternative financial measures for evaluating divisional performance were examined. However, all of the financial measure outcomes will be significantly affected when divisions transfer goods and services to each other. The established transfer price is a cost to the receiving division and revenue to the supplying division, which means that whatever transfer price is set will affect the profitability of each division. In addition, this transfer price will also significantly influence each division's input and output decisions, and thus total company profits.

In this chapter we shall examine the various approaches that can be adopted to arrive at transfer prices between divisions. Although our focus will be on transfer pricing between divisions (i.e. profit or investment centres), transfer pricing can also apply between cost centres (typically support/service centres) or from cost centres to profit/investment centres.

Look at Figure 12.1(b) in the previous chapter and assume that administration and shared services functional support cost centres are established that provide services to all of the other divisions. The cost of support centres might be reallocated to the division based on cost allocations, or the divisions may be charged for the services based on their usage at an appropriate transfer price. The same basic principles apply as those that apply between divisions, the only difference being that there is no need for a profit element to be included in the transfer price to reimburse the supplying cost centre.

PURPOSE OF TRANSFER PRICING

A transfer pricing system can be used to meet the following purposes:

1 To provide information that motivates divisional managers to make good economic decisions. This will happen when actions that divisional managers take to improve the reported profit of their divisions also improve the profit of the company as a whole.

2 To provide information that is useful for evaluating the managerial and economic performance of the divisions.

3 To ensure that divisional autonomy is not undermined.

4 To intentionally move profits between divisions or locations, such as moving taxable profits to divisions located in different countries.

Providing information for making good economic decisions

Goods transferred from the supplying division to the receiving division are known as **intermediate products**. The products sold by a receiving division to the outside world are known as **final products**. The objective of the receiving division is to subject the intermediate product to further processing before it is sold as a final product in the outside market. The transfer price of the intermediate product represents a cost to the receiving division and a revenue to the supplying division. Therefore transfer prices are used to determine how much of the intermediate product will be produced by the supplying division and how much will be acquired by the receiving division. In a centralized company the decision as to whether an intermediate product should be sold or processed further is determined by comparing the incremental cost of, and the revenues from, further processing. In a divisionalized organization structure, however, the manager of the receiving division will treat the price at which the intermediate product is transferred as an incremental cost, and this may lead to incorrect decisions being made.

For example, let us assume that the incremental cost of the intermediate product is €100, and the additional further processing costs of the receiving division are €60. The incremental cost of producing the final product will therefore be €160. Let us also assume that the supplying division has a temporary excess capacity, which is being maintained in order to meet an expected resurgence in demand, and that the market price of the final product is €200. To simplify the illustration, we assume there is no market for the intermediate product. The correct short-term decision would be to convert the intermediate product into the final product. In a centralized company this decision would be taken, but in a divisionalized organization structure where the transfer price for the intermediate product is €150 based on full cost plus a profit margin, the incremental cost of the receiving division will be €210 (€150 + €60). The divisional manager would therefore incorrectly decide not to purchase the intermediate product for further processing. This problem can be overcome if the transfer price is set at the incremental cost of the supplying division, which in this example is €100.

Evaluating divisional performance

When goods are transferred from one division to another, the transfer price represents revenue to the supplying division and a cost to the receiving division. Consequently, the prices at which goods are transferred can influence each division's reported profits, and there is a danger that an unsound transfer price will result in a misleading performance measure that may cause divisional managers to believe that the transfer price is affecting their performance rather unfairly. This may lead to disagreement and negative motivational consequences.

Conflict of objectives

Unfortunately, no single transfer price is likely to perfectly serve all of the specified purposes. They often conflict and managers are forced to make trade-offs. In particular, the decision-making and the performance evaluation purposes may conflict with each other. For example, in some situations the transfer price that motivates the short-run optimal economic decision is incremental cost. If the supplier in our earlier example has excess capacity, this cost will probably equal variable cost. The supplying division will fail to cover any of its fixed costs when transfers are made at variable cost, and will therefore report a loss. Furthermore, if a transfer price equal to variable cost (€100 in the above example) is imposed on the manager of the supplying division, the concept of divisional autonomy and decentralization is undermined. On the other hand, a transfer price that may be satisfactory for evaluating divisional performance (€150 in the above example) may lead divisions to make suboptimal decisions when viewed from the overall company perspective.

ALTERNATIVE TRANSFER PRICING METHODS

The management accounting literature identifies many different types of transfer prices that companies can use to transfer goods and services. The most notable ones are:

1 market-based transfer prices
2 cost plus a profit mark-up transfer prices
3 marginal/variable cost transfer prices
4 full cost transfer prices
5 negotiated transfer prices
6 marginal/variable cost plus opportunity cost transfer prices.

Exhibit 13.1 indicates that transfer pricing is widely used. The majority of firms use full cost-based transfer pricing and only around 10 per cent of the responding firms used variable cost-based transfer pricing.

EXHIBIT 13.1 Surveys of company practice

The international survey by the Chartered Institute of Management Accountants (2009) reported that around 70 per cent of large manufacturing companies and 40 per cent of service companies used transfer pricing. A UK survey by Abu-Serdaneh (2004) based on responses from 170 companies reported the percentage of companies that used particular transfer pricing methods to a considerable extent. The percentage usage was as follows:

	%	%
Prevailing market price	16	
Adjusted market price	15	31
Unit full manufacturing cost	24	
Unit full manufacturing cost plus a profit margin	38	62
Unit variable manufacturing cost	2	
Unit variable manufacturing cost plus a profit margin	6	
Unit variable manufacturing cost plus a fixed fee	1	9
Negotiated transfer price		8

The findings indicated that a minority of companies used more than one transfer price.

MARKET-BASED TRANSFER PRICES

In most circumstances, where a **perfectly competitive market** for an intermediate product exists it is optimal for both decision-making and performance evaluation purposes to set transfer prices at competitive market prices. A perfectly competitive market exists where products sold are all the same and no individual buyer or seller can affect market prices.

When transfers are recorded at market prices, divisional performance is more likely to represent the real economic contribution of the division to total company profits. If the supplying division did not exist, the intermediate product would have to be purchased on the outside market at the current market price. Alternatively, if the receiving division did not exist, the intermediate product would have to be sold on the outside market at the current market price. Divisional profits are therefore likely to be similar to the profits that would be calculated if the divisions were separate organizations. Consequently, divisional profitability can be compared directly with the profitability of similar companies operating in the same type of business.

Where the selling costs for internal transfers of the intermediate product are identical with those that arise from sales in the outside market, it will not matter whether the supplying division's output is sold internally or externally. To illustrate this we shall consider two alternatives. First, assume initially that the output of the supplying division is sold *externally* and that the receiving division purchases its requirements *externally*. Now consider a second situation where the output of the intermediate product is transferred *internally* at the market price and is not sold on the outside market. You should now refer to Exhibit 13.2. The aim of this diagram is to show that divisional and total profits are not affected, whichever of these two alternatives is chosen.

Exhibit 13.2 illustrates a situation where the receiving division sells 1000 units of the final product in the external market. The incremental costs of the supplying division for the production of 1000 units of the intermediate product are €5000, with a market price for the output of

EXHIBIT 13.2   Profit impact using market-based transfer prices

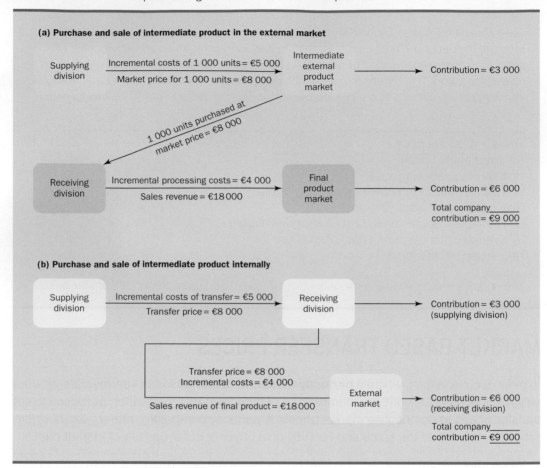

€8000. The incremental costs of the receiving division for the additional processing of the 1000 units of the intermediate product are €4000. This output can be sold for €18 000. You will see that it does not matter whether the intermediate product is transferred internally or sold externally – profits of each division and total company profits remain unchanged.

COST PLUS A MARK-UP TRANSFER PRICES

Before we discuss different cost-based transfer prices read Example 13.1 and then look at Exhibit 13.3. This exhibit shows the profit for the Baltic Group as a whole using the data given in Example 13.1. The profit maximizing output is 5000 units. The aim of the transfer pricing system should be to motivate both the supplying division (Oslo) and the receiving division (Bergen) to operate at the optimum output level of 5000 units. Assuming that the cost base for the cost plus a mark-up transfer price is full cost the fixed costs of the supplying division will be unitized by dividing the fixed costs of €60 000 for the period by the estimated output. The resulting unitized fixed cost will be added to the unit variable cost to derive a full cost per unit of output. A profit mark-up is then added to full cost to derive the transfer price. Let us assume that €35 per unit (or €35 000 per 1000 units) is the full cost plus a mark-up transfer price based on a unit fixed cost of €12 derived from dividing €60 000 fixed costs

EXAMPLE 13.1

The Oslo division and the Bergen division are divisions within the Baltic Group. One of the products manufactured by the Oslo division is an intermediate product for which there is no external market. This intermediate product is transferred to the Bergen division where it is converted into a final product for sale on the external market. One unit of the intermediate product is used in the production of the final product. The expected units of the final product which the Bergen division estimates it can sell at various selling prices are as follows:

Net selling price (€)	Quantity sold (units)
100	1 000
90	2 000
80	3 000
70	4 000
60	5 000
50	6 000

The costs of each division are as follows:

(€)	Oslo (€)	Bergen (€)
Variable cost per unit	11	7
Fixed costs attributable to the products	60 000	90 000

EXHIBIT 13.3   Profit computations for the Baltic Group

Note that the following profit computations for the company as a whole do not incorporate the transfer price since it represents inter-company trading with the transfer pricing revenues of the supplying division cancelling out the transfer pricing costs incurred by the receiving division.

Whole company profit computations

Output level (units)	Total revenues	Company variable costs	Company fixed costs	Company profit/(loss)
1 000	100 000	18 000	150 000	(68 000)
2 000	180 000	36 000	150 000	(6 000)
3 000	240 000	54 000	150 000	36 000
4 000	280 000	72 000	150 000	58 000
5 000	300 000	90 000	150 000	60 000
6 000	300 000	108 000	150 000	42 000

by an estimated output of 5000 units plus a unit variable cost of €11 plus a profit mark-up of €12. At this transfer price the profit computations for each division will be as follows:

Oslo division (Supplying division)

Output level (units)	Transfer price revenues	Variable costs	Fixed costs	Total profit/(loss)
1 000	35 000	11 000	60 000	(36 000)
2 000	70 000	22 000	60 000	(12 000)
3 000	105 000	33 000	60 000	12 000
4 000	140 000	44 000	60 000	36 000
5 000	175 000	55 000	60 000	60 000
6 000	210 000	66 000	60 000	84 000

Bergen division (Receiving division)

Output level (units)	Total revenues	Variable costs	Total cost of transfers	Fixed costs	Total profit/(loss)
1 000	100 000	7 000	35 000	90 000	(32 000)
2 000	180 000	14 000	70 000	90 000	6 000
3 000	240 000	21 000	105 000	90 000	24 000
4 000	280 000	28 000	140 000	90 000	22 000
5 000	300 000	35 000	175 000	90 000	0
6 000	300 000	42 000	210 000	90 000	(42 000)

The supplying division maximizes profits at an output level of 6000 units, whereas the receiving division maximizes profits at 3000 units so neither division will be motivated to operate at the optimal output level for the company as a whole of 5000 units. The receiving division will therefore choose to purchase 3000 units from the supplying division. This is because the Bergen division will compare its net marginal revenue with the transfer price and expand output as long as the **net marginal revenue** of the additional output exceeds the transfer price. Note that net marginal revenue is defined as the marginal (incremental) revenue from the sale of an extra unit (or a specified number of incremental units) of the final product less the marginal/incremental conversion costs (excluding the transfer price). The calculations of net marginal revenues are as follows for increments of 1000 units:

Units	Net marginal revenue (€)
1 000	93 000 (100 000 – 7 000)
2 000	73 000 (80 000 – 7 000)
3 000	53 000 (60 000 – 7 000)
4 000	33 000 (40 000 – 7 000)
5 000	13 000 (20 000 – 7 000)
6 000	–7 000 (0 – 7 000)

If you refer to the receiving division (Bergen) in the schedule of profit calculations you will see that expanding output from 1000 to 2000 units results in total revenues increasing from €100 000 to €180 000 so the marginal revenue is €80 000. Also variable conversion costs increase from €7000 to €14 000 so marginal cost is €7000. Therefore net marginal revenue is €73 000 (€80 000 – €7000). Faced with a transfer price of €35 000 per 1000 units the Bergen division will not expand output beyond 3000 units because the transfer price paid for each batch (€35 000) exceeds the net marginal revenue.

MARGINAL/VARIABLE COST TRANSFER PRICES

Marginal cost is a term that is used by economists. It refers to the additional cost of one extra unit of output. Accountants generally assume that marginal cost is the same as variable cost. When the market for the intermediate product is imperfect or non-existent, transfer prices set at the variable/marginal cost of the supplying division can motivate both the supplying and receiving division managers to operate at output levels that will maximize overall company profits. Using the data given in Example 13.1, the variable cost transfer price is €11 per unit or €11 000 for each batch of 1000 units. The receiving division will expand output as long as net marginal revenue exceeds the transfer price. Now look at the net marginal revenue that we calculated for the receiving division in the previous section to illustrate cost plus a mark-up transfer pricing. You will see that the net marginal revenue from expanding output from 4000 to 5000 units is €13 000 and the transfer price that the receiving division must pay to acquire this batch of 1000 units is €11 000. Therefore expanding the output will increase the profits of the receiving division. Will the manager of the receiving division be motivated to expand output from 5000 to 6000 units? The answer is no because the net marginal revenue (–€7000) is less than the transfer price of purchasing the 1000 units.

Setting the transfer price at the unit variable cost of the supplying division will motivate the divisional managers to operate at the optimum output level for the company as a whole provided that the supplying division manager is instructed to meet the demand of the receiving division at this transfer price. Although the variable cost transfer price encourages overall company optimality it is a poor measure of divisional performance. At a variable cost transfer price of €11 per unit the profit computations for each division will be as follows:

Oslo division (Supplying division)

Output level (units)	Transfer price revenues	Variable costs	Fixed costs	Total profit/(loss)
1 000	11 000	11 000	60 000	(60 000)
2 000	22 000	22 000	60 000	(60 000)
3 000	33 000	33 000	60 000	(60 000)
4 000	44 000	44 000	60 000	(60 000)
5 000	55 000	55 000	60 000	(60 000)
6 000	66 000	66 000	60 000	(60 000)

Bergen division (Receiving division)

Output level (units)	Total revenues	Variable costs	Total cost of transfers	Fixed costs	Total profit/(loss)
1 000	100 000	7 000	11 000	90 000	(8 000)
2 000	180 000	14 000	22 000	90 000	54 000
3 000	240 000	21 000	33 000	90 000	96 000
4 000	280 000	28 000	44 000	90 000	118 000
5 000	300 000	35 000	55 000	90 000	120 000
6 000	300 000	42 000	66 000	90 000	102 000

You can see that the supplying division reports a loss equal to €60 000 at all output levels. In the short term fixed costs are unavoidable and therefore the division manager is no worse off since fixed costs will still be incurred. Note also that the Oslo division also produces other products so the overall divisional profit (excluding the inter-divisional transfers with Bergen) may be positive. In contrast, the receiving division maximizes its profits at the optimal output level of 5000 units with a reported profit of €120 000. We can conclude that the variable cost transfer price motivates managers to choose the optimal output level for the company as a whole but it results in a poor measure of divisional performance since the allocation of the €60 000 profits from inter-divisional profits results in the supplying division reporting a loss of €60 000 and the receiving division reporting a profit of €120 000.

FULL COST TRANSFER PRICES WITHOUT A MARK-UP

In Chapter 7 it was pointed out that full costs require that predetermined fixed overhead rates should be established. Let us assume that the 5000 units optimal output level for the company as a whole is used to determine the fixed overhead rate per unit. Therefore, the fixed cost per unit for the intermediate product will be €12 per unit (€60 000 fixed costs/5000 units) giving a full cost of €23 (€11 variable cost plus €12 fixed cost). If the transfer price is set at €23 per unit (i.e. €23 000 per 1000 batch) the receiving division manager will expand output as long as net marginal revenue exceeds the transfer price. If you refer to the net marginal revenue schedule shown in the section describing cost plus a mark-up transfer prices you will see that the receiving division manager will choose to purchase 4000 units. For each 1000 units increment in output up to 4000 units net marginal revenue exceeds the transfer cost of €23 000 per 1000 unit batch. The manager will choose not to expand output to the 5000 units optimal level for the company as a whole because the transfer cost of €23 000 exceeds the net marginal revenue of €13 000. Also, at the selected output level of 4000 units the total transfer price revenues of the supplying division will be €92 000 (4000 units at €23), but you will see from the profit calculations shown earlier for the Oslo division that the total costs are €104 000 (€44 000 variable cost + €60 000 fixed cost). Therefore, the supplying division will report a loss because all of its fixed costs have not been recovered. Hence the transfer price is suitable for neither performance evaluation nor ensuring that optimal output decisions are made.

NEGOTIATED TRANSFER PRICES

The difficulties encountered in establishing a sound system of transfer pricing have led to suggestions that negotiated transfer prices should be used. Negotiated transfer prices are most appropriate in situations where some market imperfections exist for the intermediate product, such as where there are several different market prices. When there are such imperfections in the market, the respective divisional managers must have the freedom to buy and sell outside the company to enable them to engage in a bargaining process. It is claimed that if this is the case then the friction and bad feeling that may arise from a centrally controlled market transfer price will be eliminated without incurring a mis-allocation of resources.

For negotiation to work effectively it is important that managers have equal bargaining power. If the receiving division has many sourcing possibilities for the intermediate product or service, but the supplying division has limited outlets, the bargaining power of the managers will be unequal. Unequal bargaining power can also occur if the transfers are a relatively small proportion of the business for one of the divisions and a relatively large proportion of the business of the other. Negotiated transfer prices also have other limitations. A further difficulty with negotiation is that it is time-consuming for the managers concerned, particularly where a large number of transactions are involved.

Would the managers of the Baltic Group be able to negotiate a transfer price that meets the decision-making and performance evaluation requirements of a transfer pricing system? If the manager of the supplying division cannot avoid the fixed costs in the short run, he or she will have no bargaining power because there is no external market for the intermediate product. The manager would therefore accept any price as long as it is not below variable cost. Meaningful negotiation is not possible. If the fixed costs are avoidable the manager has some negotiating power since he or she can avoid €60 000 by not producing the intermediate product. The manager will try and negotiate a selling price in excess of full cost. If an output level of 5000 units is used to calculate the full cost the unit cost from our earlier calculations was €23 and the manager will try and negotiate a price in excess of €23. If you examine the net marginal revenue of the receiving division shown on page 339 you will see that the manager of the receiving division will not expand output to 5000 units if the transfer price is set above €23 per unit. As indicated earlier, negotiation is only likely to work when there is an imperfect external market for the intermediate product.

MARGINAL/VARIABLE COST PLUS OPPORTUNITY COST TRANSFER PRICES

Setting transfer prices at the marginal/variable cost of the supplying division per unit transferred plus the opportunity cost per unit of the supplying division is often cited as a general rule that should lead to optimum decisions for the company as a whole. Opportunity cost is defined as the contribution foregone by the supplying division from transferring internally the intermediate product. This rule will result in the transfer price being set at the variable cost per unit when there is no market for the intermediate product. Why? If the facilities are dedicated to the production of the intermediate product they will have no alternative use, so the opportunity cost will be zero. Consider now a situation where there is a perfectly competitive external market for the intermediate product. Assume that the market price for the intermediate product is €20 per unit and the variable cost per unit of output is €5. If the supplying division has no spare capacity the contribution foregone from transferring the intermediate product is €15. Adding this to the variable cost per unit will result in the transfer price being set at the market price of €20 per unit. What is the transfer price if the supplying division has temporary spare capacity? In this situation there will be no foregone contribution and the transfer price will be set at the variable cost per unit of €5.

You should have noted that applying the above general rule leads to the same transfer price as was recommended earlier in this chapter. In other words, if there is a perfectly competitive external market for the intermediate product, the market price is the optimal transfer price. When there is no market for the intermediate product, transfers should be made at the variable cost per unit of output of the intermediate product. Thus, the general rule is merely a restatement of the principles that have been established earlier. The major problem with this general rule is that it is difficult to apply in more complex situations such as when there is an imperfect market for the intermediate product.

COMPARISON OF COST-BASED TRANSFER PRICING METHODS

Figure 13.1 enables us to compare the cost-based transfer pricing methods in terms of whether they result in the optimal output levels for the company as a whole. Note that it is assumed that there is no market for the intermediate product. You will see that the variable cost of the intermediate product is assumed to be constant throughout the entire production range and that the net marginal revenue for the final product declines to reflect the fact that to sell more the price must be lowered. Remember that it was pointed out earlier that term 'net marginal revenue' refers to the marginal revenue of the final product less the marginal/variable conversion costs (excluding the transfer price) incurred by the receiving division. Economic theory indicates that the optimal output for the company as a whole is where the marginal cost of producing the intermediate product is equal to the net marginal revenue from the sale of the final product. That is an output level of Q_2.

If the transfer price is set at the variable cost per unit of the intermediate product the receiving division will purchase the intermediate product up to the point where net marginal revenue equals its marginal/variable costs. It will therefore result in the optimal output from the overall company perspective (Q_2). If a higher transfer price is set (as indicated by the green line) to cover full cost, or a mark-up is added to full cost, then the supplying division will restrict output to suboptimal levels such as Q_1.

It is apparent from our discussion of the different transfer pricing methods using the data in Example 13.1 and the diagrammatic presentation in Figure 13.1 that the theoretically correct transfer to encourage divisions to choose the optimal output for the company as a whole is the variable/marginal cost of producing the intermediate product. To simplify our analysis we have assumed that there is no market for the

FIGURE 13.1

A comparison of marginal cost and full cost or cost-plus transfer pricing

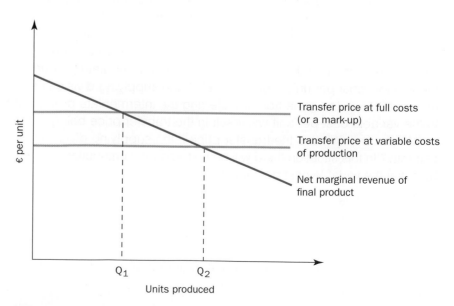

Transfer price at full costs (or a mark-up)

Transfer price at variable costs of production

Net marginal revenue of final product

intermediate product. Transfer pricing becomes even more complex when we introduce an imperfect market for the intermediate product. You should note, however, that *where there is an imperfect market for the intermediate product the theoretically correct transfer price is still the variable/marginal cost of producing the intermediate product at the optimal output for the company as a whole* (see Drury, 2018, Chapter 20 for a more detailed explanation).

PROPOSALS FOR RESOLVING TRANSFER PRICING CONFLICTS

Our discussion so far has indicated that in the absence of a perfect market for the intermediate product none of the transfer pricing methods can perfectly meet both the decision-making and performance evaluation requirements and also not undermine divisional autonomy. It has been suggested that if the external market for the intermediate product is imperfect or non-existent, transfers at marginal/variable cost should motivate decisions that are optimal from the overall company's perspective. However, transfers at marginal/variable cost are unsuitable for performance evaluation because they do not provide an incentive for the supplying division to transfer goods and services internally. This is because they do not contain a profit margin for the supplying division. Central headquarters intervention may be necessary to instruct the supplying division to meet the receiving division's demand at the marginal cost of the transfers. Thus divisional autonomy will be undermined. Transferring at cost plus a mark-up creates the opposite conflict. Here the transfer price meets the performance evaluation requirement but will not induce managers to make optimal decisions.

A solution that has been proposed to resolve the above conflicts is to charge all transfers at variable cost and for the supplying division to also charge the receiving division a fixed fee for the privilege of obtaining these transfers at short-run variable cost. This approach is sometimes described as a **two-part transfer pricing system**. With this system, the receiving division acquires additional units of the intermediate product at the variable cost of production. Therefore when it equates its marginal (variable) costs with its net marginal revenues to determine the optimum profit-maximizing output level, it will use the appropriate variable costs of the supplying division. The supplying division can recover its fixed costs and earn a profit on the inter-divisional transfers through the fixed fee charged each period. The fixed fee is intended to compensate the supplying division for tying up some of its fixed capacity for providing products or services that are transferred internally. The fixed fee should cover a share of fixed costs of the supplying division and also provide a return on capital. The advantage of this approach is that transfers will be made at the variable cost of the supplying division, and both divisions should also be able to report profits from inter-divisional trading. Furthermore, the receiving divisions are made aware, and charged for the full cost of obtaining intermediate products from other divisions, through the two components of the two-part transfer pricing system.

If you refer back to Example 13.1 you will see that this proposal would result in a transfer price at a variable cost of €11 per unit for the intermediate product plus a fixed fee lump-sum payment of €60 000 to cover the fixed costs of the capacity allocated to producing the intermediate product. In addition, a fixed sum to reflect the required return on the capital employed would be added to the €60 000. Adopting this approach the receiving division

REAL WORLD VIEWS 13.1

How a multinational pharmaceutical company solved its transfer pricing problems using ABC

Teva Pharmaceutical Industries Ltd reorganized its pharmaceutical operations into decentralized cost and profit centres. Teva proposed a transfer pricing system based on marginal costs. But the proposed transfer pricing system generated a storm of controversy. First, some executives observed that the marketing divisions would report extremely high profits because they were being charged for the variable costs only. Second, the operations division would get 'credit' only for the variable expenses. There would be little pressure and motivation to control non-variable expenses. Third, if Teva's plants were less efficient than outside manufacturers of the pharmaceutical products, the marginal cost transfer price would give the marketing divisions no incentive to shift their source of supply. An alternative approach had to be found.

Teva's managers considered, but rejected, several traditional methods for establishing a new transfer pricing system. Market price was not feasible because no market existed for Teva's manufactured and packaged pharmaceutical products that had not been marketed to customers. Senior executives also believed strongly that negotiated transfer prices would lead to endless arguments among managers in the different divisions, which would consume excessive time on non-productive discussions.

Teva solved its transfer pricing problem by using ABC. Transfer prices are calculated in two different procedures. The first one assigns unit and batch-level costs, and the second assigns product-specific and plant-level costs. The marketing divisions are charged for unit-level costs (principally materials and labour) based on the actual quantities of each individual product they acquire. In addition, they are charged batch-level costs based on the actual number of production and packaging batches of each product they order. The product-specific and plant-level expenses are charged to marketing divisions annually in lump sums based on budgeted information.

What about unused capacity? To foster a sense of responsibility among marketing managers for the cost of supplying capacity resources, Teva charges the marketing division that experienced the decline in demand a lump-sum assignment for the cost of maintaining the unused production capacity in an existing line. The assignment of the plant-level costs receives much attention, particularly from the managers of the marketing divisions. They want to verify that these costs do indeed stay 'fixed' and don't creep upward each period. The marketing managers make sure that increases in plant-level costs occur only when they request a change in production capacity.

Marketing managers now distinguish between products that cover all manufacturing costs versus those that cover only the unit and batch-level expenses but not their annual product-sustaining and plant-level expenses. Because of the assignment of unused capacity expenses to the responsible marketing division, the marketing managers incorporate information about available capacity when they make decisions about pricing, product mix and product introduction.

Questions

1 How does the transfer pricing system overcome the limitations of marginal cost transfer pricing?
2 Why is it important that capacity costs are taken into account when making pricing and product mix decisions?

Reference

Kaplan, R.S., Weiss, D. and Deseh, E. (1997) Transfer pricing with ABC, *Management Accounting (USA)*, May, 20–28.

REAL WORLD VIEWS 13.2

UK tax authority doubles its tax income from investigations of multinational transfer pricing

According to an article in the *Financial Times* the UK tax authority (HMRC – HM Revenue & Customs) raised £1.1bn from challenging the pricing of multinational companies' internal deals in 2013–14 – more than twice as much as in the previous year. The increase came as HMRC stepped up its 'transfer-pricing' investigations – scrutinizing the prices charged on transactions between different parts of the same company – following a public outcry over multinational tax planning. The Treasury has intensified action against multinationals' tax avoidance by launching a new 'diverted profits tax' as well as contributing to an overhaul of the transfer-pricing rules by the OECD group of mostly wealthy nations.

The transfer-pricing rules permit HMRC to adjust the profits on transactions between companies in the same corporate group where it appears that the transaction did not take place at 'arm's length', on the same terms as for an unrelated company. In the year to 2014, the amount of extra tax secured from transfer-pricing inquiries aimed at large businesses more than tripled.

Questions

1 Do you think it is always possible to establish an arm's length/market price?
2 Would an arms' length price be more difficult to establish in the provision of services?

References

Houlder, V. (2015, Mar 06). 'HMRC nets pound(s)1.1bn as it doubles take from pricing probes at multinationals'. *Financial Times*, 3. ISSN 03071766.

will use the short-run variable cost to equate with its net marginal revenue and choose to purchase the optimal output level for the company as a whole (5000 units). For longer-term decisions the receiving division will be made aware that the revenues must be sufficient to cover the full cost of producing the intermediate product (€11 unit variable cost plus €60 000 fixed costs plus the opportunity cost of capital). When the lump-sum fixed fee is added to the short-run transfer price you will see that the supplying division will report a profit at all output levels. Assume, for example that the fixed fee is €75 000 (€60 000 fixed costs plus €15 000 to provide a satisfactory return on capital). Now refer back to the divisional profit calculations shown on pages 339–340 for the variable cost transfer pricing system. You will see that the supplying division will report a profit of €15 000 (the revenues from the fixed fee of €75 000 less the €60 000 loss equal to the fixed costs). The receiving division's reported profits will be reduced by the €75 000 fixed fee for all output levels but its profits will still be maximized at the optimal output level of 5000 units.

INTERNATIONAL TRANSFER PRICING

The rise of multinational organizations introduces additional issues that must be considered when setting transfer prices. When the supplying and the receiving divisions are located in different countries with different taxation rates, and the taxation rates in one country are much lower than those in the other, it would be in the company's interest if most of the profits were allocated to the division operating in the low taxation country. For example, consider an organization that manufactures products in country A, which has a marginal tax rate of 25 per cent, and sells those products to country B, which has a marginal tax rate of 40 per cent. It is in the company's best interests to

REAL WORLD VIEWS 13.3

How Nike substantially reduces its global taxation profits

An article published in *The Guardian* newspaper illustrates how Nike substantially reduced its global taxable profits. Money from shoe sales across Europe, the Middle East and Africa all flow into Nike's European headquarters in the Netherlands. The amount of tax due is determined by a company's taxable profits (i.e. Revenues – costs = taxable profit, taxable profit – taxes = net profit). However, by establishing a subsidiary company that charges the Netherlands headquarters for intellectual property rights, taxable profits can be significantly reduced (i.e. Revenues – costs – payments to subsidiary = taxable profit, taxable profit – taxes = net profit).

Nike shoes are made in countries such as Vietnam and Indonesia. From there, they are shipped to the company's European warehouse. The money from sales in Europe flows out of the specific country to the Netherlands headquarters. They pay some tax on the revenues they receive from Nike sales across Europe, the Middle East and Africa.

From 2005 until 2014, Nike was able to shift vast sums of money out of the Netherlands to Bermuda, which is an offshore tax haven with zero tax. Nike did this through a Bermudan subsidiary, Nike International Ltd, which held the company's intellectual property rights for its sneaker brands. They charged large trademark royalty fees each year to Nike's European HQ for selling its trainers. The fees allowed Nike to legally shift profits away from Europe to Nike International Ltd. For the companies that know how to work the system, this is sensible, legal and above board as far as tax authorities are concerned. For campaigners who insist the system is unfair, it is ridiculous.

In 2014, with the deal from the Netherlands due to expire, the company came up with a new plan, again with the agreement of Dutch authorities. This involved moving the company's intellectual property from Nike International Ltd in Bermuda to yet another subsidiary, Nike Innovate CV. This entity is not based in Bermuda. It is not actually based anywhere. The 'CV' model allows Nike Innovate to avoid paying local taxes in the Netherlands. Nike Innovate is not being taxed anywhere else, either as Nike Innovate does not seem to have tax residency anywhere in the world. The CV model, and the one that preceded it in Bermuda, appear to have helped Nike substantially reduce its global tax rate.

The Organisation for Economic Co-operation and Development has been trying to shut down the Dutch CV model. Under the EU's anti-tax-avoidance directive, Nike may have to find a new way of funnelling its money by 2021, or pay more tax than it does at the moment.

Questions

1 Do you think management accountants are involved in tax planning decisions such as those referred to above?

2 Do you think tax avoidance is ever ethical? Is it sustainable?

Reference

Hopkins, N. and Bower, S. (2017), Revealsed: How Nike stays one step ahead of the tax man, *The Guardian*, 6 November, 2017, www.theguardian.com/news/2017/nov/06/nike-tax-paradise-papers

locate most of its profits in country A, where the tax rate is lowest. Therefore it will wish to use the highest possible transfer price so that the receiving division operating in country B will have higher costs and report lower profits whereas the supplying division operating in country A will be credited with higher revenues and thus report the higher profits. In many multinational organizations, the taxation issues outweigh other transfer pricing issues and the dominant consideration in the setting of transfer prices is the minimization of global taxes.

In an attempt to provide a worldwide consensus on the pricing of international intra-firm transactions the Organisation for Economic Cooperation and Development (OECD) issues guideline statements. These statements are important because the taxation authorities in most countries have used it as the basis for regulating transfer pricing behaviour of international intra-firm transactions. The OECD guidelines are based on the arms'-length principle, which relates to the price that would have resulted from transactions between two unrelated parties. This can be difficult to do when the 'good' being transferred is, say, a licence to exploit intellectual property in a particular country.

Nevertheless there is considerable evidence to suggest that multinational enterprises do use transfer pricing to shift income between geographical locations in response to minimizing their tax payments. For example: Apple, Facebook, Amazon, eBay and Google reported revenue of £2.6 million in the UK between 2014 and 2015, but many more billions of pounds spent by UK consumers are recorded every year, and moved around the world to their sister companies located in tax havens like Luxembourg, Ireland and Bermuda. Industry experts estimate the true UK sales of the five firms to be nearly £18 billion, but less than £100 million is paid in UK taxes.

There is a general agreement that regulation of global transfer pricing tax rules needs to be substantially improved to cope with today's intangible products such as electronic books, MP3 files, computer games and other digital media. Even the person in charge of global tax policy at the OECD, the body that crafts international rules on taxation, has stated that the current system is rotten and that aggressive tax planning needs to be replaced with firmer rules. Unfortunately, there appears to be slow progress on how this should be done.

The process of mutinational companies acting aggressively to minimize global taxes has attracted a considerable amount of negative publicity on the grounds that the behaviour is unethical. There is evidence to suggest that consumers are penalizing such behaviour by migrating from firms engaged in unethical behaviour to their competitors. For example, many consumers of Starbucks in the UK migrated to its rival, Costa, because of their perception that Starbucks did not pay a fair amount of UK taxes. Because of the concern that its customers perceived it to be engaged in unethical behaviour, Starbucks responded by volunteering to add an extra £10 million corporation tax to its tax liability.

International transfer pricing is a complex issue and is beyond the scope of this book, but you should note that there are additional considerations that must be taken into account when setting transfer prices within multinational companies.

SUMMARY

The following items relate to the learning objectives listed at the beginning of the chapter.

- **Describe the different purposes of a transfer pricing system**. Transfer pricing can be used for the following purposes: (a) to provide information that motivates divisional managers to make good economic decisions; (b) to provide information that is useful for evaluating the managerial and economic performance of a division; (c) to intentionally move profits between divisions or locations; and (d) to ensure that divisional autonomy is not undermined.

- **Identify and describe five different transfer pricing methods**. The five main transfer pricing methods are (a) market-based transfer prices; (b) marginal cost transfer prices; (c) full cost transfer prices; (d) cost plus a mark-up transfer prices; and (e) negotiated transfer prices.

- **Explain why the correct transfer price is the external market price when there is a perfectly competitive market for the intermediate product**. If there is a perfectly competitive market for the intermediate product, transfers recorded at market prices are likely to represent the real economic contribution to total company profits. If the supplying division did not exist, the intermediate product would have to be purchased on the outside market at the current market price. Alternatively, if the receiving division did not exist, the intermediate product would have to be sold on the outside market at the current market price. Divisional profits are therefore likely to be similar to the profits that would be calculated if the divisions were separate organizations. For decision-making, if the receiving division does not acquire the intermediate product internally it would be able to acquire the product at the competitive external market price. Similarly, if the supplying division does transfer internally it will be able to sell the product at the external market price. Thus, the market price represents the opportunity cost of internal transfers.

- **Explain why cost-plus transfer prices will not result in the optimum output being achieved**. If cost-plus transfer prices are used, the receiving division will determine its optimal output at the point where the marginal cost of its transfers is equal to its net marginal revenue (i.e. marginal revenue less marginal conversion costs, excluding the transfer price). However, the marginal cost of the transfers (i.e. the cost-plus transfer price) will be in excess of the marginal cost of producing the intermediate product for the company as a whole. Thus, marginal cost will be overstated and the receiving division manager will restrict output to the point where net marginal revenue equals the transfer price, rather than the marginal cost to the company of producing the intermediate product.

- **Explain a method of transfer pricing that has been advocated to resolve the conflicts between the decision-making and performance evaluation objectives**. To overcome the decision-making and performance evaluation conflicts that can occur with cost-based transfer pricing a two-part transfer pricing system is recommended. The two-part transfer pricing system involves transfers being made at the variable cost per unit of output of the supplying division plus a lump-sum fixed fee charged by the supplying division to the receiving division for the use of the capacity allocated to the intermediate product. This transfer pricing system should also motivate the receiving division to choose the optimal output level and enable the supplying division to obtain a profit on inter-divisional trading.

● **Describe the additional factors that must be considered when setting transfer prices for multinational transactions**. When divisions operate in different countries, taxation implications can be a dominant influence. The aim is to set transfer prices at levels that will ensure that most of the profits are allocated to divisions operating in low taxation counties. However, taxation authorities in the countries where the divisions are located and the OECD have introduced guidelines and legislation to ensure that companies do not use transfer prices for taxation manipulation purposes.

KEY TERMS AND CONCEPTS

Final products   Products sold by a receiving division to the outside world.

Intermediate products   Goods transferred from the supplying division to the receiving division.

Net marginal revenue   The marginal (incremental) revenue from the sale of an extra unit (or a specified number of incremental units) of the final product less the marginal/incremental conversion costs (excluding the transfer price).

Perfectly competitve market   A market where the product is homogeneous and no individual buyer or seller can affect the market prices.

Two-part transfer pricing system   A method of transfer pricing where the receiving division acquires intermediate products at the variable cost of production and the supplying division also charges a fixed fee.

ASSESSMENT MATERIAL

The review questions are short questions that enable you to assess your understanding of the main topics included in the chapter. The page numbers in parentheses provide you with the page numbers to refer to if you cannot answer a specific question.

The review problems are more complex and require you to relate and apply the content to various business problems. Solutions to review problems are provided in a separate section at the end of the book. Additional review problems

can be accessed by lecturers and students on the dedicated online support resources for this book. Solutions to these review problems are provided for lecturers in the *Instructor's Manual* accompanying this book that can be downloaded from the dedicated online instructor's resources (see Preface for details).

The dedicated online digital support resources for this book also includes over 30 case study problems.

REVIEW QUESTIONS

13.1 Distinguish between intermediate products and final products. *(p. 333)*

13.2 Explain the four purposes for which transfer pricing can be used. *(pp. 333–334)*

13.3 Explain why a single transfer pricing method cannot serve all four purposes. *(p. 334)*

13.4 If an external, perfectly competitive market exists for an intermediate product what should be the transfer price? Why? *(pp. 335–336)*

13.5 Define the term 'net marginal revenue'. *(p. 338)*

13.6 If there is no external market for the intermediate product what is the optimal transfer price? Why? *(pp. 339–340)*

13.7 Why are full cost and cost plus a mark-up transfer prices unlikely to result in the optimum output? *(p. 340)*

13.8 Why are marginal cost transfer prices not widely used in practice? *(pp. 339–340)*

13.9 Discuss the advantages and disadvantages of negotiated transfer prices. *(pp. 340–341)*

13.10 What are the circumstances that favour the use of negotiated transfer prices? *(pp. 340–341)*

13.11 Describe a proposal that has been recommended for resolving transfer pricing conflicts. *(pp. 343–345)*

13.12 What are the special considerations that must be taken into account with international transfer pricing? *(pp. 345–347)*

REVIEW PROBLEMS

13.13 X plc, a manufacturing company, has two divisions: Division A and Division B. Division A produces one type of product, ProdX, which it transfers to division B and also sells externally. Division B has been approached by another company, which has offered to supply 2500 units of ProdX for €35 each.

The following details for Division A are available:

	€
Sales revenue	
Sales to Division B @ €40 per unit	400 000
External sales @ €45 per unit	270 000
Less:	
Variable cost @ €22 per unit	352 000
Fixed costs	100 000
Profit	218 000

If Division B decides to buy from the other company, the impact of the decision on the profits of Division A and X plc, assuming external sales of ProdX cannot be increased, will be:

	Division A	X plc
(a)	€12 500 decrease	€12 500 decrease
(b)	€15 625 decrease	€12 500 increase
(c)	€32 500 decrease	€32 500 increase
(d)	€45 000 decrease	€32 500 decrease
(e)	€45 000 decrease	€45 000 decrease

(3 marks)

13.14 Determining optimal transfer prices for three different scenarios
Manuco Ltd has been offered supplies of special ingredient Z at a transfer price of €15 per kg by Helpco Ltd, which is part of the same group of companies. Helpco Ltd processes and sells special ingredient Z to customers external to the group at €15 per kg. Helpco Ltd bases its transfer price on cost plus 25 per cent profit mark-up. Total cost has been estimated as 75 per cent variable and 25 per cent fixed.

Required:

Discuss the transfer prices at which Helpco Ltd should offer to transfer special ingredient Z to Manuco Ltd in order that group profit maximizing decisions may be taken on financial grounds in each of the following situations:

(i) Helpco Ltd has an external market for all of its production of special ingredient Z at a selling price of €15 per kg. Internal transfers to Manuco Ltd would enable €1.50 per kg of variable packing cost to be avoided.

(ii) Conditions are as per (i) but Helpco Ltd has production capacity for 3000 kg of special ingredient Z for which no external market is available.

(iii) Conditions are as per (ii) but Helpco Ltd has an alternative use for some of its spare production capacity. This alternative use is equivalent to 2000 kg of special ingredient Z and would earn a contribution of €6000.

(13 marks)

13.15 Determining optimal transfer price range and volume
Mobe Co manufactures electronic mobility scooters. The company is split into two divisions: the scooter division (Division S) and the motor division (Division M). Division M supplies electronic motors to both Division S and to external customers. The two divisions run as autonomously as possible, subject to the group's current policy that Division M must make internal sales first before selling outside the group; and that Division S must always buy its motors from Division M. However, this company policy, together with the transfer price which Division M charges Division S, is currently under review.

Details of the two divisions are given below.

Division S

Division S's budget for the coming year shows that 35 000 electronic motors will be needed. An external supplier could supply these to Division S for $800 each.

Division M

Division M has the capacity to produce a total of 60 000 electronic motors per year. Details of Division M's budget, which has just been prepared for the forthcoming year, are as follows:

Budgeted sales volume (units)	60 000
Selling price per unit for external sales of motors	$850
Variable costs per unit for external sales of motors	$770

The variable cost per unit for motors sold to Division S is $30 per unit lower due to cost savings on distribution and packaging.

Maximum external demand for the motors is 30 000 units per year.

Required:

Assuming that the group's current policy could be changed, advise, using suitable calculations, the number of motors which Division M should supply to Division S in order to maximize group profits. Recommend the transfer price or prices at which these internal sales should take place.

Note: All relevant workings must be shown.

(10 marks)

13.16 Calculating the effects of a transfer pricing system on divisional and company profits

Division A of a large divisionalized organization manufactures a single standardized product. Some of the output is sold externally while the remainder is transferred to Division B where it is a sub-assembly in the manufacture of that division's product. The unit costs of Division A's product are as follows:

	(€)
Direct material	4
Direct labour	2
Direct expense	2
Variable manufacturing overheads	2
Fixed manufacturing overheads	4
Selling and packing expense – variable	1
	15

Annually 10 000 units of the product are sold externally at the standard price of €30.

In addition to the external sales, 5000 units are transferred annually to Division B at an internal transfer charge of €29 per unit. This transfer price is obtained by deducting variable selling and packing expense from the external price since this expense is not incurred for internal transfers.

Division B incorporates the transferred-in goods into a more advanced product. The unit costs of this product are as follows:

	(€)
Transferred-in item (from Division A)	29
Direct material and components	23
Direct labour	3
Variable overheads	12
Fixed overheads	12
Selling and packing expense – variable	1
	80

Division B's manager disagrees with the basis used to set the transfer price. He argues that the transfers should be made at variable cost plus an agreed (minimal) mark-up since he claims that his division is taking output that Division A would be unable to sell at the price of €30.

Partly because of this disagreement, a study of the relationship between selling price and demand has recently been made for each division by the company's sales director. The resulting report contains the following table:

Customer demand at various selling prices:

Division A

Selling price	€20	€30	€40
Demand	15 000	10 000	5 000

Division B

Selling price	€80	€90	€100
Demand	7 200	5 000	2 800

The manager of Division B claims that this study supports his case. He suggests that a transfer price of €12 would give Division A a reasonable contribution to its fixed overheads while allowing Division B to earn a reasonable profit. He also believes that it would lead to an increase of output and an improvement in the overall level of company profits.

You are required:

(a) to calculate the effect that the transfer pricing system has had on the company's profits, and

(16 marks)

(b) to establish the likely effect on profits of adopting the suggestion by the manager of Division B of a transfer price of €12.

(6 marks)

(Total 22 marks)

13.17 Inter-divisional profit statements and optimal transfer prices

Bath Co. is a company specializing in the manufacture and sale of baths. Each bath consist of a main unit plus a set of bath fittings. The company is split into two divisions, A and B. Division A manufacturers the bath and Division B manufactures sets of bath fittings. Currently, all of Division A's sales are made externally. Division B, however, sells to Division A as well as to external customers. Both of the divisions are profit centres.

The following data are available for both divisions:

Division A

Current selling price for each bath	$450
Costs per bath:	
Fittings from Division B	$75
Other materials from external suppliers	$200
Labour costs	$45
Annual fixed overheads	$7 440 000
Annual production and sales of baths (units)	80 000
Maximum annual market demand for baths (units)	80 000

Division B

Current external selling price per set of fittings	$80
Current price for sales to Division A	$75
Costs per set of fittings:	
Materials	$5
Labour costs	$15
Annual fixed overheads	$4 400 000
Maximum annual production and sales of sets of fittings (units) (including internal and external sales)	200 000
Maximum annual external demand for sets of fittings (units)	180 000
Maximum annual internal demand for sets of fittings (units)	80 000

The transfer price charged by Division B to Division A was negotiated some years ago between the previous divisional managers, who have now both been replaced by new managers. Head Office only allows Division A to purchase its fittings from Division B, although the new manager of Division A believes that he could obtain fittings of the same quality and appearance for $65 per set, if he was given the autonomy to purchase from outside the company. Division B makes no cost savings from supplying internally to Division A rather than selling externally.

Required:

(a) Under the current transfer pricing system, prepare a profit statement showing the profit for each of the divisions and for Bath Co. as a whole. Your sales and costs figures should be split into external sales and inter-divisional transfers, where appropriate.

(6 marks)

(b) Head Office is considering changing the transfer pricing policy to ensure maximization of company profits without demotivating either of the divisional managers. Division A will be given autonomy to buy from external suppliers and Division B to supply external customers in priority to supplying Division A.

Calculate the maximum profit that could be earned by Bath Co. if transfer pricing is optimized.

(8 marks)

(c) Discuss the issues of encouraging divisional managers to take decisions in the interests of the company

as a whole, where transfer pricing is used. Provide a reasoned recommendation of a policy Bath Co. should adopt.

(6 marks)

13.18 Comments on proposed transfer price policy and recommended changes

You are the management accountant of the SSA Group which manufactures an innovative range of products to provide support for injuries to various joints in the body. The group has adopted a divisional structure. Each division is encouraged to maximize its reported profit.

Division A, which is based in a country called Nearland, manufactures joint-support appliances which incorporate a 'one size fits all people' feature. A different appliance is manufactured for each of knee, ankle, elbow and wrist joints.

Budget information in respect of Division A for the year ended 31 December is as follows:

Support appliance	Knee	Ankle	Elbow	Wrist
Sales units (000s)	20	50	20	60
Selling price per unit ($)	24	15	18	9
Total variable cost of sales ($000)	200	350	160	240

Each of the four support products uses the same quantity of manufacturing capacity. This gives Division A management the flexibility to alter the product mix as desired. During the year to 31 December it is estimated that a maximum of 160 000 support products could be manufactured.

The following information relates to Division B which is also part of the SSA group and is based in Distantland:

1 Division B purchases products from various sources, including from other divisions in SSA group, for subsequent resale to customers.

2 The management of Division B has requested two alternative quotations from Division A in respect of the year ended 31 December as follows:

Quotation 1 – Purchase of 10 000 ankle supports.
Quotation 2 – Purchase of 18 000 ankle supports.

The management of the SSA Group has decided that a minimum of 50 000 ankle supports must be reserved for customers in Nearland in order to ensure that customer demand can be satisfied and the product's competitive position is maintained in the Nearland market.

The management of the SSA Group is willing, if necessary, to reduce the budgeted sales quantities of other types of joint support in order to satisfy the requirements of Division B for ankle supports. They wish, however, to minimize the loss of contribution to the Group.

The management of Division B is aware of another joint support product, which is produced in Distantland, that competes with the Division A version of the ankle support and which could be purchased at a local currency price that is equivalent to $9 per support. SSA Group policy is that all divisions are allowed autonomy to set transfer prices and purchase from whatever sources they choose. The management of Division A intends to use market price less 30 per cent as the basis for each of Quotations 1 and 2.

Required:

(a) (i) The management of the SSA Group have asked you to advise them regarding the appropriateness of the decision by the management of Division A to use an adjusted market price as the basis for the preparation of each quotation and the implications of the likely sourcing decisions by the management of Division B.

Your answer should cite relevant quantitative data and incorporate your recommendation of the prices that should be quoted by Division A for the ankle supports in respect of Quotations 1 and 2, that will ensure that the profitability of SSA Group as a whole is not adversely affected by the decision of the management of Division B.

(8 marks)

(ii) Advise the management of Divisions A and B regarding the basis of transfer pricing which should be employed in order to ensure that the profit of the SSA Group is maximized.

(4 marks)

(b) After considerable internal discussion concerning Quotation 2 by the management of SSA Group, Division A is not prepared to supply 18 000 ankle supports to Division B at any price lower than 30 per cent below market price. All profits in Distantland are subject to taxation at a rate of 20 per cent. Division A pays tax in Nearland at a rate of 40 per cent on all profit.

Advise the management of SSA Group whether the management of Division B should be directed to purchase the ankle supports from Division A, or to purchase a similar product from a local supplier in Distantland. Supporting calculations should be provided.

(8 marks)

PART FIVE

STRATEGIC PERFORMANCE AND COST MANAGEMENT AND CHALLENGES FOR THE FUTURE

P art Five focuses on strategic aspects of performance management and control. Increasing emphasis is now being placed on the need for management accounting to support an organization's competitive strategies. To encourage behaviour that is consistent with an organization's strategy, attention is focusing on an integrated framework of performance management that can be used to clarify, communicate and manage strategy. Chapter 14 describes the recent developments that seek to incorporate performance measurement and management within the strategic management process.

In Part Four, the major features of traditional management accounting control systems and the mechanisms that can be used to control costs were described. Traditional cost control systems tend to be based on the preservation of the status quo, and the ways of performing existing activities are not reviewed. The emphasis is on cost containment rather than cost reduction. In contrast, strategic cost management focuses on cost reduction rather than cost containment. Chapter 15 examines the various approaches that fall within the area of strategic cost management and value creation. Ideally, cost management should also incorporate value creation where the aims should be not only to take actions that will reduce costs but also to enhance customer satisfaction and value. Customer value may be increased by either reducing the cost without sacrificing product/service functionality or by increasing functionality without increasing cost. Reducing cost is important because it enables a company to remain competitive by reducing or maintaining selling prices and thus increasing customer satisfaction and value. Increasing customer satisfaction is generally associated with an increase in sales revenues and profits which should ultimately be reflected in creating additional shareholder value.

The content covered in chapters 14 and 15 describe practices that have only become widely used in the past two decades. In Chapter 16 we shall concentrate on the emerging issues that are likely to have an impact on management accounting and consider some potential future developments in management accounting.

14
STRATEGIC PERFORMANCE MANAGEMENT

LEARNING OBJECTIVES After studying this chapter you should be able to:

● describe three competitive strategies that a firm can adopt to achieve sustainable competitive advantage and explain how they influence management accounting practices

● describe the balanced scorecard

● explain each of the four perspectives of the balanced scorecard

● provide illustrations of performance measures for each of the four perspectives

● explain how the balanced scorecard links strategy formulation to financial outcomes

● distinguish between lead and lag measures

● outline the benefits and criticisms of the balanced scorecard.

Prior to the late 1980s, management accounting performance management systems tended to focus mainly on financial measures of performance. The inclusion of only those items that could be expressed in monetary terms motivated managers to focus excessively on cost reduction and ignore other important variables that were necessary to compete in the global competitive environment that emerged during the 1990s. Product quality, delivery, reliability, after-sales service and customer satisfaction became key competitive variables but none of these were given sufficient importance measured by the traditional management accounting performance management system.

During the late 1980s much greater emphasis was given to incorporating into the management reporting system those non-financial performance measures that provided feedback on the key variables that are required to compete successfully in a global economic environment. However, a proliferation of performance measures emerged. This resulted in confusion when some of the measures conflicted with each other and it was possible to enhance one measure at the expense of another. It was also not clear to managers how the non-financial measures they were evaluated on contributed to the whole picture of achieving success in financial terms. According to Kaplan and Norton (2001a) previous performance management systems that incorporated non-financial measurements used ad hoc collections of such measures, more like checklists of measures for managers to keep track of and improve rather than a comprehensive system of linked measurements.

During the 1990s, strategic performance management systems emerged that not only integrated financial and non-financial measures of performance but also facilitated strategy implementation and contributed to enhanced performance. The aim of this chapter is to describe the major features of these systems.

THE PERFORMANCE MANAGEMENT FRAMEWORK

Otley (1999) identifies five main sets of issues that need to be addressed in developing a framework for managing organizational performance. He suggests that these issues can be represented by the following set of questions:

1 What are the key objectives that are central to the organization's overall future success, and how does it go about evaluating its achievement for each of these objectives?

2 What strategies and plans has the organization adopted and what are the processes and activities that it has decided will be required for it to successfully implement these? How does it assess and measure the performance of these activities?

3 What level of performance does the organization need to achieve in each of the areas defined in the above two questions and how does it go about setting appropriate performance targets for them?

4 What rewards will managers (and other employees) gain by achieving these performance targets (or, conversely, what penalties will they suffer by failing to achieve them)? Because the human resources function is often responsible for the rewards systems in many organizations, the linking of rewards to performance targets tends not to be sufficiently emphasized in performance management systems.

5 What are the information flows (feedback and feed-forward loops) that are necessary to enable the organization to learn from its experience, and to adapt its current behaviour in the light of that experience? These feedback and feed-forward controls (see Chapter 10) provide information about the extent to which a company is achieving its key strategic aims. This process can range from simple corrective action through to the revision of a corporate strategy if it becomes apparent that the current strategy is proving ineffective.

STRATEGY AND STRATEGIC POSITIONING

A major aim of strategic performance management systems is to facilitate strategy implementation. Strategies can be defined as the means by which an organization plans to achieve its objectives. The chosen strategies have an important influence in determining what performance measures might be appropriate. The linking of strategies and performance measures thus promotes organizational behaviour that supports the implementation of the chosen strategies. Various typologies of strategies (known as strategic positioning) that firms may choose have been identified in the strategic management literature. Porter (1985) suggests that a firm has a choice of three generic strategies in order to achieve competitive advantage. They are:

- A **cost leadership strategy**, whereby an enterprise aims to be the lowest cost producer within the industry thus enabling it to compete on the basis of lower selling prices rather than providing unique products or services. The source of this competitive advantage may arise from factors such as economies of scale, access to favourable raw material prices and superior technology (Langfield-Smith, 1997).

- A **differentiation strategy**, whereby the enterprise seeks to offer products or services that are considered by its customers to be superior and unique relative to its competitors. Examples include the quality or dependability of the product, after-sales service, the wide availability of the product and product flexibility (Langfield-Smith, 1997).

- A **focusing strategy**, which involves seeking competitive advantage by focusing on a narrow segment of the market that has special needs that are poorly served by other competitors in the industry. A focusing strategy recognizes that differences can exist within segments (e.g. customers and geographical regions) of the same market. Competitive advantage is based on adopting either a cost leadership or product differentiation strategy within the chosen segment.

In practice, firms may choose a combination of the three strategies within the different markets in which they operate. **Strategic positioning** relates to the choice of the optimal mix of the three general strategies.

Miles and Snow (1978) distinguish between **defender and prospector strategies**. Defender organizations perceive a great deal of stability in their external environment and concentrate on a narrow and limited mix of products and customers. They compete on product price, quality and customer service rather than innovation and product and market development, and do this by focusing on making operations efficient through cost, quality and service leadership. They engage in little product/market development. Prospectors perceive high uncertainty in their environment and are continually searching for new market opportunities. They are the creators of change. They compete through new product innovations and market development. The marketing and research and development functions dominate finance and production, so efficiency and profit performance are not as important as maintaining industry leadership in product innovation.

A firm's choice of performance measures and the emphasis given to them will be influenced by the strategic position they adopt. For example, a firm pursuing a cost leadership or defender strategy will give greater emphasis to cost-based measures and quality and output/input efficiency measures. In contrast, a firm pursuing a differentiation or prospector strategy will give greater emphasis to marketing measures such as percentage market share, percentage of sales from new products, percentage of sales from new markets, etc. The performance management system is most effective when it fits with business strategy. Without such a fit, what is being measured (and communicated as important) and what is actually important to the firm are not synchronized with each other (Melnyk et al., 2014).

PERFORMANCE MEASUREMENT AND PERFORMANCE MANAGEMENT SYSTEMS

The terms 'performance measurement system' and 'performance management system' often tend to be used interchangeably in the literature but it is possible to distinguish between them. The performance measurement system encompasses the processes for setting goals and collecting, analysing and interpreting performance data. The objective of the process is to convert data into information and to assess the effectiveness and efficiency of action (Neely *et al.*, 1995).

Melnyk *et al.*, (2014) state that although performance measurement is important, it is not sufficient to manage an enterprise. There is a complementary need for a performance management system. The performance management system encompasses the processes of assessing the differences between actual and desired outcomes, identifying and flagging those differences that are critical (thereby warranting management intervention), understanding if and why the deficiencies have taken place, and, when necessary, introducing (and monitoring) corrective actions aimed at closing the significant performance gaps.

ALTERNATIVE PERFORMANCE MANAGEMENT FRAMEWORKS

Several different strategic performance management frameworks have been presented in the literature that seek to integrate financial and non-financial measures of performance and also facilitate strategy implementation and enhanced performance. The major strategic performance frameworks that have emerged are:

- A results/determinants framework (Fitzgerald *et al.*, 1991) which the authors apply to the service industry.
- The performance pyramid (Lynch and Cross,1991a and 1991b).
- The balanced scorecard (Kaplan and Norton, 1992).
- The performance prism framework (Neely *et al.*, 2002).

The balanced scorecard has become the dominant strategic performance management framework and has tended to overshadow the other frameworks that have emerged. Indeed, its diffusion was so rapid that, as early as 1997, it was labelled as one of the most influential management instruments of the twentieth century (Sibbet, 1997). Therefore, because of its widespread use and popularity, we shall concentrate on the balanced scorecard in the remainder of this chapter. The other performance management frameworks have many similarities to the balanced scorecard and describing these frameworks would tend to involve undue repetition. An understanding of these alternative frameworks is unlikely to be essential for most readers but some of the specialist accounting bodies do set examination questions requiring an understanding of these alternative performance frameworks. To meet the requirements of all readers these alternative performance management frameworks are presented in Learning note 14.1 in the digital support resources accompanying this book (see Preface for details). You should check your course curriculum to ascertain if you need to read Learning note 14.1.

REAL WORLD VIEWS 14.1

Seven myths about managing performance

The *Globe and Mail* (Canada) quotes an article written by Professor Pietro Micheli in *Industry Week* in which he listed seven myths about performance management that promote the wrong behaviours. The following is a summary of these myths:

Myth 1: Numbers. are objective

Numbers are open to interpretation and manipulation, so there is a danger that the numbers may not be accepted as valid. It is important to communicate what the numbers mean, and why they should be trusted.

Myth 2: Data are accurate

Compiling data is expensive so performance measures must meet cost/benefits criteria.

Myth 3: More measures add more value

Too many performance measures do not provide value since they can confuse and there is no time to use them. Find the measures that are important that tell you something you can act upon and then use just them.

Myth 4: Everyone should be aligned

The typical way in which managers try to create alignment can end up generating bureaucracy and negatively impacting on staff morale. Managers and employees need some discretion to adjust targets to fit their situation. For example, in a provincial health department it would be unwise to expect ambulances in urban and rural areas to hit the same targets.

Myth 5: Incentives do the trick

Managers believe that by setting targets and rewards, they will motivate employees to achieve organizational goals. There is a danger that employees become so fixated on the measures they forget the broader picture.

Myth 6: Performance measures foster change

Organizations often bring in performance indicators to point employees in new directions during periods of change. A dynamic system is required where performance measures are revised regularly.

Myth 7: Control leads to improvements

If you want to make improvements, the system must be dynamic, cost-effective, and encourage learning rather than control. If people feel the effort is really about control, they will be suspicious and disengage and will not result in improvements.

Questions

1 Provide examples of how performance measures might promote the wrong behaviours.
2 Why must performance measures be regularly reviewed and updated?

References

Micheli, P. (2012) The seven myths of performance management, 18 December, *Industry Week*. Available at www.industryweek.com/compensation-strategies/seven-myths-performance-management

Schachter, H. (2013) Seven myths about managing performance, *The Globe and Mail*, 4 February. Available at www.theglobeandmail.com/report-on-business/careers/management/seven-myths-about-managing-performance/article8122362/

THE BALANCED SCORECARD

The need to integrate financial and non-financial measures of performance and identify key performance measures that link measurements to strategy led to the emergence of the balanced scorecard. The balanced scorecard was devised by Kaplan and Norton (1992) and refined in later publications (Kaplan and Norton, 1993, 1996a, 1996b, 2001a, 2001b). Therefore, the following discussion is a summary of Kaplan and Norton's writings on this topic. Figure 14.1 illustrates how the balanced scorecard provides a framework for implementing an organization's strategy into specific objectives and linked performance measures (specified in terms of targets and actual measures) that are required to achieve each of the specific objectives.

Figure 14.1 emphasizes that the balanced scorecard philosophy creates a strategic focus by translating an organization's vision and strategy into operational objectives and performance measures for the following four perspectives:

1 **Financial perspective** (How do we look to shareholders?)
2 **Customer perspective** (How do customers see us?)
3 **Internal business perspective** (What must we excel at to satisfy our shareholders and customers?)
4 **Learning and growth perspective** (How can we continue to improve and create value?)

The **balanced scorecard** is a strategic management technique for communicating and evaluating the achievement of the mission and strategy of the organization. Kaplan and Norton define strategy as:

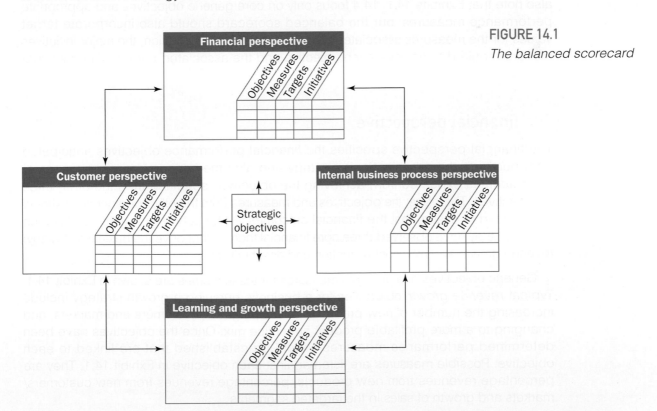

FIGURE 14.1

The balanced scorecard

Choosing the market and customer segments the business unit intends to serve, identifying the critical internal and business processes that the unit must excel at to deliver the value propositions to customers in the targeted market segments, and selecting the individual and organizational capabilities required for the internal and financial objectives.

You will see from Figure 14.1 that strategy is implemented by specifying the major *objectives* for each of the four perspectives and translating them into specific *performance measures, targets and initiatives*. There may be one or more objectives for each perspective and one or more performance measures linked to each objective. The balanced scorecard does not focus solely on achieving financial objectives. It also highlights non-financial objectives that an organization must achieve in order to meet its financial objectives in the future. Only the critical performance measures are incorporated in the scorecard. To minimize information overload and avoid a proliferation of measures each perspective ought to comprise four to five separate measures. Thus, the scorecard can provide *top* management with a fast but comprehensive view tracking the extent that the organizational unit (i.e. a division/strategic business unit) is implementing strategy. A balanced scorecard should be established for the entire organization, and also at lower levels such as divisions and responsibility centres below the divisional level. It is important that scorecards at lower levels within an organization consist of items that the responsibility centre manager can influence, and not by the actions of others, and that relate directly to the performance measures of the entire organization.

We shall now examine each of the four perspectives presented in Figure 14.1. Typical generic objectives and performance measures applicable to each perspective are presented in Exhibits 14.1–14.4, but in practice each organization will customize the objectives and performance measures to fit their own specific strategies. You should also note that Exhibits 14.1–14.4 focus only on core generic objectives and appropriate performance measures, but the balanced scorecard should also incorporate target values for the measures associated with each objective. In addition, the major initiatives that are required to achieve each objective and the associated performance measure should be described.

The financial perspective

The financial perspective specifies the financial performance objectives anticipated from pursuing the organization's strategy and also the economic consequences of the outcomes expected from achieving the objectives specified from the other three perspectives. Therefore, the objectives and measures from the other perspectives should be selected to ensure that the financial outcomes will be achieved. Kaplan and Norton state that they have observed three core financial themes that drive the business strategy: revenue growth and mix, cost reduction and asset utilization.

Generic objectives and possible measures for these themes are shown in Exhibit 14.1. Typical *revenue growth* objectives for a business pursuing a growth strategy include increasing the number of new products, developing new customers and markets, and changing to a more profitable product or service mix. Once the objectives have been determined performance measures should be established that are linked to each objective. Possible measures are listed against each objective in Exhibit 14.1. They are percentage revenues from new products, percentage revenues from new customers/markets and growth of sales in the targeted segments.

EXHIBIT 14 1 Financial perspective objectives and measures

Objectives	Measures
Revenue growth:	
Increase the number of new products	Percentage of revenues from new products
Develop new customers and markets	Percentage of revenues from new customers/markets
Change to a more profitable product (or service) mix	Sales growth percentage for targeted segments
Cost reduction:	
Reduce product/service cost per unit	Percentage reduction in cost per unit
Reduce selling/general administration costs	Percentage to total revenues of selling and administration costs
Asset utilization:	
Improve asset utilization	Return on investment Economic value added

REAL WORLD VIEW 14.2

Balanced scorecard based performance measurement of European airlines

A study by Dinçer *et al.* (2017) analysed the performance of nine European airline companies using multidimensional factors based on balanced scorecard variables in respect of four different perspectives. Dinçer *et al.* used the following 17 key factors of performance measurement, organized around the perspectives of the balanced scorecard, to analyse the performance of the airlines.

Under the financial perspective:

- return on equity
- return on assets
- growth in profit
- debt ratio
- current ratio

Under the internal business process perspective:

- flying on time
- sales performance
- number of accidents
- flights/number of employees
- number of flights/number of fleets
- number of passengers/number of employees

Under the learning and growth perspective:

- staff turnover rate (number of employees)
- increase in the number of planes
- profit per employee

Under the customer perspective:

- profit per customer
- the number of passengers/number of seats
- increasing customer retention and loyalty

Questions

1 Explain the meaning of each of the 17 variables used by the authors to measure the performance of the airlines.
2 Can you suggest other variables that might have been used instead of ones used by the authors to measure airline performance?
3 Do you think the performance measures used by the authors or the ones you have suggested are more useful to non-accountants and managers?

Reference

Dinçer, H., Hacioglu, U., Yuksel, S. (2017), Balanced scorecard based performance measurement of European airlines using a hybrid multicriteria decision making approach under the fuzzy environment, *Journal of Air Transport Management*, 63, 17–33.

The *cost reduction* objectives may include reduction in unit product costs and a reduction in selling and general and administration costs. Thus the percentage reduction in costs per unit of output for the selected cost objects and the percentage to total revenues of selling and administrative costs represent possible performance measures.

Exhibit 14.1 lists the improvement of *asset utilization* as the major objective of the asset utilization theme. Financial performance measures such as return on investment and economic value added that were described in Chapter 12 provide overall outcome measures of success for the overall financial objectives of revenue growth, cost reduction and asset utilization.

The customer perspective

The customer perspective should identify the customer and market segments in which the business unit will compete. The customer perspective underpins the revenue element for the financial perspective objectives. Therefore, the achievement of customer objectives should ensure that target revenues will be generated. Exhibit 14.2 lists five typical core or generic objectives. They are: increasing market share, increasing customer retention, increasing customer acquisition, increasing customer satisfaction and increasing customer profitability. Typical core measures for these objectives (see Exhibit 14.2) are respectively: percentage market share, percentage growth of business with existing customers, number of new customers or total sales to new customers, ratings from customer satisfaction surveys and profitability analysis by customer segments. The first four measures relate to the means required to achieve customer profitability but they do not measure the outcome. Customer profitability measures meet this requirement. In other words, a company does not want just satisfied customers, it also wants profitable customers.

EXHIBIT 14.2 Customer perspective objectives and measures

Objectives	Measures
Core:	
Increase market share	Percentage market share
Increase customer retention	Percentage growth in business from existing customers
Increase customer acquisition	Total sales to new customers
Increase customer satisfaction	Customer survey satisfaction ratings
Increase customer profitability	Customer profitability analysis
Customer value propositions:	
Improve product functionality	Customer survey product functionality rating scores
Decrease price relative to competitors	Price relative to competitors
Improve product/service quality	Percentage returns from customers
Improve delivery time	Percentage on-time deliveries

In addition to the core objectives and measures, additional measures (which Kaplan and Norton use the term **customer value propositions**) are needed which represent the attributes that drive the creation of customer value and, thus, drive the core outcomes relating to the customer perspective. Common product/service attributes encompass the functionality of the products/services, their price and quality, and for the customer dimension the delivery time attribute. Focusing on these attributes or measures has the potential to increase customer value and thus have a favourable impact on the core objectives. Typical objectives relating to the above attributes are listed in Exhibit 14.2. They are respectively: improve product functionality, decrease price relative to competitors, improve quality and improve delivery time. Possible measures for these objectives include, respectively, customer survey satisfaction scores relating to product functionality, price relative to competitors, percentage of returns from customers and percentage of on-time deliveries.

The internal business perspective

The internal business perspective requires that managers identify the critical internal processes for which the organization must excel in implementing its strategy. Critical processes should be identified that are required to achieve the organization's customer and financial objectives. Kaplan and Norton identify a generic process value chain that provides guidance for companies applying the internal process perspective. The process value chain consists of three processes: the innovation process, the operations process and the post-sales process.

In the *innovation process*, managers research the needs of customers and then create the products or services that will meet those needs. It represents the long wave of value creation in which companies first identify new markets, new customers, and the emerging and latent needs of existing customers. Then, continuing on this long wave of value creation, companies design and develop new products and services that enable them to reach these new markets and customers. Typical objectives for the innovation process are listed in Exhibit 14.3. They are increasing the number of new products, developing new markets and customers and decreasing the time taken to develop new products. Supporting performance measures are, respectively: percentage of sales from new products (also new product introductions versus competitors); percentage of sales from new markets; and development cycle time (e.g. time to the market).

The *operations process* represents the short wave of value creation. It is concerned with producing and delivering existing products and services to customers. Objectives of the operation process listed in Exhibit 14.3 include, increasing process efficiency, increasing process quality, decreasing process cost and decreasing process time. Historically, the operations process has been the major focus of most of an organization's performance management system and many possible measures exist. Typical measures associated with each of the objectives for the operations process are listed in Exhibit 14.3.

Process efficiency measures tend to focus on output/input measures such as the **production efficiency ratio** (standard hours of output/actual hours of input). Quality measures include total quality costs as a percentage of sales derived from the cost of quality report (see Chapter 15), and percentage of defective units. Process cost measures include unit cost trend measures relating to key processes, and cycle time measures have evolved that support the objective of decreasing process time.

EXHIBIT 14.3 Internal business perspective objectives and measures

Objectives	Measures
Innovation:	
Increase the number of new products	Percentage of sales from new products
	New product introductions versus competitors
Develop new markets and customers	Percentage of sales from new markets
Decrease the time taken to develop new products	Development cycle time (time to the market)
Operations:	
Increase process efficiency	Output/inputs ratios
Increase process quality	Total quality costs as a percentage of sales
	Percentage of defective output
Decrease process cost	Unit cost trends
Decrease process time	Manufacturing cycle efficiency
Post-sales service:	
Increase service quality	Percentage of customer requests that are handled with a single call
Increase service efficiency	Output/inputs ratios
Decrease service time	Cycle time in resolving customer problems
Decrease service cost	Unit cost trends

The total manufacturing cycle time consists of the sum of processing time, inspection time, wait time and move time. Only processing time adds value, and the remaining activities are non-value-added activities. The aim is to reduce the time spent on non-value-added activities and thus minimize manufacturing cycle time. A measure of cycle time that has been adopted is **manufacturing cycle efficiency (MCE)**:

$$MCE = \frac{\text{Processing time}}{\text{Processing time} + \text{Inspection time} + \text{Wait time} + \text{Move time}}$$

The generic performance measures that have been illustrated above relate to manufacturing operations but similar measures can be adopted for service companies. For example, many customers are forced to queue to receive a service. Companies that can eliminate waiting time for a service will find it easier to attract customers. Processing mortgage and loan applications by financial institutions can take a considerable time period involving a considerable amount of non-value-added waiting time. Thus, reducing the time to process the applications enhances customer satisfaction and creates the potential for increasing sales revenues. Therefore, service companies should also develop cycle time measures that support their specific customer processing activity objectives.

The *post-sales service process* represents the final item in the process value chain for the operations process perspective. It focuses on how responsive the organization is to customers after the product or service has been delivered. Post-sales services include warranty and repair activities, treatment of defects and returns, and the process and administration of customer payments. Increasing quality, increasing efficiency, and decreasing process time and cost are also objectives that apply to the post-sales service. Performance can be measured by some of the time, quality and cost measurements that have been suggested for the operations process. For example, service quality can be measured by first-pass yields defined as the percentage of customer requests that are handled with a single service call, rather than requiring multiple calls to resolve the problem. Increasing efficiency can be measured by appropriate output/input ratios and decreasing process time can be measured by cycle time where the process starts with the receipt of a customer request and ends with the ultimate resolution of the problem. Finally, the trend in unit costs can be used to measure the key post-sale service processes.

The learning and growth perspective

To ensure that an organization will continue to have loyal and satisfied customers in the future and continue to make excellent use of its resources, the organization and its employees must keep learning and developing. Hence there is a need for a perspective that focuses on the capabilities that an organization needs to create long-term growth and improvement. This perspective stresses the importance of organizations investing in their infrastructure (people, systems and organizational procedures) to provide the capabilities that enable the accomplishment of the other three perspectives' objectives. Kaplan and Norton have identified three major enabling factors for this perspective. They are: employee capabilities, information systems capabilities and the organizational climate for motivation, empowerment and alignment. Thus this perspective has three major core objectives: increase employee capabilities, increase information system capabilities and increase motivation, empowerment and alignment. The objectives and associated performance measures for this perspective are listed in Exhibit 14.4.

Core measures for the *employee capabilities* objective are concerned with employee satisfaction, employee retention and employee productivity. Many companies periodically measure employee satisfaction using surveys to derive employee satisfaction ratings. Employee retention can be measured by the annual percentage of key staff that resigns

EXHIBIT 14.4 Learning and growth perspective objectives and measures

Objectives	Measures
Increase employee capabilities	Employee satisfaction survey ratings Annual percentage of key staff leaving Sales revenue per employee
Increase information system capabilities	Percentage of processes with real-time feedback capabilities Percentage of customer-facing employees having online access to customer and product information
Increase motivation, empowerment and alignment	Number of suggested improvements per employee Number of suggestions implemented per employee Percentage of employees with personal goals aligned to the balanced scorecard Percentage of employees who achieve personal goals

and many different methods can be used to measure employee productivity. A generic measure of employee productivity that can be applied throughout the organization and compared with different divisions is the sales revenue per employee.

For employees to be effective in today's competitive environment they need accurate and timely information on customers, internal processes and the financial consequences of their decisions. Measures of *strategic information system capabilities* suggested by Kaplan and Norton include percentage of processes with real-time quality, cycle time and cost feedback capabilities available and the percentage of customer-facing employees having online access to customer and product information.

The number of suggested improvements per employee and the number of suggestions implemented per employee are proposed measures relating to the objective having *motivated and empowered employees*. Suggested measures relating to the objective of increasing individual and organizational alignment are the percentage of employees with personal goals aligned to the balanced scorecard and the percentage of employees who achieve personal goals.

Lag and lead measures

The balanced scorecard is not simply a collection of critical performance measures. The performance measures are derived from a company's strategy and objectives. The balanced scorecard consists of two types of performance measures. The first consists of **lag measures**. These are the *outcome measures* that mostly fall within the financial perspective and are the results of past actions. Outcome (lag) measures are important because they indicate whether strategy is being implemented successfully with the desired financial consequences. Outcome measures, such as economic value-added and return on investment, are normally generic and therefore tend to be common to most strategies and organizations. Lag measures generally do not incorporate the effect of decisions when they are made. Instead, they show the financial impact of the decisions as their impact materializes and this can be long after the decisions were made. The second type of performance measures are **lead measures** that are the *performance drivers* of future financial performance. They cause the outcome and usually distinguish one strategy from another. They are normally unique to a particular strategy and thus support the objective of linking measures to strategy. Lead measures tend to be the non-financial measures relating to the customer, internal business process and learning and growth perspectives.

Cause-and-effect relationships

A critical assumption of the balanced scorecard is that each performance measure is part of a cause-and-effect relationship involving a linkage from strategy formulation to financial outcomes. Cause-and-effect relationships are the means by which lead and lag measures are integrated and thus serve as the mechanism for communicating strategy. The chain of cause and effect should permeate all four perspectives of the balanced scorecard. Measures of organizational learning and growth are assumed to be the drivers of the internal business processes. The measures of these processes are in turn assumed to be the drivers of measures of customer perspective, while these measures are the driver of the financial perspective. The assumption that there is a cause-and-effect relationship is necessary because it allows the measurements relating to the non-financial perspectives to be used to predict future financial performance.

Kaplan and Norton (1996b) state that strategy can be viewed as a set of hypotheses about cause-and-effect, thus enabling a scorecard to tell the story of a business unit's strategy through a sequence of cause-and-effect relationships. The measurement system should make relationships (hypotheses) among objectives (and measures) in the various perspectives explicit so that they can be managed and validated. Every measure selected for a balanced scorecard should be an element of a chain of cause-and-effect relationships that communicates the meaning of the business unit's strategy to the organization.

Cause-and-effect relationships can be expressed by a sequence of if-then statements. For example, a link between improved training of workers to perform multiple tasks and higher profits can be established through the following sequence of if-then statements:

If employee skills are upgraded to perform multiple tasks by undertaking support activities such as duties relating to set-ups, minor repairs, preventive maintenance, quality inspection and operating different machines within the cell, then manufacturing processes can be redesigned by moving from a batch production functional layout to a cellular Just-in-time (JIT) manufacturing system (see Chapter 15 for a description of batch production and JIT manufacturing systems). If the manufacturing processes are redesigned then cycle time will decrease; if cycle time decreases, then delivery time will decrease; if delivery time decreases, then customer satisfaction will increase; if customer satisfaction increases, then market share will increase; if market share increases, then sales revenues will increase; if sales revenues increase then profits will increase.

The strategy map shown in Figure 14.2 illustrates the process redesign strategy as described by the above sequence of if-then statements, and indicates that the chain of cause-and-effect relationships encompasses all four perspectives of the balanced scorecard. Also note that a performance measure can serve as both a lag indicator and a lead indicator. For example, cycle time is an outcome measure (i.e. a lag measure) arising from improving employee skills and redesigning processes. Improvements in cycle times also serve as a lead indicator in terms of its influence on delivery time measures.

FIGURE 14.2

Strategy map

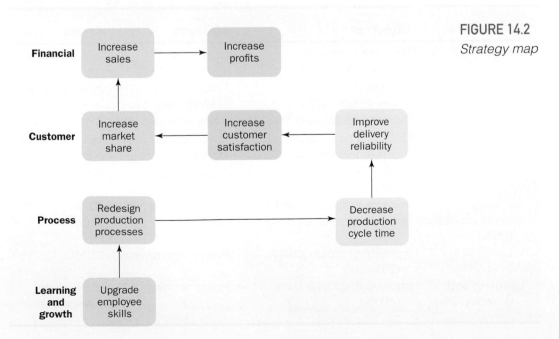

LINKING PERFORMANCE EVALUATION WITH THE BALANCED SCORECARD

Look at Figure 14.1. You will see that, besides objectives and measures, targets and initiatives are also incorporated in the balanced scorecard. Target values should be established for the measures associated with each objective. In addition, the major initiatives for each objective should be described. The scorecard objectives, initiatives and measures become the means for conveying the strategy of the organization to its employees and managers. Responsibility centre objectives and measures should also be aligned with the scorecard objectives and measures.

For feedback reporting, actual performance measures should also be added and compared with target values. The reward system should also be linked to the achievement of the scorecard objectives and measures. Failure to change the reward system may result in managers continuing to focus on short-term financial performance at the expense of concentrating on the strategic objectives of the scorecard. A US study indicates that the balanced scorecard approach is linked to incentive compensation schemes. Epstein and Manzoni (1998) reported that 60 per cent of the 100 large US organizations surveyed linked the balanced scorecard approach to incentive pay for their senior executives.

Exhibit 14.5 provides an illustration of linking the reward system with objectives, targets and performance measures. Weights expressed as percentages shown in the parentheses are used to indicate the relative importance that management has assigned to each perspective and objective. You will see that each perspective is assigned a weight of 25 per cent. Within each perspective there are multiple objectives and measures. For example, within the customer perspective there are three performance measures and management has assigned a weight of 25 per cent to increasing market

EXHIBIT 14.5   Illustration of a target and weighting incentive scheme

Perspectives	Objectives	Measures	Targets
Financial (25%)	Increase economic value-added (25%)	Economic value-added	20% increase
	Increase return on investment (25%)	Return on investment	20% increase
	Increase revenues (25%)	Sales revenues	25% increase
	Decrease process costs (25%)	Process costs	15% decrease
Customer (25%)	Increase market share (25%)	Market share	20%
	Increase customer retention (35%)	Repeat orders	60%
	Improved delivery time (40%)	On-time delivery (%)	100%
Internal processes (25%)	Improve cycle time (70%)	Cycle time	3 days
	Increase process quality (30%)	Percentage defects	0.01%
Learning and growth (25%)	Improve employee skills (100%)	Hours of training	35 hours per employee

share, 35 per cent to increasing customer retention and 40 per cent to on-time delivery. The percentage weightings are used to structure the reward system. Therefore in Exhibit 14.5, 10 per cent (40% × 25%) of the reward would be assigned to the delivery objective.

Note that the achievement of the objectives and targets shown in Exhibit 14.5 is based on cause-and-effect relationships. For example, increasing economic value, added by the targeted 20 per cent, is dependent on increasing sales revenues by a target of 25 per cent and decreasing process costs by 15 per cent. These changes are, in turn, dependent on other outcomes in other perspectives such as increasing market share and reducing cycle times by the target levels.

The actual values of the measures are compared with the target measures for a given time period. The design of a performance evaluation and reward system that is linked to multiple perspectives and objectives presents a number of difficulties such as determining what percentage weighting should be applied to each perspective?. In Exhibit 14.5 equal percentage weightings have been allocated to each perspective but there is no reason why management may choose to assign different percentage weightings.

A further problem arises when some of the target performance measures are achieved but others are not achieved. For example, in Exhibit 14.5 assume for the customer perspective that the target performance measures of 60 per cent for repeat orders and 100 per cent for on-time delivery were achieved but the actual increase in market share was 15 per cent compared with the target of 20 per cent. Should managers be given rewards when all of the measures for the objectives within the customer perspective have not been achieved? A possible solution is for the rewards to be based on the percentage achievement of each objective. Therefore, because the percentage achievement for increasing market share was 75 per cent (15 per cent actual performance compared with a target of 20 per cent) the percentage of the total reward would be 4.7 per cent (25% × 25% × 75%) compared with 6.25 per cent (25% × 25% × 100%) if the 20 per cent target market share had been achieved. There is a danger with this approach that insufficient attention will be given to all the performance measures. To avoid this, the reward system could specify that no reward will be given unless strategic measures exceed a specified minimum value.

It is also important that the linking of the balanced scorecard to a performance evaluation and reward system incorporate an appropriate time dimension. An adequate amount of time must elapse between the implementation of a strategic initiative and the ascertainment of whether the strategy has been successful. Thus, lag measures incorporated in the financial perspective can be expected to have a longer time perspective than the lead measures incorporated in the other perspectives. A possible approach is for the performance evaluation and reward system to incorporate short-term 1-year targets and longer-term targets (e.g. a 3- to 5-year time horizon).

Research evidence suggests that companies that use the balanced scorecard may continue to base their incentives mainly on financial measures. A study by Kraus and Lind (2010) of eight of Sweden's largest multinational companies that had adopted the balanced scorecard at the corporate level reported that incentives at this level were largely based on financial measures and that corporate control was also financially focused. The authors conclude that because financial markets focus on financial measures, incentives are also based on encouraging managers to focus on the same measures that are used by financial markets. Kraus and Lind point out that their research focused on the impact of the balanced scorecard on control at the corporate level and that there was a need to undertake further research to ascertain whether companies that use balance scorecards at lower business unit levels also link their reward systems mainly to financial measures at these lower levels.

BENEFITS AND LIMITATIONS OF THE BALANCED SCORECARD APPROACH

The following is a summary of the major benefits that can be attributed to the balanced scorecard approach:

1 The approach improves communications within the organization and promotes the active formulation and implementation of organizational strategy by making it highly visible through the linkage of performance measures and targets to business unit strategy.

2 It links financial and non-financial measures by identifying those non-financial measures that are leading indicators of future financial performance.

3 The balanced scorecard limits the number of measures used by focusing on the most critical. It thus avoids a proliferation of measures by focusing management's attention on only those that are vital to the implementation of strategy.

The balanced scorecard has also been subject to frequent criticisms. It is argued that the cause-and-effect relationships are merely hypotheses, that they are too ambiguous and lack theoretical underpinning or empirical support.

An important element of the balanced scorecard in guiding strategic improvement is the recognition that an adequate amount of time must elapse between the implementation of a strategic initiative and the determination of whether the strategy has been successful in increasing financial lag measures (Atkinson, 2006). A second major criticism of the balanced scorecard is the absence of any time dimension. This presents a problem when there are differences in the timing of the effects of the various lead measures, resulting in the outcomes occurring at different points in time. It is therefore difficult to determine the extent to which a particular lead indicator has had an impact on a lag measure when other lead indicators, occurring at different points in time, are also impacting on the lag measures.

A number of researchers have commented on the absence of a time dimension in the balanced scorecard (Nørreklit, 2000; Bukh and Malmi, 2005; Franco-Santos and Bourne, 2005). For example, Nørreklit argued that the absence of an explicit time dimension as part of the scorecard makes it impossible to establish cause-and-effect relationships. Several studies also suggest that causal linkages between non-financial performance drivers and financial outcome measures were often neither specified nor well understood (Ittner and Larcker, 2003; Malmi, 2001). In a study of the use of balanced scorecards in Finnish companies, Malmi (2001) found that, despite interviewees' claims to the contrary, links between strategy and balanced scorecard measures were weak and causal linkages between multiple measures were difficult to explain.

Other criticisms relate to the omission of important perspectives, the most notable being the environmental/impact on society perspective (see Chapter 16) and an employee perspective. It should be noted, however, that Kaplan and Norton presented the four perspectives as a suggested framework rather than a constraining straitjacket. There is nothing to prevent companies adding additional perspectives to meet their own requirements but they must avoid the temptation of creating too many perspectives and performance measures since one of the major benefits of the balanced scorecard is its conciseness and clarity of presentation.

Our discussion relating to the core objectives and measures of the four perspectives has concentrated mainly on the manufacturing organizations. The balance scorecard, however, has been widely adopted in service organizations. Exhibit 14.6 provides an illustration of potential balanced scorecard performance measures for different types of service organizations. You will also find it appropriate at this point to refer to Exhibit 14.7 which summarizes surveys of practice relating to the usage of the balanced scorecard.

EXHIBIT 14.6   Potential scorecard measures in different business sectors

	Generic	Health care	Airlines	Banking
Financial strength (looking back)	Market share Revenue growth Operating profits Return on equity Stock market performance Growth in margin	Patient census Unit profitability Funds raised for capital improvements Cost per care Per cent of revenue – new programmes	Revenue/cost per available passenger mile Mix of freight Mix of full fare to discounted Average age of fleet Available seat miles and related yields	Outstanding loan balances Deposit balances Non-interest income
Customer service and satisfaction (looking from the outside in)	Customer satisfaction Customer retention Quality customer service Sales from new products/ services	Patient satisfaction survey Patient retention Patient referral rate Admittance or discharge timeliness Medical plan awareness	Lost bag reports per 10 000 passengers Denied boarding rate Flight cancellation rate Customer complaints filed with the DOT	Customer retention Number of new customers Number of products per customer Face time spent between loan officers and customers
Internal operating efficiency (looking from the inside out)	Delivery time Cost Process quality Error rates on shipments Supplier satisfaction	Weekly patient complaints Patient loads Breakthroughs in treatments and medicines Infection rates Readmission rate Length of stay	Load factors (percentage of seats occupied) Utilization factors on aircraft and personnel On-time performance	Sales calls to potential customers Thank you calls or cards to new and existing customers Cross selling statistics
Learning and growth (looking ahead)	Employee skill level Training availability Employee satisfaction Job retention Amount of overtime worked Amount of vacation time taken	Training hours per caregiver Number of peer reviewed papers published Number of grants awarded (NIH) Referring MDs Employee turnover rate	Employee absenteeism Worker safety statistics Performance appraisals completed Training programme hours per employee	Test results from training knowledge of product offerings, sales and service Employee satisfaction survey

(*Source*: Learby and Wenteel, 2002)

EXHIBIT 14.7 Surveys of practice relating to balanced scorecard usage

Surveys indicate that even though the balanced scorecard did not emerge until the early 1990s it is now widely used in many countries throughout the world. A Bain & Company survey by Rigby and Biolodeau (2013) of a broad range of international executives in 1 221 firms reported a 73 per cent predicted usage rate of the balanced scorecard in 2013. In the UK a survey of 163 manufacturing companies (annual sales turnover in excess of £50 million) by Zuriekat (2005) reported that 30 per cent had implemented the balanced scorecard. Other studies in mainland Europe indicate significant usage. Pere (1999) reported a 31 per cent usage rate of companies in Finland with a further 30 per cent in the process of implementing it. In Sweden Kald and Nilsson (2000) reported that 27 per cent of major Swedish companies have implemented the approach. Oliveras and Amat (2002) report widespread usage in Spain and Speckbacher *et al.* (2003) report a usage rate of 24 per cent in German-speaking countries (Germany, Austria and Switzerland). Major companies adopting the balanced scorecard include KPMG Peat Marwick, Allstate Insurance and AT&T (Chow *et al.*, 1997).

In terms of the perspectives used, Malmi (2001) conducted a study involving semi-structured interviews in 17 companies in Finland. He found that 15 companies used the four perspectives identified by Kaplan and Norton and two companies added a fifth – an employee's perspective. The UK study by Zuriekat (2005) reported that virtually all of the balanced scorecard respondents used the financial, customer and internal business process perspectives. Other perspectives used were learning and growth, employee, supplier and the environment. The respective percentage usage rates for the balance scorecard adopters were 39 per cent, 45 per cent, 65 per cent and 26 per cent. The study also reported that 35 per cent of the adopters linked their reward systems to the balanced scorecard. A study by Olve *et al.* (2000) found that 15–20 performance measures are customarily used.

REAL WORLD VIEWS 14.3

How ZYSCO uses the balanced scorecard (BSC)

An article by Chen *et al.* (2015) published in *Strategic Finance* described how Zhongyuan Special Steel Co. (ZYSCO), a typical Chinese state-owned company, introduced a new strategic management system that would integrate its value creation strategy into everyone's day-to-day job. The BSC was the core of this new system. The foundation for implementing a balanced scorecard (BSC) was ZYSCO's strategy map. The BSC task force first drew the strategy map shown in Figure 1. Next, the BSC was developed based on ZYSCO's strategy map. Figure 2 shows the BSC and indicates how the strategic objectives were translated into performance measures.

Since the steel industry in China had large overcapacity problems, the company downplayed revenue growth and production capacity as financial measures and focused on increasing net income by controlling costs and expenses. For the customer perspective, customer satisfaction rate is based on a customer survey, which includes evaluation of product quality, on-time delivery, after-sale service and so on.

ZYSCO's BSC was then decomposed by departments creating BSCs using the company's strategy map and BSC as a guide. The authors concluded that ZYSCO's compensation system should be linked to the new system and new measures.

Questions

1 Based on ZYSCO's BSC and strategy map, create a BSC for either the finance or sales departments.
2 What problems might arise with ZYSCO seeking to link its compensation system with its new system and measures?

Reference

Chen, Y., Lu, Z. and Lin., T.W. (2015) How ZYSCO uses the balanced scorecard, *Strategic Finance*. Available at http://sfmagazine.com/wp-content/uploads/sfarchive/2015/01/How-ZYSCO-Uses-the-Balanced-Scorecard.pdf

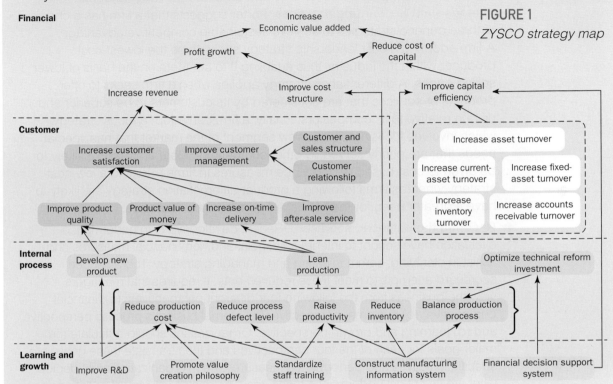

FIGURE 1
ZYSCO strategy map

FIGURE 2 *ZYSCO balanced scorecard*

KEY STRATEGIC OBJECTIVES	MEASURES	WEIGHT	TARGET
FINANCIAL PERSPECTIVE			
Increase revenue	Net income	18%	Budget
	Gross profit margin	10%	Budget
Improve cost structure	Costs and expenses	15%	Budget
Improve capital efficiency	Assets turnover	10%	Budget
CUSTOMER PERSPECTIVE			
Increase customer satisfaction	Customer satisfaction rate (based on customer survey)	6%	95%
Improve customer management	Customer retention rate	6%	100%
	Percentage of sales from high-profit products	5%	Budget
INTERNAL PROCESS PERSPECTIVE			
Develop new product	Number of new products	2%	As planned
Lean production	Implementation of lean production (evaluated by board)	5%	95%
	Manufacturing cost reduction	5%	Budget
	Capacity balance	5%	As planned
Optimize technical reform investment	Return on technical reform investment	5%	Budget
LEARNING AND GROWTH PERSPECTIVE			
Improve R&D	Number of new patents	1%	As planned
Promote value creation philosophy	Promotion of value creation (evaluated by board)	1%	95%
Standardize staff training	Training evaluation (evaluated by board)	2%	95%
Manufacture information integration system	System coverage (evaluated by board)	2%	80%
Financial decision support system	Financial decision support (evaluated by board)	2%	90%

SUMMARY

The following items relate to the learning objectives listed at the beginning of the chapter.

- **Describe three competitive strategies that a firm can adopt to achieve sustainable competitive advantage and explain how they influence management accounting practices.** Porter suggests that a firm has a choice of three generic strategies to achieve sustainable competitive advantage. A firm adopting a cost leadership strategy seeks to be the lowest-cost producer within the industry, thus enabling it to compete on the basis of lower selling prices. A differentiation strategy applies when a firm seeks to offer products or services that are considered by its customers to be superior and unique relative to its competitors. Finally, a firm can adopt a focus strategy, which involves focusing on a narrow segment of the market that has special needs that are poorly served by other competitors. More emphasis is likely to be given to cost-based performance measures in firms pursuing a low-cost strategy whereas firms following a product differentiation strategy are likely to have a greater need for market-based performance measures.

- **Describe the balanced scorecard.** Recent developments in performance evaluation have sought to integrate financial and non-financial measures and assist in clarifying, communicating and managing strategy. The balanced scorecard attempts to meet these requirements. It requires that managers view the business from the following four different perspectives: (a) financial perspective; (b) customer perspective; (c) internal business process perspective and (d) learning and growth perspective. Organizations should articulate the major goals for each of the four perspectives and then translate these goals into specific initiatives and performance measures. Each organization must decide what are its critical performance measures. The choice will vary over time and should be linked to the strategies that the organization is following.

- **Explain each of the four perspectives of the balanced scorecard.** The financial perspective provides objectives and associated performance measures relating to the financial outcomes of past actions. Thus, it provides feedback on the success of pursuing the objectives identified for the other three perspectives. In the customer perspective objectives, performance measures and initiatives should be established that track a business unit's ability to create satisfied and loyal customers. They relate to market share, customer retention, new customer acquisition, customer satisfaction and customer profitability. In the internal business perspective, managers identify the critical internal processes for which the organization must excel in implementing its strategy. The principal internal business processes include the innovation processes, operation processes and post-service sales processes. The final perspective on the balanced scorecard identifies the infrastructure that the business must build to create long-term growth and improvement.

The following three categories have been identified as falling within this perspective: employee capabilities, information system capabilities and motivation, empowerment and alignment.

● **Provide illustrations of performance measures for each of the four perspectives**. Within the financial perspective examples include economic value added and residual income. Market share and customer satisfaction ratings are generic measures within the customer perspective. Typical internal business perspective measures include percentage of sales from new products (innovation processes), cycle time measures such as manufacturing cycle efficiency (operation processes) and percentage returns from customers (post-service sales processes). Measures of employee satisfaction represent generic measures within the learning and growth perspective.

● **Explain how the balanced scorecard links strategy formulation to financial outcomes**. The balanced scorecard philosophy translates an organization's vision and strategy into operational objectives, initiatives and performance measures for each of the four perspectives. Each performance measure is part of a cause-and-effect relationship involving a linkage from strategy formulation to financial outcomes. Measures of organizational learning and growth are assumed to be the drivers of the internal business processes. The measures of these processes are in turn assumed to be the drivers of measures of customer perspective, while these measures are the drivers of the financial perspective. Measurements relating to the non-financial perspectives are assumed to be predictors of future financial performance.

● **Distinguish between lead and lag measures**. Lag measures are outcome measures that mostly fall within the financial perspective and are the results of past actions. Lag measures generally do not incorporate the effect of decisions when they are made. Instead, they show the impact of the decisions as their impact materializes and this can be long after the decisions were made. Lead measures are generally non-financial measures that are the drivers of future financial performance.

● **Outline the benefits and criticisms of the balanced scorecard**. A major benefit of the balanced scorecard is that it assists in communicating and implementing strategy throughout the organization by translating strategy into a coherent and linked set of understandable and measurable targets and performance. Criticisms relate to the cause-and-effect relationship and the absence of a time dimension. It is argued that the cause-and-effect relationships are merely hypotheses, that they are too ambiguous and lack a theoretical underpinning or empirical support. The time dimension presents a problem when there are differences in the timing of the effects of the various lead measures, resulting in the outcomes occurring at different points in time. It is therefore difficult to determine the extent to which a particular lead indicator has had an impact on a lag measure.

KEY TERMS AND CONCEPTS

Balanced scorecard A strategic management tool that integrates financial and non-financial measures of performance in a single concise report, with the aim of incorporating performance management within the strategic management process.

Cost leadership strategy A strategy adopted by an organization that aims to be the lowest cost producer within a market segment thus enabling it to compete on the basis of lower selling prices than its competitors.

Customer perspective One of the perspectives considered on the balanced scorecard, focusing on how the organization appears to its customers.

Customer value propositions The attributes that drive core objectives and measures relating to the customer perspective of an organization.

Defender strategy Firms pursuing a defender strategy perceive a great deal of stability in their external environment. They compete on product price, quality and customer service rather than innovation and product and market development.

Differentiation strategy A strategy adopted by an organization that seeks to offer products or services that are considered by its customers to be superior or unique relative to its competitors.

Financial perspective One of the perspectives considered on the balanced scorecard, focusing on how the organization looks to shareholders.

Focusing strategy A strategy which involves seeking competitive advantage by focusing on a narrow segment of the market that has

special needs that are poorly served by other competitors in the industry. Competitive advantage is based on adopting either a cost leadership or product/service differentiation strategy within the chosen segment.

Internal business perspective One of the perspectives considered on the balanced scorecard, focusing on what the organization needs to excel at.

Lag measures Outcome measures that mostly fall within the financial perspective and are the results of past actions

Lead measures Non-financial measures that are the drivers of future financial performance.

Learning and growth perspective One of the perspectives considered on the balanced scorecard, focusing on how the organization can continue to improve and create value.

Manufacturing cycle efficiency (MCE) A measure of cycle time that is calculated by dividing processing time by processing time plus the non-value-added activities of inspection time, wait time and move time.

Production efficiency ratio A process efficiency measure calculated by dividing the standard hours of output by the actual hours of input.

Prospector strategy Firms pursuing a prospector strategy perceive high uncertainty in their environment and are continually searching for new market opportunities. They compete through new product innovations and market development.

Strategic positioning The choice of strategies an organization uses to achieve sustainable competitive advantage.

ASSESSMENT MATERIAL

The review questions are short questions that enable you to assess your understanding of the main topics included in the chapter. The page numbers in parentheses provide you with the page numbers to refer to if you cannot answer a specific question.

The review problems are more complex and require you to relate and apply the content to various business problems. Solutions to review problems are provided in a separate section at the end of the book. Additional review problems can be accessed by lecturers and students on the dedicated online support resources for this book. Solutions to these review problems are provided for lecturers in the *Instructor's Manual* accompanying this book that can be downloaded from the dedicated online instructor's resources (see Preface for details).

The dedicated online digital support resources for this book also includes over 30 case study problems.

REVIEW QUESTIONS

14.1 How do different competitive strategies influence the emphasis that is given to particular management accounting techniques? *(p. 358)*

14.2 What is the purpose of a balanced scorecard? *(pp. 361–362)*

14.3 Describe the four perspectives of the balanced scorecard. *(pp. 362–368)*

14.4 Explain the differences between lag measures and lead measures. *(p. 368)*

14.5 Explain what is meant by cause-and-effect relationships within the balanced scorecard. *(pp. 368–369)*

14.6 Discuss the benefits and limitations of the balanced scorecard. *(pp. 372–373)*

14.7 Identify and describe the core objectives of the customer perspective. *(pp. 364–365)*

14.8 Describe the three principal internal business processes that can be included within the internal business perspective. *(pp. 365–367)*

14.9 What is manufacturing cycle efficiency? *(p. 366)*

14.10 Describe three principal categories within the learning and growth perspective. *(pp. 367–368)*

14.11 Provide examples of performance measures within each of the four perspectives of the balanced scorecard. *(pp. 362–368)*

REVIEW PROBLEMS

14.12 ZY is an airline operator. It is implementing a balanced scorecard to measure the success of its strategy to expand its operations. It has identified two perspectives and two associated objectives. They are:

Perspective	Objective
Growth	Fly to new destinations
Internal capabilities	Reduce time between touch down and takeoff

(i) For the 'growth perspective' of ZY, recommend a performance measure and briefly justify your choice of the measure by explaining how it will reflect the success of the strategy.

(2 marks)

(ii) For the 'internal capabilities perspective' of ZY, state data that you would gather and explain how this could be used to ensure the objective is met.

(2 marks)

14.13 Balanced scorecard
Squarize is a large company which, for many years, operated solely as a pay-tv broadcaster. However, five years ago, it started product bundling, offering broadband and telephone services to its pay-tv customers. Customers taking up the offer were then known in the business as 'bundle customers' and they had to take up both the broadband and telephone services together with the pay-tv service. Other customers were still able to subscribe to pay-tv alone but not to broadband and telephone services without the pay-tv service.

All contracts to customers of Squarize are for a minimum three-month period. The pay-tv box is sold to the customer at the beginning of the contract; however, the broadband and telephone equipment is only rented to them.

In the first few years after product bundling was introduced, the company saw a steady increase in profits. Then, Squarize saw its revenues and operating profits fall. Consequently, staff bonuses were not paid, and staff became dissatisfied. Several reasons were identified for the deterioration of results:

1   In the economy as a whole, discretionary spending had been severely hit by rising unemployment and inflation. In a bid to save cash, many pay-tv customers were cancelling their contracts after the minimum three-month period as they were then able to still keep the pay-tv box. The box comes with a number of free channels, which the customer can still continue to receive free of charge, even after the cancellation of their contract.

2   The company's customer service call centre, which is situated in another country, had been the cause of lots of complaints from customers about poor service, and, in particular, the number of calls it sometimes took to resolve an issue.

3   Some bundle customers found that the broadband service that they had subscribed to did not work. As a result, they were immediately cancelling their contracts for all services within the 14-day cancellation period permitted under the contracts.

In a response to the above problems and in an attempt to increase revenues and profits, Squarize made the following changes to the business:

1 It made a strategic decision to withdraw the pay-tv-broadband-telephone package from the market and, instead, offer each service as a standalone product.
2 It guaranteed not to increase prices for a 12-month period for each of its three services.
3 It transferred its call centre back to its home country and increased the level of staff training given for call centre workers.
4 It investigated and resolved the problem with customers' broadband service.

It is now one year since the changes were made and the finance director wants to use a balanced scorecard to assess the extent to which the changes have been successful in improving the performance of the business.

Required:

(a) For each perspective of the balanced scorecard, identify two goals (objectives) together with a corresponding performance measure for each goal which could be used by the company to assess whether the changes have been successful. Justify the use of each of the performance measures that you choose.

(16 marks)

(b) Discuss how the company could reduce the problem of customers terminating their pay-tv service after only three months.

(4 marks)

14.14 Balanced scorecard

Pharmaceutical Technologies Co. (PT) is a developer and manufacturer of medical drugs in Beeland. It is one of the 100 largest listed companies on the national stock exchange. The company focuses on buying prospective drugs that have shown initial promise in testing from small bio-engineering companies. PT then leads these through three regulatory stages to launch in the general medical market. The three stages are:

1 to confirm the safety of the drug (does it harm humans?), in small scale trials;
2 to test the efficacy of the product (does it help cure?), again in small scale trials; and
3 finally, large scale trials to definitively decide on the safety and efficacy of the product.

The drugs are then marketed through the company's large sales force to health care providers and end users (patients). The health care providers are paid by either health insurance companies or the national government dependent on the financial status of the patient.

The Beeland Drug Regulator (BDR) oversees this testing process and makes the final judgement about whether a product can be sold in the country.

Its objectives are to protect, promote and improve public health by ensuring that:

● medicines have an acceptable balance of benefit and risk
● the users of these medicines understand this risk-benefit profile; and
● new beneficial product development is encouraged.

The regulator is governed by a board of trustees appointed by the government. It is funded directly by the government and also through fees charged to drug companies when granting licences to sell their products in Beeland.

PT has used share price and earnings per share as its principal measures of performance to date. However, the share price has underperformed the market and the health sector in the last two years. The chief executive officer (CEO) has identified that these measures are too narrow and is considering implementing a balanced scorecard approach to address this problem.

A working group has drawn up a suggested balanced scorecard. It began by identifying the objectives from the board's medium term strategy:

● Create shareholder value by bringing commercially viable drugs to market.
● Improve the efficiency of drug development.
● Increase shareholder value by innovation in the drug approval process.

The working group then considered the stakeholder perspectives:

● Shareholders want a competitive return on their investment.
● Purchasers (governments, insurers and patients) want to pay a reasonable price for the drugs.
● Regulators want an efficient process for the validation of drugs.
● Doctors want safe and effective drug products.
● Patients want to be cured.

Finally, this leads to the proposed scorecard of performance measures:

● Financial – share price and earnings per share.
● Customer – number of patients using PT products.
● Internal business process – exceed industry-standard on design and testing; time to regulatory approval of a product.
● Learning and growth – training days undertaken by staff; time to market of new product; percentage of drugs bought by PT that gain final approval.

The balanced scorecard now needs to be reviewed to ensure that it will address the company's objectives and the issues that it faces in its business environment.

Required:

(a) Describe how the implementation of a balanced scorecard delivers a range of performance measures aligned with the corporate strategy

(4 marks)

(b) Evaluate the performance measures proposed for PT's balanced scorecard.

(10 marks)

(c) Identify and analyse the influence of four different external stakeholders on the regulator (BD).

(6 marks)

(d) Using your answer from part (c), describe how the application of the balanced scorecard approach at BDR would differ from the approach within PT.

(7 marks)

14.15 Balanced scorecard (customer perspective) and the reward management system.

Victoria-Yeeland Logistics (Victoria) is a logistics support business, which operates a fleet of lorries to deliver packages of goods on behalf of its customers within the country of Yeeland. Victoria collects packages from its customers' manufacturing sites or from the customers' port of importation and delivers to the final user of the goods. The lorries are run and maintained from a set of depots spread throughout Yeeland.

The overall objective of Victoria is to maximize shareholder wealth. The delivery business in Yeeland is dominated by two international companies and one other domestic business and profit margins are extremely tight. The market is saturated by these large operators and a number of smaller operators. The cost base of Victoria is dominated by staff and fuel, with fuel prices being highly volatile in the last few years.

In order to improve performance measurement and management at Victoria, the chief financial officer (CFO) plans to use the balanced scorecard (BSC). However, she has been pulled away from this project in order to deal with an issue with refinancing the business' principal lending facility. The CFO has already identified some suitable metrics but needs you, as her assistant, to complete her work and address any potential questions which might arise when she makes her presentation on the BSC to the board. The CFO has completed the identification of metrics for three of the perspectives (Appendix 1) but has yet to complete the work on the metrics for the customer perspective. This should be done using the data given in Appendix 2.

Additionally, two issues have arisen in the reward management system at Victoria, one in relation to senior management and the other for operational managers. Currently, senior management gets a fixed salary supplemented by an annual bonus awarded by the board. Shareholders have been complaining that these bonuses are not suitable. The operational managers also get bonuses based on their performance as assessed by their management superiors. The operational managers are unhappy with the system. In order to address this, it has been suggested that they should be involved in bonus target setting as otherwise there is a sense of demotivation from such a system. The CFO wants an evaluation of this system of rewards in light of the introduction of the BSC and best practice.

Required:

(a) Discuss how Victoria's success in the customer perspective may impact on the metrics given in the financial perspective.

(5 marks)

(b) Recommend, with justification, and calculate a suitable performance metric for each customer perspective success factor. Comment on the problems of using customer complaints to measure whether packages are delivered safely and on time.

(11 marks)

(c) Advise Victoria on the reward management issues outlined by the CFO.

(9 marks)

Appendix 1

Financial perspective
(How do we appear to our shareholders?)
Return on capital employed
Profit margin
Revenue growth

Customer perspective
(How do we appear to our customers?)
Success factors:
Ability to meet customers' transport needs
Ability to deliver packages quickly
Ability to deliver packages on time
Ability to deliver packages safely

Internal process perspective
(What business processes must excel?)
Time taken to load and unload
Lorry capacity utilization

Learning and growth perspective
(How do we sustain and improve our ability to grow?)
Leadership competence (qualitative judgement)
Training days per employee

Appendix 2

The process: A customer makes a transport request for a package to be collected and delivered to a given destination. The customer is supplied with a time window in which the delivery will occur. Packages are then loaded onto lorries and delivered according to a route specified by the depot's routing manager.

Total number of customer transport requests	610 000
Total number of packages transported	548 000
Total number of lorry journeys	73 000
Total package kilometres	65 760 000
Total package minutes	131 520 000
Number of delivery complaints from customers:	
from damaged packages	8 220
from late delivery (outside agreed time window)	21 920

Notes:

1 All figures are for the last financial year.
2 A package kilometre is defined as a kilometre travelled by one package.
3 A package minute is defined as a minute spent in transit by one package.

14.16 Balanced scorecard and problems with interpreting performance measures.

Soup operates passenger rail services in Deeland, a technologically advanced country, with high demand for fast reliable rail travel from business and leisure passengers. Many passengers choose train travel because they see it as less harmful to the environment than other forms of transport.

Soup's main objective is to maximize shareholder wealth. Since becoming licensed to operate routes in Regions A and B by the Deeland government five years ago, Soup has consistently delivered increased dividends and share prices for investors. In its initial appraisal of the licensing opportunity, Soup expected to operate the routes for at least 15 years, however, their licence may not be renewed when it expires in three years' time. The government has warned Soup it 'is unhappy about high returns to shareholders while there are many reports of poor passenger service, overcrowded trains and unreliable services on certain routes and at busy times'.

Soup owns its fleet of diesel powered trains. Each train in Region A has seven coaches with 70 passenger seats available per coach. In the less busy Region B, each train has six coaches each with 70 seats. As a condition of the licence, Soup runs a set number of services at both busy and quieter times in both regions. Soup has two larger rivals, both operating electric trains, which cause less harm to the environment than diesel powered trains. They run on the same routes in both regions.

The government regulates fares charged to passengers, which are the same per distance travelled for every operator in that region. The railway track, stations and other infrastructure are managed by the government which charges the operators a fee. There are several stations along the route which are only used by Soup trains and others where Soup trains do not stop at all.

Soup's trains are 25 years old, originally purchased cheaply from an operator whose licence was withdrawn by the government. Soup believes the low price it paid is a key competitive advantage enabling them to steadily increase their return on capital employed, the company's main performance measure, to a level well in excess of their rivals. The shareholders are pleased with the growth in passenger numbers over the last five years, which is the other performance measure Soup uses.

Soup's ageing trains spend increasing time undergoing preventative maintenance, safety checks or repairs. A recent television documentary also showed apparently poor conditions on board, such as defective heating and washroom facilities and dirty, torn seating. Passengers complained in the programme of difficulties finding a seat, the unreliability of accessing wireless internet services and even that the menu in the on-board cafe had not changed for five years.

Soup's CEO responded that unreliable internet access arose from the rapid growth in passengers expecting to access the internet on trains. She said Soup had never received any formal complaints about the lack of choice in the on-board cafe, nor had she heard of a recent press report that Soup's trains were badly maintained, so causing harm to the environment.

The CEO has asked you, as chief management accountant, for your advice. 'In view of the government's warning, we must develop performance measures balancing the needs of passengers with the requirements of the shareholders', she has said. 'I don't want to know how to improve the actual performance of the business; that is the job of the operational managers, nor do I just want a list of suggested performance measures. Instead I need to know why these performance measures will help to improve the performance of Soup.'

The following data applies to Soup:

	Region A	Region B
Number of services per day		
Peak times	4	4
Other times	6	8
Number of passengers per day		
Peak times	2 500	1 400
Other times	2 450	1 850

Required:

(a) Advise the CEO on how the use of the balanced scorecard could improve the performance management system of Soup.

(10 marks)

(b) Using the performance data given, evaluate the comments of the Deeland government that Soup's trains are overcrowded.

(7 marks)

(c) Assess the problems Soup may encounter in selecting and interpreting performance measures when applying the balanced scorecard to its performance management system.

(8 marks)

14.17 Financial and non-financial performance measurement in a service organization

The owners of The Eatwell Restaurant have diversified business interests and operate in a wide range of commercial areas. Since buying the restaurant they have carefully recorded the data below.

Recorded data for The Eatwell Restaurant 2016–2019

	2016	2017	2018	2019
Total meals served	3 750	5 100	6 200	6 700
Regular customers attending weekly	5	11	15	26
Number of items on offer per day	4	4	7	9
Reported cases of food poisoning	4	5	7	7
Special theme evenings introduced	0	3	9	13
Annual operating hours with no customers	380	307	187	126
Proposals submitted to cater for special events	10	17	29	38
Contracts won to cater for special events	2	5	15	25
Complimentary letters from satisfied customers	0	4	3	6
Average number of customers at peak times	18	23	37	39
Average service delay at peak time (mins)	32	47	15	35
Maximum seating capacity	25	25	40	40
Weekly opening hours	36	36	40	36
Written complaints received	8	12	14	14
Idle time	570	540	465	187
New meals introduced during the year	16	8	27	11
Financial data	€	€	€	€
Average customer spend on wine	3	4	4	7
Total turnover	83 000	124 500	137 000	185 000
Turnover from special events	2 000	13 000	25 000	55 000
Profit	11 600	21 400	43 700	57 200
Value of food wasted in preparation	1 700	1 900	3 600	1 450
Total turnover of all restaurants in locality	895 000	1 234 000	980 000	1 056 000

Required:

(a) Assess the overall performance of the business and submit your comments to the owners. They wish to compare the performance of the restaurant with their other business interests and require your comments to be grouped into the key areas of performance such as those described by Fitzgerald and Moon (see Learning Note 14.1).

(14 marks)

(b) Identify any additional information that you would consider of assistance in assessing the performance of The Eatwell Restaurant in comparison with another restaurant. Give reasons for your selection and explain how they would relate to the key performance area categories used in (a).

(6 marks)

(Total 20 marks)

14.18 Performance measurement in non-profit organizations

(a) The absence of the profit measure in not-for-profit (NFP) organizations causes problems for the measurement of their efficiency and effectiveness.

You are required to explain:

(i) why the absence of the profit measure should be a cause of the problems referred to;

(9 marks)

(ii) how these problems extend to activities within business entities that have a profit motive. Support your answer with examples.

(4 marks)

(b) A public health clinic is the subject of a scheme to measure its efficiency and effectiveness. Among a number of factors, the 'quality of care provided' has been included as an aspect of the clinic's service to be measured. Three features of 'quality of care provided' have been listed:

- clinic's adherence to appointment times;
- patients' ability to contact the clinic and make appointments without difficulty;
- the provision of a comprehensive patient health monitoring programme.

You are required to:

(i) suggest a set of quantitative measures that can be used to identify the effective level of achievement of each of the features listed;

(9 marks)

(ii) indicate how these measures could be combined into a single 'quality of care' measure.

(3 marks)

(Total 25 marks)

15
STRATEGIC COST MANAGEMENT AND VALUE CREATION

In Chapters 9–11 the major features of traditional management accounting control systems and the mechanisms that can be used to control costs were described. The focus was on comparing actual results against a pre-set standard (typically the budget), identifying and analysing variances and taking remedial action to ensure that future outcomes conform with budgeted outcomes. Traditional cost control systems tend to be based on the preservation of the *status quo* and the ways of performing existing activities are not reviewed. The emphasis is on cost containment rather than cost reduction.

Strategic cost management and value creation seeks to have a more profound effect on reducing an organization's costs and to provide a competitive advantage. It aims to provide a competitive advantage by creating better or equivalent customer satisfaction at a lower cost than that offered by competitors. In particular, strategic cost management is a future oriented approach that focuses on cost reduction, continuous improvement and changes in the ways that activities and processes are performed, rather than just focusing on cost containment. Indeed, the term cost reduction could be used instead of cost management, but the former is an emotive term. Therefore cost management is preferred. Whereas traditional cost control systems are routinely applied on a continuous basis, cost management tends to be applied on an *ad hoc* basis when an opportunity for cost reduction is identified. Also, many of the approaches that are incorporated within the area of cost management do not necessarily involve the use of accounting techniques. In contrast, cost control relies heavily on accounting techniques.

Strategic cost management consists of those actions that are taken by managers to reduce costs, some of which are prioritized on the basis of information extracted from the accounting system. Other actions, however, are undertaken without the use of accounting information. They involve process improvements, where an opportunity has been identified to perform processes more effectively and efficiently, and which have obvious cost reduction outcomes and also the potential to increase customer customer satisfaction. It is important that you are aware of all the approaches that can be used to reduce costs even if these methods do not rely mainly on accounting information. You should also note that although cost management seeks to reduce costs, it should not be at the expense of customer satisfaction. Ideally, the aim is to take actions that will both reduce costs and enhance customer satisfaction.

Ideally, cost management should also incorporate value creation, where the aims should be not only to take actions that will reduce costs but also to enhance customer satisfaction and value. Customer value may be increased by either reducing the cost without sacrificing product/service functionality or by increasing functionality without increasing cost. Reducing cost is important because it enables a company to remain competitive by reducing or maintaining selling prices and thus increasing customer satisfaction and value. Increasing customer satisfaction is generally associated with an increase in sales revenues and profits which should ultimately be reflected in creating additional shareholder value.

LIFE-CYCLE COST MANAGEMENT

Identifying the costs incurred during the different stages of a product's life cycle provides an insight into understanding and managing the total costs incurred throughout its life cycle. In particular, **life-cycle cost management** enables management to understand the cost consequences of developing and making a product and to identify areas in which cost reduction efforts are likely to be most effective.

Figure 15.1 illustrates a typical pattern of cost commitment and cost incurrence during the three stages of a product's life cycle – the planning and design stage, the manufacturing stage and the service and abandonment stage. **Committed** or **locked-in costs** are those costs that have not been incurred but that will be incurred in the future on the basis of decisions that have already been made. At this stage costs become committed and broadly determine the future costs that will be incurred during the manufacturing stage. You will see from Figure 15.1 that approximately 80 per cent of a product's costs are committed during the planning and design stage. At this stage product designers determine the product's design and the production process. In contrast, the majority of costs are incurred at the manufacturing stage, but they have already become locked in at the planning and design stage and are difficult to alter. During the service and abandonment stage further

FIGURE 15.1

Product life-cycle phase relationship between costs committed and costs incurred

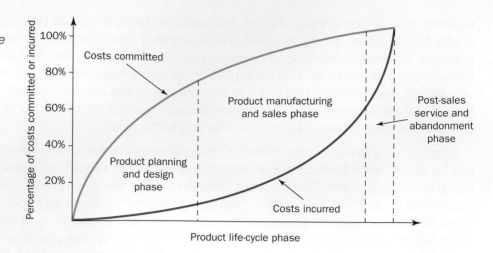

costs are incurred relating to customer support and the need for a company to discharge its environmental and sustainability responsibilities. For example, Microsoft has provided support for its Windows operating systems after the sales have ceased and mining companies have to rehabilitate the damage they have done to the environment after mining has ceased. Many of these costs also become committed at the planning and design stage.

It is apparent from Figure 15.1 that cost management can be most effectively exercised during the planning and design stage and not at the manufacturing and service and abandonment stages when the product design and processes have already been determined and costs have been committed. At this latter stage the focus is more on cost containment than cost management. An understanding of life-cycle costs and how they are committed and incurred at different stages throughout a product's life cycle led to the emergence of **target costing**, a technique that focuses on managing costs during a product's planning and design phase.

TARGET COSTING

In Chapter 5 we briefly looked at target costing as a mechanism for determining selling prices. We shall now consider how target costing can also be used as a cost management tool. Target costing originated in Japan in the early 1970s. It was mainly developed by the Japanese auto industry, particularly Toyota. Target costing involves the following stages:

Stage 1: Determine the target price which customers will be prepared to pay for the product.

Stage 2: Deduct a target profit margin from the target price to determine the target cost.

Stage 3: Estimate the actual cost of the product.

Stage 4: If estimated actual cost exceeds the target cost investigate ways of driving down the actual cost to the target cost.

The first stage requires market research to determine *the customers' perceived value* of the product, based on its functions and its attributes (i.e. its functionality), its differentiation value relative to competing products and the price of competing products. This process results in the determination of a target selling price. A target profit is deducted from the target selling price to give the target cost. The target cost is compared with the predicted actual cost. If the predicted actual cost is above the target cost intensive efforts are made to close the gap so that the predicted cost equals the target cost. Instead of designing the product and determining how much it costs, target costing reverses the procedure and determines the target cost for a product. Steps are taken to design a product that does not exceed the target cost. A major feature of target costing is that a team approach is adopted to achieve the target cost. For example the team members may include designers, engineers, purchasing, manufacturing, marketing and management accounting personnel and sometimes representatives from suppliers.

The major advantage of adopting target costing is that it is deployed during a product's design and planning stage so that it can have a maximum impact in determining the level of the locked-in costs. It is an iterative process with the design team, which ideally should result in the design team continuing with its product and process design attempts until it finds designs that give an expected cost that is equal or less than the target cost. If the target cost cannot be attained then the product should not be launched. Design teams should not be allowed to achieve target costs by eliminating desirable product functions. Thus, the aim is to design a product with an expected cost that does not exceed target cost and that also meets the target level of functionality. Design teams use reverse engineering, value analysis and process improvements to achieve the target cost.

Reverse engineering

Reverse engineering (also known as **tear down analysis**) involves examining a competitor's product in order to identify opportunities for product improvement and/or cost reduction. The competitor's product is dismantled to identify its functionality and design and to provide insights about the processes that are used and the cost to make the product. The aim is to benchmark provisional product designs with the designs of competitors and to incorporate any observed relative advantages of the competitor's approach to product design.

Value analysis

Value analysis (also known as **value engineering**) is a systematic interdisciplinary examination of factors affecting the cost of a product or service in order to devise a means of achieving the specified purpose at the required standard of quality and reliability at the target cost. The aim of value analysis is to achieve the assigned target cost by (i) identifying improved product designs that reduce the product's cost without sacrificing functionality and/or (ii) eliminating unnecessary functions that increase the product's costs and for which customers are not prepared to pay extra.

Value analysis requires the use of **functional analysis**. This process involves decomposing the product into its many elements or attributes. For example, in the case of automobiles, functions might consist of style, comfort, operability, reliability, quality, attractiveness and many others (Kato, 1993). A price, or value, for each element is determined which reflects the amount the customer is prepared to pay. To obtain this information companies normally conduct surveys and interviews with customers. The cost of each function of a product is compared with the benefits perceived by the customers.

REAL WORLD
VIEWS 15.1

EVA target costing

Taylor, Woods and Cheng Ge Fang, reported on how one UK company moved its target costing system away from profit targets and focused it on product-level economic-value added (EVA) targets. The company, which used the pseudonym Electronics for confidentiality purposes, had been using target costing since the 1990s. Electronics deducted a target EVA instead of a target profit from the selling price to determine a target cost thus ensuring that the cost of capital is considered in cost-savings programmes. The incorporation of EVA-based targets into target costing may require a larger reduction in product cost than required under traditional accounting-based profit metrics. At Electronics the reduction needed to meet EVA targets was 46 per cent. The expected selling price under EVA target costing did not change and was still determined by customer value so the change did not affect the firm's focus on customers.

Closing the gap between current and target cost involves evaluating the impact of reducing and substituting product components as well as changing assembly methods. The use of EVA extended the range of cost-reduction opportunities to include capital costs. Alternatives that required more capital were evaluated carefully in order to assess their impact on EVA. At Electronics, EVA-based measures changed how people behaved by, for example, motivating engineers to seek ways of reducing the capital base, since such savings enabled the target EVA to be achieved. Thus more attention was focused on capital costs.

Questions

1 What practical difficulties might arise from determining the target cost using EVA target costing?
2 Does the use of conventional (non-EVA) target costing mean that the cost of capital is ignored?

Reference

Taylor, G., Woods, M. and Cheng Ge Fang (2014) Electronics: A case study of economic value added in target costing, *Financial Management*, April, 55–6.

If the cost of the function exceeds the benefit to the customer, then the function should be either eliminated, modified to reduce its cost, or enhanced in terms of its perceived value so that its value exceeds the cost. Also by focusing on the product's functions, the design team will often consider components that perform the same function in other products, thus increasing the possibility of using standard components and reducing costs. It should be noted that the focus is on value to the customer rather than just cost reduction. Therefore value may be increased by either reducing the cost without sacrificing functionality or by increasing functionality without increasing cost.

Process improvements

Both reverse engineering and value analysis focus on product design to achieve cost reductions. The business processes that will be used to produce and market the product are also potential sources of cost reduction. Therefore, it is important that processes within the entire value chain (a description of value chain analysis is provided later in the chapter) are intensively studied with a view to increasing their efficiency in order to achieve the needed cost reductions.

Surveys of practice

Given that target costing was developed in Japan it is not surprising that the survey evidence suggests greater usage in Japan. A study of Tani et al. (1994) reported that 61 per cent of their sample of 180 listed Japanese manufacturing firms used some form of target costing. In the USA, Ernst & Young and The Institute of Management Accountants (IMA) (2003) reported that 26% of IMA member firms employed target costing. A survey by Dekker and Smidt (2003) of Dutch firms listed at the Amsterdam stock exchange on the adoption and use of practices that resemble the Japanese target costing concept reported that 19 out of 32 manufacturing firms claimed to use these practices, although they used different names for them. In Sweden a study by Ax *et al* (2008) reported a 25 per cent usage rate. In a comparative study of the implementation of target costing in UK, Australian and New Zealand companies Yazdifar and Askarany (2012) reported similar adoption rates for each country with approximately 18 per cent of companies adopting target costing.

In a review of the literature on the development of target costing Burrows and Chenhall (2012) point out that the target costing literature has focused on manufacturing organizations and is best suited to new products that are marketed in competitive environments having short product life cycles. However, the study by Yazdifar and Askarany (2012) reported similar usage of target costing by manufacturing and service organizations. In contrast, the survey by Dekker and Smidt (2003) reported that none of the eleven responding non-manufacturing organizations used target costing. However, they do not rule out the possibility that these organizations may have had difficulty relating the target costing definition in the survey to their situation, and that different but related methods might be used in these industries in product and service development.

An illustration of target costing

Example 15.1 is used to illustrate the target costing process. You will note from reading the information presented in this example that the projected cost of the product is €700 compared with a target cost of €560. To achieve the target cost the company establishes a project team to undertake an intense target costing exercise. Example 15.1 indicates that the end result of the target costing exercise is a projected cost of €555 which is marginally below the target cost of €560. Let us now look at how the company has achieved the target cost and also how the costs shown in Example 15.1 have been derived.

In response to the need to reduce the projected cost the project team starts by purchasing similar types of camcorders from its main competitors and undertaking reverse engineering. This process involves dismantling the camcorders to provide insights into potential design improvements for the new camcorder that will be launched. Reverse engineering is undertaken with the project team working closely with the design engineers. Their objective is to identify new designs that will accomplish the same functions at a lower cost and also to eliminate any functions that are deemed to be unnecessary. This process results in a simplified design, the reduction in the number of parts and the replacement of some customized parts with standard parts. The outcome of the reverse engineering and value analysis activities is a significant reduction in the projected direct

EXAMPLE 15.1

The Digital Electronics Company manufactures cameras and video equipment. It is in the process of introducing a 'top of the range' combined camcorder and camera that incorporates today's most advanced technologies. The company has undertaken market research to ascertain the customers' perceived value of the product, based on its special features and a comparison with competitors' products. The results of the survey, and a comparison of the new camcorder with competitors' products and market prices, have been used to establish a target selling price and projected lifetime volume. In addition, cost estimates have been prepared based on the proposed product specification. The company has set a target profit margin of 30 per cent on the proposed selling price and this has been deducted from the target selling price to determine the target cost. The following is a summary of the information that has been presented to management:

Projected lifetime sales volume	300 000 units
Target selling price	€800
Target profit margin (30% of selling price)	€240
Target cost (€800 – €240)	€560
Projected cost	€700

The excess of the projected cost over the target cost results in an intensive target costing exercise. After completing the target costing exercise the projected cost is £555 which is marginally below the target cost of €560. The analysis of the projected cost before and after the target costing exercise is as follows:

	Before		After	
	(€)	(€)	(€)	(€)
Manufacturing cost				
Direct material (bought in-parts)	390		325	
Direct labour	100		80	
Direct machining costs	20		20	
Ordering and receiving	8		2	
Quality assurance	60		50	
Rework	15		6	
Engineering and design	10	603	8	491
Non-manufacturing costs				
Marketing	40		25	
Distribution	30		20	
After-sales service and warranty costs	27	97	19	64
Total cost		700		555

materials, labour and rework costs, but the revised cost estimates still indicate that the projected cost exceeds the target cost.

Next the team engages in value analysis. They identify the different elements, functions and attributes of the camcorder and potential customers are interviewed to ascertain the values that they place on each of the functions. This process indicates that several functions that have been included in the prototype are not valued by customers. The team therefore decide to eliminate these functions. The value analysis results in further cost reductions being made, principally in the areas of materials and direct labour assembly costs but the revised cost estimates still indicate that the target cost has not been attained.

The team now turn their attention to redesigning the production and support processes. They decide to redesign the ordering and receiving process by reducing the number of suppliers and working closely with a smaller number of suppliers. The suppliers are prepared to enter into contractual arrangements whereby they are periodically given a predetermined production schedule and in return they will inspect the shipments and guarantee quality prior to delivery. In addition, the marketing, distribution and customer after-sales services relating to the product are subject to an intensive review, and process improvements are made that result in further reductions in costs that are attributable to the camcorder. The projected cost after undertaking all of the above activities is €555 compared with the target cost of €560 and at this point the target costing exercise is concluded.

Having described the target costing approach that the Digital Electronics Company has used let us now turn our attention to the derivation of the projected costs shown in Example 15.1. The projected cost for direct materials prior to the target costing exercise is €390 but reverse engineering and the functional analysis have resulted in a reduction in the number of parts that are required to manufacture the camcorder. The elimination of most of the unique parts, and the use of standard parts that the company currently purchases in large volumes, also provides scope for further cost savings. The outcome of the redesign process is a direct material cost of €325.

The simplified product design enables the assembly time to be reduced, thus resulting in the reduction of direct labour costs from €100 to €80. The direct machine costs relate to machinery that will be used exclusively for the production of the new product. The estimated cost of acquiring, maintaining and operating the machinery throughout the product's life cycle is €6 million. This is divided by the projected lifetime sales volume of the camera (300 000 units) giving a unit cost of €20. However, it has not been possible to reduce the unit cost because the machinery costs are committed, and fixed, and the target costing exercise has not resulted in a change in the predicted lifetime volume.

Prior to the target costing exercise 80 separate parts were included in the product specification. The estimated number of orders placed for each part throughout the product's life cycle is 150 and the predicted cost per order for the order and receiving activity is €200. Therefore, the estimated lifetime costs are €2.4 million (80 parts × 150 orders × €200 per order) giving a unit cost of €8 (€2.4 million/300 000 units). The simplified design, and the parts standardization arising from the functional analysis and the value engineering activities, have enabled the number of parts to be reduced to 40. The redesign of the ordering and receiving process has also enabled the number of orders and the ordering cost to be reduced (the former from 150 to 100 and the latter from €200 to €150 per order). Thus the projected lifetime ordering and receiving costs after the target costing exercise are €600 000 (40 parts × 100 orders × €150 per order) giving a revised unit cost of €2 (€600 000/300 000 units).

Quality assurance involves inspecting and testing the camcorders. Prior to the target costing exercise the projected cost was €60 (12 hours at €5 per hour) but the simplified design means that the camcorder will be easier to test, resulting in a revised cost of €50 (10 hours at €5 per hour). Rework costs of €15 represent the average rework costs per camcorder. Past experience with manufacturing similar products suggests that 10 per cent of the output will require rework. Applying this rate to the estimated total lifetime volume of 300 000 camcorders results in 30 000 camcorders requiring rework at an estimated average cost of €150 per reworked camcorder. The total lifetime rework cost is therefore predicted to be €4.5 million (30 000 × €150) giving an average cost per unit of good output of €15 (€4.5 million/300 000). Because of the simplified product design the rework rate and the average rework cost will be reduced. The predicted rework rate is now 5 per cent and the average rework cost will be reduced from €150 to €120. Thus, the revised estimate of the total lifetime cost is €1.8 million (15 000 reworked units at €120 per unit) and the projected unit cost is €6 (€1.8 million/300 000 units).

The predicted total lifetime engineering and design costs and other product sustaining costs are predicted to be €3 million giving a unit cost of €10. The simplified design and reduced number of parts enables the lifetime cost to be reduced by 20 per cent, to €2.4 million, and the unit cost to €8. The planned process improvements have also enabled the predicted marketing, distribution and after-sales service costs to be reduced. In addition, the simplified product design and the use of fewer parts has contributed to the reduction to the after-sales warranty costs. However, to keep our example brief the derivation of the non-manufacturing costs will not be presented, other than to note that the company uses an activity-based-costing system. All costs are assigned using cost drivers that are based on established cause-and-effect relationships.

ACTIVITY-BASED MANAGEMENT

The early adopters of activity-based costing (ABC) used it to produce more accurate product (or service) costs but it soon became apparent to the users that it could be extended beyond purely product costing to a range of cost management applications. The terms **activity-based management (ABM)** or **activity-based cost management (ABCM)** are used to describe the cost management applications of ABC. To implement an ABM system only the first three of the four stages described in Chapter 8 for designing an activity-based product costing system are required. They are:

1 identifying the major activities that take place in an organization (i.e. activity analysis)

2 assigning costs to cost pools/cost centres for each activity

3 determining the cost driver for each major activity.

ABM views the business as a set of linked activities that ultimately add value to the customer. It focuses on managing the business on the basis of the activities that make up the organization. ABM is based on the premise that every activity consumes costs. Therefore, by managing activities, costs will be managed in the long term. Managing activities requires an understanding of what factors cause activities to be performed and what causes activity costs to change. The goal of ABM is to enable customer needs to be satisfied while making fewer demands on organizational resources (i.e. cost reduction). Besides providing information on what activities are performed, ABM provides information on the cost of activities, why the activities are undertaken, and how well they are performed.

Traditional budget and control reports analyse costs by types of expense for each responsibility centre. In contrast, ABM analyses costs by activities and thus provides management with information on why costs are incurred and the output from the activity (in terms of cost drivers). Exhibit 15.1 illustrates the difference between the conventional analysis and the activity-based analysis in respect of customer order processing – a business process. A business process consists of a collection of activities that are linked

EXHIBIT 15.1 Customer order processing activity

	($000s)
Traditional analysis	
Salaries	320
Stationery	40
Travel	140
Telephone	40
Depreciation of equipment	40
	580
ABM analysis	
Preparing quotations	120
Receiving customer orders	190
Assessing the creditworthiness of customers	100
Expediting	80
Resolving customer problems	90
	580

together in a coordinated manner to achieve a specified objective. The major differences are that the ABM approach reports by *business processes* and *activities* whereas the traditional analysis is by *departments*.

Another distinguishing feature of ABM reporting is that it often reports information on processes and activities that cross departmental boundaries. For example, different production departments and the distribution department might undertake customer processing activities. They may resolve customer problems by expediting late deliveries. The finance department may assess customer credit worthiness and the remaining customer processing activities might be undertaken by the customer service department. Therefore, the total cost of the customer processing activity could be considerably in excess of the costs that are assigned to the customer service department. However, to simplify the presentation it is assumed in Exhibit 15.1 that the departmental and activity costs are identical but if the cost of the customer order processing activity was found to be, say, three times the amount assigned to the customer service department, this would be important information because it may change the way in which the managers view the activity. For example, the managers may give more attention to reducing the costs of the customer processing activity.

It is apparent from an examination of Exhibit 15.1 that the ABM approach provides more meaningful information. It gives more visibility to the cost of undertaking the activities that make up the organization and may raise issues for management action that are not highlighted by the traditional analysis. For example, why is $90 000 spent on resolving customer problems? Attention-directing information such as this is important for managing the cost of the activities.

Knowing costs by activities is a catalyst that eventually triggers the action necessary to become competitive. Consider a situation where salespersons, as a result of costing activities, are informed that it costs $50 to process a customer's order. They therefore become aware that it is questionable to pursue orders with a low sales value. By eliminating many small orders, and concentrating on larger value orders, the demand for customer-processing activities should decrease, and future spending on this activity should be reduced.

Prior to the introduction of ABM most organizations have been unaware of the cost of undertaking the activities that make up the organization. Knowing the cost of activities enables those activities with the highest cost to be highlighted so that they can be prioritized for detailed studies to ascertain whether they can be eliminated or performed more efficiently. In a study of a UK-based multinational bank, Soin *et al.* (2002) reported that ABM was used to establish which activities were expensive and why they were being used, and to ascertain whether increased volumes would or would not increase costs. No attempt was made to link costs to products or customers.

Value added and non-value added activities

To identify and prioritize the potential for cost reduction many organizations have found it useful to classify activities as either value added or non-value added. Definitions of what constitutes value added and non-value added activities vary. A common definition is that a **value added activity** is an activity that customers perceive as adding usefulness or value to the product or service they purchase. For example, painting a car would be a value added activity in an organization that manufactures cars. Other definitions are an activity that is being performed as efficiently as possible or an activity that supports the primary objective of producing outputs.

In contrast, a **non-value added activity** is an activity where there is an opportunity for cost reduction without reducing the product's service potential to the customer. Examples of non-value added activities include inspecting, storing and moving raw materials and performing set-ups. The cost of these activities can be reduced without reducing the value of the products to the customers. Non-value added activities are essentially those activities that customers should not be expected to pay for. Reporting the cost of non-value added activities draws management's attention to the vast amount of waste that has been tolerated by the organization. This should prioritize those activities with the greatest potential for cost reduction by eliminating or carrying them out more effectively. For example, the activity of inspecting incoming materials is necessary only because of the poor quality of deliveries by suppliers. By establishing strong relationships with nominated suppliers who can guarantee high quality deliveries, incoming inspections can be eventually eliminated. Activities can be undertaken more effectively at a lower cost by finding ways of reducing set-up times, material movements and inventory levels and also improving production flows. Taking action to reduce or eliminate non-value added activities is given top priority because by doing so the organization permanently reduces the cost it incurs without reducing the value of the product to the customer.

Our discussion so far has related to the application of ABM during the manufacturing or service phase of a product's life cycle. However, some organizations have used their activity-based costing systems to influence future costs at the design stage within the target costing process. In particular, they have opted for behaviourally orientated cost systems that may be less accurate than costing technology allows in order to induce desired behavioural responses. For example, the Portable Instruments Division of Tektronix, Inc. in the USA, assigned material support expenses using a single cost driver – number of part numbers. The company wanted to encourage design engineers to focus their attention on reducing the number of part numbers, parts and suppliers in future generations of products. Product timeliness was seen as a critical success factor

REAL WORLD VIEWS 15.2

The impact of ABC at Intel industries

Intel Industries decided to implement ABM at the Andrews, South Carolina plant. The ABM team analysed operations and identified 12 business processes involving a total of 146 activities. The ABM study revealed that the 20 most expensive activities accounted for 87 per cent of Andrews' total physical and people resource of $21.4 million. Activities were further classified into value added and non-value added. Nearly $4.9 million was spent on non-value added activities such as reactive maintenance, dealing with scrap, moving materials, reworking products and managing customer complaints. Those activities, within the 20 most expensive, were targeted for cost reduction and process improvement.

The company estimates that within a year of the first ABM study, $1.8 million had been saved in quality costs, mainly through a reduction of scrap and reactive maintenance costs. Freight costs were reduced $555 000 in a year in the Andrews plant alone. Non-value added activities were reduced from 22 per cent of activity costs to 17 per cent.

The ABM study prompted Intel to start tracking freight cost per pound shipped. This directed attention to ways in which these costs could be reduced. By changing the layout of boxes within each truck, the Andrews plant was able to ship 7400 pounds more per truckload.This represented a 20 per cent reduction in freight expense. When Intel realized how much they were actually incurring in quality costs, the team probed deeper into understanding better what was causing the quality costs to be incurred and for suggesting steps to reduce them. Intel realized that certain foreign suppliers of rods were lower in price but supplied poorer-quality rods that caused breakdowns in Intel's manufacturing process. The lower price of those suppliers did not compensate for the quality costs. Intel switched to higher-quality rod suppliers. Intel also realized that smaller diameter wire products were more likely to break and disrupt the manufacturing process. Intel migrated its product mix to more large diameter wire products. Such initiatives led to reduction in quality costs from $6.7 million to $4.9 million in the following year. It is hard to estimate how much of these savings would have been realized had Intel not conducted an ABM analysis. The activity analysis gave them an appreciation of the scope and quantified the magnitude of the improvement potential, thereby allowing them to prioritize among various process improvement possibilities. Clearly ABM served as a focusing device by providing cost data by activities, directing attention to the top 20 activities, and by labelling some of them as non-value added activities.

Question

1 How might activity costs for Intel differ from departmental costs?

Reference

Narayanan, V.G. and Sarkar, R.G. (2002) The impact of activity-based costing on managerial decisions at Intel Industries: a field study, *Journal of Economics and Management Strategy*, 11(2), 257–288.

and this was facilitated by designs that simplified parts procurement and production processes. The cost system motivated engineers to design simpler products requiring less development time because they had fewer parts and part numbers. The cost system designers knew that most of the material support expenses were not incurred in direct proportion to the single cost driver chosen, but the simplified and imprecise cost system focused attention on factors deemed to be most critical to the division's future success.

BENCHMARKING

In order to identify the best way of performing activities and business processes, organizations are turning their attention to **benchmarking**, which involves comparing key activities or processes with best practices found within and outside the organization. External benchmarking attempts to identify a process, such as customer order processing, that needs to be improved and finding a non-rival organization that is considered to represent world-class best practice for the process and studying how it performs the process. The objective is to find out how the process can be improved and ensure that the improvements are implemented. In contrast, internal benchmarking compares different business units within an organization that performs the same processes. The unit that is considered to represent best practice becomes the target to achieve.

Benchmarking is often used to measure performance compared to others using specific performance metrics such as cost, productivity or cycle time per unit of measure. Sometimes it is carried out collaboratively by comparing subsidiaries of multinational companies in different countries or through their industry trade associations. For example, the UK construction industry has carried out benchmarking since the late 1990s through its industry association.

Benchmarking is widely used in public sector organizations. Unlike private sector organizations the government acts as a governing body that can force public sector organizations to disclose the relevant information for benchmarking exercises. League tables summarizing selected metrics into a weighted overall score are widely used in the public sector to present the results of benchmarking. For example, published data provide rankings of universities by various metrics that may influence the choice of potential students.

League tables enable many different areas of performance to be summarized into one final score thus providing an indication of how well the organization has performed overall. Ideally, league tables should improve competition among the organizations, and provide an incentive for organizations to improve and move up the table.

League tables are often criticized because they do not take into account differences between the organizations being measured. For example, the performance of schools may be influenced more by demographics of the area where the schools are located (with schools in poorer areas typically appearing towards the bottom of the table) rather than the quality of education provided. There is also a danger that too much stress on performance measures and benchmarking can encourage dysfunctional behaviour such as manipulating the performance measures or organizations taking actions to improve their measured scores without improving underlying performance. For example, universities may over-concentrate on improving short-term examination performance in the league tables at the expense of providing a challenging and high quality education. Another criticism of comparing metrics is that they can become a measuring exercise rather than a learning process because they over-concentrate comparisons with the benchmark when the focus should be on learning from, and implementing best practice.

A major advantage of benchmarking is that it is cost beneficial since an organization can save time and money avoiding mistakes that other companies have made and/or the organization can avoid duplicating the efforts of other companies. The overall aim should be to find and implement best practice.

BUSINESS PROCESS RE-ENGINEERING

Business process re-engineering involves examining business processes and making substantial changes to how the organization currently operates. It involves the redesign of how work is done through activities. A business process consists of a collection of activities that are linked together in a coordinated manner to achieve a specific objective. For example, material handling might be classed as a business process consisting of separate activities relating to scheduling production, storing materials, processing purchase orders, inspecting materials and paying suppliers.

The aim of business process re-engineering is to improve the key business processes in an organization by focusing on simplification, cost reduction, improved quality, enhanced customer satisfaction and become a world-class competitor. Business process re-engineering can be applied not only to manufacturing processes but also to administrative processes. Consider the materials handling process outlined in the above paragraph. The process might be re-engineered by sending the production schedule direct to nominated suppliers and entering into contractual agreements to deliver the materials in accordance with the production schedule and also guaranteeing their quality by inspecting them prior to delivery. The end result might be the elimination, or a permanent reduction, of the storing, purchasing and inspection activities. These activities are non-value added activities since they represent an opportunity for cost reduction without reducing the products' service potentials to customers.

A distinguishing feature of business process re-engineering is that it involves radical and dramatic changes in processes by abandoning current practices and reinventing completely new methods of performing business processes. The focus is on major changes rather than marginal improvements. A further example of business process re-engineering is moving from a traditional functional plant layout to a just-in-time (JIT) cellular product layout and adopting a JIT philosophy. Adopting a JIT system and philosophy has important implications for cost management and performance reporting. It is therefore important that you understand the nature of such systems and how they differ from traditional systems. This topic is discussed in the next section.

JUST-IN-TIME SYSTEMS

In the previous section it was pointed out that reorganizing business processes and adopting a JIT system was an illustration of business process engineering. Given that implementing a JIT system is a mechanism for reducing non-value added costs and long-run costs it is important that you understand the nature of such a system and its cost management implications.

The success of Japanese firms in international markets in the 1980s and 1990s generated interest among many Western companies as to how this success was achieved. The implementation of **JIT production methods** (also known as **lean manufacturing systems**) was considered to be one of the major factors contributing to this success. The aims of JIT are to reduce waste by producing the required items, at the required quality and in the required quantities, at the precise time they are required. In other words, nothing is purchased or produced until just before it is needed. JIT manufacturing is a demand pull manufacturing system that pulls products through the manufacturing process. Each operation produces only what is necessary to meet the demand of the following operation. Production is not undertaken until there is a signal from the following process indicating a need to produce. The demand pull process starts with customer demand for a finished product and works all the way back to the demand for direct materials that arrive JIT to be used in the production process. JIT production aims to keep the materials moving in a continuous flow with no stoppages and no storage.

The major features of a JIT production system are:

1 The rearrangement of the production process into **production cells** consisting of different types of equipment that are used to manufacture a given product.

2 Reducing set-up times (i.e. the amount of time required to adjust equipment settings and to retool for the production of a different product).

REAL WORLD VIEWS 15.3

Management accounting and control practices in a lean manufacturing environment

Using data from 244 US companies with an interest in lean manufacturing, Fullarton *et al.*, found that the extent of lean manufacturing implementation positively influenced value stream costing, employee empowerment, visual performance measurement information, and a simplified strategic reporting system; and negatively influenced inventory tracking. They identified the following practices as elements of a lean manufacturing strategy - statistical process control, just-in-time inventory management (JIT), total quality management (TQM), and total preventive maintenance (TPM).

Firms operating in a lean manufacturing environment are likely to reorganize into cells/value streams that allows them to focus on the value generated by products or product families across all functions. The change to a cell/value stream structure also influences the nature of accounting practices, since costing and reporting of variances, overhead allocations, and budgeting are performed at the value stream level rather than at a product or functional department level. Average unit cost can be calculated by dividing value stream costs by the number of units shipped.

In a lean manufacturing environment, shop-floor workers rely on visual, easy-to-use performance measurements (e.g. visual boards and charts) that communicate real-time results. Therefore there is greater reliance on a visual performance measurement system comprising of operational measures that identify production needs and problems that are required to achieve lean strategic objectives.

In a lean environment, accountants are also encouraged to interact more with shop-floor personnel to better understand their information needs and provide that information in a more simplified format.

Detailed inventory tracking relying on absorption costing systems can actually impede lean implementations by encouraging firms to build more inventory. This is exactly opposite the intent of lean manufacturing. Furthermore, the focus in lean manufacturing to minimize inventory levels reduces the emphasis that needs to be given to tracking inventory.

Questions

1 What are the advantages and disadvantages of a company that adopts a JIT philosophy?
2 Besides the items mentioned above what should be the main features of a management information system for a company that adopts a lean manufacturing strategy?

Reference

Fullarton, R.R., Kennedy, F.A. and Widener, S.K. (2013), Management accounting and control practices in a lean manufacturing environment, *Accounting, Organizations and Society*, 38, 50–71.

3 Increased emphasis on total quality management that seeks to eliminate defective production.

4 Production cell workers are trained to multi-task so that they can perform a variety of operations and tasks.

5 The adoption of JIT purchasing techniques, whereby the delivery of materials immediately precedes demand or use.

6 The modification of management accounting performance measures and product costing systems so that they support the JIT production systems.

Rearrangement of the production process

The first stage in implementing JIT manufacturing techniques is to rearrange the production process away from a **batch production functional layout** towards a product layout using flow lines. With a batch production functional plant layout, products pass through a number of specialist departments that normally contain a group of similar machines. Products are processed in large batches so as to minimize the set-up times when machine settings are changed between processing batches of different products. Batches move via different and complex routes through the various departments, travelling over much of the plant before they are completed. Each process normally involves a considerable amount of waiting time. In addition, much time is taken transporting items from one process to another. A further problem is that it is not easy at any point in time to determine what progress has been made on individual batches. Therefore, detailed cost accumulation records are necessary to track work in progress. The consequences of this complex routing process are high work in progress inventory levels, long manufacturing cycle times and high material handling costs.

The JIT solution is to reorganize the production process by dividing the many different products that an organization makes into families of similar products or components. All of the products in a particular group will have similar production requirements and routings. Production is rearranged so that each product family is manufactured in a well-defined production cell based on flow line principles. In a **product flow line**, specialist departments containing *similar* machines no longer exist. Instead groups of *dissimilar* machines are organized into product or component family flow lines that function like an assembly line. For each product line the machines are placed close together in the order in which they are required by the group of products to be processed. Items in each product family can now move, one at a time, from process to process more easily, thereby reducing work in progress inventories and lead times. The ideal layout of each flow line is normally U-shaped. This layout is called **cellular manufacturing**.

JIT manufacturing aims to produce the right parts at the right time, only when they are needed, and only in the quantity needed, using a **pull manufacturing system**. The pull system is implemented by monitoring the consumption of parts at each operation stage and using various types of visible signalling systems (known as *Kanbans*) to authorize production and movement of the part to the using location. The producing cell cannot run the parts until authorized to do so. The signalling mechanism usually involves the use of *Kanban* containers. These containers hold materials or parts for movement from one work centre to another. The capacity of *Kanban* containers tends to vary from two to five units. They are just big enough to permit the production line to operate smoothly despite minor interruptions to individual work centres within the cell. To illustrate how the system works consider three machines forming part of a cell where the parts are first processed by machine A before being further processed on machine B and then machine C. The *Kanbans* are located between the machines. As long as the *Kanban* container is not full, the worker at machine A continues to produce parts, placing them in the *Kanban* container. When the container is full the worker stops producing and recommences when a part has been removed from the container by the worker operating machine B. A similar process applies between the operations of machines B and C. This process can result in idle time within certain locations within the cell, but the JIT philosophy considers that it is more beneficial to absorb short-run idle time rather than add to inventory during these periods. During idle time the workers perform preventive maintenance on the machines.

With a pull system problems arising in any part of the system will immediately halt the production line because work centres at the earlier stages will not receive the pull signal (because the *Kanban* container is full) if a problem arises at a later stage. Alternatively, work centres at a later stage will not have their pull signal answered (because of empty *Kanban* containers) when problems arise with work centres at the earlier stages of the production cycle. Thus attention is drawn immediately to production problems so that appropriate remedial action can be taken. This is deemed to be preferable to the approach adopted in a traditional manufacturing system where large inventory levels provide a cushion for production to continue.

In contrast, the traditional manufacturing environment is based on a **push manufacturing system**. With this system, machines are grouped into work centres based on the similarity of their functional capabilities. Each manufactured part has a designated routing, and the preceding process supplies parts to the subsequent process without any consideration being given to whether the next process is ready to work on the parts or not. Hence the use of the term 'push-through system'.

Demand-pull JIT systems are also applied in non-manufacturing organizations. For example, fast food restaurants such as McDonald's and Burger King use a demand-pull system to control their finished inventories. When a customer orders a burger, it is taken from the shelf of completed burgers and the chef does not cook any new burgers until the inventories begin to run out. Customer demand thus pulls the burgers through the system.

Reduced set-up times

Set-up time is the amount of time required to adjust equipment settings and to retool for the production of a different product. Long set-up and changeover times make the production of batches with a small number of units uneconomic. Why? Because larger batches enable the costs of a set-up to be spread over a larger number of units thus reducing the set-up cost per unit. However, the production of large batches leads to substantial throughput delays and the creation of high inventory levels. Throughput delays arise because several lengthy production runs are required to process larger batches through the factory. A further problem with large batches is that they often have to wait for lengthy periods before they are processed by the next process or before they are sold.

The JIT philosophy is to substantially reduce or eliminate the need for set-ups. Set-up times can be reduced by training workers to perform set-ups more quickly. Alternatively, set-ups can be minimized or eliminated entirely by establishing manufacturing cells that are dedicated to the manufacture of a single product or a family of single products rather than multiple dissimilar products. Many firms have also reduced set-up times by investing in advanced manufacturing technologies that enable machine settings to be adjusted automatically instead of manually. By significantly reducing set-up times, small batch sizes become economical. Small batch sizes, combined with short throughput times, also enable a firm to adapt more readily to short-term fluctuations in market demand and respond faster to customer requests, since production is not dependent on long planning lead times.

Total quality management

With a JIT system a defective part can stop the entire demand pull production flow line. Defective parts represent waste that cannot be tolerated in a production environment that operates without inventories. Therefore total quality management (TQM) with a never-ending quest to a goal of zero-defects is an essential part of a JIT production system. In contrast, with a traditional batch production system work in progress inventories are available at each production stage to meet the demands of succeeding operations so defective units are unlikely to halt the production process. Compared with a JIT system there is less need to eliminate defective output and therefore the same emphasis may not be placed on total quality management.

Multiple-task workforce

Producing on demand can result in workers having free time when there is no demand pull signal from the following operation. There is also a need to respond quickly to any production problems in the flow line, so there is a greater emphasis on employee empowerment so employees can take actions without requiring authorization at higher management levels. Therefore, workers are trained to perform multiple tasks by undertaking support activities such as duties relating to set-ups, minor repairs, preventive maintenance, quality testing and inspection. Workers are also trained to operate different machines within the cell. The ability of workers to multi-task enables a smooth production flow within the cell to be achieved.

JIT purchasing arrangements

The JIT philosophy also extends to adopting **JIT purchasing techniques**, whereby the delivery of materials immediately precedes demand or use. By arranging with suppliers for more frequent deliveries of small batches just before the supplies are needed, inventories can be cut to a minimum. Considerable savings in material handling expenses can be obtained by requiring suppliers to inspect materials before their delivery and guaranteeing their quality. This improved service is obtained by giving more business to fewer highly reliable suppliers and placing longer-term purchasing orders. Therefore the supplier has an assurance of long-term sales, and can plan to meet this demand. Thus, a critical component of JIT purchasing is that strong long-term relationships are established with reliable suppliers, based on trust and cooperation.

Companies that have implemented JIT purchasing techniques claim to have substantially reduced their investment in raw materials and work in progress inventories. Other advantages include a substantial saving in factory space, large quantity discounts, savings in time from negotiating with fewer suppliers and a reduction in paperwork arising from issuing blanket long-term orders to a few suppliers rather than individual purchase orders to many suppliers.

JIT and management accounting

Management accountants in many organizations have been strongly criticized because of their failure to alter the management accounting system to reflect the move from a traditional manufacturing to a JIT manufacturing system. Conventional management accounting systems can encourage behaviour that is inconsistent with a JIT manufacturing philosophy. Management accounting must support JIT manufacturing by monitoring, identifying and communicating to decision-makers any delay, error and waste in the system. Modern management accounting systems are now placing greater emphasis on providing information on supplier reliability, set-up times, throughput cycle times, percentage of deliveries that are on time and defect rates.

In a traditional manufacturing environment many different unrelated products may be subject to processing in a single department. After the products have been processed they are transferred to other processes located in different departments. Because many products are processed in each department the costs of each department are common to all products passing through each department. These departmental costs are mostly indirect product costs that are allocated to products using the approaches described in Chapters 7 and 8. In a JIT manufacturing system all of the processes necessary for the manufacture of a single product (or family of similar products) are undertaken in a single cell. Therefore, the costs of operating the cell can be directly assigned to the cell's product or family of similar products.

QUALITY COST MANAGEMENT

To compete successfully in today's global competitive environment companies have become 'customer-driven' and have made customer satisfaction an overriding priority. Customers now demand ever-improving levels of service regarding cost, quality, reliability, delivery and the choice of innovative new products. Quality has become a key competitive variable in both service and manufacturing organizations and this has created the need for management accountants to become more involved in the provision of information relating to the quality of products and services and activities that produce them. Various studies suggest that costs of quality can be substantial ranging from 10 per cent to 20 per cent of total sales. Eliminating inferior quality by implementing quality improvement initiatives can therefore result in substantial cost savings and higher revenues and value creation. Companies that do not focus on continuous quality improvement programmes are likely to suffer a decline in market shares, revenues and value. The emphasis on quality has been a key competitive weapon for many years, resulting quality having now shifted from a source of strategic advantage to a competitive necessity.

Total quality management (TQM), a term used to describe a situation where all business functions are involved in a process of continuous quality improvement, has been adopted by many companies. TQM practices emerged as an increasingly fashionable management innovation in response to the lack of competitiveness in Western manufacturing industries during the 1980s, and the perceived superiority of Japanese firms in delivering high quality products and services. It is a customer-oriented process of continuous improvement that focuses on delivering products or services of consistent

REAL WORLD VIEWS 15.4

Cost of quality – BP and Toyota

In recent years, two global companies have had to deal with some quite large costs as a result of quality control failures. First, take the example of Toyota cars in the USA. In late 2009 and early 2010, Toyota recalled several of its US models, the Camry in particular, after several accidents occurred due to a faulty accelerator pedal. The recall involved over 5 million vehicles, and sales and production were suspended for a time in the USA. According to author Paul Ingrassia, the problem occurred because Toyota broke one of its key principles called the 'three nevers' at its US manufacturing plants: never build a new product, in a new facility, with a new workforce. In the case of the Camry in the USA, all three were broken. This cost the company $2 billion before any legal costs. Toyota was fined $1.2 billion in March 2014 by the US Justice Department. The recall woes continued, with a recall of over 6 million vehicles in April 2014, costing the company at least $600 million in repair costs.

In April 2010, the Deepwater Horizon drilling rig, which was ultimately under the control of British Petroleum (BP), exploded in the Gulf of Mexico. An oil slick resulted, which lasted for approximately 3 months and caused extensive damage to the environment and coastlines around the Gulf of Mexico. By September 2010, the total costs had risen to almost $10 billion, with BP setting aside a provision of $20 billion. In January 2011, a US presidential commission squarely laid the blame for the disaster at the door of BP and its contractors. The report cited several systemic failures, short-cuts and sub-standard materials and workmanship as the cause, all of which it attributed to management failures. By 2016, BP published its final estimate of the total cost at just under $62 billion.

Questions

1 Can management accountants do anything to help engineers and designers focus more on considering the cost of failures in quality and quality control?
2 Can you list some of the internal and external failure costs for the two issues described above?

References

BP Press Release, 14 July 2016, available at www.bp.com/en/global/corporate/press/press-releases/bp-estimates-all-remaining-material-deepwater-horizon-liabilitie.html

CNNMoney (2014) Toyota's huge fine won't dent its $60 billion cash pile. Available at money.cnn.com/2014/03/19/news/companies/toyota-cash-pile/?iid=EL

Ingrassia, P. (2010) Crash Course: The American Automobile Industry's Road from Glory to Disaster, Random House.

Kollewe, J. (2010) 'BP oil spill cost hits nearly $10bn', 20 September, *The Guardian*. Available at www.guardian.co.uk/environment/2010/sep/20/bp-oil-spill-deepwater-horizon-costs-10bn

Toyota Recalls More Than 6 Million Vehicles Worldwide, Bloomberg, www.bloomberg.com/news/articles/2014-04-09/toyota-recalls-6-76-million-vehicles-worldwide-including-rav4, accessed 4 December, 2016.

high quality in a timely fashion. In the past most European and American companies considered quality to be an additional cost of manufacturing, but in the 1990s they realized that focusing on TQM saves money. Prior to the 1990s companies focused on emphasizing production volume over quality resulting in high levels of inventories at each production stage in order to protect against shortages caused by inferior quality at previous stages. This approach results in excessive expenditure on inspection, rework, scrap and warranty repairs. In the 1990s many companies discovered that it was cheaper to produce the items correctly the first time rather than wasting resources by making substandard items that have to be detected, reworked, scrapped or returned by customers.

In recent years international quality standards have been introduced. The International Organization for Standardization has introduced five standards, known as the ISO 9000 family of standards, that provide a certification that a company's quality systems meets certain quality standards. The process of obtaining certification is subject to a detailed audit of quality systems and is lengthy and expensive. Many companies now require their suppliers to hold ISO certification and certification has become necessary to compete in the global market. The ISO quality standards have been adopted worldwide by approximately 1.14 million companies.

Cost of quality reports

In the 1990s it became apparent that quality practices had become so important that management accounting could no longer ignore TQM. Traditional management accounting focused on cost and production analysis, but ignored quality analysis. Management accounting systems emerged that helped organizations to achieve their quality goals by providing a variety of reports and measures that motivated and evaluated managerial efforts to improve quality. These include financial and non-financial measures. Many companies were not aware of how much they were spending on quality because the costs were incurred across many different departments and not accumulated as a separate cost object within the costing system. Managers need to know the costs of quality and how they are changing over time. A **cost of quality report** should be prepared to indicate the total cost to the organization of producing products or services that do not conform with quality requirements. Four categories of costs should be reported:

1 **Prevention costs** are the costs incurred in preventing the production of products or services that do not conform to specification. They include the costs of preventive maintenance, quality planning and training, quality reporting and supplier evaluation and selection.

2 **Appraisal costs** are the costs incurred to ensure that materials, products and services meet quality conformance standards. They include the costs of inspecting purchased parts, work in process and finished goods, quality audits and field tests.

3 **Internal failure costs** are the costs incurred when products and services fail to meet quality standards or customer needs. They include costs incurred before the product is despatched to the customer, such as the costs of scrap, repair, downtime and work stoppages caused by defects.

4 **External failure costs** are the costs incurred when products or services fail to conform to requirements or satisfy customer needs after they have been delivered. They include the costs of handling customer complaints, warranty replacement, repairs of returned products, lost market share and the costs arising from a damaged company reputation. Costs within this category can have a dramatic impact on future sales.

Exhibit 15.2 presents a typical cost of quality report. By expressing each category of costs as a percentage of sales revenues comparisons can be made with previous periods, other organizations and divisions within the same group. Trends in absolute amounts and percentages can therefore be observed and acted upon. Such comparisons can highlight problem areas. For example, comparisons of external failure costs with other companies can provide an indication of the current level of customer satisfaction.

EXHIBIT 15.2 Cost of quality report

	($000s)	% of sales ($100 million)
Prevention costs		
Quality training	1 000	
Supplier reviews	300	
Quality engineering	400	
Preventive maintenance	500	
	2 200	2.2
Appraisal costs		
Inspection of materials received	500	
Inspection of WIP and completed units	1 000	
Testing equipment	300	
Quality audits	800	
	2 600	2.6
Internal failure costs		
Scrap	800	
Rework	1 000	
Downtime due to quality problems	600	
Retesting	400	
	2 800	2.8
External failure costs		
Returns	2 000	
Recalls	1 000	
Warranty repairs	800	
Handling customer complaints	500	
Forogone contribution from lost sales	3 000	
	7 300	7.3
	14 900	14.9

The cost of quality report can be used as an attention-directing device to make the top management of a company aware of how much is being spent on quality-related costs and the areas where they should focus their attention. Exhibit 15.2 shows that significant savings can be made by reducing the costs of scrap and rework. The report can also draw management's attention to the possibility of reducing total quality costs by a wiser allocation of costs among the four quality categories. For example, by spending more on the prevention costs, the amount of spending in the internal and external failure categories can be substantially reduced, and therefore total spending can be lowered. Also, by designing quality into the products and processes, appraisal costs can be reduced, since far less inspection is required.

Non-financial measures of quality and customer satisfaction

In addition to financial measures organizations need non-financial measures relating to the quality of the products and services and the activities that produce them. Typical measures provided by the management accounting information system relating to internal processes include:

- process parts per million (PPM) defect rates for each product line
- the number and percentage of defects for each product line
- process yields (ratio of good items produced to good items entering the process)
- supplier performance measures such as percentage of defects of incoming materials and the number of late deliveries.

Non-financial measures relating to customer satisfaction include:

- number and percentage of defective goods delivered to customers
- number and percentage of customer complaints
- percentage of products that do not meet the warranty requirements
- percentage of deliveries that are not on time.

In addition, many companies conduct surveys to measure customer satisfaction in relation to product or service quality. In general, cost of quality reports are produced annually but non-financial measures should be reported at more frequent intervals in order to provide earlier warnings of potential quality problems so that remedial actions can be quickly taken. Managers should examine trends over time and use the measures to highlight areas that require action to improve quality performance.

COST MANAGEMENT AND THE VALUE CHAIN

The **value chain** is the linked set of value creating activities all the way from basic raw material sources for component suppliers through to the ultimate end use product or service delivered to the customer. The value chain is illustrated in Figure 15.2. It consists of those activities that add value to customers, products and services. There are two types of linkages: *internal linkages* and *external linkages*. Internal linkages are relationships among activities that are performed within the firm and external linkages relate to activities that are performed with a firm's suppliers and customers. It is important that a company focuses on the entire value chain and not just the internal linkages. Effective management of the value chain is essential to increase customer value at the lowest possible cost.

A **value chain analysis** is used to analyse, coordinate and optimize linkages in the value chain. Coordinating the individual parts of the value chain together creates the conditions to improve customer satisfaction, particularly in terms of cost efficiency, quality and

FIGURE 15.2
The value chain

delivery. A firm which performs the value chain activities more efficiently, and at a lower cost than its competitors, will gain a competitive advantage. Therefore it is necessary to understand how value chain activities are performed and how they interact with each other. The activities are not just a collection of independent activities but a system of inter-dependent activities in which the performance of one activity affects the performance and cost of other activities.

The linkages in the value chain express the relationships between the performance of one activity and its effects on the performance of another activity. A linkage occurs when interdependence exists between activities and the higher the interdependence between activities the greater is the required coordination. Thus it is appropriate to view the value chain from the customer's perspective, with each link being seen as the customer of the previous link. If each link in the value chain is designed to meet the needs of its customers, then end-customer satisfaction should ensue. Furthermore, by viewing each link in the value chain as a supplier–customer relationship, the opinions of the customers can be

---

REAL WORLD VIEWS 15.5

Inter-organizational Cost Management in Supply Chains

Traditionally, companies have focused on costs that they can control from within, which is known as internal cost management. With the advent of technology capable of measuring and tracking costs along a supply chain, there is an emerging trend to manage costs associated with supply chain partners, too.

Fayard *et al* provide examples of areas of how inter-organizational cost management can be applied based on the findings from a survey from 76 American firms. For example, ABC focuses on identifying the relevant internal activities or business processes in order to trace activity costs to the appropriate products, suppliers, distribution channels or customers. They found that it was a natural evolution for companies to take what they have been doing internally and extend it to their partnerships.

Another technique that can be applied in an inter-organizational context is target costing. Target costing often affects a product's design and its production process. Traditionally, target costing did not actively involve a partner company. More and more companies, however, are now extending target costing to include costs outside the organization.

A further example of an internal cost management technique being extended to the wider organizational context is Kaizen costing, a system of incremental or continuous improvements used to reduce the costs associated with manufacturing a product. Kaizen costing generally accepts the design of the product as fixed and seeks ways to manage or reduce manufacturing and delivery costs. Now, however, there is evidence that companies can also use Kaizen costing to identify and set cost reduction objectives for suppliers.

Other internal cost management techniques frequently used include the development of common demand and sales forecasts, the joint management of quality costs, inventory management procedures and the sharing of common assets.

Questions

1 How can an organization reduce its own costs and that of other organizations by sharing information within the value chain?
2 What do you think are the factors that may motivate firms to engage in inter-organizational cost management activities?

Reference

Fayard, D., Lee, L.S., Leitch, R.A. and Kettinger, W.J. (2014), Interorganizational Cost Management in Supply Chains: Practices and Payoffs, *Management Accounting Quarterly*, 15,3, 1–9.

used to provide useful feedback information on assessing the quality of service provided by the supplier. Opportunities are thus identified for improving activities throughout the entire value chain.

In the value chain shown in Figure 15.2 the design process activities occur before the production process. Product designs affect production costs and production costs are determined by product cost drivers, so that knowing the cost driver rates of the activities required to produce the products is essential for exploiting the linkages between design and production. If designers are made aware that the number of parts is a major cost driver of the various product-related activities, then they will focus on producing products with standard parts thus reducing the number of parts required and the cost of production activities. The design activity is also linked to the customer service activity in the value chain. Producing a product with fewer parts and relying on standard parts reduces the likelihood of product failure and the associated warranty costs, besides enhancing customer satisfaction and value.

A cost management system should also provide performance measures relating to the wide variety of activities that span the value chain. Information on supplier reliability, throughput cycle times and percentage of deliveries that are on time provides the feedback that contributes to timely customer deliveries thus increasing customer value at the lowest possible cost.

Managing linkages in the value chain is also the central idea of the concept of **supply chain management**. By examining potential linkages with suppliers and understanding supplier costs it may be possible for the buying organization to change its activities in order to reduce the suppliers' costs. For example, cost generating activities in the supplying organizations are often triggered by purchasing parameters (e.g. design specifications, lot size, delivery schedule, number of shipments, design changes and level of documentation). However, the buying organization can only be sensitive to these issues if it understands how supplier costs are generated (Seal *et al.*, 1999). Shank and Govindarajan (1992) illustrated how an American automobile company failed to use the entire value chain approach to exploit links with suppliers and enhance profitability. The company had made significant internal savings from introducing JIT manufacturing techniques, but, at the same time, price increases from suppliers more than offset these internal cost savings. A value chain perspective revealed that 50 per cent of the firm's costs related to purchases from parts suppliers. As the automobile company reduced its own need for buffer inventories, it placed major new strains on the manufacturing responsiveness of suppliers. The increase in the suppliers' manufacturing costs was greater than the decrease in the automobile company's internal costs:

> For every dollar of manufacturing cost the assembly plants saved by moving towards JIT management concepts, the suppliers' plant spent much more than 1 dollar extra because of schedule instability arising from the introduction of JIT. Because of its narrow value added perspective, the auto company had ignored the impact of its changes on its suppliers' costs. Management had ignored the idea that JIT involves a partnership with suppliers. (Shank, 1989).

Similarly, by developing linkages with customers mutually beneficial relationships can be established. For example, Shank and Govindarajan (1992) reported that some container producers in the USA have constructed manufacturing facilities near beer breweries and deliver the containers through overhead conveyers directly onto the customers' assembly lines. This practice results in significant cost reductions for both the container producers and their customers by expediting the transport of empty containers, which are bulky and heavy.

SUMMARY

The following items relate to the learning objectives listed at the beginning of the chapter.

- **Distinguish between the features of a traditional management accounting control system and cost management.** A traditional management accounting control system tends to be based on the preservation of the status quo and the ways of performing existing activities are not reviewed. The emphasis is on cost containment rather than cost reduction. Cost management focuses on cost reduction rather than cost containment. Whereas traditional cost control systems are routinely applied on a continuous basis, cost management tends to be applied on an *ad hoc* basis when an opportunity for cost reduction is identified. Also many of the approaches that are incorporated within the area of cost management do not involve the use of accounting techniques. In contrast, cost control relies heavily on accounting techniques.

- **Describe the typical pattern of cost commitment and cost incurrence during the three stages of a product's life cycle.** Three stages of a product's life cycle can be identified – the planning and design stage, the manufacturing stage and the service and abandonment stage. Approximately 80 per cent of a product's costs are committed during the planning and design stage. Cost management can be most effectively exercised during the planning and design stage and not at the manufacturing stage when the product design and processes have already been determined and costs have been committed.

- **Describe the target costing approach to cost management.** Target costing is a customer-oriented technique that is widely used by Japanese companies and which has recently been adopted by companies in Europe and the USA. The first stage requires market research to determine the target selling price for a product. Next a standard or desired profit margin is deducted to establish a target cost for the product. The target cost is compared with the predicted actual cost. If the predicted actual cost is above the target cost intensive efforts are made to close the gap. Value engineering and functional analysis are used to drive the predicted actual cost down to the target cost. The major advantage of adopting target costing is that it is deployed during a product's design and planning stage so that it can have a maximum impact in determining the level of the locked-in costs.

- **Describe activity-based cost management.** Activity-based management (ABM) focuses on managing the business on the basis of the activities that make up the organization. It is based on the premise that activities consume costs. Therefore, by managing activities, costs will be managed in the long term. The goal of ABM is to enable customer needs to be satisfied while making fewer demands on organization resources. Knowing the cost of activities enables those activities with the highest cost to be highlighted so that they can be prioritized for detailed studies to ascertain whether they can be eliminated or performed more efficiently.

● **Distinguish between value added and non-value added activities**. A value added activity is an activity that customers perceive as adding usefulness to the product or service they purchase, whereas a non-value added activity is an activity where there is an opportunity for cost reduction without reducing the product's service potential to the customer. Taking action to reduce or eliminate non-value added activities is given top priority because by doing so the organization permanently reduces the cost it incurs without reducing the value of the product to the customer.

● **Explain the role of benchmarking and business process engineering within the cost management framework**. Benchmarking involves comparing key activities and processes with world-class best practices by identifying an activity or process that needs to be improved, finding a non-rival organization that is considered to represent world-class best practice for the process, and studying how it performs the process. The objective is to establish how the activity or process can be improved and ensure that the improvements are implemented. The aim of business process re-engineering is to improve the key business processes in an organization by focusing on simplification, cost reduction, improved quality and enhanced customer satisfaction.
A distinguishing feature of business process re-engineering is that it involves radical and dramatic changes in processes by abandoning current practices and reinventing completely new methods of performing business processes.

● **Outline the main features of a just-in-time philosophy**. Many companies seek to eliminate and/or reduce the costs of non-value added activities by introducing just-in-time (JIT) systems. The aims of a JIT system are to produce the required items, at the required quality and in the required quantities, at the precise time they are required. In particular, JIT aims to eliminate waste by minimizing inventories and reducing cycle or throughput times (i.e. the time elapsed from when customers place an order until the time when they receive the desired product or service). Adopting a JIT manufacturing system involves moving from a batch production functional layout to a cellular flow line manufacturing system. The JIT philosophy also extends to adopting JIT purchasing techniques, whereby the delivery of materials immediately precedes their use. By arranging with suppliers for more frequent deliveries, inventories can be cut to a minimum.

● **Explain the purpose of a cost of quality report**. A cost of quality report indicates the total cost to the organization of producing products or services that do not conform with quality requirements. Quality costs are analysed by four categories for reporting purposes (prevention, appraisal, and internal and external failure costs). The report draws management's attention to the possibility of reducing total quality costs by a wiser allocation of costs among the four quality categories.

● **Describe how value chain analysis can be used to increase customer satisfaction and manage costs more effectively**. Increasing attention is now being given to value chain analysis as a means of increasing customer satisfaction and value, and managing costs more effectively. The value chain is the linked set of value-creating activities all the way from basic raw material sources from component suppliers through to the ultimate end-use product or service delivered to the customer. Understanding how value chain activities are performed and how they interact with each other creates the conditions to improve customer satisfaction and value, particularly in terms of cost efficiency, quality and delivery.

KEY TERMS AND CONCEPTS

Activity-based cost management (ABCM)   The cost management applications applied to activity-based costing, without the need to assign activity costs to products, also known as activity-based management.

Activity-based management (ABM)   The cost management applications applied to activity-based costing, without the need to assign activity costs to products, also known as activity-based cost management.

Appraisal costs   The costs incurred to ensure that materials, products and services meet quality conformance standards.

Batch production functional layout   A plant layout in which products pass in batches through a number of specialist departments that normally contain a group of similar machines.

Benchmarking   A mechanism for achieving continuous improvement by measuring products, services or activities against those of other best performing organizations.

Business process re-engineering   Examining business processes and making substantial changes to how the organization operates and the redesign of how work is done through activities.

Cellular manufacturing   A plant layout based on product flow lines, which are normally U-shaped.

Committed costs   Costs that have not yet been incurred but that will be incurred in the future on the basis of decisions that have already been made, also known as locked-in costs.

Cost of quality report   A report indicating the total cost to the organization of producing products or services that do not conform with quality requirements.

External failure costs   The costs incurred when products or services fail to conform to requirements or satisfy customer needs after they have been delivered.

Functional analysis   A process that involves decomposing a product into its many elements or attributes and determining a price or value for each element that reflects the amount the customer is prepared to pay.

Internal failure costs   The internal costs incurred when products and services fail to meet quality standards or customer needs.

Just-in-time (JIT) production methods   The design of the production process that involves producing the required items, at the required quality and in the required quantities, at the precise time they are required.

Just-in-time (JIT) purchasing arrangements   Strategic partnerships with suppliers that involve the delivery of materials and goods immediately before they are required.

Kanbans   Visible signalling systems that authorize the production of parts and their movement to the location where they will be used.

Lean manufacturing systems   Systems that seek to reduce waste in manufacturing by implementing just-in-time production systems, focusing on quality, simplifying processes and investing in advanced technologies.

Life-cycle cost management   The estimation of costs over a product's entire life cycle in order to determine whether profits made during the manufacturing phase will cover the costs incurred during the pre- and post-manufacturing stages.

Locked-in costs   Costs that have not yet been incurred but that will be incurred in the future on the basis of decisions that have already been made, also known as committed costs.

Non-value added activities Activities that can be reduced or eliminated without altering the product's service potential to the customer.

Prevention costs The costs incurred in preventing the production of products or services that do not conform to specification.

Product flow line A plant layout in which groups of dissimilar machines are organized into product or component family flow lines so that individual items can move from process to process more easily.

Production cells Self-contained areas in which a team works on a product family.

Pull manufacturing system A system that pulls products through the manufacturing process so that each operation produces only what is necessary to meet the demand of the following operation.

Push manufacturing system A system in which machines are grouped into work centres based on the similarity of their functional capabilities and one process supplies parts to the subsequent process without any consideration as to whether the next process is ready to work on the parts or not.

Reverse engineering The dismantling and examination of a competitor's product in order to identify opportunities for product improvement and/or cost reduction, also known as tear-down analysis.

Supply chain management Managing linkages in the supply chain by examining supplier costs and modifying activities to reduce these costs.

Target costing A technique that focuses on managing costs during a product's planning and design phase by establishing the target cost for a product or service that is derived from starting with the target selling price and deducting a desired profit margin.

Tear-down analysis The dismantling and examination of a competitor's product in order to identify opportunities for product improvement and/or cost reduction, also known as reverse engineering.

Total quality management (TQM) A customer-oriented process of continuous improvement that focuses on delivering products or services of consistent high quality in a timely fashion.

Value added activity An activity that customers perceive as adding usefulness to the product or service they purchase.

Value analysis A systematic interdisciplinary examination of factors affecting the cost of a product or service in order to devise means of achieving the specified purpose at the required standard of quality and reliability at the target cost, also known as value engineering.

Value engineering A systematic interdisciplinary examination of factors affecting the cost of a product or service in order to devise means of achieving the specified purpose at the required standard of quality and reliability at the target cost, also known as value analysis.

Value-chain analysis The analysis, coordination and optimization of the linked set of value-creating activities all the way from basic raw material sources for component suppliers through to the ultimate end-use product or service delivered to the customer.

ASSESSMENT MATERIAL

The review questions are short questions that enable you to assess your understanding of the main topics included in the chapter. The numbers in parentheses provide you with the page numbers to refer to if you cannot answer a specific question.

The review problems are more complex and require you to relate and apply the content to various business problems. Solutions to review problems are provided in a separate section at the end of the book. Additional review problems can be accessed by lecturers and students on the dedicated online support resources for this book. Solutions to these review problems are provided for lecturers in the *Instructor's Manual* accompanying this book that can be downloaded from the dedicated online instructor's resources (see Preface for details).

The dedicated online digital support resources for this book also includes over 30 case study problems.

REVIEW QUESTIONS

15.1 How does cost management differ from traditional management accounting control systems? *(pp. 384–385)*

15.2 What are committed (locked-in) costs? *(p. 385)*

15.3 Explain the essential features of life-cycle costing. *(pp. 385–386)*

15.4 Describe the stages involved with target costing. Describe how costs are reduced so that the target cost can be achieved. *(pp. 386–389)*

15.5 What are the distinguishing features of activity-based management? *(pp. 392–395)*

15.6 Distinguish between value added and non-value added activities. *(p. 394)*

15.7 What is business process re-engineering? *(p. 397)*

15.8 Identify and discuss the four kinds of quality costs that are included in a cost of quality report. Give examples of costs that fall within each category. *(p. 404)*

15.9 Discuss the value of a cost of quality report. *(pp. 404–405)*

15.10 Explain what is meant by value-chain analysis. Illustrate how value-chain analysis can be applied. *(pp. 406–408)*

15.11 Explain how benchmarking can be used to manage costs and improve activity performance. *(p. 396)*

15.12 What are the major features of a just-in-time manufacturing philosophy? *(pp. 397–399)*

15.13 Distinguish between a pull and push manufacturing system. *(pp. 399–400)*

15.14 What are the essential features of just-in-time purchasing arrangements? *(p. 401)*

REVIEW PROBLEMS

15.15 Target costing and value chain

PBB is a toy manufacturer and retailer. PBB sells toys to consumers through its large network of retail outlets in its home country and via the company's website.

PBB purchases the materials and components that it needs to manufacture toys from a number of different suppliers. All of the purchases are delivered to PBB's raw material store at its factory and are held there until they are needed for production.

Finished toys are transported from the factory to PBB's retail outlets by PBB's fleet of vehicles. The vehicles follow the same schedule each week irrespective of the load they are carrying. Finished toys that are destined for sale via the company's website are transported to PBB's distribution centre.

PBB has recently won the contract to manufacture and sell a new toy. The new toy, Toy Z, is a doll based on a character from a very popular international children's film. PBB is free to set the selling price of Toy Z as it sees fit, but must pay a royalty fee of 15 per cent of the selling price to the film company. PBB intends to sell Toy Z through its network of retail outlets.

PBB plans to adopt a target costing approach for Toy Z. Market research has determined that the selling price will be $25 per Toy Z. PBB requires a profit margin of 25 per cent of the selling price of Toy Z.

The forecast costs per Toy Z are:

	$
Component A	2.15
Component B	1.75
Other materials	see note below for additional information
Labour (0.4 hours at $15 per hour)	6.00
Product-specific production overhead cost	1.89
Product-specific selling and distribution cost	2.38

Note: Each Toy Z requires 0.6kg of 'other materials'. These 'other materials' are purchased from a supplier at a cost of $4 per kg and 4 per cent of all materials purchased are found to be substandard.

Required:

(a) Calculate the cost gap that exists between the forecast total cost per unit and the target cost per unit of Toy Z.

(3 marks)

(b) Discuss how PBB could reduce costs in THREE primary activities in its value chain.

(7 marks)

15.16 Cost of quality reporting

JMM is a car manufacturer. It is a relatively new company and the directors are keen to establish a reputation for high quality. The management of JMM recognizes the need to establish a culture of Total Quality Management (TQM) at the company.

The management accounting team at JMM has collected the following actual information for the most recent quarter of the current year:

Cost data

	$
Customer support centre cost per hour	58
Equipment testing cost per hour	30
Manufacturing rework cost per car	380
Warranty repair cost per car	2 600

Volume and activity data

Cars requiring manufacturing rework	800 cars
Cars requiring warranty repair	650 cars
Customer support centre time	500 hours
Production line equipment testing time	400 hours

Additional information

JMM undertook a quality review of its existing suppliers during the quarter at a cost of $60 000.

Due to the quality issues in the quarter, the car production line experienced periods of unproductive 'down time' which cost $375 000.

Required:

(a) Produce a Cost of Quality report for JMM using the four recognized quality cost headings.

(6 marks)

(b) Explain how a Cost of Quality report would support the development of a TQM culture at JMM.

(4 marks)

15.17 Benchmarking

Ganymede University (GU) is one of the three largest universities in Teeland, which has eight universities in total. All of the universities are in the public sector. GU obtains the vast majority of its revenue through government contracts for academic research and payments per head for teaching students. The economy of Teeland has been in recession in the last year and this has caused the government to cut funding for all the universities in the country.

In order to try to improve efficiency, the chancellor of the university, who leads its executive board, has asked the head administrator to undertake an exercise to benchmark GU's administration departments against the other two large universities in the country, AU and BU. The government

education ministry has supported this initiative and has required all three universities to cooperate by supplying information.

The following information has been collected regarding administrative costs for the most recent academic year:

	GU $000	AU $000	BU $000
Research			
Contract management	14 430	14 574	14 719
Laboratory management	41 810	42 897	42 646
Teaching facilities management	26 993	27 263	26 723
Student support services	2 002	2 022	2 132
Teachers' support services	4 005	4 100	4 441
Accounting	1 614	1 571	1 611
Human resources	1 236	1 203	1 559
IT management	6 471	6 187	6 013
General services	17 049	16 095	18 644
Total	115 610	115 912	118 488
Drivers:			
Student numbers	28 394	22 783	29 061
Staff numbers	7 920	7 709	8 157
Research contract value $m	185	167	152

The key drivers of costs and revenues have been assumed to be research contract values supported, student numbers and total staff numbers. The head administrator wants you to complete the benchmarking and make some preliminary comments on your results.

Required:

(a) Assess the progress of the benchmarking exercise to date, explaining the actions that have been undertaken and those that are still required.

(8 marks)

(b) Evaluate, as far as possible, Ganymede University's benchmarked position.

(9 marks)

ACCA P5 Advanced Performance Management

15.18 Preparations of a cost of quality statement

Telecoms At Work (TAW) manufactures and markets office communications systems. During the year ended 31 May TAW made an operating profit of $30 million on sales of $360 million. However, the directors are concerned that products do not conform to the required level of quality and TAW is therefore not fulfilling its full potential in terms of turnover and profits achieved.

The following information is available in respect of the year ended 31 May:

1 Production data:

Units manufactured and sold	18 000
Units requiring rework	2 100
Units requiring warranty repair service	2 700
Design engineering hours	48 000
Process engineering hours	54 000
Inspection hours (manufacturing)	288 000

2 Cost data:

	$
Design engineering per hour	96
Process engineering per hour	70
Inspection per hour (manufacturing)	50
Rework per communication system reworked (manufacturing)	4 800
Customer support per repaired unit (marketing)	240
Transportation costs per repaired unit (distribution)	280
Warranty repairs per repaired unit (customer service)	4 600

3 Staff training costs amounted to $180 000 and additional product testing costs of $72 000.

4 The marketing director has estimated that sales of 1 800 units were lost as a result of public knowledge of poor quality at TAW. The average contribution per communication system is estimated at $7200.

Required:

(a) Prepare a cost analysis which shows actual prevention costs, appraisal costs, internal failure costs, and external failure costs for the year ended 31 May. Your statement should show each cost heading as a per cent of turnover and clearly show the total cost of quality. Comment briefly on the inclusion of opportunity costs in such an analysis.

(11 marks)

(b) A detailed analysis has revealed that the casings in which the communications systems are housed are often subject to mishandling in transit to TAW's manufacturing premises. The directors are considering two alternative solutions proposed by the design engineering team which are aimed at reducing the quality problems that are currently being experienced. These are as follows:

Option 1 – Increase the number of immediate physical inspections of the casings when they are received from the supplier. This will require an additional 10 000 inspection hours.

Option 2 – Redesign and strengthen the casings and the containers used to transport them to better withstand mishandling during transportation. Redesign will require an additional 2000 hours of design engineering and an additional 5000 hours of process engineering.

Internal failure costs of rework for each reworked communication system are as follows:

		$
Variable costs	(including direct materials, direct labour rework and supplies)	1 920
Allocated fixed costs	(equipment, space and allocated overhead)	2 880
Total costs (as per note 2 on cost data)		4 800

The directors of TAW believe that, even if it is able to achieve improvements in quality, it will be unable to save any of the fixed costs of internal and external failure.

If TAW chooses to inspect the casings more carefully, it expects to eliminate re-work on 720 communication systems whereas if it redesigns the casings it expects to eliminate rework on 960 communication systems.

If incoming casings are inspected more carefully, TAW estimates that 600 fewer communication systems will require warranty repair and that it will be able to sell an additional 300 communication systems. If the casing is redesigned, the directors estimate that 840 fewer communication systems will require warranty repair and that an additional 360 communication systems will be sold.

External failure costs of repair for each repaired communication system are as follows:

	Variable costs $	Fixed costs $	Total costs $
Customer support costs	96	144	240
Transportation costs	210	70	280
Warranty repair costs	1 700	2 900	4 600

Required:

Prepare an estimate of the financial consequences of each option and advise the directors of TAW which option should be chosen.

(9 marks)

15.19 Traditional and activity-based budget statements and life-cycle costing

The budget for the production, planning and development department of Obba plc, is currently prepared as part of a traditional budgetary planning and control system. The analysis of costs by expense type for the period ended 30 November where this system is in use is as follows:

Expense type	Budget %	Actual %
Salaries	60	63
Supplies	6	5
Travel cost	12	12
Technology cost	10	7
Occupancy cost	12	13

The total budget and actual costs for the department for the period ended 30 November are €1 000 000 and €1 060 000 respectively.

The company now feels that an activity-based budgeting approach should be used. A number of activities have been identified for the production, planning and development department. An investigation has indicated that total budget and actual costs should be attributed to the activities on the following basis:

Activities	Budget %	Actual %
1 Routing/scheduling – new products	20	16
2 Routing/scheduling – existing products	40	34
3 Remedial re-routing/scheduling	5	12
4 Special studies – specific orders	10	8
5 Training	10	15
6 Management and administration	15	15

Required:

(a) (i) Prepare *two* budget control statements for the production planning and development department for the period ended 30 November which compare budget with actual cost and show variances using:
  1 a traditional expense based analysis and
  2 an activity based analysis.

(6 marks)

(ii) Identify and comment on *four* advantages claimed for the use of activity based budgeting over traditional budgeting using the production planning and development example to illustrate your answer.

(12 marks)

(iii) Comment on the use of the information provided in the activity based statement which you prepared in (i) in activity based performance measurement and suggest additional information which would assist in such performance measurement.

(8 marks)

(b) Other activities have been identified and the budget quantified for the three months ended 31 March as follows:

Activities	Cost driver unit basis	Units of Cost driver	Cost (€000)
Product design	design hours	8 000	2 000 (see note 1)
Purchasing	purchase orders	4 000	200
Production	machine hours	12 000	1 500 (see note 2)
Packing	volume (cu.m.)	20 000	400
Distribution	weight (kg)	120 000	600

Note 1: this includes all design costs for new products released this period.
Note 2: this includes a depreciation provision of €300 000 of which €8000 applies to 3 months' depreciation on a straight line basis for a new product (NPD). The remainder applies to other products.

New product NPD is included in the above budget. The following additional information applies to NPD:

(i) Estimated total output over the product life cycle: 5000 units (four years life cycle).
(ii) Product design requirement: 400 design hours
(iii) Output in quarter ended 31 March: 250 units
(iv) Equivalent batch size per purchase order: 50 units
(v) Other product unit data: production time 0.75 machine hours: volume 0.4 cu. metres; weight 3 kg.

Required:

Prepare a unit overhead cost for product NPD using an activity based approach which includes an appropriate share of life-cycle costs using the information provided in (b) above.

(9 marks)

(Total 35 marks)

15.20 Cost management
Navier Aerials Co (Navier) manufactures satellite dishes for receiving satellite television signals. Navier supplies the major satellite TV companies who install standard satellite dishes for their customers. The company also manufactures and installs a small number of specialized satellite dishes to individuals or businesses with specific needs resulting from poor reception in their locations.

The chief executive officer (CEO) wants to initiate a programme of cost reduction at Navier. His plan is to use activity-based management (ABM) to allocate costs more accurately and to identify non-value adding activities. The first department to be analysed is the customer care department, as it has been believed for some time that the current method of cost allocation is giving unrealistic results for the two product types.

At present, the finance director (FD) absorbs the cost of customer care into the product cost on a per unit basis using the data in Table 1. He then tries to correct the problem of unrealistic costing by making rough estimates of the costs to be allocated to each product, based on the operations director's impression of the amount of work of the department. In fact, he simply adds $100 above the standard absorbed cost to the cost of a specialized dish to cover the assumed extra work involved at customer care.

The cost accountant has gathered information for the customer care department in Table 2 from interviews with the finance and customer care staff. She has used this information to correctly calculate the total costs of each activity using activity-based costing in Table 3. The CEO wants you, as a senior management accountant, to complete the work required for a comparison of the results of the current standard absorption costing to activity-based costing for the standard and specialized dishes.

Once this is done, the CEO wants you to consider the implications for management of the customer care process of the costs of each activity in that department. The CEO is especially interested in how this information may impact on the identification of non-valued added activities and quality management at Navier.

Navier Dishes (information for the year ending 31 March)
Customer care (CC) department

Table 1: Existing costing data

	$000
Salaries	400
Computer time	165
Telephone	79
Stationery and sundries	27
Depreciation of equipment	36
	707

Note:

(i) CC cost is currently allocated to each dish based on 16 000 orders a year, where each order contains an average of 5.5 dishes.

Table 2: Activity-costing data

Activities of CC dept	Staff time	Comments
Handling enquiries and preparing quotes for potential orders	40%	relates to 35 000 enquiries/quotes per year
Receiving actual orders	10%	relates to 16 000 orders in the year
Customer credit checks	10%	done once an order is received
Supervision of orders through manufacture to delivery	15%	
Complaints handling	25%	relates to 3200 complaints per year

Notes:

1 Total department cost is allocated using staff time as this drives all of the other costs in the department.

2 90 per cent of both enquiries and orders are for standard dishes. The remainder are for specialized dishes.

3 Handling enquiries and preparing quotes for specialized dishes takes 20 per cent of staff time allocated to this activity.

4 The process for receiving an order, checking customer credit and supervision of the order is the same for both a specialized dish order and a standard dish order.

5 50 per cent of the complaints received are for specialized dish orders.

6 Each standard dish order contains an average of six dishes.

7 Each specialized dish order contains an average of one dish.

Table 3: Activity-based costs

	Total $	Standard $	Specialized $
Handling enquiries and preparing quotes	282 800	226 240	56 560
Receiving actual orders	70 700	63 630	7 070
Customer credit checks	70 700	63 630	7 070
Supervision of order through manufacture to delivery	106 050	95 445	10 605
Complaints handling	176 750	88 375	88 375
Total	707 000	537 320	169 680

Required:

(a) Evaluate the impact of using activity-based costing, compared to the existing costing system for customer care, on the cost of both types of product.

(13 marks)

(b) Assess how the information on each activity can be used and improved upon at Navier in assisting cost reduction and quality management in the customer care department.

Note: There is no need to make comments on the different product types here.

(12 marks)

16
CHALLENGES FOR THE FUTURE

LEARNING OBJECTIVES After studying this chapter you should be able to:

- explain the meaning of sustainable development and shared value
- describe environmental management accounting
- explain the role of the management accountant in avoiding unethical behaviour
- explain how today's information technology is changing the role of the management accountant
- discuss whether globalization causes management accounting practices to differ across national borders
- explain the meaning of intellectual capital
- describe integrated reporting.

In Chapter 1 the important changes that have taken place in the business environment over the past few decades were described. It was pointed out how these changes significantly altered the ways in which firms operated and, throughout the book, the ways in which these changes have influenced management accounting practices were described. In this chapter we shall concentrate on the emerging issues that are likely to have an impact on management accounting and consider some potential future developments in management accounting. To fully understand future developments it is helpful to understand how management accounting has evolved over the years. The chapter therefore begins with a brief history of management accounting.

A BRIEF HISTORICAL REVIEW OF MANAGEMENT ACCOUNTING

The origins of today's management accounting can be traced back to the Industrial Revolution of the nineteenth century. During the late 1980s criticisms of current management accounting practices were widely publicized in the professional and academic accounting literature. In 1987 Johnson and Kaplan's book, entitled *Relevance Lost: The Rise and Fall of Management Accounting*, was published. An enormous amount of publicity was generated by this book as a result of the authors' criticisms of management accounting. Many other commentators also concluded that management accounting was in crisis and that fundamental changes in practice were required.

According to Johnson and Kaplan (1987), most of the management accounting practices that were in use in the mid-1980s had been developed by 1925, and for the next 60 years there was a slow down, or even a halt, in management accounting innovation. They argue that this stagnation could be attributed mainly to the demand for product cost information for external financial accounting reports. The separation of the ownership and management of organizations created a need for the owners of a business to monitor the effective stewardship of their investment. This need led to the development of financial accounting. Statutory obligations were established requiring companies to publish audited annual financial statements. In addition, there was a requirement for these published statements to conform to a set of rules known as generally accepted accounting principles (GAAP), which were developed by regulators.

The preparation of published external financial accounting statements required that costs be allocated between cost of goods sold and inventories. Cost accounting emerged to meet this requirement. Simple procedures were established to allocate costs to products that were objective and verifiable for financial accounting purposes. Such costs, however, were not sufficiently accurate for decision-making purposes and for distinguishing between profitable and unprofitable products and services. Johnson and Kaplan argue that the product costs derived for financial accounting purposes were also being used for management accounting purposes. They conclude that managers did not have to yield the design of management accounting systems to financial accountants and auditors. Separate systems could have been maintained for managerial and financial accounting purposes, but the high cost of information collection meant that the costs of maintaining two systems exceeded the additional benefits. Thus companies relied primarily on the same information as that used for external financial reporting to manage their internal operations.

Johnson and Kaplan claim that, over the years, organizations had become fixated on the cost systems of the 1920s. Furthermore, when the information systems were automated in the 1960s, the system designers merely automated the manual systems that were developed in the 1920s. Johnson and Kaplan conclude that the lack of management accounting innovation over the decades, and the failure to respond to its changing environment, resulted in a situation in the mid-1980s where firms were using management accounting systems that were obsolete and no longer relevant to the changing competitive and business environment.

Since the mid-1980s management accounting practitioners and academics have sought to modify and implement new techniques that are relevant to today's environment that will ensure that management accounting regains its relevance. Many new management accounting tools such as activity-based costing, activity-based management and the balanced scorecard emerged in the late 1980s and early 1990s and over the years they have been refined and modified. By the mid-1990s Kaplan (1994) stated that:

> The past ten years have seen a revolution in management accounting theory and practice. The seeds of the revolution can be seen in publications in the early to mid-1980s that identified the failings and obsolescence of existing cost and performance measurement systems. Since that time we have seen remarkable

innovations in management accounting; even more remarkable has been the speed with which the new concepts have become widely known, accepted and implemented in practice and integrated into a large number of educational programmes.

Nevertheless many of the techniques that were developed decades ago such as budgeting, variance analysis, cost-volume-profit analysis and payback investment appraisal are still widely used today. Indeed, if you were to compare the content of the first edition of this book published in 1985 with the current edition you would find a significant overlap in the content of both books. One reason for this is that the techniques have been adapted to respond to the changing environment. What will be the future of management accounting? In the following sections the emerging issues and their possible impact on management accounting are discussed.

ENVIRONMENTAL AND SUSTAINABILITY ISSUES

Increasing attention is now being given to making companies accountable for ethical, social and environmental issues and the need for organizations to be managed in a sustainable way. There is now a general recognition that environmental resources are limited and should be preserved for future generations. Social factors relating to a company's impact on the community, the provision of employment and safe working conditions and a concern for society as a whole have also emerged as important issues that companies should concentrate on.

Recently more attention has been given to social responsibility reporting relating to ethical, social and environmental issues within company's published annual *external* reports, possibly due to pressures from stakeholders and government regulations requiring more social responsibility reporting. Different terms are often used to describe social responsibility reporting such as sustainability reporting, eco-reporting and corporate accountability reporting. Social disclosures may be mandatory (a legal requirement to deliver this information) or voluntary. The United Nations is recommending that all large firms be mandated to publish sustainability reports by 2030.

According to Bernardi and Stark (2018) the preferred format for social responsibility reporting has typically been a stand-alone report, but a concern with stand-alone reports relating to environmental and social activities is that they provide non-financial information which is non-integrated and compartmentalized. Therefore, they are not capable of providing stakeholders with the required links and connections that are fundamental to effectively evaluating business performance, strategy and potential for future value creation. Integrated reporting is a response to this criticism. Integrated reporting is described later in this chapter, but at this point you should note that it aims to provide information on financial and non-financial/social performance in a single document, showing the relationship between financial and non-financial performance and how these inter-related dimensions are creating or destroying value for shareholders and other stakeholders.

Even though more attention has been given to has been given to social responsibility within company's annual *external* reports, it has been argued by some that the reporting has been cosmetic, based on public relations campaigns to publicize the company's social and environmental good deeds. For example, Hopper and Bui (2016) state that

REAL WORLD VIEWS 16.1

BP Gulf of Mexico oil accident

According to a US Congressional enquiry, this accident apparently partly resulted from local decisions within the oil multinational BP and its contractors to save relatively immaterial costs by cutting corners in oil exploration safety measures (National Commission on the BP Deepwater Horizon Oil Spill & Offshore Drilling, 2011). The ensuing accident might have been prevented had more robust safety measures been in place. It directly killed 11 workers employed on the oil drilling exploration rig. It also directly caused large-scale oil pollution in the Gulf of Mexico and directly incurred large economic costs for BP and its partners in extinguishing the fire, stopping the oil leak and cleaning up some of the spilt oil.

These direct (and fairly immediate) external impacts on social, environmental and economic factors themselves then caused many other negative impacts in these areas. Thus, for example, the oil pollution killed many fish, prevented many fishermen going to sea to catch fish for a period and damaged the tourist industry in states close to the oil spill (National Commission on the BP Deepwater Horizon Oil Spill &

Offshore Drilling, 2011). The negative environmental impact from the oil spill therefore caused other social and economic impacts on communities in coastal areas close to the oil spill. Several of these and other impacts then fed through into further economic impacts for BP and its contractors who were required to pay compensation to those affected and who suffered reputation damage. In total, BP reported costs of US$40.9 billion in 2010 associated with the Gulf oil spill.

Questions

1 Do you think environmental costs and benefits can be accurately measured?
2 Do issues such as the environment help management accountants become more strategically important members of the organization?

References

Unerman, J. and Chapman, C. (2014) 'Academic contributions to enhancing accounting for sustainable development', *Accounting, Organizations and Society*, 39(6), 385–94.
National Commission on the BP Deepwater Horizon Oil Spill and Offshore Drilling (2011). Deep Water: The Gulf Oil Disaster and the Future of Offshore Drilling: Report to the President, Washington DC, US Independent Agencies and Commissions.

for some external corporate reporting will only produce 'greenwashing' that gives the impression of adoption of sustainability practices to gain external legitimacy and to mitigate pressures for environmental reform.

The social responsibility reporting literature has tended to focus on reporting within company's published annual *external* reports, but to manage corporate, environmental and social activities more effectively there is a need for an appropriate *internal* management accounting system that supports a company's strategic environmental, social and ethical objectives. Management accounting has also been criticized for not giving sufficient attention to how social, environmental and sustainability issues can be incorporated within management accounting information systems. In 2013 a major international management accounting research journal (*Management Accounting Research*) published a special issue titled 'Sustainable development, management and accounting: Boundary crossing', edited by Bebbington and Thomson (2013). The editors stated that the aim of the special issue was to provide an impetus for the evolution of a sustainable development-orientated management accounting.

The principle of sustainability requires that companies should operate in ways that secure long-term economic performance by avoiding short-term behaviour that is socially detrimental or environmentally wasteful. The most widely quoted definition of sustainable development is 'An approach to progress which meets the needs of the present without compromising the ability of future generations to meet their own needs' (World Commission on Environment and Development, 1987).

Porter and Kramer (2006) argue that companies that pursue their economic objectives at the expense of the society in which they operate will find that their success will be illusory and temporary. Conversely a healthy society needs successful companies to create jobs, wealth and improved living standards.

In a later article Porter and Kramer (2011) argue that neither a business nor a society should pursue policies that benefit their interests at the expense of the other since a temporary gain for one will undermine the long-term prosperity of both. They recommend that companies should follow the principle of **shared value**, which they define as policies and operating practices that enhance the competitiveness of a company while simultaneously advancing economic and social conditions in the communities in which it operates. Porter and Kramer provide the following examples of how shared value thinking is transforming the value chain:

Energy use and logistics: Some companies are redesigning their logistical systems to reduce transportation systems. Marks and Spencer has overhauled its supply chain by stopping the purchase of supplies from one hemisphere and transporting to another. This was expected to result in £175 million annual savings by 2016, while hugely reducing carbon emissions.

Resource usage: Advances in technology are providing opportunities for companies to develop new approaches for reducing the usage of water, raw materials and packaging. Coca-Cola reduced its worldwide consumption of water by nearly 20 per cent between 2004 and 2012.

Procurement: Nestlé required a reliable supply of specialized coffees and redesigned its procurement by working intensively with local growers, providing advice on farming practices, guaranteeing bank loans and helping to secure inputs such as pesticides and fertilizers. The company has succeeded over the years in improving the standard of living of local farmers while ensuring itself a stable supply of high quality commodities at a competitive cost.

Distribution: Re-examining distribution practices provides opportunities for creating shared value. Kindle, iTunes and the publishing and newspaper industry have established alternative electronic distribution approaches that reduce paper and transportation usage.

Further examples of how some companies are using opportunities throughout the value chain to create shared value and sustainability by increasing revenues, controlling costs, building trust and managing risk are illustrated in a report by Accenture and the Chartered Institute of Management Accountants (2011) (see Exhibit 16.1).

Environmental cost management

Management accounting systems have given insufficient attention to creating shared value. Instead, the response has been reactive rather than proactive by focusing on

EXHIBIT 16.1   Business benefits from sustainability

Company value chain	Revenue generation	Cost control	Building trust	Risk management
Procurement and logistics • Supply chain • Warehousing • Equipment • Inbound logistics	The **Co-operative** switched its own-label chocolate to Fairtrade suppliers in 2002, resulting in a 50% sales volume uplift in the following 12 months.	**Walmart** substantially exceeded a target of 25% improvement in fleet efficiency against 2005 baseline within one year.	**Walmart's** ethical standards programme for sourcing merchandise is recognized as one of the 'gold standards' in the industry.	In July 2009, energy drink manufacturer **Red Bull** was ordered to pay over £270 000 in fines and costs for breaking recycling laws.
Operations • Products • Services • Operations • Buildings • Manufacturing	**Philips** earns 38% of total revenue from 'green product' sales (up from 31% in 2009). **M&S's** 'Plan A' generated £50m profit from new products – such as M&S Energy which provides insulation and solar panels for 300 000 customers – and reduced costs in only the third year of its operation in 2009–10.	**IKEA** saved £1m by removing plastic bags from checkouts in the UK in 30 months. Its stores are 9% more energy efficient compared to 2005. Japanese pharmaceutical firm **Tanabe Seiyaku** hit annual savings of ¥33m with new environmental accounting techniques.	**GE's** brand value increased by 17% after the launch of 'Ecomagination', a business initiative to meet customer demand for more energy-efficient products.	**Taylerson's Malmesbury Syrup** realized that sales of their products were linked to cold weather and would decline within the next 20 years as winters become milder. The product range was reviewed and they now provide syrups to be used with ice creams and cold frappes.
Marketing, sales and service • Marketing • Sales • CRM • Retail • Customer service • Outbound logistics	**Vodafone's** 'Carbon Connections' report demonstrates a potential for 113Mt reduction in CO$_2$e and €43bn in cost reductions through 1bn new mobile connections.	**M&S's** 'Marks and Start' programme (work experience for disadvantaged adults) has lower attrition rates than comparable schemes for new employees.	77% of consumers have, in the past year, refused to buy products/services from companies they do not trust. Trust must be built or sales are put at risk.	The **Co-operative Bank** showed the risk associated with a loss of trust, citing the 'flight to trust' after the banking crisis as one of the key drivers of a 38% increase in their own current account sales in 2009.
Support activities • Finance • Technology • R&D • HR • Legal • Firm infrastructure	**Novo Nordisk** bring products to market faster by including environmental, social and economic impacts in new drug applications.	**Fife Council** have identified additional cost avoidance opportunities of £75m that can be achieved by improving its carbon reductions by a further 3% per annum between 2007 and 2021.	Graduating MBAs from leading **North American and European business schools** are willing to forgo financial benefits to work for a more ethical employer.	**Ribena** noticed that local weather patterns have been changing, affecting their blackcurrant harvests. They have been developing new varieties of blackcurrants that will thrive in a changing climate.

Source: Sustainability performance management. Copyright © 2011 Accenture and Chartered Institute of Management Accountants. All rights reserved.

managing escalating environmental costs arising from meeting regulatory requirements and seeking to avoid litigation and fines. Environmental costs are large in some industrial sectors. For example, Ranganathan and Ditz (1996) reported that Amoco's environmental costs at its Yorktown refinery were at least 22 per cent of operating costs. Henri et al. (2014) have also reported that industry's total environmental protection expenditure for the European Union is now more than 45 billion euros representing approximately 0.4 per cent of gross domestic product. Therefore, selecting the least costly method of compliance has become a major objective. These developments have resulted in some companies focusing on measuring, reporting and monitoring environmental costs. In 2005 the International Federation of Accountants (IFAC) issued a guidance document that provides a general framework and set of definitions for environmental management accounting (see www.ifac.org).

Nevertheless, there is evidence to suggest that many companies have not been able to identify their total environmental costs and do not recognize that they can be controlled and reduced (Epstein and Roy, 1997). A study by Bartolomeo et al. (2000) involving interviews with accountants and environmental managers in 84 companies in Germany, Italy, the Netherlands and the UK reported that only 50 per cent of the European companies were explicitly tracking any of a number of named environmental costs. They concluded that opportunities existed for many companies to become more active in environmental management accounting and that the pressures on them to do so will increase. A more recent study by Henri et al. (2014 and 2016) of 319 Canadian manufacturing firms concluded that many of the sampled firms did not track environmental costs extensively.

Henri et al. also reported that there was a statistical positive relationship between the tracking of environmental costs and the implementation of environmental initiatives. They attribute their findings to the fact that the tracking of environmental costs provides feedback that focuses organizational attention on the search for innovative ways to reduce environmental costs and their impacts. More specifically, the tracking of environmental costs facilitates the understanding of the links between costs and output, and provides insights into possible cost reductions through specific actions on cost drivers, such as the reduction in the material and energy intensity of goods or services, the reduction in the dispersion of toxic materials and improvement in recyclability by product and process redesign. They conclude that the tracking of environmental costs acts (i) as a catalyst for efficiency improvements *within the same cost structure*; and (ii) it acts as a catalyst for new initiatives which help to create a *different cost structure*.

In most cost accounting systems, environmental costs are hidden within general overheads and are either not allocated to cost objects or are allocated on an arbitrary basis within the allocation of general overheads. Thus crucial relationships are not identified between environmental costs and the responsible products, processes and underlying activities. For example, Ranganathan and Ditz (1996) point out that the principal environmental issue facing Spectrum Glass, a major manufacturer of speciality sheet glass, is the use and release of cadmium. It discovered that only one product (ruby red glass) was responsible for all of its cadmium emissions, but the cost accounting system allocated a portion of this cost to all products. This process resulted in ruby red glass being undercosted and other products being overcosted.

Environmental costs should be accumulated by separate cost pools, analysed by appropriate categories and traced to the products or processes that caused the costs using ABC concepts. Knowledge of the amount and categories of environmental costs, and their causes, provides the information that managers need to not only manage environmental costs more effectively by process redesign but to also reduce the pollutants emitted to the environment.

The United Nations Division for Sustainable Development (UNDSD) identified **input/output analysis** as a technique that could be used to reduce the usage of environmental resources and costs. Inflows of resources such as water, materials and energy are recorded and balanced with outflows on the basis that, what comes in, must go out. For example if 10 000kg/litres of a resource has been acquired but only 9000kg/litres have been used in the productive process then the 1000kg/litres difference must be accounted for. The balance may represent avoidable waste, so actions should be taken to eliminate in the future. By accounting for inputs and outputs in this way, both in terms of physical quantities and, at the end of the process, in monetary terms too, businesses can seek to reduce environmental costs.

Hansen and Mendoza (1999) point out that environmental costs are incurred because of poor environmental quality controls and thus are similar in nature to quality costs discussed in Chapter 15. They advocate that an environmental cost report should be periodically produced, based on the principles of a cost of quality report (see Exhibit 15.2) to indicate the total environmental costs to the organization associated with the creation, detection, remedy and prevention of environmental degradation. Adopting a similar classification as that used for quality costs, the following four categories of environmental costs can be reported:

1 **Environmental prevention costs** are the costs of activities undertaken to prevent the production of waste that could cause damage to the environment. Examples include the costs associated with the design and operation of processes to reduce contaminants, training employees, recycling products and obtaining certification relating to meeting the requirements of international and national standards.

2 **Environmental detection costs** are the costs incurred to ensure that a firm's activities, products and processes conform to regulatory laws and voluntary standards. Examples include inspection of products and processes to ensure regulatory compliance, auditing environmental activities and performing contamination tests.

3 **Environmental internal failure costs** are the costs incurred from performing activities that have produced contaminants and waste that have not been discharged into the environment. Such costs are incurred to eliminate or reduce waste to levels that comply with regulatory requirements. Examples include the costs of disposing of toxic materials and recycling scrap.

4 **Environmental external failure costs** are the costs incurred on activities performed after discharging waste into the environment. Examples include the costs of cleaning up contaminated soil, restoring land to its natural state and cleaning up oil spills and waste discharges. Clearly this category of costs has the greatest impact on a company in terms of adverse publicity. For example, the cost to BP of the oil leak arising from the Deepwater Horizon oil disaster was estimated to be $61bn. The disaster has had a dramatic negative impact on BP's image (see Real World Views 16.1).

The environmental cost report should be similar in format to the cost of quality report (see Exhibit 15.2) with each category of costs expressed as a percentage of sales revenues (or operating costs) so that comparisons can be made with previous periods, other organizations and divisions within the same group. The environmental cost report should be used as an attention directing device to make top management aware of how much is being spent on environmental costs and the relative amount in each category. The report also draws management's attention to those areas that have the greatest potential for cost reduction. The same principles as those described for quality cost reporting also apply. That is, investing more in prevention and detection activities has the potential to significantly reduce environmental failure costs. A major limitation of environmental cost reports is that they only report those environmental costs for which the company is responsible. The report does not include externality costs that are caused by a firm but borne by society. Examples include losing land for recreational use and damaging ecosystems from solid waste disposal. Attempts should be made to develop non-financial and/or qualitative measures that draw attention to how an organization is contributing to becoming environmentally responsible and a good social citizen.

Managing and reporting carbon emissions

Managing and reporting carbon emissions have become increasingly popular among large corporations. Ernst and Young's (2012) survey reported that more than 75 per cent of large global companies have set carbon emission reduction targets and disclosed carbon emission information, with another 16 per cent indicating that they plan to do so in five years. Similarly, a survey by KPMG (2015) revealed that 73 per cent of the top 100 companies across 45 countries report their social and environmental responsibility activities publicly. The Carbon Disclosure Project (CDP) reported that by 2016, 97 per cent of world-leading companies had established carbon emission reduction initiatives, and 85 per cent had formulated and reported absolute or relative carbon emission reduction targets (CDP, 2016 a and b).

A more fundamental question, however, is whether the reporting of carbon emissions is associated with improvements in carbon performance. A study by Qian and Schaltegger (2017) of Global Fortune 500 companies in the Carbon Disclosure Project (CDP), of their carbon emission and disclosure data released during 2008 and 2012 found that changes in carbon disclosure levels were positively associated with subsequent changes in carbon performance.

A study by Kumarasiri and Gunasekarage (2017) examined how perceptions of climate change uncertainties and external pressure for disclosure of emissions information influenced Australian companies to use management accounting in managing climate change risk. They interviewed 39 emissions management executives representing 18 randomly chosen companies. They found that companies used techniques such as target setting and measurement to a great extent. The majority of interviewees believed that emission targets helped their companies to focus clearly on the emission management goals, while all interviewees felt that measurement of carbon emissions assisted them in better understanding emissions drivers and enabled their companies to take effective actions on reducing their carbon footprints.

The role of management accounting in supporting the creation of shared value and sustainable development

In addition to managing and controlling environmental costs, management accounting systems should support the creation of shared value and sustainable development.

A report titled 'Sustainability Performance Management' by Accenture and the Chartered Institute of Management Accountants (2011) identified that the two major sustainability roles for the finance function were assisting in providing information for making the business case for creating shared value by reconfiguring the value and developing new products and tracking sustainability related key performance indicators. The environmental consequences of products should be evaluated using the life-cycle cost management approach described in Chapter 15. In other words, the environmental consequences and opportunities for creating shared value should be managed at the planning and design stage and not at the manufacturing stage when a substantial proportion of the environmental costs and outcomes will already have been determined.

Incorporating a society/environmental perspective within a balanced scorecard framework has been adopted by some companies to link their environmental strategy to concrete performance measures. The balanced scorecard framework requires that within the scorecard the environmental objectives are clearly specified. Typical objectives include minimizing the use of hazardous materials, minimizing energy requirements, minimizing the release of pollutants and other opportunities for creating shared value. These objectives should be translated into specific performance measures. In addition, within the scorecard, firms should describe the major initiatives for achieving each objective and also establish targets for each performance measure. For feedback reporting, actual performance measures should also be added.

FOCUS ON ETHICAL BEHAVIOUR

Management accounting practices have developed to provide information that assists managers to maximize future profits. It is too simplistic, however, to assume that the only objective of a business firm is to maximize profits. The profit maximization objective should be constrained by the need for firms to also give high priority to their social responsibilities and ensure that their employees adopt high standards of **ethical behaviour**. Managers have responsibility to avoid the narrow pursuit of profits at any cost.

Identification of what is acceptable ethical behaviour has attracted much attention in recent years with numerous examples of companies attracting negative coverage for ethical failings and their impact on reported profits. For example, Volkswagen (VW), Europe's biggest car maker, has suffered a dramatic decline in its reputation after the revelation that it fitted software designed to cheat emission tests to 11 million cars worldwide. VW has set aside €18.4 billion to cover the costs of legal action, compensation and refits. Commentators predict that the scam could end up costing the company more than twice this amount. The final bill for BP's 2010 Deepwater Horizon disaster amounted to $61.6 billion. Unethical behaviour can have drastic effects on the companies, employees, the society, and the environment in general. Public distrust and protests against corporate misdemeanours have resulted in calls for increased regulation and the need to focus on improving ethical behaviour.

Ethics represent a system of rules or principles that guide people in making decisions in various situations. An organization's code of ethics represents a statement setting down its corporate principles, rules of conduct, codes of practice or company philosophy concerning its responsibility to employees, shareholders, consumers, the environment, or any other aspects of society external to the company (Singh, 2011). A global survey of business ethics by the Chartered Global Management Accountant (CGMA, 2012) reported that approximately 80 per cent of the responding organizations provided a code of ethics or similar document to guide staff about ethical standards in their work. Although the existence of organizations' ethical codes can, to a certain extent, reduce unethical behaviours within an organization there is no guarantee that their existence will do so. One of the key messages to emerge from the CGMA (2012) survey was an 'ethics divide' whereby there was a stated strong commitment to ethical codes and behaviour, but in practice high pressure to act unethically. Approximately 30 per cent of the respondents stated that they sometimes or always felt under pressure to compromise their organization's standards of ethical conduct. Pressures were most apparent in some emerging economies.

The CGMA (2012) survey concluded that, based on their skills and roles, management accountants have a critical part to play in the management of ethical performance and an obligation to uphold ethical standards. Professional accounting organizations play an important role in promoting a high standard of ethical behaviour by their members. Both of the professional bodies representing management accountants, in the UK (Chartered Institute of Management Accountants), and in the USA (The American Institute of Certified Public Accountants), have issued codes of ethical guidelines for their members and established mechanisms for monitoring and enforcing professional ethics. The guidelines are concerned with ensuring that accountants follow fundamental principles relating to:

- integrity (being honest and not being a party to any falsification)
- objectivity (not being biased or prejudiced)
- confidentiality and professional competence and due care (maintaining the skills required to ensure a competent professional service)
- compliance with relevant laws and regulations.

You can view each organization's ethical standards at www.cimaglobal.com/ Professionalism/Ethics/CIMA-code-of-ethics-for-professional-accountants/ and www. aicpa.org/research/standards/codeofconduct.html. A new code of ethics for professional accountants (www.ethicsboard.org/restructured-code-easier-navigate-use-enforce) that takes effect from June 2019 has also been issued by the International Ethics Standards Board for Accountants to identify, evaluate, and address threats to compliance with the fundamental principles and independence.

The above discussion suggests that management accountants will be faced with increasingly ethical challenges in the future and are at risk of being pressurized to act unethically. You will remember from Chapter 13 that transfer pricing can be used to enable one division of a multinational to sell products and services to another division at an artificial price in order to make profits seem higher in a low-tax country and lower in a high-tax one. This process has attracted a considerable amount of negative publicity on the grounds that the behaviour is unethical, and there is evidence to suggest that consumers are penalizing firms they perceive as engaging in unethical behaviour by migrating to their competitors. For example, many consumers at Starbucks in the UK migrated to its rival, Costa, because of their perception that Starbucks did not pay a fair amount of UK taxes.

We also noted in Chapter 10 that flaws in the performance measurement systems used by banks contributed to the financial crisis in the banking sector in 2008. Bonuses and performance measures were based on short-term, rather than long-term performance that did not take risk into account. Managers were paid large commissions for selling mortgage loans to customers that were a large risk to the banks due to their low credit worthiness. In many cases, the employees of the banks were paid commissions on the date that the loan agreements were signed, while the loans lasted for 25 years, but if the borrowers defaulted the employees were not required to repay the commission. This practice resulted in many banks having a high volume of questionable loans with a high probability of default. This raises the question as to whether the managers were engaging in unethical behaviour or did the system of performance evaluation encourage the behaviour? So where should the blame be assigned? Is the reward system at fault or the unethical behaviour? Or both?

It is apparent from the above illustrations debate about what is right or wrong or ethical or unethical can be subject to different views and all the management accountant can do is refer to a company's and professional accountancy bodies for guidance. However, where actions are proposed that are illegal or contrary to regulatory requirements the management accountant should present documentary evidence that such actions should not be undertaken.

INFORMATION TECHNOLOGY

During the past two decades advances in information technology (IT) have had a profound impact on business activities including management accounting practices and the role of the management accountant. Prior to the 1990s companies developed their own company specific stand alone information systems such as an accounting information system, a materials procurement system and a production system that were applicable only to specific parts of the organization. These systems were not integrated with each other.

During the late 1980s and the 1990s larger companies replaced these with commercially available software integrated packages called **enterprise resource planning systems (ERPS)**. An ERPS is a single system comprising of a set of integrated sub-systems software modules specializing in particular business functions that aim to control all information flows within a company. Users can use their personal computers (PCs) to access the organization's single database and follow developments almost as they happen. Using real time data enables managers to analyse information quickly and thus continually improve the efficiencies of processes. A major feature of ERPS systems is that all data are entered only once, typically where they originate. There are ERPS packages on the market provided by companies such as SAP, Baan, Oracle and J.D. Edwards. ERPS have been implemented in most large companies and are also widely used in medium- and smaller-sized companies with SAP being the market leader.

Companies installed software such as ERPS on their own servers (a large powerful computer that responds to a request across a computer network to provide a network or data services). The emergence of **cloud computing** enables software to be located on servers outside the company owned by an external IT provider. The provider then makes the software available over the Internet to the companies. With cloud computing, resources are provided in return for monthly subscriptions or on a pay-as-you go basis. In the latter case this results in some IT costs becoming variable instead of fixed and in the former case capital expenditure relating to the acquisition of the software is replaced with monthly rental type payments. Therefore cost considerations can significantly

REAL WORLD VIEWS 16.2

Management accounting in the future

In the March 2012 edition of CIMA's *Financial Management* journal, Christian Doherty asks what will management accountants ten years on be grappling with? This question has been posed before (see, for example, Scapens *et al.*, 2003) and technology is a factor which is often cited as being something which will change management accounting. Doherty (2012) mentions a number of trends which are likely to affect how business is done and, thus, how management accountants do their work.

Technology is viewed by Doherty as a potential 'liberator', allowing management accountants to become more influential in decision-making. Technology developments such as Big Data have become a key tool in the provision of decision-making information (see CGMA, 2014). However, management accountants need to be cautious that increasing amounts of data do not overwhelm them. A second factor mentioned by Doherty (2012) is the need to provide insight, not information. Put simply, reporting may not be enough; rather, management accountants of the future must be able to provide professional insightful advice to other managers and directors. Third, while the BRICS (Brazil, Russia, India, China, South Africa) economies receive a lot of attention as some of the fastest growing, these are likely to be joined by others such as Columbia, Indonesia, Vietnam and Turkey. These new markets may present new opportunities for many firms, either in increasing sales or a manufacturing base, for example. Again, management accountants need to be centre stage to help take advantage of any opportunities. Finally, reporting is likely to become increasingly broad, with issues like sustainability, risk assessment and business valuation coming to the fore. More recently, in 2016 the IMA CEO reinforced the analytical skills needed of management accountants to provide 'predictive analytics (forecasting future events) and prescriptive analytics (actions and interventions, based on historical and future trends)'.

Questions

1 Do you think technological developments will always be an issue for management accountants?

2 Based on the brief summary above, what kinds of skills other than technical accounting training do management accountants need?

References

AccountingWeb (2016) Why the Future of Management Accounting Looks Bright, available at www .accountingweb.com/practice/growth/why-the-future -of-management-accounting-looks-bright

CGMA (2014) The Big Data Pathway, *CGMA*, November 2014. Available at www.cgma.org/Resources /Reports/Pages/big-data.aspx

Doherty, C. (2012) Management accounting in 2022, *Financial Management*, March, CIMA. Available at www.fm-magazine.com

Scapens, R., Ezzamel, M., Burns, J. and Baldvinsdottir, G. (2003) *The Future Direction of UK Management Accounting*, London, CIMA.

influence the decision as to whether to adopt cloud computing. Other factors to be taken into account relate to the fact that software updates are implemented by the provider so there is no need for companies to update their own software. A potential disadvantage, however, of cloud computing is that security and data protection risks are beyond the company's control and determined by the external cloud provider.

Recently the term 'Big Data' has been widely publicized. **Big data** is a term that describes the large volume of raw data, both structured and unstructured, that inundates a business on a daily basis. It includes information such as email messages, social media postings, phone calls, purchase transactions, website traffic and video streams. Approximately 90 per cent of the data is estimated to be unstructured. The amount of data that is being created is so voluminous they cannot be reasonably analysed using database management systems or traditional software programs (Warren *et al.*, 2015). The challenge is to explore and analyse this raw data to obtain meaningful information that is useful for decision-making.

It is important to understand the difference between data and information. **Data** are mere records of raw facts that are not organized to be meaningful whereas **information** is data that has been organized in a way so that it becomes understandable and useful for a particular purpose. For example, management accounting systems record data that is structured and aggregated into performance reports. Information, however, on its own only becomes valuable when it is transformed into knowledge which guides managers to make correct decisions.

The volume of information has exploded in recent years but it is not the volume of information that matters but what is done with the available information. Users of information must perceive it as being useful and helpful. An important role of management accounting is to ensure that users are not faced with **information overload** whereby users are provided with too much information to the extent that it becomes unmanageable and no longer useful.

The above IT developments have had a significant impact on the work of management accountants. In particular, it substantially reduces routine information gathering and the processing of information that was traditionally done by management accountants. Prior to the 1990s accountants were considered to be the information managers, but this role relating to the design and implementation of IT systems has now been taken over by IT specialists. In addition, non-accounting managers often have a Masters degree in business administration and have a greater understanding of accounting information. Instead of managers asking management accountants for information, they can access the system to derive the information they require directly from personal computers, laptops and tablets from different locations anywhere in the world and do their own analyses.

These developments have freed up management accountants from undertaking the routine and mundane tasks and enabled them to adopt the role of advisers and internal consultants to the business. Management accountants are now becoming more involved in interpreting the information generated from the IT systems and providing business support for managers. In addition, management accountants will also need to be aware of the latest developments in IT in order to assess what can be achieved from these developments.

GLOBALIZATION AND MANAGEMENT ACCOUNTING INTERNATIONAL PRACTICES

Globalization and developments in information technology have had a significant impact on management accounting. The growth in multinational companies has resulted in management accountants being responsible for overseeing the operation of management accounting systems in many different countries. Do management accounting practices differ across national borders?

Granlund and Lukka (1998) argue that there is a strong current tendency towards global homogenization of management accounting practices within the industrialized parts of the world. They distinguish between management accounting practices at the macro and micro levels. The macro level relates to concepts and techniques; in other words, it relates mainly to the content of this book. In contrast, the micro level is concerned with the behavioural patterns relating to how management accounting information is actually *used*. At the macro level, Granlund and Lukka suggest that the convergence of management accounting practices in different countries has occurred because of intensified global competition, developments in information technology, the increasing tendency of transnational companies to standardize their practices, the global consultancy industry and the use of globally applied textbooks and teaching.

Firms throughout the world are adopting similar integrated enterprise resource planning systems or standardized software packages that have resulted in the standardization of data collection formats and reporting patterns of accounting information. In multinational companies, this process has resulted in the standardization of the global flow of information, but it has also limited the ability to generate locally relevant information. Besides the impact of integrated IT systems, it is common for the headquarters/parent company of a transnational enterprise to force foreign divisions to adopt similar accounting practices to those of the headquarters/parent company. Global consultancy companies tend to promote the same standard solutions globally. Finally, the same textbooks are used globally and university and professional accounting syllabuses tend to be similar in different countries.

At the micro level, Granlund and Lukka acknowledge that differences in national and corporate culture can result in management accounting information being *used* in different ways across countries. For example, there is evidence to suggest that accounting information is used in a more rigorous/rigid manner to evaluate managerial performance in cultures exhibiting certain national traits, and in a more flexible way in cultures exhibiting different national traits.

INTELLECTUAL CAPITAL AND THE KNOWLEDGE BASE ECONOMY

During the past two decades the world's economy has rapidly changed from an industrial to a knowledge base. In the new knowledge economy, wealth is created by developing and managing knowledge (Ricceri and Guthrie, 2009). These value creating knowledge resources are commonly referred to as intellectual capital.

The term **intellectual capital** has been defined as the intangible benefits accessible by a firm from its workforce, and more broadly, from its established relationships with groups such as customers, suppliers and competitors (Gowthorpe, 2009). It is often used interchangeably with other terms such as 'knowledge capital', 'knowledge economy' and 'intangible assets'. Examples of items that represent intellectual capital include resources such as the organization's reputation, the morale of its staff, customer satisfaction, knowledge and skills of employees, established relationships with suppliers etc.

Recently, increased attention has been given to the importance of intellectual capital arising from the observed dramatic differences between the book and market values of

REAL WORLD VIEWS 16.3

Seismic shift from tangible to intangible value

In the March 2016 edition of CIMA's *Financial Management* journal, Lawrie Homes interviewed Noel Togoe, CIMA'S director of Education. Togoe stated that value measurement has been an area of dramatic change affecting the financial management landscape. The shift from tangible to intangible value has been seismic. It's something that makes us think differently about management accounting. As recently as 30 years ago, the balance sheet represented about 80 per cent of the value of quoted firms on average. Today it's about 17 per cent. It's common knowledge that products will give your firm a competitive edge for only a limited time, because it's possible for your rivals to copy them. But you can often derive a sustainable competitive advantage from relationships. These cannot be reverse-engineered or replicated, because you need all the right cultural conditions.

It is intangible factors – culture, reputation, relationships, processes and the innovative potential of the workforce – that give an organization its long-term advantage. If part of the work of managers is to enhance the value of the organization, preserve the value of the organzation and ensure that stakeholders get value from the organization, they need to pay attention to the drivers of value. If the drivers of value are intangible, you need to pay attention to them, but we don't seem to have got to that.

Questions

1 Provide examples of companies where most of their value can be attributed to intellectual capital rather than physical assets.
2 What do you think are the key intellectual capital drivers of corporate value?

Reference

Holmes, L. (2016), Insight track, *Financial Management*, March, 32–4.

many companies, particularly the dotcom companies in the late 1990s. Successful companies today tend to be those that continually innovate, relying on new technologies and the skills and knowledge of their employees rather than just their tangible physical assets.

Although it is problematic as to whether monetary values can be assigned to most internally generated intangible assets representing intellectual capital, it is important that they are considered in order to provide a greater understanding of the process of value creation. Otherwise there is a danger that a firm will be unable to assess the value of future business opportunities. This presents a challenge as to how to identify, measure and report on the value of intellectual capital.

One approach that has been suggested to calculate the value of an organization's intellectual capital is to take the difference between its market value (the number of shares in issue multiplied by the market value of the share) and the net book value of its assets. The gap between the two figures represents the market-to-book ratio and provides an indication of the value of intellectual capital assets that are not reflected in its financial statements. The problem with this approach is that it values intellectual capital as one asset and makes no attempt to separate the items that might comprise it. In addition, the market value of a company is subject to wide fluctuations due to factors unrelated to changes in intellectual capital. Another approach is to disclose information relating to intellectual capital, without attempting to assign any monetary value to it. For a review of some of the approaches that can be used to measure and value intellectual capital you should refer to Starovic and Marr (2010).

At present there is no consensus as to what represents a recommended approach to managing and reporting intellectual capital. Management accountants should be at the forefront of this process, using their skills and expertise in measurement and control to develop systems capable of accommodating intellectual capital. It may take some time to reach agreement on what constitutes the best approach and experimentation will be necessary in order to determine the best way forward.

INTEGRATED REPORTING

Recently, a new type of external corporate reporting called **integrated reporting** has been advocated. Integrated reporting has been rapidly gaining international recognition and is now being widely implemented in South Africa. Current corporate reports tend to focus on detailed *historical financial* information, ignoring the social and environmental impact made by an entity. Critics have argued that there is a need for a report that provides a bigger picture of a company's short and long-term performance. The Integrated Reporting Committee (IRC) of South Africa (2011) defined integrated reporting as the bringing together of material information about an organization's strategy, governance, performance and prospects in a way that reflects the commercial, social and environmental context within which it operates.

The International Integrated Reporting Council (IIRC) advocates that integrated reporting should become the worldwide norm for corporate reporting to investors, but to date only in South Africa has integrated reporting been mandated, with South African listed firms being required to publish an integrated report from March, 2011. Nevertheless, worldwide interest in integrated reporting continues to grow. According to the IIRC, more than 1500 firms currently prepare an integrated report, including AES Brasil, Clorox, GE, Mitsubishi, Novo Nordisk, Tata Steel, and Vivendi. There also has been strong support for integrated reporting from the large accounting firms as well as standard setters and professional accounting bodies in various countries. Richard Howitt, the IIRC Chief Executive Officer, has identified 2018 as the start of a 'global adoption phase,' the goal of which is to make integrated reporting the norm (Howitt, 2017).

Integrated reporting aims to give a forward-looking assessment of the business by providing information on financial and non-financial performance in a single document, showing the relationship between financial and non-financial performance and how these inter-related dimensions are creating or destroying value for shareholders and other stakeholders. The IRC discussion paper suggested that the following key elements should be included in an integrated report:

- a concise overview of the organization's structure, including governance and its main activities
- a description of material risks and opportunities, based on a review of financial, social, environmental, economic, and governance issues
- a description of the strategic objectives of the business as influenced by an assessment of the external environment and internal resource constraints
- an account of the organization's performance based on its strategic objectives in terms of key performance and risk indices.

Increasingly, businesses are expected to report not just on profit but on their impact on the wider perspectives relating to the economy, society and the environment. A study by Adams *et al.* (2016) examined the published accounts of Heineken, Unilever, GlaxoSmithKline and the National Australia Bank, and found that these companies were starting to think about their social investment activities in terms of value creation and are linking them to strategy. They concluded that integrated reporting offers significant potential for changing how organizations think about their social investments.

Integrated reporting aims to provide an overview of an organization's activities and performance in this broader context by communicating the mission and strategy of the organization and linking performance measurement to strategy. Integrated *external* corporate reporting therefore has many similarities with the balanced scorecard approach (see Chapter 14) that is used for *internal* performance management. Where integrated reporting is adopted it is likely that it will draw off internal management accounting information, performance management and non-financial measures. It is therefore likely that management accounting will have a greater input into *external* corporate reporting in those companies that adopt integrated reporting.

SUMMARY

The following items relate to the learning objectives listed at the beginning of the chapter.

● **Explain the principles of sustainable development and shared value.** Sustainable development is an approach to progress which meets the needs of the present without compromising the ability of future generations to meet their own needs. Shared value relates to operating practices that enhance the competitiveness of a company while simultaneously advancing economic and social conditions in the communities in which it operates.

● **Describe environmental management accounting.** Environmental management accounting has been reactive rather than proactive by focusing on managing escalating environmental costs arising from meeting regulatory requirements and seeking to avoid litigation and fines. It includes the tracking and reporting of environmental costs, input–output analysis and periodically producing an environmental cost report analysed by environmental prevention costs, detection costs, internal failure costs and external failure costs. Management accounting should also assist in making the business case for creating shared value by reconfiguring the value chain. Some companies have incorporated a society/environmental perspective within a balanced scorecard framework in order to link their environmental strategy to concrete performance measures.

● **Explain the role of the management accountant in avoiding unethical behaviour.** The management accountant should ensure that any business practices that they are a party to conform with their organization's code of ethics and the guidelines established by their professional accountancy body. Where actions are proposed that are illegal or contrary to regulatory requirements the management accountant should present documentary evidence indicating that such actions should not be undertaken.

- **Explain how today's information technology is changing the role of the management accountant.** IT developments have freed up management accountants from undertaking the routine and mundane tasks and enabled them to adopt the role of advisers and internal consultants to the business. Management accountants are now becoming more involved in interpreting the information generated from the IT systems and providing business support for managers.

- **Discuss whether globalization causes management accounting practices to differ across national borders.** At the macro level there has been a convergence of management accounting practices across different countries arising from developments in information technology, the increasing tendency of transnational companies to standardize their practices, the global consultancy industry and the use of globally applied textbooks and teaching.

- **Explain the meaning of intellectual capital.** Intellectual capital has been defined as the intangible benefits accessible by a firm from its workforce, and more broadly, from its established relationships with groups such as customers, suppliers and competitors. It is often used interchangeably with other terms such as 'knowledge capital', 'knowledge economy' and 'intangible assets'.

- **Describe integrated reporting.** Integrated reporting aims to provide information on the financial and non-financial performance in a single document that reports on an organization's impact on the wider perspectives relating to the economy, society and the environment.

KEY TERMS AND CONCEPTS

Big data A term that describes the large volume of raw data, both structured and unstructured, that inundates a business on a daily basis. It includes information such as email messages, social media postings, phone calls, purchase transactions, website traffic and video streams.

Cloud computing Enables software to be located on servers outside the company owned by an external IT provider. The provider then makes the software available over the internet to the companies.

Data Mere records of raw facts that are not organized to be meaningful.

Enterprise resource planning system (ERPS) A set of integrated software application modules that aim to control all information flows within a company.

Environmental detection costs The costs incurred to ensure that a firm's activities, products and processes conform to regulatory laws and voluntary standards.

Environmental external failure costs The costs incurred on activities performed after discharging waste into the environment.

Environmental internal failure costs The costs incurred from performing activities that have produced contaminants and waste that have not been discharged into the environment.

Environmental prevention costs The costs of activities undertaken to prevent the production of waste that could cause damage to the environment.

Ethical behaviour Behaviour that is consistent with the standards of honesty, fairness and social responsibility that have been adopted by the organization.

Information   Data that has been organized in a way so that it becomes understandable and useful for a particular purpose.

Information overload   A situation that arises when users are provided with too much information to the extent that it becomes unmanageable and no longer useful.

Input/output analysis   A technique that can be used to reduce the usage of environmental resources and costs. Inflows of resources such as water, materials and energy are recorded and balanced with outflows on the basis that, what comes in, must go out.

Integrated reporting   An external report that aims to provide information on the financial and non-financial performance in a single document relating to the economy, society and the environment.

Intellectual capital   The intangible benefits accessible by a firm from its workforce, and more broadly, from its established relationships with groups such as customers, suppliers and competitors. It is often used interchangeably with other terms such as 'knowledge capital', 'knowledge economy' and 'intangible assets.'

Shared value   Policies and operating practices that enhance the competitiveness of a company while simultaneously advancing economic and social conditions in the communities in which it operates.

RECOMMENDED READING

The entire publication of the March 2016 issue of *Financial Management* is devoted to the future of management accounting. This publication can be accessed at www.fm-magazine.com. For a discussion of environmental and sustainability issues you should refer to special issues of *Management Accounting Research* (2013, volume 24, issue 4), *Accounting, Organizations and Society* (2014, volume 39, issue 6) and *British Accounting Review* (2014, volume 46, issue 4). A report by the Chartered Global Management Accountants discusses how management accounting can contribute to shared value. The report is titled 'Sustainable business: shared value in practice' and can be accessed at www.cgma.org/resources/reports/pages/sustainablebusiness.aspx. Finally, you should note that the entire publication of the June 2017 issue of *Financial Management* (www.fm-magazine.com) is devoted to issues relating to ethical behaviour and management accounting.

ASSESSMENT MATERIAL

The review questions are short questions that enable you to assess your understanding of the main topics included in the chapter. The numbers in parentheses provide you with the page numbers to refer to if you cannot answer a specific question.

The review problems are more complex and require you to relate and apply the content to various business problems. Solutions to review problems are provided in a separate section at the end of the book. Additional review problems can be accessed by lecturers and students on the dedicated online support resources for this book. Solutions to these review problems are provided for lecturers in the *Instructor's Manual* accompanying this book that can be downloaded from the dedicated online instructor's resources (see Preface for details).

The dedicated online digital support resources for this book also includes over 30 case study problems.

REVIEW QUESTIONS

16.1 Why was there virtually no innovation in management accounting practices until the mid 1980s. *(p. 419)*

16.2 Explain what is meant by the term shared value and provide examples of how shared value can be created. *(p. 422)*

16.3 Describe input/output analysis. *(p. 425)*

16.4 Discuss the value of an environmental cost report. *(pp. 425–426)*

16.5 Describe how management accounting can support shared value and sustainable development. *(pp. 426–427)*

16.6 Provide examples of unethical behaviour in an organization. *(p. 427)*

16.7 Describe enterprise resource planning systems and their impact on management accountants. *(pp. 429–431)*

16.8 What factors influence the decision as to whether to adopt cloud computing? *(p. 429)*

16.9 Describe the meaning of the term Big Data. *(pp. 430–431)*

16.10 Distinguish between data and information. *(p. 431)*

16.11 Explain why management accounting practices tend not to differ across countries. *(pp. 431–432)*

16.12 Explain the meaning of intellectual capital and its implications for management accounting. *(pp. 432–434)*

REVIEW PROBLEMS

16.13 Environmental management is considered to be one of the most important issues facing companies today. An effective environmental costing system will not only support a company's environmental management but may also improve the financial performance of the organization.

Required:

Explain THREE ways in which an environmental costing system can lead to improved financial performance.

(5 marks)

16.14 P plc is a multinational conglomerate company with manufacturing divisions, trading in numerous countries across various continents. Trade takes place between a number of the divisions in different countries, with partly completed products being transferred between them. Where a transfer takes place between divisions trading in different countries, it is the policy of the board of P plc to determine centrally the appropriate transfer price without reference to the divisional managers concerned. The board of P plc justifies this policy to divisional managers on the grounds that its objective is to maximize the conglomerate's post-tax profits and that the global position can be monitored effectively only from the head office.

Required:

(a) Explain and critically appraise the possible reasoning behind P plc's policy of centrally determining transfer prices for goods traded between divisions operating in different countries.

(10 marks)

(b) Discuss the ethical implications of P plc's policy of imposing transfer prices on its overseas divisions in order to maximize post-tax profits.

(10 marks)

16.15 Environmental reporting and life cycle costing
PLX Refinery Co is a large oil refinery business in Kayland. Kayland is a developing country with a large and growing oil exploration and production business which supplies PLX with crude oil. Currently, the refinery has the capacity to process 200 000 barrels of crude oil per day and makes profits of $146m per year. It employs about 2000 staff and contractors. The staff are paid $60 000 each per year on average (about twice the national average pay in Kayland).

The government of Kayland has been focused on delivering rapid economic growth over the last 15 years. However, there are increasing signs that the environment is paying a large price for this growth with public health suffering. There is now a growing environmental pressure group, Green Kayland (GK), which is organizing protests against the companies that it sees as being the major polluters.

Kayland's government wishes to react to the concerns of the public and the pressure groups. It has requested that companies involved in heavy industry contribute to a general improvement in the treatment of the environment in Kayland.

As a major participant in the oil industry with ties to the nationalized oil exploration company (Kayex), PLX believes it will be strategically important to be at the forefront of environmental developments. It is working with other companies in the oil industry to improve environmental reporting since there is a belief that this will lead to improved public perception and economic efficiency of the industry. PLX has had a fairly good compliance record in Kayland, with only two major fines being levied in the last eight years for safety breaches and river pollution ($1m each).

The existing information systems within PLX focus on financial performance. They support financial reporting obligations and allow monitoring of key performance metrics such as earnings per share and operating margins. Recent publications on environmental accounting have suggested there are a number of techniques [such as input/output analysis, activity-based costing (ABC) and a life cycle view] that may be relevant in implementing improvements to these systems.

PLX is considering a major capital expenditure programme to enhance capacity, safety and efficiency at the refinery. This will involve demolishing certain older sections of the refinery and building on newly acquired land adjacent to the site. Overall, the refinery will increase its land area by 20 per cent.

Part of the refinery extension will also manufacture a new plastic, Kayplas. Kayplas is expected to have a limited market life of five years after which it will be replaced by Kayplas2. The refinery accounting team has forecast the following data associated with this product and calculated PLX's traditional performance measure of product profit for the new product:

All figures are $m

	2020	2021	2022	2023	2024
Revenue costs	25.0	27.5	30.1	33.2	33.6
Production costs	13.8	15.1	16.6	18.3	18.5
Marketing costs	5.0	4.0	3.0	3.0	2.0
Development costs	5.6	3.0	0.0	0.0	0.0
Product profit	0.6	5.4	10.5	11.9	13.1

Subsequently, the following environmental costs have been identified from PLX's general overheads as associated with Kayplas production.

	2020	2021	2022	2023	2024
Waste filtration	1.2	1.4	1.5	1.9	2.1
Carbon dioxide exhaust extraction	0.8	0.9	0.9	1.2	1.5

Additionally, other costs associated with closing down and recycling the equipment in Kayplas production are estimated at $18m in 2024.

The board wishes to consider how it can contribute to the oil industry's performance in environmental accounting, how it can implement the changes that this might require and how these changes will benefit the company,

Required:

(a) Discuss different cost categories that would aid transparency in environmental reporting both internally and externally at PLX.

(4 marks)

(b) Explain and evaluate how the three environmental accounting techniques mentioned can assist in managing the environmental and strategic performance of PLX.

(9 marks)

(c) Evaluate the costing approach used for Kayplas's performance compared to a life cycle costing approach, performing appropriate calculations.

(7 marks)

16.16 Environmental reporting

FGH Telecom (FGH) is one of the largest providers of mobile and fixed line telecommunications in Ostland. The company has recently been reviewing its corporate objectives in the light of its changed business environment. The major new addition to the strategic objectives is under the heading: 'Building a more environmentally friendly business for the future'. It has been recognized that the company needs to make a contribution to ensuring sustainable development in Ostland and reducing its environmental footprint. Consequently, it adopted

a goal that, by 2025, it would have reduced its environmental impact by 60 per cent (compared to year 2009).

The reasons for the board's concern are that the telecommunications sector is competitive and the economic environment is increasingly harsh, with the markets for debt and equities being particularly poor. On environmental issues, the government and public are calling for change from the business community. It appears that increased regulation and legislation will appear to encourage business towards better performance. The board has recognized that there are threats and opportunities from these trends. It wants to ensure that it is monitoring these factors and so it has asked for an analysis of the business environment with suggestions for performance measurement.

Additionally, the company has a large number of employees working across its network. Therefore, there are large demands for business travel. FGH runs a large fleet of commercial vehicles in order to service its network along with a company car scheme for its managers. The manager in charge of the company's travel budget is reviewing data on carbon dioxide emissions to assess FGH's recent performance.

Recent initiatives within the company to reduce emissions have included:

(a) the introduction in 2018 of a homeworking scheme for employees in order to reduce the amount of commuting to and from their offices; and

(b) a drive to increase the use of teleconferencing facilities by employees.

Data on FGH Telecom:
Carbon dioxide emissions

Measured in millions of kgs	2009 Base year	2017	2018
Commercial fleet diesel	105.4	77.7	70.1
Commercial fleet petrol	11.6	0.4	0.0
Company car diesel	15.1	14.5	12.0
Company car petrol	10.3	3.8	2.2
Other road travel (diesel)	0.5	1.6	1.1
Other road travel (petrol)	3.1	0.5	0.3
Rail travel	9.2	9.6	3.4
Air travel (short haul)	5.0	4.4	3.1
Air travel (long haul)	5.1	7.1	5.4
Hire cars (diesel)	0.6	1.8	2.9
Hire cars (petrol)	6.7	6.1	6.1
Total	172.6	127.5	106.6

Required:

(a) Evaluate the data given on carbon dioxide emissions using suitable indicators. Identify trends from within the data and comment on whether the company's behaviour is consistent with meeting its targets.

(9 marks)

(b) Suggest further data that the company could collect in order to improve its analysis and explain how this data could be used to measure the effectiveness of the reduction initiatives mentioned.

(3 marks)

BIBLIOGRAPHY

Abernethy, M.A., Lillis, A.M., Brownell, P. and Carter, P. (2001) Product diversity and costing system design: Field study evidence, *Management Accounting Research*, **12**(3), 261–80.

Abu-Serdaneh, J. (2004) Transfer Pricing in UK Manufacturing Companies, PhD dissertation, University of Huddersfield.

Accenture and the Chartered Institute of Management Accountants, (2011) *Sustainability performance management: How CFO'S can unlock value,* Chartered Institute of Management Accountants.

Adams, C.A., Potter, B., Singh, P.A. and York, J. (2016) Exploring the implications of integrated reporting for social investment (disclosures), *British Accounting Review*, **48**(3), 283–296.

Al-Omiri, M. and Drury, C. (2007) A survey of the factors influencing the choice of product costing systems in UK organizations, *Management Accounting Research,* **18**(4), 399–424.

Al-Sayed, M. and Dugdale, D. (2016) Activity-based innovations in the UK manufacturing sector: Extent, adoption process patterns and contingency factors, *The British Accounting Review,* **48**, 38–58.

Ask, U., Ax, C. and Jonsson, S. (1996) Cost management in Sweden: From modern to post-modern, in Bhimani, A. (ed.) *Management Accounting: European Perspectives*, Oxford University Press, 199–217.

Atkinson, H. (2006) Strategy implementation: A role for the balanced scorecard? *Management Decision*, **44**(10), pp. 1441–1460.

Ax, C., Greve, J. and Nilsson, U. (2008) The impact of competition and uncertainty on the adoption of target costing, *International Journal of Production Economics*, **115**(1), 92–103.

Ballas, A. and Venieris, G. (1996) A survey of management accounting practices in Greek firms, in Bhimani, A. (ed.) *Management Accounting: European Perspectives*, Oxford University Press, 123–39.

Bartolomeo, M., Bennett, Bouma, J., Heydkamp, P., James, P. and Wolters, T. (2000) Environmental management accounting in Europe: Current practice and future potential, *European Accounting Review,* **9**(1), 31–52.

Bartelsman, E.J. and Beetsma, R.M. (2003) Why pay more? Corporate tax avoidance through transfer pricing in OECD countries, *Journal of Public Economics,* (87), pp.2225–52.

Barth, M. E., Steven, F. Cahan, S.F, Chen, L and Venter, E.R. (2017) The economic consequences associated with integrated report quality: Capital market and real effects, *Accounting, Organizations and Society,* (62), 43–64.

Baxter, W.T. and Oxenfeldt, A.R. (1961) Costing and pricing: The cost accountant versus the economist, *Business Horizons*, Winter, 77–90; also in *Studies in Cost Analysis*, 2nd edn (ed. D. Solomons) Sweet and Maxwell (1968) 293–312.

Bebbington, J. and Thomson, I. (2013) Sustainable development, management and accounting: Boundary crossing, Management Accounting Research, **24**(4), 277–83.

Bernardi, C. and Stark, A.W. (2018) Environmental, social and governance disclosure, integrated reporting, and the accuracy of analyst forecasts *The British Accounting Review*, **50**(1), 16–31.

Bjornenak, T. (1997) Conventional wisdom and accounting practices, *Management Accounting Research*, **8**(4), 367–82.

Bourmistrov, A. and Kaarbøe, K. (2013) From comfort to stretch zones: A field study of two multinational companies applying beyond budgeting, *Management Accounting Research* **24**(3), 196–211.

Brounen, D., de Jong, A. and Koedijk, K. (2004) Corporate finance in Europe: Confronting theory with practice, *Financial Management*, **33**(4), 71–101.

Bukh, P.N. and Malmi, T. (2005) Re-examining the cause-and-effect principle of the balanced scorecard. In: Jönsson, S., Mouritsen, J. (Eds.), *Accounting in Scandinavia — The Northern Lights*, Malmö, Liber, pp. 87–113.

Burrows, G. and Chenhall, R.H. (2012) Target costing: First and second comings, *Accounting History Review*, **22**(2), 127–42.

Carbon Disclosure Project (CDP). (2016a) Out of the starting blocks: Tracking progress on corporate climate action. UK: Carbon Disclosure Project.

Carbon Disclosure Project. (2016b) Carbon disclosure project report 2016 Australia and New Zealand. https://www.cdp.net/CDPResults/CDP-Australia-NZClimate-Change-Report-2016.pdf.

Chartered Global Management Accountant (CGMA, 2012) *Sustainable business: shared value in practice,* Chartered Institute of Management Accountants.

Chartered Institute of Management Accountants (2009) *Management accounting tools for today and tomorrow*, Chartered Institute of Management Accountants, www.cimaglobal.com/managementaccountingtools.

Chartered Institute of Management Accountants (2014) *Rethinking the value chain – the extended value chain,* Chartered Institute of Management Accountants.

Chow, C., Haddad, K. and Williamson, J. (1997) Applying the balanced scorecard to small companies, *Management Accounting*, August, 21–7.

Committee on Cost Concepts and Standards. (1956) Tentative statement of cost concepts underlying reports for management purposes. *The Accounting Review* (April): 182–193.

Cools, M. and Emmanuel, C. (2007) Transfer pricing, the implications of fiscal compliance, in Chapman, C.S., Hopwood, A.G. and Shields, M. D. (eds), *Handbook of Management Accounting Research*, Elsevier, Vol.**2**, pp.573–85.

Cooper, R. (1990a) Cost classifications in unit-based and activity-based manufacturing cost systems, *Journal of Cost Management*, Fall, 4–14.

Cooper, R. (1990b) Explicating the logic of ABC, *Management Accounting*, November, 58–60.

Cooper, R. (1997) Activity-based costing: Theory and practice, in Brinker, B.J. (ed.), *Handbook of Cost Management*, Warren, Gorham and Lamont, B1–B33.

Cooper, R. and Kaplan, R.S. (1987) How cost accounting systematically distorts product costs, in W.J. Bruns and R.S. Kaplan (eds) *Accounting and Management: Field Study Perspectives*, Harvard Business School Press, Ch. 8.

Cooper, R. and Kaplan, R.S. (1988) Measure costs right: Make the right decisions, *Harvard Business Review*, September/October, 96–103.

Cooper, R. and Kaplan, R.S. (1991) *The Design of Cost Management Systems: Text, Cases and Readings*, Prentice Hall.

Cooper, R. and Kaplan, R.S. (1992) Activity based systems: Measuring the costs of resource usage, *Accounting Horizons*, September, 1–13.

Dekker, H.C. (2003) Value chain analysis in interfirm relationships: A field study, *Management Accounting Research*, **14**(1), 1–23.

Dekker, H. and Smidt, P. (2003) A survey of the adoption and use of target costing in Dutch firms, *International Journal of Production Economics*, **84**(3), 293–306.

Drucker, P.F. (1964) Controls, control and management, in *Management Controls: New Directions in Basic Research* C.P. Bonini, R. Jaedicke and H. Wagner (eds), McGraw-Hill.

Drury, C. (2018) *Management and Cost Accounting*, Cengage EMEA.

Drury, C. and El-Shishini, H. (2005) *Divisional Performance Measurement,* Chartered Institute of Management Accountants.

Drury, C. and Tayles, M. (1994) Product costing in UK manufacturing organisations, *The European Accounting Review*, **3**(3), 443–69.

Drury, C. and Tayles, M. (2000) *Cost System Design and Profitability Analysis in UK Companies*, Chartered Institute of Management Accountants.

Drury, C. and Tayles M. (2005) Explicating the design of overhead absorption procedures in UK organizations, *British Accounting Review*, **37**(1), 47–84.

Drury, C. and Tayles, M. (2006) Profitability analysis in UK organizations: An exploratory study, *British Accounting Review*, **38**(4), 405–25.

Drury, C., Braund, S., Osborne, P. and Tayles, M. (1993) A Survey of Management Accounting Practices in UK Manufacturing Companies, ACCA Research Paper, Chartered Association of Certified Accountants.

Dugdale, D. and Lyne, S. (2006) Are budgets still needed?, *Financial Management*, November, 32–5.

Dugdale, D., Colwyn-Jones, T. and Green, S. (2006) *Contemporary Management Accounting Practices in UK Manufacturing Companies*, Chartered Institute of Management Accountants.

Ekholm, B-G. and Wallin, J. (2000) Is the annual budget really dead?, *The European Accounting Review*, **9**(4), 519–39.

El-Shishini, H. and Drury, C. (2001) Divisional Performance Measurement in UK Companies, Paper presented to the Annual Congress of the European Accounting Association, Athens.

Emmanuel, C., Otley, D. and Merchant, K. (1990) *Accounting for Management Control,* International Thomson Business Press.

Epstein, M. and Manzoni, J.F. (1998) Implementing corporate strategy: From tableaux de bord to balanced scorecards, *European Management Journal*, **16**(2), 190–203.

Epstein, M. and Roy, M.J. (1997) Environmental management to improve corporate profitability, *Journal of Cost Management*, November–December, 26–34.

Ernst & Young and The Institute of Management Accountants (2003) *The Ernst & Young and IMA Survey of Management Accounting,* Ernst & Young LLP, New York, NY.

Ernst, & Young. (2012) Six growing trends in corporate sustainability. EYGM Limited.

Ezzamel, M., Willmott, H. and Worthington, F. (2008) Manufacturing shareholder value: The role of accounting in organizational transformation, *Accounting, Organization and Society* **33**, 107–140.

Fitzgerald, L., Johnston, R., Brignall, T.J., Silvestro, R. and Voss, C. (1991) *Performance Measurement in Service Businesses*, Chartered Institute of Management Accountants.

Fitzgerald, L., Johnston, R., Silvestro, R. and Steele, A. (1989) Management control in service industries, *Management Accounting*, April, 44–6.

Fitzgerald, L. and Moon, P. (1996) *Performance Management in Service Industries*, Chartered Institute of Management Accountants.

Franco-Santos, M. and Bourne, M. (2005) An examination of the literature relating to issues affecting how companies manage through measures, *Production Planning and Control*, **16**(2), pp. 114–124.

Fremgen, J.M. and Liao, S.S. (1981) *The Allocation of Corporate Indirect Costs*, National Association of Accountants, New York.

Gowthorpe, C. (2009) Wider still and wider? A critical discussion of intellectual capital recognition, measurement and control in a boundary theoretical context, *Critical Perspective on Accounting*, **20**, 823–834.

Granlund, M. and Lukka, K. (1998) It's a small world of management accounting practices, *Journal of Management Accounting Research*, **10**, 151–79.

Guilding, C., Drury, C. and Tayles, M. (2005) An empirical investigation of the importance of cost-plus pricing, *Managerial Auditing Journal*, **20**(2), 125–37.

Guilding, C., Lamminmaki, D. and Drury, C. (1998) Budgeting and standard costing practices in New Zealand and the United Kingdom, *The International Journal of Accounting*, **33**(5), 41–60.

Hansen, D.R. and Mendoza, R. (1999) Costos de Impacto Ambiental: Su Medicion, Asignacion, y Control, *INCAE Revista*, **X**(2).

Hassan, Y. and Davood, D. (2012) A comparative study of the adoption and implementation of target costing in the UK, Australia and New Zealand, *International Journal of Production Economics* **135**(1), 382–92.

Henri, J.F., Boiral, O. and Roy, M-J (2014) The Tracking of Environmental Costs: Motivations and Impacts, *European Accounting Review*, **23**(4), 647–669.

Henri, J.F., Boiral, O. and Roy, M-J (2016) Strategic cost management and performance: The case of environmental costs, *British Accounting Review*, **48**, 269–282.

Hope, J. and Fraser, R. (1999a) Beyond budgeting: Building a new management model for the information age, *Management Accounting*, January, 16–21.

Hope, J. and Fraser, R. (1999b) Take it away, *Accountancy*, May, 66–67.

Hope, J. and Fraser, R. (2001) Figures of hate, *Financial Management*, February, 22–5.

Hope, J. and Fraser, R. (2003a) Who needs budgets? *Harvard Business Review*, February, 42–48.

Hope, J. and Fraser, R. (2003b) New Ways of Setting Rewards: The Beyond Budgeting Model, *Californian Management Review*, Vol **45**, No.2 Winter 2003, 104–119.

Hopper, T. and Bui, B. (2016) Has Management Accounting Research been critical? Management Accounting Research, **31**(1), 10–30.

Howitt, R. (2017) Interview: Richard Howitt, chief executive of the international integrated reporting Council. AB magazine (1 may). Available at: http://www.accaglobal.com/in/en/member/member/accounting-business/2017/05/interviews/richard-howitt.html. Institute of Directors (IoD). (2009) King (Howitt, 2017).

Innes, J. and Mitchell, F. (1995) A survey of activity-based costing in the UK's largest companies, *Management Accounting Research*, June, 137–54.

Innes, J., Mitchell, F. and Sinclair, D. (2000) Activity-based costing in the UK's largest companies: A comparison of 1994 and 1999 survey results, *Management Accounting Research*, **11**(3), 349–62.

Integrated Reporting Committee (IRC) of South Africa (2011) *Framework for Integrated Reporting and the Integrated Report*, SAICA.

International Federation of Accountants (2005) *International Guidance Document: Environmental Management Accounting*, International Federation of Accountants. Available at: https://www.ifac.org/publications-resources/international-guidance-document-environmental-management-accounting.

Ittner, D and Larcker, D. (2003) Coming up short on non-financial performance Measurement, *Harvard Business Review*, **70** (January–February), 71–79.

Johnson, G., Scholes, K. and Whittington, R. (2017) *Exploring Strategy*, Pearson Education.

Johnson, H.T. (1990) Professors, customers and value: Bringing a global perspective to management accounting education, in P. Turney (ed.) *Performance Excellence in Manufacturing and Services Organizations*, American Accounting Association.

Johnson, H.T. and Kaplan, R.S. (1987) *Relevance Lost: The Rise and Fall of Management Accounting*, Harvard Business School Press.

Joseph, N., Turley, S., Burns, J., Lewis, L., Scapens, R.W. and Southworth, A. (1996) External financial reporting and management information: A survey of UK management accountants, *Management Accounting Research* **7**(1), 73–94.

Kald, M. and Nilsson, F. (2000) Performance measurement at Nordic companies, *European Management Journal*, **1**, 113–27.

Kaplan, R.S. (1994) Management accounting (1984–1994): Development of new practice and theory, *Management Accounting Research*, September and December, 247–60.

Kaplan, R.S. and Cooper, R. (1998) *Cost and Effect: Using Integrated Systems to Drive Profitability and Performance*, Harvard Business School Press.

Kaplan, R.S. and Norton, D.P. (1992) The balanced scorecard: Measures that drive performance, *Harvard Business Review*, January–February, 71–9.

Kaplan, R.S. and Norton, D.P. (1993) Putting the balanced scorecard to work, *Harvard Business Review*, September–October, 134–47.

Kaplan, R.S. and Norton, D.P. (1996a) Using the balanced scorecard as a strategic management system, *Harvard Business Review*, January–February, 75–85.

Kaplan, R.S. and Norton, D.P. (1996b) *The Balanced Scorecard: Translating Strategy Into Action*, Harvard Business School Press.

Kaplan, R.S. and Norton, D.P. (2001a) *The Strategy-focused Organization*, Harvard Business School Press.

Kaplan, R.S. and Norton, D.P. (2001b) Balance without profit, *Financial Management*, January, 23–6.

Kaplan, R.S. and Norton, D.P. (2001c) Transforming the balanced scorecard from performance measurement to strategic management: Part 1, *Accounting Horizons*, March, 87–104.

Kaplan, R.S. and Norton, D.P. (2001d) Transforming the balanced scorecard from performance measurement to strategic management: Part 2, *Accounting Horizons*, June, 147–60.

Kaplan, R. and Anderson, S. (2004) Time-driven activity-based costing. *Harvard Business Review,* **82**, 11, pp. 131–138.

Kaplan, R. and Anderson, S. (2007) The innovation of time-driven activity-based costing. *Journal of Cost Management,* **21**, 2 pp. 5–15.

Kato, Y. (1993) Target costing support systems: Lessons from leading Japanese companies, *Management Accounting Research*, March, 33–48.

Kohli, C. and Suri, R., (2011) The price is right? Guidelines for pricing to enhance profitability. *Business Horizons,* **54**(6), pp. 563.

KPMG (2011) Transfer pricing issues and solutions for digital media, http://www.kpmg.com/global/en/issues and insights/articlespublications/pages/transfer-pricing-digital-media-2011.

KPMG. (2015) KPMG International survey of corporate responsibility reporting 2015. KPMG International.

Kraus, K. and Lind, J. (2010) The impact of the corporate balanced scorecard on corporate control—A research note, *Management Accounting Research,* **21**(4), 265–277.

Kumarasiri, J. and Gunasekarage, A. (2017) Risk regulation, community pressure and the use of management accounting in managing climate change risk: Australian evidence, *British Accounting Review*, **49**(1), 25–38.

Langfield-Smith, K. (1997) Management control systems and strategy: A critical review, *Accounting, Organizations and Society*, **22**, 207–32.

Learby, B.A. and Wenteel, K. (2002) Know the score: The balanced scorecard approach to strategically assist clients, *Pennsylvania CPA Journal*, Spring, 29–32.

Libby, T. and Lindsay, R.M. (2010) Beyond budgeting or budgeting reconsidered? A survey of North American budgeting practice, *Management Accounting Research*, **21**(1), 56–75.

Lukka, K. and Granlund, M. (1996) Cost accounting in Finland: Current practice and trends of development, *The European Accounting Review*, **5**(1), 1–28.

Lynch, R.L. and Cross, K.F. (1991a) *Measure Up! How to Measure Corporate Performance*, Blackwell, Boston, MA.

Lynch, R.L., Cross, K.F., (1991b) Measure Up—*The Essential Guide to Measuring Business Performance*. Mandarin, London.

Malmi, T. (2001) Balanced scorecards in Finnish companies: A research note, *Management Accounting Research*, **12**(2), 207–20.

Melnyk, S.A., Bititci, U., Platts, K, Tobias, J. and Andersene, B. (2014) Is performance measurement and management fit for the future? *Management Accounting Research, 25*(2), 173–186

Merchant, K.A. and van der Stede, W. (2017) *Modern Management Control Systems: Text and Cases*, Pearson Education.

Miles, R.E. and Snow, C.C. (1978) *Organizational Strategies, Structure and Process, New York*, McGraw-Hill.

Moon, P. and Fitzgerald, L. (1996) *Performance Measurement in Service Industries: Making it Work*, Chartered Institute of Management Accountants.

Neely, A., Adams, C. and Crowe, P. (2001) "The performance prism in practice", *Measuring Business Excellence,* Vol. **5** No. 2, pp. 6–12.

Neely, A.D., Adams, C. and Kennerley, M., (2002) *The Performance Prism: The Scorecard for Measuring and Managing Business Success*, Pearson Education Ltd., London, UK.

Neely, A.D., Gregory, M.J. and Platts, K.W. (1995) Performance measurement system design—a literature review and research agenda, *International Journal of Operations & Production Management* **15**(4), 80–116.

Nørreklit, H. (2000) The balance on the balanced scorecard – a critical analysis of some of its assumptions, *Management Accounting Research*, **11**, 65–88.

Nørreklit, H. (2003) The balanced scorecard: What is the score? A rhetorical analysis of the balanced scorecard, *Accounting, Organizations and Society*, **28**, 591–619.

OECD (2010) *OECD Transfer Pricing Guidelines for Multinational Enterprises and Tax Administrations 2010*, OECD Publishing, Paris.DOI: http://dx.doi.org/10.1787/tpg-2010-en.

Oliveras, E. and Amat, O. (2002) The Balanced Scorecard Assumptions and the Drivers of Business Growth, Paper presented at the 25th Annual Congress of the European Accounting Association, Copenhagan, Denmark.

Olve, N., Roy, J. and Wetter, M. (2000) *Performance Drivers: A Practical Guide to Using the Balanced Scorecard*, John Wiley & Sons.

Otley, D. (1999) Performance management: A framework for management control systems research. *Management Accounting Research* **10**(4), 363–382.

Ouchi, W.G. (1979) A conceptual framework for the design of organizational control mechanisms, *Management Science*, 833–48.

Pere, T. (1999) How the Execution of Strategy is Followed in Large Organisations Located in Finland, Master's Thesis (Helsinki School of Economics and Business Administration).

Phyrr, P.A. (1976) Zero-based budgeting – where to use it and how to begin, *S.A.M. Advanced Management Journal*, Summer, 5.

Porter, M. (1985) *Competitive Advantage*, New York, Free Press.

Porter, M. E. and Kramer, M. R. (2006) Strategy and society: The link between competitive advantage and social responsibility, *Harvard Business Review, 84*(12), 78–92.

Porter, M. E. and Kramer, M. R. (2011) Creating shared value, *Harvard Business Review, 89*(1/2), 62–77.

Qian, W. and Schaltegger, S. (2017) Revisiting carbon disclosure and performance: Legitimacy and management views, *British Accounting Review*, **49**(4), 365–379.

Ranganathan, J. and Ditz, D. (1996) Environmental accounting: A tool for better management, *Management Accounting*, February, 38–40.

Reece, J.S. and Cool, W.R. (1978) Measuring investment centre performance, *Harvard Business Review*, May/June 29–49.

Ricceri, F., & Guthrie, J. (2009) Critical analysis of international guidelines for the management of knowledge resources, in Jemielniak, D, and Kociatkiewicz, J (Eds.), *Handbook on research on knowledge intensive organisations.* PA: Information Science Press.

Rigby, D. and Biolodeau (2013) Executive Guide—Management Tools 2007 (Bain & Company Publishing). http://www.bain.com/publications/articles/management-tools-and-trends-2013.aspx.

Scapens, R., Ezzamel, M., Burns, J. and Baldvinsdottir, G. (2003) *The Future Direction of UK Management Accounting*, London, CIMA.

Seal, W., Cullen, J., Dunlop, D., Berry, T. and Ahmed, M. (1999) Enacting a European supply chain: a case study on the role of management accounting, *Management Accounting Research*, **10**(3), 303–22.

Shank, J.K. (1989) Strategic cost management: New wine or just new bottles?, *Journal of Management Accounting Research* (USA), Fall, 47–65.

Shank, J. and Govindarajan, V. (1992) Strategic cost management: The value chain perspective, *Journal of Management Accounting Research*, **4**, 179–97.

Sibbet, D. (1997) 75 years of management ideas and practice 1922–1997, *Harvard Business Review*, **75**(5), pp. 2–12.

Simon, H.A. (1959) Theories of decision making in economics and behavioural science, *The American Economic Review*, June, 233–83.

Singh, J.B. (2011) Determinants of the Effectiveness of Corporate Codes of Ethics: An Empirical Study, *Journal of Business Ethics, 101*(3), 385–395. Available at: https://link.springer.com/journal/10551.

Sizer, J. (1989) *An Insight into Management Accounting*, Penguin, Chs 11–12.

Skinner, R.C. (1990) The role of profitability in divisional decision making and performance, *Accounting and Business Research*, Spring, 135–41.

Solomons, D. (1965) *Divisional Performance: Measurement and Control*, R.D. Irwin.

Soin, K., Seal, W. and Cullen, J. (2002) ABC and organization change: an institutional perspective, *Management Accounting Research*, 13(2), 151–72.

Speckbacher, G., Bischof, J. and Pfeiffer, T. (2003) A descriptive analysis on the implementation of balanced scorecards in German-speaking countries, *Management Accounting Research*, 14(4), 361–88.

Starovic, D. and Marr, B. (2010) *Understanding corporate value, managing and reporting intellectual capital,* Chartered Institute of Management Accountants.

Stern, J., Stewart, G., Chew, D. (1995) The EVA Financial Management system. *Journal of Applied Corporate Finance,* Summer, 32–46.

Tani, T., Okano, H., Shimizu, N., Iwabuchi, Y., Fukuda, J. and Cooray, S. (1994) Target cost management in Japanese companies: Current state of the art, *Management Accounting Research*, 5(1), 67–82.

The Economist (1997) The EVA brew, July 31st 1997.

Thompson, J.L. and Martin, F. (2014) *Strategic Management*, London, Cengage EMEA.

United Nations (2013) UN panel call for global sustainability reporting. Available at: http://www.post2015hlp.org/wp-content/uploads/2013/05/UN-Report.pdf.

Warren J.D, Moffitt K.C., and Byrnes, P. (2015) *Accounting Horizons,* American Accounting Association, 29(2) 397–407.

World Commission on Environment and Development (1987) *Tokyo Declaration*, Tokyo. WCED.

Yazdifar, H. and Askarany, D. (2012) A comparative study of the adoption and implementation of target costing in the UK, Australia and New Zealand, *International Journal of Production Economics* 135(2012) 382–392.

Zuriekat, M. (2005) Performance Measurement Systems: An Examination of the Influence of Contextual Factors and Their Impact on Performance with Specific Emphasis on the Balanced Scorecard Approach, PhD dissertation, University of Huddersfield.

APPENDICES

APPENDIX A: PRESENT VALUE OF £1 AFTER n YEARS = $£1/(1 + k)^n$

Years hence	1%	2%	4%	6%	8%	10%	12%	14%	15%	16%
1	0.990	0.980	0.962	0.943	0.926	0.909	0.893	0.877	0.870	0.862
2	0.980	0.961	0.925	0.890	0.857	0.826	0.797	0.769	0.756	0.743
3	0.971	0.942	0.889	0.840	0.794	0.751	0.712	0.675	0.658	0.641
4	0.961	0.924	0.855	0.792	0.735	0.683	0.636	0.592	0.572	0.552
5	0.951	0.906	0.822	0.747	0.681	0.621	0.567	0.519	0.497	0.476
6	0.942	0.888	0.790	0.705	0.630	0.564	0.507	0.456	0.432	0.410
7	0.933	0.871	0.760	0.665	0.583	0.513	0.452	0.400	0.376	0.354
8	0.923	0.853	0.731	0.627	0.540	0.467	0.404	0.351	0.327	0.305
9	0.914	0.837	0.703	0.592	0.500	0.424	0.361	0.308	0.284	0.263
10	0.905	0.820	0.676	0.558	0.463	0.386	0.322	0.270	0.247	0.227
11	0.896	0.804	0.650	0.527	0.429	0.350	0.287	0.237	0.215	0.195
12	0.887	0.788	0.625	0.497	0.397	0.319	0.257	0.208	0.187	0.168
13	0.879	0.773	0.601	0.469	0.368	0.290	0.229	0.182	0.163	0.145
14	0.870	0.758	0.577	0.442	0.340	0.263	0.205	0.160	0.141	0.125
15	0.861	0.743	0.555	0.417	0.315	0.239	0.183	0.140	0.123	0.108
16	0.853	0.728	0.534	0.394	0.292	0.218	0.163	0.123	0.107	0.093
17	0.844	0.714	0.513	0.371	0.270	0.198	0.146	0.108	0.093	0.080
18	0.836	0.700	0.494	0.350	0.250	0.180	0.130	0.095	0.081	0.069
19	0.828	0.686	0.475	0.331	0.232	0.164	0.116	0.083	0.070	0.060
20	0.820	0.673	0.456	0.312	0.215	0.149	0.104	0.073	0.061	0.051

Years hence	18%	20%	22%	24%	25%	26%	28%	30%	35%
1	0.847	0.833	0.820	0.806	0.800	0.794	0.781	0.769	0.741
2	0.718	0.694	0.672	0.650	0.640	0.630	0.610	0.592	0.549
3	0.609	0.579	0.551	0.524	0.512	0.500	0.477	0.455	0.406
4	0.516	0.482	0.451	0.423	0.410	0.397	0.373	0.350	0.301
5	0.437	0.402	0.370	0.341	0.328	0.315	0.291	0.269	0.223
6	0.370	0.335	0.303	0.275	0.262	0.250	0.227	0.207	0.165
7	0.314	0.279	0.249	0.222	0.210	0.198	0.178	0.159	0.122
8	0.266	0.233	0.204	0.179	0.168	0.157	0.139	0.123	0.091
9	0.225	0.194	0.167	0.144	0.134	0.125	0.108	0.094	0.067
10	0.191	0.162	0.137	0.116	0.107	0.099	0.085	0.073	0.050
11	0.162	0.135	0.112	0.094	0.086	0.079	0.066	0.056	0.037
12	0.137	0.112	0.092	0.076	0.069	0.062	0.052	0.043	0.027
13	0.116	0.093	0.075	0.061	0.055	0.050	0.040	0.033	0.020
14	0.099	0.078	0.062	0.049	0.044	0.039	0.032	0.025	0.015
15	0.084	0.065	0.051	0.040	0.035	0.031	0.025	0.020	0.011
16	0.071	0.054	0.042	0.032	0.028	0.025	0.019	0.015	0.008
17	0.060	0.045	0.034	0.026	0.023	0.020	0.015	0.012	0.006
18	0.051	0.038	0.028	0.021	0.018	0.016	0.012	0.009	0.005
19	0.043	0.031	0.023	0.017	0.014	0.012	0.009	0.007	0.003
20	0.037	0.026	0.019	0.014	0.012	0.010	0.007	0.005	0.002

APPENDIX B: PRESENT VALUE OF AN ANNUITY OF £1 RECEIVED ANNUALLY FOR n YEARS $= \frac{£1}{K}\left(1 - \frac{1}{(1+K)^n}\right)$

Years hence	1%	2%	4%	6%	8%	10%	12%	14%	15%	16%	18%
1	0.990	0.980	0.962	0.943	0.926	0.909	0.893	0.877	0.870	0.862	0.847
2	1.970	1.942	1.886	1.833	1.783	1.736	1.690	1.647	1.626	1.605	1.566
3	2.941	2.884	2.775	2.673	2.577	2.487	2.402	2.322	2.283	2.246	2.174
4	3.902	3.808	3.630	3.465	3.312	3.170	3.037	2.914	2.855	2.798	2.690
5	4.853	4.713	4.452	4.212	3.993	3.791	3.605	3.433	3.352	3.274	3.127
6	5.795	5.601	5.242	4.917	4.623	4.355	4.111	3.889	3.784	3.685	3.498
7	6.728	6.472	6.002	5.582	5.206	4.868	4.564	4.288	4.160	4.039	3.812
8	7.652	7.325	6.733	6.210	5.747	5.335	4.968	4.639	4.487	4.344	4.078
9	8.566	8.162	7.435	6.802	6.247	5.759	5.328	4.946	4.772	4.607	4.303
10	9.471	8.983	8.111	7.360	6.710	6.145	5.650	5.216	5.019	4.833	4.494
11	10.368	9.787	8.760	7.887	7.139	6.495	5.937	5.453	5.234	5.029	4.656
12	11.255	10.575	9.385	8.384	7.536	6.814	6.194	5.660	5.421	5.197	4.793
13	12.134	11.343	9.986	8.853	7.904	7.103	6.424	5.842	5.583	5.342	4.910
14	13.004	12.106	10.563	9.295	8.244	7.367	6.628	6.002	5.724	5.468	5.008
15	13.865	12.849	11.118	9.712	8.559	7.606	6.811	6.142	5.847	5.575	5.092
16	14.718	13.578	11.652	10.106	8.851	7.824	6.974	6.265	5.954	5.669	5.162
17	15.562	14.292	12.166	10.477	9.122	8.022	7.120	6.373	6.047	5.749	5.222
18	16.398	14.992	12.659	10.828	9.372	8.201	7.250	6.467	6.128	5.818	5.273
19	17.226	15.678	13.134	11.815	9.604	8.365	7.366	6.550	6.198	5.877	5.316
20	18.046	16.351	13.590	11.470	9.818	8.514	7.469	6.623	6.259	5.929	5.353

Years hence	20%	22%	24%	25%	26%	28%	30%	35%	36%	37%
1	0.833	0.820	0.806	0.800	0.794	0.781	0.769	0.741	0.735	0.730
2	1.528	1.492	1.457	1.440	1.424	1.392	1.361	1.289	1.276	1.263
3	2.106	2.042	1.981	1.952	1.923	1.868	1.816	1.696	1.673	1.652
4	2.589	2.494	2.404	2.362	2.320	2.241	2.166	1.997	1.966	1.935
5	2.991	2.864	2.745	2.689	2.635	2.532	2.436	2.220	2.181	2.143
6	3.326	3.167	3.020	2.951	2.885	2.759	2.643	2.385	2.339	2.294
7	3.605	3.416	3.242	3.161	3.083	2.937	2.802	2.508	2.455	2.404
8	3.837	3.619	3.421	3.329	3.241	3.076	2.925	2.598	2.540	2.485
9	4.031	3.786	3.566	3.463	3.366	3.184	3.019	2.665	2.603	2.544
10	4.192	3.923	3.682	3.571	3.465	3.269	3.092	2.715	2.649	2.587
11	4.327	4.035	3.776	3.656	3.544	3.335	3.147	2.752	2.683	2.618
12	4.439	4.127	3.851	3.725	3.606	3.387	3.190	2.779	2.708	2.641
13	4.533	4.203	3.912	3.780	3.656	3.427	3.223	2.799	2.727	2.658
14	4.611	4.265	3.962	3.824	3.695	3.459	3.249	2.814	2.740	2.670
15	4.675	4.315	4.001	3.859	3.726	3.483	3.268	2.825	2.750	2.679
16	4.730	4.357	4.033	3.887	3.751	3.503	3.283	2.834	2.757	2.685
17	4.775	4.391	4.059	3.910	3.771	3.518	3.295	2.840	2.763	2.690
18	4.812	4.419	4.080	3.928	3.786	3.529	3.304	2.844	2.767	2.693
19	4.844	4.442	4.097	3.942	3.799	3.539	3.311	2.848	2.770	2.696
20	4.870	4.460	4.110	3.954	3.808	3.546	3.316	2.850	2.772	2.698

ANSWERS TO REVIEW PROBLEMS

Chapter 2

2.14 (a) SV (or variable if direct labour can be matched exactly to output)
   (b) F
   (c) F
   (d) V
   (e) F (Advertising is a discretionary cost. See Chapter 9, Zero-based budgeting for an explanation of this cost.)
   (f) SV
   (g) F
   (h) SF
   (i) V

2.15 Controllable c, d, f
   Non-controllable a, b, e, g, h

2.16 Answer = (b)

2.17 Answer = (b)

2.18 Answer = (d)

2.19 Answer = (b)

2.20 Variable costs are constant per unit of output. The costs per unit of output are as follows:

	Cost per unit 125 units (£)	Cost per unit 180 units (£)
T1	8.00	7.00
T2	14.00	14.00
T3	19.80	15.70
T4	25.80	25.80

Answer = (c)

2.21 (a) (i) Schedule of annual mileage costs

	5 000 miles (£)	10 000 miles (£)	15 000 miles (£)	30 000 miles (£)
Variable costs:				
Spares	100	200	300	600
Petrol	380	760	1 140	2 280
Total variable cost	480	960	1 440	2 880
Variable cost per mile	0.096	0.096	0.096	0.096
Fixed costs				
Depreciation[a]	2 000	2 000	2 000	2 000
Maintenance	120	120	120	120
Vehicle licence	80	80	80	80
Insurance	150	150	150	150
Tyres[b]	—	—	75	150
	2 350	2 350	2 425	2 500
Fixed cost per mile	0.47	0.235	0.162	0.083
Total cost	2 830	3 310	3 865	5 380
Total cost per mile	0.566	0.331	0.258	0.179

Notes:

[a]Annual depreciation = $\dfrac{\text{£5 500 (cost)} - \text{£1 500 (trade-in price)}}{\text{2 years}}$ = £2 000

[b]At 15 000 miles per annum tyres will be replaced once during the 2-year period at a cost of £150. The average cost per year is £75. At 30 000 miles per annum tyres will be replaced once each year.

Comments
Tyres are a semi-fixed cost. In the above calculations they have been regarded as a step-fixed cost. An alternative approach would be to regard the semi-fixed cost as a variable cost by dividing £150 tyre replacement by 25 000 miles. This results in a variable cost per mile of £0.006.
   Depreciation and maintenance cost have been classified as fixed costs. They are likely to be semi-variable costs, but in the absence of any additional information they have been classified as fixed costs.

   (ii) See Figure 2.21.
   (iii) The respective costs can be obtained from the vertical dashed lines in the graph (Figure 2.21).

   (b) The *cost per mile* declines as activity increases. This is because the majority of costs are fixed and do not increase when mileage increases. However, *total cost* will increase with increases in mileage.

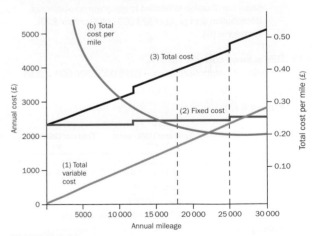

FIGURE 2.21

The step increase in fixed cost is assumed to occur at an annual mileage of 12 500 and 25 000 miles, because tyres are assumed to be replaced at this mileage

2.22 (a) For an explanation of sunk and opportunity costs see Chapter 2. The down payment of €5000 represents a sunk cost. The lost profit from subletting the shop of €1600 p.a. ((€550 × €12) – €5000) is an example of an opportunity cost. Note that only the €5000 additional rental is included in the opportunity cost calculation. (The €5000 sunk cost is excluded from the calculation.)

(b)   The relevant information for running the shop is:

	(€)
Net sales	100 000
Costs (€87 000 – €5 000 sunk cost)	82 000
	18 000
Less opportunity cost from subletting	1 600
Profit	16 400

The above indicates that €16 400 additional profits will be obtained from using the shop for the sale of clothing. It is assumed that Mrs Johnston will not suffer any other loss of income if she devotes half her time to running the shop.

Chapter 3

3.11   (a)   Answer = (i)

(b)   The increase in fixed costs will result in an increase in the break-even point. The only correct alternative that is listed is item (iii). This indicates an increase in the break-even point sales value.

3.12   (a)   An increase in fixed costs will result in a lower break-even point (i.e. the number of units sold to break even). Therefore t will decrease. Answer = (iii)

(b)   The slope of the profit line is represented by the change in contribution per unit. The diagram indicates that sales are 800 units in excess of the break-even point (represented by t) and these 800 units generate a profit of $16 000 (represented by w). Profit is equal to contribution above the break-even point so the contribution per unit is $20 ($16 000/800 units). Additional sales can thus be expected to generate an additional contribution and profit of $28 000 (1400 units × $20). Answer = (iii)

3.13   BEP = Fixed costs/PV ratio

PV ratio = Contribution/Sales = £275 000/£500 000 = 0.55

BEP = £165 000/0.55 = £300 000

Answer = (d)

3.14

	Total cost (1000 units) (£)	Total cost (2000 units) (£)
Production overhead	3 500 (£3.50 × 1 000)	5 000 (£2.50 × 2 000)
Selling overhead	1 000 (£1 × 1 000)	1 000 (£0.5 × 2 000)

$$\text{Variable cost per unit} = \frac{\text{Change in cost}}{\text{Change in activity}}$$

Production overhead = £1500/1000 units = £1.50

Selling overhead = Fixed cost since total costs remain unchanged.

The unit costs of direct materials are constant at both activity levels and are therefore variable.

Production overheads fixed cost element = Total cost (£3500) – Variable cost (1000 × £1.50) = £2000

Total fixed cost = £2000 + £1000 = £3000

Unit variable cost £4 + £3 + £1.50 = £8.50

Answer = E

3.15   Contribution per unit = 40% × €20 = €8

$$\text{Break-even point} = \frac{\text{Fixed costs (€60 000)}}{\text{Contribution per units (€8)}} = 7500 \text{ units}$$

Answer = (e)

3.16   Break-even point in units = £18 000 sales/unit selling price (£15) = 1200 units

Contribution per unit sold = £15 × 0.4 = £6

Profit when 1500 units are sold = (1500 – 1200) × £6 = £1800

Answer = (b)

3.17   At the break-even point, contribution is equal to fixed costs so the contribution to sales ratio is 40 per cent ($320 000/$800 000)

To earn a profit of $200 000 the required contribution is equal to the fixed costs plus the required profit ($320 000 + $200 000)/0.40 = $1 300 000

Answer = (b)

3.18   Variable costs are 60% of the selling price and the variable cost per unit is £24 so the selling price per unit is £24/0.6 = £40

Contribution per unit = £16 (£40 × 0.4)

Break-even point = Fixed costs (£720 000) / contribution per unit (£16) = 45 000 units

Answer = (d)

3.19   *Preliminary calculations:*

	Sales (units)	Profit/(loss)
November	30 000	£40 000
December	35 000	£60 000
Increase	5 000	£ 20 000

An increase in sales of 5000 units increases contribution (profits) by £20 000. Therefore contribution is £4 per unit. Selling price is £10 per unit (given) and variable cost per unit will be £6.

At 30 000 unit sales:

Contribution	minus Fixed costs	= Profit
£120 000	minus ?	= £40 000

$\therefore$ Fixed costs = £80 000

The above information can now be plotted on a graph.

A break-even chart or a profit–volume graph could be constructed. A profit–volume graph avoids the need to calculate the profits since the information can be read directly from the graph. (See Figure 3.19a for a break-even chart and Figure 3.19b for a profit–volume graph.)

(a)   (i)   Fixed costs = £80 000.

(ii)   Variable cost per unit = £6.

(iii) Profit–volume =

$$\frac{\text{Contribution per unit (£4)}}{\text{Selling price per unit (£10)}} \times 100 = 40\%$$

(iv)   Break-even point = 20 000 units.

(v)   The margin of safety represents the difference between actual or expected sales volume and the break-even point. Therefore the margin of safety will be different for each month's sales. For example, the margin of safety in November is 10 000 units (30 000 units – 20 000 units). The margin of safety can be read from Figure 3.19b for various sales levels.

(b) and (c) See the section 'Linear CVP relationships' in Chapter 3 for the answers.

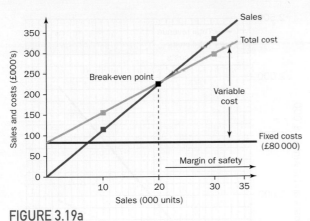

FIGURE 3.19a

Break-even chart

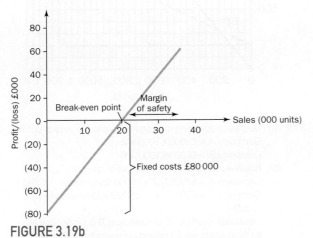

FIGURE 3.19b

Profit–volume graph

3.20 (a) Let *x* = number of units of output
Total cost for 30 000 units or less = $50 000 + 5*x* (where
5 = variable cost per unit)
Total cost for more than 30 000 units = $100 000 + 5*x*

(b)

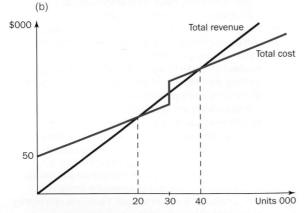

(c) There are two break-even points resulting in the
production plan being profitable only between
20 000 and 30 000 units and above 40 000 units.
The production plan should be set based on these
considerations.

3.21

Workings:	(000)
Sales	1 000
Variable costs	600
Contribution	400
Fixed costs	500
Profit/(loss)	(100)

Unit selling price = £20   (£1m/50 000)
Unit variable cost = £12   (£600 000/50 000)
Unit contribution = £8

(a) Sales commission will be £2 per unit, thus reducing the
contribution per unit to £6. The break-even point will be
83 333 units (£500 000/£6) or £1 666 666 sales value.
This requires an increase of 67 per cent on previous
sales and the company must assess whether or not
sales can be increased by such a high percentage.

(b) A 10 per cent decrease in selling price will decrease
the selling price by £2 per unit and the revised unit
contribution will be £6:

	(£)
Revised total contribution (65 000 × £6)	390 000
Less fixed costs	500 000
Profit/(loss)	(110 000)

The estimated loss is worse than last year and the
proposal is therefore not recommended.

(c) Wages will increase by 25 per cent – that is, from
£200 000 to £250 000 – causing output to increase by
20 per cent.

		(£)
Sales		1 200 000
Direct materials and variable overheads	480 000	
Direct wages	250 000	730 000
Contribution		470 000
Less fixed costs		550 000
Profit/(loss)		(80 000)

This represents an improvement of £20 000 on last
year's loss of £100 000.

(d) Revised selling price = £24
Let X = Revised sales volume
∴ sales revenue less (variable costs + fixed costs)= Profit

24X less (12X + 800 000)	= 0.1 (24X)
∴ 9.6X	= 800 000
∴ X	= 83 333 units

Clearly this proposal is preferable since it is the only
proposal to yield a profit. However, the probability of
increasing sales volume by approximately 67 per cent
plus the risk involved from increasing fixed costs by
£300 000 must be considered.

3.22 (i) Contribution per unit = $24.00 − $8.60 − $1.20 = $14.20
Break-even point = $880 400/$14.20 = 62 000 units

(ii) Margin of safety = (90 000 − 62 000) / 90 000 = 31.1%

(iii) Revised contribution per unit = $25.00 − $8.60 −
$2.00 = $14.40
Break-even point = $890 400/$14.40 = 61 833 units

3.23

$$\text{Break-even point} = \frac{\text{Fixed costs}}{\text{Contribution per unit}}$$

Product X 25 000 units (£100 000/£4)

Product Y 25 000 units (£200 000/£8)

Company as a whole 57 692 units (£300 000/£5.20[a])

Note:

[a]Average contribution per unit

$$= \frac{(70\,000 \times £4) + (30\,000 \times £8)}{100\,000 \text{ units}}$$

$= £5.20$

The sum of the product break-even points is less than the break-even point for the company as a whole. It is incorrect to add the product break-even points because the sales mix will be different from the planned sales mix. The sum of the product break-even points assumes a sales mix of 50 per cent to X and 50 per cent to Y. The break-even point for the company as a whole assumes a planned sales mix of 70 per cent to X and 30 per cent to Y. CVP analysis will yield correct results only if the planned sales mix is equal to the actual sales mix.

3.24 (a)

	T	C	R	Total
Unit selling price ($)	1 600	1 800	1 400	
Unit variable cost ($)	628	716	531	
Unit contribution ($)	972	1 084	869	
Sales volume	420	400	380	
Total contribution ($)	408 240	433 600	330 220	1 172 060
Total sales ($)	672 000	720 000	532 000	1 924 000

Note

The unit variable cost includes 40 per cent of the direct labour cost

Weighted average contribution/sales ratio = $1 172 060/$1 924 000 = 60.92%.

(b) Fixed labour costs = [(420 × $220) + (400 × $240) + (380 × $190)] × 0.6 = $156 360

Total fixed costs = $156 360 + $55 000 = $211 360.

Breakeven sales revenue = fixed costs/weighted average contribution/sales ratio

= $211 360/60.92% = $346 947

Margin of safety = Budgeted sales revenue ($1 924 000) – breakeven sales revenue ($346 947)

= $1 577 053.

(c) Total variable cost = (420 × $628) + (400 × $716) + (380 × $531) = $751 940

Total cost = $751 940 variable cost + $211 360 fixed costs = $963 300

Total sales revenue $1 924 000

The above total figures are plotted on the graph below for a sales volume of 100 units

(d) If the more profitable products are sold first the company will cover its fixed costs more quickly resulting in the breakeven point being lower. This is because a lower sales volume will be required to cover fixed costs and break even.

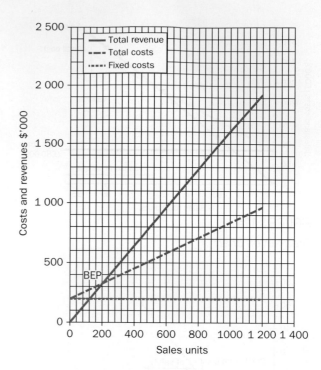

3.25 (a) Degree of operating leverage = Contribution margin/profit

Company A = €2000/€1000 = 2

Company B = €6000/€1000 = 6

(b) Break-even point = Fixed costs/PV ratio

Company A = €1000/0.2 = €5000 (expressed in 000s)

Company B = €5000/0.6 = €8 333.333 (expressed in 000s)

The break-even point for Company B is higher because its fixed costs are €5 million compared with €1 million for company A. Company A generates a contribution of €0.20 per €1 of sales whereas Company B generates a contribution of €0.60. However, to cover its fixed costs of €5 million Company B must achieve a higher level of sales (€8.33 million sales at €0.60 per €1 of sales) whereas to cover fixed costs of €1 million Company A only needs to achieve sales of €5 million at a contribution of €0.20 per €1 of sales.

(c) Revised profits for Company A = €15 million sales yielding a contribution of €3 million less fixed costs of €1 million giving a profit of €2 million.

Revised profits for Company B = €15 million sales yielding a contribution of €9 million less fixed costs of €5 million giving a profit of €4 million.

Company A's profits have increased from €1 million to €2 million representing an increase of 100 per cent. In contrast, Company B's profits have increased from €1 million to €4 million representing an increase of 300 per cent. The degree of operating leverage for Company A is 2, which means that an increase in sales of 50 per cent will result in an increase in profits of 100 per cent (50% × 2). In contrast, the degree of operating leverage for Company B is 6 so that an increase in sales of 50 per cent results in an increase in profits of 300 per cent (50% × 6). The degree of operating leverage measures the sensitivity of profits to changes in sales. A degree of operating leverage (DOL) of 2 means that profits change by two times more than the change in sales whereas a DOL of 6 means that profits change by six times more than the change in sales.

3.26 (a) $\text{BEP} = \dfrac{400\,000 \text{ (fixed costs)} \times £1\,000\,000 \text{ (sales)}}{£420\,000 \text{ (contribution)}}$

= 952 380

(b) (i)

	(£)	(£)
Revised selling price		9.00
Less variable costs:		
Direct materials	1.00	
Direct labour	3.50	
Variable overhead	0.60	
Delivery expenses	0.50	
Sales commission	0.18	
(2% of selling price)		5.78
Contribution per unit		3.22
Number of units sold		140 000
Total contribution (140 000 × 3.22)		450 800
Fixed costs		400 000
Profit from proposal (i)		50 800

(ii)

Desired contribution	= 480 000
Contribution per unit for present proposal	= 3.22
Required units to earn large profit	= 149 068

(c) (i) The variable cost of selling to the mail order firm is:

	(£)
Direct material	1.00
Direct labour	3.50
Variable overhead	0.60
Delivery expenses	—
Sales commission	—
Additional package cost	0.50
	5.60

To break even, a contribution of £1.20 is required (60 000 fixed cost/50 000 units sold). Therefore selling price to break even is £6.80 (£5.60 + £1.20).

(ii) To earn £50 800 profit, a contribution of £110 800 (£60 000 + £50 800) is required. That is, a contribution of £2.22 per unit is required. Therefore required selling price is £7.82 (£5.60 + £2.22).

(iii) To earn the target profit of £80 000, a contribution of £140 000 is required. That is, £2.80 per unit. Therefore required selling price = £8.40 (£5.60 + £2.80).

(d) Contribution per unit is £3.22 per (B)

Unit sold		160 000
Total contribution		£515 200
Fixed costs		£430 000
	Profit	£85 200

Chapter 4

4.13 The relevant cost of the skilled labour is the hourly wage rate of £8 per hour plus the lost contribution of £10 per hour

(£25/2.5 hours) giving £18 per hour. The labour hours required to produce one unit of output is derived from dividing the labour cost (£25) by the hourly wage rate. The total relevant cost of labour is £1620 (90 hours × £18).

Answer = (c)

4.14 The relevant cost of regularly used materials that will be replaced is the replacement cost (600 × £27) = £16 200

Answer = (c)

4.15

Product	A	B	C	D
Selling price per unit	$160	$214	$100	$140
Raw material cost	$24	$56	$22	$40
Direct labour cost at $11 per hour	$66	$88	$33	$22
Variable overhead cost	$24	$18	$24	$18
Contribution per unit	$46	$52	$21	$60
Direct labour hours per unit	6	8	3	2
Contribution per labour hour	$7.67	$6.50	$7	$30
Rank	2	4	3	1
Normal monthly hours (total units × hours per unit)	1 800	1 000	720	800

If the strike goes ahead only 2160 labour hours will be available so the company should make all of D, then allocate the remaining 1360 hours to A (2160 − 800 hrs).

Answer = A

4.16 If the company uses the equipment on the contract it will lose its current sale value of €2000 and incur additional disposal costs of €800 giving a total relevant cost of €2800.

Answer = (d)

4.17 Incremental cost of new employees = R40 000 × 4 = R160 000

Supervision is not an incremental cost.

Incremental costs of retraining

= R15 000 + R100 000 replacement cost = R115 000

Retraining is the cheaper alternative and therefore the relevant cost of the contract is R115 000.

Answer = (b)

4.18

Component	Additional cost of buying-in per unit £	Hours per unit to manufacture	Additional cost per hour £
A	48	4	12
B	60	6	10
C	45	5	9
D	39	3	13

Component C should be purchased because it has the lowest additional cost per hour saved.

Answer = (c)

4.19 Apportioned fixed costs = €120 000 (0.6 × €200 000)

Fixed costs apportioned to Shop

S = €40 000 (500/1500 × €120 000)

Specific avoidable fixed cost for Shop

S = €30 000 (€70 000 − €30 000)

Shop S therefore provides a contribution of €30 000 (variable cost contribution of €60 000 less specific fixed costs of €30 000) to general apportioned fixed costs. The effect of closing down shop S is that total budgeted profit will decline by the lost contribution from S to €50 000.

Answer = (a)

4.20   (a)

The relevant costs of the order are as follows:

	$
Lunch[a]	0
Engineers' costs[b]	500
Technical advisor[c]	480
Site visits[d]	0
Training costs[e]	125
Handsets[f]	2 184
Control system[g]	7 600
Cable[h]	1 300
Total relevant cost	12 189

Notes:
[a]This is a sunk cost and is therefore not relevant to the decision.
[b]One of the engineers has spare capacity so there will be no additional cost in undertaking the contract. Undertaking the contract will result in Contract X being delayed by 1 week so that T's costs will increase by $500.
[c]The overtime costs represent the additional costs that will be incurred if the contract is undertaken ($60 × 8 hours).
[d]This cost will be paid by the customer so no additional site visit costs will be incurred by T Co.
[e]The monthly salary cost is irrelevant since it will be paid whether or not the contract is undertaken. However, the commission of $125 is an incremental cost associated with the contract.
[f]The handsets are in regular use and undertaking the contract will necessitate replacement of 80 handsets at $18.20 each. The remaining 40 handsets will be purchased at £18.20 so the relevant cost is $2 184 (120 × $18.20).
[g]The original cost of the Swipe 1 is a sunk cost and not relevant. However, since the company could sell it for $3000 if it did not use it for this contact. It represents an opportunity cost. The current market price of Swipe 1 is not relevant since the company does not intend to replace it. In order to use Swipe 1 on the contract it must be converted at a cost of $4600. The relevant cost is $7600 since this is less than the cost of a new Swipe 2 ($10 800).
[h]The cost of the inventory represents a sunk cost and is not relevant. The replacement cost of $1.30 per metre is the relevant cost.

(b)   You should refer to 'Identifying relevant costs and revenues', 'Determining the relevant costs of direct labour and materials' and 'opportunity costs' in Chapter 4 for discussing the principles used in part (a). The explanation of the implications of the minimum price should point out that the relevant cost represents the minimum price and starting point for determining a price. It represents a price at which T Co. will be no better or worse off if it did not carry out the work. The answer should also point out that prices based on covering relevant costs represent short-run prices but that the final agreed price should be attractive enough to encourage repeat orders. For additional points you should refer to the four factors referred to in 'Special pricing decisions' in Chapter 4 and 'A price-setting firm facing short-run pricing decisions' in Chapter 5.

4.21   (a)   (i)

Product	A ($)	B ($)	C ($)
Selling price	15	12	11
Less variable costs:			
Materials	(5)	(4)	(3)
Labour	(3)	(2)	(1.5)
Variable overhead (1)	(3.50)	(2)	(1.5)
Contribution	3.50	4	5

Note:
(1) Fixed overheads are apportioned to products on the basis of sales volume and the remaining overheads are variable with output.

(ii)

Product	B ($)	C ($)
Selling price	12	9.50
Less variable costs:		
Materials	(4)	(3)
Labour	(2)	(1.80)
Variable overhead	(2)	(1.50)
Contribution	4	3.20

(b)   (i)

Product	A	B	C	Total
Total contribution	350 000	480 000	400 000	1 230 000
Less fixed costs:				
Labour				(220 000)
Fixed administration				(900 000)
Profit				110 000

(ii)

Product	B	C	Total
Total contribution[a]	480 000	576 000	1 056 000
Less fixed costs:			
Labour[b]			(160 000)
Fixed administration[c]			(850 000)
Profit			46 000

Notes:
[a]B = 120 000 units × $4 contribution, C = 18 000 units × $3.20 contribution.
[b](25% × $320 000 for B) plus (25% × $160 000 × 2 for C).
[c]Fixed administration costs will decline by 1/6 of the amount apportioned to Product A (100/300 × $900 000). Therefore fixed overheads will decline from $900 000 to $850 000.

(c)   Product A should not be eliminated even though a loss is reported for this product. If product A is eliminated the majority of fixed costs allocated to it will still continue and will be borne by the remaining products. Product A generates a contribution of $350 000 towards fixed costs but the capacity released can be used to obtain an additional contribution from product C of $176 000 ($576 000 – $400 000). This will result in a net loss in contribution of $174 000. However, fixed cost savings of $110 000 ($50 000 administration

apportioned to product A plus $100 000 labour for
A less an extra $40 000 labour for product C) can be
obtained if product A is abandoned. Therefore there
will be a net loss in contribution of $64 000 ($174 000 –
$110 000) and profits will decline from $110 000 to
$64 000.

4.22 (a)

The relevant costs are as follows:

	Keypads $	Display screens $
Direct materials[a]	164 000	118 320
Direct labour	40 000	60 000
Heat and power avoidable costs[b]	44 000	58 000
Machine avoidable fixed costs[c]	4 000	6 000
Machine variable batch set-up costs[d]	27 500	30 000
Avoidable depreciation and insurance costs[e]	33 600	38 400
Total relevant cost	313 100	310 720
Cost of buying-in[f]	328 000	344 000

The above figures indicate it is cheaper to manufacture the
components.

Notes:

[a]Keypads = $80 000 + ($80 000 × 1.05). Display screens =
$116 000 × 1.02

[b]Keypads = $64 000 – $20 000. Display screens = $88 000 –
$30 000

[c]Fixed costs are assumed to be avoidable.
Current number of batches = 160 for both components
(80 000/500). Current cost per batch: Keypads = $22 000/160
= $137.50. Display screens = $24 000/160 = $150
New number of batches = 200 for both components
(80 000/400).
New batch related costs: Keypads = 200 × $137.50. Display
screens = 200 × $150

[d]It is assumed that 40 percent of depreciation and insurance
costs are avoidable that assets depreciate according to units of
output.

[e]Keypads = 80 000 × $4.10. Display screens = 80 000 × $4.30

(b) Both products are cheaper to produce internally.
Producing the maximum demand of either product
will not utilize all of the available labour hours so both
products will be produced internally. Therefore
avoidable fixed costs will be incurred irrespective of
the decision and only variable costs will be relevant for
determining the allocation of the output.

	Keypads $	Display screen $
Buy	4.1	4.3
Variable cost of making ($231 500/80 000) ($208 320/80 000)	2.89	2.6
Saving from making per unit	1.21	1.7
Labour hour per unit	0.5	0.75
Saving from making per unit of limiting factor	2.42	2.27
Ranking	1	2

Since keypads produce the larger saving per scarce
factor (labour hours) the maximum supply of keypads
should be produced internally. The production of
100 000 keypads requires 50 000 labour hours resulting
in the remaining 50 000 hours being allocated to the
production of 66 666 display screens (50 000 hours/0.75
hours per unit). Therefore 33 334 display screens
(100 000 – 66 666) should be purchased.

(c) The following non-financial factors should be considered:

- The reliability of the supplier. The supplier is a new
  company and may not be able to meet demand.
  Outsourcing is high risk since the failure rate of new
  companies is high. The company needs to ascertain if
  there is a competitive market with alternative suppliers
  to ensure that it is not totally reliant on the supplier.
- The contracted price is for 2 years and after this
  the supplier may significantly increase prices if the
  manufacturer no longer has the facilities to produce
  internally. Again it is necessary to ensure that there is a
  competitive market for the supply of the components.
- The quality of the components provided by the
  supplier. Poor quality of components may lead to a
  future loss of sales or increased warranty costs.
- Reliability in meeting promised delivery dates.
  Late deliveries may result in lost sales of the final
  products arising from customers migrating to
  competitors.

4.23 The following information represents a comparison of
alternatives 1 and 2 with the sale of material XY.

Alternative 1: Conversion versus immediate sale

		(£)	(£)	(£)
1.	Sales revenue (900 units at £400 per unit)			360 000
	Less Relevant costs:			
2.	Material XY opportunity cost		21 000	
3.	Material A (600 units at £90)		54 000	
4.	Material B (1000 units at £45)		45 000	
5.	Direct labour:			
	Unskilled (5000 hrs at £8)	40 000		
	Semi-skilled	—		
	Skilled (5000 hrs at £16)	80 000	120 000	
6.	Variable overheads (15 000 hrs at £1)		15 000	
7.	Selling and delivery expenses		27 000	
	Advertising		18 000	
8.	Fixed overheads		—	300 000
	Excess of relevant revenues			60 000

Alternative 2: Adaptation versus immediate sale

		(£)	(£)	(£)
9.	Saving on purchase of sub-assembly:			
	Normal spending (1200 units at £900)		1 080 000	
	Revised spending (900 units at £950)		855 000	225 000
	Less relevant costs:			
2.	Material XY opportunity cost		21 000	
10.	Material C (1000 units at £55)		55 000	
5.	Direct labour:			
	Unskilled (4000 hrs at £8)	32 000		
	Semi-skilled	—		
	Skilled (4000 hrs at £16)	64 000	96 000	
6.	Variable overheads (9000 hrs at £1)		9 000	
8.	Fixed overheads		—	181 000
	Net relevant savings			44 000

1   There will be additional sales revenue of £360 000 if
alternative 1 is chosen.

2   Acceptance of either alternative 1 or 2 will mean a loss
of revenue of £21 000 from the sale of the obsolete material XY.

This is an opportunity cost, which must be covered whichever alternative is chosen. The original purchase cost of £75 000 for material XY is a sunk cost and is irrelevant.

3 Acceptance of alternative 1 will mean that material A must be replaced at an additional cost of £54 000.

4 Acceptance of alternative 1 will mean that material B will be diverted from the production of product Z. The excess of relevant revenues over relevant cost for product Z is £180 and each unit of product Z uses four units of material. The lost contribution (excluding the cost of material B which is incurred for both alternatives) will therefore be £45 for each unit of material B that is used in converting the raw materials into a specialized product.

5 Unskilled labour can be matched exactly to the company's production requirements. The acceptance of either alternative 1 or 2 will cause the company to incur additional unskilled labour costs of £8 for each hour of unskilled labour that is used. It is assumed that the semi-skilled labour would be retained and that there would be sufficient excess supply for either alternative at no extra cost to the company. In these circumstances semi-skilled labour will not have a relevant cost. Skilled labour is in short supply and can only be obtained by reducing production of product L, resulting in a lost contribution of £24 or £6 per hour of skilled labour. We have already established that the relevant cost for labour that is in short supply is the hourly labour cost plus the lost contribution per hour, so the relevant labour cost here will be £16 per hour.

6 It is assumed that for each direct labour hour of input variable overheads will increase by £1. As each alternative uses additional direct labour hours, variable overheads will increase, giving a relevant cost of £1 per direct labour hour.

7 As advertising selling and distribution expenses will be different if alternative 1 is chosen, these costs are clearly relevant to the decision.

8 The company's fixed overheads will remain the same whichever alternative is chosen, and so fixed overheads are not a relevant cost for either alternative.

9 The cost of purchasing the sub-assembly will be reduced by £225 000 if the second alternative is chosen, and so these savings are relevant to the decision.

10 The company will incur additional variable costs of £55 for each unit of material C that is manufactured, so the fixed overheads for material C are not a relevant cost.

When considering a problem such as this one, there are many different ways in which the information may be presented. The way we have dealt with the problem here is to compare each of the two stated alternatives with the other possibility of selling off material XY for its scrap value of £21 000. The above answer sets out the differential (relevant) cash flows arising from choosing alternative 1 or 2 instead of selling material XY, and shows that of the three possibilities alternative 1 is to be preferred.

An alternative presentation of this information, which you may prefer, is as follows:

	Sale of obsolete materials for scrap	Alternative 1	Alternative 2
Relevant revenues less relevant costs	£21 000	£81 000	£65 000

Difference in favour of Alternative 1 £60 000 (£81 000 – £21 000)
Difference in favour of Alternative 2 £44 000 (£65 000 – £21 000)

We show here *the sale of the obsolete materials as a separate alternative*, and so the opportunity cost of material XY, amounting to £21 000 (see item 2 in the answer) is not included in either alternative 1 or 2, since it is brought into the analysis as a separate alternative under the heading 'Sale of obsolete materials for scrap' in the above alternative presentation. Consequently, in both alternatives 1 and 2 the relevant revenues less relevant costs figure is increased by £21 000. The differences between alternative 1 and 2 and the sale of the obsolete materials are still, however, £60 000 and £44 000 respectively, which gives an identical result to that obtained in the above solution.

4.24 (a) *Preliminary calculations*

Variable costs are quoted per acre, but selling prices are quoted per tonne. Therefore, it is necessary to calculate the planned sales revenue per acre. The calculation of the selling price and contribution per acre is as follows:

	Potatoes	Turnips	Parsnips	Carrots
(a) Yield per acre in tonnes	10	8	9	12
(b) Selling price per tonne	€100	€125	€150	€135
(c) Sales revenue per acre, (a) × (b)	€1 000	€1 000	€1 350	€1 620
(d) Variable cost per acre	€470	€510	€595	€660
(e) Contribution per acre	€530	€490	€755	€960

(a) (i)

(i) Profit statement for current year

	Potatoes	Turnips	Parsnips	Carrots	Total
(a) Acres	25	20	30	25	
(b) Contribution per acre	€530	€490	€755	€960	
(c) Total contribution (a × b)	€13 250	€9 800	€22 650	€24 000	€69 700
			Less fixed costs		€54 000
			Profit		€15 700

(ii) Profit statement for recommended mix

	Area A (45 acres)		Area B (55 acres)		Total
	Potatoes	Turnips	Parsnips	Carrots	
(a) Contribution per acre	€530	€490	€755	€960	
(b) Ranking	1	2	2	1	
(c) Minimum sales requirements in acres[a]		5	4		
(d) Acres allocated[b]	40			51	
(e) Recommended mix (acres)	40	5	4	51	
(f) Total contribution, (a) × (e)	€21 200	€2 450	€3 020	€48 960	€75 630
			Less fixed costs		€54 000
			Profit		€21 630

Notes:
[a]The minimum sales requirement for turnips is 40 tonnes, and this will require the allocation of 5 acres (40 tonnes/8 tonnes yield per acre). The minimum sales requirement for parsnips is 36 tonnes, requiring the allocation of 4 acres (36 tonnes/9 tonnes yield per acre).
[b]Allocation of available acres to products on basis of a ranking that assumes that acres are the key factor.

(b) (i) Production should be concentrated on carrots, which have the highest contribution per acre (€960).

	(£)
(ii) Contribution from 100 acres of carrots (100 × €960)	96 000
Fixed overhead	54 000
Profit from carrots	42 000

(iii) Break-even point in acres for carrots = $\dfrac{\text{Fixed costs (€54000)}}{\text{Contribution per acre (€960)}}$

= 56.25 acres

Contribution in sales value for carrots

= €91 125 (56.25 acres at €1 620 sales revenue per acre).

Chapter 5

5.13

Units	Total variable costs (€)	Selling price per unit (€)	Total sales revenue (€)	Total contribution (€)
10	40 000	6 500	65 000	25 000
11	44 400	6 350	69 850	25 450
12	49 200	6 200	74 400	25 200
13	54 400	6 050	78 650	24 250

It is apparent from the cost and revenue functions that contribution declines beyond an output of 11 units so there is no need to compute the contribution for 14 and 20 units. The most profitable output is 11 units.

Answer = (b)

5.14

Profits will be increased up to the point where incremental cost equals incremental revenue (see Chapter 2 for a definition of incremental cost and incremental revenue). The following schedule shows the calculation of incremental cost and incremental revenues for different output levels.

Demand Units	Selling Price per unit £	Total Revenue £ units × unit selling price	Incremental Revenue £	Cost per unit £ units × cost per unit	Total Cost £	Incremental Cost £
1 100	48	52 800	52 800	22	24 200	24 200
1 200	46	55 200	2 400	21	25 200	1 000
1 300	45	58 500	3 300	20	26 000	800
1 400	42	58 800	300	19	26 600	600

Incremental cost exceeds incremental revenue at output levels above 1300 units. Therefore profits are maximized at an output level of 1300 units and a selling price of £45 per unit.

5.15

(a) Variable cost plus 20% = £37 × 1.20 = £44.40
Total cost plus 20% = £44 × 1.20 = £52.80

Advantages of variable costs include that it avoids arbitrary allocations, identifies short-term relevant costs, simplicity and mark-up can be increased to provide a contribution to fixed costs and profit. The disadvantages are that it represents only a partial cost, it is short-term oriented and ignores price/demand relationships.

Advantages of total cost include that it attempts to include all costs, reduces the possibility that fixed costs will not be covered, and simplicity. The disadvantages are that total cost is likely to involve some arbitrary apportionments and the price/demand relationship is ignored.

(b) See 'Pricing policies' in Chapter 5 for the answer to this question. The answer should point out that price skimming is likely to lead to a higher initial price whereas a pricing penetration policy is likely to lead to a lower initial price.

5.16

(a) For the answer to this question you should refer to Chapter 5. In particular the answer should discuss the role of cost information in the following situations:

1 a price-setting firm facing short-run pricing decisions
2 a price-setting firm facing long run decisions
3 a price-taking firm facing short-run product mix decisions
4 a price-taking firm facing long-run decisions.

(b) *Calculation of variable overhead absorption rates*

	Moulding (£000)	Finishing (£000)	General factory (£000)
Allocated overheads	1 600	500	1 050
Reallocation of general factory based on machine hours	600	450	(1 050)
	2 200	950	
Machine hours	800	600	
Variable overhead rate per hour	£2.75	£1.583	

Calculation of fixed overhead absorption rates

	Moulding (£000)	Finishing (£000)	General factory (£000)
Allocated overheads	2 500	850	1 750
Reallocation of general factory based on machine hours	1 050	700	(1 750)
	3 550	1 550	
Machine hours	800	600	
Variable overhead rate per hour	£4.4375	£2.583	

Calculation of full manufacturing cost

		(£)
Direct material		9.00
Direct labour	10.00 (1 × £10)	
	16.50 (2 × £8.25)	26.50
Variable overheads	11.00 (4 × £2.75)	
	4.75 (3 × £1.583)	15.75
Variable manufacturing cost		51.25
Fixed overheads	17.75 (4 × £4.4375)	
	7.75 (3 × £2.583)	25.50
Full manufacturing cost		76.75

Prices based on full manufacturing cost
25% mark up = £95.94
30% mark up = £99.78
35% mark up = £103.61

Minimum prices based on short-term variable cost and incremental cost are as follows:

Variable cost = £51.25

Incremental cost = £59.60 (£51.25 plus specific fixed costs of £8.35)

The specific fixed cost per unit is calculated by dividing the fixed costs of £167 000 by the estimated sales volume (10% × 200 000).

(c) The cost information is more likely to provide a general guide to the pricing decision but the final pricing decision will be influenced by the prices of competitors' products (£90–£100). The full cost prices indicate prices within a range of £96–£104. The variable/incremental price indicates a minimum short-run price that may be appropriate if the company wishes to pursue a price-skimming policy. Given that the product is an improvement on competitors, a price in the region of £100 would seem to be appropriate but the final decision should be based on marketing considerations drawing off the knowledge of the marketing staff. The role of the cost information has been to indicate that a price within this range should provide a reasonable margin and contribution to general fixed costs.

5.17 (a)

	$	Note
Food and drink at meeting	–	1
Material Z	78 000	2
Construction workers	–	3
Engineers	4 485	4
Specialist machine	15 250	5
Windows	1 500	6
Other materials	6 000	7
Fixed overhead	–	8
Profit margin	–	9
Total relevant cost	105 235	

Notes:
[1] The food and drink costs are sunk and therefore do not represent relevant costs.
[2] The 550kg currently in inventory will need to be replaced and therefore should be valued at replacement cost. The remaining 650kg will also need to be replaced so the relevant cost is $78 000 (1200 × $65).
[3] Spare capacity exists and no additional costs will be incurred so the relevant cost is zero.
[4] Additional costs of $4680 ($52 × 90 hours) will be incurred if the engineers work overtime whereas a profit contribution of $4485 ($1495 × 3 units of product Y) will be lost if production of product Y is reduced. The relevant cost is the lower of the two options ($4485).
[5] The incremental rental cost is $15 250 whereas the net cost of purchase is $20 000 so the additional relevant cost is the lower of the two alternatives.
[6] The cost of producing the windows is sunk and irrelevant. If the windows are not used for the conference the sales will not be lost since the chief executive will visit the client to secure the sale. The chief executive's time is not a relevant cost since he is paid a fixed salary. If the windows are used for the contract an additional conference non-attendance fee of $1500 will be incurred. Therefore the relevant cost is $1500.
[7] The incremental/relevant cost is $6000.
[8] The fixed cost will be incurred whether or not the contract is undertaken so it is not a relevant cost.
[9] The profit mark-up is not relevant since the objective is to establish a minimum price to cover the relevant cost.

(b) See 'A price-setting firm facing a short-run pricing decision' in Chapter 5 for the answer to this question. The answer should also point out that the quoted minimum price does not include a profit margin.

(c) A market skimming pricing strategy is likely to be appropriate to launch the houses in the new country.

A market skimming pricing policy charges a high price for the product initially where the product is unique and there are significant barriers to entry for competitors. The price is reduced as new competitors enter the market with a similar product. The high quality materials and unique energy saving technology used in the houses should enable high prices to be initially set as this provides a differential advantage for sales to customers who would like to have houses with this technology. This market skimming approach will allow DLW to recover the research and development costs incurred to develop the energy saving technology.

5.18 (a) (i) The following tabular approach can be used to find the profit maximizing combination of selling price per room and quantity of double rooms demanded.

Selling price per room per night ($)	Quantity demanded	Variable costs per room per night ($)	Contribution per night ($)
380	1 520	200	273 600
390	1 480	200	281 200
400	1 440	200	288 000
410	1 400	200	294 000
420	1 360	200	299 200
430	1 320	200	303 600
440	1 280	200	307 200
450	1 240	200	310 000
460	1 200	200	312 000
470	1 160	200	313 200
480	1 120	200	313 600
490	1 080	200	313 200

(ii) The profit attributable to the tournament is as follows:

Sales revenue:		No of rooms	Fee/room	Nights	Total $000
Double		1 120	480	5	2 688
Single	15%	360	300	5	540
Family	10%	240	600	5	720
Total revenue					3 948
Variable costs (W1):					
Double	2 ×	1 120 × 100 × 5			= 1 120
Single	1 ×	360 × 100 × 5			= 180
Family	4 ×	240 × 100 × 5			= 480
Total variable costs:					1 780
Incremental fixed costs:					
Double rooms					516 000
Single & family rooms					300 000
Profit					1 352 000

(W1) Number of guests per room × number of rooms × variable cost per guest night × number of nights.

(b) The tabular approach illustrated in (a) above can be used to find the profit maximizing combination of selling price per room and quantity of double rooms demanded. The revised profit attributable to staging the Robyn Cup is as follows:

Sales revenue:		No of rooms	Fee	Nights	Total $000
Double		1 200	460	5	2 760
Single	15%	360	300	5	540
Family	10%	240	600	5	720
Total revenue					4 020

Variable costs:				
Double	2 ×	1 200 × 80 × 5	=	960
Single	1 ×	360 × 80 × 5	=	144
Family	4 ×	240 × 80 × 5	=	384
Total variable costs:				1 488
Incremental fixed costs:				
Double rooms				516
Single & family rooms				300
Additional fixed costs				200
Profit				1 516

Management would be advised to undertake changes in proposed operational activities on purely financial grounds as this would result in an increased profit of ($1 516 000 – $1 352 000) = $164 000.

(c) The following actions might be considered:

- Management could sell a range of souvenirs etc. to visitors to the golf tournament.

- Management could offer guests a price reduction for staying extra nights at the hotel either before or after the golf tournament.

Chapter 6

6.13 Using the interpolation method the IRR is:

$$15\% + \frac{£3\,664}{(£3\,664 + £21\,451)} \times (20\% - 15\%) = 15.7\%$$

Answer = (a)

6.14 Because the same amount is paid each period the cumulative (annuity) discount tables in Appendix B can be used. For 12 periods at 3 per cent the annuity factor is 9.954. The present value 3 months from now will be £2986 (300 × 9.954). Assuming that the first payment is made at the beginning of month 3 this is the equivalent to the end of month 2 for discounting purposes. Therefore it is necessary to discount the present value back 2 months (periods) to today (time zero). Using the discount factor for 3 per cent and 2 periods the present value at time zero is £2 816 (£2 986 × 0.9426). Therefore the answer is (a).

6.15

Time	Cash flow (€000)	Discount factor value at 8%	Present (€000)
0	(20 000)	1.0	(20 000)
1–4	3 000	3.312	9 936
5–8	7 000	2.435 (5.747 – 3.312)	17 045
10	(10 000)	0.463	(4 630)
		NPV	2 351

Note that the discount factors for periods 1–4 and 5–8 are derived from the annuity tables since the cash flows are constant per period for the time period involved.

Answer = (d)

6.16 The annual percentage rate (APR) is 12.68 per cent, which is based on annual payments.

Monthly interest rate = $\sqrt[12]{1.1268} - 1 = 0.01$ so that $r = 1\%$

In other words a monthly interest rate compounded for 12 periods at 1 per cent is equivalent to an annual rate of 12.68 per cent. This is derived from using the compound interest formula used in the chapter = $(1 + 0.01)^{12} - 1$ = 0.1268 = 12.68%

To determine the future value of an annuity where a constant amount is invested each period the future value

$$= A\left[\frac{(1+r)^n - 1}{r}\right]$$ where r is the rate of interest per period and A is the annuity amount.

$$\text{Future value} = 50 \times \left[\frac{1.01^{13\times12} - 1}{.01}\right] = \$18\,610$$

Answer = (d)

6.17 Because the investment is a constant amount each period we can use the annuity future value formula shown in the answer to question 6.16:

$$\text{Future value} = A\left[\frac{(1+r)^n - 1}{r}\right]$$ where r is the rate of interest per period and A is the annuity amount.

$$£7\,000 = A \times \left[\frac{1.005^{12\times5} - 1}{.005}\right]$$

£7 000 = 69.77A
A = £100.33
Answer = (c)

6.18 The loan represents the present value of a series of repayments over a three-year period. Since the payments are constant per period we can use the following annuity present value formula:

$$\text{Present value} = \frac{A}{r}\left[1 - \frac{1}{(1+r)^n}\right]$$

where A is the annuity amount and r is the interest rate per period.

The annual interest rate must be converted to a monthly rate since we are dealing with monthly repayments.

Monthly interest rate = $\sqrt[12]{1.10} - 1 = .0079$ (i.e. 0.79%)

$$\text{Present value (2 000)} = \frac{A}{0.0079}\left[1 - \frac{1}{1.0079^{36}}\right]$$

$$2\,000 = \frac{A}{0.0079}(0.2467)$$

2 000 (0.0079) = 0.2467A
A = 15.8/.2467 = €64.04
Answer = (b)

6.19 (a) (i) Average capital invested

$$= \frac{£50\,000 + £10\,000}{2} = £30\,000$$

For an explanation of why the project's scrap value is added to the initial cost to calculate the

average capital employed, you should refer to
Note 1 at the end of Chapter 6.
   Note that the mid-point of the project's life is
2 years and the written down value at the end of
year 2 is £30 000.

Average annual profit (Project A)

$$= \frac{£25\,000 + £20\,000 + £15\,000 + £10\,000}{4}$$

$$= £17\,500$$

Average annual profit (Project B)

$$= \frac{£10\,000 + £10\,000 + £14\,000 + £26\,000}{4}$$

$$= £15\,000$$

Average annual return:

$$A \quad 58.33\% \left(\frac{£17\,500}{£30\,000} \times 100\right)$$

$$B \quad 50\% \left(\frac{£15\,000}{£30\,000} \times 100\right)$$

(ii) Payback period:

Project A $\left(1 + \dfrac{£15\,000}{£30\,000}\right)$
1.5 years

Project B $\left(2 + \dfrac{£10\,000}{£24\,000}\right)$
2.4 years

(iii) Net present value

Year	Project A Cash inflows (W1) (£)	Project B Cash inflows (W1) (£)	Discount factor	Project A PV (£)	Project B PV (£)
1	35 000	20 000	0.909	31 815	18 180
2	30 000	20 000	0.826	24 780	16 520
3	25 000	24 000	0.751	18 775	18 024
4	20 000	36 000	0.683	13 660	24 588
4	10 000	10 000	0.683	6 830	6 830
				95 860	84 142
		Investment cost		(50 000)	(50 000)
		NPV		45 860	34 142

Workings:
(W1) Cash flows = Profit + depreciation.
Note that the estimated resale value is included as a year
4 cash inflow.

(b) See Chapter 6 for the answer to this section of the
problem.
(c) Project A is recommended because it has the highest
NPV and also the shortest payback period.

6.20 Net cash flows per annum = $101\,000 – $30\,000 –
$5000 = $66\,000
PV of net cash flows = $66\,000 × 3.605 = $237\,930
NPV = $237\,930 – $150\,000 = $87\,930
The PV of the sales revenue = $101\,000 × 3.605
= $364\,105
The percentage change in the selling price that will result
in the project being rejected is:
$87\,930/$364\,105 = 24.15\%

6.21 (a) (i) This is a relevant incremental cost
         (ii) Depreciation is reflected in the investment outlay
              and disposable value at the end of a project's life.
              Therefore depreciation is not a relevant cost.
         (iii) The further training costs are incremental and
              relevant
         (iv) This is a relevant and incremental cost
         (v) This is a sunk and irrelevant cost
         (vi) This is irrelevant because it is already reflected in
              the discounting process within the NPV calculation

    (b) (i) Increase in sales = ($11m – $10m) = $1m
              Increase due to the project = ($1m – $0.2m) =
              $800\,000
         (ii) Total sales in year 1 = $11m
              Savings ($11m × 0.01) = $110\,000
         (iii) Present value ($75\,000 × 3.791 annuity factor for
              5 years) = $284\,325

6.22 (a) The IRR is where:

         annual cash inflows × discount factor = investment cost

         i.e.   £4000 × discount factor = £14 000

         Therefore   discount factor = $\dfrac{£14\,000}{£4\,000}$

                                          = 3.5

         We now work along the five-row table of the cumulative
         discount tables to find the discount rate with a
         discount factor closest to 3.5. This is 13 per cent.
         Therefore the IRR is 13 per cent.

    (b) The annual saving necessary to achieve a 12 per cent
         internal rate of return is where:
         annual savings × 12% discount factor = investment cost
         i.e. annual savings × 3.605   = £14 000

         Therefore annual savings $= \dfrac{£14\,000}{3.605}$

                                          = £3 883

    (c) NPV is calculated as follows:
         £4000 received annually from years 1–5:   (£)
         £4000 × 3.791 discount factor   15 164
            Less investment cost   14 000
         NPV   1 164

6.23 (a) *Project 1*
         Internal failure cost savings
         Current expected value of savings ($000s) = ($300 ×
         0.5) + ($500 × 0.3) + ($700 × 0.2) = $440
         Expected savings ($000s) in year 1 = $440 × 1.04 ×
         80% = $366.08

         External failure cost savings
         Current expected value of savings ($000s) = ($1300
         × 0.6) + ($1900 × 0.3) + ($3000 × 0.1) = $1650
         Expected savings ($000s) in year 1 = ($1650 × 1.04 ×
         80%) = $1 372.8

         Raw material cost future savings
         Expected savings ($000s) in year 1 = 50 000 × $62 ×
         1.04 = $3224

Net cash flows in year1
$366 080 + $1 372 800 + $3 224 000 = $4 962 880

(b) (i) *Project 2 NPV*

Expected savings in year 1 = $110 ($370 − $260) × 50 000 × $110 × 1.04 = $5 720 000

Additional annual fixed costs = $5m − $15m/5 depreciation = $2m

Net Present Value

	Year 0 $000	Year 1 $000	Year 2 $000	Year 3 $000	Year 4 $000	Year 5 $000
Initial Investment	(15 000)					
Working capital	(1 000)					1 000
Cost savings		5 720	5 949	6 187	6 434	6 691
Fixed costs		(2 000)	(2 000)	(2 000)	(2 000)	(2 000)
Net cash flows	(16 000)	3 720	3 949	4 187	4 434	5 691
Discount factor @ 8%	1 000	0.926	0.857	0.794	0.735	0.681
Present value	(16 000)	3 445	3 384	3 324	3 259	3 876

NPV = 1 288 000

Note that the cost savings increase at 4% per annum because of the increased production.

(ii) *Project 2 IRR*

Using a higher discount rate of 12 per cent to apply the trial and error process the NPV is - $503 000 as shown in the following calculation:

	Year 0 $000	Year 1 $000	Year 2 $000	Year 3 $000	Year 4 $000	Year 5 $000
Net cash flows	(16 000)	3 720	3 949	4 187	4 434	5 691
Discount factor @ 12%	1.000	0.893	0.797	0.712	0.636	0.567
Present value	(16 000)	3 322	3 147	2 981	2 820	3 227

Based on discount rates of 8 per cent and 12 per cent and using interpolation IRR

8% + (1288/(1288 + 503)) × 4% = 10.9%

(c) Capital rationing applies. Project 1 requires $4m more investment funds than project 2. If the $4m could be invested to yield a NPV in excess of the NPV of $1 338 000 from project 1 less the NPV of $1 288 000 from project 2 then project 2 should be chosen.

(d) See 'comparison of NPV and IRR' in Chapter 6 for the answer to this question.

6.24 (a) The expected value of year 1 car parking charges is: ($60 × 40%) + ($50 × 25%) + ($70 × 35%) = $61 × 1.05 inflation factor = $64.05
Year 1 sales revenue = (600 × 0.75) × $64.05 × 52 weeks = $1499k
Year 1 contribution = $1499k × 0.8 = $1199k
Fixed costs
Year 1 staff costs = $350k × 1.04 inflation factor = $364k
Year 1 security system costs = $100k × 1.04 inflation = $104k
The above cash flows are entered in year 1 of the following cash flow statement and the cash flows for the remaining years are adjusted by the appropriate inflation rate.

Cash flows

	Year 1 $000	Year 2 $000	Year 3 $000	Year 4 $000	Year 5 $000
Contribution	1 199	1 259	1 322	1 388	1 457
Leasing costs	(50)	(50)	(50)	(50)	(50)
Staff costs	(364)	(379)	(394)	(409)	(426)
Security system costs	(104)	(108)	(112)	(117)	(122)
Net cash flows	681	722	766	812	859

Taxation

	Year 1 $000	Year 2 $000	Year 3 $000	Year 4 $000	Year 5 $000
Net cash flows	681	722	766	812	859
Taxation @ 30%	(204)	(217)	(230)	(244)	(258)

Net present value

	Year 0 $000	Year 1 $000	Year 2 $000	Year 3 $000	Year 4 $000	Year 5 $000	Year 6 $000
Land purchase and development	(8 000)					10 000	
Net cash flows		681	722	766	812	859	
Tax payment		(102)	(108)	(115)	(122)	(129)	
Tax payment		0	(102)	(109)	(115)	(122)	(129)
Net cash flow after tax	(8 000)	579	512	542	575	10 608	(129)
Discount factors @ 8%	1.000	0.926	0.857	0.794	0.735	0.681	0.630
Present value	(8 000)	536	439	430	423	7 224	(81)

The project has a positive NPV of $971k and therefore should be accepted.

(b) NPV at 12%

	Year 0 $000	Year 1 $000	Year 2 $000	Year 3 $000	Year 4 $000	Year 5 $000	Year 6 $000
Net cash flow after tax	(8 000)	579	512	542	575	10 608	(129)
Discount factors @ 12%	1.000	0.893	0.797	0.712	0.636	0.567	0.507
Present value	(8 000)	517	408	386	366	6015	(65)

Net present value = −$373k

IRR = 8% + (($971k/($971k + $373k))×(12% − 8%))
= 8% + 2.9%
= 10.9%

(c) The three elements of the time value of money are risk, the opportunity cost arising from the delay in inflows/outflows and inflation. You should refer to 'The opportunity cost of an investment' in Chapter 6 for an explanation of risk and 'Compounding and discounting' in Chapter 6 for the opportunity cost arising from the delay in inflows/outflows. The inflation element relates to the fact that if there is inflation then investors also need to be compensated for the loss in purchasing power.

6.25 (a) Project A = 3 years + $\dfrac{350 - 314}{112}$ = 3.32 years

Project B = 3.0 years

Project C = 2.00 years

(b) Accounting rate of return = average profit/average investment

Project A = 79/175 = 45%

Project B = 84/175 = 48%

Project C = 70/175 = 40%

Note that average profit = (sum of cash flows – investment cost)/project's life.

(c) The report should include:

(i) NPVs of each project (project A = £83 200 (W1), project B = £64 000 (W2), project C = £79 000 (W3). A simple description of NPV should also be provided. For example, the NPV is the amount over and above the cost of the project that could be borrowed, secure in the knowledge that the cash flows from the project will repay the loan.

(ii) The following rankings are based on the different evaluation procedures:

Project	IRR	Payback	ARR	NPV
A	2	3	2	1
B	3	2	1	3
C	1	1	3	2

(iii) A discussion of each of the above evaluation procedures.

(iv) IRR is subject to the following criticisms:

1 Multiple rates of return can occur when a project has unconventional cash flows.

2 It is assumed that the cash flows received from a project are reinvested at the IRR and not the cost of capital.

3 Inability to rank mutually exclusive projects.

4 It cannot deal with different sized projects. For example, it is better to earn a return of 35 per cent on £100 000 than 40 per cent on £10 000.

Note that the above points are explained in detail in Chapter 6.

(v) Payback ignores cash flows outside the payback period, and it also ignores the timing of cash flows within the payback period. For example, the large cash flows for project A are ignored after the payback period. This method may be appropriate for companies experiencing liquidity problems who wish to recover their initial investment quickly.

(vi) Accounting rate of return ignores the timing of cash flows, but it is considered an important measure by those who believe reported profits have a significant impact on share prices.

(vii) NPV is generally believed to be the theoretically correct evaluation procedure. A positive NPV from an investment is supposed to indicate the increase in the market value of shareholders' funds, but this claim depends upon the belief that the share price is the discounted present value of the future dividend stream. If the market uses some other method of valuing shares then a positive NPV may not represent the increase in market value of shareholders' funds. Note that the cash flows have been discounted at the company's cost of capital. It is only suitable to use the company's cost of capital as the discount rate if projects A, B and C are equivalent to the average risk of all the company's existing projects. If they are not of average risk then project risk-adjusted discount rates should be used.

(viii) The projects have unequal lives. It is assumed that the equipment will not be replaced.

(ix) It is recommended that NPV method is used and project A should be selected.

(d) Stadler prefers project C because it produces the highest accounting profit in year 3. Stadler is assuming that share prices are influenced by short-run reported profits. This is in contrast with theory, which assumes that the share price is the discounted present value of the future dividend stream. Stadler is also assuming that the market only has access to reported historical profits and is not aware of the future benefits arising from the projects. The stock market also obtains company information on future prospects from sources other than reported profits. For example, press releases, chairman's report and signals of future prosperity via increased dividend payments.

Workings

(W1) Project A = (100 × 0.8333) + (110 × 0.6944) + (104 × 0.5787) + (112 × 0.4823) + (138 × 0.4019) + (160 × 0.3349) + (180 × 0.2791) – £350

(W2) Project B = (40 × 0.8333) + (100 × 0.6944) + (210 × 0.5787) + (260 × 0.4823) + (160 × 0.4019) – £350

(W3) Project C = (200 × 0.8333) + (150 × 0.6944) + (240 × 0.5787) + (40 × 0.4823) – £350

Chapter 7

7.12 Overhead absorbed (£714 000) = Actual hours (119 000) × Pre-determined overhead rate.

Pre-determined overhead rate = £714 000/119 000 = £6.

Budgeted overheads (£720 000) = Budgeted machine hours × Budgeted overhead rate (£6).

Budgeted machine hours = £720 000/£6 = 120 000 hours.

Answer = (c)

7.13 Overhead absorbed (30 000 × $3.50) = £105 000

Overhead incurred = $108 875

Under-absorbed = $3875

Answer = (a)

7.14 (i) Budgeted overhead rates and not actual overhead rates should be used as indicated in Chapter 7.

Overhead rate = $148 750/8500 hours = $17.50 per hour.

Answer = A

(ii)

	($)
Actual overheads incurred	146 200
Overheads absorbed (7928 × $17.50)	138 740
Under-absorbed overheads	7 460

Answer = D

7.15 (i) It is assumed that labour cost is to be used as the allocation base.

Total labour cost = €14 500 + €3500 + €24 600 = €42 600

Overhead recovery rate = €126 000/€42 600 = €2.9578 per €1 of labour

Overhead charged to Job CC20 = €24 600 × €2.9578 = €72 761

Answer = C

(ii)

	(€)
Opening WIP	42 790
Direct labour	3 500
Overhead (€3500 × €2.9578)	10 352
	56 642
Selling price (€56 642/0.667)	84 921
or €56 642 divided by 2/3 =	€84 963

Answer = C

(iii) Closing WIP = Total cost of AA10 and CC20

	Total (€)	AA10 (€)	CC20 (€)
Opening WIP		26 800	0
Materials in period		17 275	18 500
Labour in period		14 500	24 600
Overheads in period:			
2.9577465 × €14 500		42 887	
2.9577465 × €24 600			72 761
	217 323	101 462	115 861

Answer = D

7.16 Answer = (d)

7.17 Because production is highly automated it is assumed that overheads will be most closely associated with machine hours. The predetermined overhead rate will therefore be £18 derived from dividing budgeted overheads (£180 000) by the budgeted machine hours (10 000). Therefore the answer is (b).

7.18 (a)

	Total ($)	Departments A ($)	B ($)	C ($)	X ($)	Y ($)
Rent and rates[a]	12 800	6 000	3 600	1 200	1 200	800
Machine insurance[b]	6 000	3 000	1 250	1 000	500	250
Telephone charges[c]	3 200	1 500	900	300	300	200
Depreciation[b]	18 000	9 000	3 750	3 000	1 500	750
Supervisors' salaries[d]	24 000	12 800	7 200	4 000		
Heat and light[a]	6 400	3 000	1 800	600	600	400
	70 400					
Allocated		2 800	1 700	1 200	800	600
		38 100	20 200	11 300	4 900	3 000
Reapportionment of X		2 450 (50%)	1 225 (25%)	1 225 (25%)	(4 900)	(3 000)
Reapportionment of Y		600 (20%)	900 (30%)	1 500 (50%)		
		$41 150	$22 325	$14 025		
Budgeted D.L. hours[e]		3 200	1 800	1 000		
Absorption rates		$12.86	$12.40	$14.02		

Notes:
[a]Apportioned on the basis of floor area.
[b]Apportioned on the basis of machine value.
[c]Should be apportioned on the basis of the number of telephone points or estimated usage. This information is not given and an alternative arbitrary method of apportionment should be chosen. In the above analysis telephone charges have been apportioned on the basis of floor area.

[d]Apportioned on the basis of direct labour hours.
[e]Machine hours are not given but direct labour hours are. It is assumed that the examiner requires absorption to be on the basis of direct labour hours.

(b)

	Job 123 ($)	Job 124 ($)
Direct material	125.00	79.70
Direct labour:		
Department A	88.00	70.40
Department B	51.00	42.50
Department C	42.00	58.80
Total direct cost	306.00	251.40
Overhead:		
Department A	257.20	205.76
Department B	148.80	124.00
Department C	140.20	196.28
Total cost	852.20	777.44
Profit	284.07	259.15

(c) Listed selling price 1 136.27 1 036.59
Note
Let SP represent selling price.
Cost + 0.25SP = SP
Job 123: $852.20 + 0.25SP = 1SP
$$0.75SP = \$852.20$$
Hence SP = $1 136.27
For Job 124: $$0.75SP = \$777.44$$
Hence SP = $1 036.59

7.19 (a) (i) Calculation of budgeted overhead absorption rates:

Apportionment of overheads to production departments

	Machine shop (£)	Fitting section (£)	Canteen (£)	Machine maintenance section (£)	Total (£)
Allocated overheads	27 660	19 470	16 600	26 650	90 380
Rent, rates, heat and light[a]	9 000	3 500	2 500	2 000	17 000
Depreciation and insurance of equipment[a]	12 500	6 250	2 500	3 750	25 000
	49 160	29 220	21 600	32 400	132 380
Service department apportionment					
Canteen[b]	10 800	8 400	(21 600)	2 400	—
Machine maintenance section	24 360	10 440	—	(34 800)	—
	84 320	48 060	—	—	132 380

Calculation of absorption bases

Product	Budgeted production	Machine shop Machine hours per product	Total machine hours	Fitting section Direct labour cost per product (£)	Total direct wages (£)
X	4 200 units	6	25 200	12	50 400
Y	6 900 units	3	20 700	3	20 700
Z	1 700 units	4	6 800	21	35 700
			52 700		106 800

Budgeted overhead absorption rates

Machine shop

$$\frac{\text{Budgeted overheads}}{\text{Budgeted machine hours}} = \frac{£84\,320}{52\,700}$$
= £1.60 per machine hour

Fitting section

$$\frac{\text{Budgeted overheads}}{\text{Budgeted direct wages}} = \frac{£48\,060}{106\,800}$$
= 45% of direct wages

Notes:

[a]Rents, rates, heat and light are apportioned on the basis of floor area. Depreciation and insurance of equipment are apportioned on the basis of book value.

[b]Canteen costs are reapportioned according to the number of employees. Machine maintenance section costs are reapportioned according to the percentages given in the question.

(ii) The budgeted manufacturing overhead cost for producing one unit of product X is as follows:

	(£)
Machine shop: 6 hours at £1.60 per hour	9.60
Fittings section: 45% of £12	5.40
	15.00

(b) The answer should discuss the limitations of blanket overhead rates and actual overhead rates. See 'Blanket overhead rates' and 'Budgeted overhead rates' in Chapter 7 for the answer to this question.

7.20 (a) The calculation of the overhead absorption rates are as follows:

Forming department machine hour rate = €6.15 per machine hour (€602 700/98 000 hours)

Finishing department labour hour rate = €2.25 per labour hour (€346 500/154 000 hours)

The forming department is mechanized, and it is likely that a significant proportion of overheads will be incurred as a consequence of employing and running the machines. Therefore a machine hour rate has been used. In the finishing department several grades of labour are used. Consequently the direct wages percentage method is inappropriate, and the direct labour hour method should be used.

(b) The decision should be based on a comparison of the incremental costs with the purchase price of an outside supplier if spare capacity exists. If no spare capacity exists then the lost contribution on displaced work must be considered. The calculation of incremental costs requires that the variable element of the total overhead absorption rate must be calculated. The calculation is:

Forming department variable machine hour rate = €2.05 (€200 900/98 000 hours)

Finishing department variable direct labour hour rate = €0.75 (€115 500/154 000 hours)

The calculation of the variable costs per unit of each component is:

	A (€)	B (€)	C (€)
Prime cost	24.00	31.00	29.00
Variable overheads: Forming	8.20	6.15	4.10
Finishing	2.25	7.50	1.50
Variable unit manufacturing cost	34.45	44.65	34.60
Purchase price	€30	€65	€60

On the basis of the above information, component A should be purchased and components B and C manufactured. This decision is based on the following assumptions:

(i) Variable overheads vary in proportion to machine hours (forming department) and direct labour hours (finishing department).

(ii) Fixed overheads remain unaffected by any changes in activity.

(iii) Spare capacity exists.

For a discussion of make-or-buy decisions see Chapter 4.

(c) Production overhead absorption rates are calculated in order to ascertain costs per unit of output for stock valuation and profit measurement purposes. Such costs are inappropriate for decision-making and cost control. For an explanation of this see the section in Chapter 7 entitled 'Different costs for different purposes'.

Chapter 8

8.13 (a) (i) Fixed production overheads = $15 400 000
Budgeted material cost = $22 000 000
Fixed production overhead absorption rate
= $15 400 000 / 22 000 000 = 70%

	Anti-ageing cream $000	Facial masks $000	Collagen fillers $000	Total $000
Fixed production overhead	8 260	4 340	2 800	15 400

(ii) Calculation of cost driver quantities

	Anti-ageing cream	Facial masks	Collagen fillers
Budgeted production per annum (units)	1 000 000	1 200 000	600 000
Batch size (units)	1 000	2 000	1 500
Number of batches	1 000	600	400
Number of machine set-ups	3 000	1 800	1 600
Number of purchase orders	2 000	1 200	400
Processing time (minutes)	2 000 000	3 600 000	2 400 000

Calculation of cost driver rates

Activity	Activity cost $000	Cost driver	Cost driver rate
Machine set up	3 600	Number of machine set ups	$3 600 000/6 400 = $562.50 per set-up
Quality inspection	1 200	Number of quality inspections	$1 200 000/2 000 = $600 per inspection
Processing	6 500	Processing time	$6 500 000/8 000 000 = $0.8125 per minute
Purchasing	1 800	Number of purchase orders	$1 800 000/3 600 = $500 per purchase order
Packaging	2 300	Number of units	$2 300 000/2 800 000 = $0.821 per unit

Assignment of overheads to products

	Anti-ageing cream $000	Facial masks $000	Collagen fillers $000	Total $000
Sales	60000	38000	22000	120000
Direct material	11800	6200	4000	22000
Direct labour	3700	2400	1900	8000
Machine set ups	(3000 × $562.50) 1688	(1800 × $562.50) 1012	(1600 × $562.50) 900	3600
Quality inspections	(1000 × $600) 600	(600 × $600) 360	(400 × $600) 240	1200
Processing	(2000000 × $0.8125) 1625	(3600000 × $0.8125) 2925	(2400000 × $0.8125) 1950	6500
Purchasing	(2000 × $500) 1000	(1200 × $500) 600	(400 × $500) 200	1800
Packaging	(1000000 × $0.821) 821	(1200000 × $0.821) 986	(600000 × $0.821) 493	2300
Gross profit	38766	23517	12317	74600

8.14 (a) Annual activity per cost driver

	A	B	Total
No. of procedures	14600	22400	37000
Admin time per procedure (hours)	14600	33600	48200
Patient hours	350400	1075200	1425600
Number of meals	14600	89600	104200

Cost driver rates

Administrative costs	$1870160/48200 = $38.80 per admin hour
Nursing costs	$6215616/1425600 = $4.36 per patient hour
Catering costs	$966976/104200 = $9.28 per meal
General facility costs	$8553600/1425600 = $6 per patient hour

Overhead allocation procedure

	A	B
Administrative costs	38.80	58.20
Nursing costs	104.64	209.28
Catering costs	9.28	37.12
General facility costs	144.00	288.00
	296.72	592.60
Add direct costs:		
Surgical	1 200.00	2640.00
Anaesthesia	800.00	1 620.00
Total cost per procedure	2 296.72	4 852.60

(b) When activity-based costing (ABC) is used the cost for Procedure A is approximately $2297 compared with $2476 calculated by the current blanket overhead system. For Procedure B, the cost using ABC is approximately $4853 compared and $4736 with the current system resulting in the cost of Procedure A decreasing and the cost of Procedure B increasing with ABC. This is mainly due to the fact that the largest proportion of the overhead costs is the nursing and general facility costs. These costs are driven by the number of patient hours. Procedure B has double the number of patient hours compared with Procedure A and thus allocates double the amount of costs. This is not taken into account with the current system which assumes that all overheads are driven by the number of procedures and allocates

approximately 40 per cent of the overheads to Procedure A (14600/37000 procedure) and the remaining 60 per cent to Procedure B. Therefore the ABC system assigns the costs based on the use of resources driving the overheads.

The major disadvantage of using ABC is that it is more costly to implement and operate. Given that the majority of the overhead costs consist of nursing costs and general facility costs, and both are driven by the number of patient hours, similar costs will be reported if all overhead costs are allocated on the basis of number of patient hours. Using this allocation base would result in an absorption rate of $12.35 per hour ($17606352/1425600 hours). Therefore the overhead costs allocated to Procedure A would be $296 (24 × $12.35) and $592 (48 × $12.35) giving virtually identical results to the more expensive ABC system. It is recommended that this more accurate, but simplistic system, replace the existing system.

8.15 (a) (i) *Conventional absorption costing profit statement:*

	XYI	YZT	ABW
(1) Sales volume (000 units)	50	40	30
	$	$	$
(2) Selling price per unit	45	95	73
(3) Prime cost per unit	32	84	65
(4) Contribution per unit	13	11	8
(5) Total contribution in $000s (1 × 4)	650	440	240
(6) Machine department overheads[a]	120	240	144
(7) Assembly department overheads[b]	288.75	99	49.5
Profit ($000)	241.25	101	46.5
Total profit = $388 750			

Notes:
[a]XYI = 50 000 × 2 hrs × $1.20, YZT = 40 000 × 5 hrs × $1.20
[b]XYI = 50 000 × 7 hrs × $0.825, YZT = 40 000 × 3 hrs × $0.825

(ii) *Cost pools:*

	Machining services	Assembly services	Set-ups	Order processing	Purchasing
$000	357	318	26	156	84
Cost drivers	420 000 machine hours	530 000 direct labour hours	520 set-ups	32 000 customer orders	11 200 suppliers' orders
Cost driver rates	$0.85 per machine hour	$0.60 direct labour hour	$50 per set-up	$4.875 per customer order	$7.50 per suppliers' order

ABC profit statement:

	XYI ($000)	YZT ($000)	ABW ($000)
Total contribution	650	440	240
Less overheads:			
Machine department at $0.85 per hour	85	170	102
Assembly at $0.60 per hour	210	72	36
Set-up costs at $50 per set-up	6	10	10
Order processing at $4.875 per order	39	39	78
Purchasing at $7.50 per order	22.5	30	31.5
Profit (Loss)	287.5	119	(17.5)

Total profit = $389 000

(b) See the sections on 'Comparison of traditional and ABC systems' and 'Volume-based and non-volume-based cost drivers' in Chapter 8 for the answer to this question.

8.16 (a) Absorption costing production cost per unit

Product	X	Y	Z	Total
Budgeted annual production (units)	20 000	16 000	22 000	
Labour hours per unit	2.5	3	2	
Total labour hours	50 000	48 000	44 000	142 000

Overhead absorption rate = $1 377 400/142 000 = $9.70 per hour.

Product	X $ per unit	Y $ per unit	Z $ per unit
Direct materials	25	28	22
Direct labour	30	36	24
Overhead ($9.70 × 2.5/3/2)	24.25	29.10	19.40
Full cost per unit	79.25	93.10	65.40

(b) ABC production cost per unit

Product	X	Y	Z	Total
Budgeted annual production (units)	20 000	16 000	22 000	
Batch size	500	800	400	
Number of batches	40	20	55	115
Number of purchase orders per batch	4	5	4	
Total number of orders	160	100	220	480
Machine hours per unit	1.5	1.25	1.4	
Total machine hours	30 000	20 000	30 800	80 800

Cost driver rates:
Cost per machine set up $280 000/115 = $2 434.78
Cost per order $316 000/480 = $658.33
Cost per machine hour ($420 000 + $361 400)/80 800 = $9.67

Allocation of overheads to each product:

Product	X $	Y $	Z $	Total
Machine set up costs	97 391	48 696	133 913	280 000
Material ordering costs	105 333	65 833	144 834	316 000
Machine running and facility costs	290 100	193 400	297 836	781 336
Total	492 824	307 929	576 583	1 377 336
Number of units produced	20 000	16 000	22 000	
Overhead cost per unit	$24.64	$19.25	$26.21	

Total cost per unit:	$ per unit	$ per unit	$ per unit
Direct materials	25	28	22
Direct labour	30	36	24
Overhead	24.64	19.25	26.21
ABC cost per unit	79.64	83.25	72.21

The failure to allocate $64 of the machine running and facility costs is due to rounding differences.

(c) The cost of product X is similar for both systems and the selling price will thus be unchanged. Product Y is overcosted by $10 and product Z is undercosted by approximately $7 with the traditional absorption costing system. This will result in a reduction in selling price of product Y and an increase in the price of product Z using cost-plus pricing. Given that demand for product Y is elastic the reduction in price should result in an increase in demand whereas the inelastic demand for product Z may result in demand remaining unchanged.

8.17 (a) Calculation of cost driver quantities

	Tablets	Convertible laptops	All-in-one PCs	Total
Budgeted production per annum (units)	10 000	12 000	6 000	28 000
Average number of units per order	10	6	4	
Number of orders	1 000	2 000	1 500	4 500
Parts per unit	20	35	25	
Total number of parts	200 000	420 000	150 000	770 000
Assembly time per unit (minutes)	20	40	30	
Total assembly time (minutes)	200 000	480 000	180 000	860 000
Software applications per unit	2	3	4	
Total number of software applications	20 000	36 000	24 000	80 000

Calculation of cost driver rates

Activity	Activity cost $000	Cost driver	Cost driver rate
Manufacturing scheduling	162	Number of orders	$162 000/4 500 = $36 per order
Parts handling	2 464	Number of parts	$2 464 000/770 000 = $3.20 per part
Assembly	4 472	Assembly time	$4 472 000/860 000 = $5.20 per minute
Software installation and testing	2 000	Number of software applications	$2 000 000/80 000 = $25.00 per application
Packaging	1 302	Number of units	$1 302 000/28 000 = $46.50 per unit

Assignment of overheads to products

	Tablets $000	Convertible Laptops $000	All-in-one PCs $000	Total $000
Manufacturing scheduling	(1 000 × $36) 36	(2 000 × $36) 72	(1 500 × $36) 54	162
Parts handling	(200 000 × $3.20) 640	(420 000 × $3.20) 1 344	(150 000 × $3.20) 480	2 464
Assembly	(200 000 × $5.20) 1 040	(480 000 × $5.20) 2 496	(180 000 × $5.20) 936	4 472
Software installation and testing	(20 000 × $25) 500	(36 000 × $25) 900	(24 000 × $25) 600	2 000
Packaging	(10 000 × $46.50) 465	(12 000 × $46.50) 558	(6 000 × $46.50) 279	1 302
Total production overhead costs	2 681	5 370	2 349	10 400

Activity-based costing gross profit analysis

	Tablets $000	Convertible laptops $000	All-in-one PCs $000	Total $000
Sales	3640	12480	9880	26000
Direct material	800	2800	2200	5800
Direct labour	300	1200	800	2300
Production overheads	2681	5370	2349	10400
Gross profit	(141)	3110	4531	7500

(b) Gross profits per unit

	Tablets	Convertible laptops	All-in-one PCs
Current absorption costing system	$108 ($1084k/10k)	$291	$488
ABC	($14) (–$141K/10k)	$259	$755

Under the traditional absorption costing system each of the products was making a profit whereas a loss is reported with ABC. Under the traditional absorption costing system production overheads were charged to products based on sales revenue resulting in Tablets, which have a relatively low proportion of the total sales revenue (14 per cent), being charged with a relatively low level of fixed production overheads. ABC assigns costs on the basis of the actual consumption of activities resulting in Tablets being charged significantly more production overheads than before.

(c) ABC provides information for decisions relating to product pricing and product mix. ABC also provides information about the various activities and the cost drivers for each activity. This enables the company to focus on those activities with the highest costs in order to determine whether they can be eliminated or performed more efficiently. Activities can be classified as value-added and non-value added so that the focus can be on action to reduce or eliminate the non-value added activities.

8.18 (a) The following profitability statement is based on the hierarchical approach:

Product	W $	X $	Y $	Z $	Total $
Sales	1 300 000	2 260 000	2 120 000	1 600 000	7 280 000
Direct materials	300 000	910 000	940 000	500 000	2 650 000
Direct labour	400 000	1 040 000	640 000	600 000	2 680 000
Overhead:					
Machine related	80 000	78 000	32 000	120 000	310 000
Batch related	50 000	65 000	40 000	75 000	230 000
Gross contribution	470 000	167 000	468 000	305 000	1 410 000
Overhead:					
Product specific	500 000	50 000	100 000	50 000	700 000
Net contribution	(30 000)	117 000	368 000	255 000	710 000
General overhead					310 000
Profit					400 000

Note:
Machine related costs are $0.40 per hour ($310 000/775 000) and are assigned to products on the basis of machine hours used. Production is in 100 usage batches. The cost per batch is $50

($230 000/4 600) and costs are assigned on the basis of batch usage (e.g. 1000 batches of W, 1300 batches of X etc.).

(b) (i) The profit statement shown in the question is unsuitable for decision-making because it is based on the arbitrary allocation of fixed costs rather than cause-and-effect allocations. Also some of the allocated fixed overheads are facility sustaining costs that are common and unavoidable to all alternatives so dropping an individual product will not result in a decline in these costs. The profit statement in (a) overcomes these criticisms by using only cause-and-effect allocations and not allocating general fixed overheads to individual products.

(ii) The profit statement shows that W has a negative net contribution and unless there are important qualitative factors this product should be discontinued since this would increase the company's profits by $30 000. This differs from the original profit statement which showed that products W and Y were profitable and products X and Z were loss making. Products X, Y and Z should be continued because they all have a positive net contribution.

(c) The specific fixed cost of product W is $500 000 and the contribution to sales ratio is 0.36154 ($470 000 / $1 300 000). Therefore, the break-even sales value is $500 000 / 0.36154 = $1 382 973 so the break-even sales volume is $1 382 973 / $13 = 106 383 units. Since production must be in batches of 100 units then to break even 1064 batches must be produced and sold.

(d) For the answer to this question see 'Value Analysis' in Chapter 15. The answer should point out that the company should compare its products with those provided by its competitors to ascertain if their products have superior features, and whether these features are important to their customers. If they are, these features should be incorporated in WTL's products. The company should also review the design of its products to ascertain if redesign can reduce costs without reducing the value of the products to its customers.

8.19 (a) Large-scale service organizations have a number of features that have been identified as being necessary to derive significant benefits from the introduction of ABC:

(i) they operate in a highly competitive environment
(ii) they incur a large proportion of indirect costs that cannot be directly assigned to specific cost objects
(iii) products and customers differ significantly in terms of consuming overhead resources
(iv) they market many different products and services.

Furthermore, many of the constraints imposed on manufacturing organizations, such as also having to meet financial accounting stock valuation requirements, or a reluctance to change or scrap existing systems, do not apply. Many service organizations have only recently implemented cost systems for the first time. This has occurred at the same time as when the weaknesses of existing systems and the benefits of ABC systems were being widely publicized. These conditions have provided a strong incentive for introducing ABC systems.

(b)   The following may create problems for the application of ABC:

   (i)   Facility sustaining costs (such as property rents etc.) represent a significant proportion of total costs and may only be avoidable if the organization ceases business. It may be impossible to establish appropriate cost drivers.

   (ii) It is often difficult to define products where they are of an intangible nature. Cost objects can therefore be difficult to specify.

   (iii) Many service organizations have not previously had a costing system and much of the information required to set up an ABC system will be non-existent. Therefore introducing ABC is likely to be expensive.

(c)   The uses for ABC information for service industries are similar to those for manufacturing organizations:

   (i)   It leads to more accurate product costs as a basis for pricing decisions when cost-plus pricing methods are used.

   (ii) It results in more accurate product and customer profitability analysis statements that provide a more appropriate basis for decision-making.

   (iii) ABC attaches costs to activities and identifies the cost drivers that cause the costs. Thus ABC provides a better understanding of what causes costs and highlights ways of performing activities more effectively by reducing cost driver transactions. Costs can therefore be managed more effectively in the long term. Activities can also be analysed into value-added and non-value-added activities and by highlighting the costs of non-value-added activities attention is drawn to areas where there is a potential for cost reduction without reducing the products' service potential to customers.

(d)   The following aspects would be of most interest to a regulator:

   (i)   The costing method used (e.g. marginal, traditional full cost or ABC). This is of particular importance to verify whether or not reasonable prices are being set and that the organization is not taking advantage of its monopolistic situation. Costing information is also necessary to ascertain whether joint costs are fairly allocated so that cross-subsidization from one service to another does not apply.

   (ii) Consistency in costing methods from period to period so that changes in costing methods are not used to distort pricing and profitability analysis.

   (iii) In many situations a regulator may be interested in the ROI of the different services in order to ensure that excessive returns are not being obtained. A regulator will therefore be interested in the methods and depreciation policy used to value assets and how the costs of assets that are common to several services (e.g. corporate headquarters) are allocated. The methods used will influence the ROI of the different services.

Chapter 9

9.17   This is an example of feedforward control because the manager is using a forecast to assist in making a future decision

Answer = (a)

9.18   (a)   Production budget

Product	A	B
Sales	2 000	1 500
Opening inventory	(100)	(200)
Closing inventory		
(10% × sales level)	200	150
	2 100	1 450

(b)   Materials usage budget

Material type	X kg	Y litres
Usage		
(2 100 × 2) + (1450 × 3)	8 550	
(2 100 × 1) + (1450 × 4)		7 900

(c)   Materials purchases budget

Usage	8 550	7 900
Opening inventory	(300)	(1 000)
Closing inventory[a]	850	800
	9 100	7 700
	× £10	× £7
	£91 000	£53 900

(d)   Labour budget

	Skilled hours	Semi-skilled hours
(2 100 × 4) + (1 450 × 2)	11 300	
(2 100 × 2) + (1 450 × 5)		11 450
	× £12	× £8
	£135 600	£91 600

Note:
[a]Material closing inventory: Material X (2000 × 2 + 1500 × 3) × 10% = 850
Material Y (2000 × 1 + 1500 × 4) × 10% = 850

9.19

Task 1

   Alderley Ltd Budget Statements 13 weeks to 4 April

(a)   Production budget

	Elgar units	Holst units
Budgeted sales volume	845	1 235
Add closing inventory[a]	78	1 266
Less Opening inventory	(163)	(361)
Units of production	760	1 140

(b)   Material purchases budget

	Elgar kg	Holst kg	Total kg
Material consumed	5 320 (760 × 7)	9 120 (1 140 × 8)	14 440
Add raw material closing inventory[b]			2 888
Less raw material opening inventory			(2 328)
Purchases (kg)			15 000

(c) Purchases (£) (1500 × £12)   £180 000

(d) Production labour budget

	Elgar hours	Holst hours	Total hours
Standard hours produced[c]	6 080	5 700	11 780
Productivity adjustment (5/95 × 11 780)			620
Total hours employed			12 400
Normal hours employed[d]			11 544
Overtime hours			856

(e) Labour cost

	£
Normal hours (11 544 × £8)	92 352
Overtime (856 × £8 × 125%)	8 560
Total	100 912

Notes:
[a]Number of days per period = 13 weeks × 5 days = 65
 Stock: Elgar = (6/65) × 845 = 78, Holst = (14/65) × 1235 = 266
[b](13/65) × (5320 + 9120) = 2888
[c]Elgar 760 × 8 hours = 6080, Holst 1140 × 5 hours = 5700
[d]24 employees × 37 hours × 13 weeks = 11 544

Task 2

(a) Four ways of forecasting future sales volume are:

   (i)   Where the number of customers is small it is possible to interview them to ascertain what their likely demand will be over the forecasting period.

   (ii) Produce estimates based on the opinion of executives and sales personnel. For example, sales personnel may be asked to estimate the sales of each product to their customers, or regional sales managers may estimate the total sales for each of their regions.

   (iii) Market research may be necessary where it is intended to develop new products or new markets. This may involve interviews with existing and potential customers in order to estimate potential demand.

   (iv) Estimates involving statistical techniques that incorporate general business and market conditions and past growth in sales.

(b) Interviewing customers and basing estimates on the opinions of sales personnel are likely to be more appropriate for existing products and customers involving repeat sales. Market research is appropriate for new products or markets and where the market is large and anticipated revenues are likely to be sufficient to justify the cost of undertaking the research.

   Statistical estimates derived from past data are likely to be appropriate where conditions are likely to be stable and past demand patterns are likely to be repeated through time. This method is most suited to existing products or markets where sufficient data are available to establish a trend in demand.

(c) The major limitation of interviewing customers is that they may not be prepared to divulge the information if their future plans are commercially sensitive. There is also no guarantee that the orders will be placed with Alderley Ltd. They may place their orders with competitors.

Where estimates are derived from sales personnel there is a danger that they might produce over-optimistic estimates in order to obtain a favourable performance rating at the budget setting stage. Alternatively, if their future performance is judged by their ability to achieve the budgeted sales they may be motivated to underestimate sales demand.

Market research is expensive and may produce unreliable estimates if inexperienced researchers are used. Also small samples are often used which may not be indicative of the population and this can result in inaccurate estimates.

Statistical estimates will produce poor demand estimates where insufficient past data is available, demand is unstable over time and the future environment is likely to be significantly different from the past. Statistical estimates are likely to be inappropriate for new products and new markets where past data are unavailable.

9.20 (a) (i) *Cash budget for weeks 1–6*

	Week 1 (£)	Week 2 (£)	Week 3 (£)	Week 4 (£)	Week 5 (£)	Week 6 (£)
Receipts from debtors[a]	24 000	24 000	28 200	25 800	19 800	5 400
Payments:						
To material suppliers[b]	8 000	12 500	6 000	—	—	—
To direct workers[c]	3 200	4 200	2 800	—	—	—
For variable overheads[d]	4 800	3 200	—	—	—	—
For fixed overhead[e]	8 300	8 300	6 800	6 800	6 800	6 800
Total payments	24 300	28 200	15 600	6 800	6 800	6 800
Net movement	(300)	(4 200)	12 600	19 000	13 000	(1 400)
Opening balance (week 1 given)	1 000	700	(3 500)	9 100	28 100	41 100
Closing balance	700	(3 500)	9 100	28 100	41 100	39 700

Notes:
[a]Debtors:

	Week 1	Week 2	Week 3	Week 4	Week 5	Week 6
Units sold*	400	500	400	300	—	—
Sales (£)	24 000	30 000	24 000	18 000	—	—
Cash received (70%)		16 800	21 000	16 800	12 600	
(30%)			7 200	9 000	7 200	5 400
Given	24 000	7 200				
Total receipts (£)	24 000	24 000	28 200	25 800	19 800	5 400

*Sales in week 4 = opening stock (600 units) + production in weeks 1 and 2 (1000 units) less sales in weeks 1–3 (1 300 units) = 300 units.
[b]Creditors:

	Week 1 (£)	Week 2 (£)	Week 3 (£)	Week 4	Week 5	Week 6
Materials consumed at £15	9 000	6 000	—	—	—	—
Increase in stocks	3 500	—				
Materials purchased	12 500	6 000				
Payment to suppliers	8 000 (given)	12 500	6000	—	—	—

[c]Wages:

	Week 1 (£)	Week 2 (£)	Week 3 (£)	Week 4	Week 5	Week 6
Wages consumed at £7	4 200	2 800	—	—	—	—
Wages paid	3 200 (given)	4 200	2 800	—	—	—

[d]Variable overhead payment = budgeted production × budgeted cost per unit.
[e]Fixed overhead payments for weeks 1–2 = fixed overhead per week (£9000) less weekly depreciation (£700).
Fixed overhead payments for weeks 3–6 = £8300 normal payment less £1500 per week.

(ii) *Comments*
   1 Finance will be required to meet the cash deficit in week 2, but a lowering of the budgeted material stocks at the end of

week 1 would reduce the amount of cash to be borrowed at the end of week 2.

2 The surplus cash after the end of week 2 should be invested on a short-term basis.

3 After week 6, there will be no cash receipts, but cash outflows will be £6800 per week. The closing balance of £39 700 at the end of week 6 will be sufficient to finance outflows for a further 5 or 6 weeks (£39 700/£6800 per week).

(b) The answer should include a discussion of the matching concept, emphasizing that revenues and expenses may not be attributed to the period when the associated cash inflows and outflows occur. Also, some items of expense do not affect cash outflow (e.g. depreciation).

9.21 (a) For the answer to this question you should refer to 'rolling budgets' in Chapter 9. The answer should point out that instead of a 12 month period remaining static it would be updated by 1 month on a monthly basis so that a 12 monthly budget is always available. When the budget is initially prepared for year ending 30th November the first month (December) is prepared in detail, and the later months in less detail because of the greater uncertainty about the future. At the end of the first month the budget for the next month (January) is prepared in detail and the remaining 11 months updated based on updated information.

(b) The major problem with rolling budgets is that they are very time-consuming to administer. This is a major problem in this company that only employs one part-qualified accountant that is already overworked and may not have the time or experience to operate a system of monthly rolling budgets. Rolling budgets are more appropriate for businesses that face rapid change but the question indicates that the business is very stable from year to year. Rather than implementing monthly rolling budgets quarterly rolling budgets would be preferable but annual budgeting may be preferred because of the stable operating environment.

With the present system the sales managers have been set targets that are easy to achieve and so are likely to react badly to the new system that requires them to work hard all year round. A further problem is that the sales managers will not know the target for the whole year in advance and having met the target for the month may be encouraged to defer seeking extra work for the month until the next month thus obtaining easier targets.

(c) The major problem with the current scheme is that the reward system is stepped with the first $1.5m of fee income target being too easy to reach and the second $1.5m being too difficult. Therefore managers are not motivated to earn additional fees once the initial target has been reached. An alternative approach would be to replace the current system with a commission given to managers based on a percentage of fee income rather than a percentage of salary. Currently the company is paying each of the three sales managers a bonus of $30 000 (20% of $150 0000) representing 2 percent of the fee income target of $1 500 000.

Therefore an alternative system would be to pay 2% commission on all sales.

(d) The use of the accountant's own spreadsheets involve keying in a large amount of data from existing records so there is a high probability of errors if the data that are entered are not checked. Also the use of any formulae in the spreadsheets will result in the generation of incorrect data if the formulae are wrong. Rolling budgets are far more complex and this significantly increases the chance of errors in the spreadsheets. If spreadsheets are used data entry and any changes in the variables should be carefully checked.

9.22 (a) *Budgeted income*
Income from pupils registered on 1 June $724 500
Expected number of new joiners: $(0.2 \times 50) + (0.3 \times 20) + (0.5 \times 26) = 29$
Expected income from new joiners at $(29 \times \$900) = \$26 100$
Total expected income = $750 600.
Budgeted expenditure
Repairs and maintenance: $30 000 \times 1.03 = \$30 900$.
Salaries: $[(\$620 000 - \$26 000)/2] + [(\$620 000 - \$26 000) \times 1.02)/2]$
$= \$297 000 + \$302 940 = \$599 940$.
Expected capital expenditure = $(0.7 \times \$145 000) + (0.3 \times \$80 000) = \$125 500$.
Total expected expenditure = $756 340.
Budget deficit = $5740 ($750 600 - $756 340)

(b) The main advantages of incremental budgets are simplicity and speed of budget preparation. Incremental budgeting is more appropriate for organizations that have stable activities where changes in revenue and expenditure are mainly attributable to inflation. The major disadvantages of incremental budgeting are that they encourage inefficiency because incremental budgets use the preceding year's data (which may contain inefficiencies) as the base for determining the budget. Therefore errors from one year are carried forward to the next year. Managers may also be motivated to attempt to use their entire budget up for one year, even if they do not need to, just to ensure that the budget is maintained again the next year.

(c) See 'Zero-based budgeting' in Chapter 9 for the answer to this question.

(d) A simplistic form of ZBB may be appropriate for the school if it is applied to selective areas. For areas where budgeting is straightforward such as staff salaries, which are likely to be fixed over the budget period, incremental budgeting should still be used. ZBB is more appropriate for discretionary expenses. For example, the extent to which sports education is provided involves discretionary activities and it would be appropriate to establish decision packages for various levels of packages of activities in order to prioritize which activities should be undertaken.

9.23 (a) In the public sector precise objectives are difficult to define in a quantifiable way, and the actual accomplishments are even more difficult to measure. In most situations outputs cannot be measured in monetary terms. By 'outputs' we mean the quality and amount of the services rendered. Quality is difficult to define and measure in a quantifiable way. In profit-oriented organizations output can be measured in terms of sales revenues and profits. The effect of this is that budgets in the public sector tend to be mainly concerned with the input of resources (i.e. expenditure), whereas budgets in profit organizations focus on the relationships between inputs (expenditure) and outputs (sales revenue). In the public sector there is unlikely to be the same emphasis on what was intended to be achieved for a given input of resources. The budgeting process tends to compare what is happening in cash input terms with the estimated cash inputs rather than the relationship between inputs and outputs. In other words, there is little emphasis on measures of managerial performance in terms of the results achieved. The reason for this is that there is no clear relationship between resource inputs and the benefits flowing from the use of these resources. Finally, the budget process tends to more difficult in the public sector because their limited resources makes it difficult to achieve the desired results. Any shortcomings in the results tend to be highly publicized and may often be subject to political scrutiny by different pressure groups.

(b) See 'incremental budgeting' and 'zero-base budgeting' in Chapter 9.

(c) See 'zero-base budgeting' in Chapter 9 for the answer to this question.

(d) Incremental budgeting, as with all planning and control mechanisms, is subject to a number of limitations (see 'incremental budgets' in Chapter 9) but the comment that there is no longer a place for incremental budgeting in most organizations represents an extreme view. Zero-budgeting is subject to a number of limitations and these should be carefully considered before concluding that there is no place for incremental budgeting. The limitations of zero-based budgeting are:

- ZBB has never achieved the widespread adoption that the proponents envisaged since its introduction many years ago. It does not appear to have been widely accepted in practice.
- The major reason for the lack of adoption of ZBB is that it is considered to be too costly and time-consuming to implement and operate.
- The process of identifying decision packages and determining their purpose, cost and benefits is extremely time-consuming.
- There are often too many decision packages to evaluate and there is frequently insufficient information to enable them to be ranked.
- Managers may not have the skills to implement and operate ZBB unless they have had appropriate training.

ZBB is most appropriate for discretionary expenses. Such expenses tend to be the dominant ones in the public sector. Incremental budgeting is more appropriate in commercial organizations where well defined input/output relationships exist that can easily be quantified. Incremental budgeting is simple to operate and easy to understand where these circumstances apply. Rather than seeking to implement ZBB in the public sector it may be preferable to implement priority-based incremental budgeting (see Chapter 9 for an explanation).

9.24 (a) *Cumbersome process*
The answer to the first comment in the question should include a very brief summary of 'Stages in the budgeting process' in Chapter 9. The process involves detailed negotiations between the budget holders and their superiors and the accountancy staff. Because the process is very time-consuming it must be started well before the start of the budget year. Subsequent changes in the environment, and the fact that the outcomes reflected in the master budget may not meet financial targets, may necessitate budget revisions and a repeat of the negotiation process. The renegotiating stage may well be omitted because of time constraints. Instead, across the board cost reductions may be imposed to meet the budget targets.

Concentration on short-term financial control
Short-term financial targets are normally set for the budget year and the budget is used as the mechanism for achieving the targets. Budget adjustments are made to ensure that the targets are achieved often with little consideration being given to the impact such adjustments will have on the longer-term plans.

Undesirable motivation effects on managers
Managers are often rewarded or punished based on their budget performance in terms of achieving or exceeding the budget. There is a danger that the budget will be viewed as a punitive device rather than as an aid to managers in managing their areas of responsibility. This can result in dysfunctional consequences such as attempting to build slack into the budgeting system by overstating costs and understating revenues. Alternatively, cuts may be made in discretionary expenses, which could have adverse long-term consequences. The overriding aim becomes to achieve the budget, even if this is done in a manner that is not in the organization's best interests.

Emphasizing formal organizational structure
Budgets are normally structured around functional responsibility centres, such as departments and business units. A functional structure is likely to encourage bureaucracy and slow responses to environmental and competitive changes. There is a danger that there will be a lack of goal congruence and that managers may focus on their own departments to the detriment of the organization. Also if budgets are extended to the lower levels of the organization employees will focus excessively on meeting the budget and this may constrain their activities in terms of the flexibility that is required when dealing with customers.

(b) *Cumbersome process*
Managers could be given greater flexibility on how they will meet their targets. For example, top management might agree specific targets with the managers and the managers could be given authority to achieve the targets in their own way. Detailed budgets are not required and the emphasis is placed on managers achieving their overall targets.

Another alternative is to reduce the budget planning period by implementing a system of continuous or rolling budgets.

Concentration on short-term financial control
This might be overcome by placing more stress on a manager's long-term performance and adopting a profit-conscious style of budget evaluation and also placing more emphasis on participative budgeting (see 'Determining how much influence managers should have in setting targets' in Chapter 10). Attention should also be given to widening the performance measurement system and focusing on key result areas that deal with both short-term and long-term considerations. In particular a balanced scorecard approach (see Chapter 14) might be adopted.

Undesirable motivation effects on managers
The same points as those made above (i.e. profit-conscious style of evaluation, participative budgeting and a broader range of performance measures) also apply here. In addition, the rewards and punishment system must be changed so that it is linked to a range of performance criteria rather than being dominated by short-term financial budget performance. Consideration could also be given to changing the reward system from focusing on responsibility centre performance to rewards being based on overall company performance.

Emphasizing formal organizational structure
Here the answer could discuss activity-based budgeting with the emphasis being on activity centres and business processes, rather than functional responsibility centres that normally consist of departments. For a discussion of these issues you should refer to 'Activity-based budgeting' in Chapter 9 and 'Activity-based cost management' in Chapter 15. Consideration should also given to converting cost centres to profit centres and establishing a system of internal transfer prices. This would encourage managers to focus more widely on profits rather than just costs. Finally, budgets should not be extended to lower levels of the organization and more emphasis should be given to empowering employees to manage their own activities.

Chapter 10

10.17 *Task 1*

Reclamation Division Performance Report – 4 weeks to 31 May:

Original budget	250 tonnes	
Actual output	200 tonnes	

	Budget based on 200 tonnes	Actual	Variance	Comments
Controllable expenses:				
Wages and social security costs[a]	43 936	46 133	2 197A	
Fuel[b]	15 000	15 500	500A	
Consumables[c]	2 000	2 100	100A	
Power[d]	1 500	1 590	90A	
Directly attributable overheads[e]	20 000	21 000	1 000A	
	82 436	86 323	3 887A	
Non-controllable expenses:				
Plant maintenance[e]	5 950	6 900	950A	
Central services[e]	6 850	7 300	450A	
	12 800	14 200	1 400A	
Total	95 236	100 523	5 287A	

Notes:
[a]6 employees × 4 teams × 42 hours per week × £7.50 per hour × 4 weeks = £30 240.
[b]200 tonnes × £75
[c]200 tonnes × £10
[d]£500 + (£5 × 200) = £1 500
[e]It is assumed that directly attributable expenses, plant maintenance and central services are non-variable expenses.

Task 2

(a) (i) Past knowledge can provide useful information on future outcomes but ideally budgets ought to be based on the most up-to-date information. Budgeting should be related to the current environment and the use of past information that is 2 years old can only be justified where the operating conditions and environment are expected to remain unchanged.

   (ii) For motivation and planning purposes budgets should represent targets based on what we are proposing to do. For control purposes budgets should be flexed based on what was actually done so that actual costs for actual output can be compared with budgeted costs for the actual output. This ensures that valid comparisons will be made.

   (iii) For variable expenses the original budget should be reduced in proportion to reduced output in order to reflect cost behaviour. Fixed costs are not adjusted since they are unaffected in the short term by output changes. Flexible budgeting ensures that like is being compared with like so that reduced output does not increase the probability that favourable cost variances will be reported. However, if less was produced because of actual sales being less than budget this will result in an adverse sales variance and possibly an adverse profit variance.

   (iv) Plant maintenance costs are apportioned on the basis of capital values and therefore newer equipment (with higher written down values) will be charged with a higher maintenance cost. Such an approach does not provide a meaningful estimate of maintenance resources consumed by departments since older equipment is likely to be more expensive to maintain. The method of recharging should be reviewed and ideally based on estimated usage according to maintenance records. The charging of the overspending by the maintenance department to user departments is questionable since this masks inefficiencies. Ideally, maintenance department costs should be recharged based on actual usage at budgeted cost and the maintenance department made accountable for the adverse spending (price) variance.

   (v) The comments do not explain the causes of the variances and are presented in a negative tone. No comments are made, nor is any praise given, for the favourable variances.

   (vi) Not all variances should be investigated. The decision to investigate should depend on both their absolute and relative size and the likely benefits arising from an investigation.

   (vii) Central service costs are not controllable by divisional managers. However, even though the divisional manager cannot control these costs there is an argument for including them as non-controllable costs in the performance report. The justification for this is that divisional managers are made aware of central service costs and may put pressure on central service staff to control such costs more effectively. It should be made clear to divisional managers that they are not accountable for any non-controllable expenses that are included in their performance reports.

10.18 (a) (i) Activity varies from month to month, but quarterly budgets are set by dividing total annual expenditure by 4.

(ii) The budget ought to be analysed by shorter intervals (e.g. monthly) and costs estimated in relation to monthly activity.

(iii) For control purposes monthly comparisons and cumulative monthly comparisons of planned and actual expenditure to date should be made.

(iv) The budget holder does not participate in the setting of budgets.

(v) An incremental budget approach is adopted. A zero-based approach would be more appropriate.

(vi) The budget should distinguish between controllable and uncontrollable expenditure.

(b) The information that should flow from a comparison of the actual and budgeted expenditure would consist of the variances for the month and year to date analysed into the following categories:

(i) controllable and uncontrollable items

(ii) price and quantity variances with price variance analysed by inflationary and non-inflationary effects.

(c) (i) Flexible budgets should be prepared on a monthly basis. Possible measures of activity are number of patient days or expected laundry weight.

(ii) The laundry manager should participate in the budgetary process.

(iii) Costs should be classified into controllable and non-controllable items.

(iv) Variances should be reported and analysed by price and quantity on a monthly and cumulative basis.

(v) Comments should be added explaining possible reasons for the variances.

10.19

Task 1

Performance Statement – Month to 31 October
Number of guest days = Original budget   9 600
Flexed budget   11 160

	Flexed budget (€)	Actual (€)	Variance (€)
Controllable expenses			
Food (1)	23 436	20 500	2 936F
Cleaning materials (2)	2 232	2 232	0
Heat, light and power (3)	2 790	2 050	740F
Catering staff wages (4)	8 370	8 400	30A
	36 828	33 182	3 646F
Non-controllable expenses			
Rent, rates, insurance and depreciation (5)	1 860	1 860	0

Notes:
(1) €20 160/9600 × 11 160.
(2) €1920/9600 × 11 160.
(3) €2400/9600 × 11 160.
(4) €11 160/40 × €130.
(5) Original fixed budget based on 30 days but October is a 31-day month (€1800/30 × 31).

Task 2

(a) See the sections on the multiple functions of budgets (motivation) in Chapter 9, and 'Setting financial performance targets' in Chapter 10 for the answers to this question.

(b) Motivating managers ought to result in improved performance. However, besides motivation, improved performance is also dependent on managerial ability, training, education and the existence of a favourable environment. Therefore motivating managers is not guaranteed to lead to improved performance.

(c) The use of a fixed budget is unlikely to encourage managers to become more efficient where budgeted expenses are variable with activity. In the original performance report actual expenditure for 11 160 guest days is compared with budgeted expenditure for 9600 days. It is misleading to compare actual costs at one level of activity with budgeted costs at another level of activity. Where the actual level of activity is above the budgeted level adverse variances are likely to be reported for variable cost items. Managers will therefore be motivated to reduce activity so that favourable variances will be reported. Therefore it is not surprising that Susan Green has expressed concern that the performance statement does not reflect a valid reflection of her performance. In contrast, most of Brian Hilton's expenses are fixed and costs will not increase when volume increases. A failure to flex the budget will therefore not distort his performance.

To motivate, challenging budgets should be set and small adverse variances should normally be regarded as a healthy sign and not something to be avoided. If budgets are always achieved with no adverse variances this may indicate that undemanding budgets may have been set that are unlikely to motivate best possible performance. This situation could apply to Brian Hilton who always appears to report favourable variances.

10.20 (a) Recommendations are as follows:

(i) For cost control and managerial performance evaluation, expenses should be separated into their controllable and non-controllable categories. Two separate profit calculations should be presented: controllable profit, which is appropriate for measuring managerial performance, and a 'bottom-line' net profit, which measures the economic performance of each store rather than the manager.

(ii) The report should be based on an *ex post* basis. In other words, if the environment is different from that when the original budget was set, actual performance should be compared with a budget that reflects any changed conditions. For example, the budget should be adjusted to reflect the effect of the roadworks.

(iii) Actual expenses should be compared with flexed budgets and not the original budget.

(iv) Each store consists of three departments. The report should therefore analyse gross profits by departments. Selling prices and the cost of goods sold are beyond the control of the stores' managers, but each departmental manager can influence sales volume. An analysis of gross profits by departments and a comparison with previous periods should provide useful feedback on sales performance and help in deciding how much space should be allocated to each activity.

(v) Stock losses should be minimized. Such losses are controllable by departmental managers. The cost of stock losses should therefore be monitored and separately reported.

(vi) The budget should include cumulative figures to give an indication of trends, performance to date and the potential annual bonus.

(vii) Any imputed interest charges should be based on economic values of assets and not historic costs.

(b) The report should include a discussion of the following:

(i) *Review of delegation policies:* Head office purchases the goods for sale, fixes selling prices, appoints permanent staff and sets pay levels. Stores managers are responsible for stores' running expenses, employment of temporary staff and control of stocks.

Purchasing is centralized, thus enabling the benefits of specialized buying and bulk purchasing to be obtained. Purchasing policies are coordinated with expected sales by consultation between head office buyers and stores and departmental managers. It is wise to make store managers responsible for controlling stocks because they are in the best position to assess current and future demand.

Managers are responsible for sales volume but they cannot fix selling prices. There are strong arguments for allowing stores to set selling prices, and offer special discounts on certain goods. Central management may wish to retain some overall control by requiring proposed price changes beyond certain limits to be referred to them for approval. There are also strong arguments for allowing the stores' managers to appoint permanent staff. The stores' managers are likely to be in a better position to be able to assess the abilities necessary to be a successful member of their own team.

(ii) *Strengths of the management control system:*

1 Sales targets are set after consultation between head office and the departmental managers.

2 The budgets are prepared well in advance of the start of the budget year, thus giving adequate time for consultation.

3 Performance reports are available 1 week after the end of the period.

4 Budgets are adjusted for seasonal factors.

5 Significant variations in performance are investigated and appropriate action is taken.

(iii) *Weaknesses of the management control system:*

1 There is no consultation in the setting of expense budgets.

2 Actual costs are compared with a fixed budget and not a flexible budget.

3 Costs are not separated into controllable and non-controllable categories.

4 Budgets are set on an incremental basis with budgets set by taking last year's base and adjusting for inflation.

5 Budgets are not revised for control purposes. Targets set for the original budget before the start of the year may be inappropriate for comparison with actual expenses incurred towards the end of the budget year.

6 Using a budget that does not include *ex post* results and that is not linked to controllable profit is likely to be demotivating, and results in managers having little confidence in the budget system.

(iv) *Recommendations:*

1 Compare actual costs with a flexed budget.

2 The performance report should separate costs into controllable and uncontrollable categories, and controllable profit should be highlighted. Any bonus payments should be related to controllable profit and not 'bottom-line' profits.

3 Introduce monthly or quarterly rolling budgets.

4 Ensure that the store's managers participate in setting the budget and accept the target against which they will be judged.

5 Set targets using a zero-based approach.

6 Consider extending the bonus scheme to departmental managers.

10.21 (a) *Meeting only the lowest budget targets.* This implies that once the budget has been agreed the budget holder will be satisfied just with achieving only the budgeted level of performance and not exceeding it.

Using more resources than necessary. This may arise when a manager is aware that the budget could be achieved by using less resources but continues to use excess resources in order not to be seen to over-achieve and thus preserve the budget allowance for future budgets.

Making the bonus–whatever it takes. Budgetees may view the maximization of bonuses as their main priority and focus on achieving the targets even if this leads to a lack of goal congruence (see 'harmful side-effects of controls' in Chapter 10 for a more detailed answer).

Competing against other divisions, business units and departments. Managers may focus on maximizing their own performance even if this is at the expense of other departments or the company as a whole.

Ensuring that what is in the budget is spent. Managers may consider that they can only preserve their budget allowance for various items of expenses for the following year by ensuring that the budget is spent. This may be particularly applicable to discretionary expenses.

Providing inaccurate forecasts. Budget holders may seek to provide inaccurate forecasts to build in some slack into the budget targets in order to avoid what they perceive as difficult targets.

Meeting the target but not beating it. This relates to budgetees considering that the incentive is only to achieve the budget and not exceed it.

Avoiding risks. Managers may prefer to avoid uncertainty in setting or achieving targets because by avoiding risks they have greater control in achieving the budget.

(b) *Meeting only the lowest targets and using more resources than necessary.*

Variable costs of $200 per tonne have been agreed so there is no incentive to achieve a better level of performance. Also more resources than necessary may be used to achieve the variable cost because of the lack of incentive.

Making the bonus–whatever it takes and meeting the budget target but not beating it. A bonus is paid for achieving an output of 100 000 units so managers may ignore waste, quality and on-time delivery as long as they achieve the targeted output.

Competing against other divisions etc. At present, the division obtains its materials from selected suppliers who have been used for some years but there is evidence that similar materials could be obtained from another division but this does not appear to have been considered, because there is no incentive to do so.

Ensuring that what is in the budget is spent. There is a fixed budget allowance of $50m so there will be a reluctance to under-spend since this may result in a reduced budget allowance next year.

Providing inaccurate forecasts. There is no external reference point relating to the 15 per cent processing loss because of ageing machinery. The manager may have deliberately biased this information to reduce the pressure in meeting the budget requirements.

Avoiding risks. The fact that none of the items listed in note 5 of the question have been pursued may be due to risk avoidance.

(c) *Meeting only the lowest targets and meeting the target but not beating it.* The bonus system could be changed so that an extra bonus can be obtained arising from increments in meeting demand over 100 000 units, or base the bonus on the ability to always meet the demands of the receiving division. Alternatively, consider making the division a profit centre so that they are rewarded with extra profits for meeting demand in excess of 100 000 units.

Using more resources than necessary. There is no mention of the managers being evaluated on the basis of variances from standard. Using more resources than necessary would be reflected in unfavourable variances that should be incorporated into the performance evaluation process.

Making the bonus–whatever it takes. Again it may be preferable to base the bonus on the ability to be able to meet the demand of the receiving divisions without any delivery delays.

Competing against other divisions etc. Implement a requirement within the group that divisions should give priority to internal sourcing where divisions are prepared to supply at the same price and quality as outside suppliers.

Ensuring that what is in the budget is spent and providing inaccurate forecasts. Providing assurance to managers that under-spending will not automatically result in a reduced budget allowance next year and also allowing greater participation in the budget negotiation process. Ensuring that a flexible style of budget evaluation is applied.

Avoiding risk. Providing a guarantee to management that any adverse effects from undertaking the initiatives listed in note 5 will be taken into account in the budget evaluation process and guaranteeing that managers will not suffer a reduction in bonus arising from adverse effects of new initiatives, provided they have had top management approval. In other words, ensuring that a flexible style of evaluation is applied.

10.22 (a) The current traditional budgeting method does not appear appropriate for a company that faces a rapidly changing external environment and has corporate objectives that focus on innovation and continuous product development. The budgeting system is subject to the following weaknesses:

● The budgets are only prepared annually which is inappropriate given the company's objectives and environment in which it operates. The company faces considerable uncertainty in costs (e.g. silver prices), exchange rates, selling prices and sales volume which makes it extremely difficult to forecast on an annual basis. Rolling budgets are likely to be more appropriate for a rapidly changing environment.

● A rigid budget constrained style of budget evaluation is used where deviations from planned targets are not tolerated. This approach is inappropriate for companies operating in an uncertain environment. Using only rigid, annual budgets has resulted in P Division being unable to cope with changes in demand or one-off events such as the factory fire. It has also resulted in short-term cost cutting to achieve the budgeted net profit (e.g. by closing one of the research and development (R&D) facilities even though R&D is a key competitive advantage of the company). G Division also did not take on additional staff to cope with increased demand following reopening of their customer's factory. This also may be due to the managers being constrained by the budget. This action has been to the long-term detriment of the company because it has resulted in the loss of the preferred supplier status with its main customer.

● The budget process appears to be very bureaucratic and time consuming. Approval of the budgets often occurs after the start of the budget period resulting in the budgets already being out of date. Managers therefore find the budgeting process demotivating. Also the fact that the directors revise the budgets after they have been prepared has a demotivational effect. There is a need for managers to have greater participation and be involved in negotiation process prior to the authorization of the annual budget.

● The controllability principle has not been applied and fixed budgets rather than flexible budgets appear to be used. Managers are discouraged from deviating from the original fixed budget and are evaluated on factors which are outside their control. No attempt is made to distinguish between planning and operating variances. For example, the manager of P Division did not make technical modifications to its components because of the extra costs. This resulted in a failure to supply components for use in the new model of smartphone and the company having to heavily discount the inventories of the old version in order to achieve planned sales volumes.

● The absence of information relating to the frequency of feedback reporting suggests infrequent feedback resulting in a failure to respond to deviations from plan.

● Performance reporting is internally focused despite the rapidly changing environment. More emphasis should be given to relative performance evaluation (see Chapter 10) using information from external sources to enable performance to be assessed in a more meaningful way.

● The current system does not encourage goal congruence or coordination and communication between divisions. Divisional managers are evaluated on the financial performance of their own division and are therefore likely to prioritize the interests of their own division rather than the company as a whole. For example, P Division did not re-allocate its manufacturing facilities to G Division, even though G Division needed these facilities to cope with the extra demand following reopening of the customer's factory.

(b) The answer should describe the main features of beyond budgeting (see 'Beyond budgeting' in Chapter 9). The likely impact of the company moving to beyond budgeting will be as follows:

● The company operates in a rapidly changing environment resulting in the need to quickly respond and develop new products. The company will therefore be able to change its budget plans frequently by replacing annual incremental budgeting with regular rolling budgets. Short-term performance measures should be replaced with key performance measures that focus on the long-term success of the organization.

● Beyond budgeting places greater emphasis on longer-term non-financial targets using relative performance evaluation involving external benchmarks to analyse it to assess performance. The ability to be seen as the preferred supplier with key customers could be a key objective and performance measure of the divisional managers.

● Beyond budgeting places greater emphasis on empowering managers make decisions that are in the long-term interests of the business. It therefore allows managers to respond quickly to changes in the external environment by implementing innovative actions to external change.

● The company currently applies a top-down approach to budgeting. Adopting beyond budgeting will require a bottom-up budget setting process with a more devolved decision-making structure.

● Beyond budgeting requires that resources should be made available for managers to take advantage of opportunities in the market, such as the smartphone designed for playing games. This would enable managers to react to changes in material prices and foreign currency exchange rates by having the authority to purchase silver at times when the prices are low.

● Presently divisional managers compete for resources when setting budgets and this has resulted in a lack of goal congruence. Beyond budgeting encourages managers to work together for the good of the business and to share knowledge and resources. This is particularly important where product innovation is a key success factor. Each division has its own IT systems but effectively sharing knowledge and responding to the changing external environment requires shared IT facilities.

● Appropriate training and the implementation of appropriate information systems will be required to implement the above changes.

10.23 See 'determining how much influence managers should have in setting targets' in Chapter 10 for the answer to this question. In addition, to the advantages and disadvantages listed in Chapter 10 the answer could draw attention to the positive motivational impact arising from staff feeling that they are being respected because of their knowledge and experience relating to running the college. The following additional disadvantages could also be included in the answer:

● senior staff may spend a great deal of time arguing with each other and top management relating to the content and level of difficulty of the budget

● the participative process can be very time-consuming

● senior staff may be excellent in their chosen area but lack the knowledge and skills to engage in the management of the budget process.

10.24 (a) Although the senior managers appear to be involved in the budget process it is clear that they do not have any real impact in the process since the budgets they have been involved in are amended without any consultation. They are involved in what is called pseudo participation. This approach will probably have a worse impact than not involving the partners at all since staff will feel that they have wasted their time in preparing the budget which is then ignored. The benefit of participation leading to ownership of the budget and thus feeling personally responsible in achieving the budget is lost, and the partners will not be motivated to achieve the budgeted cost. There is also the additional possibility that the managers may be motivated to deliberately fail to achieve the budgeted costs in order to prove that their own budget was correct and that the changes implemented by the senior partner were wrong.

(b) The following non-financial indicators could be used:

● amount of staff time spent on developing new products and services and details of the number of new products and services developed

● response time between an enquiry and the first meeting of the client in order to measure response time

● number of staff training days which will provide an indication of the firm's investment in people.

10.25   (i)   Budgets are used for a variety of purposes, one of which is to evaluate the performance of budgetees. When budgets form the basis for future performance evaluation, there is a possibility that budgetees will introduce bias into the process for personal gain and self-protection. Factors that are likely to cause managers to submit budget estimates that do not represent their best estimates include:

1   *The reward system:* If managers believe that rewards depend upon budget attainment then they might be encouraged to underestimate sales budgets and overestimate cost budgets.

2   *Past performance:* If recent performance has been poor, managers may submit favourable plans so as to obtain approval from their supervisors. Such an approach represents a trade-off advantage of short-run security and approval against the risk of not being able to meet the more optimistic plans.

3   *Incremental budgeting:* Incremental budgeting involves adding increments to past budgets to reflect expected future changes. Consequently, the current budget will include bias that has been built into previous budgets.

4   *External influences:* If managers believe that their performance is subject to random external influences then, from a self-protection point of view, they might submit budgets that can easily be attained.

5   *Style of performance evaluation:* A budget-constrained style of evaluation might encourage the budgetee to meet the budget at all costs. Consequently, budgetees will be motivated to bias their budget estimates.

(ii)   The following procedures should be introduced to minimize the likelihood of biased estimates:

1   Encourage managers to adopt a more flexible profit-conscious style of evaluation.

2   Adopt a system of zero-based budgeting.

3   Key figures in the budget process (e.g. sales estimates) should be checked by using information from different sources.

4   Planning and operating variances should be segregated. Managers might be motivated to submit more genuine estimates if they are aware that an *ex post* budget will be used as a basis for performance appraisal.

5   Participation by the budgetees in the budget process should be encouraged so as to secure a greater commitment to the budget process and improve communication between budgetees, their superior and the budget accountants.

10.26   (a)   The answer should include a discussion of the following points:

(i)   Constant pressure from top management for greater production may result in the creation of anti-management work groups and reduced efficiency, so that budgetees can protect themselves against what they consider to be increasingly stringent targets.

(ii)   Non-acceptance of budgets if the budgetees have not been allowed to participate in setting the budgets.

(iii)   Negative attitudes if the budget is considered to be a punitive control device instead of a system to help managers do a better job. The negative attitudes might take the form of reducing cooperation between departments and also with the accounting department. Steps might be taken to ensure that costs do not fall below budget, so that the budget will not be reduced next year. There is a danger that data will be falsified, and more effort will be directed to finding excuses for failing to achieve the budget than trying to control or reduce costs.

(iv)   Managers might try and achieve the budget at all costs even if this results in actions that are not in the best interests of the organization, e.g. delaying maintenance costs.

(v)   Organizational atmosphere may become one of competition and conflict rather than one of cooperation and conciliation.

(vi)   Suspicion and mistrust of top management, resulting in the whole budgeting process being undermined.

(vii)   Belief that the system of evaluation is unjust and widespread worry and tension by the budgetees. Tension might be relieved by falsifying information, blaming others or absenteeism.

(b)   For the answer to this question see 'Dealing with the distorting effects of uncontrollable factors before (and after) the measurement period' in Chapter 10.

Chapter 11

11.11   Materials price variance = (Standard price − Actual price) × Actual quantity
= (Actual quantity × Standard price) − Actual cost
= (8200 × £0.80) − £6888
= £328 Adverse

Material usage variance = (Standard quantity − Actual quantity) × Standard price
= (870 × 8 kg − 0960 − 7150) × £0.80
= £152 Adverse

Answer = D

11.12   Fixed overhead variance = Budgeted cost (not flexed) − Actual cost
= £10 000 per month − £9 800
= £200 Favourable

Answer = B

11.13   Sales volume variance = (Actual sales volume − Budgeted sales volume) × Standard contribution margin
= (4500 − 5000) $4.40
= $2200 Adverse

Answer = B

11.14   (a)   Total materials cost variance = (actual production × standard material cost per unit of production) − actual materials cost
= (26 000 × £20) − £532 800
= £12 800A

Total variable overhead variance = (actual production × standard variable overhead rate per unit) − actual variable overhead cost
= (26 000 × £24) − £614 000
= £10 000F

Wage rate variance = (standard wage rate per hour – actual wage rate) × actual labour hours worked
= (£8 – £1 221 000/150 000) × 150 000
= £21 000A

Labour efficiency variance = (standard quantity of labour hours for actual production – actual labour hours) × standard wage rate
= [(26 000 × 6 hours) – 150 000] × £8
= £48 000F

(b)

	£	£
Budgeted contribution [25 000 × (£120 – £920]		700 000
Sales price variance (W1)		5 000A
Direct materials		12 800A
Total variable overhead production		10 000F
Direct labour rate	21 000A	
Direct labour efficiency	48 000F	
Total direct labour		2 700F
Actual contribution (W2)		719 200

Workings

W1 Sales margin price variance = (actual selling price – standard selling price) × actual sales volume

= [(£2995 000/25 000) – £120] × 25 000

= £5000A

W2	£	£
Actual sales		2 995 000
Actual costs:		
Materials	532 800	
Labour	1 221 000	
Production overhead	614 000	
	2 367 800	
Less closing stock at standard cost (1000 × £92)	92 000	
Variable cost of sales		2 275 800
Actual contribution		719 200

(c) The two variances may be related if more skilled labour, paid at a higher wage rate than that planned, was used. Higher skilled labour may have been more efficient resulting in a favourable efficiency variance, but the higher wage rate would also have resulted in an adverse wage rate variance.

11.15 (a) Sales margin price variance = (actual selling price – standard selling price) × actual sales volume

= [(£731 000/34 000) – £22] × 34 000

= £17 000A

Sales margin volume variance = (actual sales volume – budgeted sales volume) × standard contribution margin

= (34 000 – 32 000) × £13

= £26 000F

(b) The actual selling price was £0.50 less than the budgeted selling price resulting in an adverse sales margin price variance, whereas the actual sales volume was 2000 units in excess of the budget resulting in a favourable volume variance. The increase in sales volume may have been due to the reduction in the selling price. Therefore the two variances are interrelated and should be considered together rather than in isolation.

11.16 *Preliminary calculations*

The standard product cost and selling price are calculated as follows:

	(€)
Direct materials	
X (10 kg at €1)	10
Y (5 kg at €5)	25
Direct wages (5 hours × €8)	40
Standard variable cost	75
Profit/contribution margin	75
Selling price	150

The actual profit for the period is calculated as follows:

	(€)	(€)
Sales (9500 at €160)		1 520 000
Direct materials: X	115 200	
Y	225 600	
Direct wages (46 000 × €8.20)	377 200	
Fixed overhead	290 000	1 008 000
Actual profit		512 000

It is assumed that the term 'using a fixed budget' refers to the requirement to reconcile the actual results with the original fixed budget.

	(€)	(€)
Material price variance: (Standard price – Actual price) × Actual quantity		
X: (€1 – €1.20) × 96 000	19 200 A	
Y: (€5 – €4.70) × 48 000	14 440 F	4 800 A
Material usage variance: (Standard quantity – Actual quantity) × Standard price		
X: (9500 × 10 = 95 000 – 96 000) × €1	1 000 A	
Y: (9500 × 5 = 47 500 – 48 000) × €5	2 500 A	3 500 A

The actual materials used are in standard proportions. Therefore there is no mix variance.

	(€)	(€)
Wage rate variance: (Standard rate – Actual rate) × Actual hours (€8 – €8.20) × 46 000	9 200 A	
Labour efficiency variance: (Standard hours – Actual hours) × Standard rate (9500 × 5 = 47 500 – 46 000) × €8	12 000 F	2 800 F
Fixed overhead expenditure: Budgeted fixed overheads – Actual fixed overheads (10 000 × €30 = €300 000 – €290 000)		10 000 F
Sales margin price variance: (Actual margin – Standard margin) × Actual sales volume (€85 – €75) × 9500	95 000 F	
Sales margin volume variance: (Actual sales volume – Budgeted sales volume) × Standard margin (9500 – 10 000) × €75	37 500 A	57 500 F
Total variance		62 000 F

	(€)
Budgeted profit contribution (10 000 units at €75)	750 000
Less budgeted fixed overheads	300 000
Budgeted profit	450 000
Add favourable variances (see above)	62 000
Actual profit	512 000

11.17 *Standard product cost for one unit of product XY*

	(£)
Direct materials (8 kg (W2) at £1.50 (W1) per kg)	12.00
Direct wages (2 hours (W4) at £10 (W3) per hour)	20.00
Variable overhead (2 hours (W4) at £1 (W5) per hour)	2.00
	34.00

Workings

(W1) Actual quantity of materials purchased at standard price is £225 000 (actual cost plus favourable material price variance). Therefore standard price = £1.50 (£225 000/150 000 kg).

(W2) Material usage variance = 6000 kg (£9000/£1.50 standard price). Therefore standard quantity for actual production = 144 000 kg (150 000 – 6000 kg). Therefore, standard quantity per unit = 8 kg (144 000 kg/18 000 units).

(W3) Actual hours worked at standard rate = £320 000 (£328 000 – 8000). Therefore standard rate per hour = £10 (£320 000/32 000 hours).

(W4) Labour efficiency variance = 4000 hours (£32 000/£8). Therefore standard hours for actual production = 36 000 hours (32 000 + 4000). Therefore standard hours per unit = 2 hours (36 000 hours/18 000 units).

(W5) Actual hours worked at the standard variable overhead rate is £32 000 (£38 000 actual variable overheads less £6000 favourable expenditure variance). Therefore, standard variable overhead rate = £1 (£32 000/32 000 hours).

11.18 (a) The favourable material price variance suggests that the wood was cheaper than the standard saving $5100 on the standard. The concern is that this may be due to obtaining cheaper lower quality wood. The material usage variance indicates that the waste levels of wood are worse than standard. It is possible that the lower grade labour could have also contributed to the waste level. There is an overall adverse variance of $2400 when both the price and usage variances are taken together so it appears that it has been a poor decision to outsource the wood from a different supplier. The production manager is responsible for both decisions and is therefore accountable for the variances arising from the decision. When the new labour is trained it may be that the wood usage improves but this will only become apparent in the next few months.

The impact that the new wood might have had on sales should also be taken into account. Variances should not be viewed as impacting on one department and no one department should be viewed in isolation to another. Sales are down and returns are up and this is likely to be due to the purchase of poor quality wood.

The company uses traditional manual techniques that normally requires skilled labour. The labour was paid less, saving the company $43 600 in wages but the adverse efficiency and idle time variances total $54 200.

Thus the decision had a negative impact on profits during the first month. The efficiency variance indicates that it took longer to produce the bats than expected. The new labour was being trained in April and so it is possible that the situation may improve next month because of the learning effects.

(b) Material price variance ($5 – $196 000/40 000) × 40 000 = $4000 F

Material usage variance ((19 200 × 2) – 40 000) × $5/kg = $8 000 Adv

Wage rate variance ($12 – $694 000/62 000) × 62 000 hours = $50 000 Fav

Labour efficiency variance (19 000 × 3 = 57 000 – 61 500) × $12 = $46 800 Adv

Labour idle time variance 500 × $12 = $6 000 Adv

Sales price variance (65 – 68) × 18 000 = $54 000 Adv

Sales volume contribution variance (18 000 – 19 000) × $22 = $22 000 Adv

11.19 (a) Wage rate variance = (SP – AP)AH = (SP × AH) – (AP × AH)

= (€9 × 53 workers × 13 weeks × 40 hrs) – €248 740
= €700A

Labour efficiency = (SH – AH)SP

SH (Standard hours) = (35 000 × 0.4 hrs) + (25 000 × 0.56 hrs) = 28 000

AH (Actual hours) = 53 workers × 13 weeks × 40 hrs = 27 560

Variance = (28 000 – 27 560) × €9 = €3 960A

(b)

Material price variance	= (SP – AP)AQ
	= (AQ × SP) – (AQ × AP)
€430F (given)	= 47 000 SP – €85 110
SP (Standard price)	= $\dfrac{€430 + 85\ 110}{47\ 000}$
	= €1.82

Material usage variance	= (SQ – AQ)SP
	= (SQ × SP) – (AQ × SP)
€320.32A (given)	= €1.82 SQ – (33 426 × €1.82) –
€320.32A	= €1.82 SQ – €60 835.32
€1.82 SQ	= €60 515
SQ	= €60 515/€1.82 = 33 250
Note that SQ	= Actual production (35 000 units) × Standard usage

Therefore 35 000 × Standard usage = 33 250

Standard usage	= 33 250/35 000
	= 0.95 kg per unit of component X

(c) For the answer to this question you should refer to the detailed illustration of the budget process shown in Chapter 9. In particular, the answer should indicate that if sales are the limiting factor the production budget should be linked to the sales budget. Once the production budget has been established for the two components, the production quantity of each component multiplied by the standard usage of material A per unit of component output determines the required quantity of material to meet the production requirements. The budgeted purchase quantity of material A consists of the quantity to meet the production usage requirements plus or minus an adjustment to take account of any planned change in the level of raw material stock.

Chapter 12

12.13 Divisional managers do not control the cash function. Therefore, controllable net assets should exclude the cash overdraft so controllable net assets are R125 000 (R101 000 + R24 000).

Controllable residual income = R69 000 (Profit before interest and tax)

Less cost of capital	= 12 500 (10% × 125 000)
Residual income	= 56 500

Answer = (b)

12.14

	£m
Profit	89.20
Add back:	
Current depreciation (120 × 20%)	24.00
Development costs ((£9.60 × 2/3)	6.40
Less: Replacement depreciation (£168 × 20%)	33.60
Adjusted profit	86.00
Less: Cost of capital charge (13% × £168)[a]	21.84
EVA	64.16

Note:

[a]13% × [Fixed assets (£168 – £33.6) + Working capital (£27.2) + Development costs (£6.4)]

Answer = (a)

12.15

	£m	£m
Net profit after tax		8.6
Add:		
Interest	2.3	
Development costs	6.3	
Advertising	1.6	10.2
Less development costs (1/3)		(2.1)
		16.7
Less cost of capital charge (£30m × 13%)		(3.9)
EVA		12.8

12.16 Divisional profit before depreciation = $2.7m × 15% = $405 000 per annum.
Less depreciation = $2.7m × 1/50 = $54 000 per annum.
Divisional profit after depreciation = $351 000
Imputed interest = $2.7m × 7% = $189 000
Residual income = $162 000.
Answer = (c)

12.17 (a) Return on investment (ROI)

Division A	£
Profit	35 000
Net assets	150 000
Return on investment = 35 000/150 000 = 23.3%	

Division B	£
Profit	70 000
Net assets	325 000
Return on investment = 70 000/325 000% = 21.5%	

Residual income (RI)
Division A = £35 000 – (150 000 × 0.15) = £12 500
Division B = £70 000 – (325 000 × 0.15) = £21 250

Division A has a higher ROI but a lower residual income.

(b) Return on investment would be the better measure when comparing divisions as it is a relative measure (i.e. based on percentage returns).

(c) Appropriate aspects of performance include:
- competitiveness
- financial performance
- quality of service
- flexibility
- innovation
- resource utilization efficiency.

12.18 (a)

Return on investment = net profit/net assets

Division B = ($311 000 × 12)/$23 200 000 = 16.09%

Division C = ($292 000 × 12)/$22 600 000 = 15.5%

(b)

	B	C
	$	$
Net profit (monthly profit x 12)	3 732	3 504
Less: imputed interest charges:		
$23.2m × 10%	2 320	
$22.6m × 10%		2 260
Residual income	1 412	1 244

(c) Both divisions have ROI's below the target of 20% suggesting that they have not performed well but this is because non-controllable head office costs are being allocated before calculating ROI. The ROI's using the old method before allocating head office expenses are:

B: ($311 000 + $155 000) × 12/$23.2m = 24.1%

C: ($292 000 + $180 000) × 12/$22.6m = 25.06%

From this it can be seen that both divisions have actually improved their performance.

The residual income figures indicate that both divisions have performed well by reporting positive figures, even when using net profit rather than controllable profit are used as the bases for the calculations. The cost of capital of the company is significantly lower than the target return on investment that the company is setting thus indicating that the divisions are adding value.

(d) Depreciation = ($2 120 000 – $200 000)/48 months = $40 000 per month.

Net profit for July = $311 000 + ($600 000 × 8.5%) – $40 000 = $322 000

Annualized net profit: $322 000 × 12 = $3 864 000

Net assets after investment = $23.2m + $2.12m = $25.32m.

ROI = $3.864m/25.32m = 15.26%

Therefore, Division B will not proceed with the investment, since it will cause a decrease in its ROI.

If RI is used the result is as follows:

	$000
Annualized net profit after investment	3 864
Less imputed cost of capital (10% × $25.32m)	2 532
Residual income	1 332

Since the residual income is lower with the investment the divisional manager will be reluctant to invest if he or she focuses on the short-term.

To ascertain whether the investment is in the best interests for the company as whole the NPV should be calculated:

	$000
PV of annual cash inflows ($600 000 × 8.5% × 12 months = $612 000) × annuity factor at 10% for 4 years (3.170)	1 940
PV of sale proceeds in year 4 ($200 000 × 0.909)	182
	2 112
Investment cost	2 120
NPV	–8

The project has a negative NPV and should be rejected. Therefore both performance measures encourage goal congruence.

(e) The staff in both divisions have been used to achieving the targets and being rewarded for this. Suddenly, they find that even though divisional performance has improved, neither division is achieving its ROI target. This is a result of including the allocation of head office costs in the performance measure. Managerial evaluation should not be based on the allocation of uncontrollable costs but if senior management have reasons for doing so (see 'surveys of practice' in Chapter 12 for possible reasons) the target ROI should be revised upwards. Staff are likely to become demotivated with the new system which is clearly unfair. This is likely to result in the dysfunctional behavioural consequences described in Chapters 10 and 12.

12.19 (a) To compute EVA$^{(TM)}$, adjustments must be made to the conventional after-tax profit measures of $44 million and $55 million shown in the question. Normally an adjustment is made to convert conventional financial accounting depreciation to an estimate of economic depreciation, but the question indicates that profits have already been computed using economic depreciation. Non-cash expenses are added back since the adjusted profit attempts to approximate cash flow after taking into account economic depreciation. Net interest is also added back because the returns required by the providers of funds will be reflected in the cost of capital deduction. Note that net interest is added back because interest will have been allowed as an expense in determining the taxation payment.

The capital employed used to calculate EVA$^{(TM)}$ should be based on adjustments that seek to approximate book economic value at the start of each period. Because insufficient information is given, the book value of shareholders' funds plus medium- and long-term loans at the end of 2018 is used as the starting point to determine economic capital employed at the beginning of 2019.

	2018 ($m)	2019 ($m)
Adjusted profit	56.6 (44 + 10 + (4 × 0.65))	68.9 (55 + 10 + (6 × 0.65))
Capital employed	233 (223 + 10)	260 (250 + 10)

The weighted average cost of capital should be based on the target capital structure. The calculation is as follows:

2018 = (15% × 0.6) + (9% × 0.65 × 0.4) = 11.34%

2019 = (17% × 0.6) + (10% × 0.65 × 0.4) = 12.8%

EVA 2018 = 56.6 – (233 × 0.1134) = $30.18m

EVA 2019 = 68.9 – (260 × 0.128) = $35.62

The EVA$^{(TM)}$ measures indicate that the company has added significant value in both years and achieved a satisfactory level of performance.

(b) Advantages of EVA$^{(TM)}$ include:
1 because some discretionary expenses are capitalized the harmful side-effects of financial measures described in Chapters 10 and 12 are reduced
2 EVA$^{(TM)}$ is consistent with maximizing shareholders' funds
3 EVA$^{(TM)}$ is easily understood by managers
4 EVA$^{(TM)}$ can also be linked to managerial bonus schemes and can motivate managers to take decisions that increase shareholder value.

Disadvantages of EVA$^{(TM)}$ include:
1 the EVA$^{(TM)}$ computation can be complicated when many adjustments are required
2 EVA$^{(TM)}$ is difficult to use for inter-firm and inter-divisional comparisons because it is not a ratio measure
3 if economic depreciation is not used, the short-term measure can conflict with the long-term measure
4 economic depreciation is difficult to estimate and conflicts with generally accepted accounting principles, which may hinder its acceptance by financial managers.

12.20 (a) Value based management (VBM) is based on the principle that the primary objective of companies whose shares are traded in the stock market is to maximize shareholder wealth. VBM seeks to maximize shareholder wealth by aligning performance measurement and evaluation with this objective. The principle measure used at the strategic level is economic value added (EVA™). This measure was developed with the aim of producing an overall financial measure that encourages senior managers to concentrate on the delivery of shareholder value. EVA™ is equivalent in the long term to the present value of future cash flows which is the theoretical basis for share valuation. It is therefore important that the key financial measure that is used to measure divisional or company performance should be congruent with shareholder value. It is claimed that EVA™ is more likely to meet this requirement and also to reduce dysfunctional behaviour.

(b)   *Calculation of EVA™*

	2018 $m	2019 $m
Profit after interest and tax	35.00	26.80
Add back interest after tax[b]		
[interest × (1 – tax rate)]	3.00	5.85
Adjusted profit	38.00	32.65
Cost of capital[a]	8.38	9.99
EVA™	29.62	22.66

Notes:

[a]Cost of capital charge = (Capital employed at the start of the year) × (Weighted average cost of capital)

WACC:

2018 (50% × 12.7%) + (50% × 4.2%) = 8.45%

2019 (50% × 15.3%) + (50% × 3.9%) = 9.60%

Capital employed at the start of the year:

2018 = $99.2m

2019 = $104.1m

Cost of capital charge:

2018 = 8.45% × $99.2m = $8.38m

2019 = 9.60% × $104.1m = $9.99m

[b]Net interest is added back to reported profit because the tax benefits of interest are allowed for as an expense in the computation of the tax liability.

[c]It is assumed that economic and accounting depreciation are the same, the taxation paid is the same as the tax included in the profits after tax calculation and that there are no non-cash expenses to adjust in the above calculation of adjusted profit.

Calculation of earning per share (profits after interest and tax/average number of shares)

2018 21.875 cents ($35m/160m)

2019 16.75 cents ($26.8m/160m)

Comments

The above figures and the data in the question indicate that there has been a percentage decline in the following measures when 2019 is compared with 2018:

EVA™ = 23.5%

EPS = 23.4%

Main market index = 34.9%

Retailing sector index = 26.0%

Company share price = 12.3%

All of the company based measures have declined but the company share price fall of 12% is lower than the sector decline (26%) and the market as a whole (35%). Market comparisons suggest that the market has a more favourable view of the company when compared with market/sector data. This view is consistent with the positive EVA™ for 2019. Although EVA™ has fallen from 2018 it has remained positive so the company continues to create value for its shareholders even in the poor economic environment. The positive EVA™ indicates that shareholder investment has been worthwhile even though the market has been falling.

(c)   Value measures are considered to be superior to profit measures because they take into consideration the capital employed and cost of capital and also attempt to adjust profit measures to provide a better approximation of economic income. The major difficulty with using value-based measures like EVA™ compared to profit measures is that it is difficult to obtain a reasonable estimate for some of the EVA™ adjustments. For example, accurate calculations of the cost of capital and economic depreciation are difficult to determine. EVA™ can also be subject to manipulation by choosing projects with high initial earnings but which are not justifiable on the basis of a long-term evaluation.

12.21 (a)   Examples of the types of decisions that should be transferred to the new divisional managers include:

(i)   Product decisions such as product mix, promotion and pricing.

(ii)   Employment decisions, except perhaps for the appointment of senior managers.

(iii)   Short-term operating decisions of all kinds. Examples include production scheduling, subcontracting and direction of marketing effort.

(iv)   Capital expenditure and disinvestment decisions (with some constraints).

(v)   Short-term financing decisions (with some constraints).

(b)   The following decisions might be retained at company head office:

(i)   Strategic investment decisions that are critical to the survival of the company as a whole.

(ii)   Certain financing decisions that require that an overall view be taken. For example, borrowing commitments and the level of financial gearing should be determined for the group as a whole.

(iii)   Appointment of top management.

(iv)   Sourcing decisions such as bulk buying of raw materials if corporate interests are best served by centralized buying.

(v)   Capital expenditure decisions above certain limits.

(vi)   Common services that are required by all profit centres. Corporate interests might best be served by operating centralized service departments such as an industrial relations department. Possible benefits include reduced costs and the extra benefits of specialization.

(vii)   Arbitration decisions on transfer pricing disputes.

(viii) Decisions on items that benefit the company rather than an individual division, e.g. taxation and computer applications.

(c)   The answer to this question should focus on the importance of designing performance reports which encourage goal congruence. For a discussion of this topic see Chapter 12.

12.22 (a)   For the answer to this question see 'Return on investment' and 'Residual income' in Chapter 12. Note that discounted future earnings are the equivalent to discounted future profits.

(b) The existing ROCE is 20 per cent and the estimated ROCE on the additional investment is 15 per cent (£9000/£60 000). The divisional manager will therefore reject the additional investment, since adding this to the existing investments will result in a decline in the existing ROCE of 20 per cent.

The residual income on the additional investment is £600 (£9000 average profit for the year less an imputed interest charge of 14% × £6000 = £8400). The manager will accept the additional investment, since it results in an increase in residual income.

If the discounted future earnings method is used, the investment would be accepted, since it will yield a positive figure for the year (that is, £9000 × 3.889 discount factor).

Note that the annual future cash flows are £19 000 (£9000 net profit plus £10 000 depreciation provision). The project has a 6-year life. The annual cash inflow must be in excess of £15 428 (£60 000/3.889 annuity factor – 6 years at 14%) if the investment is to yield a positive NPV. If annual cash flows are £19 000 each year for the next 6 years, the project should be accepted.

The residual income and discounted future earnings methods of evaluation will induce the manager to accept the investment. These methods are consistent with the correct economic evaluation using the NPV method. If ROCE is used to evaluate performance, the manager will incorrectly reject the investment. This is because the manager will only accept projects that yield a return in excess of the current ROCE of 20 per cent.

Note that the above analysis assumes that the cash flows/profits are constant from year to year.

Chapter 13

13.13 The loss of contribution (profits) in division A from lost internal sales of 2500 units at €18 (€40 – €22) is €45 000.

The impact on the whole company is that the external purchase cost is €87 500 (2 500 × €35) compared with the incremental cost of manufacture of €55 000 (2500 × €22). Therefore the company will be worse off by €32 500.

Answer = (d)

13.14 (i) The proposed transfer price of €15 is based on cost plus 25 per cent implying that the total cost is €12. This comprises €9 variable cost (75 per cent) and €3 fixed cost. The general transfer pricing guideline described in Chapter 13 can be applied to this question. That is the transfer price that should be set at marginal cost plus the opportunity cost. It is assumed in the first situation that transferring internally will result in Helpco having a lost contribution of €6 (€15 external market price less €9 variable cost for the external market). The marginal cost of the transfer is €7.50 (€9 external variable cost less €1.50 packaging costs not required for internal sales). Adding the opportunity cost of €6 gives a transfer price of €13.50 per kg. This is equivalent to applying the market price rule where the transfer price is set at the external market price (€15) less selling costs avoided (€1.50) by transferring internally.

(ii) For the 3000 kg where no external market is available the opportunity cost will not apply and transfers should be at the variable cost of €7.50. The remaining output should be transferred at €13.50 as described above.

(iii) The lost contribution for the 2000 kg is €3 per kg (€6000/2000 kg) giving a transfer price of €10.50 (€7.50 variable cost plus €3 opportunity cost). The remaining 1000 kg for which there is no external market should be transferred at €7.50 variable cost and the balance for which there is an external market transferred at €13.50.

13.15 Division M generates a contribution to profit of $80 ($850 – $770) for the group as a whole for every motor sold externally. The incremental cost for every motor which Division S has to buy from outside of the group is $60 per unit ($800 – [$770 – $30]). Therefore, from the group's perspective as many external sales as possible should be made before any internal transfers are made. Division M's total capacity is 60 000 units so 30 000 units should be sold externally and the remaining 30 000 units transferred to Division S. From the group's perspective, the cost of supplying these internally is $60 per unit ($800 – $740) cheaper than buying externally. Division S's remaining demand of 5000 units should be bought form the external supplier at $800 per unit.

Therefore the group's current policy will need to be changed. In order to determine the transfer price which should be set for the internal sales of 30 000 motors, the perspective of both divisions should be considered. Division M can only sell the motors to Division S and the lowest price it would be prepared to charge is the marginal cost of $740 of making these units but it will also wish to make a profit on each unit transferred. From Division S's perspective it can buy as many external motors as it needs from outside the group at a price of $800 per unit so this will be the maximum price which it is prepared to pay. Therefore, the transfer price should be set somewhere between $740 and $800. The total group profit will be the same irrespective of where in this range the transfer price is set.

13.16 (a) The variable costs per unit of output for sales *outside* the company are €11 for the intermediate product and €49 [€10(A) + €39(B)] for the final product. Note that selling and packing expenses are not incurred by the supplying division for the transfer of the intermediate product. It is assumed that the company has sufficient capacity to meet demand at the various selling prices.

Optimal output of intermediate product for sale on external market

Selling price (€)	20	30	40
Unit contribution (€)	9	19	29
Demand (units)	15 000	10 000	5 000
Total contribution (€)	135 000	190 000	145 000

Optimal output is 10 000 units at a selling price of €30.

Optimal output for final product

Selling price (€)	80	90	100
Unit contribution (€)	31	41	51
Demand (units)	7 200	5 000	2 800
Total contribution (€)	223 200	205 000	142 800

Optimal output is 7 200 units at a selling price of €80.

Optimal output of Division B based on a transfer price of €29

Division B will regard the transfer price as a variable cost. Therefore total variable cost per unit will be €68 (€29 + €39), and division B will calculate the following contributions:

Selling price (€)	80	90	100
Unit contribution (€)	12	22	32
Demand (units)	7 200	5 000	2 800
Total contribution (€)	86 400	110 000	89 600

The manager of division B will choose an output level of 5000 units at a selling price of €90. This is sub-optimal for the company as a whole. Profits for the *company as a whole* from the sale of the final product are reduced from €223 200 (7 200 units) to €205 000 (5000 units). The €205 000 profits would be allocated as follows:

Division A €95 000 [5000 units at (€29 – €10)]

Division B €110 000

(b) At a transfer price of €12, the variable cost per unit produced in division B will be €51 (€12 + €39). Division B will calculate the following contributions:

Selling price (€)	80	90	100
Unit contribution (€)	29	39	49
Demand (units)	7 200	5 000	2 800
Total contribution (€)	208 800	195 000	137 200

The manager of division B will choose an output level of 7200 units and a selling price of €80. This is the optimum output level for the company as a whole. Division A would obtain a contribution of €14 400 [7200 × (€12 – €10)] from internal transfers of the intermediate product, whereas division B would obtain a contribution of €208 800 from converting the intermediate product and selling as a final product. Total contribution for the company as a whole would be €223 200. Note that division A would also earn a contribution of €190 000 from the sale of the intermediate product to the external market.

13.17 (a) In this situation head office only allows Division A will sell 80 000 baths and purchase its fittings from Division B. Division A will therefore purchase 80 000 units from Division B and Division B will use the balance of its production capacity to sell 120 000 units externally at $80.

Profit statement

	Division A $000	Division B $000	Company $000
Sales revenue:			
External (1)	36 000	9 600	45 600
Inter-divisional transfers	0	6 000	
Total	36 000	15 600	45 600
Variable costs:			
External material costs (2)	(16 000)	(1 000)	(17 000)
Inter-divisional transfers (3)	(6 000)	0	
Labour costs (4)	(3 600)	(3 000)	(6 600)
Total	(25 600)	(4 000)	(23 600)
Fixed costs	(7 440)	(4 400)	(11 840)
Profit	2 960	7 200	10 160

Workings ($000)
(1) External sales and inter-divisional transfers
Div A: 80 000 × $450 = $36 000

Div B: 120 000 × $80 = $9600
Div B inter-divisional transfers: 80 000 × $75 = $6000

(2) External material costs
Div A: 80 000 × $200 = $16 000
Div B: 200 000 × $5 = $1000

(3) Inter-divisional transfers
Div A: 80 000 × $75 = $6000

(4) Labour costs
Div A: 80 000 × $45 = $3600
Div B: 200 000 × $15 = $3000

(b) and (c)
The manger of Division A will maximize his/her profits by purchasing 80 000 bath fittings at the lowest price (the outside the company's price of $65 per unit). The manager of Division B will wish to sell the maximum demand (180 000 units) of bath fittings to the external market at $80 per unit and transfer the remaining capacity (20 000) units at a transfer price above variable cost. Since Division B can sell 180 000 bath fittings at $80 per unit the most profitable choice for the company as a whole is for Division B to sell 180 000 units externally at $80 and for Division A to buy similar type of fittings outside at $65 per unit. Division B will have unutilized capacity of 20 000 units and since its variable cost is $20 per unit it is best for the company as a whole if these 20 000 units are transferred internally rather than purchased outside for $65 per unit. Therefore the optimum output is for Division B to sell 180 000 units externally and transfer 20 000 units internally and for Division A to sell 80 000 units externally (buying 60 000 units externally and 20 000 units internally).

To encourage the divisional managers to make the above decisions the transfer price should be set above Division B's variable cost of $20 and not higher than the outside price faced by Division A ($65). Therefore the optimum transfer price is within the range is from $20 to $65. Instead of head office imposing a transfer price within the above range divisional autonomy could be promoted by allowing the divisional managers to negotiate a transfer price, given the circumstances presented in the question. Provided that the managers are competent if would be rational for them to agree a transfer price within the above range. The following profit statements are based on a transfer price of $65 but statements could be prepared for any transfer price within the optimal range.

	Division A $000	Division B $000	Company $000
Sales revenue:			
External (1)	36 000	14 400	50 400
Internal sales (2)		1 300	
Total	36 000	15 700	50 400
Variable costs:			
External material costs (3)	(19 900)	(1 000)	(20 900)
Inter-divisional transfers (2)	(1 300)		
Labour costs	(3 600)	(3 000)	(6 600)
Total	(24 800)	(4 000)	(27 500)
Fixed costs	(7 440)	(4 400)	(11 840)
Profit	3 760	7 300	11 060

Workings ($000)

(1) External sales
Div A: 80 000 × $450 = $36 000
Div B: 180 000 × $80 = $14 400

(2) Internal sales/inter-divisional transfers
20 000 × $65 = $1 300

(3) Material costs
Div A: 60 000 × $65 for outside purchase of fittings +
(80 000 × $200) = $19 900
Div B: 200 000 × $5 = $1 000

13.18 (a) (i) With Quotation 1 the proposed internal transfer price is $10.50 ($15 less 30%) and the locally available price is $9. Division B would therefore purchase ankle supports from a local supplier in order to increase its profitability. Division A has spare production capacity of 10 000 units (the maximum capacity is 160 000 units and total demand is 150 000 units). Division A could, therefore, supply 10 000 units of ankle supports at its variable cost of $7 per unit ($350 000/50 000) giving a total cost of $70 000. The cost of purchasing 10 000 units from the local supplier is $90 000. In order to maximize group profits, Division A should quote its variable cost of $7 per unit for each of the 10 000 units required by Division B and group profit will increase by $20 000.

As regards Quotation 2 Division B would again wish to purchase from a local supplier in order to increase its reported profits Division A quotes a transfer price of $10.50. Division A could potentially supply 18 000 ankle supports by using its spare capacity for 10 000 units and switching production of 8000 units from sales of the type of support that earns the lowest contribution per unit. The 10 000 units of spare capacity can be supplied at a variable cost of $7 per unit and the additional 8000 units would have to be diverted from the type of existing support that yields the lowest contribution per unit. The calculations are as follows:

Product	Knee support	Ankle support	Elbow support	Wrist support
Selling price per unit ($)	24	15	18	9
Variable cost per unit ($)	10	7	8	4
Contribution per unit ($)	14	8	10	5

Division A should offer to transfer the additional 8000 ankle supports at $12 per unit [variable cost ($7) + contribution foregone ($5)]. Division B would reject the offer and buy externally at $9 per unit. This would ensure that the profit of the group is not adversely affected by any transfer decision.

(ii) The answer should draw attention to the general rule for transfer pricing, which is that the transfer price should be set at the variable cost per unit of the supplying division plus the opportunity cost per unit of the supplying division. You should refer to 'marginal/variable cost plus opportunity cost transfer prices' in Chapter 13 for a more detailed explanation.

(b) Because the two divisions operate in different countries that are subject to different tax rates it is necessary to work out the impact on profits and taxes arising from the decision whether Division B buys from Division A or buys locally. If division B buys locally the implications for SSA group are as follows.

	$
Division A sales:	
60 000 wrist supports at a contribution of $5 per unit	300 000
Taxation at 40%	120 000
After tax benefit of sales	180 000
Division B purchases:	
18 000 ankle supports at a cost of $9 per unit	162 000
Taxation benefit at 20%	32 400
After tax cost of purchases	129 600
Net benefit to SSA Group – $180 000 – $129 600	$50 400

If Division B buys internally from Division A the financial implications for SSA group are as follows.

	$
Division A sales:	
External:	
52 000 wrist supports at a contribution of $5 per unit	260 000
18 000 ankle supports to Division B at a contribution of ($15 × 70%) – $7 = $3.5 per unit	63 000
	323 000
Taxation at 40%	129 200
After tax benefit of sales	193 800
Division B purchases:	
18 000 ankle supports at cost of $10.50 per unit	189 000
Taxation benefit at 20%	37 800
After tax cost of purchases	151 200
Net benefit to SSA Group	$42 600

Therefore SSA group will be $7800 worse off ($50 400 – $42 600) if Division B purchases the ankle supports from Division A instead of the local supplier.

Chapter 14

14.12 (i) The percentage of occupancy on flights to new destinations should provide feedback on how successful this policy is in terms of meeting the growth objective.

(ii) Measures of baggage loading/unloading times, aircraft cleaning times and fuel loading times can be used to implement a policy of continuous improvement and thus contribute to the achievement of the internal capabilities objective.

14.13 (a)

Objectives	Performance measures	Justification
Financial perspective		
Improve operating profit margins (or asset utilization)	Percentage increase in profit/sales or economic value added (EVA).	The question indicates that the changes have been implemented partly in an attempt to increase profit so it is appropriate to incorporate this measure. If the investment base has changed significantly it may be preferable to use EVA.
Increase revenue	Percentage increase in total revenue	The question also indicates that the changes have been implemented partly in an attempt to increase revenues so it is also appropriate to incorporate this measure.
Customer perspective		
Increase customer acquisition	Total sales to new customers	The changes were made to attract new customers so the proposed measure provides feedback on the impact of the changes that were made.
Increase customer retention	Number of customers cancelling their contacts each period.	Measures were introduced in an attempt to retain customers. This proposed measure also provides feedback on the impact of the changes that were made.
Internal business perspective		
Improve after sales service quality	Number of complaints each period or percentage of total calls that are not resolved after one call.	The company transferred its call centre back to the home country in order to reduce the number of complaints and also reduce the number of calls to resolve an issue. Either of the proposed performance measures should provide feedback on the action that has been taken.
Reduce number of broadband contracts cancelled.	Number of broadband contracts cancelled each period.	This measure should provide feedback on the impact of the attempt to improve the broadband service quality.
Learning and growth perspective		
Increase employee satisfaction	Percentage of staff leaving per period	This measure should result in an improvement in customer service since it focuses on the retention of experienced staff. The end result should help to attract new customers and thus increase revenues.
Employee skill levels	Training hours per employee	This measure should also encourage an improvement in customer service thus helping to attract new customers and maintain existing customers.

(b) The company should consider increasing the minimum contract period from 3 months to 12 months. Significant set-up costs will be incurred for new customers and it is unlikely that profits will be earned from customers that leave soon after the three-month period has expired.

Pay-tv customers own the boxes so they can cancel their contract after the first three months and can use the set-top box with its free channels after cancellation. The company should consider renting the boxes rather than selling them and also provide an option to introduce a purchase charge for the boxes if they choose to cancel.

14.14 (a) See 'The balanced scorecard' in Chapter 14 for the answer to this question.

(b) The measures proposed for the financial perspective (share price and earnings per share) are identical to the existing performance measures that have been used. They represent historical short-term measures and it is claimed that economic value added provides a better measure of the economic value added to shareholder wealth. If earnings per share and share price are also retained it is preferable to show the growth in these measures over time.

The customer perspective focuses only on the patients but does not take into account other customers who pay for the products (e.g. government and insurers). Measures of cost comparisons and customer satisfaction with competitors would be appropriate.

The internal process perspective measure appear to directly address one of the objectives from the board's strategy (improve the efficiency of drug development) by incorporating appropriate measures of manufacturing excellence and efficiency in the testing process.

The learning and growth perspective focuses on the innovation objective. Appropriate measures include time to the market and the percentage of drugs that are finally improved. The trend in improvements in these measures and comparisons with industry competitors should also be reported for these measures.

(c) The key stakeholders are the government, the drug companies, the healthcare providers and their funders, and the patients. The government is an influential stakeholder because it has the power (by the appointment of trustees) over senior appointments and the funding of BDR. The drug companies have influence over BDR since they determine the testing environment for the products. Although BDR must be seen to be independent of the drug companies it is in BDR's interest to have a successful drug development industry in order to achieve its goal of encouraging new drug development. The healthcare providers will have an interest in the quality of the approval process so they can have confidence in the medication that they prescribe. The patients will have an interest in development in new innovative treatments being quickly and safely brought to market.

(d) The objectives at BDR are more qualitative and more of a non-financial nature when compared with PT. It will therefore be more difficult to set quantifiable measures. There is also the danger that any quantifiable measures that are established will be focused on to a greater extent than the qualitative objectives. BDR will have a more complex balanced scorecard compared with PT due to the diverse nature of its important stakeholders. The principal stakeholder is the government and this presents political dimensions that will influence performance measurement. The primary objective at PT is financial whereas BDR has are several key objectives that are difficult to prioritize. Stakeholders may also have conflicting objectives so it will be more difficult to prioritize the measures that are incorporated in the balanced scorecard.

14.15 (a) Success within areas focusing on the customer perspective will lead to improved customer satisfaction. This should improve the customer perception of services provided by the company and thus lead to an increase in market share and also the potential to increase selling prices if the company is perceived to offer a better service. This in turn should lead to an increase in sales revenues and the increase in selling prices should improve the profit margins. Increased volumes should improve capacity utilization by increasing the loads delivered by the vehicles. The end result should be an increase in return on capital employed arising from an improvement in operating profit without additional capital expenditure.

(b) In order to meet customers' transport needs it is necessary to be able to meet all delivery requests. This can be measured as follows:

$$\frac{\text{Total number of packages transported (548 000)}}{\text{Total number of customer transport requests (610 000)}}$$
= 89.8%

Ability to deliver packages quickly will depend on the distances travelled for the different packages so it is inevitable that long distance deliveries will take longer than short distance deliveries. Therefore, a measure based on time taken per kilometre which a package travels should be used:

$$\frac{\text{Total minutes spent in transit by each package (131 520 000)}}{\text{Total package kilometres travelled (65 760 000)}}$$
= 2.0

Ability to deliver packages on time requires that the packages are delivered within the time window given to the customer. This can be measured as follows:

$$\frac{\text{Deliveries within window (548 000 − 21 920)}}{\text{Total number of packages transported (548 000)}}$$
= 96%

The ability to deliver packages safely can be measured by the number of undamaged packages delivered within the time window given to the customer:

$$\frac{\text{Deliveries of undamaged packages (548 000 − 8 220)}}{\text{Total number of packages transported (548 000)}}$$
= 98.5%

The obvious danger of measuring performance using the number of complaints is that some customers may not bother to complain when a package is not delivered safely or on time. Instead they may migrate to competitors resulting in the company losing repeat business. This could be avoided by introducing a system that monitors late deliveries and also providing some form of compensation for late deliveries for both customers that complain and do not complain. Some customers may also make unreasonable complaints or complaints may arise because of factors that are beyond the company's control. The measure records all complaints without distinguishing whether they are reasonable or not. This can be overcome by using the number or customers that have been compensated because of delivery problems rather than the total number of complaints.

(c) It is assumed that senior management are members of the board resulting in them being involved in setting their own rewards. Therefore there is a danger that easily achievable targets will be set, resulting in potential large bonuses that will reduce profits that could be distributed to shareholders or reinvested in the business to increase shareholder value. The bonus scheme should be linked to the BSC to ensure that the objectives of the senior management are congruent with those of the shareholders. At present, return on capital represents a key performance measure within the financial perspective but a value based measure such as economic value added is preferable since this measure is more closely linked to shareholder value.

The current method of performance evaluation is too subjective and it is proposed that managers should be involved in setting their own bonus targets. Given that the targets are used to set the financial rewards, there is a danger that easily achievable standards will be set. Challenging targets should be set at a higher management level. Targets are set that are easily achievable or very difficult to achieve will not motivate the managers. At the operational level attempts should be made to ensure that the targets mainly include items that are controllable by the managers. Ideally measures applicable to the operation managers should cascade down from the strategic measures in the BSC. These measures will normally fall within the customer and process perspectives.

14.16 (a) The answer should provide a description of the four perspectives of the balanced scorecard (BSC) as described in Chapter 14. In particular, the description should emphasize that an organization's strategy is implemented by specifying the major objectives for each of the four objectives and translating them into specific targets, performance measures and initiatives.

Within the financial perspective Soup currently uses return on capital employed (ROCE) as its key financial performance measure, but as indicated in Chapter 12 (see 'Return on investment') this can encourage short-term decisions to be taken at the expense of long-term success. It is apparent that Soup has purchased old trains and not invested in new trains. The question indicates that the trains are becoming unreliable and their condition is deteriorating and in the long term this will reduce customer satisfaction and financial performance. This may account for soup's high ROCE (see 'Impact of depreciation' in Chapter 12). Maximizing ROCE may have encouraged Soup not to reinvest. Replacing ROCE with EVA provides a more suitable measure of increasing shareholder value (see Chapter 12 for an explanation).

Within the customer perspective Soup currently measures growth in passenger numbers which does provide some indication of customer satisfaction but in many situations passengers may have no alternative but to travel with Soup because of the lack of competition in some geographical areas. Soup could obtain more forward looking qualitative performance measures by using customer surveys to ascertain the importance and quality of the services provided by Soup (e.g. frequency and reliability of trains, overcrowding, comfort, wireless access etc.). The responses to the customer survey will enable Soup to focus on improving performance in the key areas identified by the survey.

Measures within the internal business perspective are likely to focus on reliability and overcrowding. The number of train journeys not arriving on time (analysed by the time length of the delay) and the number of train journeys cancelled could be used as measures of reliability. Overcrowding can be measured by the percentage of seats occupied, analysed by different routes and time periods. These measures also provide a measure of the utilization of services. High levels of utilization are necessary to support the measures within the financial perspective.

The innovation and learning perspective should focus on forward looking measures. Typical measures relate to the quality of online information systems available to customers and displayed on the trains, staff absenteeism, number of training hours, number of suggested improvements per employee, etc.

(b) Seat occupancy measured by the number of seats occupied expressed as a percentage of the total number of seats available can be used to measure the extent of overcrowding. Seats available per train is 490 (7 coaches × 70 seats) in Region A and 420 (7 coaches × 60 seats) in Region B.

	Region A	Region B
Seats available per train	490 (7 coaches × 70 seats)	420 (6 coaches × 70 seats)
Seats available per day:		
Peak times	1 960 (490 × 4)	1 680 (420 × 4)
Other times	2 940 (490 × 6)	3 360 (420 × 8)
Seat occupancy:		
Peak times	128% (2 500/1 960)	83% (1 400/1 680)
Other times	83% (2 450/2 940)	55% (1 850/3 360)

Total seat occupancy = Number of passengers (8 200)/ Total seats available (9 940) = 82.5%

The total seat occupancy ratio of 82.5 per cent indicates that on average the number of seats are not fully utilized. However, this measure is misleading since overcrowding may exist during peak times. Indeed, the above ratios indicate that 22 per cent of the passengers (i.e. 540) travelling at peak times in Region A are unable to obtain a seat. This represents 7 per cent (540/8 200) of all passengers. There are significant variations between regions and times travelled but overcrowding only occurs at peak times in Region A. The above analysis suggests that the claim that Soup's trains are overcrowded appears to be exaggerated.

(c) Care must be taken to avoid a proliferation of measures. It is important that the BSC does not become a long list of measures and objectives resulting in information overload. Another problem that Soup may encounter relates to the weighting that should be given to the performance measures in order to assess the relative importance that management assigns to each performance measure. Determining the weighting, however, is difficult but in the absence of weighting each measure will be viewed as being of equal importance.

Also some objectives are easier to measure than others. For example, it is apparent from the answer to part (b) that seat occupancy as a measure of overcrowding is easy to measure whereas measuring customer satisfaction is far more subjective and difficult to measure.

The measures chosen may also conflict. Passengers wish to avoid overcrowded trains but high levels of utilization of seat capacity and running fully occupied trains contributes to improved short-term financial measures.

14.17 (a) The key areas of performance referred to in the question are listed in Exhibit LN14.1 in Learning Note 14.1 that can be accessed on the digital online resources – financial, competitiveness, quality of service, flexibility, resource utilization and innovation.

Financial
- There has been a continuous growth in sales turnover during the period – increasing by 50 per cent in 2017, 10 per cent in 2018 and 35 per cent in 2019.
- Profits have increased at a higher rate than sales turnover – 84 per cent in 2017, 104 per cent in 2018 and 31 per cent in 2019.
- Profit margins (profit/sales) have increased from 14 per cent in 2016 to 31 per cent in 2019.

Competitiveness
Market share (total turnover/total turnover of all restaurants) has increased from 9.2 per cent in 2016 to 17.5 per cent in 2019. The proposals submitted to cater for special events has increased from 2 in 2016 to 38 in 2019. This has also been accompanied by an increase in the percentage of contracts won, which has increased over the years (20 per cent in 2016, 29 per cent in 2017, 52 per cent in 2018 and 66 per cent in 2019). Although all of the above measures suggest good performance in terms of this dimension, the average service delay at peak times increased significantly in 2019. This area requires investigating.

Quality of service
The increasing number of regular customers attending weekly suggests that they are satisfied with the quality of service. Other factors pointing to a high-level quality of service are the increase in complimentary letters from satisfied customers. Conversely the number of letters of complaint and reported cases of food poisoning have not diminished over the years. Therefore the performance measures do not enable a definitive assessment to be made on the level of quality of service.

Innovation/flexibility
Each year the restaurant has attempted to introduce a significant number of new meals. There has also been an increase each year in the number of special theme

evenings introduced and the turnover from special events has increased significantly over the years. These measures suggest that the restaurant has been fairly successful in terms of this dimension.

Resource utilization
The total meals served have increased each year. Idle time and annual operating hours with no customers have also decreased significantly each year. There has also been an increase in the average number of customers at peak times. The value of food wasted has varied over the years but was at the lowest level in 2019. All of the measures suggest that the restaurant has been particularly successful in terms of this dimension.

(b) *Financial*
Details of the value of business assets are required to measure profitability (e.g. return on investment). This is important because the seating capacity has been increased. This may have resulted in an additional investment in assets and there is a need to ascertain whether an adequate return has been generated. Analysis of expenditure by different categories (e.g. food, drinks, wages, etc.) is required to compare the trend in financial ratios (e.g. expense categories as a percentage of sales) and with other restaurants.

Competitiveness
Comparison with other restaurants should be made in respect of the measures described in (a) such as percentage of seats occupied and average service delay at peak times.

Quality of service
Consider using mystery shoppers (i.e. employment of outsiders) to visit this and competitor restaurants to assess the quality of service relative to competitors and to also identify areas for improvement.

Innovation/flexibility
Information relating to the expertise of the staff and their ability to perform multi-skill activities is required to assess the ability of the restaurant to cope with future demands.

Resource utilization
Data on the number of employees per customer served, and the percentage of tables occupied at peak and non-peak times would draw attention to areas where there may be a need to improve resource utilization.

14.18 (a) (i) Efficiency measures focus on the relationship between outputs and inputs. Optimum efficiency levels are achieved by maximizing the output from a given input or minimizing the resources used in order to achieve a particular output. Measures of effectiveness attempt to measure the extent to which the outputs of an organization achieve the latter's goals. An organization can be efficient but not effective. For example, it can use resources efficiently but fail to achieve its goals.
In organizations with a profit motive, effectiveness can be measured by return on investment. Inputs and outputs can be measured. Outputs represent the quality and amount of service offered. In profit-orientated organizations output can be measured in terms of sales revenues. This provides a useful proxy measure of the quality and amount of services offered. In non-profit-making organizations outputs cannot be easily measured in monetary terms. Consequently, it is difficult to state the objectives in quantitative terms and thus measure the extent to which objectives are being achieved.

If it is not possible to produce a statement of a particular objective in measurable terms, the objectives should be stated with sufficient clarity that there is some way of judging whether or not they have been achieved. However, the focus will tend to be on subjective judgements rather than quantitative measures of effectiveness. Because of the difficulty in measuring outputs, efficiency measures tend to focus entirely on input measures such as the amount of spending on services or the cost per unit of input.

(ii) Similar problems to those of measuring effectiveness and efficiency in non-profit-making organizations arise in measuring the performance of non-manufacturing activities in profit-orientated organizations. This is because it is extremely difficult to measure the output of non-manufacturing activities.

(b) (i) *Adherence to appointment times*
1   Percentage meeting appointment times.
2   Percentage within 15 minutes of appointment time.
3   Percentage more than 15 minutes late.
4   Average delay in meeting appointments.

Ability to contact and make appointments
It is not possible to obtain data on all those patients who have had difficulty in contacting the clinic to make appointments. However, an indication of the difficulties can be obtained by asking a sample of patients at periodic intervals to indicate on a scale (from no difficulty to considerable difficulty) the difficulty they experienced when making appointments. The number of complaints received and the average time taken to establish telephone contact with the clinic could also provide an indication of the difficulty patients experience when making appointments.

Monitoring programme
1   Comparisons with programmes of other clinics located in different regions.
2   Questionnaires asking respondents to indicate the extent to which they are aware of monitoring facilities currently offered.
3   Responses on level of satisfaction from patients registered on the programme.
4   Percentage of population undertaking the programme.

(ii)   Combining the measures into a 'quality of care' measure requires that weights be attached to each selected performance measure. The sum of the performance measures multiplied by the weights would represent an overall performance measure. The problems with this approach are that the weights are set subjectively, and there is a danger that staff will focus on those performance measures with the higher weighting and pay little attention to those with the lower weighting.

Chapter 15

15.15 (a)

	$
Sales price	25.00
25% profit margin	6.25
Target cost	18.75

	$	Working
Component A	2.15	
Component B	1.75	
Materials	2.50	1
Labour (0.4 hours at $15 per hour)	6.00	
Production overhead cost	1.89	
Distribution and sales cost	2.38	
Royalty fee	3.75	2
Forecast cost	20.42	
Cost gap	1.67	

Workings:
1 0.6kg × $4 per kg = $2.40/0.96 = $2.50
2 $25 × 0.15 = $3.75

(b)   Inbound logistics includes purchasing, receipt and storage of components and materials from a number of suppliers. Adopting just-in-time (JIT) purchasing may significantly reduce storage costs. The JIT supplier takes the responsibility for the quality of products supplied and meeting the required delivery schedules (see 'JIT purchasing arrangements' in Chapter 15 for a more detailed answer).

Scheduled deliveries fall within the outbound logistics category. Following the same schedule each week irrespective of load appears to be inefficient because the delivery process does not take into account the toy requirements at retail stores. Therefore the company may be delivering to retail outlets that do not require toys and thus incurring excessive transportation costs. A data processing system needs implementing that ensures that deliveries are matched with demand and that avoids small inefficient deliveries.

The company sells toy Z through its network of retail outlets. It may be possible to reduce costs by offering the toy for sale via the PBB website.

15.16 (a) *Cost of quality report*

	Volume	Rate $	Cost $
Prevention costs			
Supplier review			60 000
Appraisal costs			
Equipment testing	400	30	12 000
Internal failure costs			
Down time			375 000
Manufacturing rework	800	380	304 000
Total internal failure costs			679 000
External failure costs			
Customer support	500	58	29 000
Warranty repair	650	2 600	1 690 000
Total external failure costs			1 719 000
Total quality costs			2 470 000

(b)   See 'Cost of quality reports' in Chapter 15 for the answer to this question.

15.17 (a) Benchmarking involves the following:

1   Identify an activity that needs to be improved and identify organizations that are prepared to participate in the process.
    (GU has identified administration operations relating to teaching and research and the government has selected two large universities, rather than smaller universities, that are comparable for benchmarking. If possible it would be appropriate to include overseas universities in the exercise since they might adopt different approaches to practices that are uniform in Teeland.)

2   Identify key drivers of costs and revenues and appropriate performance indicators.
    (The key drivers have been identified and information extracted based on the activity per driver.)

3   Measure performance of the activities for all of the organisations participating in the benchmarking process.
    (The appropriate data has been gathered as requested by the government education ministry. This stage will more difficult in the private sector where there is no regulatory body and information may be commercially sensitive.)

4   Compare performances
    (This is the stage that is required in part (b) of the question.)

5   Identify and implement areas for improvement.
    (The procedures used at the benchmarked universities should be studied in detail and best practice should be implemented at GU.)

6   Monitor improvements
    (After completion the benchmarking process should be subject to review to ascertain if the improvements have been achieved.)

(b) Below details of the performance comparison arising from the benchmarking exercise are presented:

	GU $	AU $	BU $
Research			
contract management	78	87	97
laboratory management	226	257	281
Teaching facilities management	951	1 197	920
Student support services	71	89	73
Teachers support services	506	532	544
Accounting	204	204	197
Human resources	156	156	191
IT management	817	803	737
General services	2 153	2 088	2 286

Note:

It is assumed that the performance drivers are as follows:

Research categories – Research contract values supported
Teaching facilities and student support – Student numbers
Remaining categories – Staff numbers

Therefore the performance comparison for the research categories is per $000 of contract value supported, teaching facilities and student support services per student and the remaining items per staff member.

Comments
The performance comparison indicates that GU is the most successful university in controlling costs associated with research contracts. AU spends most per student on its teaching facilities and student support although it has the smallest number of students. Higher student pass rates and future success in gaining employment may reflect the more expensive teaching environment at AU but these quality measures are not incorporated in the benchmarking exercise. In accounting and general services, all the universities are similar and in human resources management, BU is 22% per cent higher than the other universities. In IT management BU's costs are 10% lower than GU's. It should be noted, however, that comparing performance is difficult because of differences such as the mix of subjects taught and researched.

15.18 (a)

Prevention costs:	Quantity	Rate $	Total costs $000	% of sales
Design engineering	48 000	96	4 608	1.28
Process engineering	54 000	70	3 780	1.05
Training			180	0.05
Total prevention costs			8 568	2.38
Appraisal costs:				
Inspection (manufacturing)	288 000	50	14 400	4.00
Product testing			72	0.02
Total appraisal costs			14 472	4.02
Internal failure costs:				
Rework (Manufacturing)	2 100	4 800	10 080	2.80
Total internal failure costs			10 080	2.80
External failure costs:				
Customer support (Marketing)	2 700	240	648	0.18
Transportation costs (Distribution)	2 700	280	756	0.21
Warranty repair (Customer service)	2 700	4 600	12 420	3.45
Total external failure costs			13 824	3.84
Total costs for all 4 categories			46 944	13.04
Opportunity costs	1 800	7 200	12 960	3.60
Total quality costs			59 904	16.64

Quality cost statements frequently exclude opportunity costs such as the foregone contribution on lost sales arising from poor quality. This is because the lost sales are very difficult to estimate. Because of this many companies omit the opportunity costs arising from lost sales from their cost of quality reports. A compromise is to report opportunity costs separately (as in the above statement) and draw management's attention that estimates of such costs may be subject to a significant margin of error.

(b)

Option:	Rate	Option 1 $	Option 2 $
Cost of quality items:	$		
Additional design engineering costs	2 000	96	192 000
Additional process engineering costs	5 000	70	350 000
Additional inspection and testing costs	10 000	50	500 000
Savings in rework costs:			
Option 1	720	1 920	–1 382 400
Option 2	960	1 920	–1 843 200
Savings in customer support costs:			
Option 1	600	96	–57 600
Option 2	840	96	–80 640
Saving in transportation costs:			
Option 1	600	210	–126 000
Option 2	840	210	–176 400
Savings in warranty repair costs:			
Option 1	600	1 700	–1 020 000
Option 2	840	1 700	–1 428 000
Additional sales:			
Option 1	300	7 200	–2 160 000
Option 2	360	7 200	–2 592 000
Incremental savings		–4 246 000	–5 578 240

Option 2 is preferable since it provides the greater incremental savings.

15.19 (a) (i) *Performance report for period ending 30 November (traditional analysis)*

Expenses

	Budget (€)	Actual (€)	Variance (€)
Salaries	600 000	667 800	67 800A
Supplies	60 000	53 000	7 000F
Travel cost	120 000	127 200	7 200A
Technology cost	100 000	74 200	25 800F
Occupancy cost	120 000	137 800	17 800A
Total	1 000 000	1 060 000	60 000A

Performance report for period ending 30 November (activity-based analysis)

Activities

	(€)	(€)	(€)
Routing/scheduling – new products	200 000	169 600	30 400F
Routing/scheduling – existing products	400 000	360 400	39 600F
Remedial re-routing/scheduling	50 000	127 200	77 200A
Special studies – specific orders	100 000	84 800	15 200F
Training	100 000	159 000	59 000A
Management and administration	150 000	159 000	9 000A
Total	1 000 000	1 060 000	60 000A

(ii) See 'Activity-based budgeting' in Chapter 9 for the answer to this question. In particular, the answer should stress:

(i) The enhanced visibility of activity-based budgeting (ABB) by focusing on outcomes (activities) rather than a listing by expense categories.

(ii) The cost of activities are highlighted thus identifying high-cost non-value-added activities that need to be investigated.

(iii) ABB identifies resource requirements to meet the demand for activities whereas traditional budgeting adopts an incremental approach.

(iv) Excess resources are identified that can be eliminated or redeployed.

(v) ABB enables more realistic budgets to be set.

(vi) ABB avoids arbitrary cuts in specific budget areas in order to meet overall financial targets.

(vii) It is claimed that ABB leads to increased management commitment to the budget process because it enables management to focus on the objectives of each activity and compare the outcomes with the costs that are allocated to the activity.

(iii) The ABB statement shows a comparison of actual with budget by activities. All of the primary value-adding activities (i.e. the first, second and fourth activities in the budget statement) have favourable variances. Remedial re-routing is a non-value-added activity and has the highest adverse variance. Given the high cost, top priority should be given to investigating the activity with a view to eliminating it, or to substantially reducing the cost by adopting alternative working practices. Training and management and administration are secondary activities that support the primary activities. Actual training expenditure exceeds budget by 50 per cent and the reason for the over-spending should be investigated.

For each activity it would be helpful if the costs were analysed by expense items (such as salaries, supplies, etc.) to pinpoint the cost build-up of the activities and to provide clues indicating why an overspending on some activities has occurred.

Cost driver usage details should also be presented in a manner similar to that illustrated in Exhibit 9.2 in Chapter 9. Many organizations that have adopted ABC have found it useful to report budgeted and actual cost driver rates. The trend in cost driver rates is monitored and compared with similar activities undertaken within other divisions where a divisionalized structure applies. As indicated in Chapter 15, care must be taken when interpreting cost driver rates.

For additional points to be included in the answer see 'Activity-based management' in Chapter 15.

(b) The cost driver rates are as follows:

Product design = €250 per design hour (€2m/8000 hours)

Purchasing = €50 per purchase order (€200 000/4000 orders)

Production (excluding depreciation) = €100 per machine hour ((€1 500 000 – €300 000)/12 000 hours)

Packing = €20 per cubic metre (€400 000/20 000)

Distribution = €5 per kg (€600 000/120 000)

The activity-based overhead cost per unit is as follows:

		(€)
Product design	(400 design hours at €250 per hour = €100 000 divided by life-cycle output of 5000 units)	20.00
Purchasing	(5 purchase orders at 50 units per order costing a total of €250 for an output of 250 units)	1.00
Production	(0.75 machine hours at €100 per machine hour)	75.00
Depreciation	(Asset cost over life cycle of 4 years = 16 quarters' depreciation at €8000 per quarter divided by life-cycle output of 5000 units)	25.60
Packing	(0.4 cubic metres at €20)	8.00
Distribution	(3 kg at €5)	15.00
Total cost		144.60

15.20 (a) The absorption cost per dish for the customer repair department is $8.03 ($707 000/ (16 000 × 5.5 dishes). This cost is added to other direct costs that are incurred to obtain a total cost per dish. In addition, the financial director (FD) adds an additional $100 per specialized dish in order to compensate for the extra work involved. This results in an over-absorption of total cost since $8.03 fully absorbs the costs so an extra $160 000 (1600 specialized dishes at $100) of costs will absorbed.

The ABC cost per dish is computed as follows:

	Standard dishes	Specialized dishes
Activity cost assignment	$537 320	$169 680
Number of orders	14 400	1 600
Average dish per order	6	1
Total number of dishes	86 400	1 600
ABC cost per dish	$6.22	$106.05

The company sells two different types of dish that utilize different quantities of resources resulting in the ABC system highlighting customer care costs of $106.05 per unit for specialized dishes and $6.22 for standard dishes. Therefore the current system overcosts the standard dishes and understates the profit contribution. The cost of specialized dishes of $106.05 using ABC is similar to the finance director's estimate of $108.03 but no attempt has been made to adjust the cost of standard dishes to reflect the over-absorption of overheads outlined above arising from the FD's adjustment.

The major activities that contribute to this higher cost of specialized dishes are handling sales enquiries/preparing quotes and handling complaints. The cost per dish for these activities for specialized dishes is significantly higher than the unit costs for standard dishes. This is not surprising, as the specialized dishes require a customized service which cannot be standardized.

ABC highlights the activities that are causing the higher product/service costs thus highlighting the potential for cost reduction or ensuring that customers pay for the resources consumed. It should, however be questioned whether the ABC analysis meets the cost/benefit criterion given that the FD's estimate of resource consumption is similar to the ABC analysis provided that a correction for the over-allocation of total costs is made.

(b) The ABC analysis indicates that handling enquiries and quotes and post-sale complaints handling are the high cost activities that in total consume 65 per cent of the resources of the customer care department. These activities therefore have the potential for significantly reducing total costs. Approximately 46 per cent (16 000/35 000) of enquiries are converted to orders. Ideally, this ratio should be benchmarked with competitors but this may be difficult given the commercially sensitive nature of this information.

Complaints handling is a non-value added activity which should be prioritized for further investigation in order to minimize these activities. The ABC analysis highlights the high costs of this activity, accounting for approximately 25 per cent of total costs of the customer care department. The number of complaints is high accounting for 20 per cent (3200/16 000) of orders. The high cost and level of complaints is of particular concern given that they have been identified by customers and thus represent external failure costs. The causes of the complaints should be investigated and eliminated.

Chapter 16

16.13

1 Cost reductions arising from a reduction in wastage and disposal costs and any possible additional revenues as a result of recycling waste.

2 By meeting the environmental concerns of customers the company's image will be improved and this may generate increased sales.

3 A lack of awareness of environmental costs can result in environmental penalty and clean-up costs (e.g. the BP oil spill in the Gulf of Mexico has cost the company billions of dollars in penalties and fines).

16.14 (a) See 'International transfer pricing' in Chapter 13 for the answer to this question. Besides the ethical issues and legal considerations other criticisms relate to the distortions in the divisional profit reporting system. Also divisional autonomy will be undermined if the transfer prices are imposed on the divisional managers.

(b) The ethical limitations relate to multinational companies using the transfer pricing system to reduce the amount paid in custom duties, taxation and the manipulation of dividends remitted. Furthermore, using the transfer prices for these

purposes is likely to be illegal, although there is still likely to be some scope for manipulation that is within the law. It is important that multinational companies are seen to be acting in a socially responsible manner. Any bad publicity relating to using the transfer pricing system purely to avoid taxes and custom duties will be very harmful to the image of the organization. Nevertheless tax management and the ability to minimize corporate taxes is an important task for management if it is to maximize shareholder value. Thus it is important that management distinguish between tax avoidance and tax evasion. Adopting illegal practices is not acceptable and management must ensure that their transfer pricing policies do not contravene the regulations and laws of the host countries in which they operate.

16.15 (a) Environmental costs can be categorized as environmental prevention, detection and internal and external failure costs. Periodically, an environmental cost report should be presented with costs reported by these four cost categories (see 'Environmental cost management' in Chapter 16 for an explanation of the report and the four cost categories).

(b) In an input/output analysis, all incoming and outgoing materials and energy flows are summarized over the entire production site and represented on a table. With this approach, an approximate evaluation of the environmental relevance of a company's operations can be made. One major difficulty is that the analysis does not support the allocation of the material flows to the products or specific processes resulting in the origins of the inputs and outputs cannot be identified.

ABC analyses cost by activities rather than departments and thus reports information on activities that cross departmental boundaries. ABC thus gives visibility to the cost of undertaking the environmental activities that make up the organization. With traditional costing systems environmental costs tend to be hidden in the overhead costs across many different departments. This will assist the company in identifying and controlling environmental costs.

A life cycle view estimates and accumulates costs and revenues over a product's entire life cycle rather than one accounting period in order to determine whether the profits earned during the manufacturing phase will cover the costs incurred during the pre- and post-manufacturing stages. Identifying the costs incurred during the different stages of a product's life cycle provides an insight into understanding and managing the total costs incurred throughout its life cycle. In particular, life cycle costing helps management to understand the cost consequences of developing and making a product and to identify areas in which cost reduction efforts are likely to be most effective.

(c) The costing approach used by the company ignores capital costs, environmental costs and the cost of decommissioning. A life cycle analysis aims to capture the costs over the entire life cycle of the product. The life cycle analysis is as follows:

	$m
Production costs	82.3
Marketing costs	17
Development costs	8.6
	107.9
Environmental costs	
Waste filtration	8.1
Carbon dioxide exhaust extractor	5.3
	13.4
Other costs	
Decommissioning costs	18
Total costs	139.3

Total revenues are $149.4m giving a lifetime profit of $10.1m. Life cycle costing provides visibility at the design stage of the costs that will be incurred at each stage of the production process and identifies in advance important costs that need to be focused on (e.g. the high costs of decommissioning). The traditional product profit analysis shows a surplus of $41.5m over the life of the product but it does not incorporate environmental and decommissioning costs.

16.16 (a) *Workings in millions of kg*

	2009 Base year	2017	2018	Change on base year
Commercial Fleet Diesel	105.4	77.7	70.1	−33%
Commercial Fleet Petrol	11.6	0.4	0.0	−100%
Company Car Diesel	15.1	14.5	12.0	−21%
Company Car Petrol	10.3	3.8	2.2	−79%
Other road travel (Diesel)	0.5	1.6	1.1	120%
Other road travel (Petrol)	3.1	0.5	0.3	−90%
Rail travel	9.2	9.6	3.4	−63%
Air Travel (short haul)	5.0	4.4	3.1	−38%
Air Travel (long haul)	5.1	7.1	5.4	6%
Hire Cars (Diesel)	0.6	1.8	2.9	383%
Hire Cars (Petrol)	6.7	6.1	6.1	−9%
Total	172.6	127.5	106.6	
Index	100%	74%	62%	

The following is an analysis by the three main categories (road, air and rail travel):

	2009 Base year	2017	2018	Change on base year
Road travel	153.3	106.4	94.7	−38%
Air travel	10.1	11.5	8.5	−16%
Rail travel	9.2	9.6	3.4	−63%
Total	172.6	127.5	106.6	−38%

The company's goal is that by 2025, it will have reduced its environmental impact by 60 per cent (compared to 2009). Overall, it has cut emissions by 38 per cent in the first nine years (from 100 per cent in the base year to 62 per cent nine years later). There was a reduction of 16 per cent in the last year of measurement. If this rate of improvement is maintained then the company will reduce its emissions by approximately 80 per cent) by the end of the target period. The analysis by the three main categories indicates that the largest cut has been in rail-related emissions (63 per cent). Road emissions are the dominant category and they have fallen by 38 per cent but it appears that they will meet the target reduction of 60 per cent in nine years' time. Air travel is not falling at the same pace but this may be due to greater globalization of the industry requiring managers to visit overseas suppliers and clients. Rail travel has the largest percentage reduction. The major change shown in the above workings is the move from petrol to diesel-powered motor vehicles, which, in the commercial fleet, is almost complete.

(b) The analysis could be improved by collecting data on the total distances travelled so that the effect of switching away from physical meetings and using teleconferencing facilities can be measured. Data relating to overseas travel could be monitored since cutting air travel appears to be an area where improvements can be made. The collection of data relating to distance travelled will enable the average emission per km travelled to be measured.

GLOSSARY

Absorption costing system   A costing system that allocates all manufacturing costs, including fixed manufacturing costs, to products and values unsold stocks at their total cost of manufacture.

Accounting rate of return   A method of appraising capital investments where the average annual profits from a project are divided into the average investment cost, also known as return on investment and return on capital employed.

Action controls   Observing the actions of individuals as they go about their work, also known as behavioural controls.

Activity   The aggregation of different tasks, events or units of work that cause the consumption of resources.

Activity cost centres   Cost centres in which costs are accumulated by activities.

Activity cost drivers   A cost driver used to assign the costs assigned to an activity cost centre to products.

Activity measure   Any factor whose change causes a change in the total cost of an activity, also known as a cost driver.

Activity-based budgeting (ABB)   An approach to budgeting that takes cost objects as the starting point, determines the necessary activities and then estimates the resources that are required for the budget period.

Activity-based cost management (ABCM)   The cost management applications applied to activity-based costing, without the need to assign activity costs to products, also known as activity-based management.

Activity-based costing (ABC)   A system of cost allocation that aims to use mainly cause-and-effect cost allocations by assigning costs to activities.

Activity-based management (ABM)   The cost management applications applied to activity-based costing, without the need to assign activity costs to products, also known as activity-based cost management.

Allocation base   The basis used to allocate costs to cost objects.

Annual percentage rate (APR)   A discount or interest rate quoted as a rate per annum.

Annuity   An asset that pays a fixed sum each period for a specific number of periods.

Appraisal costs   The costs incurred to ensure that materials, products and services meet quality conformance standards.

Arbitrary allocation   The allocation of costs using a cost base that is not a significant determinant of cost.

Aspiration level   The level of performance that the person responsible for the budget hopes to attain.

Assignable causes   Factors that can be assigned to a known cause, which may or may not be worth investigating further.

Avoidable costs   Costs that may be saved by not adopting a given alternative.

Balanced scorecard   A strategic management tool that integrates financial and non-financial measures of performance in a single concise report, with the aim of incorporating performance management within the strategic management process.

Batch production functional layout   A plant layout in which products pass in batches through a number of specialist departments that normally contain a group of similar machines.

Batch-related activities   Activities that are performed each time a batch of goods is produced.

Behavioural controls   Controls that involve observing the actions of individuals as they go about their work, also known as action controls.

Benchmarking   A mechanism for achieving continuous improvement by measuring products, services or activities against those of other best performing organizations.

Beyond budgeting   A term used to describe alternative approaches, such as rolling forecasts, that can be used instead of annual budgeting.

Big data   A term that describes the large volume of raw data, both structured and unstructured, that inundates a business on a daily basis. It includes information such as email messages, social media postings, phone calls, purchase transactions, website traffic and video streams.

Bill of materials   A document stating the required quantity of materials for each operation to complete the product.

Blanket overhead rate   An overhead rate that assigns indirect costs to cost objects using a single overhead rate for the whole organization, also known as plant-wide rate.

Bottom-up budget setting Allowing individuals to participate in the setting of budgets and targets.

Break-even chart A chart that plots total costs and total revenues against sales volume and indicates the break-even point.

Break-even point The level of output at which costs are balanced by sales revenue and neither a profit nor loss will occur.

Budget A financial plan for implementing management decisions.

Budgetary control process The process of comparing actual and planned outcomes, and responding to any deviations from the plan.

Budgeted costs Expected costs for an entire activity or operation.

Budgeted overhead rate An overhead rate based on estimated annual expenditure on overheads and levels of activity.

Budgeting The implementation of the long-term plan for the year ahead through the development of detailed financial plans.

Business process re-engineering Examining business processes and making substantial changes to how the organization operates and the redesign of how work is done through activities.

Business-sustaining activities Activities performed to support the organization as a whole, also known as facility-sustaining activities.

Cash budget A budget that aims to ensure that sufficient cash is available at all times to meet the level of operations that are outlined in all other budgets.

Cause-and-effect allocation The use of an allocation base that is a significant determinant of cost, also known as driver tracing.

Cellular manufacturing A plant layout based on product flow lines, which are normally U-shaped.

Cloud computing Enables software to be located on servers outside the company owned by an external IT provider. The provider then makes the software available over the Internet to the companies.

Committed costs Costs that have not yet been incurred but that will be incurred in the future on the basis of decisions that have already been made, also known as locked-in costs.

Compounding interest The concept of adding the interest earned to the original capital invested so that further interest is generated.

Consumption ratio The proportion of each activity consumed by a product.

Continuous budgeting An approach to budgeting in which the annual budget is broken down into months for the first three months and into quarters for the rest of the year, with a new quarter being added as each quarter ends, also known as rolling budgeting.

Continuous improvement An ongoing search to reduce costs, eliminate waste and improve the quality and performance of activities that increase customer value or satisfaction.

Contribution graph A graph that plots variable costs and total costs against sales volume, and fixed costs represent the difference between the total cost line and the variable cost line.

Contribution margin The margin calculated by deducting variable expenses from sales revenue.

Contribution margin ratio The proportion of sales available to cover fixed costs and provide for profit, calculated by dividing the contribution margin by the sales revenue, also known as profit-volume ratio.

Control The process of ensuring that a firm's activities conform to its plan and that its objectives are achieved.

Control process The process of comparing actual and planned outcomes, and responding to any deviations from the plan.

Controllability principle The principle that it is appropriate to charge to an area of responsibility only those costs that are significantly influenced by the manager of that responsibility centre.

Controllable investment The net asset base that is controllable or strongly influenced by divisional managers.

Controllable profit A profit figure that is computed by deducting from divisional revenues all those costs that are controllable by a divisional manager.

Controls Measurement and information used to help determine what control action needs to be taken.

Conversion cost The sum of direct labour and manufacturing overhead costs; it is the cost of converting raw materials in to finished products.

Corporate objectives Specific, measurable statements, often expressed in financial terms, of what the organization as a whole wishes to achieve.

Cost accounting Accounting concerned with cost accumulation for inventory valuation to meet the requirements of external reporting and internal profit measurement.

Cost allocation The process of assigning costs to cost objects where a direct measure of the resources consumed by these cost objects does not exist.

Cost centres A location to which costs are assigned, also known as a cost pools and responsibility centres such as when managers are normally accountable for only those costs that are under their control (also known as expense centres).

Cost driver The basis used to allocate costs to cost objects in an ABC system.

Cost leadership strategy A strategy adopted by an organization that aims to be the lowest cost producer within a market segment thus enabling it to compete on the basis of lower selling prices than its competitors.

Cost object Any activity for which a separate measurement of costs is desired.

Cost of capital The financial return that an organization could receive if, instead of investing cash in a capital project, it invested the same amount in securities on the financial markets, also known as the opportunity cost of an investment, the minimum required rate of return, the discount rate and the interest rate.

Cost of quality report A report indicating the total cost to the organization of producing products or services that do not conform with quality requirements.

Cost pool A location to which overhead costs are assigned, also known as a cost centre.

Cost-benefit analysis (CBA) An investment appraisal technique developed for use by non-profit-making organizations that defines the costs and benefits of a project in much wider terms than those included in investment appraisals undertaken in the pursuit of profit maximization.

Cost-plus pricing An approach to pricing customized products and services that involves calculating product costs and adding the desired profit margin.

Cultural controls A set of values, social norms and beliefs that are shared by members of the organization and that influence their actions.

Customer perspective One of the perspectives considered on the balanced scorecard, focusing on how the organization appears to its customers.

Customer profitability analysis The analysis of profits by individual customers or customer categories.

Customer value propositions The attributes that drive core objectives and measures relating to the customer perspective of an organization.

Customer-sustaining activities Activities that are performed to support the relationship with customers.

Cycle time The length of time from start to completion of a product or service and is the sum of processing time, move time, wait time and inspection time.

Data Mere records of raw facts that are not organized to be meaningful.

Decision packages A decision package represents the incremental packages reflecting different levels of effort that may be expended to undertake a specific group of activities within an organization.

Decreasing returns to scale A situation that arises when unit costs rise as volume increases.

Defender strategy Firms pursuing a defender strategy perceive a great deal of stability in their external environment. They compete on product price, quality and customer service rather than innovation and product and market development.

Degree of operating leverage The contribution margin divided by the profit for a given level of sales.

Differential cash flows The cash flows that will be affected by a decision that is to be taken, also known as incremental cash flows.

Differential costs The difference between the costs of each alternative action under consideration, also known as incremental costs.

Differentiation strategy A strategy adopted by an organization that seeks to offer products or services that are considered by its customers to be superior or unique relative to its competitors.

Direct cost tracing The process of assigning a cost directly to a cost object.

Direct costing A costing system that assigns only direct costs, to products or services.

Direct costing system A costing system that assigns only direct manufacturing costs, not fixed manufacturing costs, to products or services, also known as variable costing system or marginal costing system.

Direct labour costs Labour costs that can be specifically and exclusively identified with a particular cost object.

Direct labour hour rate An hourly overhead rate calculated by dividing the cost centre overheads by the number of direct labour hours.

Direct material costs Material costs that can be specifically and exclusively identified with a particular cost object.

Discount rate The financial return that an organization could receive if, instead of investing cash in a capital project, it invested the same amount in securities on the financial markets, also known as the opportunity cost of an investment, the minimum required rate of return, the cost of capital and the interest rate.

Discounted cash flow (DCF) A technique used to compare returns on investments that takes account of the time value of money.

Discounted payback method A version of the payback method of appraising capital investments in which future cash flows are discounted to their present values.

Discounted present value The value today of cash to be received in the future, calculated by discounting.

Discounted rate of return A technique used to make capital investment decisions that takes into account the time value of money, representing the true interest rate earned on an investment over the course of its economic life, also known as internal rate of return (IRR).

Discounting The process of converting cash to be received in the future into a value at the present time by the use of an interest rate.

Discretionary costs Costs such as advertising and research where management has some discretion as to the amount it will budget.

Discretionary expense centres Cost centres where output cannot be measured in quantitative terms and there are no clearly observable relationships between inputs and outputs.

Diversification strategy A strategy of investing in a range of different projects in order to minimize risk.

Divisional net profit before taxes A profit figure obtained by allocating all general and administrative expenses to divisions.

Divisional profit contribution Controllable profit, less any non-controllable expenses that are attributable to a division, and which would be avoidable if the division was closed.

Divisionalized organizational structure A decentralized organizational structure in which a firm is split into separate divisions.

Driver tracing The use of an allocation base that is a significant determinant of cost, also known as cause-and-effect allocation.

Duration drivers A cost driver used to assign the costs assigned to an activity cost centre to products that is based on the amount of time required to perform an activity.

e-Business The use of information and communication technologies to support any business activities, including buying and selling.

e-Commerce The use of information and communication technologies to support the purchase, sale and exchange of goods.

Economic value added (EVA(TM)) A refinement of the residual income measure that incorporates adjustments to the divisional financial performance measure for distortions introduced by generally accepted accounting principles, trademarked by the Stern Stewart consulting organization.

Employee empowerment Providing employees with relevant information to allow them to make continuous improvements to the output of processes without the authorization by superiors.

Engineering methods Methods of analyzing cost behaviour that are based on the use of engineering analyses of technological relationships between inputs and outputs.

Engineering studies Detailed studies of each operation, based on careful specifications of materials, labour and equipment and on controlled observations of operations.

Enterprise resource planning system (ERPS) A set of integrated software application modules that aim to control all information flows within a company.

Environmental detection costs The costs incurred to ensure that a firm's activities, products and processes conform to regulatory laws and voluntary standards.

Environmental external failure costs The costs incurred on activities performed after discharging waste into the environment.

Environmental internal failure costs The costs incurred from performing activities that have produced contaminants and waste that have not been discharged into the environment.

Environmental prevention costs The costs of activities undertaken to prevent the production of waste that could cause damage to the environment.

Ethical behaviour Behaviour that is consistent with the standards of honesty, fairness and social responsibility that have been adopted by the organization.

***Ex post* budget adjustments** The adjustment of a budget to the environmental and economic conditions that the manager's actually faced during the period.

***Ex post* variance analysis approach** An approach to variance analysis in which actual results are compared with adjusted standards based on the conditions in which managers actually operated during the period.

Expense centres Responsibility centres whose managers are normally accountable for only those costs that are under their control, also known as cost centres.

External failure costs The costs incurred when products or services fail to conform to requirements or satisfy customer needs after they have been delivered.

Facility sustaining costs Common costs that are incurred to support the organization as a whole and are which are normally not affected by a decision that is to be taken.

Facility-sustaining activities Activities performed to support the organization as a whole, also known as business-sustaining activities.

Feedback control Monitoring outputs achieved against desired outputs and taking whatever corrective action is necessary if a deviation exists.

Feedback loops Parts of a control system that allow for review and corrective action to ensure that actual outcomes conform with planned outcomes.

Feed-forward control Comparing predictions of expected outputs with the desired outputs and taking prior corrective action to minimize any differences.

Final products Products sold by a receiving division to the outside world.

Financial accounting Accounting concerned with the provision of information to parties that are external to the organization.

Financial perspective One of the perspectives considered on the balanced scorecard, focusing on how the organization looks to shareholders.

First stage allocation bases The various bases, such as area, book value of machinery and number of employees, used to allocate indirect costs to production and service centres.

Fixed costs Costs that remain constant for a specified time period and which are not affected by the volume of activity.

Fixed overhead expenditure variance The difference between the budgeted fixed overheads and the actual fixed overhead spending.

Flexible budgets Budgets in which the uncontrollable volume effects on cost behaviour are removed from the manager's performance reports.

Focusing strategy A strategy which involves seeking competitive advantage by focusing on a narrow segment of the market that has special needs that are poorly served by other competitors in the industry. Competitive advantage is based on adopting either a cost leadership or product/service differentiation strategy within the chosen segment.

Full cost The estimated sum of all resources that are committed to a product in the long run, also known as long-run cost.

Full costing system A costing system that allocates all manufacturing costs, including fixed manufacturing costs, to products and values unsold stocks at their total cost of manufacture.

Functional analysis A process that involves decomposing a product into its many elements or attributes and determining a price or value for each element that reflects the amount the customer is prepared to pay.

Functional organizational structure An organization in which all activities of a similar type within a company are placed under the control of the appropriate departmental head, who is responsible for only that part of the organization's activities.

Goal congruence The situation that exists when controls motivate employees to behave in a way that is in tune with the organization's goals.

High–low method A method of analysing cost behaviour that consists of selecting the periods of highest and lowest activity levels and comparing the changes in costs that result from the two levels in order to separate fixed and variable costs.

Increasing returns to scale A situation that arises when unit costs fall as volume increases

Incremental budgeting An approach to budgeting in which existing operations and the current budgeted allowance for existing activities are taken as the starting point for preparing the next annual budget and are then adjusted for anticipated changes.

Incremental cash flows The cash flows that will be affected by a decision that is to be taken, also known as differential cash flows.

Incremental costs The difference between the costs of each alternative action under consideration, also known as differential costs.

Indirect costs Costs that cannot be identified specifically and exclusively with a given cost object, also known as overheads.

Information Data that has been organized in a way so that it becomes understandable and useful for a particular purpose.

Information overload A situation that arises when users are provided with too much information to the extent that it becomes unmanageable and no longer useful.

Input/output analysis A technique that can be used to reduce the usage of environmental resources and costs. Inflows of resources such as water, materials and energy are recorded and balanced with outflows on the basis that, what comes in, must go out.

Integrated reporting An external report that aims to provide information on the financial and non-financial performance in a single document relating to the economy, society and the environment.

Intellectual capital The intangible benefits accessible by a firm from its workforce, and more broadly, from its established relationships with groups such as customers, suppliers and competitors. It is often used interchangeably with other terms such as 'knowledge capital', 'knowledge economy' and 'intangible assets.'

Interest rate The financial return that an organization could receive if, instead of investing cash in a capital project, it invested the same amount in securities on the financial markets, also known as the opportunity cost of an investment the minimum required rate of return, the cost of capital and the discount rate.

Intermediate products Goods transferred from the supplying division to the receiving division.

Internal business perspective One of the perspectives considered on the balanced scorecard, focusing on what the organization needs to excel at.

Internal failure costs The internal costs incurred when products and services fail to meet quality standards or customer needs.

Internal rate of return (IRR) A technique used to make capital investment decisions that takes into account the time value of money, representing the true interest rate earned on an investment over the course of its economic life, also known as discounted rate of return.

Internet commerce The buying and selling of goods and services over the Internet.

Investment centre Responsibility centres whose managers are responsible for both sales revenues and costs and also have responsibility and authority to make capital investment decisions.

Irrelevant costs and revenues Future costs and revenues that will not be affected by a decision.

Job cards A source document that records the amount of time spent on a particular job, together with the employee's hourly rate, so that direct labour costs can be assigned to the appropriate cost object.

Job-order costing system A system of assigning costs to products or services that is used in situations where many different products or services are produced.

Just-in-time (JIT) production methods The design of the production process that involves producing the required items, at the required quality and in the required quantities, at the precise time they are required.

Just-in-time (JIT) purchasing arrangements Strategic partnerships with suppliers that involve the delivery of materials and goods immediately before they are required.

Kanbans Visible signalling systems that authorize the production of parts and their movement to the location where they will be used.

Labour efficiency variance The difference between the standard labour hours for actual production and the actual labour hours worked during the period multiplied by the standard wage rate per hour.

Lag measures Outcome measures that mostly fall within the financial perspective and are the results of past actions

Lead measures Non-financial measures that are the drivers of future financial performance.

Lead time The time that elapses between placing an order and the actual delivery of stocks.

Lean manufacturing systems Systems that seek to reduce waste in manufacturing by implementing just-in-time production systems, focusing on quality, simplifying processes and investing in advanced technologies.

Learning and growth perspective One of the perspectives considered on the balanced scorecard, focusing on how the organization can continue to improve and create value.

Life-cycle cost management The estimation of costs over a product's entire life cycle in order to determine whether profits made during the manufacturing phase will cover the costs incurred during the pre- and post-manufacturing stages.

Limiting factors Scarce resources that constrain the level of output.

Linear programming A mathematical technique used to determine how to employ limited resources to achieve optimum benefits.

Locked-in costs Costs that have not yet been incurred but that will be incurred in the future on the basis of decisions that have already been made, also known as committed costs.

Long-run cost The estimated sum of all resources that are committed to a product or service in the long run, also known as full cost.

Long-term plan A top level plan that sets out the objectives that an organization's future activities will be directed towards, also known as a strategic plan.

Machine hour rate An hourly overhead rate calculated by dividing the cost centre overheads by the number of machine hours.

Management accounting Accounting concerned with the provision of information to people within the organization to aid decision-making and improve the efficiency and effectiveness of existing operations.

Management by exception A system in which a manager's attention and effort can be concentrated on significant deviations from the expected results.

Management control system The entire array of controls used by an organization.

Manufacturing cycle efficiency (MCE) A measure of cycle time that is calculated by dividing processing time by processing time plus the non-value-added activities of inspection time, wait time and move time.

Margin of safety The amount by which sales may decrease before a loss occurs

Marginal cost The additional cost of one extra unit of output.

Marginal costing system A costing system that assigns only variable manufacturing costs, not fixed manufacturing costs, to products and includes them in the inventory valuation, also known as variable costing system or direct costing system.

Marginal revenue The additional revenue from one extra unit of output.

Master budget A document that brings together and summarizes all lower level budgets and which consists of a budgeted profit and loss account, a balance sheet and cash flow statement.

Material price variance The difference between the standard price and the actual price per unit of materials multiplied by the quantity of materials purchased.

Material usage variance The difference between the standard quantity required for actual production and the actual quantity used multiplied by the standard material price.

Minimum required rate of return The financial return that an organization could receive if, instead of investing cash in a capital project, it invested the same amount in securities of equal risk on the financial markets, also known as the opportunity cost of an investment, the cost of capital, the discount rate and the interest rate.

Mission statement A statement that provides in very general terms what the organization does to achieve its vision, its broad purpose and reason for its existence, the nature of the business(es) it is in and the customers it seeks to serve and satisfy.

Mixed costs Costs that contain both a fixed and a variable component, also known as semi-variable costs.

Mutually exclusive In the context of comparing capital investments, a term used to describe projects where the acceptance of one project excludes the acceptance of another.

Net marginal revenue The marginal (incremental) revenue from the sale of an extra unit (or a specified number of incremental units) of the final product less the marginal/incremental conversion costs (excluding the transfer price).

Net present value (NPV) The present value of the net cash inflows from a project less the initial investment outlay.

Non-financial factors Non-monetary factors that may affect a decision.

Non-value added activities Activities that can be reduced or eliminated without altering the product's service potential to the customer.

Non-volume-based cost drivers A method of allocating indirect costs to cost objects that uses alternative measures instead of assuming that a product's consumption of overhead resources is directly related to the number of units produced.

Operating leverage A measure of the sensitivity of profits to changes in sales.

Opportunity cost Cost that measures the opportunity that is sacrificed when the choice of one course of action requires that an alternative is given up.

Opportunity cost of an investment The financial return that an organization could receive if, instead of investing cash in a capital project, it invested the same amount in securities of equal risk on the financial markets, also known as the minimum required rate of return, the cost of capital, the discount rate and the interest rate.

Output controls Collecting and reporting information about the outcomes of work effort, also known as results controls.

Outsourcing The process of obtaining goods or services from outside suppliers instead of producing the same goods or providing the same services within the organization.

Overhead analysis sheet A document used to assign manufacturing overheads to production and service cost centres.

Overheads Costs that cannot be identified specifically and exclusively with a given cost object, also known as indirect costs.

Pareto analysis A type of analysis based on the observation that a very small proportion of items account for the majority of value.

Participation The extent that individuals are able to influence the figures that are incorporated in their budgets or targets.

Payback method A simple method to appraise capital investments, defined as the length of time that is required for a stream of cash proceeds from an investment to recover the original cash outlay.

Penetration pricing policy An approach to pricing that involves charging low prices initially with the intention of gaining rapid acceptance of the product.

Perfectly competitive market A market where the product is homogeneous and no individual buyer or seller can affect the market prices.

Performance reports Performance reports show budget and actual performance (normally listed by items of expenses) at frequent intervals (normally monthly) for each responsibility centre.

Period cost adjustment The record of under- and over-recovery of fixed overheads at the end of a period.

Period costs Costs that are not included in the inventory valuation of goods and which are treated as expenses for the period in which they are incurred.

Personnel controls Helping employees to perform well through the use of selection and placement, training, job design and the provision of necessary resources.

Plant-wide rate An overhead rate that assigns indirect costs to cost objects using a single overhead rate for the whole organization, also known as a blanket overhead rate.

Present value The value today of cash to be received in the future.

Prevention costs The costs incurred in preventing the production of products or services that do not conform to specification.

Price setters Firms that have some discretion over setting the selling price of their products or services.

Price takers Firms that have little or no influence over setting the selling price of their products or services.

Price-skimming policy An approach to pricing that attempts to exploit sections of the market that are relatively insensitive to price changes.

Prime cost   The sum of all direct manufacturing costs.

Priority-based budgeting   An approach to budgeting in which projected expenditure for existing activities starts from base zero rather than last year's budget, forcing managers to justify all budget expenditure, also known as zero-based budgeting.

Priority-based incremental budgets   Budgets in which managers specify what incremental activities or changes would occur if their budgets were increased or decreased by a specified percentage, leading to budget allocations being made by comparing the change in costs with the change in benefits.

Product costs   Costs that are identified with goods purchased or produced for resale and which are attached to products and included in the inventory valuation of goods.

Product flow line   A plant layout in which groups of dissimilar machines are organized into product or component family flow lines so that individual items can move from process to process more easily.

Product's life cycle   The period of time from initial expenditure on research and development to the withdrawal of support to customers.

Product line-sustaining expenses   Expenses relating to supporting a product line and not to any brand or product within that product line.

Production cells   Self-contained areas in which a team works on a product family.

Production efficiency ratio   A process efficiency measure calculated by dividing the standard hours of output by the actual hours of input.

Product-sustaining activities   Support activities that are performed to enable the production and sale of individual products and which are not related to the volume of each product.

Profit centres   A Responsibility centres where managers are accountable for both revenues and costs.

Profit–volume graph   A graph that plots profit/losses against volume.

Profit–volume ratio   The proportion of sales available to cover fixed costs and provide for profit, calculated by dividing the contribution margin by the sales revenue, also known as contribution margin ratio.

Prospector strategy   Firms pursuing a prospector strategy perceive high uncertainty in their environment and are continually searching for new market opportunities. They compete through new product innovations and market development.

Pull manufacturing system   A system that pulls products through the manufacturing process so that each operation produces only what is necessary to meet the demand of the following operation.

Push manufacturing system   A system in which machines are grouped into work centres based on the similarity of their functional capabilities and one process supplies parts to the subsequent process without any consideration as to whether the next process is ready to work on the parts or not.

Qualitative factors   Non-monetary factors that may affect a decision.

Relative performance evaluation   The evaluation of the performance of a responsibility centre relative to the performance of similar centres within the same company or of similar units outside the organization.

Relevant costs and revenues   Future costs and revenues that will be changed by a particular decision, whereas irrelevant costs and revenues will not be affected by that decision.

Relevant range   The output range at which an organization expects to be operating with a short-term planning horizon.

Residual income   Controllable profit less a cost of capital charge on the investment controllable by the divisional manager.

Resource cost driver   A cause-and-effect cost driver used to allocate shared resources to individual activities.

Responsibility accounting   Accounting that involves tracing costs and revenues to responsibility centres.

Responsibility centres   Units or departments within an organization for whose performance a manager is held responsible.

Results controls   Collecting and reporting information about the outcomes of work effort, also known as output controls.

Return on capital employed   A method of appraising capital investments where the average annual profits from a project are divided into the average investment cost, also known as the accounting rate of return and return on investment.

Return on investment (ROI)   A method of appraising capital investments where the average annual profits from a project are divided into the average investment cost, also known as the accounting rate of return and return on capital employed.

Revenue centres   Responsibility centres where managers are mainly accountable for financial outputs in the form of generating sales revenues.

Reverse engineering   The dismantling and examination of a competitor's product in order to identify opportunities for product improvement and/or cost reduction, also known as tear-down analysis.

Risk A term applied to a situation where there are several possible outcomes and there is relevant past experience to enable statistical evidence to be produced for predicting the possible outcomes.

Risk-free gilt-edged securities Bonds issued by governments in many countries for set periods of time with fixed interest rates.

Rolling budgeting An approach to budgeting in which the annual budget is broken down into months for the first three months and into quarters for the rest of the year, with a new quarter being added as each quarter ends, also known as continuous budgeting.

Sales margin price variance The difference between the actual contribution margin and the standard margin multiplied by the actual sales volume.

Sales margin volume variance The difference between the actual sales volume and the budgeted volume multiplied by the standard contribution margin.

Semi-fixed costs Costs that remain fixed within specified activity levels for a given amount of time but which eventually increase or decrease by a constant amount at critical activity levels; also known as step-fixed costs.

Semi-variable costs Costs that contain both a fixed and a variable component, also known as mixed costs.

Sensitivity analysis Analysis that shows how a result will be changed if the original estimates or underlying assumption changes.

Service departments Departments that exist to provide services to other units within the organization, also known as support departments.

Service-sustaining activities Support activities that are performed to enable the production and sale of individual services and which are not related to the volume of each service provided.

Shared value Policies and operating practices that enhance the competitiveness of a company while simultaneously advancing economic and social conditions in the communities in which it operates.

Social or cultural controls The selection of people who have already been socialized into adopting particular norms and patterns of behaviour to perform particular tasks.

Special studies A detailed non-routine study that is undertaken relating to choosing between alternative courses of action.

Stakeholders Various parties that have an interest in an organization. Examples include managers, shareholders and potential investors, employees, creditors and the government.

Standard cost centres Cost centres where output can be measured and the input required to produce each unit of output can be specified.

Standard costs Target costs that are predetermined and should be incurred under efficient operating conditions.

Standard hours The number of hours a skilled worker should take working under efficient conditions to complete a given job.

Standard hours produced A calculation of the amount of time, working under efficient conditions, it should take to make each product.

Step-fixed costs Costs that remain fixed within specified activity levels for a given amount of time but which eventually increase or decrease by a constant amount at critical activity levels; also known as semi-fixed costs.

Strategic control Control that focuses outside the organization, looking at how a firm can compete with other firms in the same industry.

Strategic plan A top level plan that sets out the objectives that an organization's future activities will be directed towards, also known as a long-term plan.

Strategic positioning The choice of strategies an organization uses to achieve sustainable competitive advantage.

Strategies Courses of action designed to ensure that objectives are achieved.

Subjective judgements Judgements made by senior managers of a responsibility head's performance based on the senior manager's own experience, knowledge and interpretation of the performance level achieved.

Sunk costs Costs that have been incurred by a decision made in the past and that cannot be changed by any decision that will be made in the future.

Supply chain management Managing linkages in the supply chain by examining supplier costs and modifying activities to reduce these costs.

Support departments Departments that exist to provide services to other units within the organization, also known as service departments.

Target costing A technique that focuses on managing costs during a product's planning and design phase by establishing the target cost for a product or service that is derived from starting with the target selling price and deducting a desired profit margin.

Target rate of return on invested capital An approach to pricing that involves estimating the amount of investment attributable to a product and setting a price that ensures a satisfactory return on investment for a given volume.

Tear-down analysis The dismantling and examination of a competitor's product in order to identify opportunities for product improvement and/or cost reduction, also known as reverse engineering.

Time value of money The concept that a specific amount of cash is worth more now than it will be in the future.

Top-down budget setting Imposing budgets and targets from above, without the participation of the individuals involved.

Total labour variance The difference between the standard labour cost for the actual production and the actual labour cost.

Total material variance The difference between the standard material cost for the actual production and the actual cost.

Total quality management (TQM) A customer-oriented process of continuous improvement that focuses on delivering products or services of consistent high quality in a timely fashion.

Total sales margin variance The difference between actual sales revenue less the standard variable cost of sales and the budgeted contribution.

Total variable overhead variance The difference between the standard variable overheads charged to production and the actual variable overheads incurred.

Traditional costing systems Widely used costing systems that tend to use arbitrary allocations to assign indirect costs to cost objects.

Transaction drivers A cost driver used to assign the costs assigned to an activity cost centre to products that is based on the number of times an activity is performed.

Transactions motive Holding stock in order to meet future production and sales requirements.

Two-part transfer pricing system A method of transfer pricing where the receiving division acquires intermediate products at the variable cost of production and the supplying division also charges a fixed fee.

Unavoidable costs Costs that cannot be saved, whether or not an alternative is adopted.

Uncertainty A term applied to a situation where there are several possible outcomes and but there is little previous statistical evidence to enable possible outcomes to be predicted.

Under- or over-recovery of overheads The difference between the overheads that are allocated to products or services during a period and the actual overheads that are incurred.

Unit objectives Specific, measurable statements, often expressed in financial terms, of what individual units within an organization wish to achieve.

Unit-level activities Activities that are performed each time a unit of the product or service is produced.

Value added activity An activity that customers perceive as adding usefulness to the product or service they purchase.

Value analysis A systematic interdisciplinary examination of factors affecting the cost of a product or service in order to devise means of achieving the specified purpose at the required standard of quality and reliability at the target cost, also known as value engineering.

Value engineering A systematic interdisciplinary examination of factors affecting the cost of a product or service in order to devise means of achieving the specified purpose at the required standard of quality and reliability at the target cost, also known as value analysis.

Value-based-management (VBM) A management principle that states that management should first and foremost consider the interests of shareholders in its business decisions.

Value-chain analysis The analysis, coordination and optimization of the linked set of value-creating activities all the way from basic raw material sources for component suppliers through to the ultimate end-use product or service delivered to the customer.

Variable costing system A costing system that assigns only variable manufacturing costs, not fixed manufacturing costs, to products and includes them in the inventory valuation, also known as marginal costing system or direct costing system.

Variable costs Costs that vary in direct proportion to the volume of activity.

Variable overhead efficiency variance The difference between the standard hours of output and the actual hours of input for the period multiplied by the standard variable overhead rate.

Variable overhead expenditure variance The difference between the budgeted flexed variable overheads for the actual direct labour hours of input and the actual variable overhead costs incurred.

Variance The difference between the actual cost and the standard cost.

Variance analysis The analysis of factors that cause the actual results to differ from pre-determined budgeted targets.

Vision statement A statement that clarifies the beliefs and governing principles of an organization, what it wants to be in the future or how it wants the world in which it operates to be.

Volume-based cost drivers A method of allocating indirect costs to cost objects that correlates a product's consumption of overhead resources with the number of units produced.

Volume variance   The difference between actual production and budgeted production for a period multiplied by the standard fixed overhead rate.

Wage rate variance   The difference between the standard wage rate per hour and the actual wage rate multiplied by the actual number of hours worked.

Weighted average cost of capital   The overall cost of capital to an organization, taking into account the proportion of capital raised from debt and equity.

Written down value   The original cost of an asset minus depreciation.

Zero-based budgeting   An approach to budgeting in which projected expenditure for existing activities starts from base zero rather than last year's budget, forcing managers to justify all budget expenditure, also known as priority-based budgeting.

CREDITS

Chapter 1

Page 11 © audioundwerbung/ Thinkstock
Page 12 © Kristen Prahl/ Shutterstock
Page 17 © monkeybusinessimages/ Thinkstock

Chapter 2

Page 28 © monkeybusinessimages/ Thinkstock
Page 32 © nicostock/ Shutterstock
Page 38 © Jim West / Alamy Stock Photo
Page 39 © jacoblund/ Getty Images

Chapter 3

Page 53 © onlyyouqj/ Thinkstock
Page 61 © oatz stocker/ Shutterstock
Page 66 © Grassetto/ Thinkstock

Chapter 4

Page 85 © Creatas/Thinkstock
Page 91 © AKP Photos / Alamy Stock Photo

Chapter 5

Page 108 © Belekekin/iStock/Thinkstock
Page 116 © Betoon/iStock/Getty Images
Page 118 © Jacek Lasa / Alamy Stock Photo

Chapter 6

Page 131 © Hhakim/iStock/Getty Images
Page 139 © Mahroch/iStock/Thinkstock
Page 143 © Shutter_M/iStock/Thinkstock
Page 145 © cookelma/Thinkstock
Page 149 © Mouse_sonya/iStock/Getty Images

Chapter 7

Page 178 © BrandX Pictures/Thinkstock

Chapter 8

Page 203 © Dmitry Kalinovsky/ Shutterstock
Page 204 © Thomas Northcut/digitalvision/ Thinkstock

Chapter 9

Page 234 © NicoElNino/ Thinkstock

Chapter 10

Page 256 © piotr290/ Thinkstock
Page 266 © John Birdsall / Alamy Stock Photo

Chapter 11

Page 282 © Shironosov/iStock/Thinkstock
Page 284 © Image Source White/Thinkstock

Chapter 12

Page 312 © Clynt Garnham Business / Alamy Stock Photo
Page 323 © Robert Convery / Alamy Stock Photo
Page 324 © jgroup/ Thinkstock

Chapter 13

Page 344 © Thomas Northcut/Thinkstock
Page 345 © Violinconcertono3/iStock/Getty Images

Chapter 14

Page 360 © Sharpshutter/iStock/Thinkstock

Chapter 15

Page 388 © Wavebreakmedia Ltd/Thinkstock
Page 395 © Goto_Tokyo/iStock/Thinkstock

Chapter 16

Page 430 © Mckyartstudio/iStock/Getty Images

INDEX